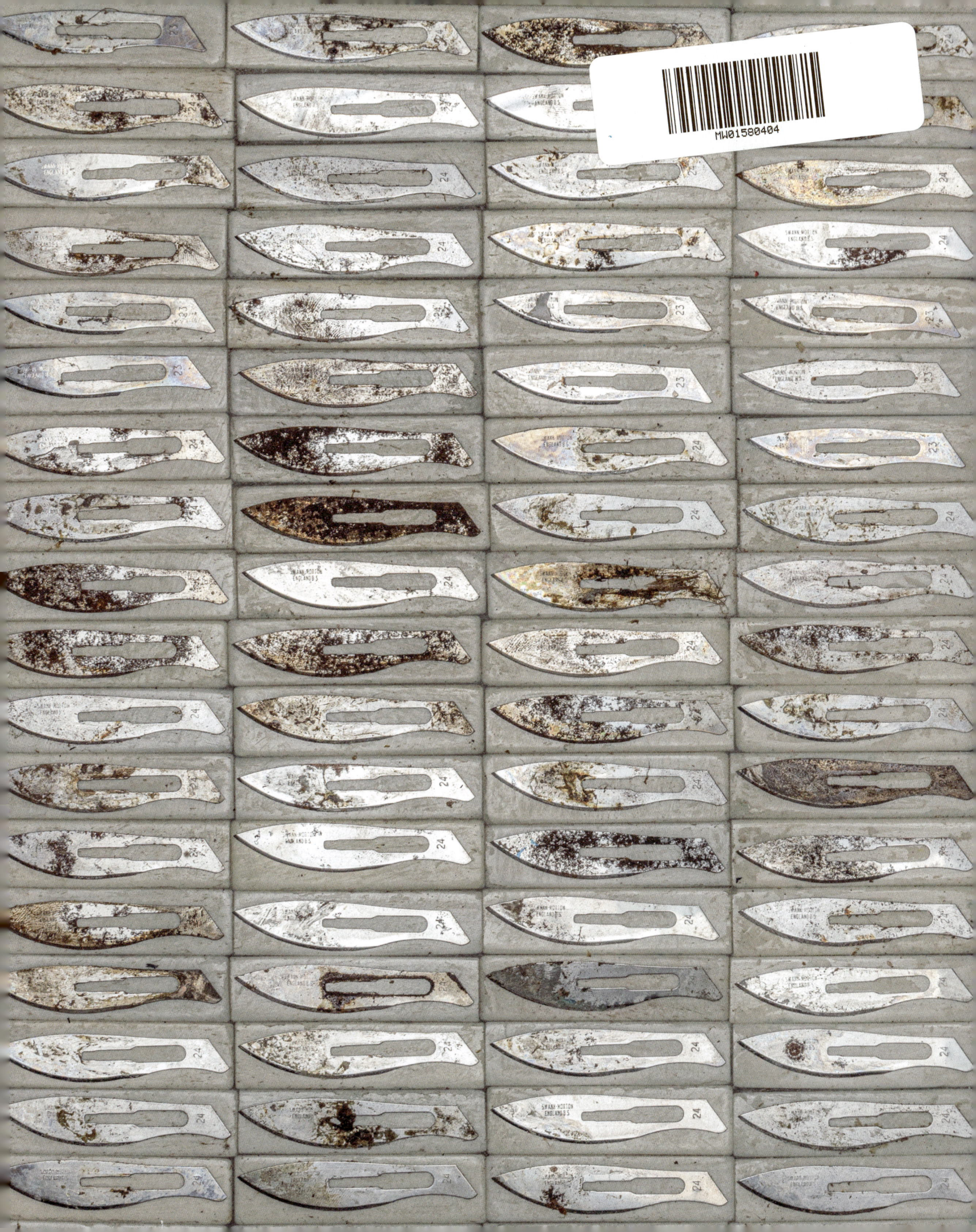

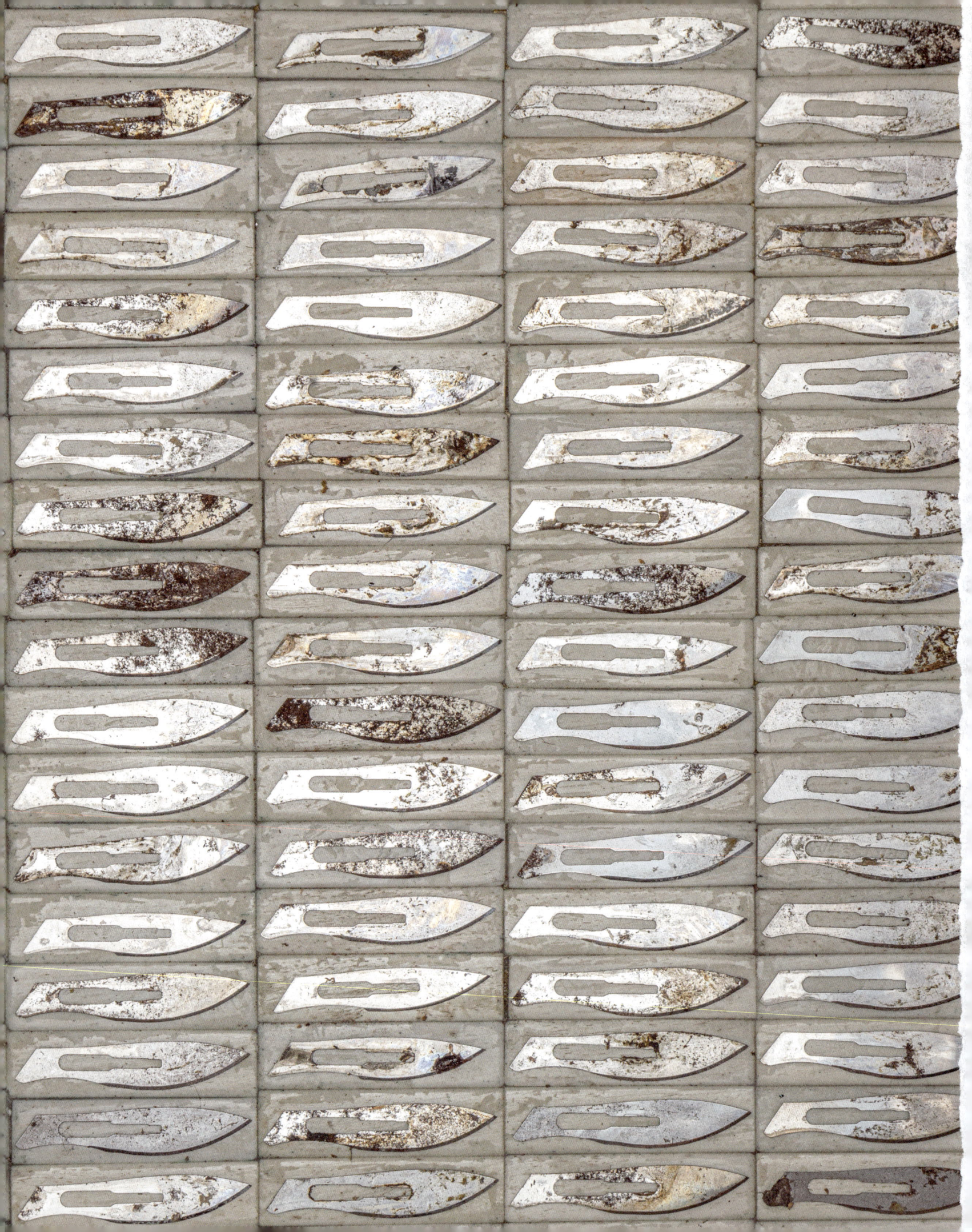

OUR GOLDEN RULE

None of our animals
have been taken from the wild.
All animals died
of natural causes.

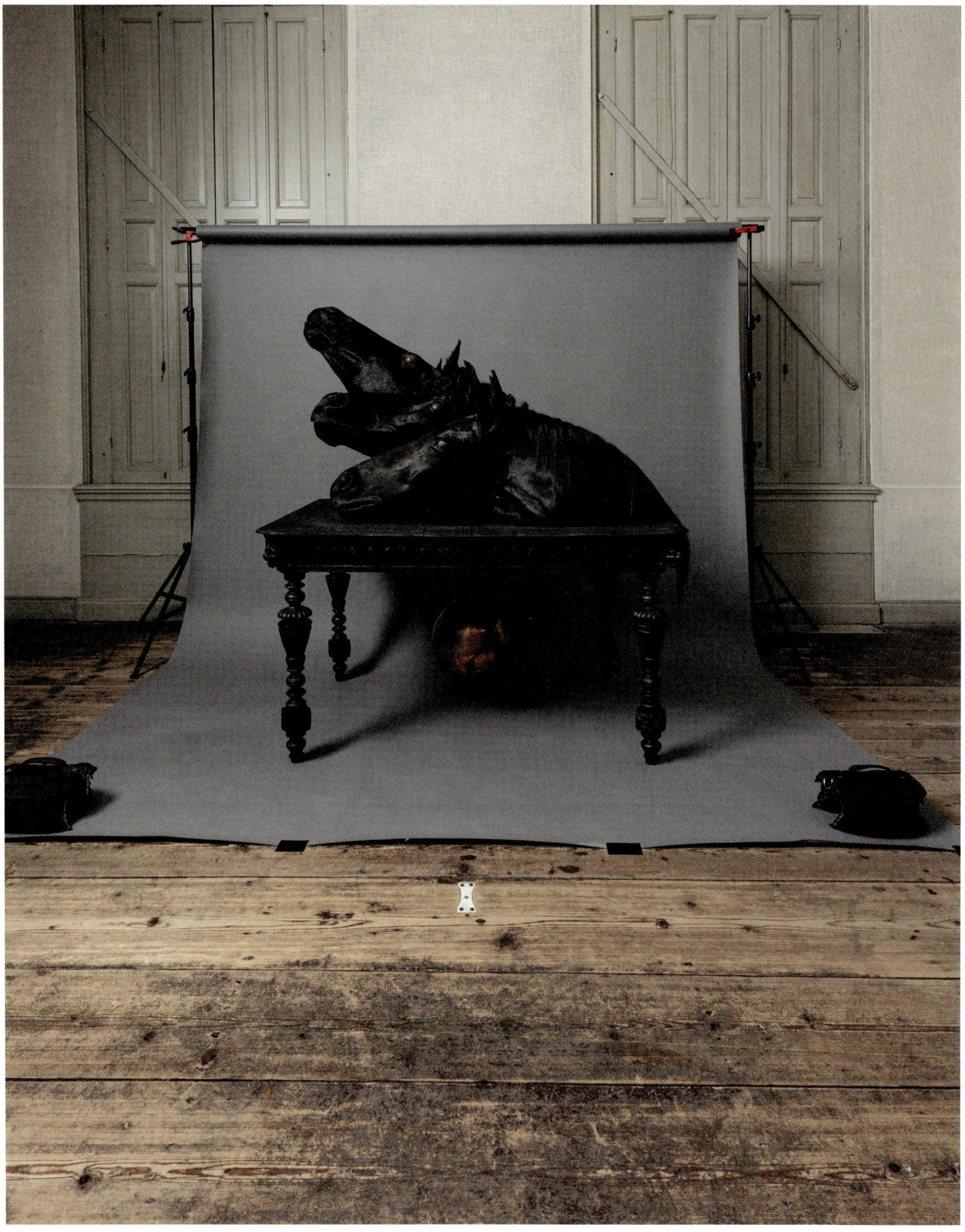

Words by Darwin, Sinke & van Tongeren

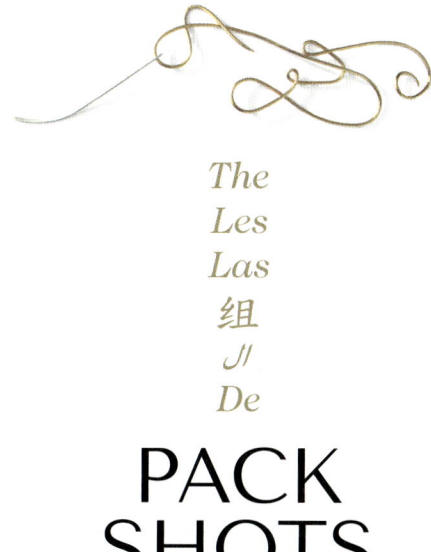

The
Les
Las
组
儿
De

PACK SHOTS

Lannoo

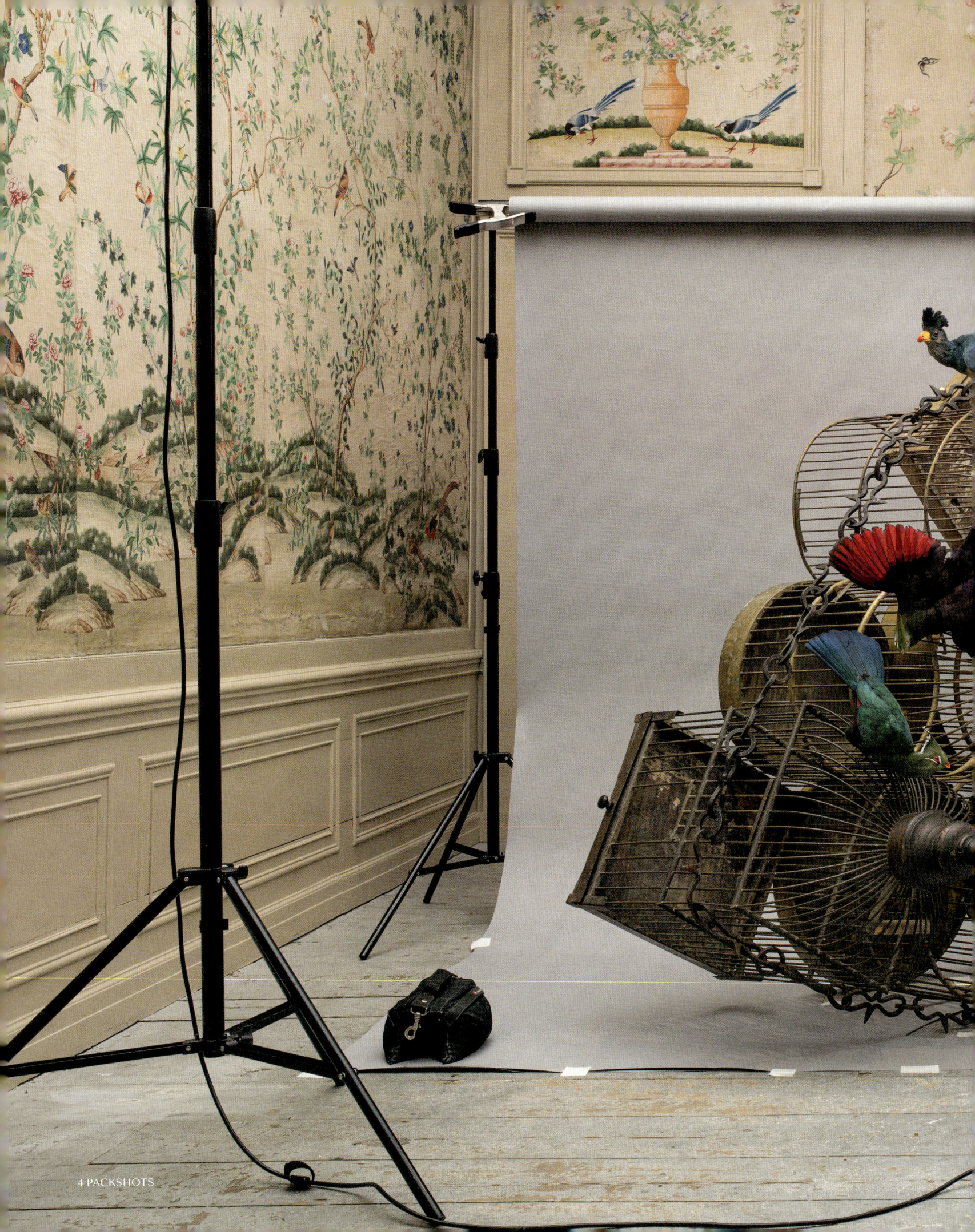

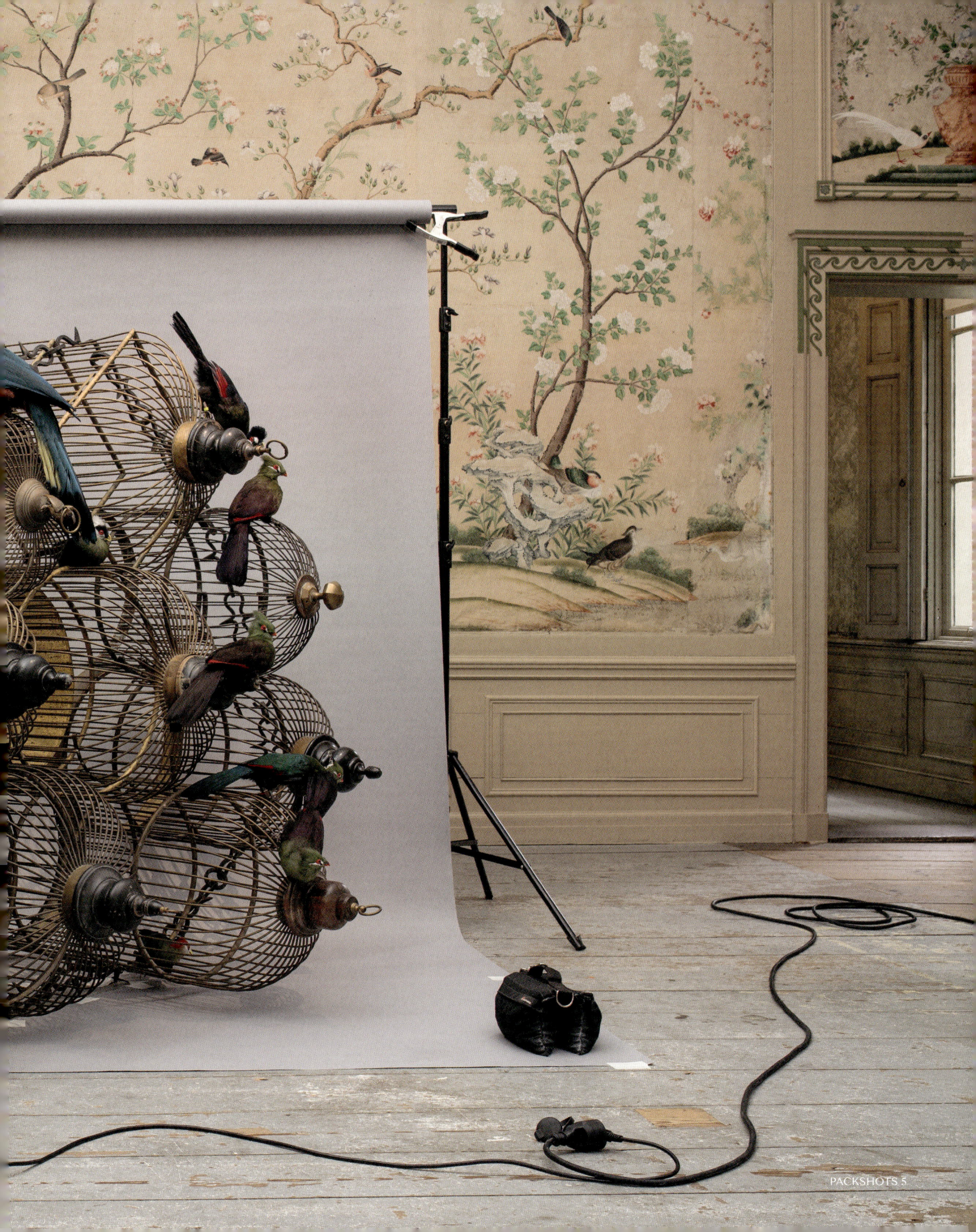

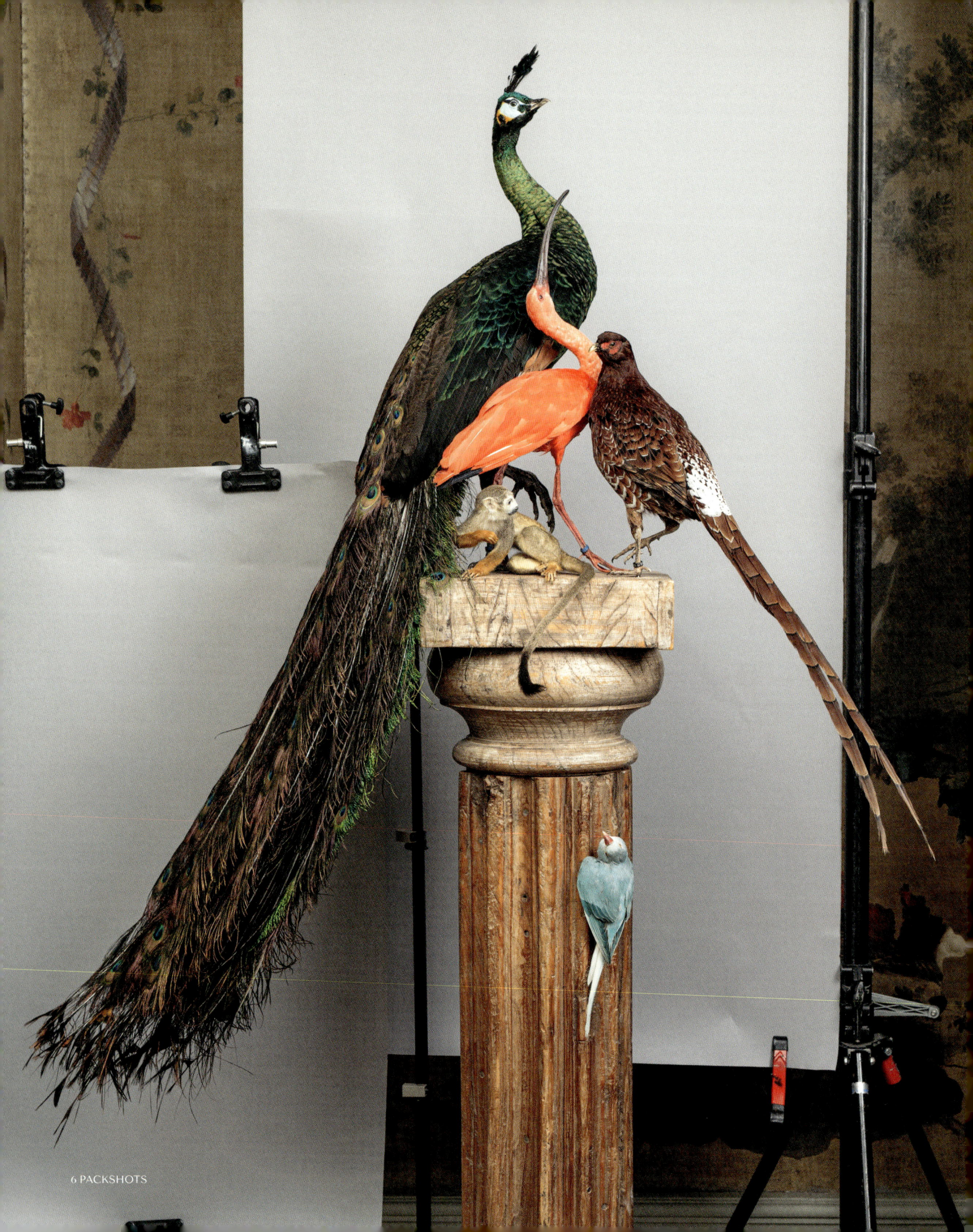

6 PACKSHOTS

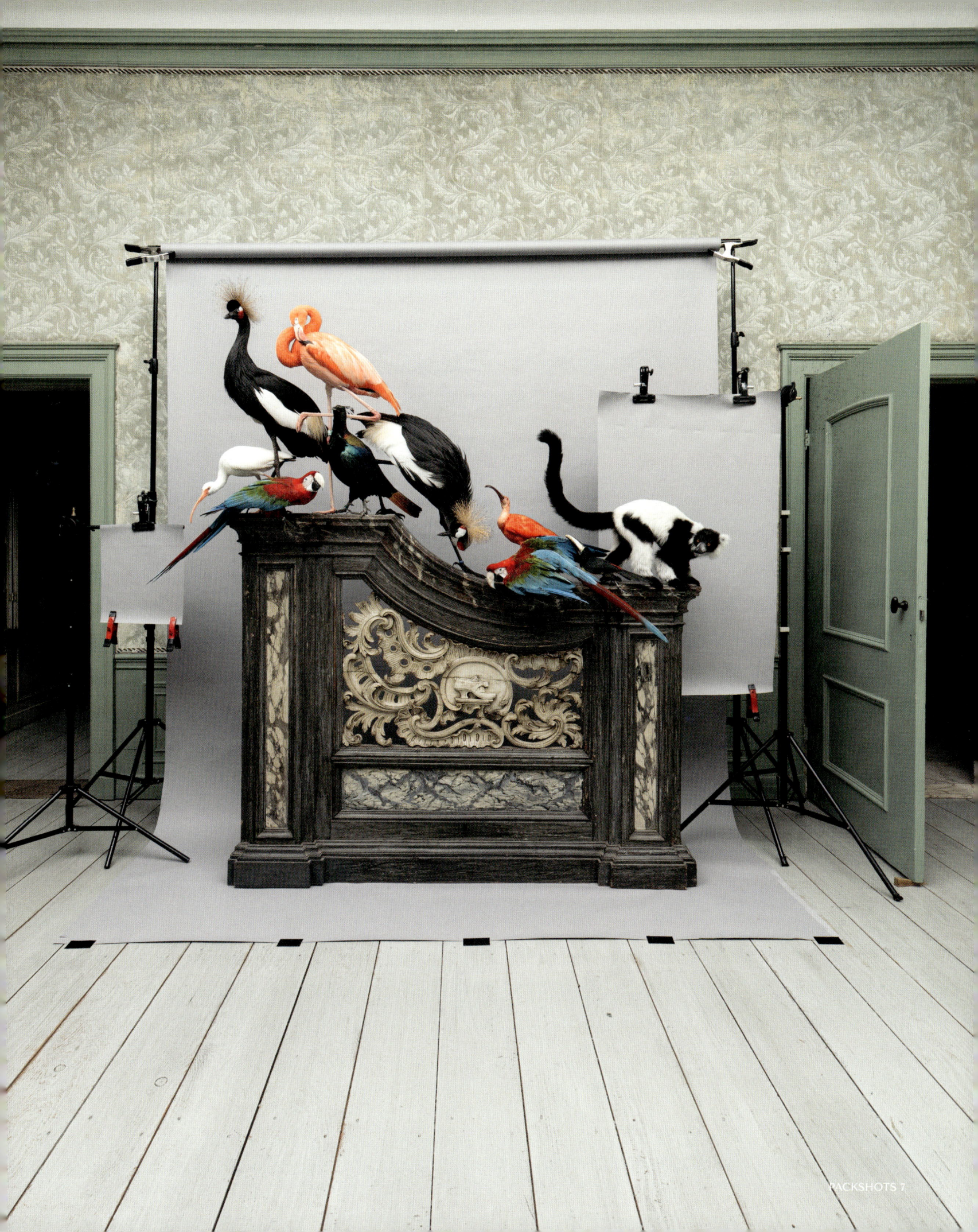

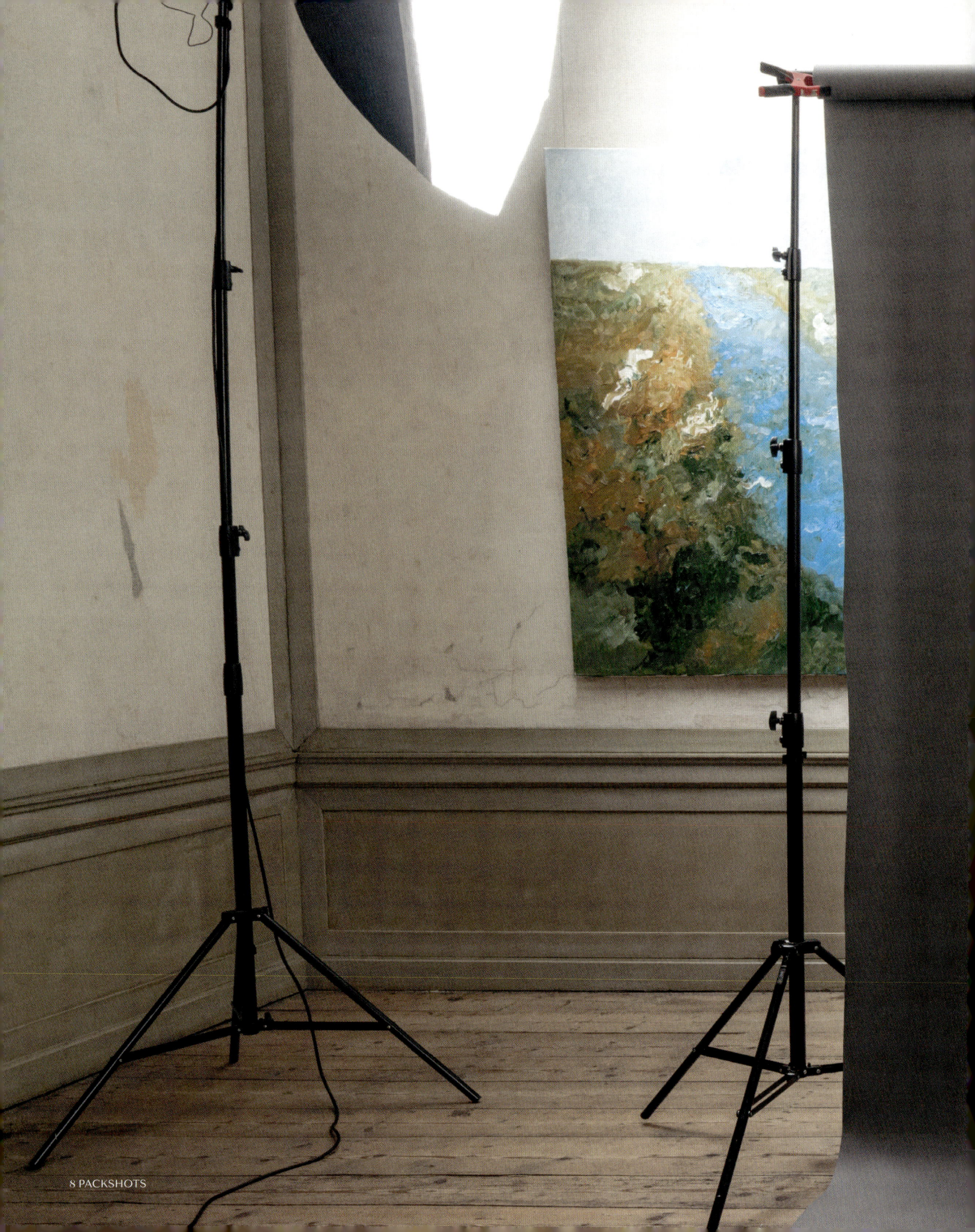

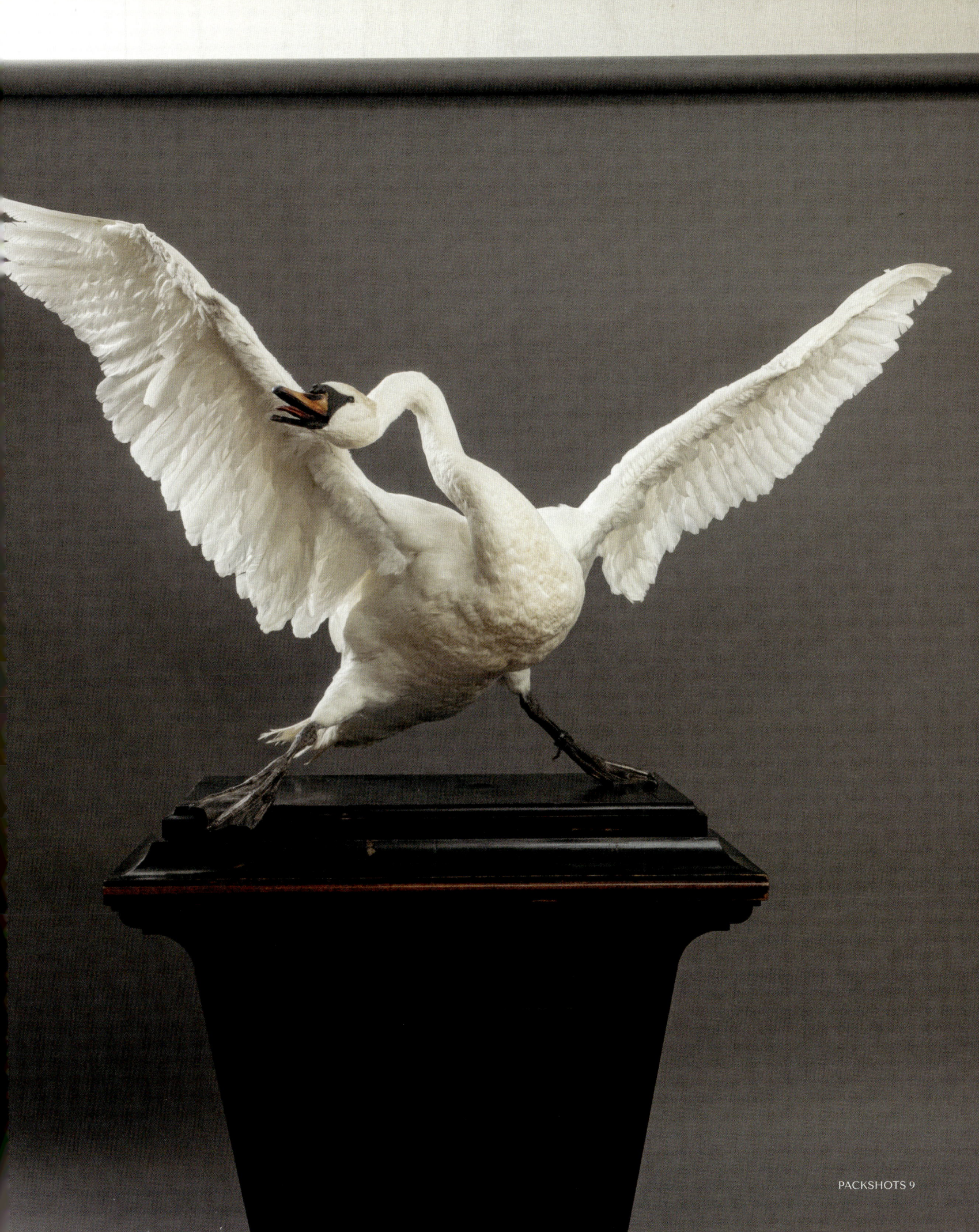

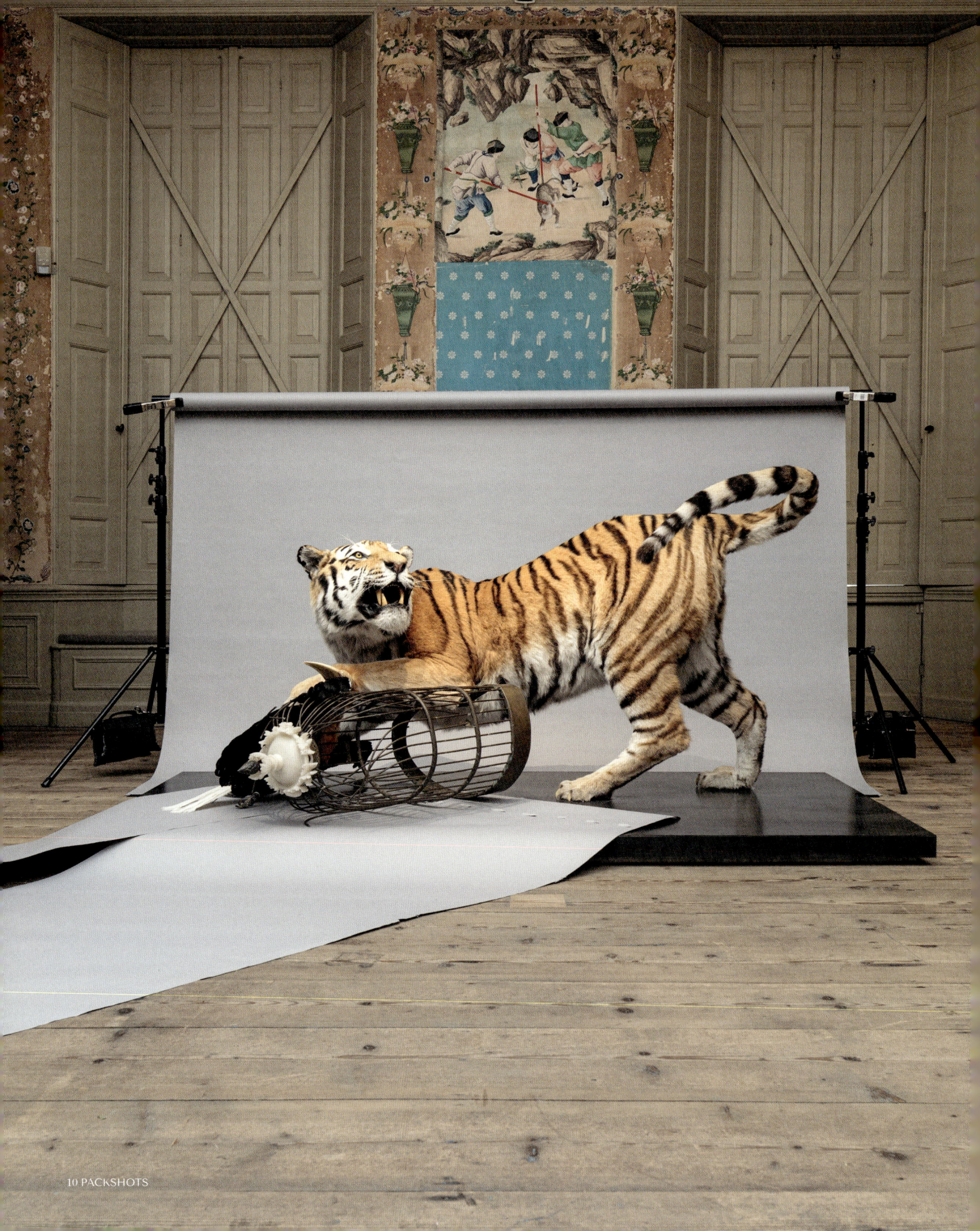

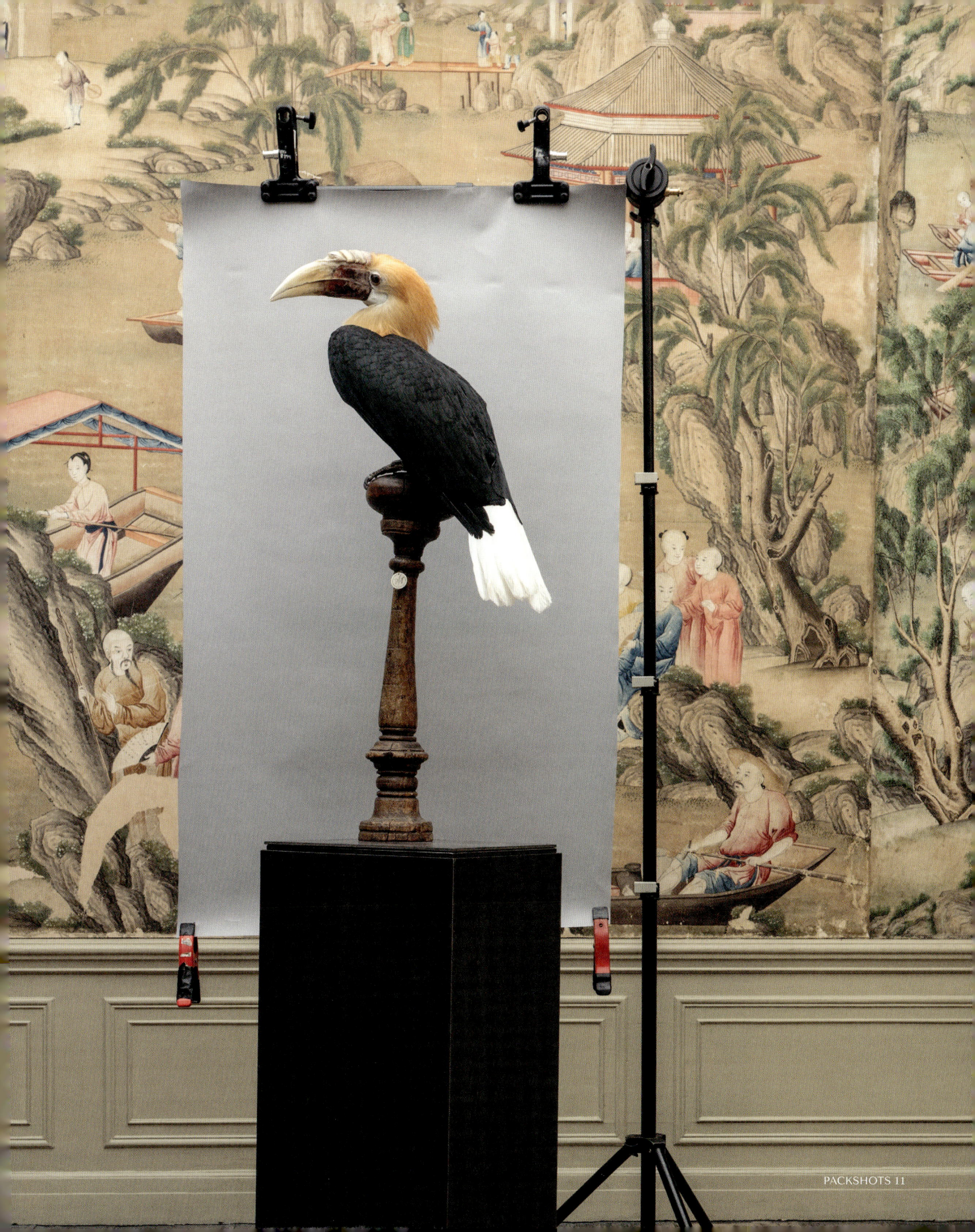

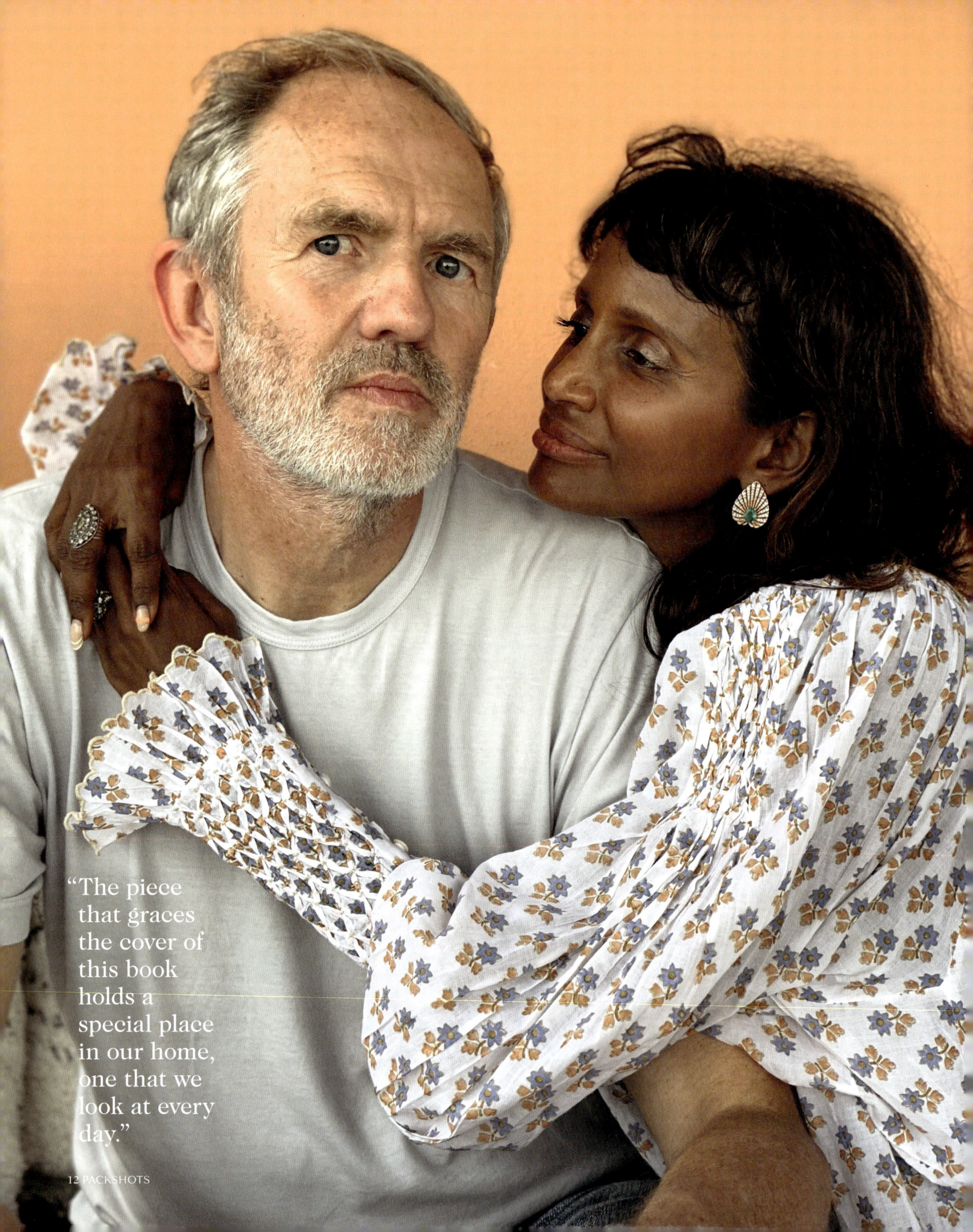

"The piece that graces the cover of this book holds a special place in our home, one that we look at every day."

Foreword

NIMI & ANTON CORBIJN

World-renowned fashion designer and photographer couple

Portrait by Morleigh Steinberg

In art, we have always been drawn to works that make us feel something beyond the surface, something visceral and alive. When we first encountered the art of Darwin, Sinke & van Tongeren, we were struck by the quiet intensity of their pieces — a world where life, death, beauty, and decay exist in perfect balance. Each piece felt like a moment suspended in time, a pause that invites you to look closer, to think deeper.

As a collector, you develop relationships not just with the artworks but also with the artists behind them. Over the years, we've had the pleasure of getting to know them both as creators and as people. Their passion, their precision, their eye for the natural world — these are qualities that not only define their work but also the way they approach life. It is rare to find such dedication to the details, such respect for nature, and such boldness in vision.

The piece that graces the cover of this book holds a special place in our home, one that we look at every day. It's a constant reminder of why we fell in love with their work in the first place — the way they breathe life into nature, capturing its raw beauty, which creates something eternal from what is, by nature, fleeting. "Our" bird feels transcendent, between life and death; thanks to the creativity of the makers, this is not merely a dead animal that we are looking at.

This book is a testament to the journey that Darwin, Sinke & van Tongeren have taken over the past decade. It's a journey of exploration, of pushing boundaries, and of creating something truly extraordinary. As you turn these pages, you'll see the mastery of their work, and you'll feel, as we do, the deep connection that they have to their art and the world around them. We are honoured to write this foreword, not just as collectors, but as folks who deeply respect their vision. Their work continues to inspire us, and we hope it will inspire you too!

Anton & Nimi

CONTENTS

Foreword by Nimi & Anton Corbijn	p. 12–13
Introduction	p. 15
About	p. 16–17
Packshots Fine Taxidermy	p. 18–275
Lunch Break With Two of Our Masterpieces	p. 276–293
Page Index	p. 294–300
Species Index	p. 301–303
Credits	p. 304

Introduction

TO OUR READERS:

Darwin, Sinke & van Tongeren officially came to life in 2013, but our journey as artists began long before that. We, Ferry van Tongeren and Jaap Sinke, first met in 1994 while working in advertising in Amsterdam. What started off as a shared passion for art, nature and 17th-century aesthetics gradually grew into something much larger. In 2014, we launched our first collection, La Vie de L'Eden, and we were incredibly honoured when Damien Hirst purchased the entire exhibition. That moment was a significant milestone for us, but it also reminded us of how much more we wanted to explore and express through our work.

This book is in many ways a visual diary of that exploration over the past ten years. It is not just a collection of our taxidermy and photography — it is a way of documenting our ongoing curiosity about and fascination with the intersection of art, nature and science. Through these images, we have tried to capture the delicate balance between preserving the beauty of the natural world and transforming it into something that resonates on a deeper emotional and artistic level.

Our photography, like our art, is an extension of that process. We did not set out to become photographers, but through experimentation and observation, we have taught ourselves how to capture our work in the most honest way we know.

Natural light is at the heart of our photography, giving each image a softness and depth that artificial lighting can't replicate. In this way, our studio becomes an ever-changing canvas, bathed in sunlight that brings out the true textures and colours of each piece. We use long lenses to focus on the intricate details — every feather, every curve — without distortion, often setting our works against antique panelled walls that add a timeless quality to the shots.

But this book is not just about our art; it is also about how our work has shaped our lives and the lives of those closest to us. In these pages, you will find an intimate lunch conversation with our daughters. It was a moment to pause and reflect on how our art has not only defined us but has also influenced our daughters' childhoods and their views on life. This discussion about our past, present and future adds another layer to this book, reminding us that our creative journey is inseparable from our personal one.

As you turn the pages, we invite you to join us in looking back, not just to see where we have been, but to share in the excitement of what is ahead. This book is a window into our world. It is filled with the wonder and complexity of nature and the joy we have found in preserving it through our work.

Jaap & Ferry

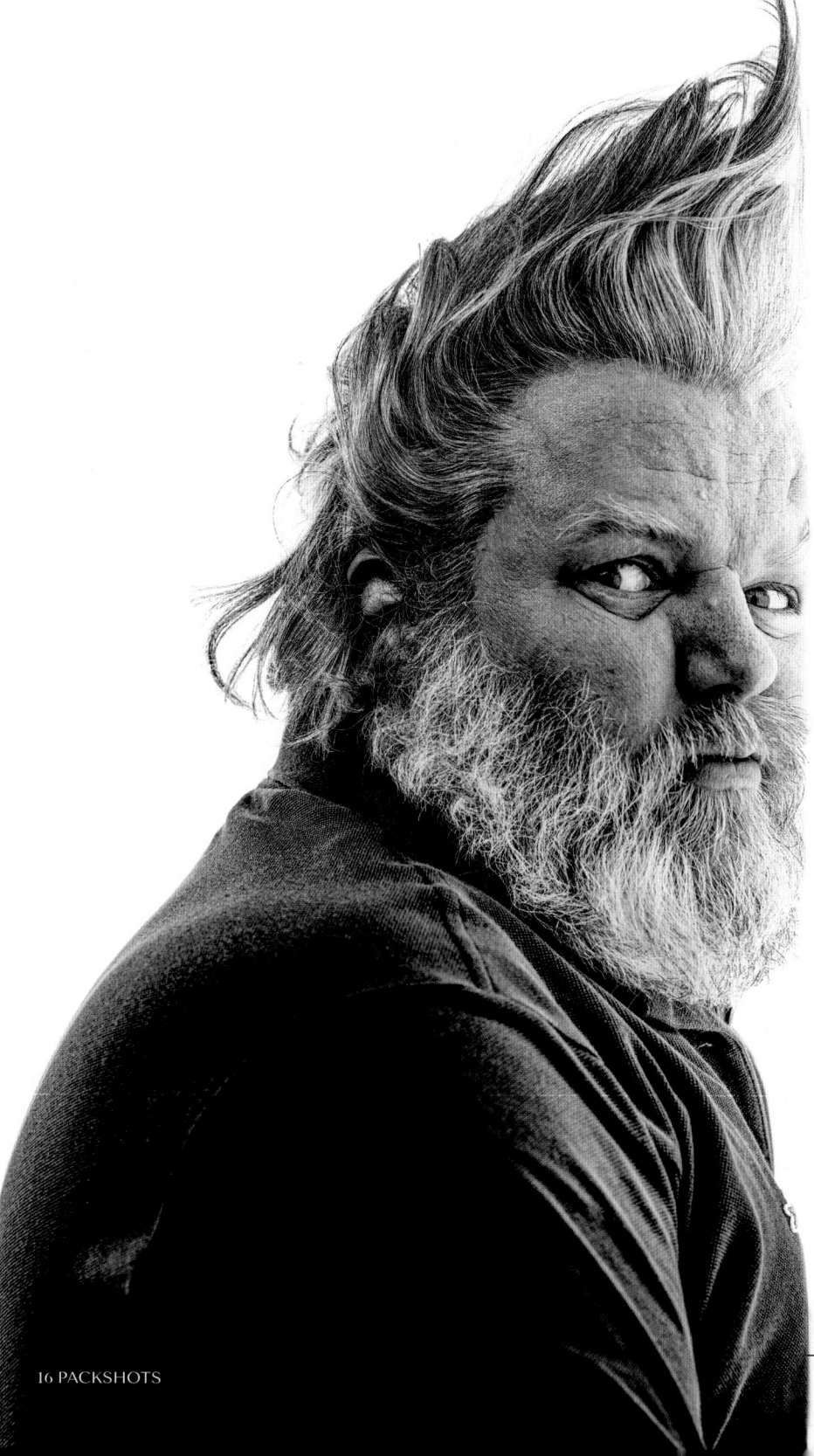

Jaap Sinke

I have always had a profound respect for animals, a bond forged in my youth growing up as the son of a vet. That early connection shaped my sensitivity to the natural world, and it is that sensitivity which drives our art today. For me, working with animals in our art isn't just about recreating what was lost — it's about capturing the soul of the creature, its movement, its essence. My aim is to breathe life back into the animals we work with, one careful brushstroke at a time. Our art is not just about creating beauty; it's about honouring the stories that nature tells.

About

Ferry van Tongeren

I was always a seeker of new perspectives. I was always driven by curiosity. After years in the advertising world, I felt a need to step away and find a more meaningful connection to the natural world. My love for animals and fascination with their forms led me to taxidermy, but my vision went far beyond preservation. For me, every composition is a way to give nature a voice, to reimagine the beauty and fragility of life in ways that inspire and provoke. Our work is a tribute to the animals I revere, urging us to reflect on our responsibility to the world around us.

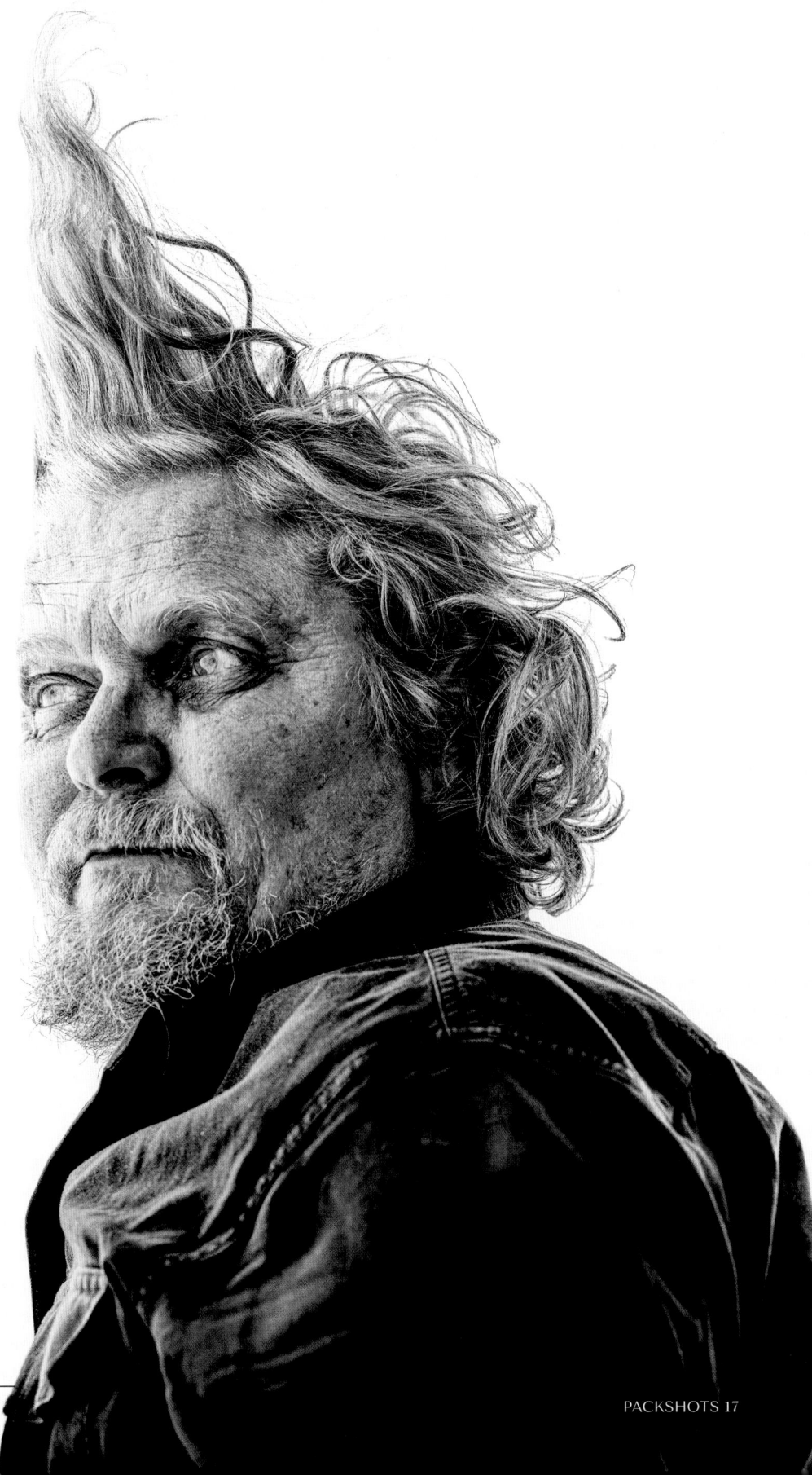

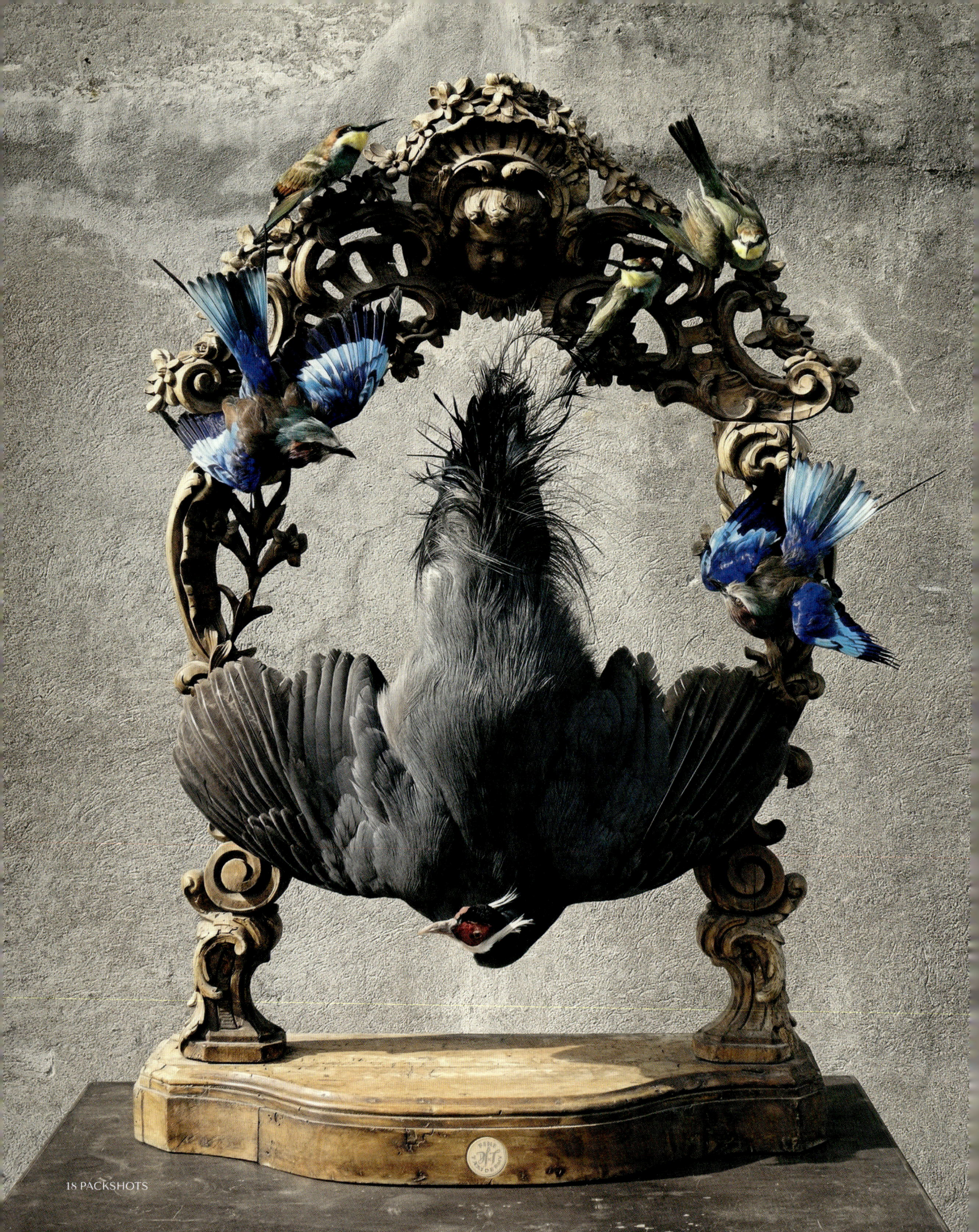

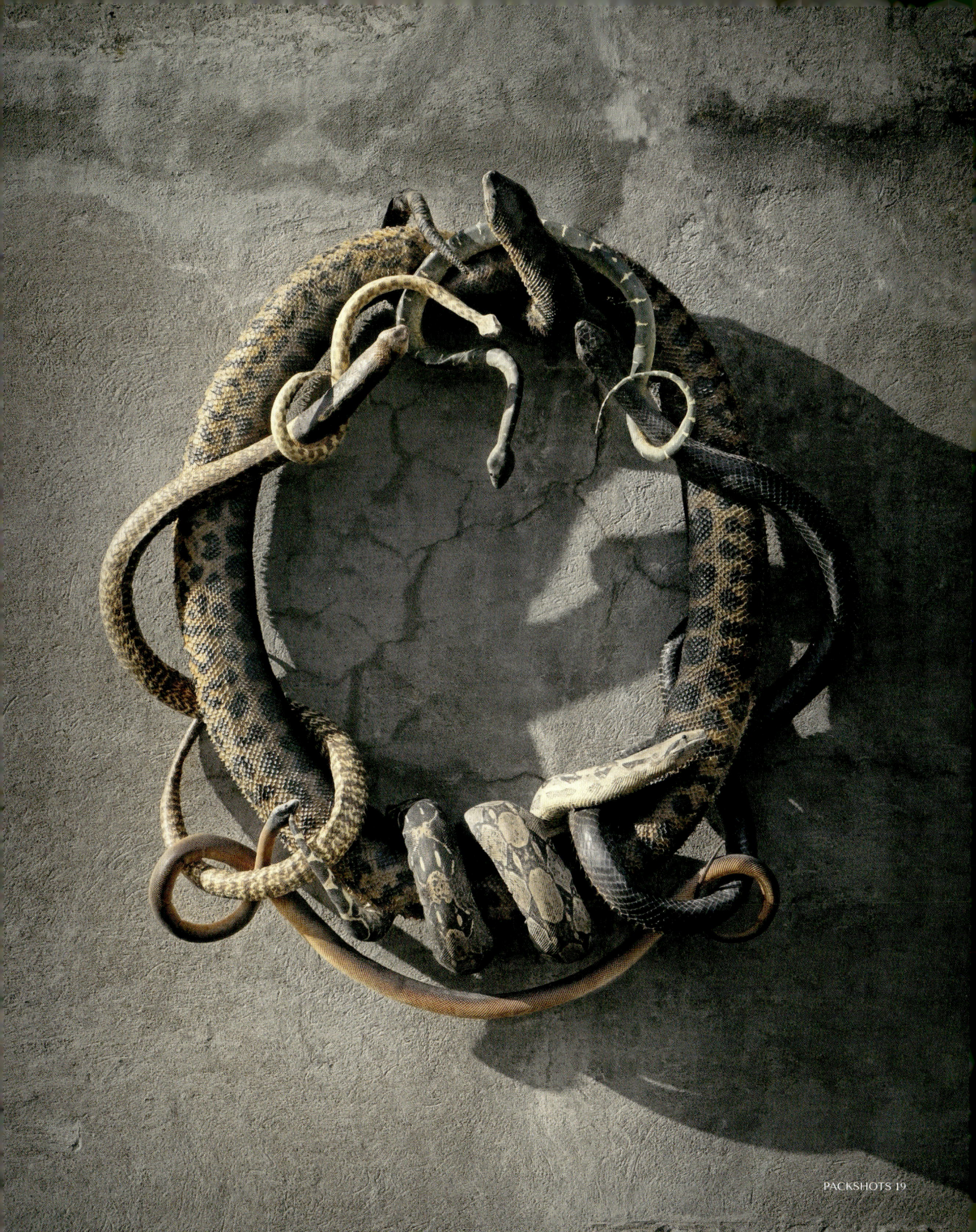

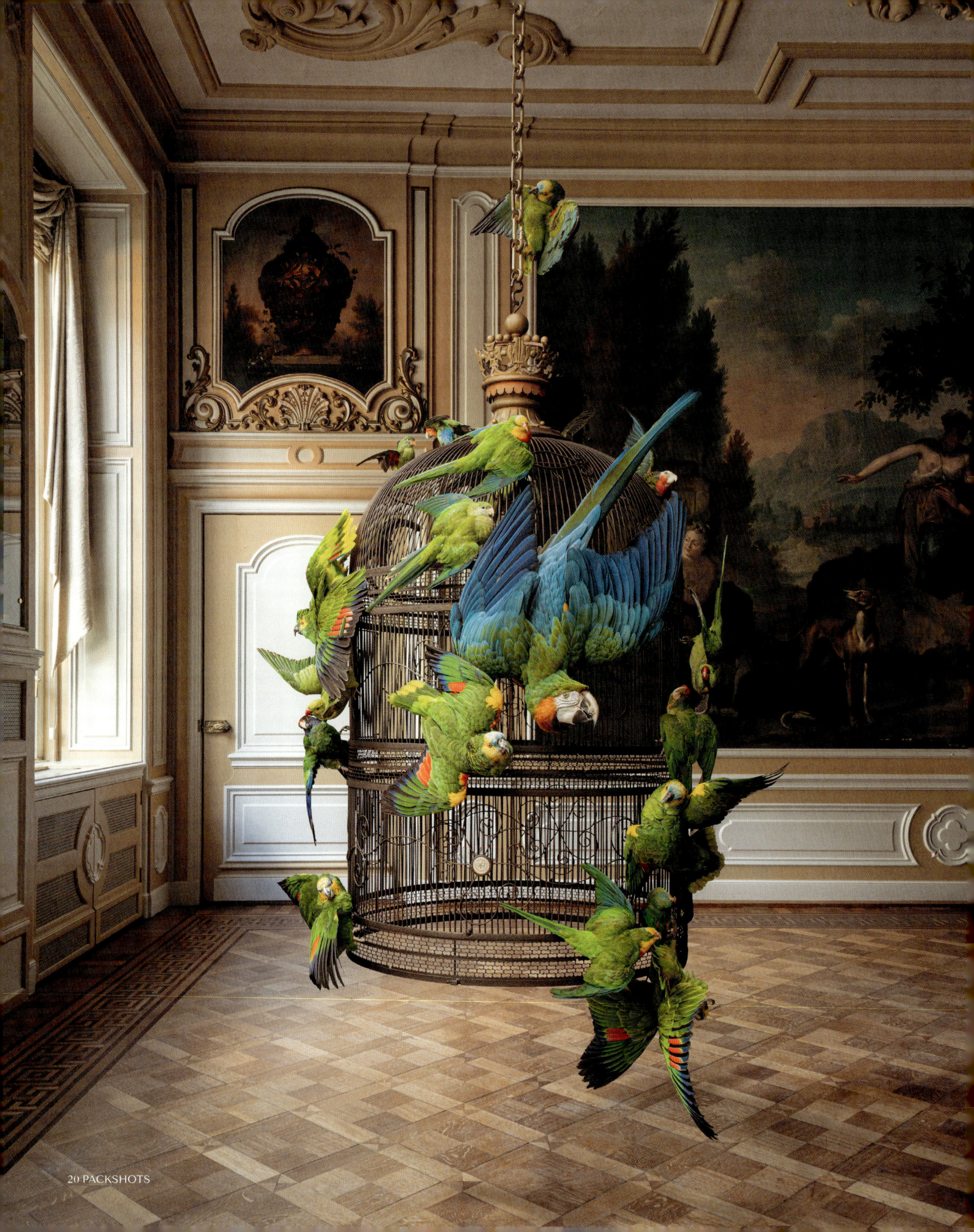

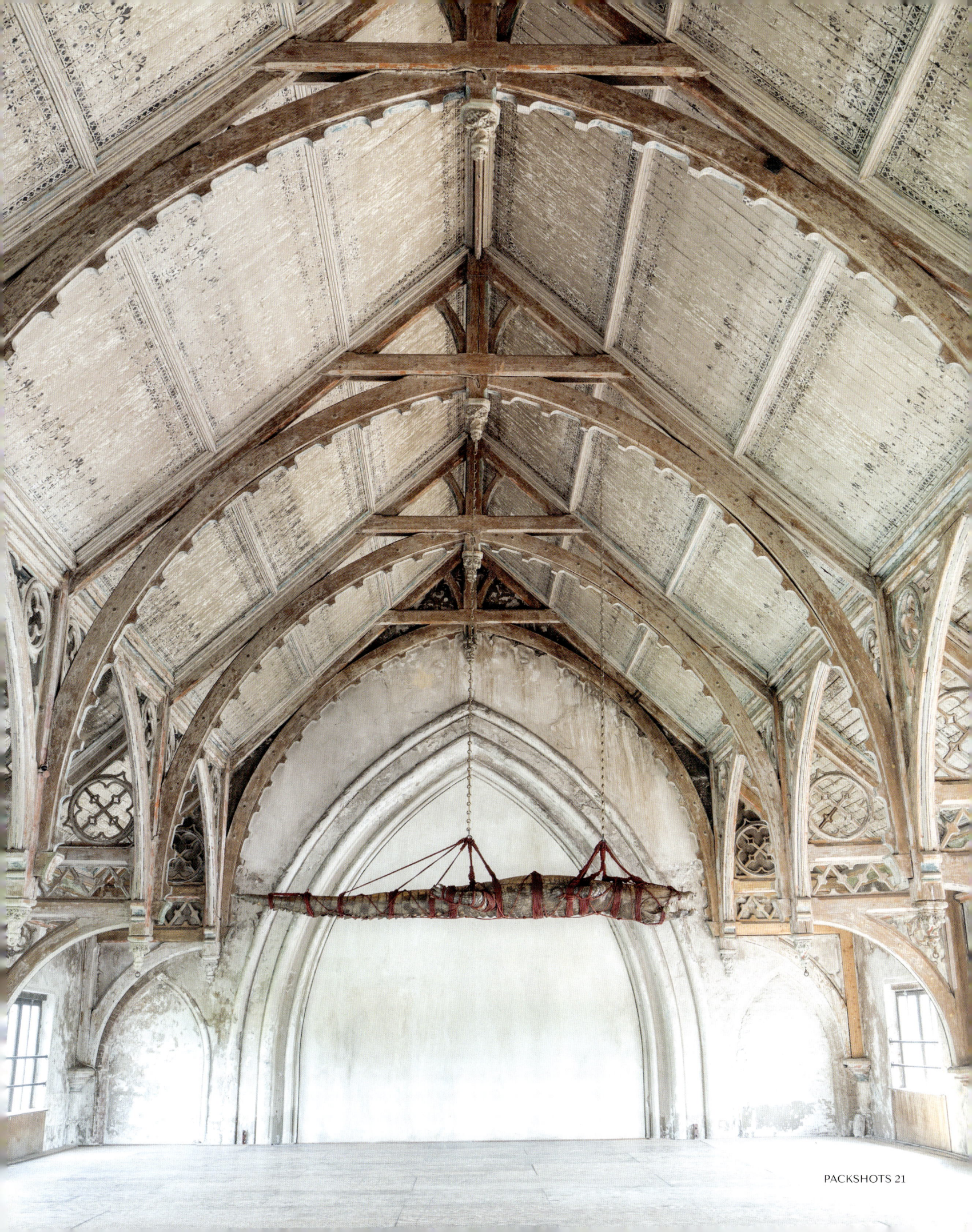

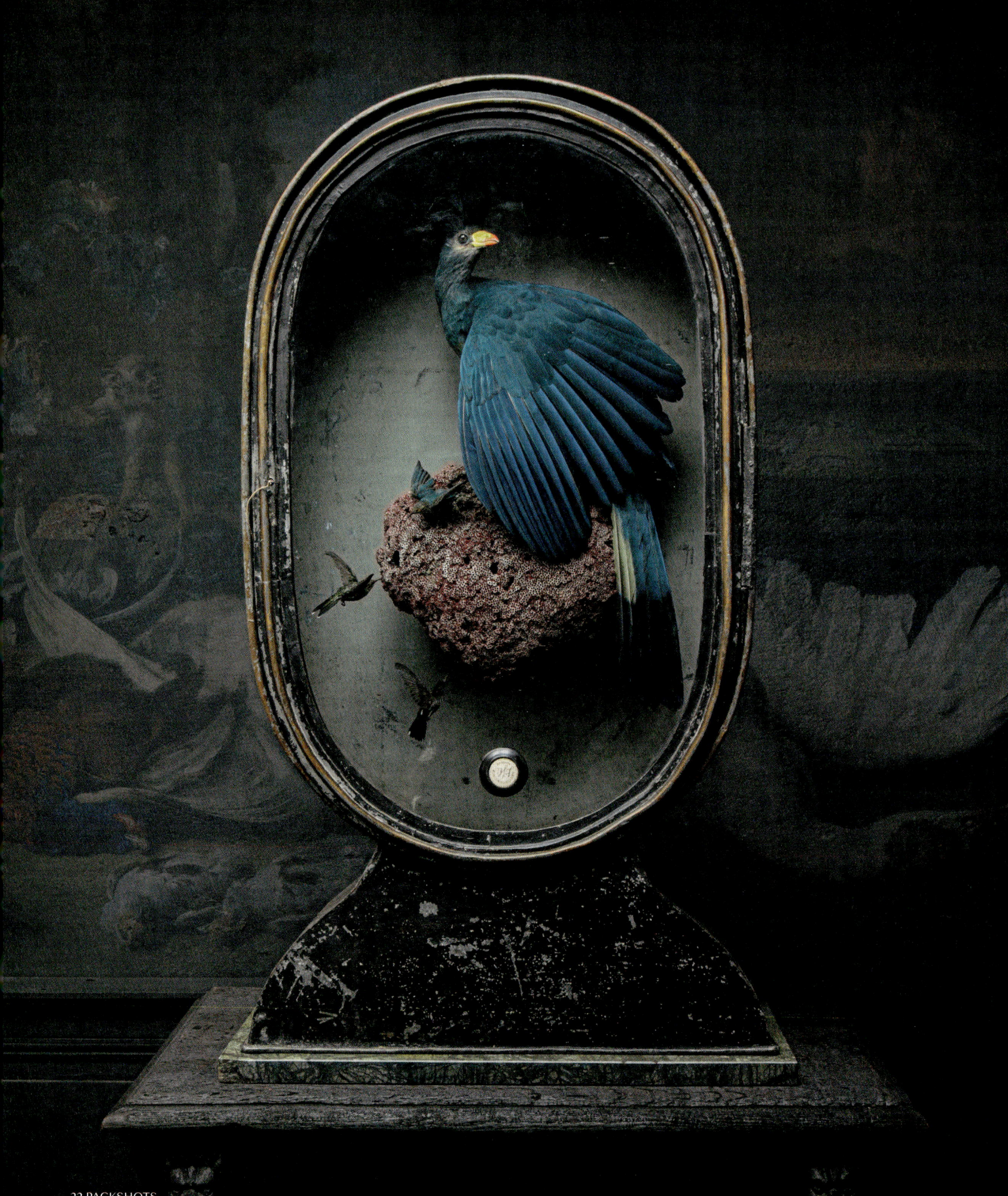

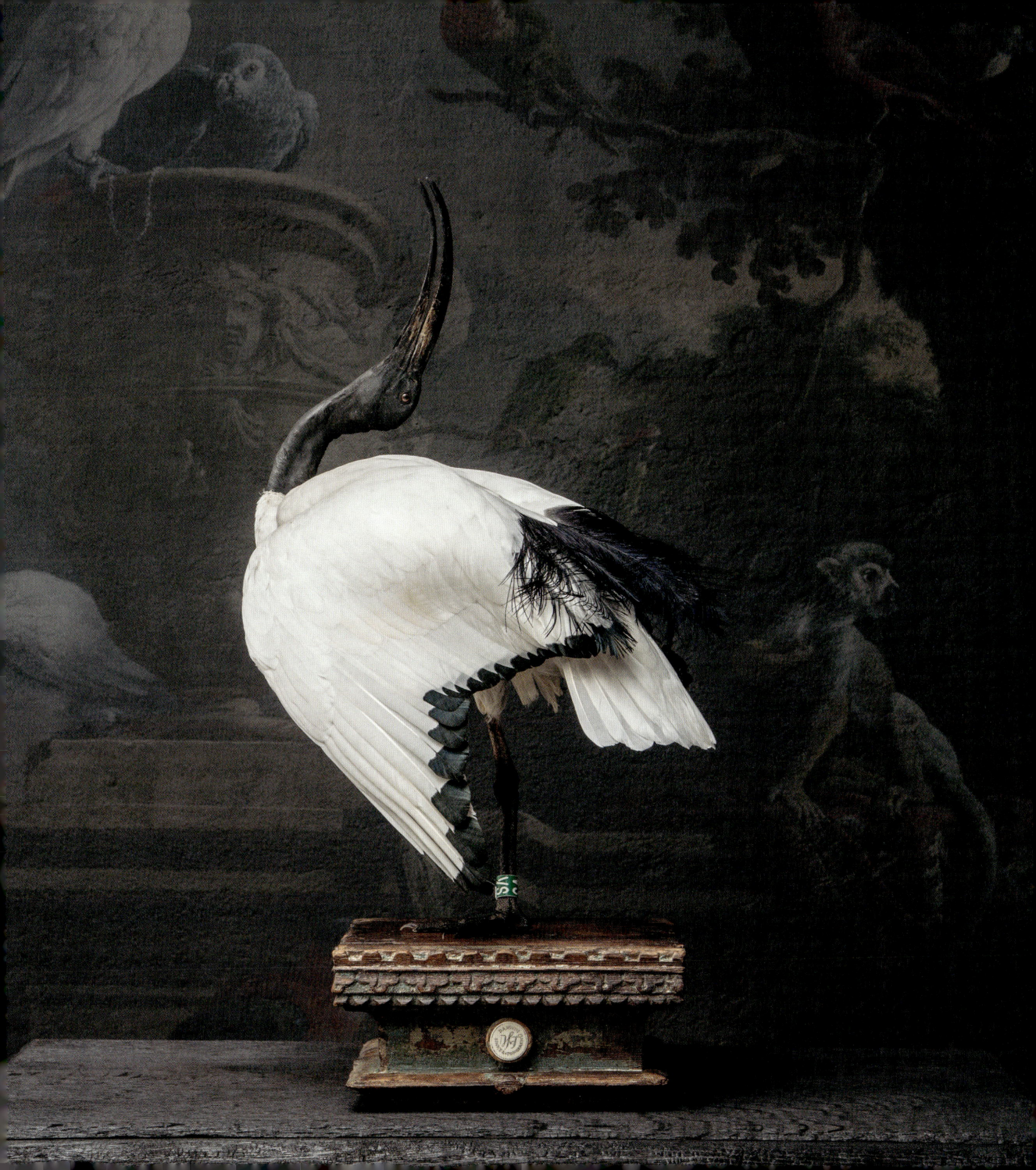

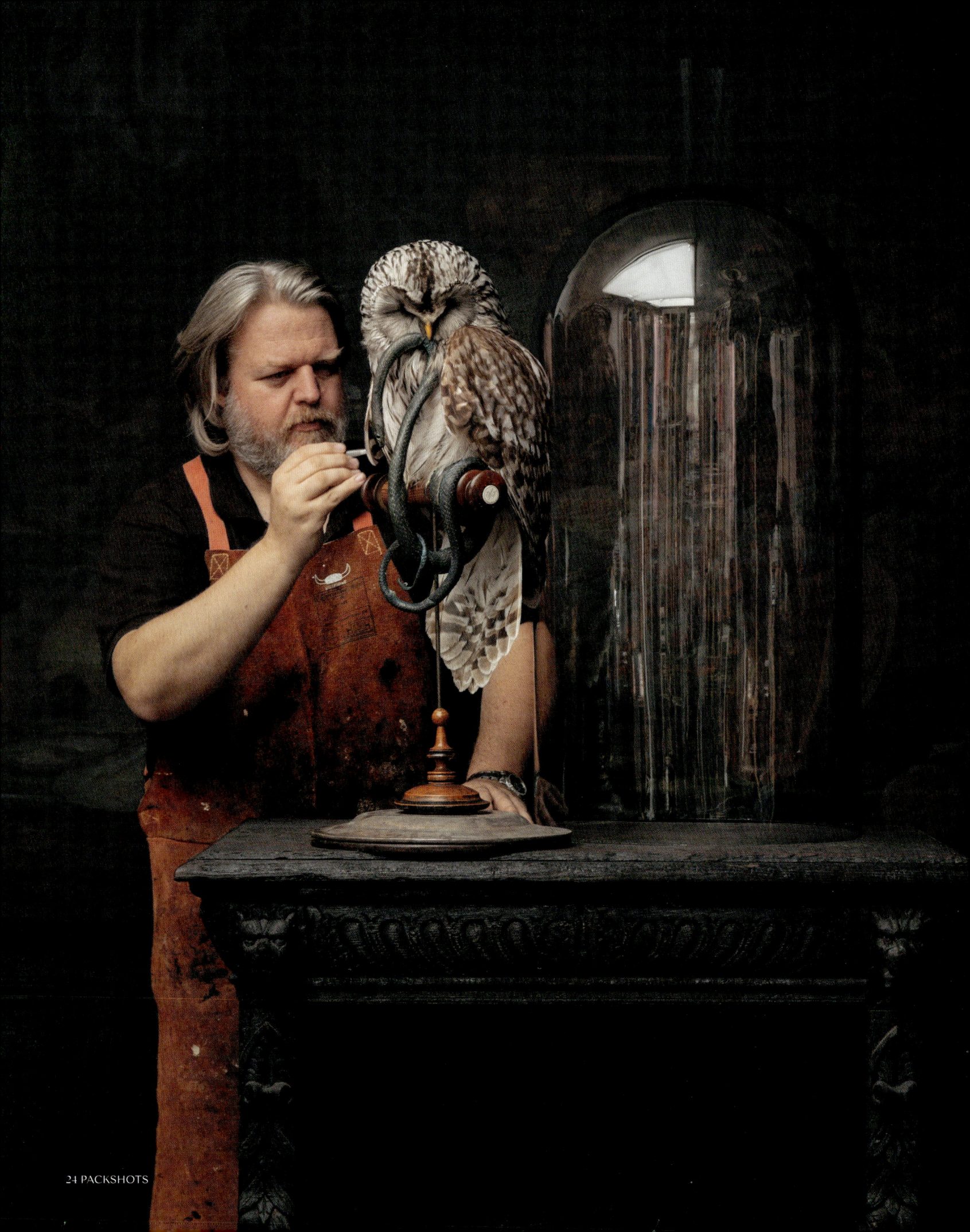

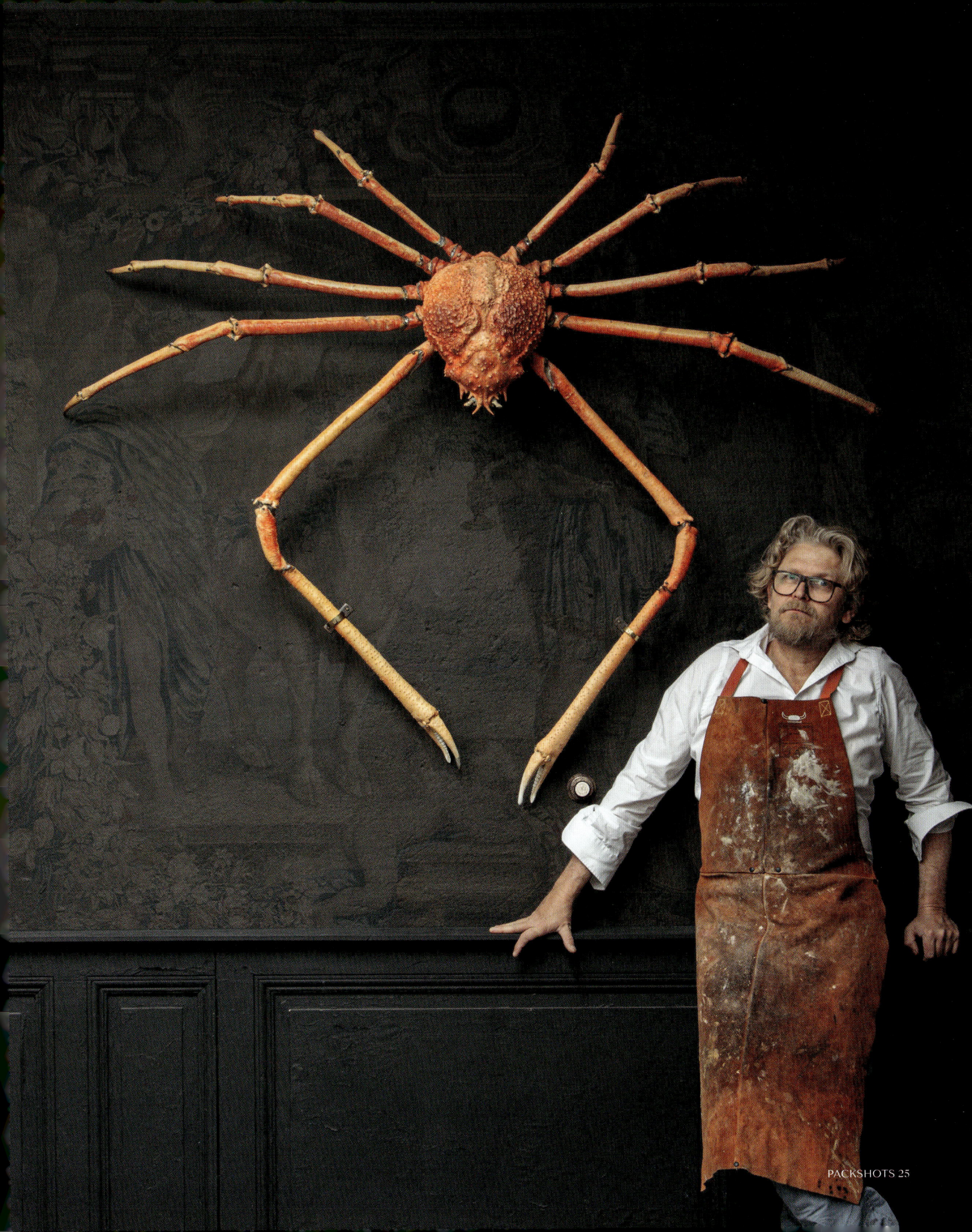

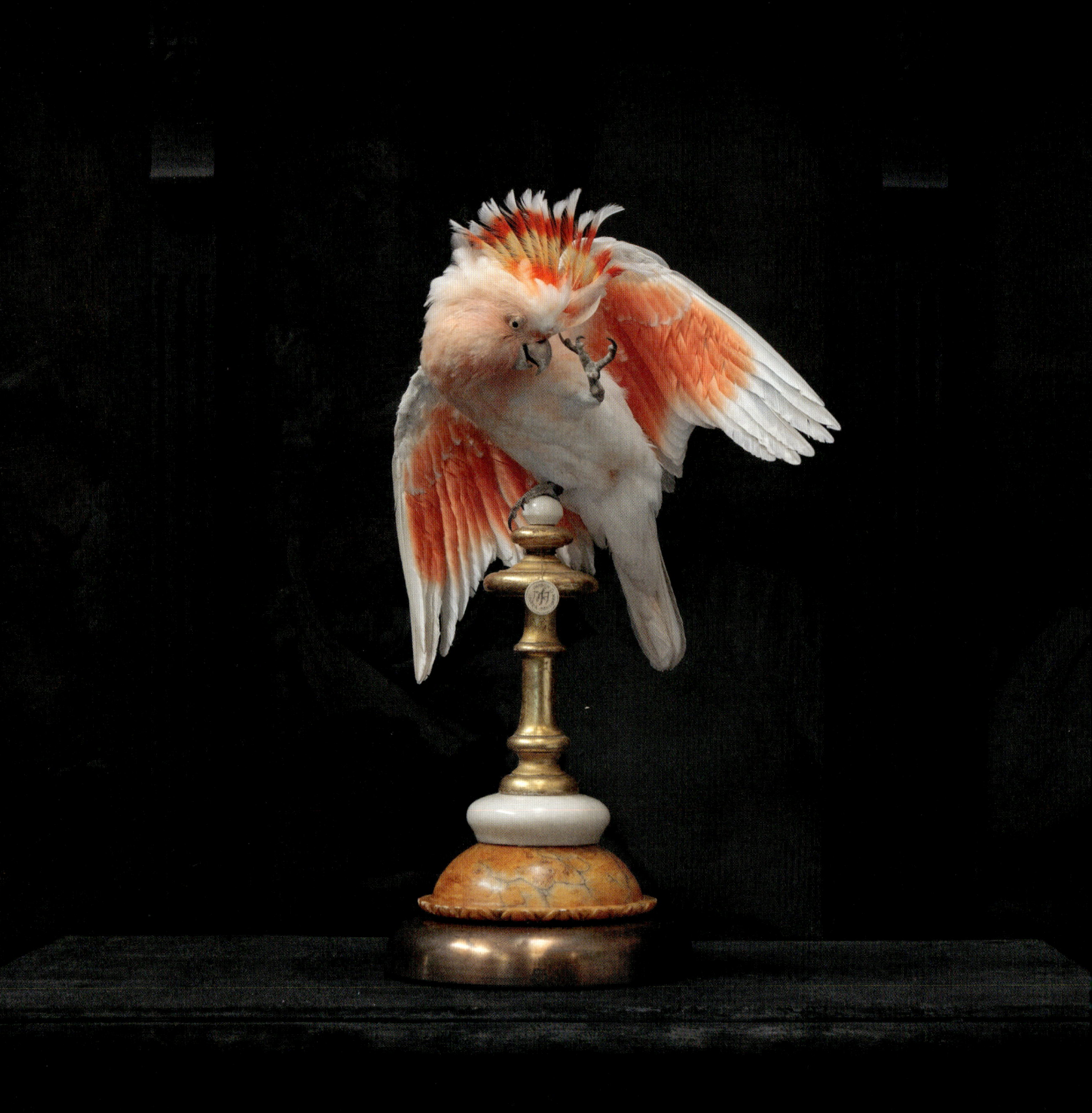

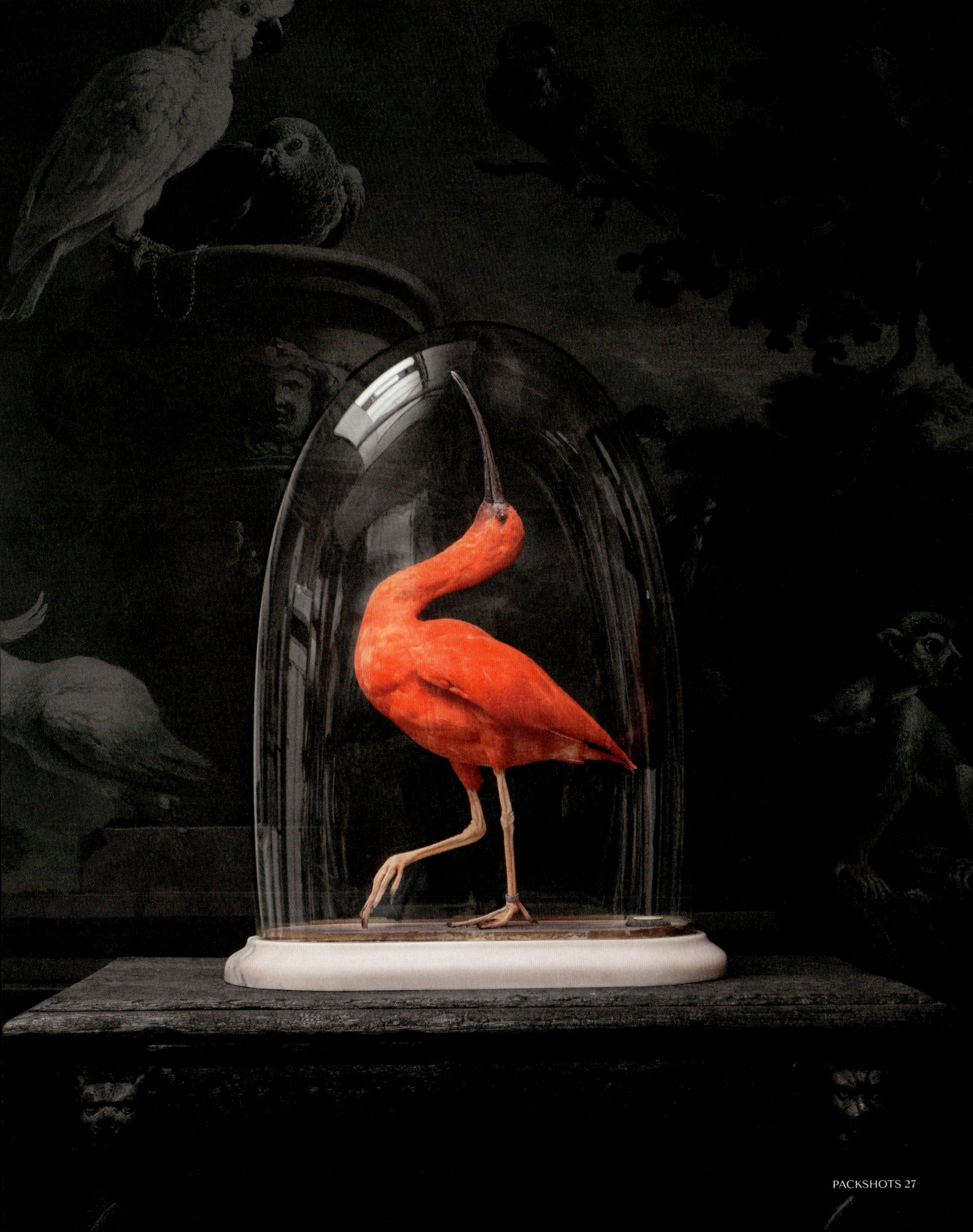

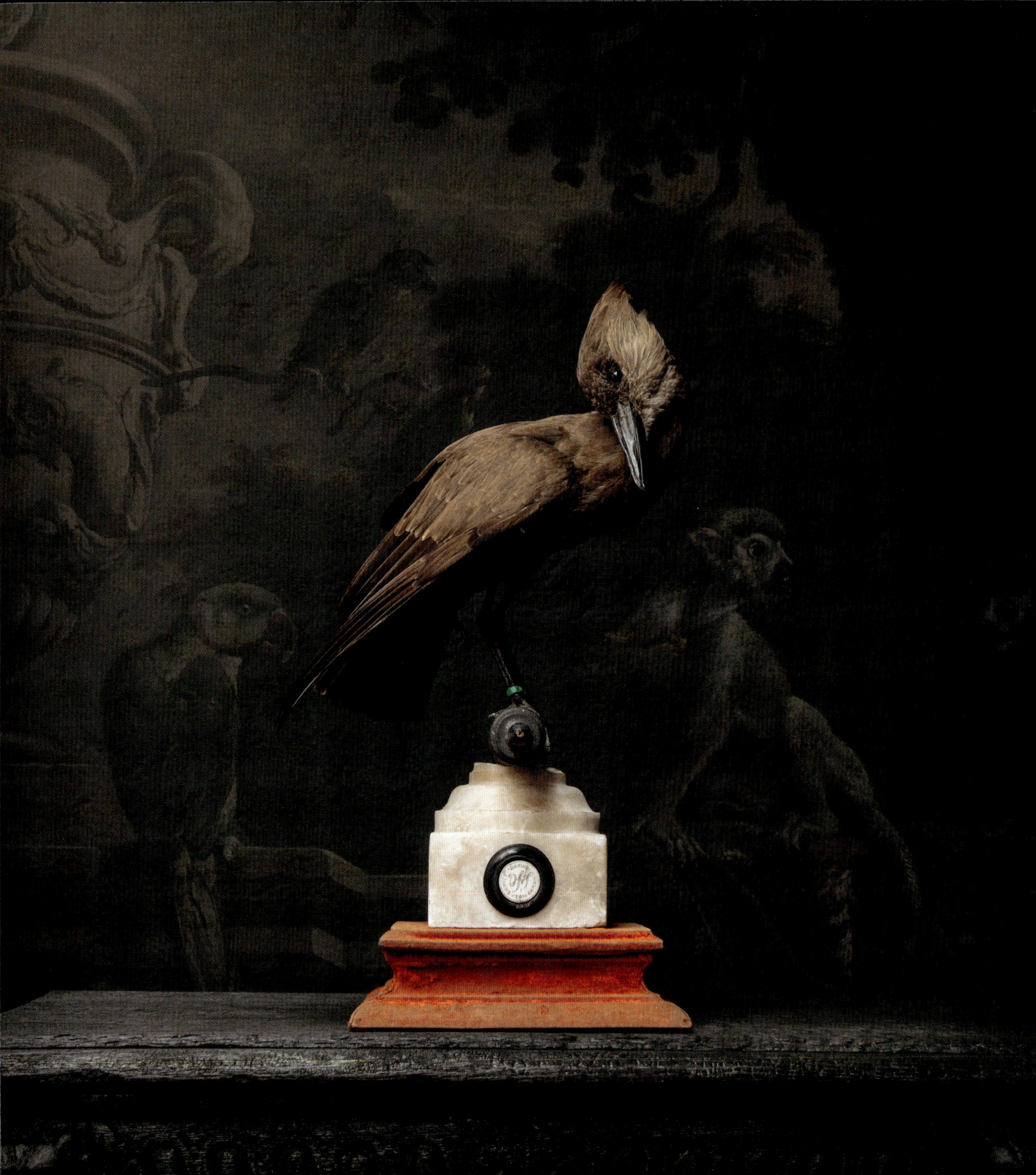

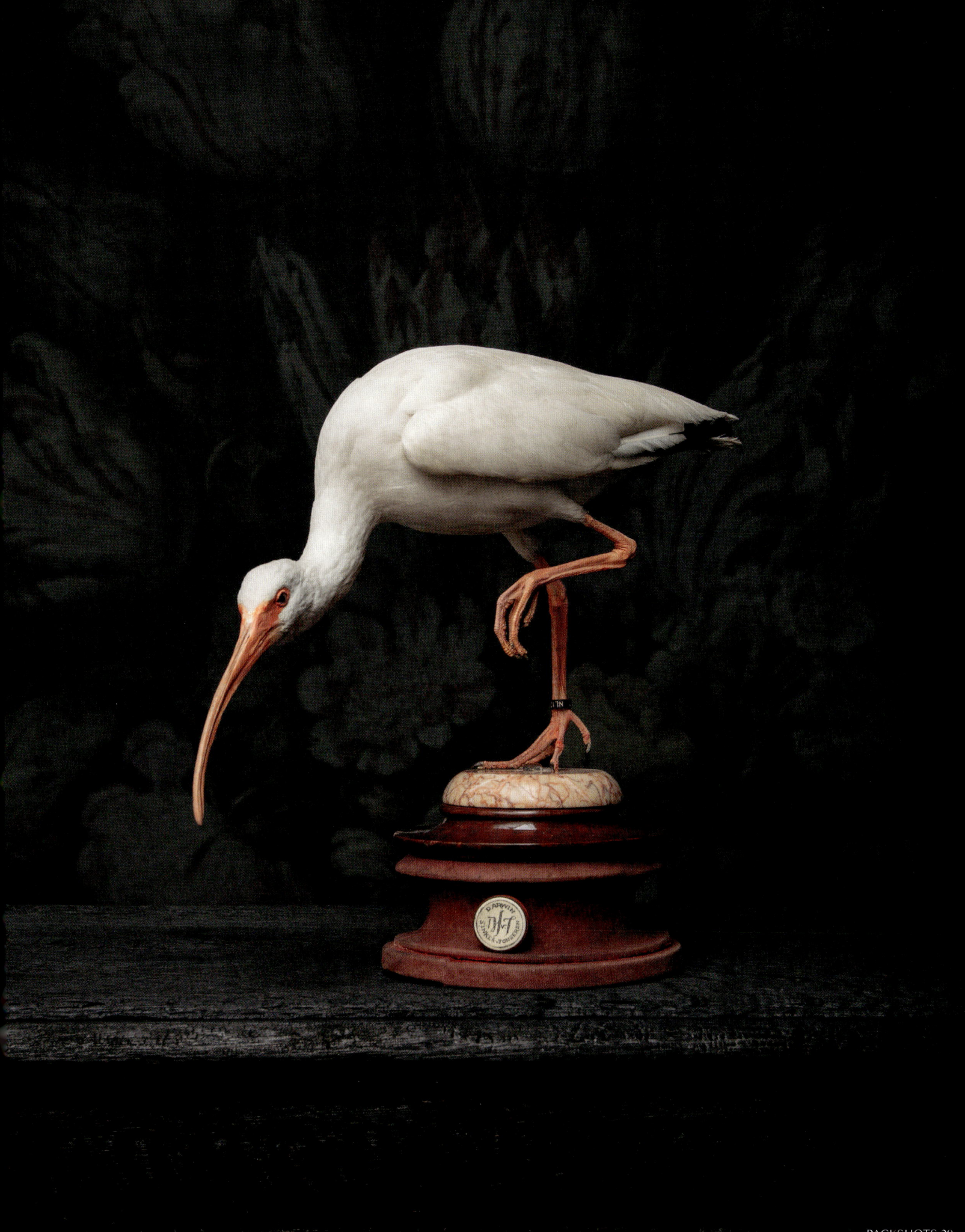

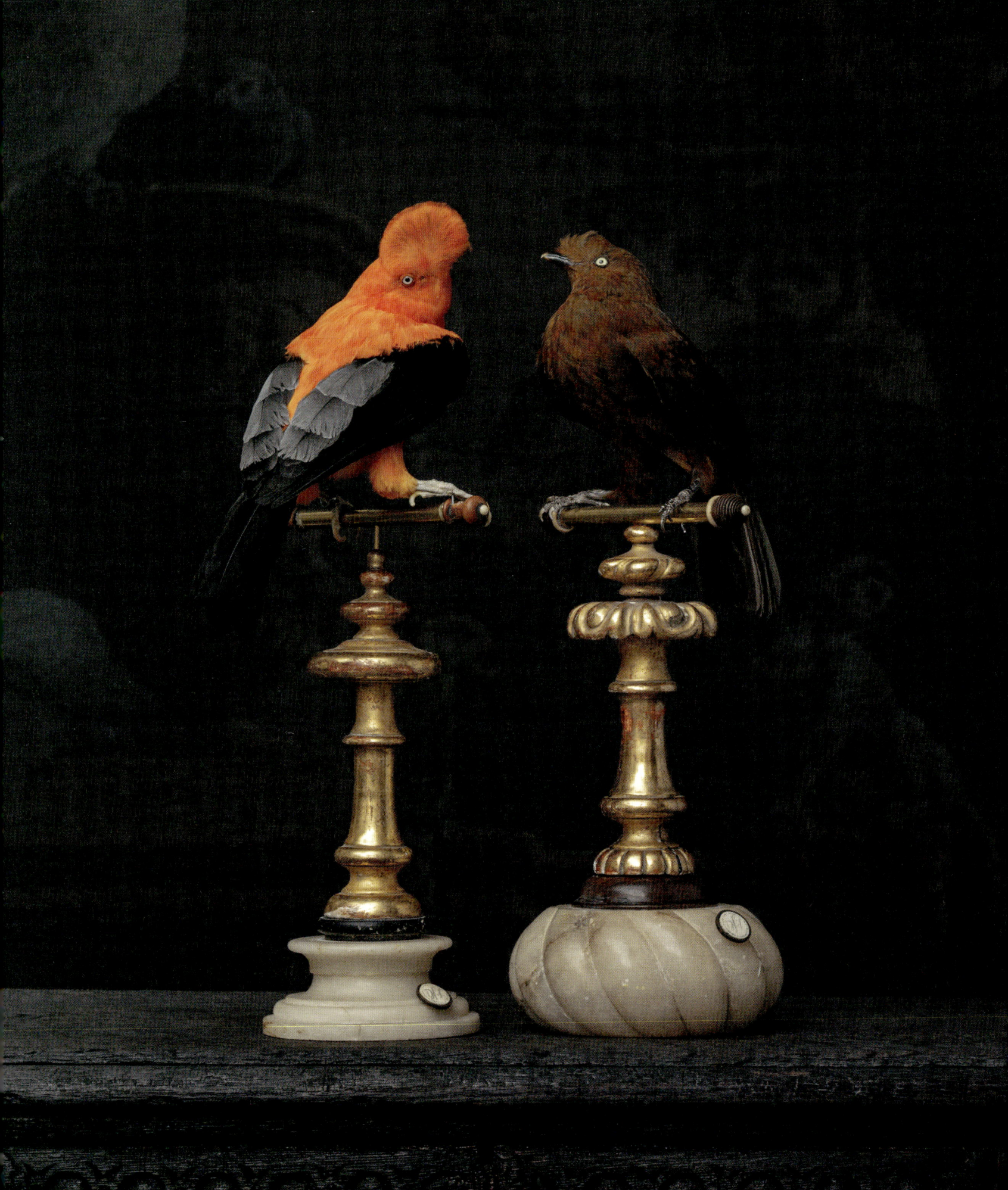

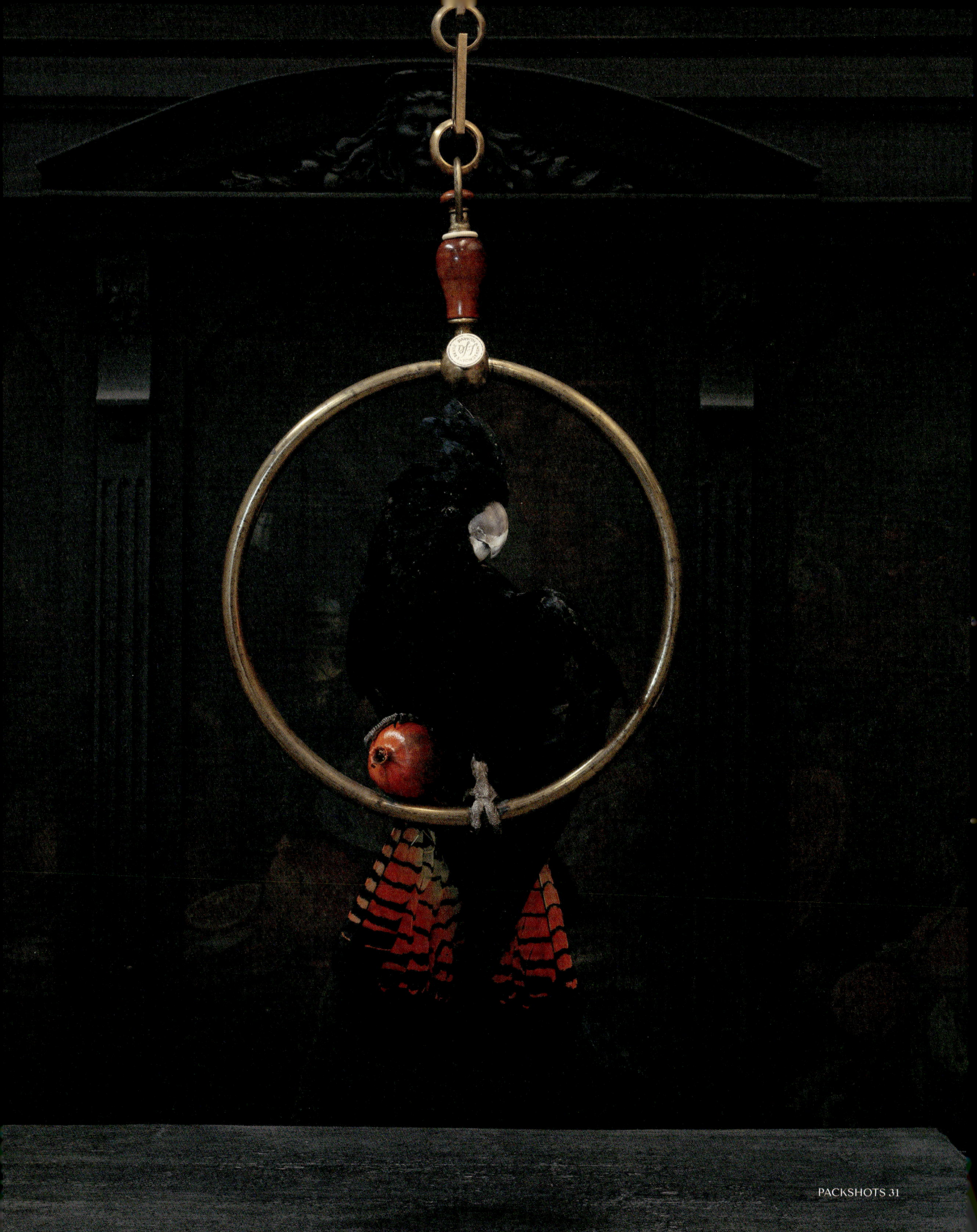

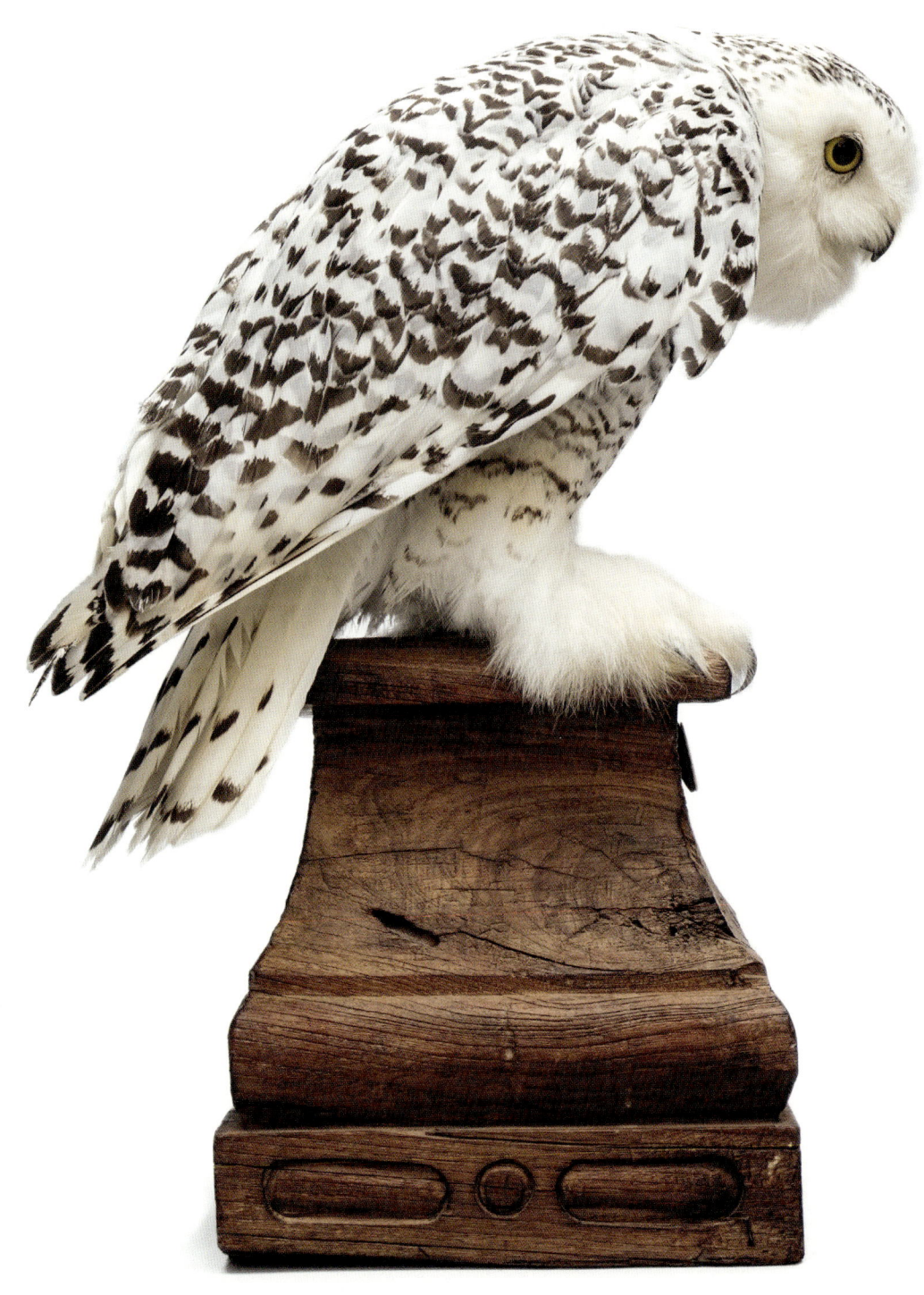

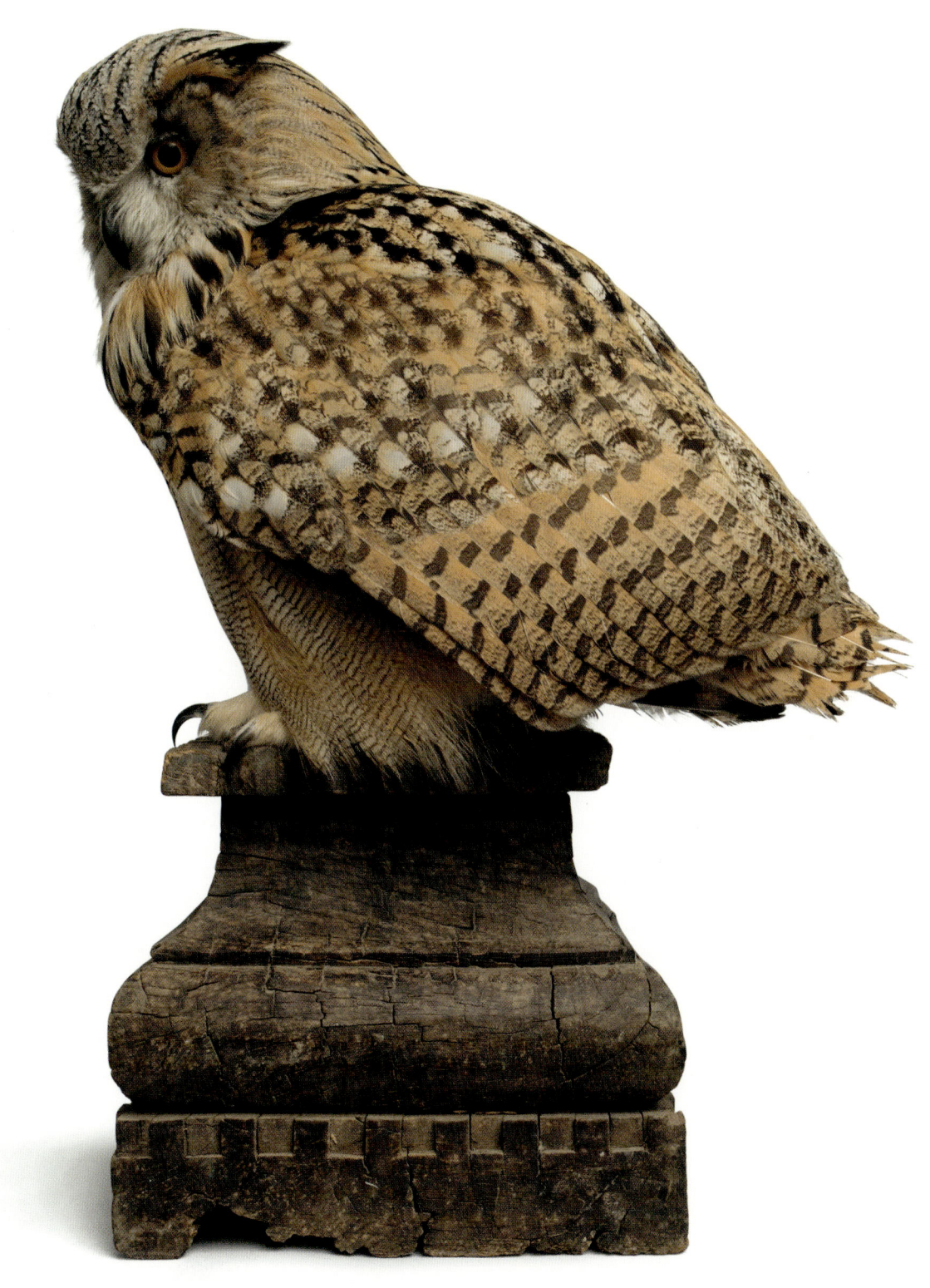

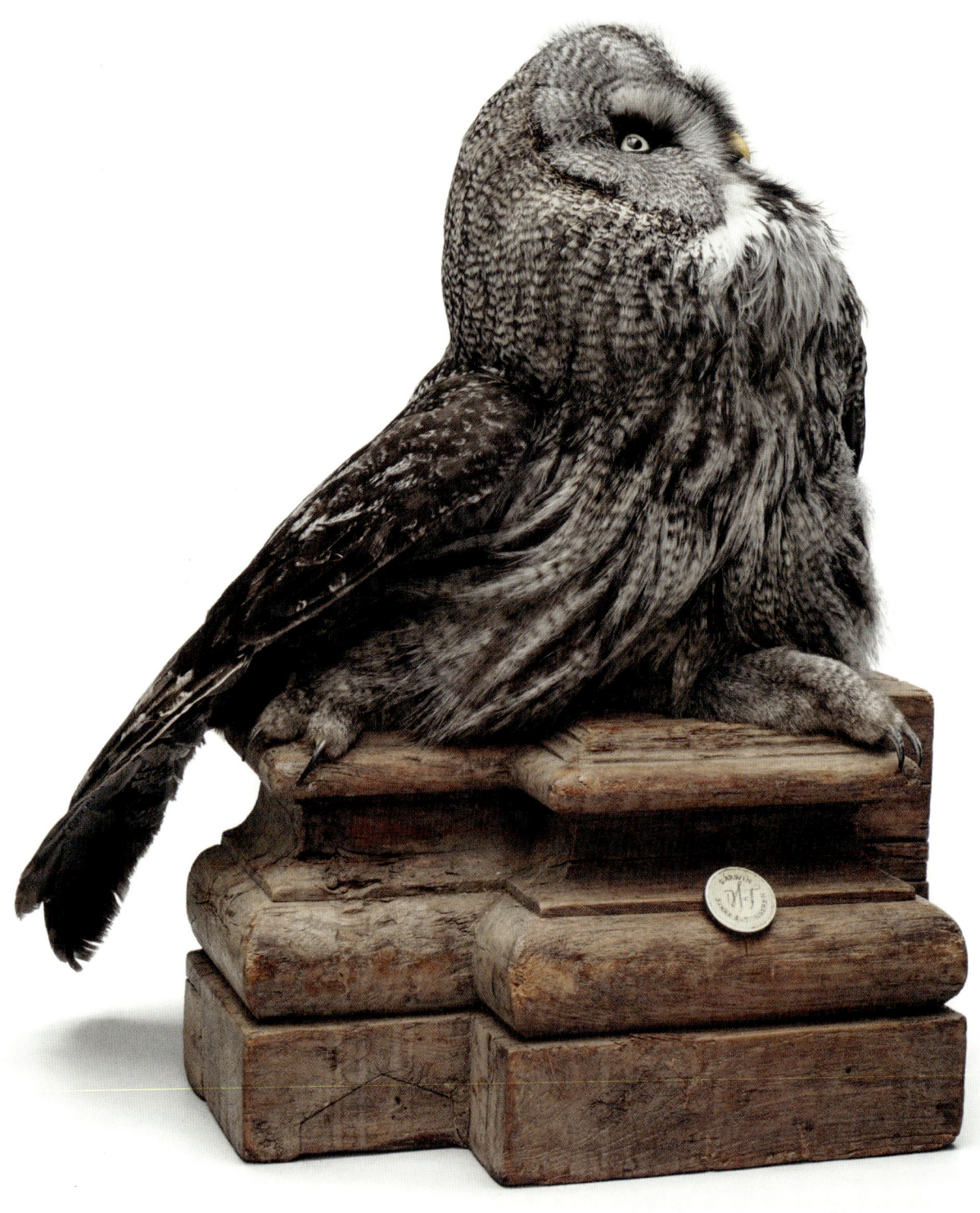

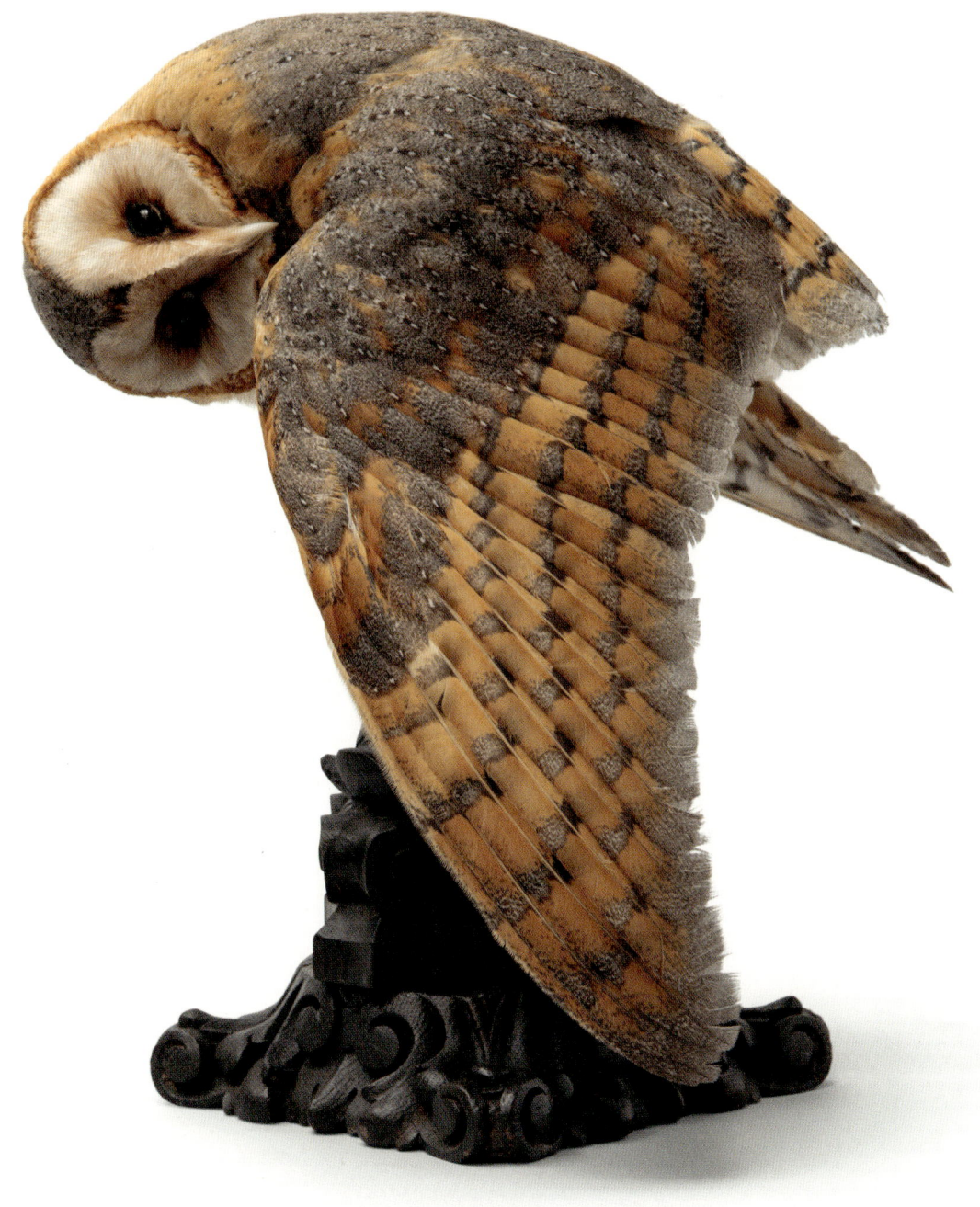

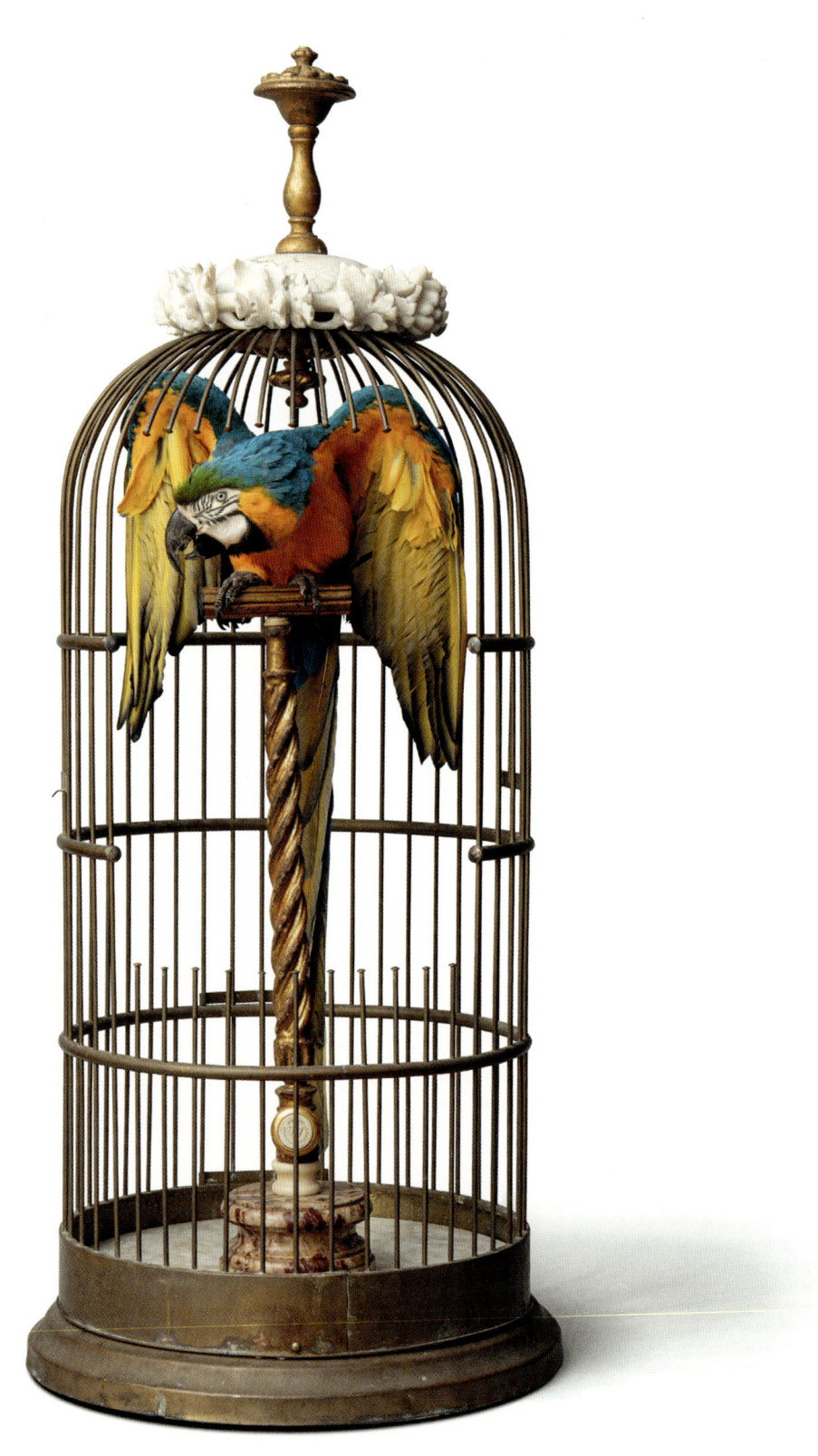

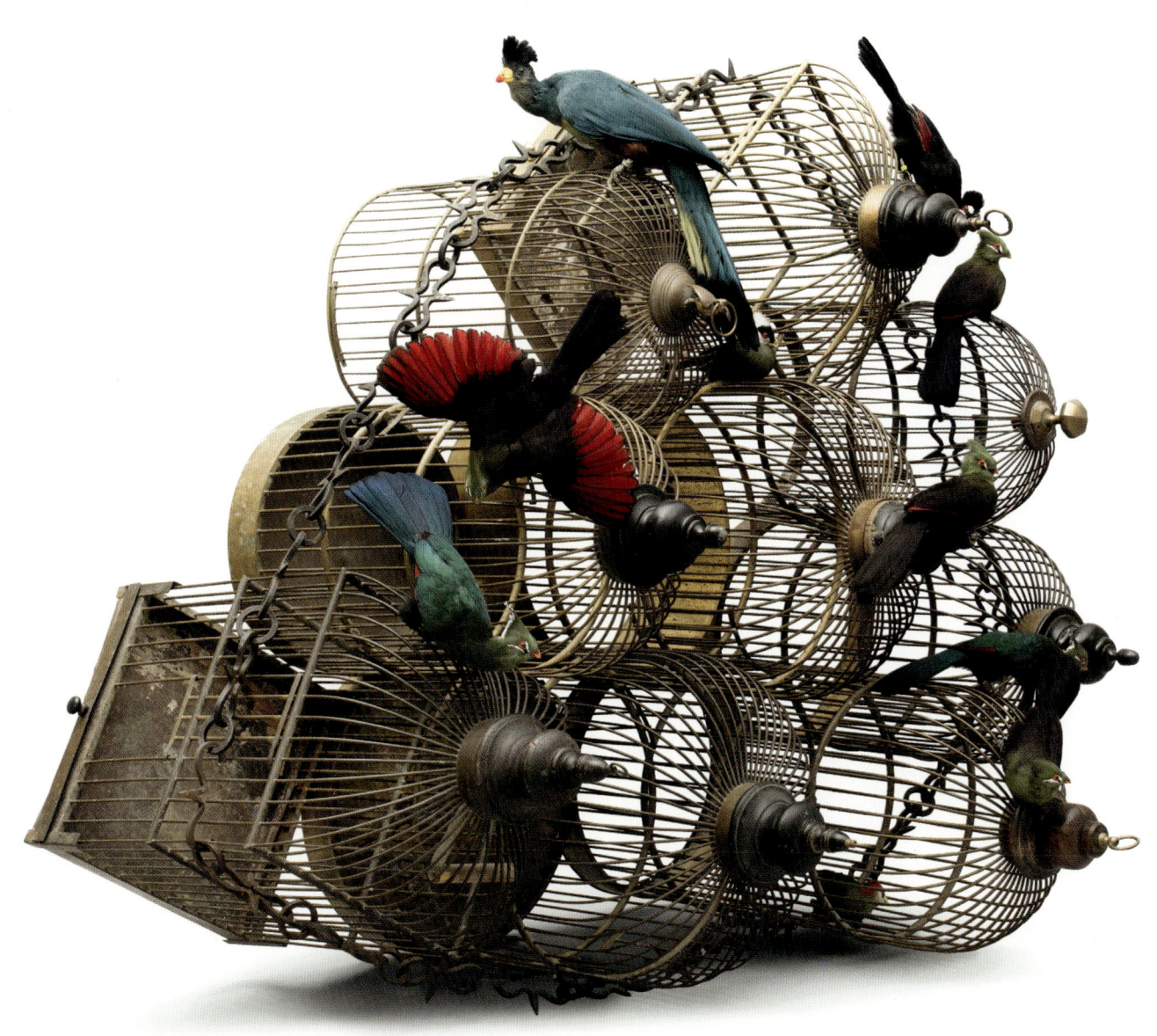

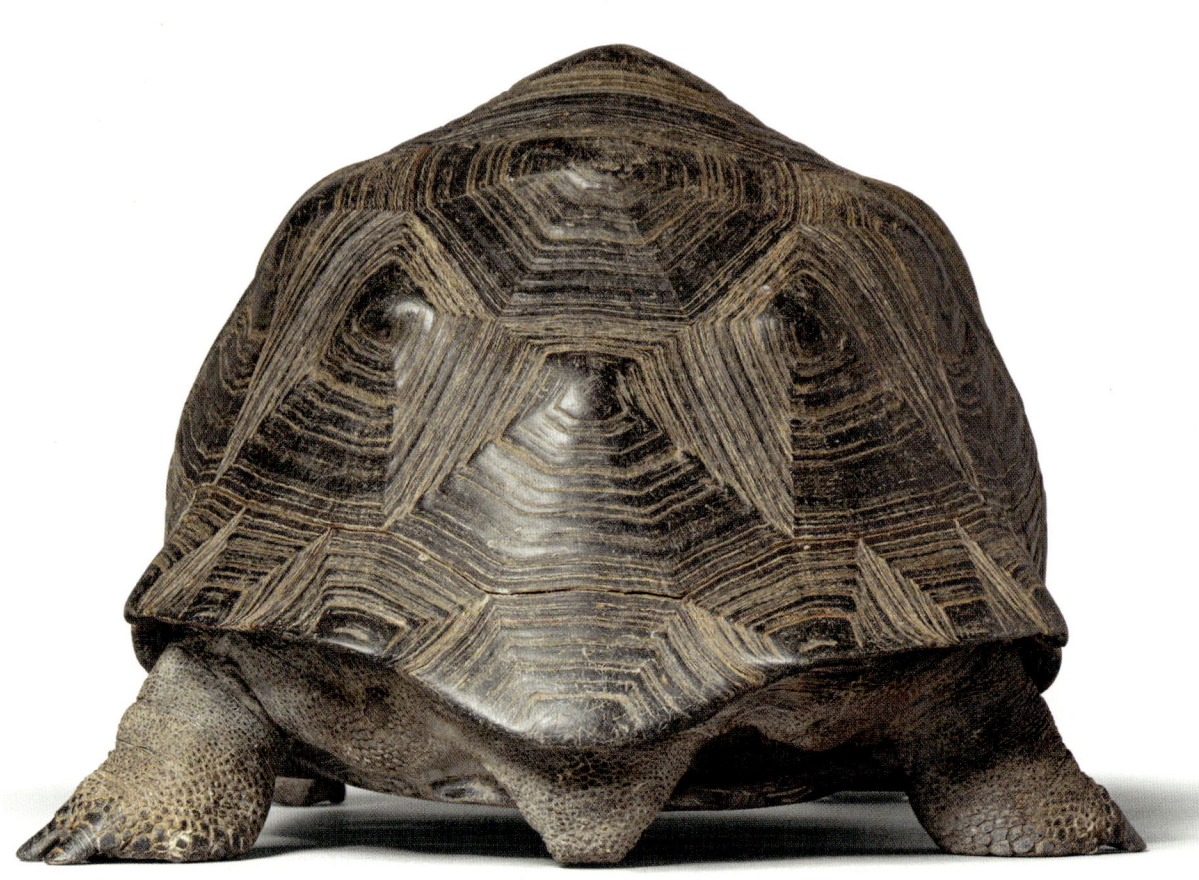

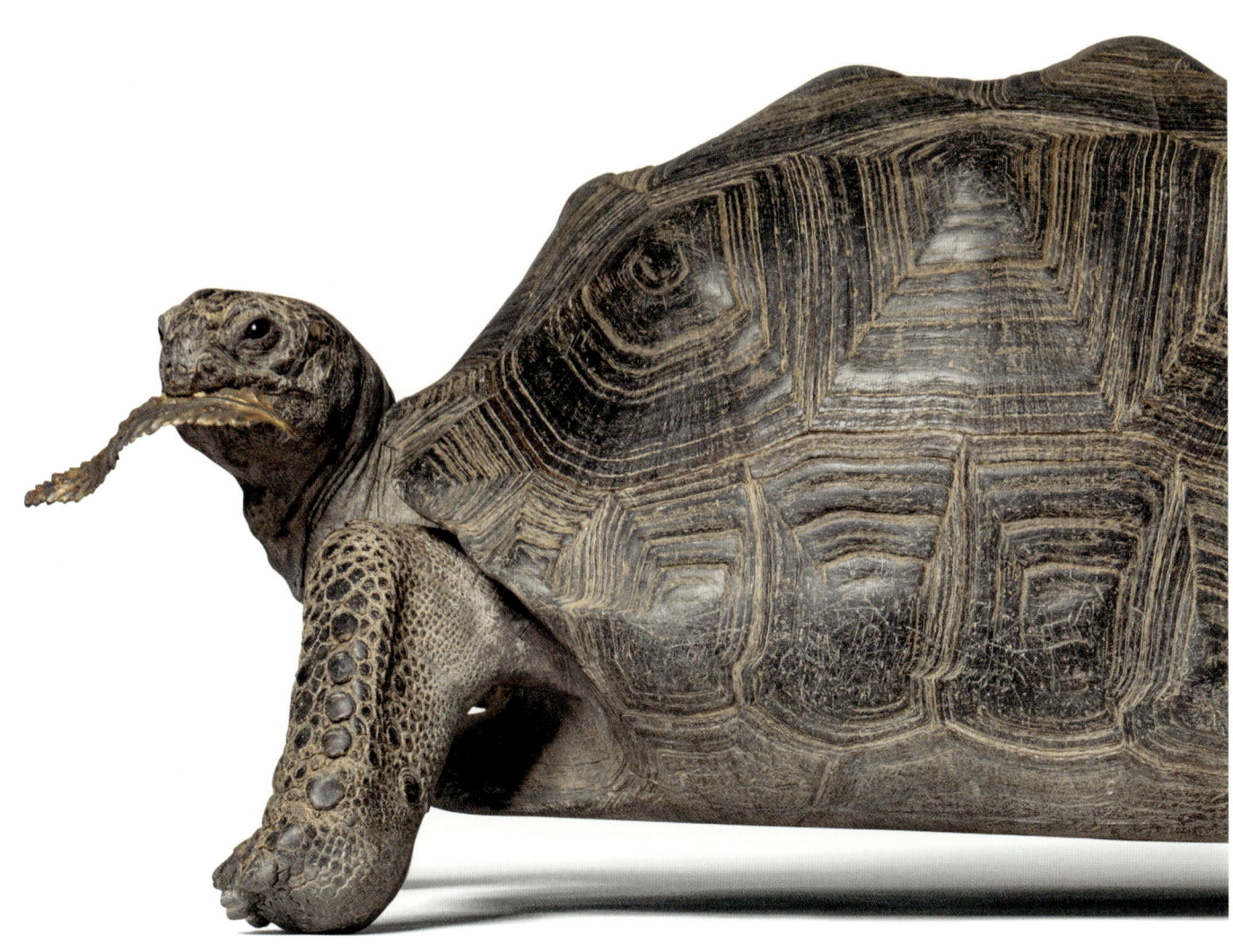

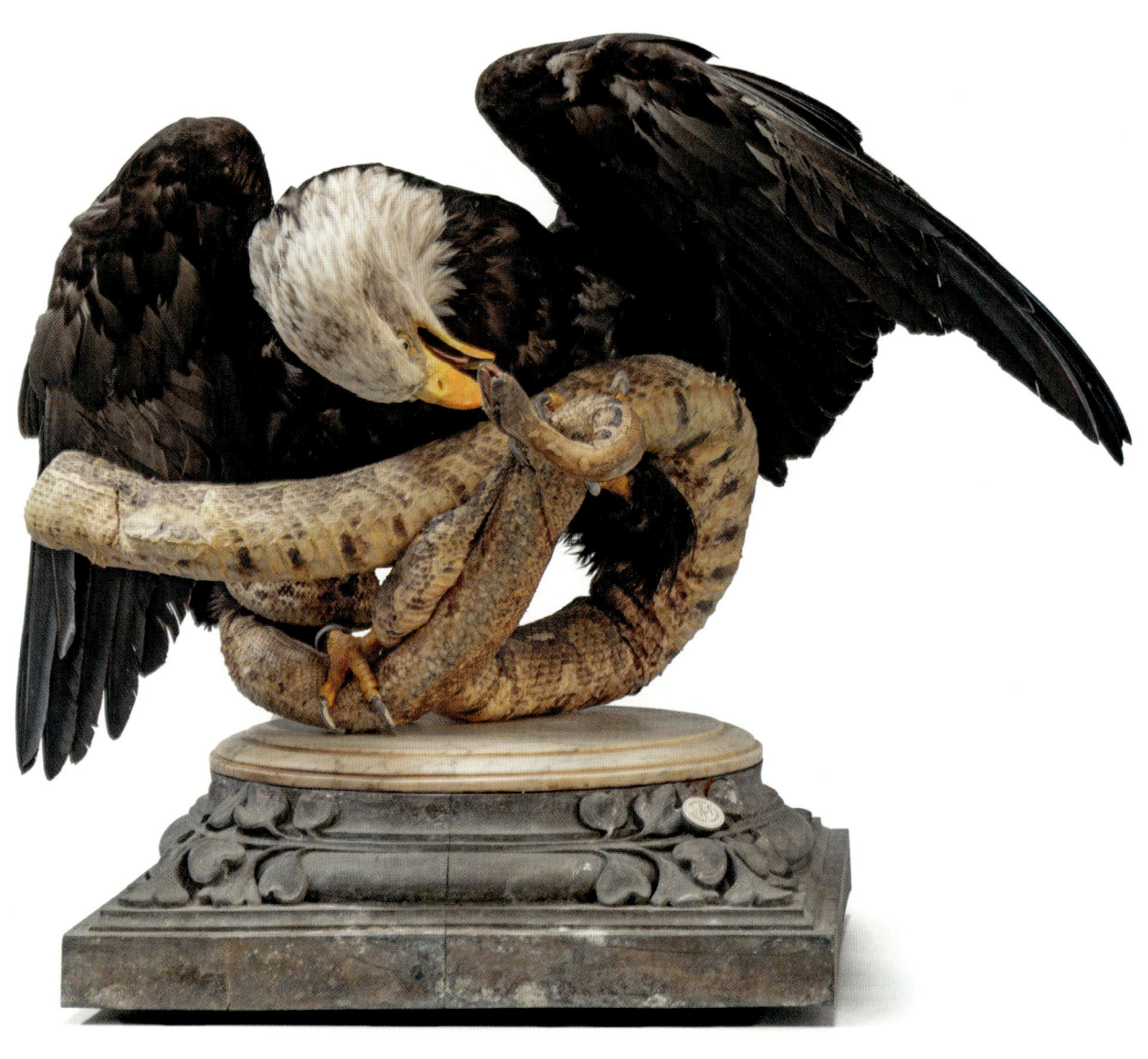

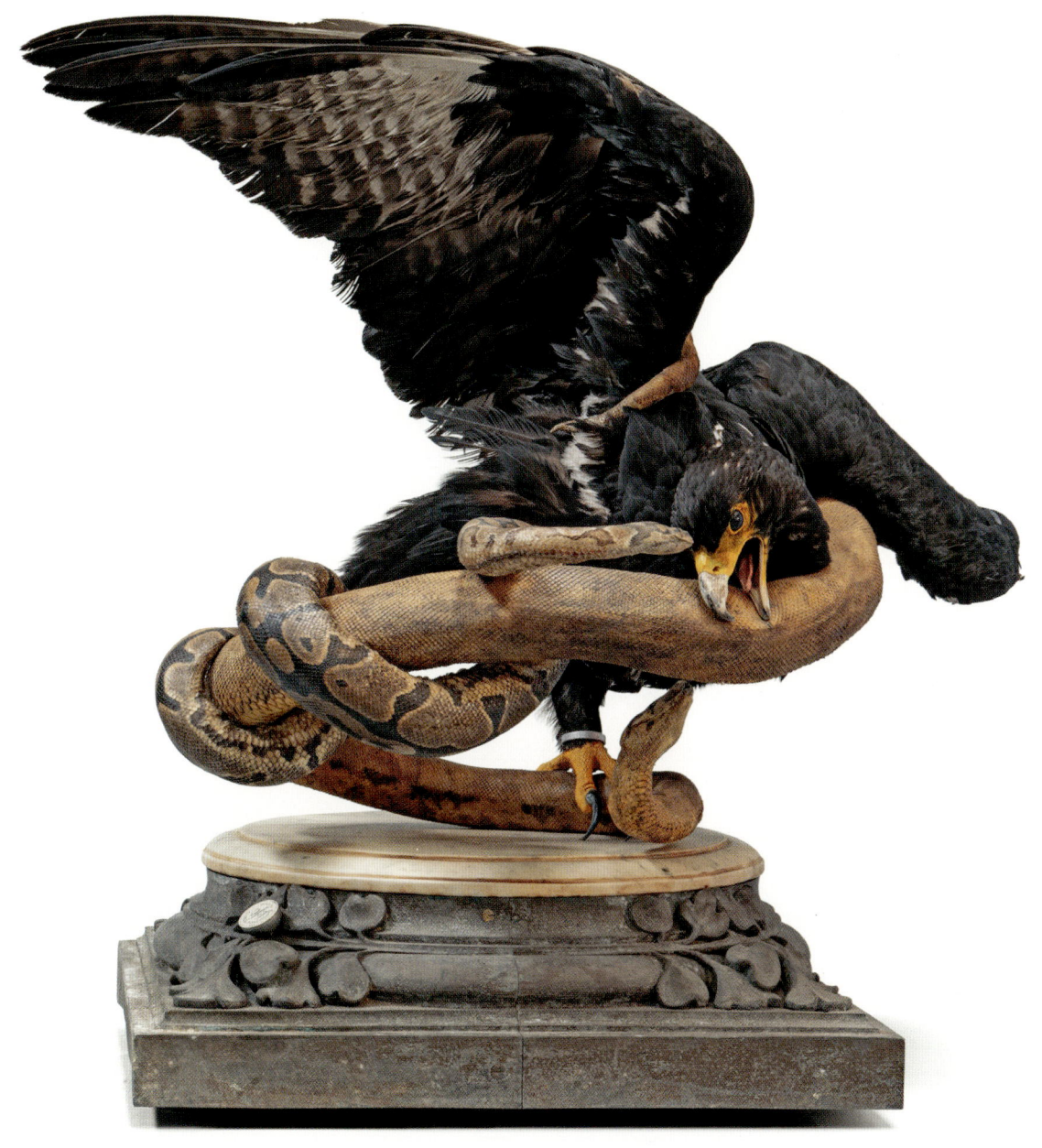

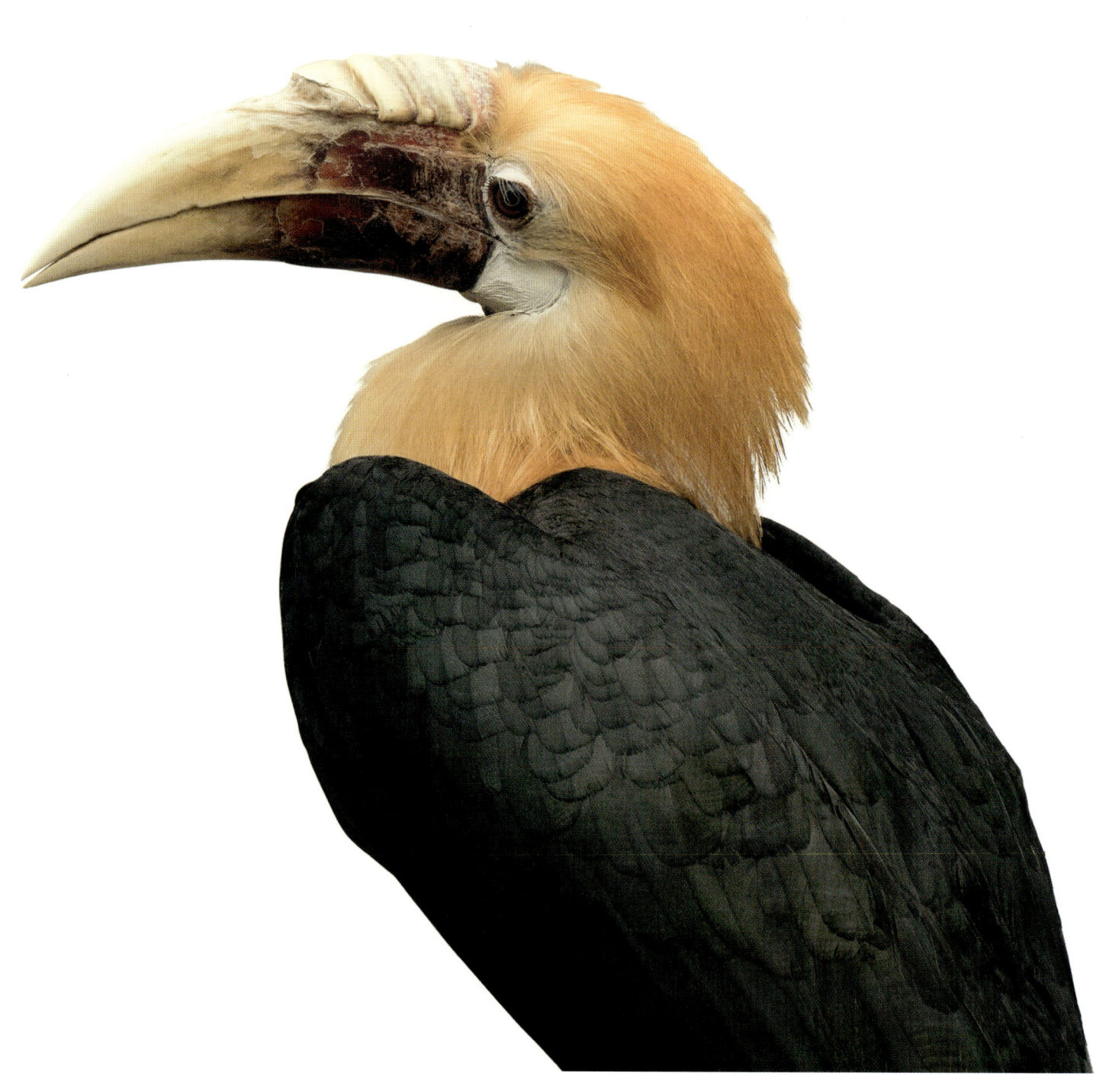

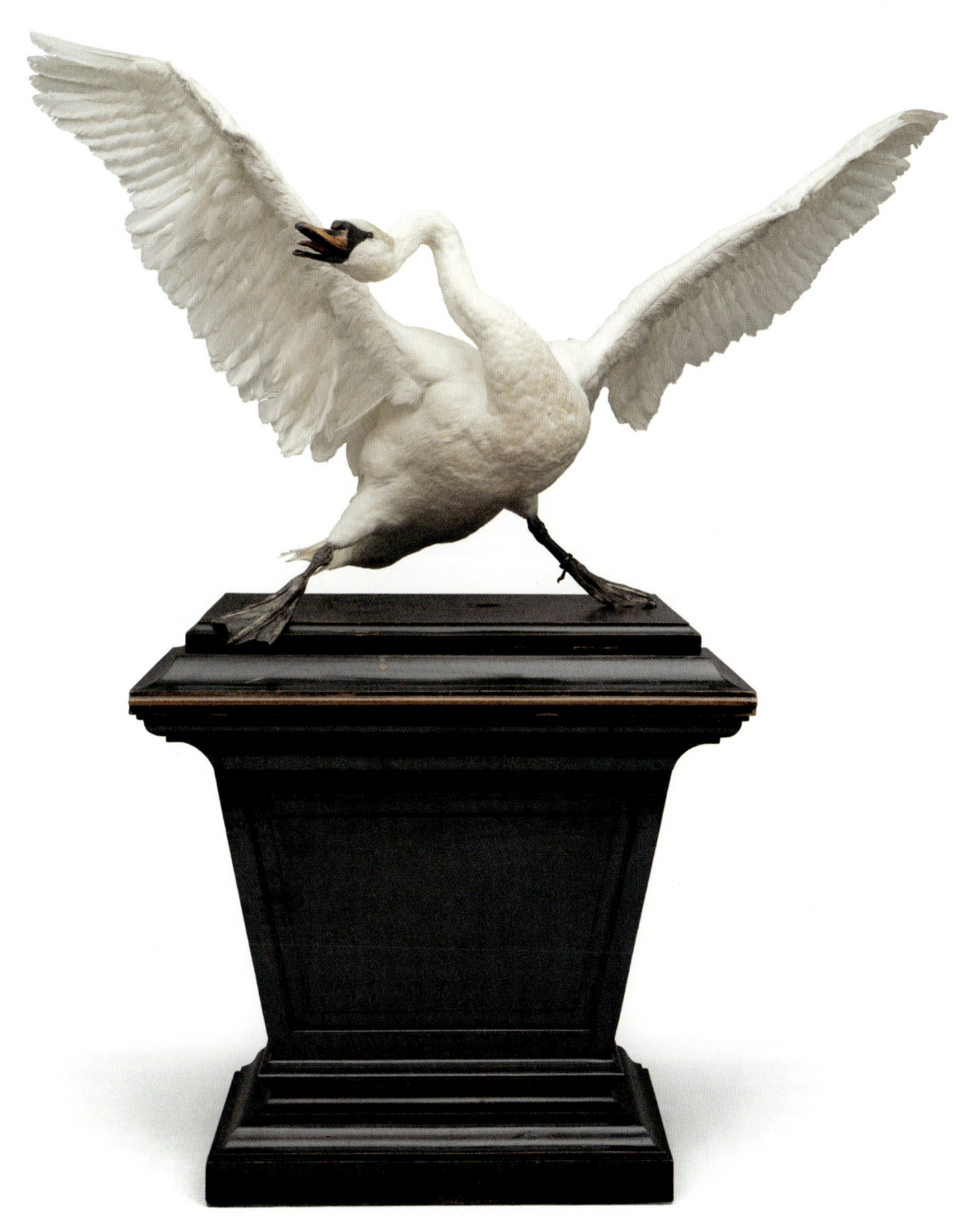

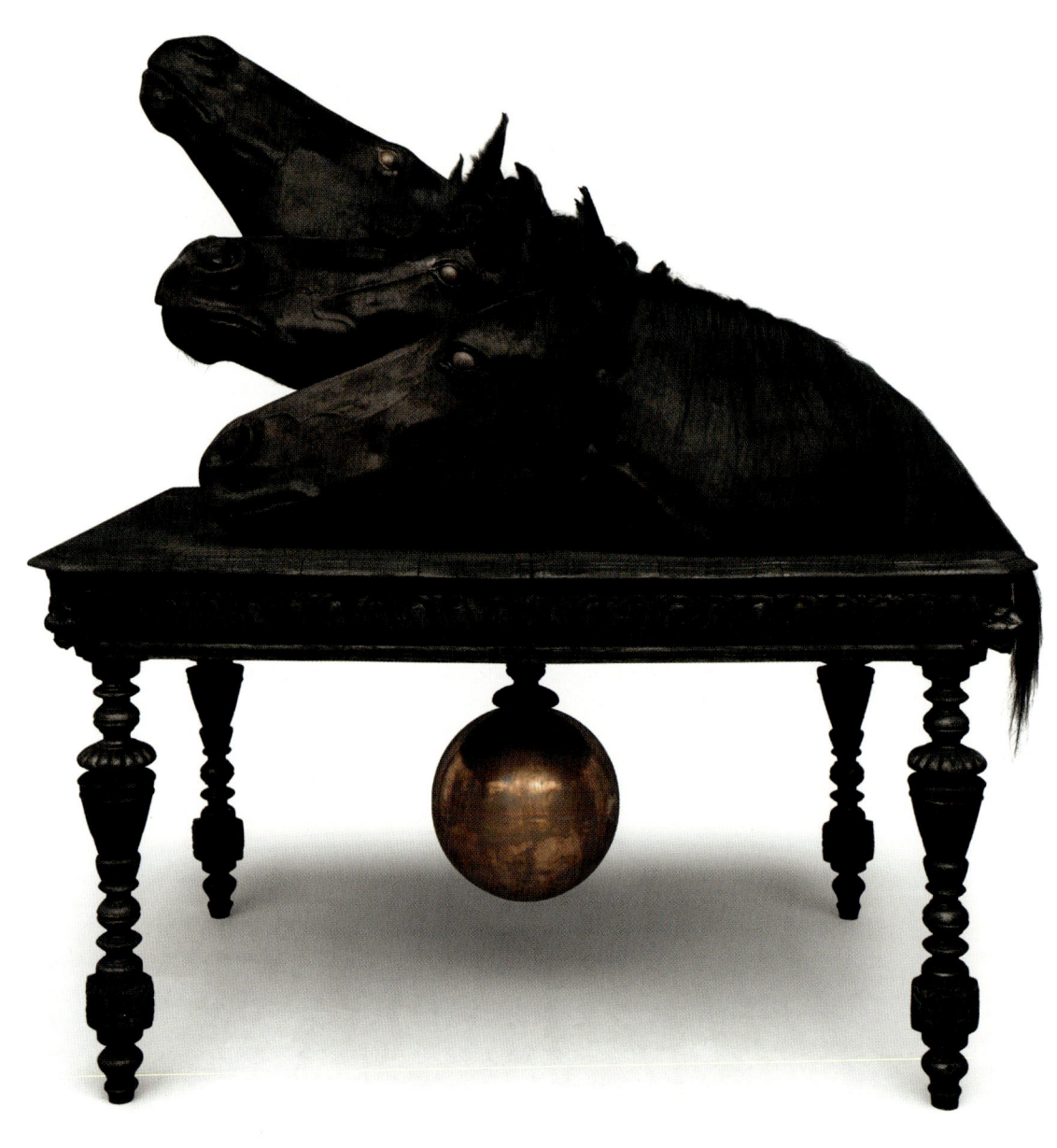

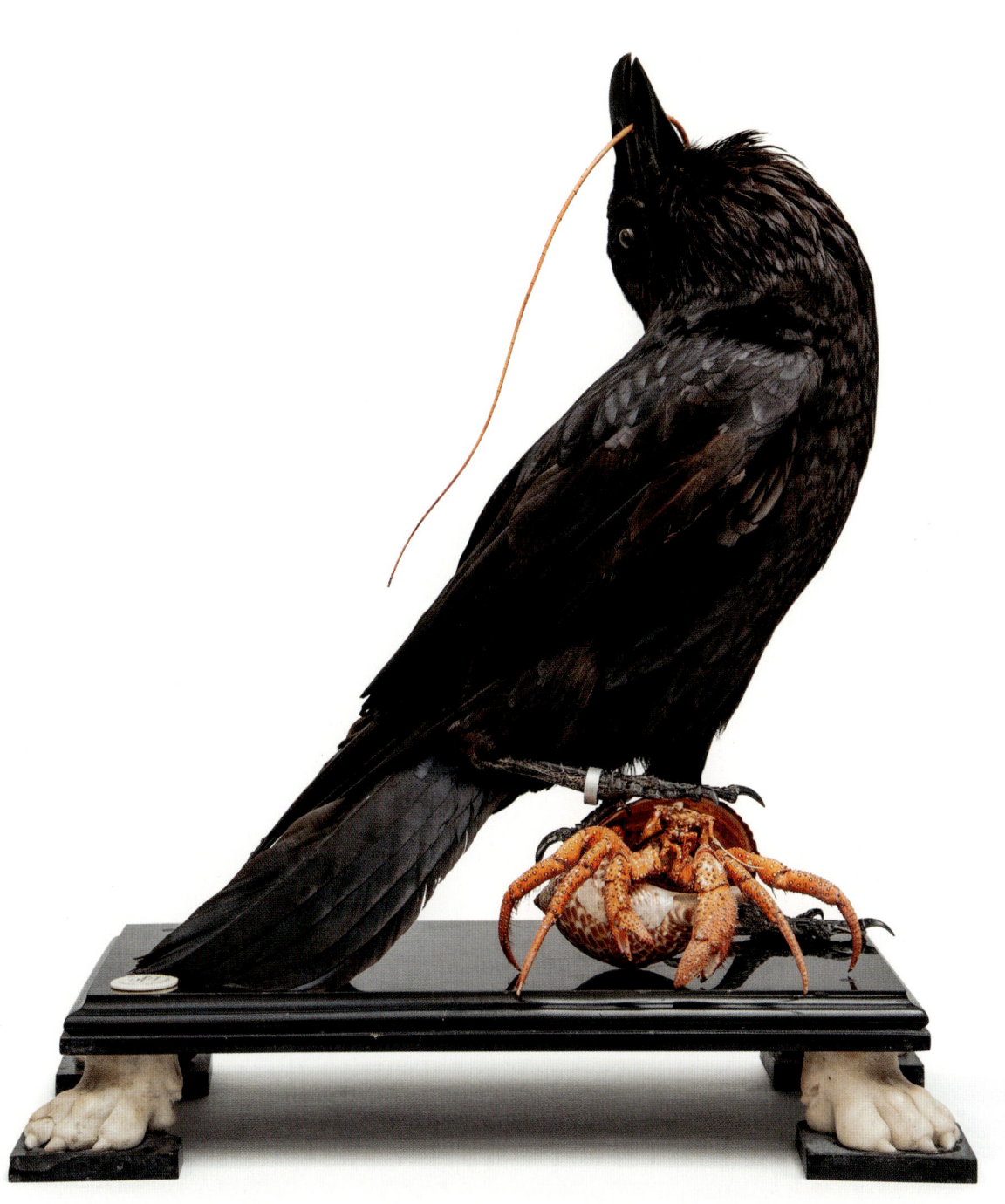

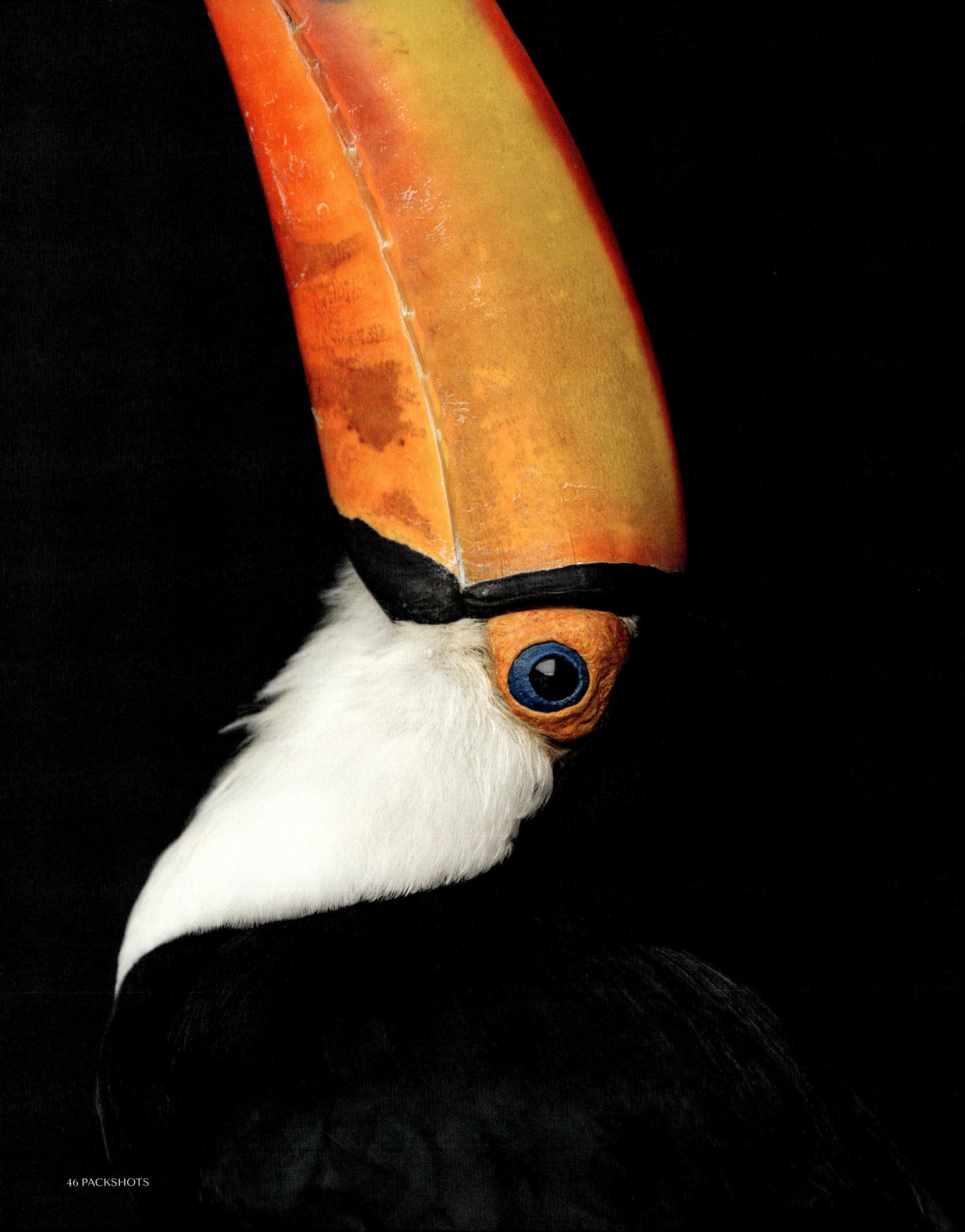

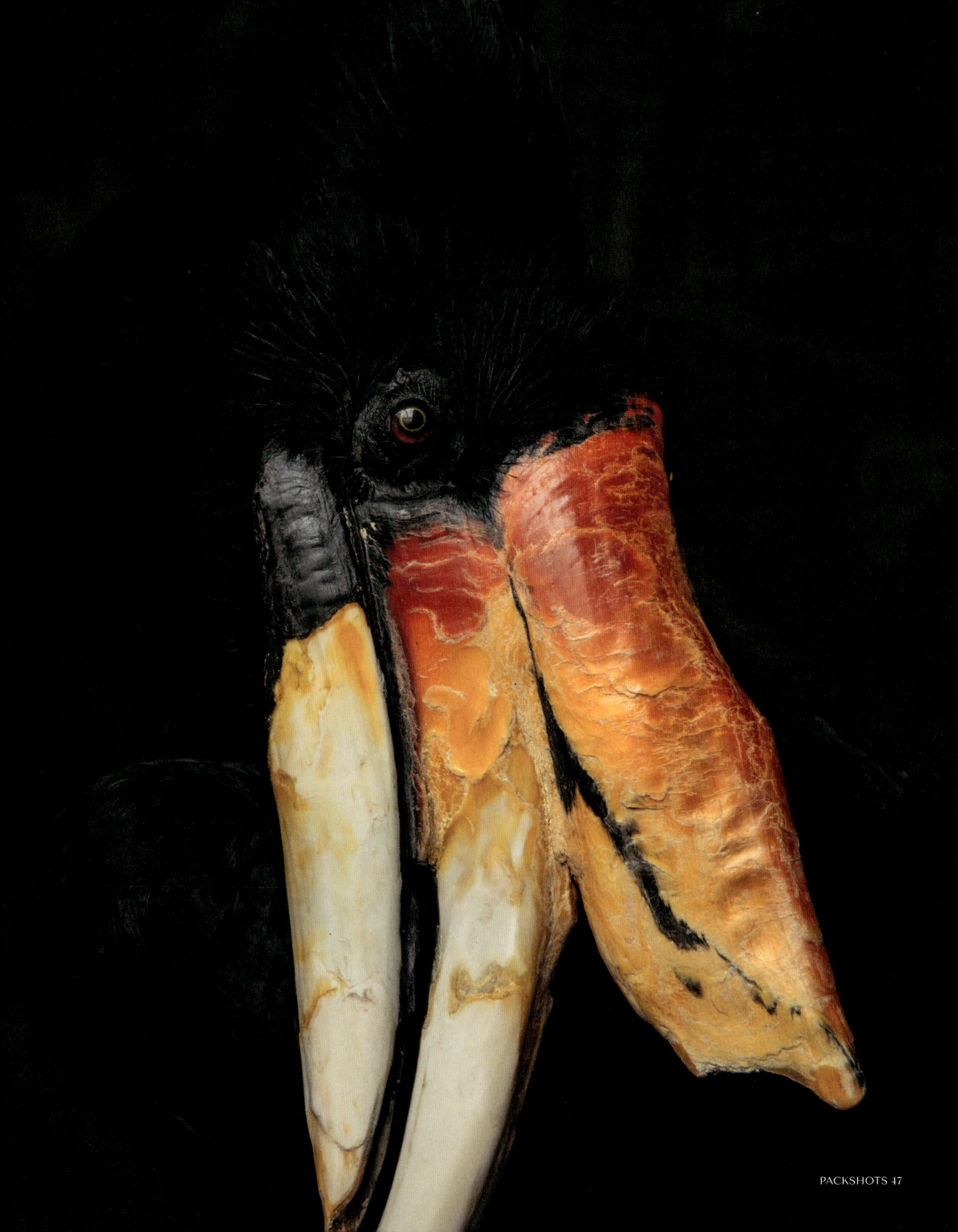

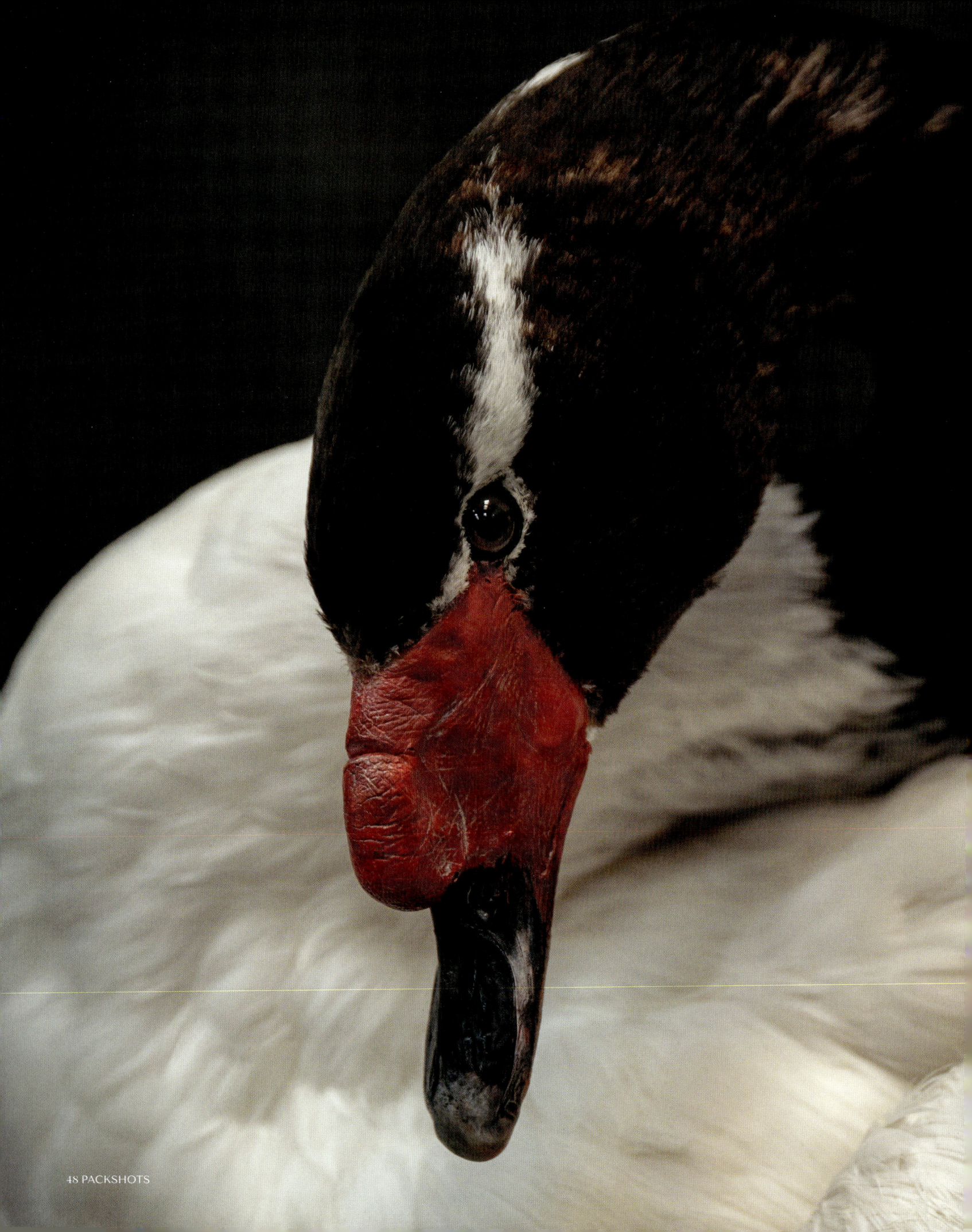

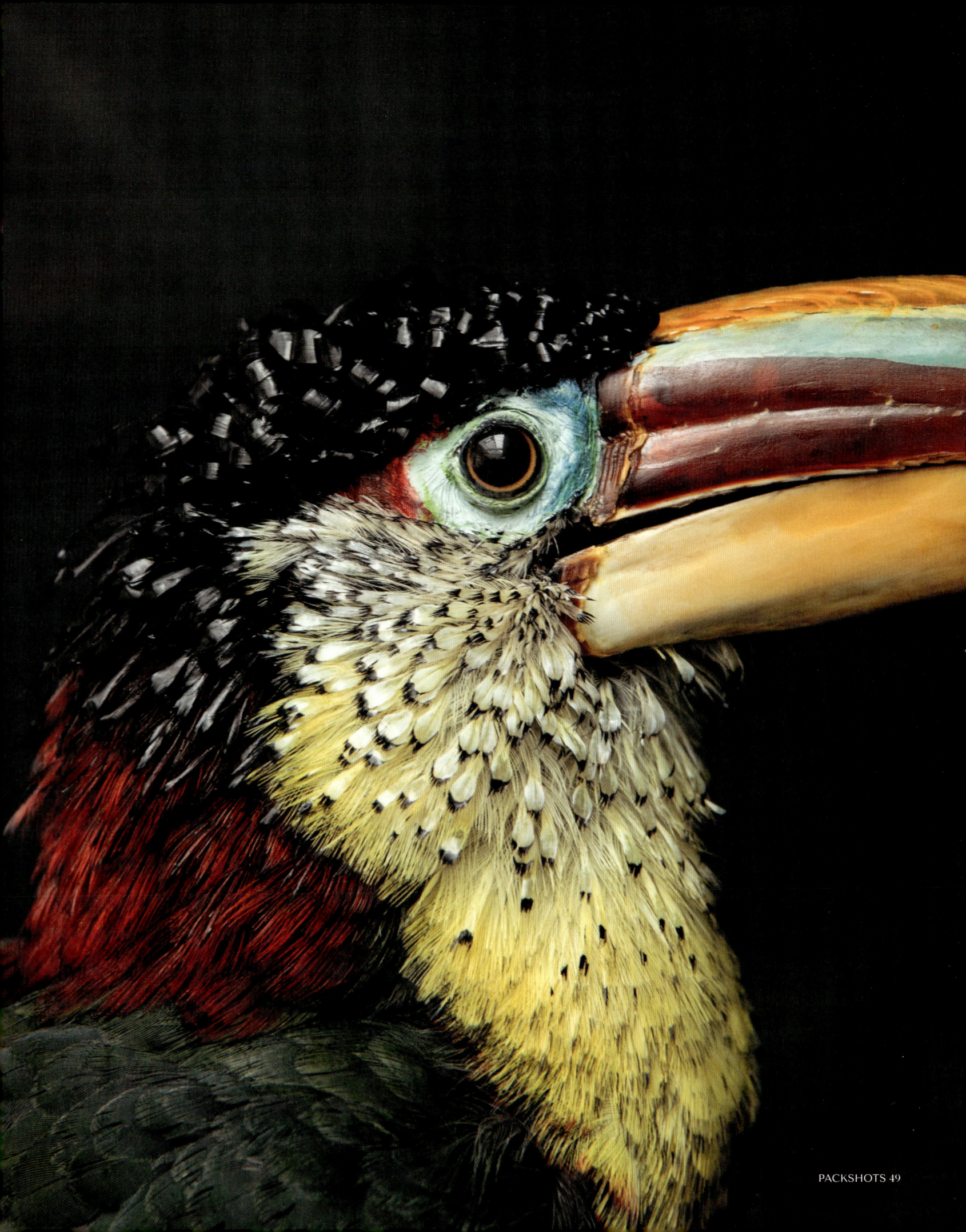

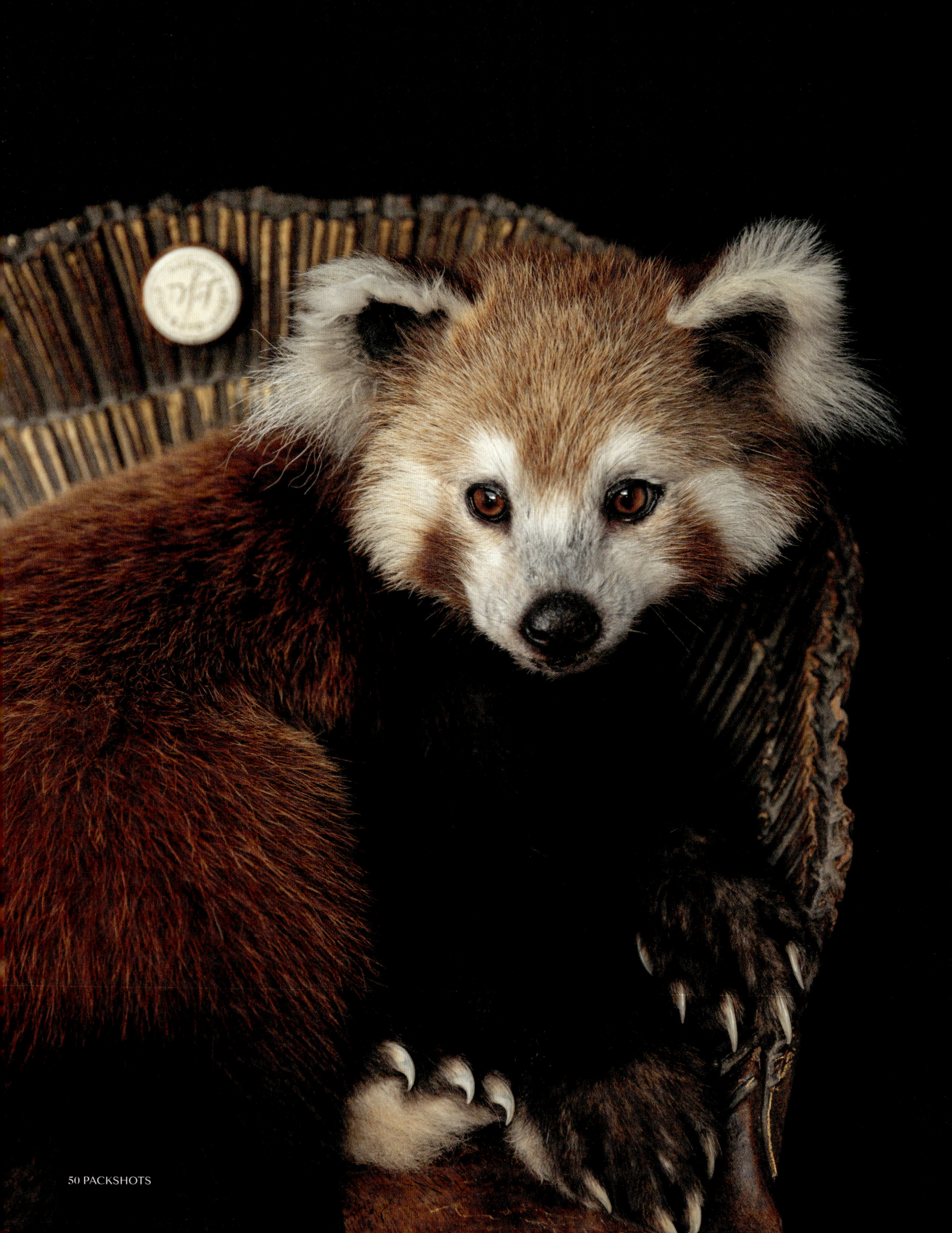

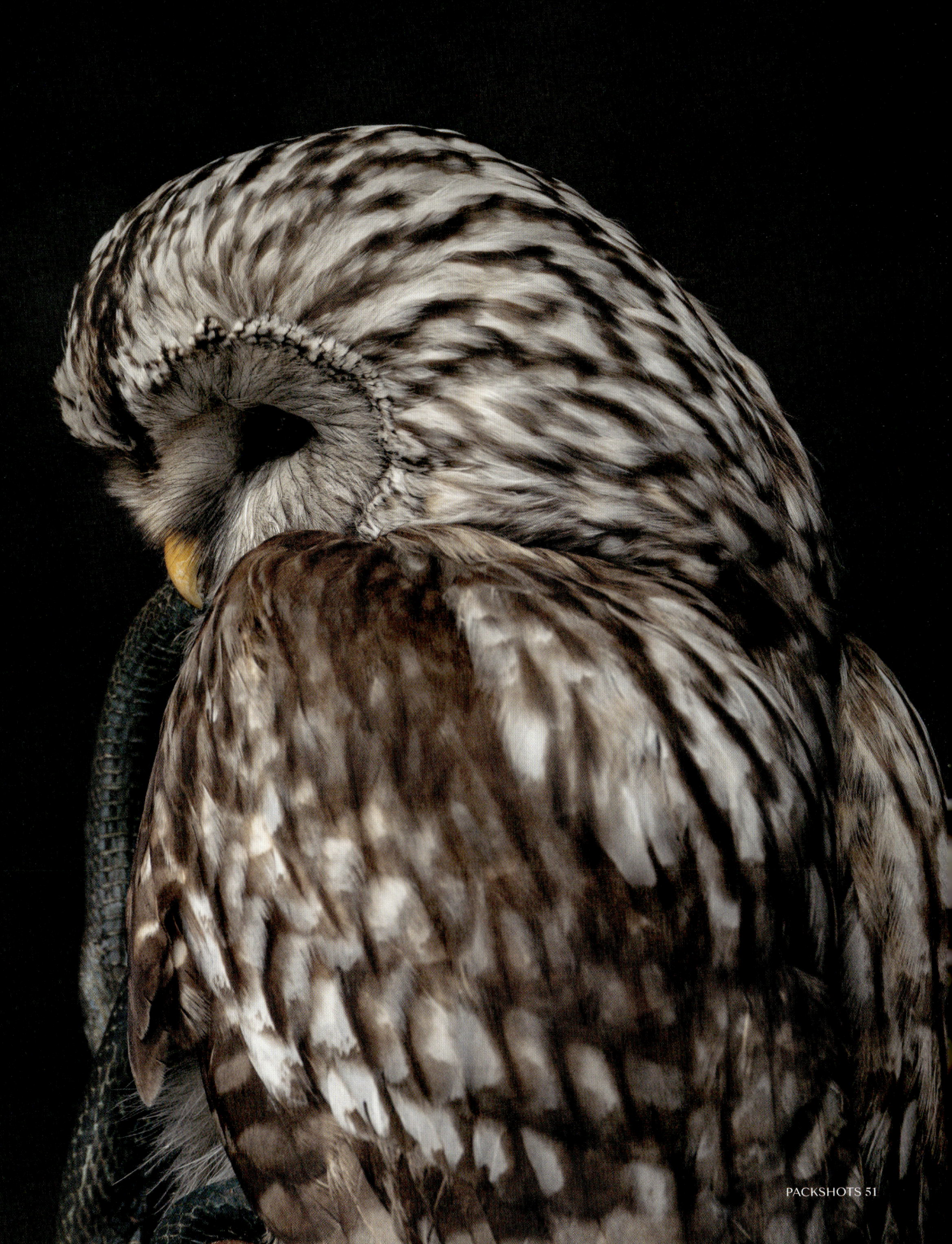

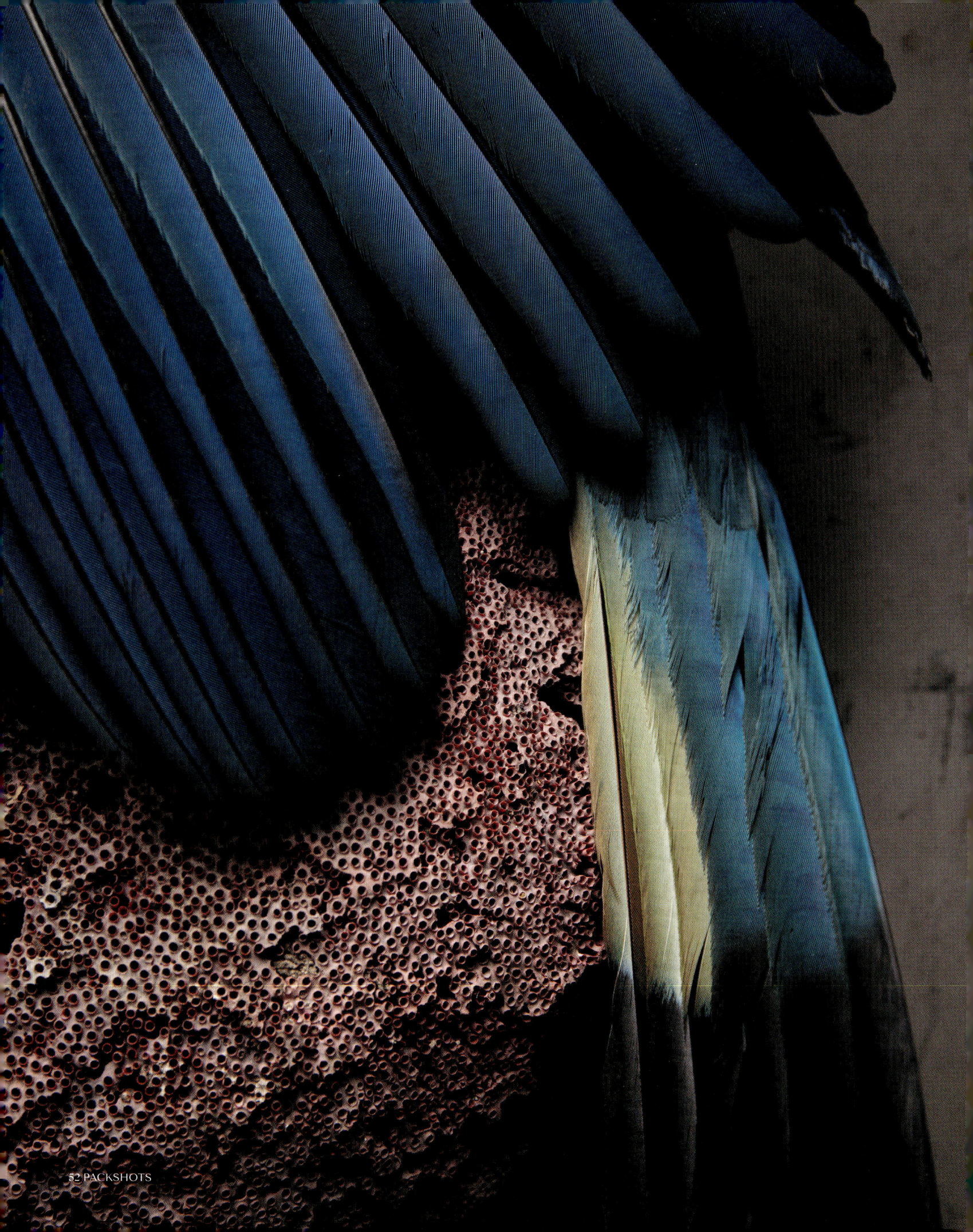

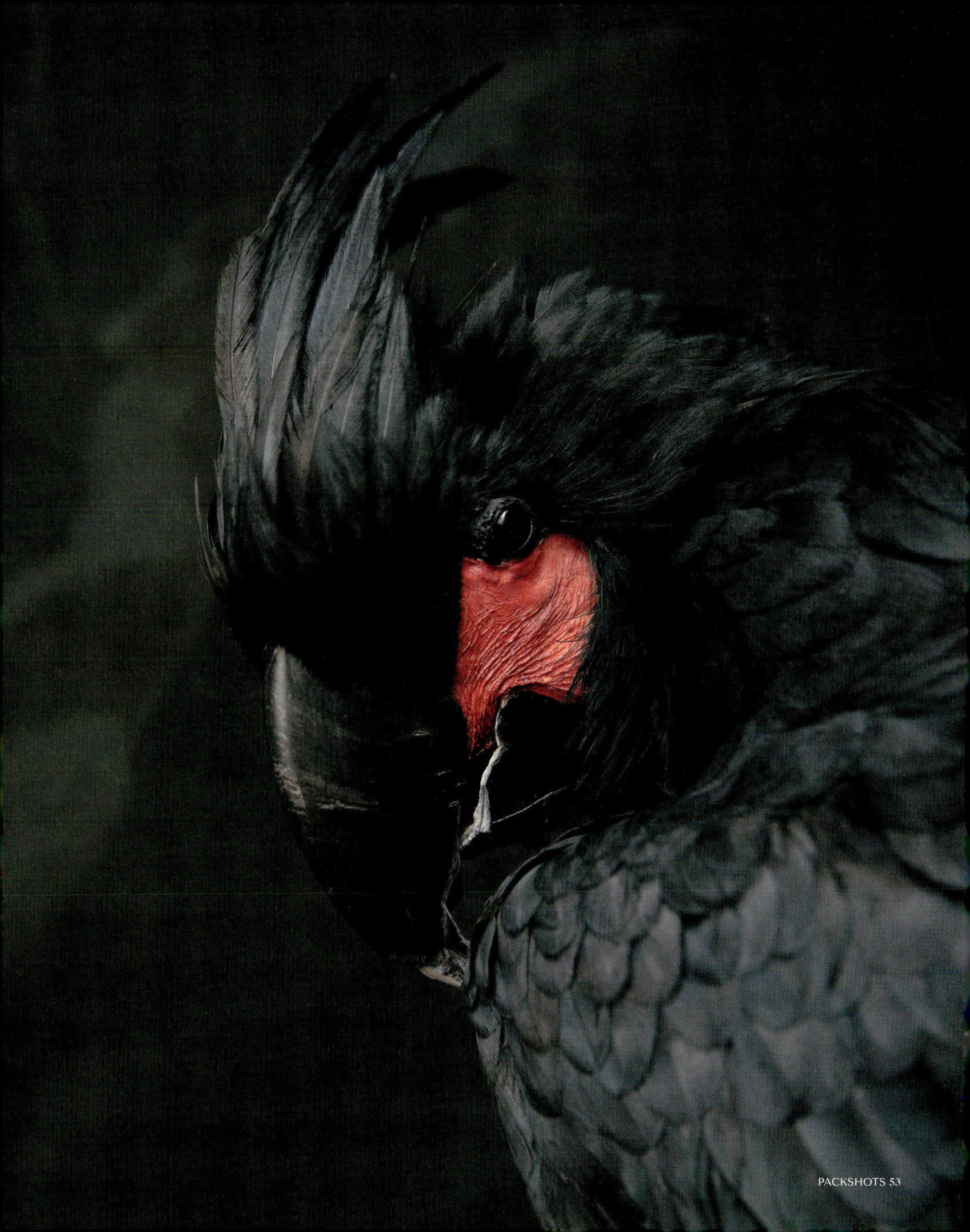

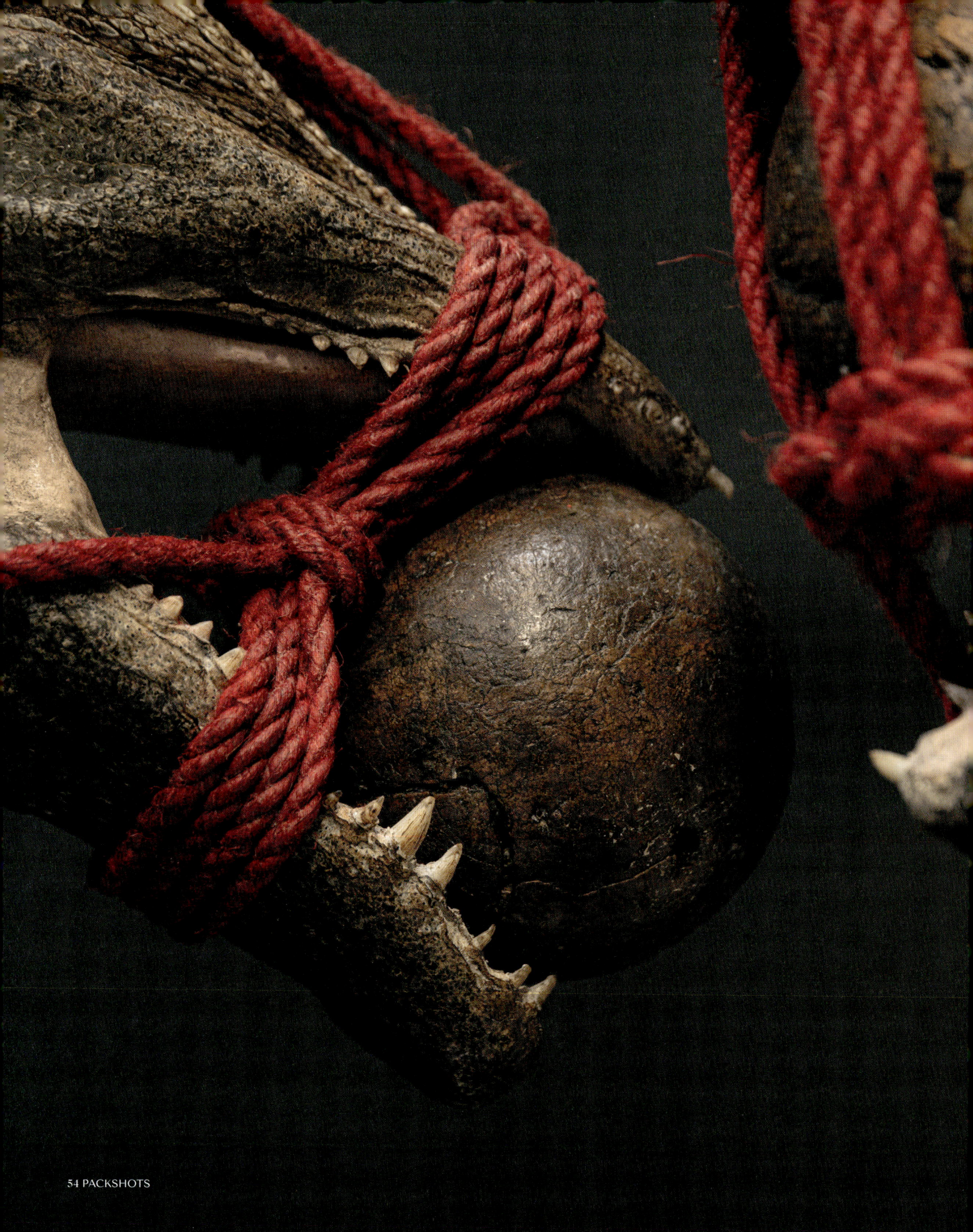

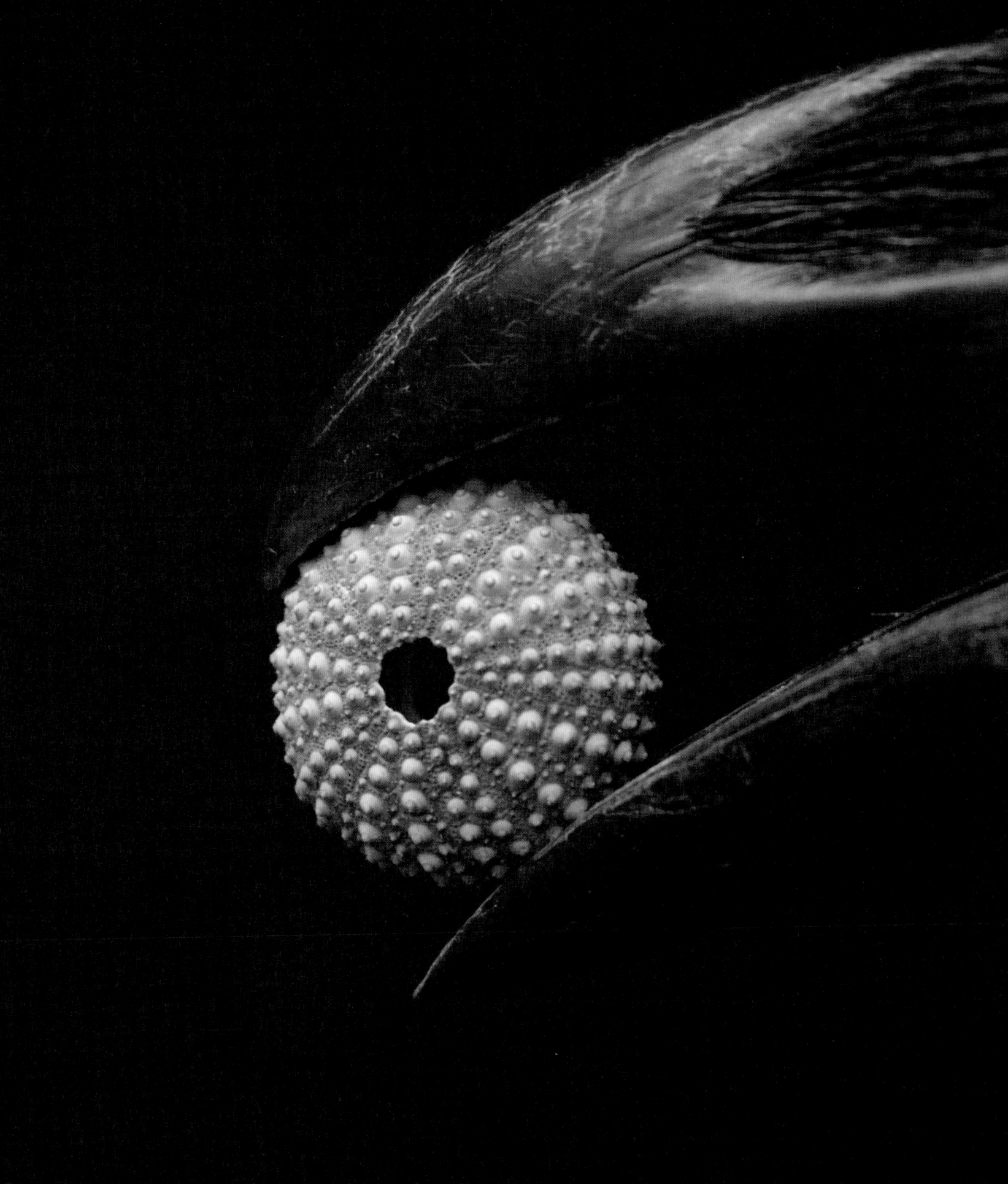

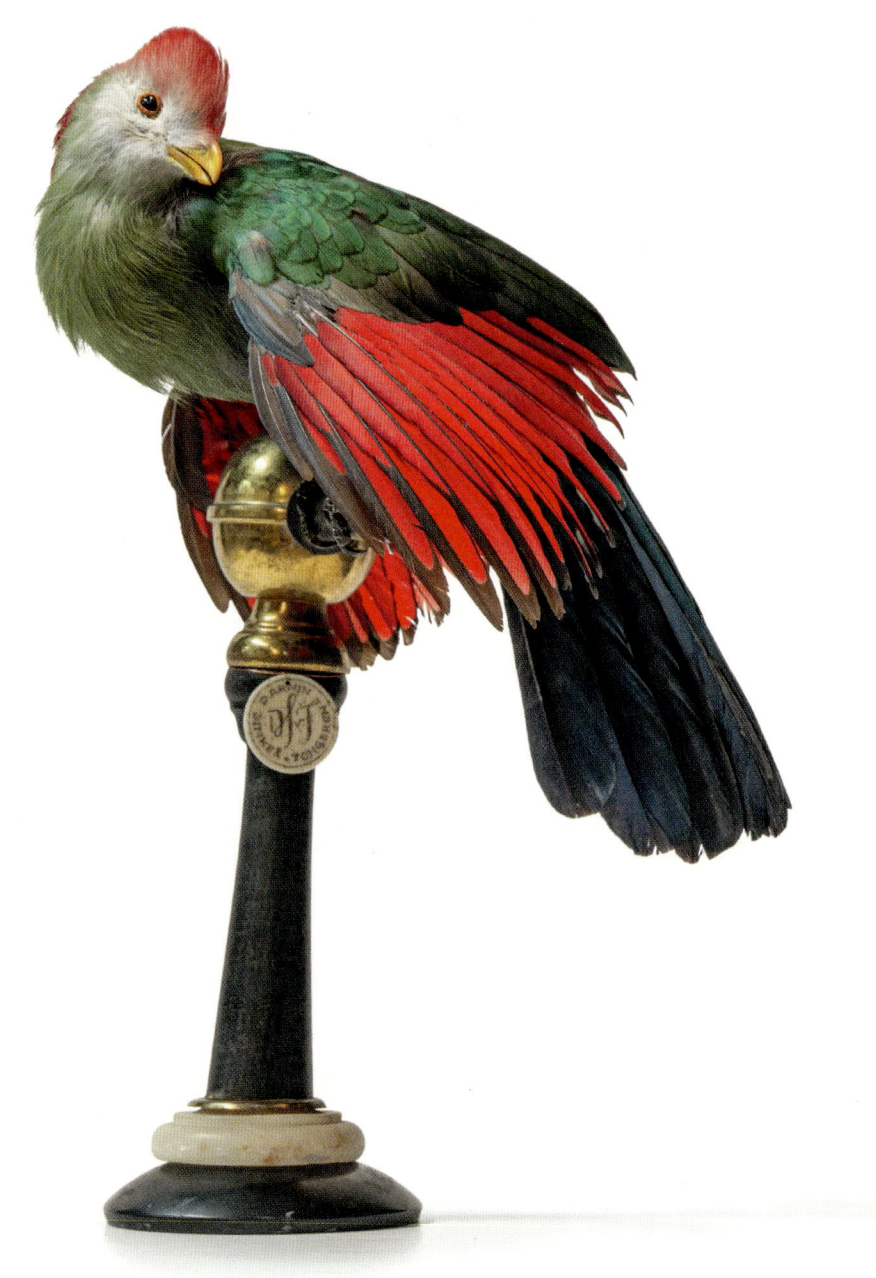

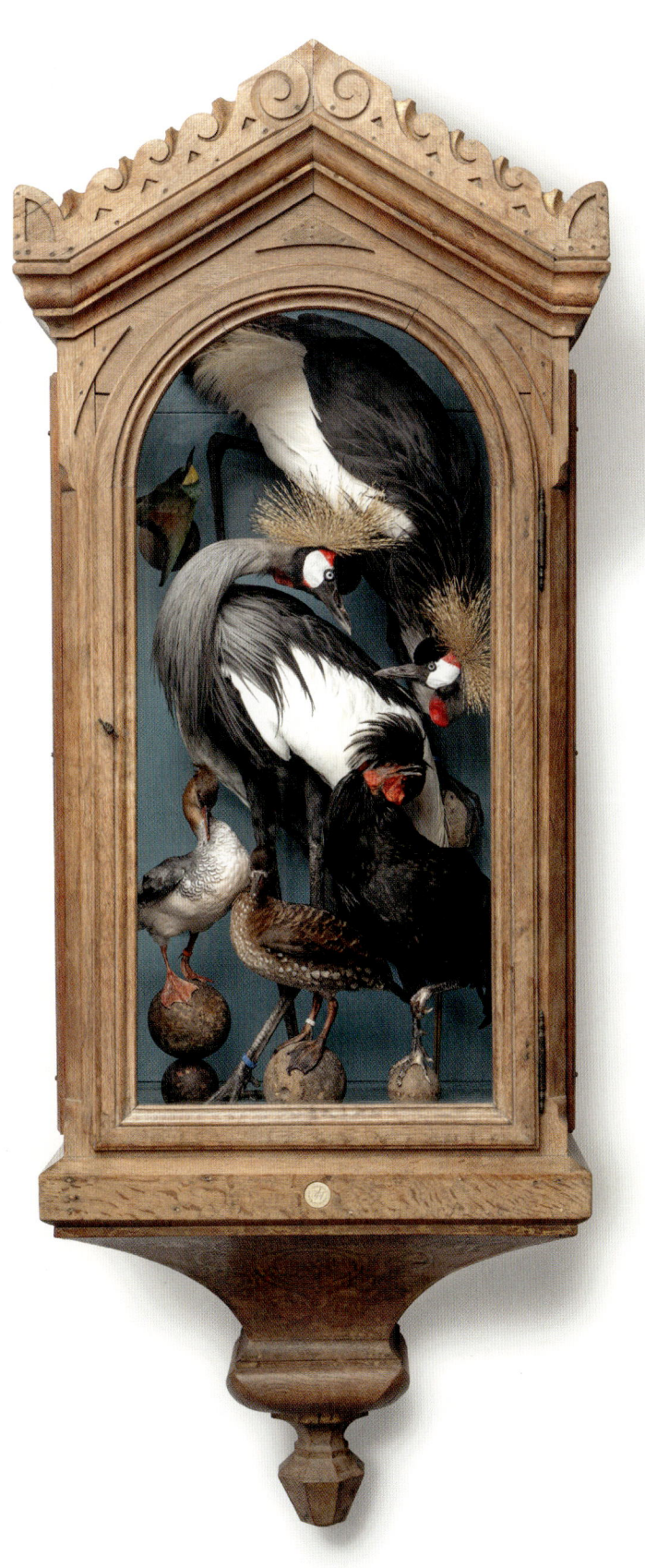

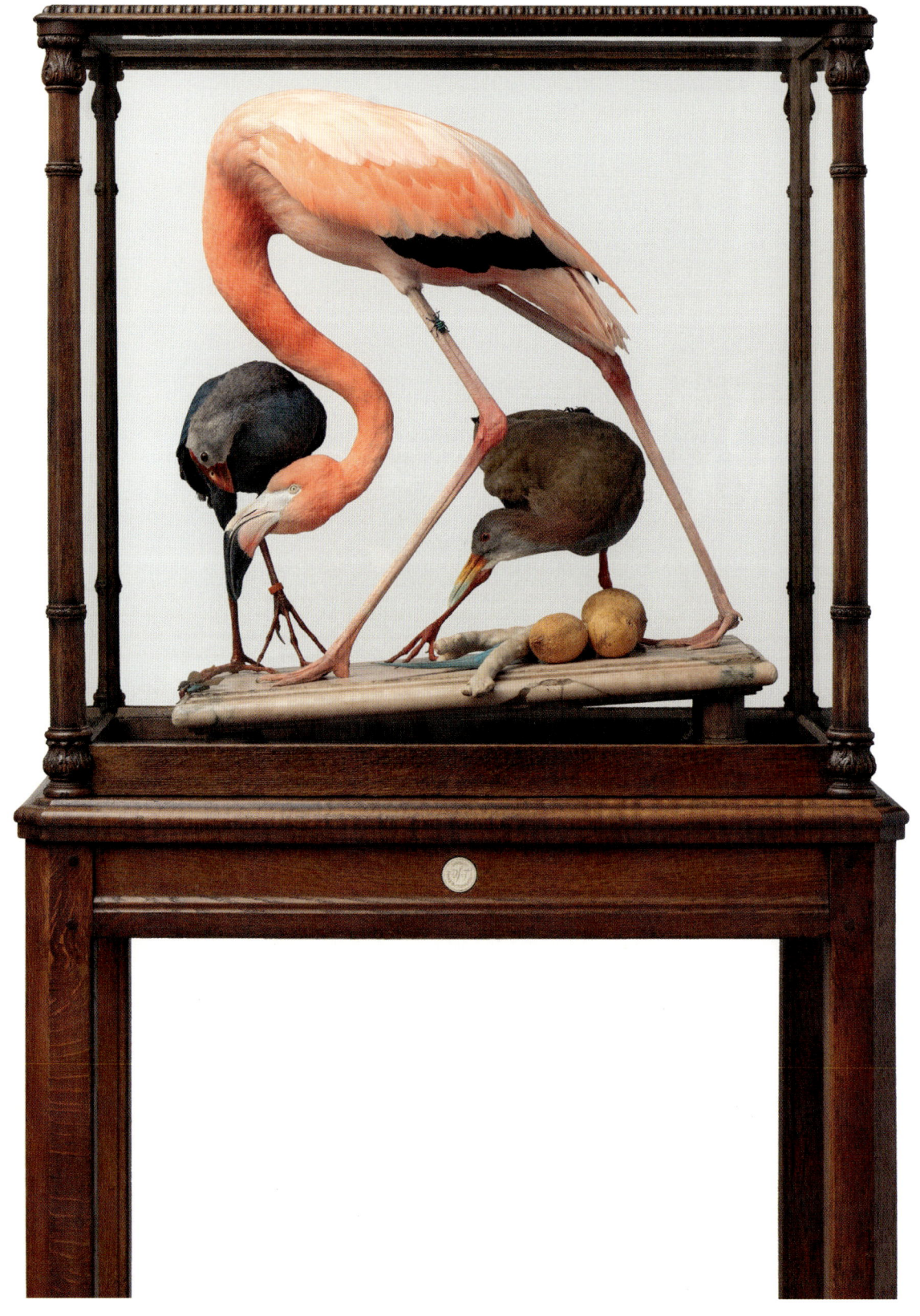

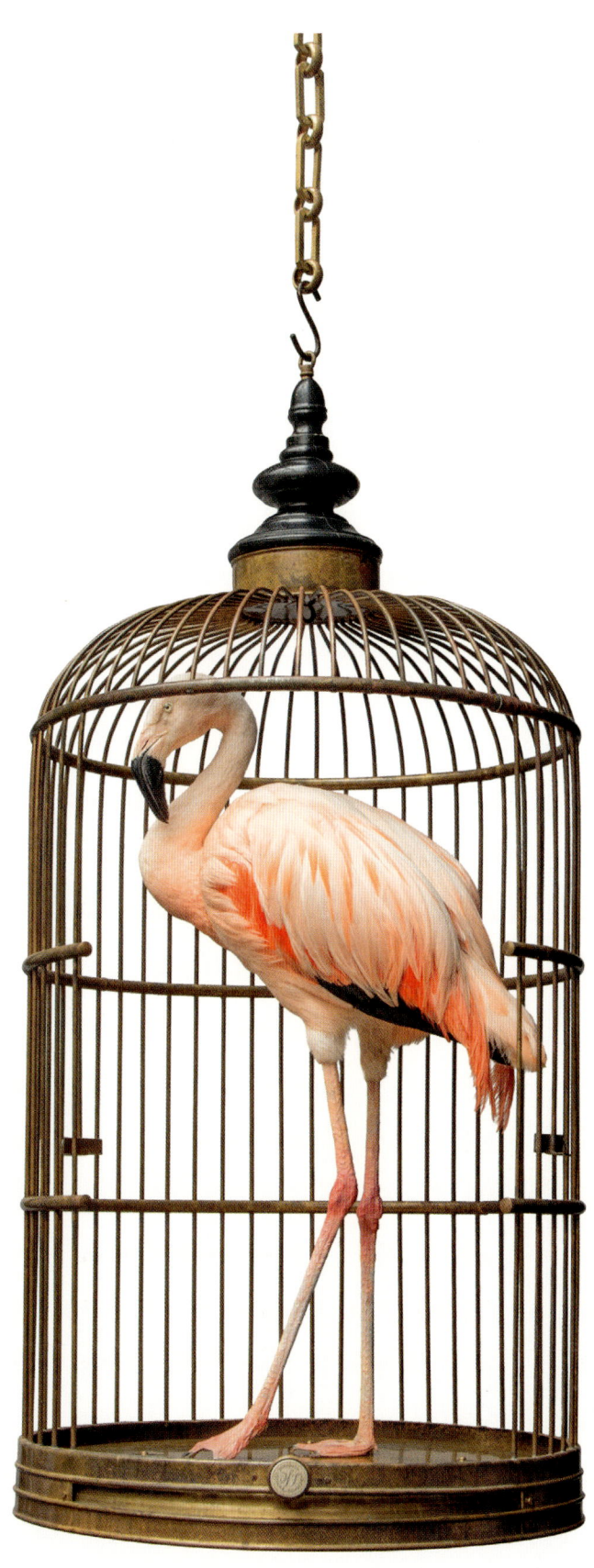

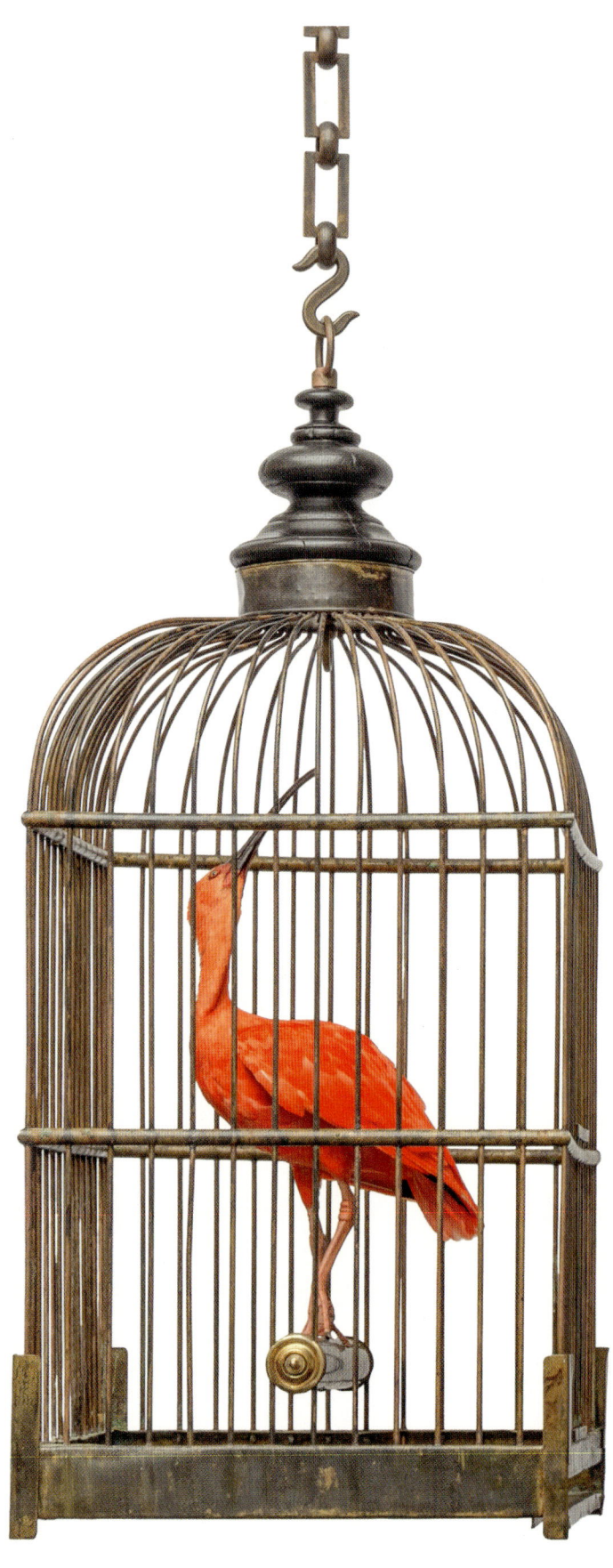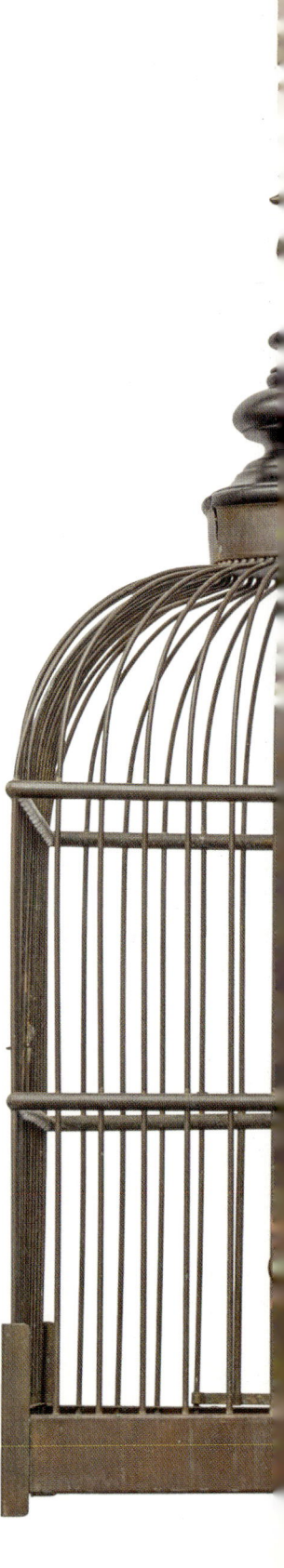

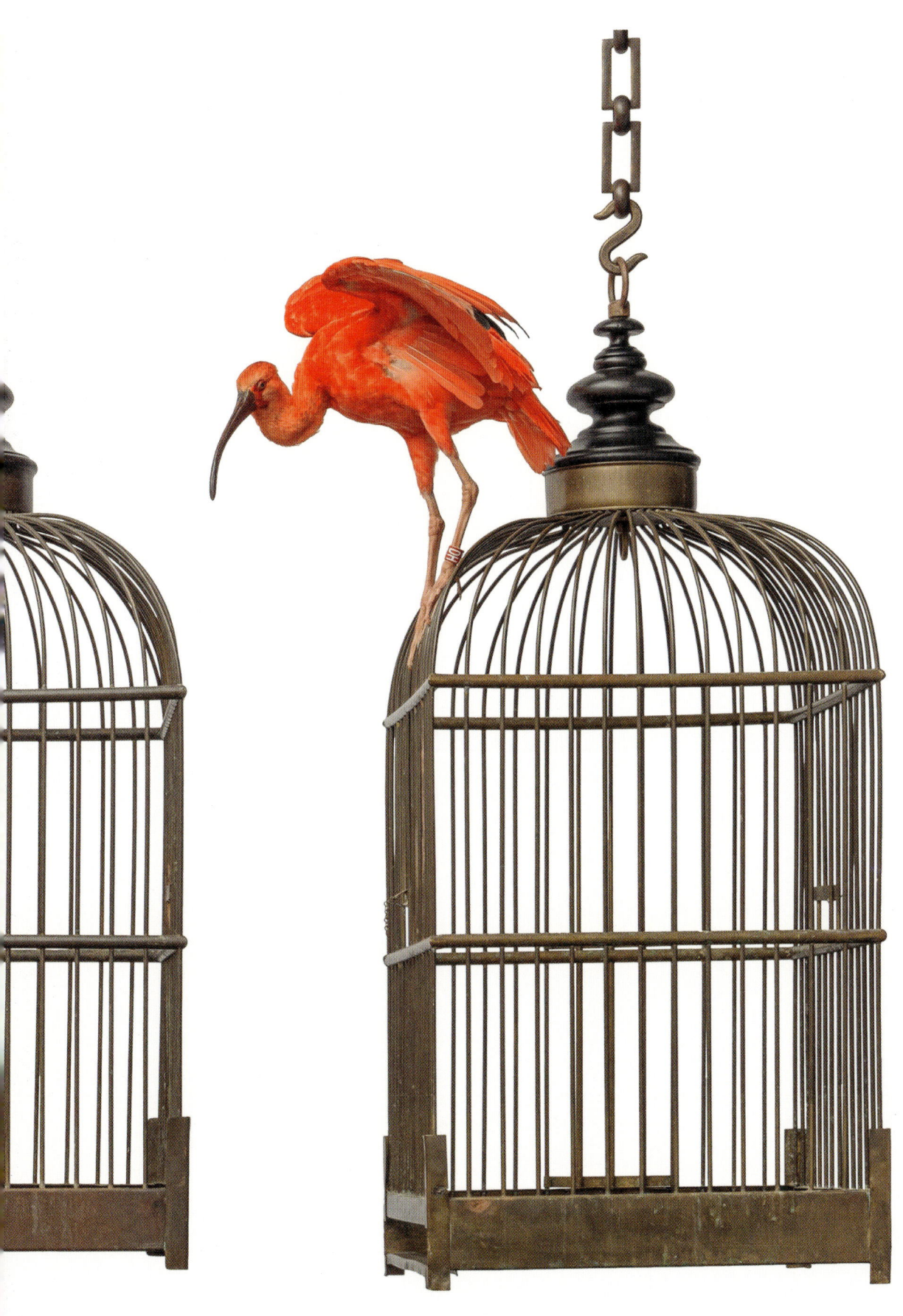

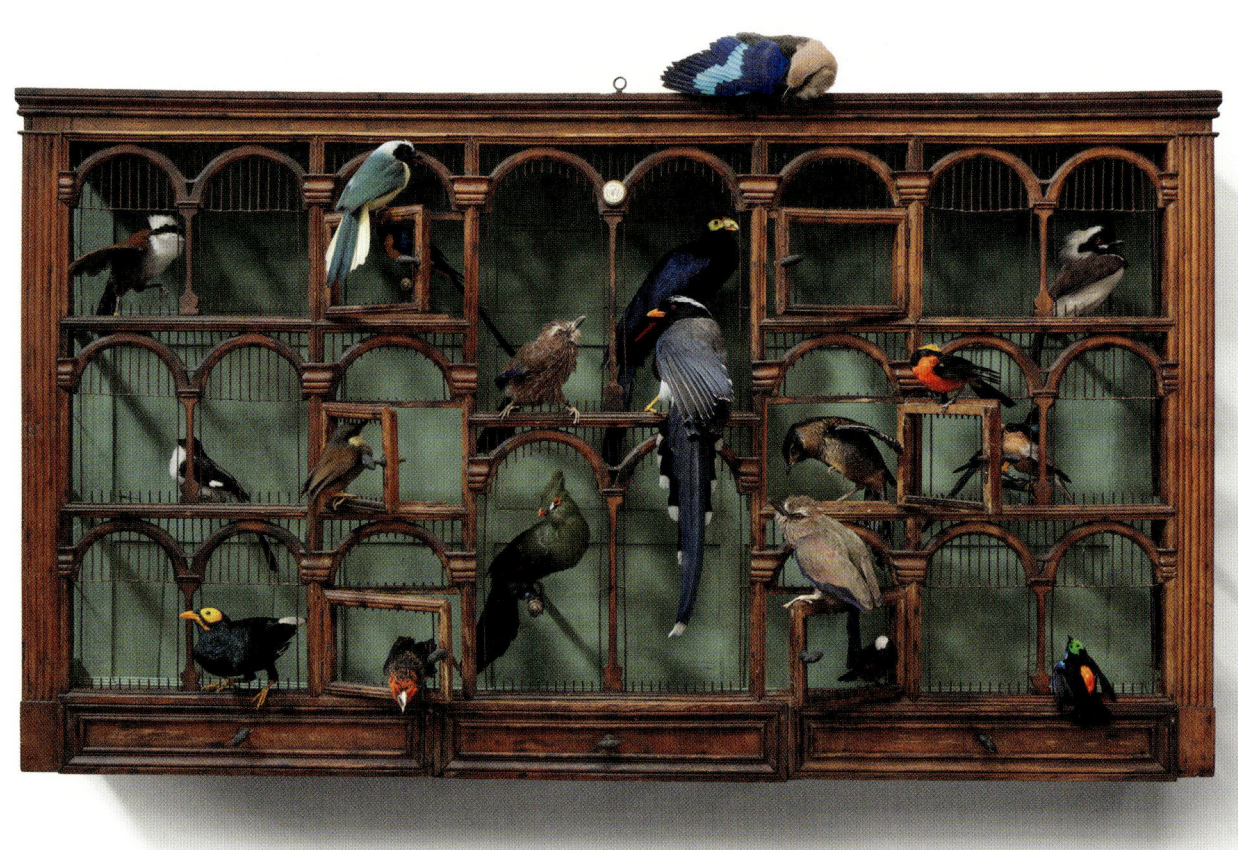

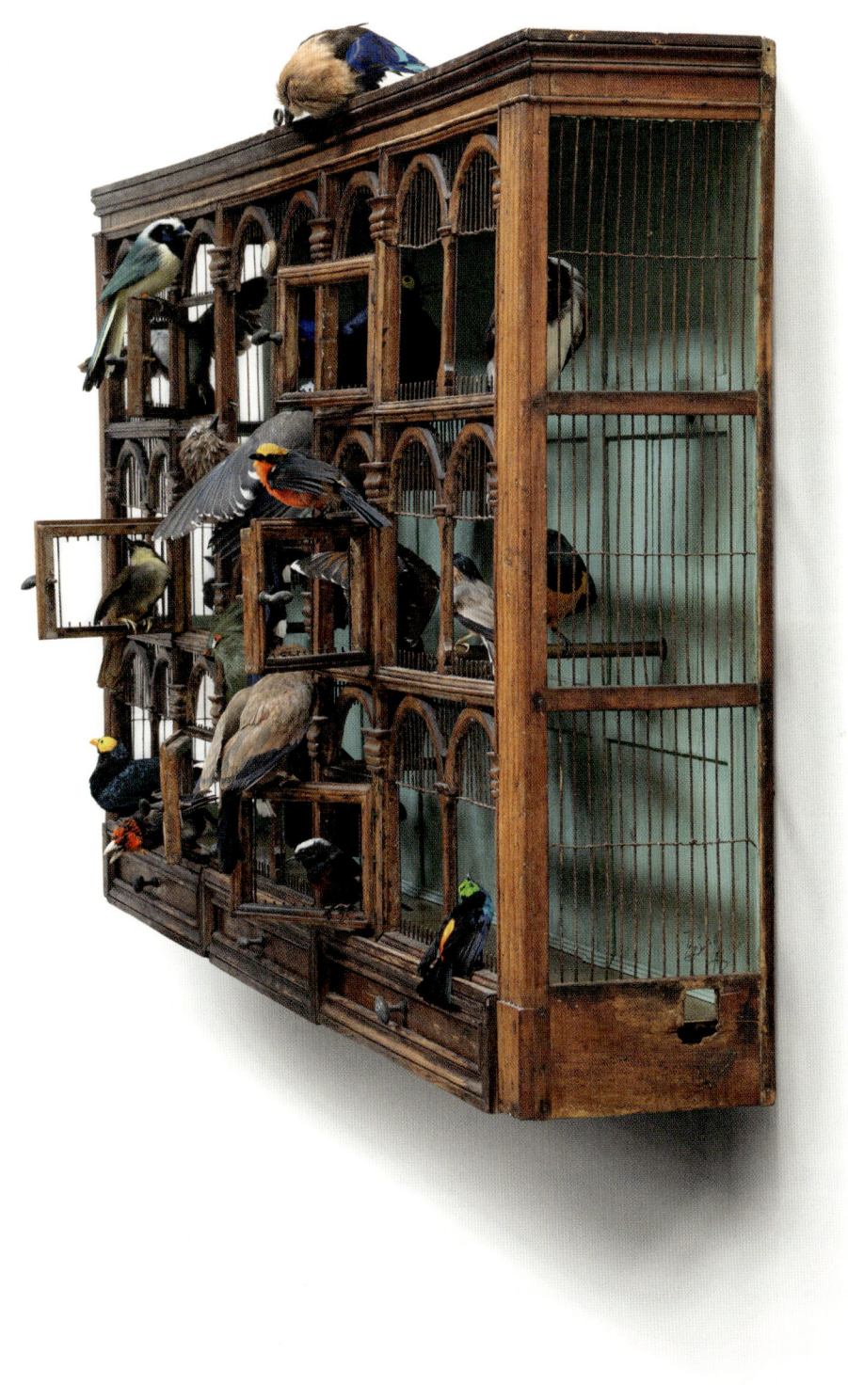

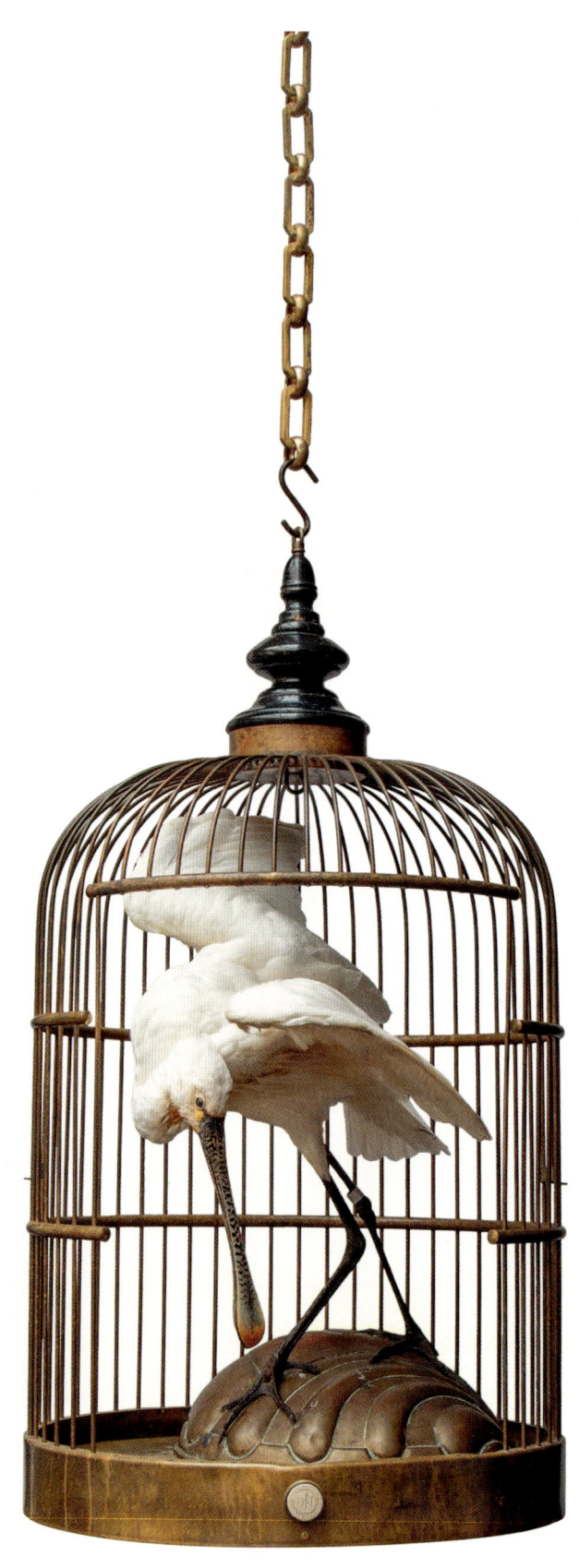

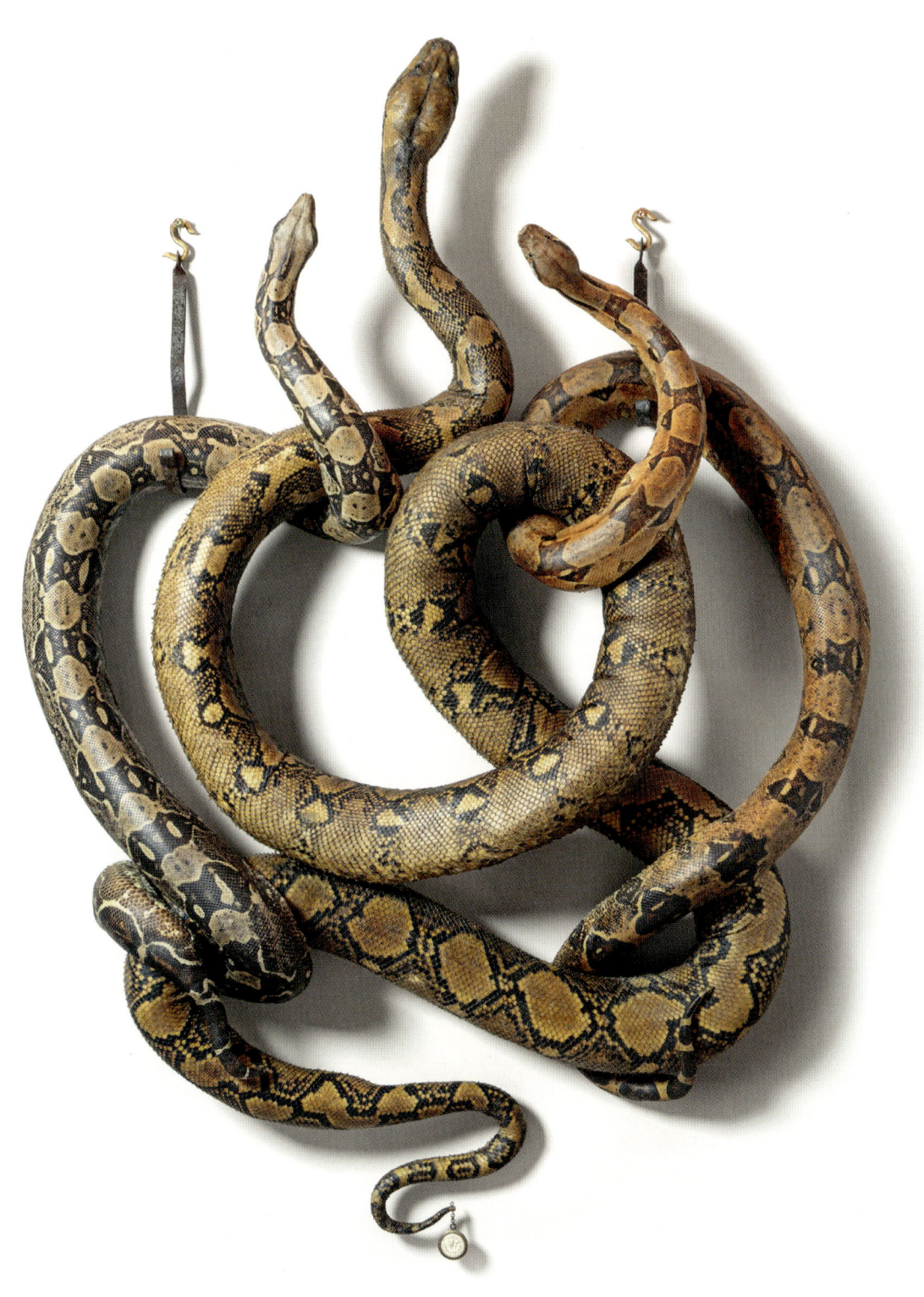

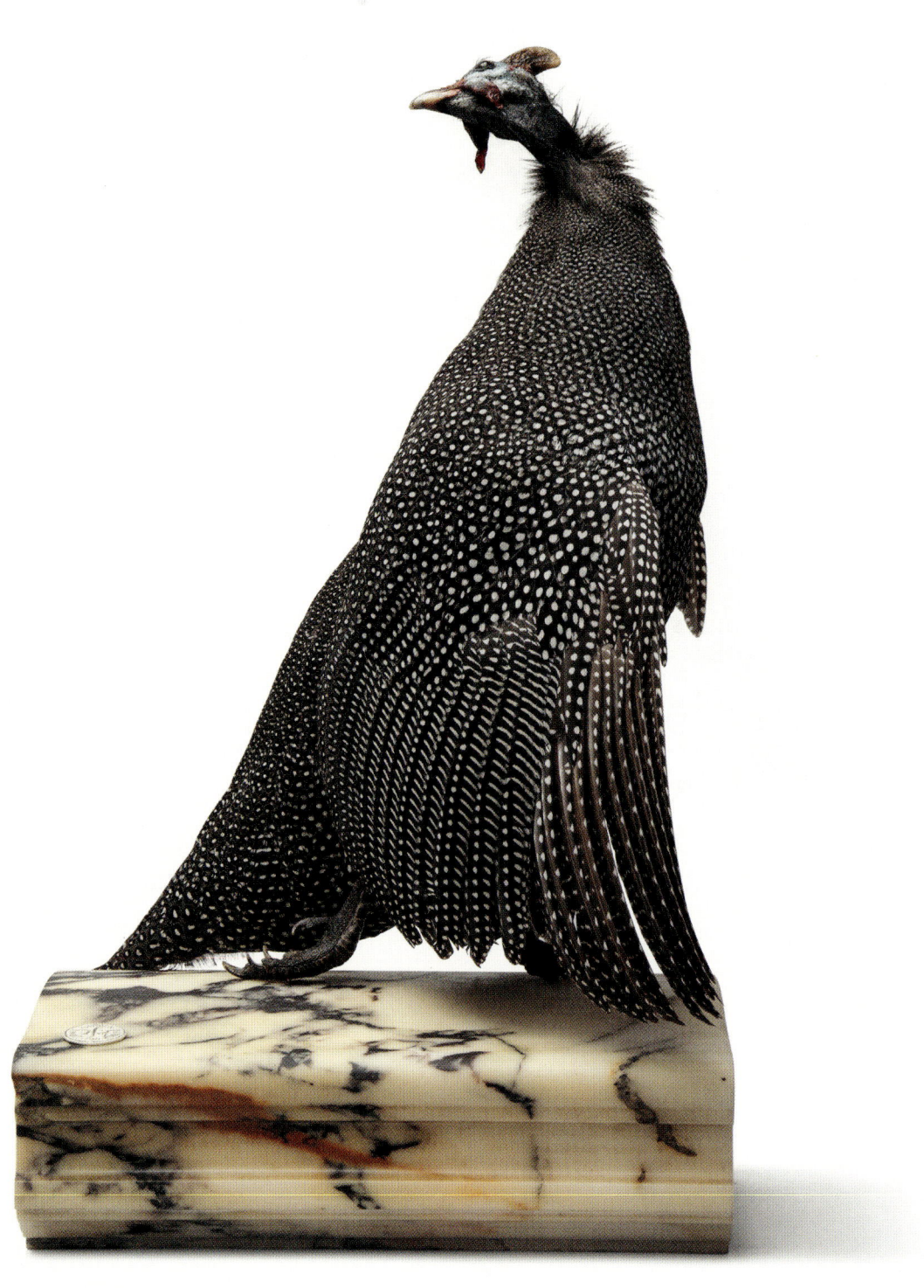

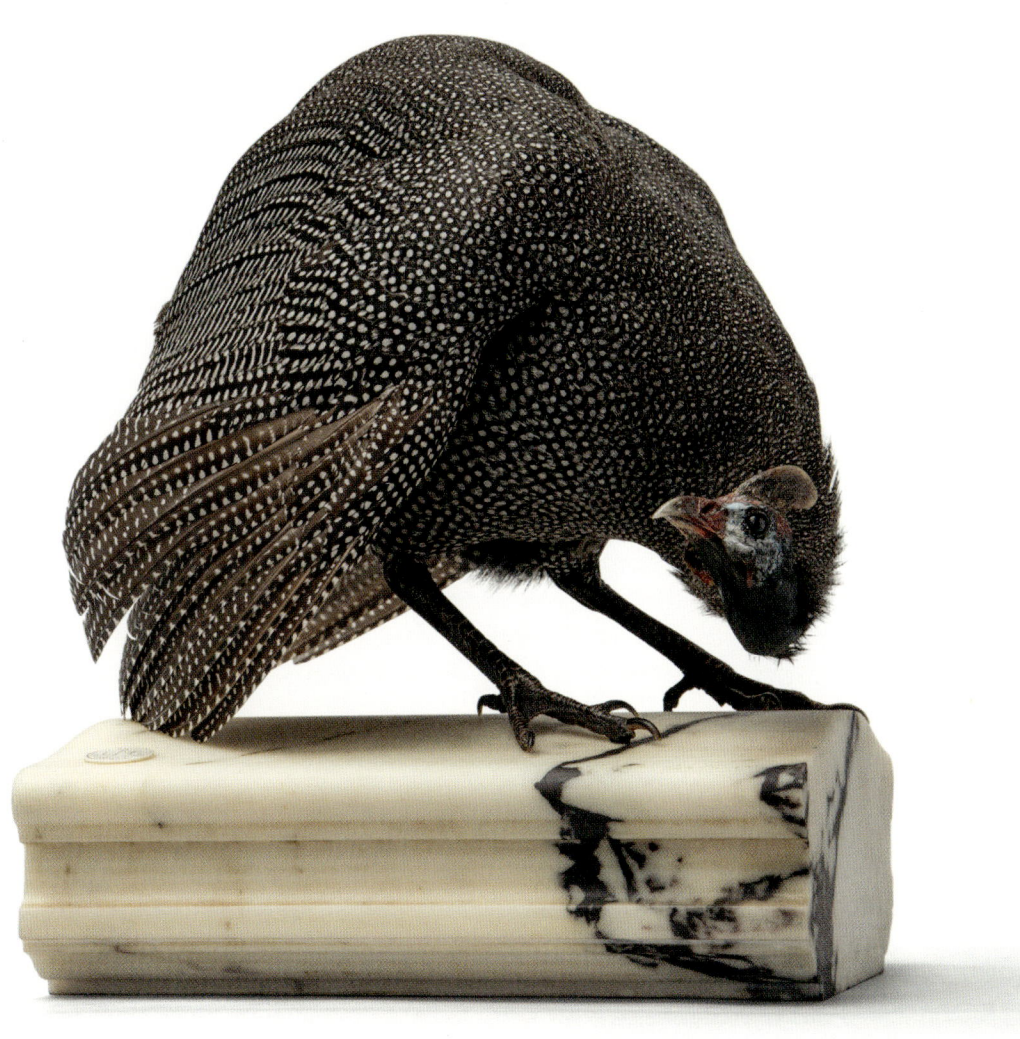

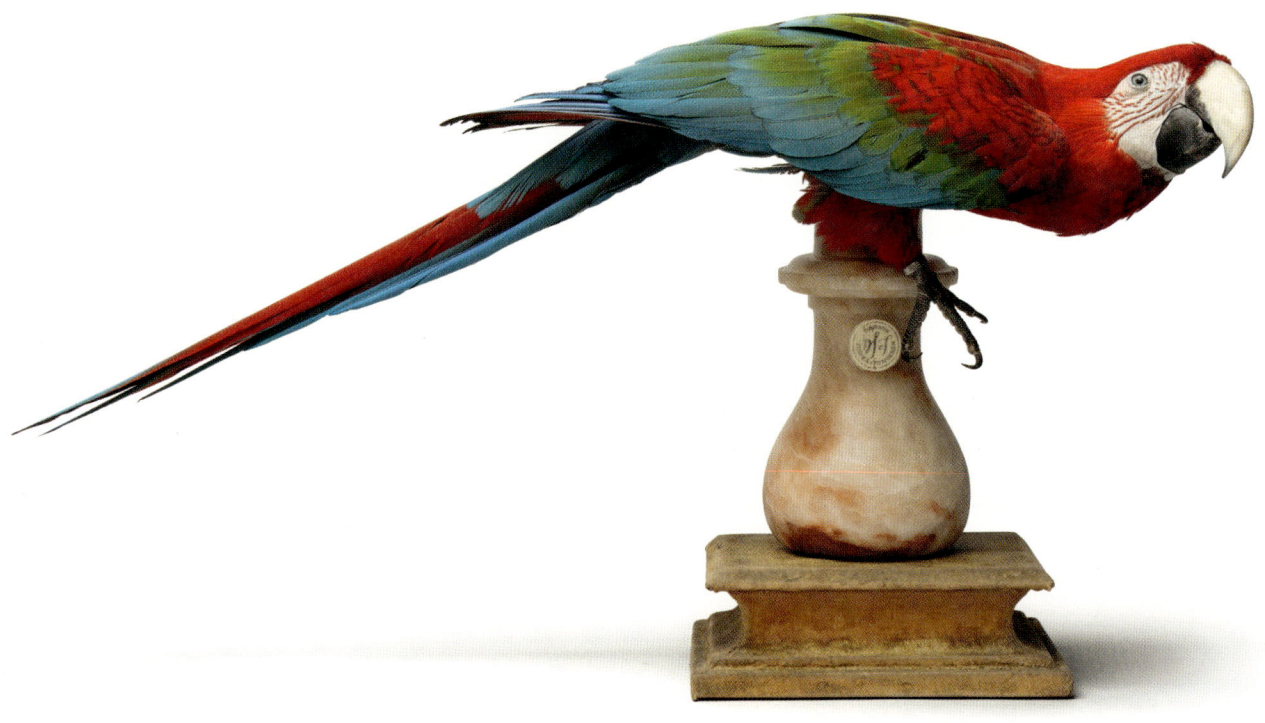

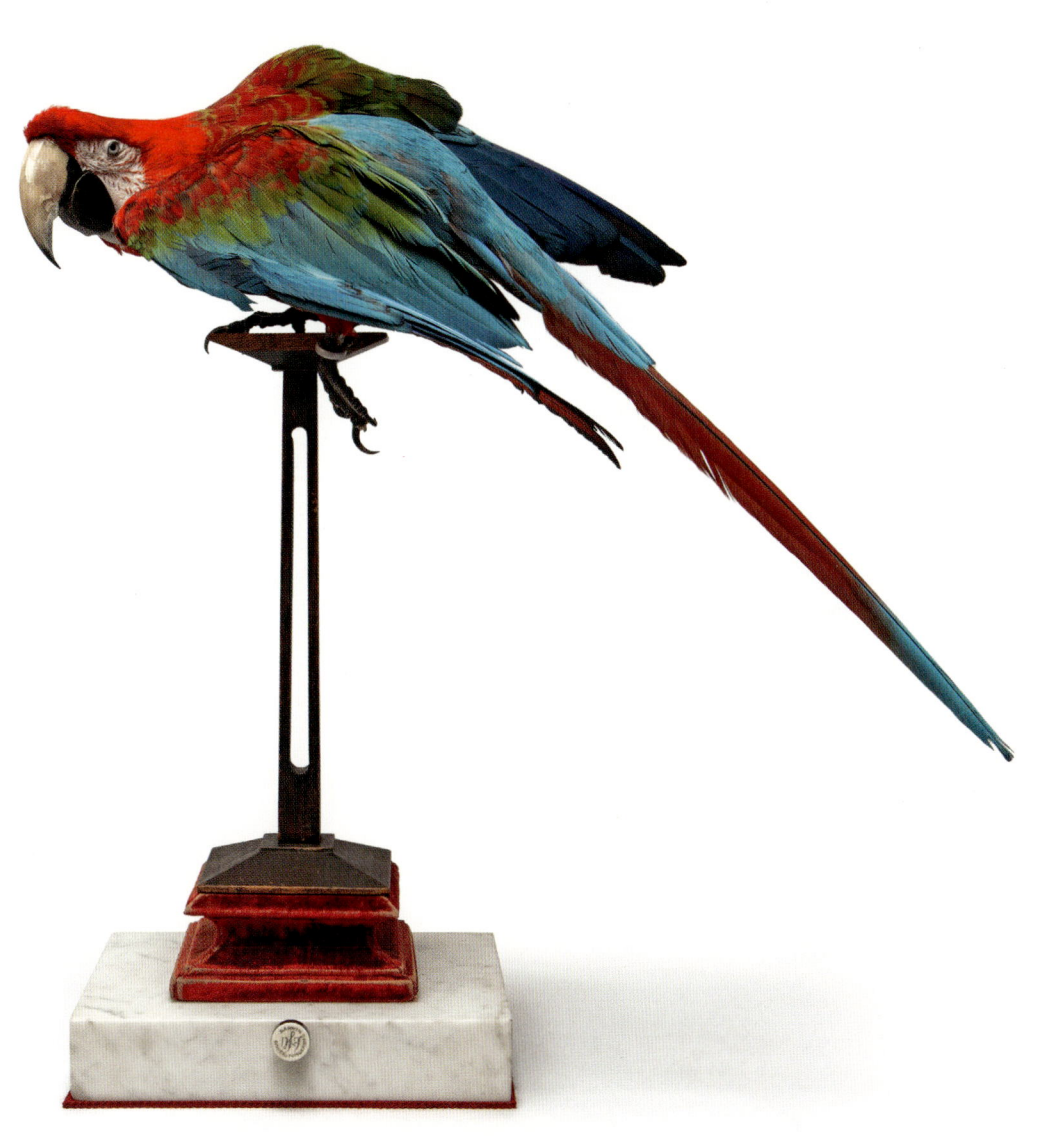

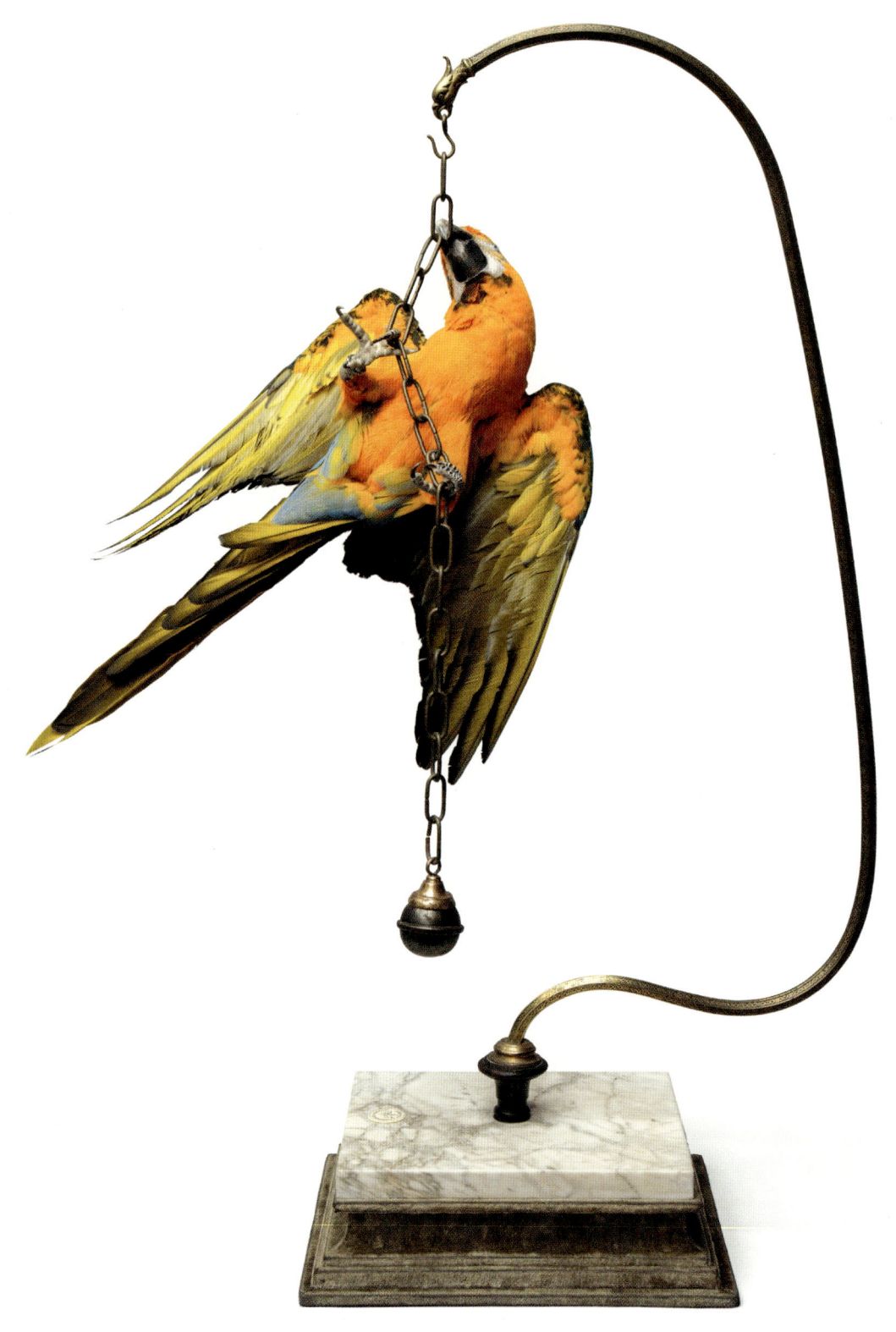

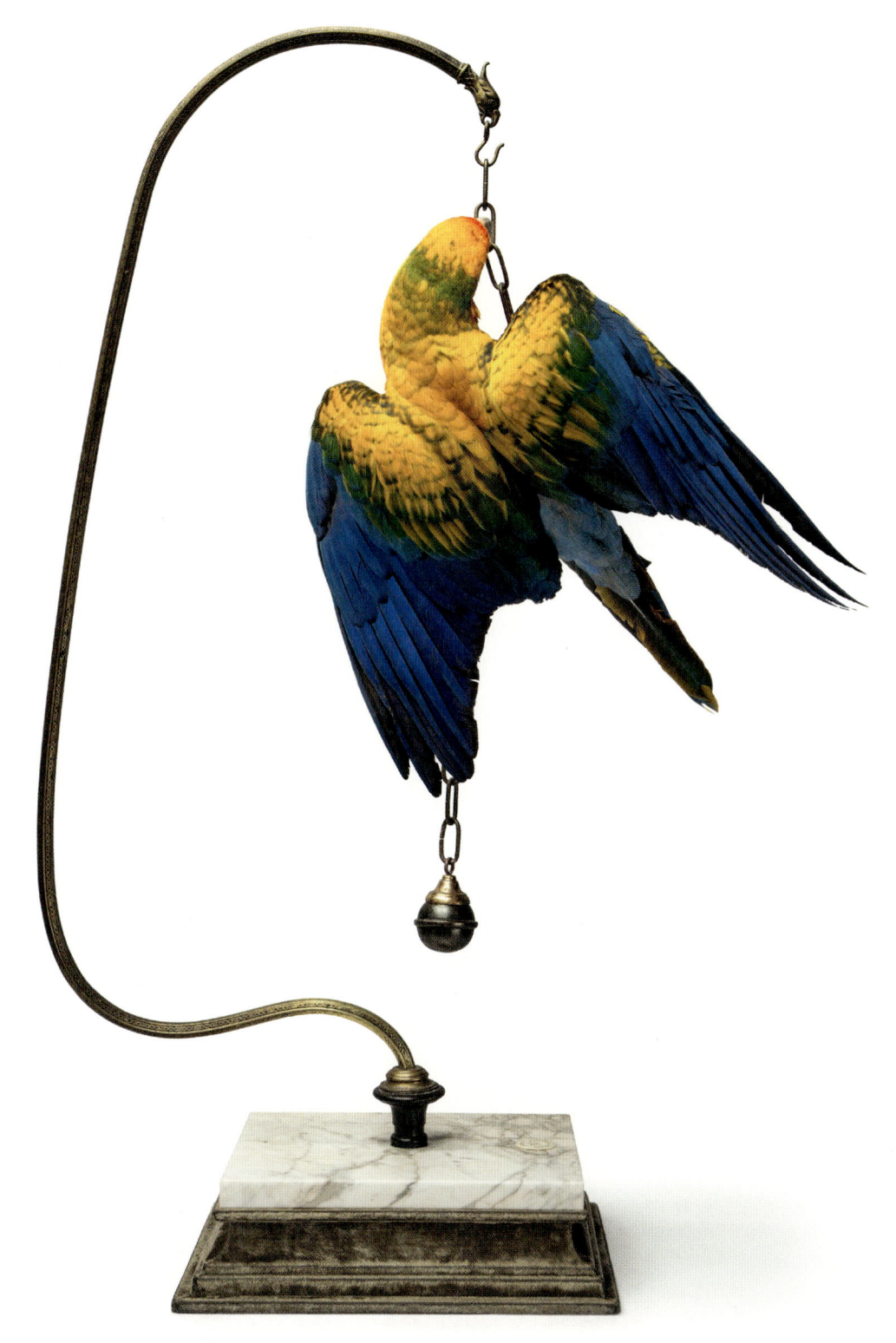

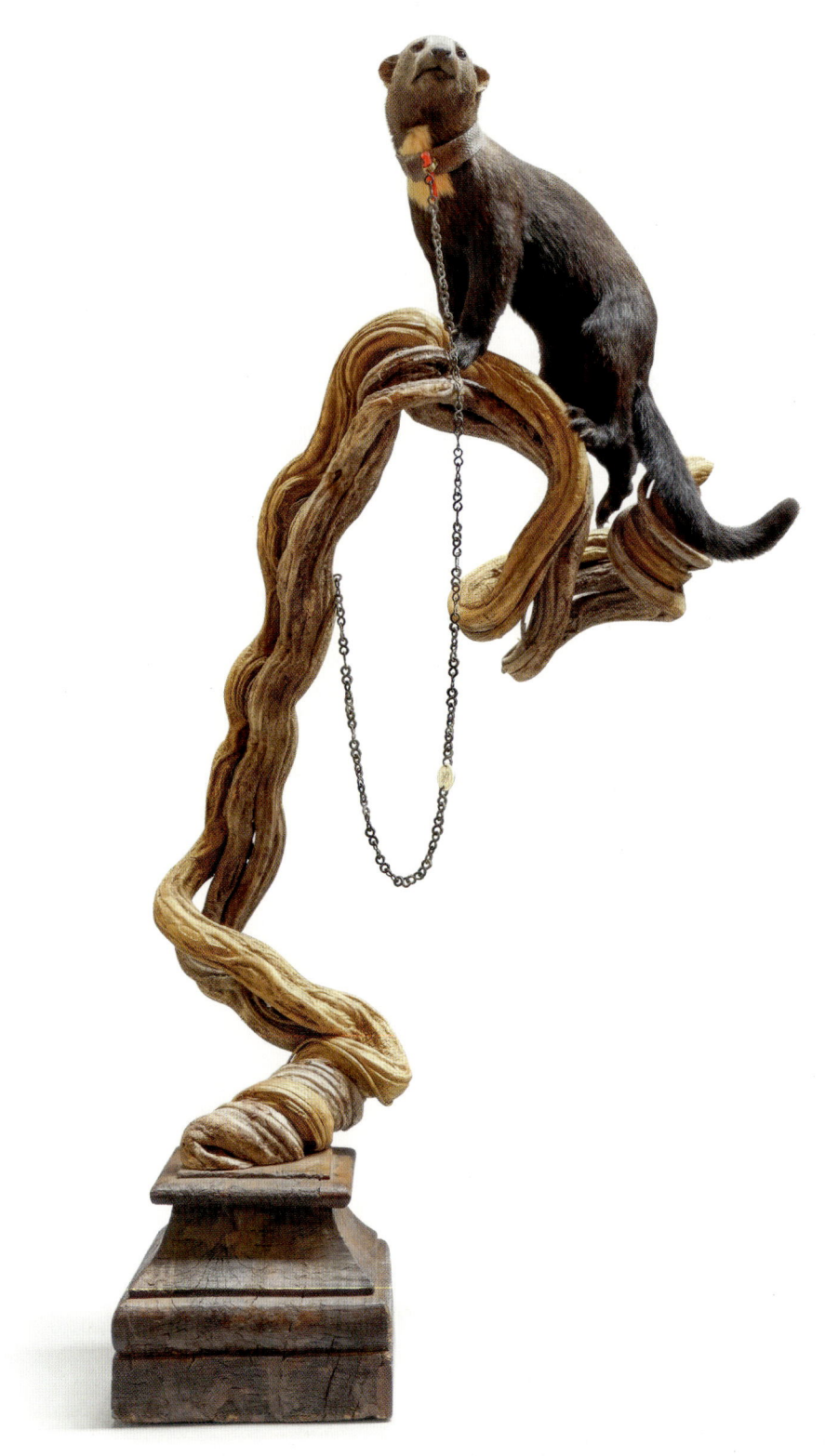

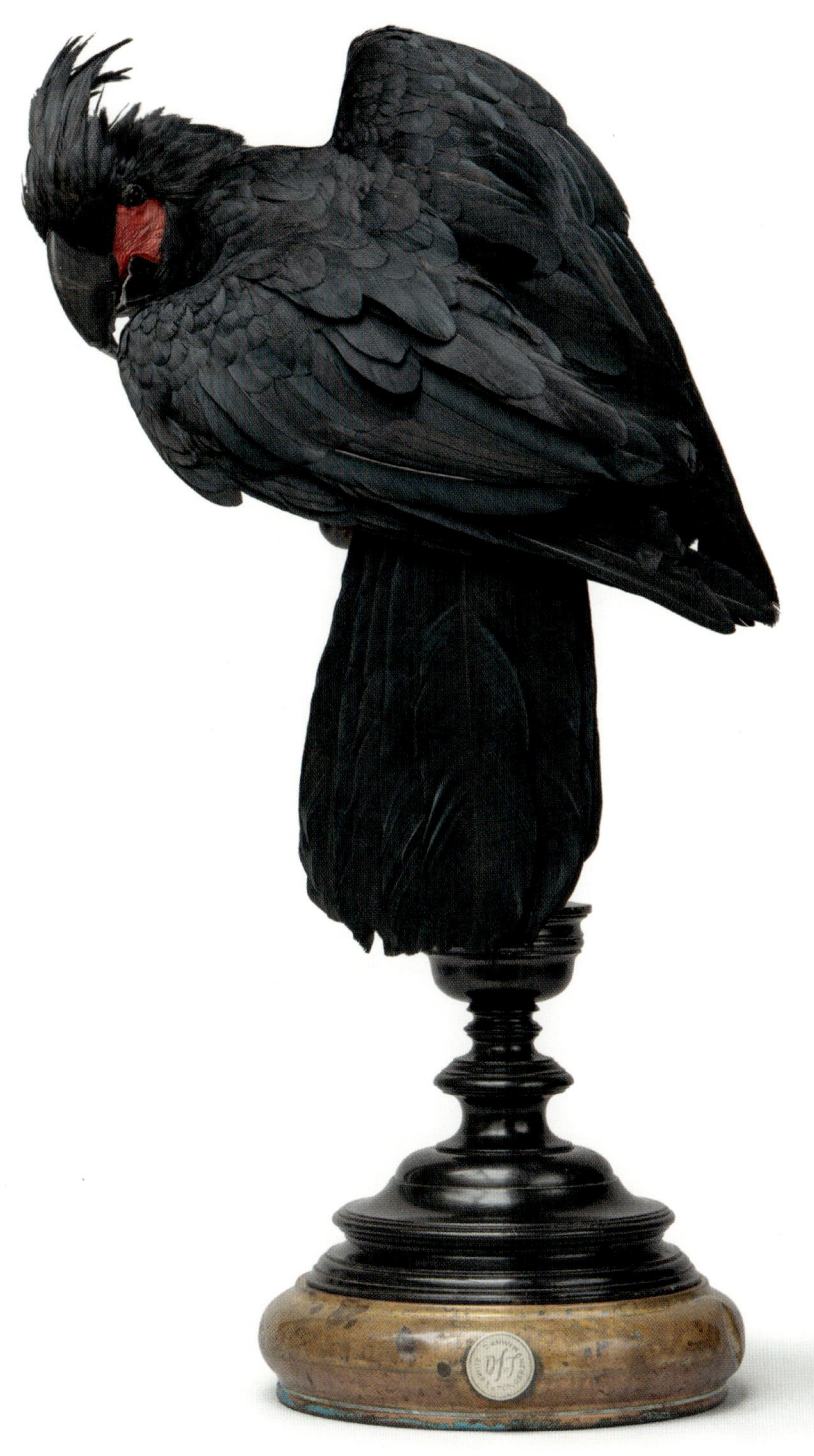

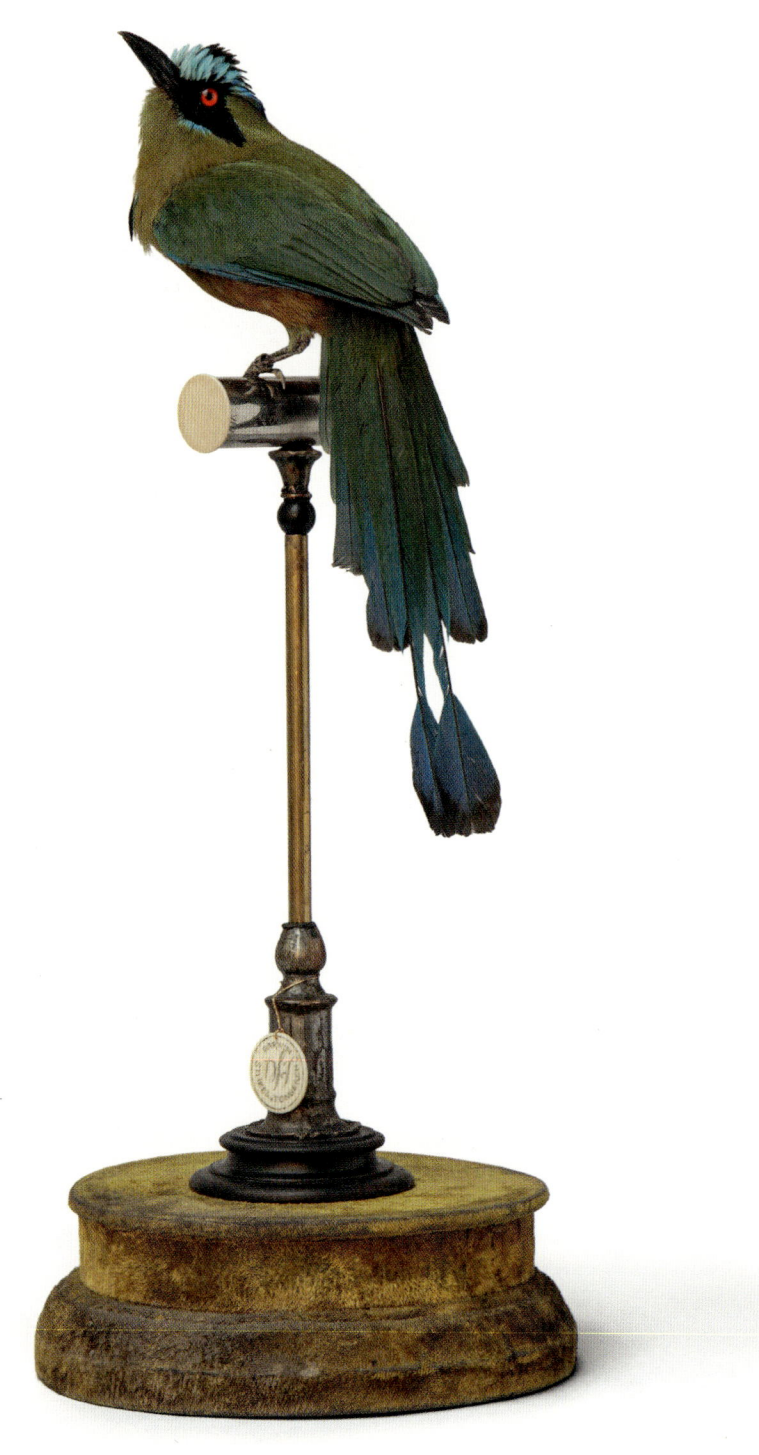

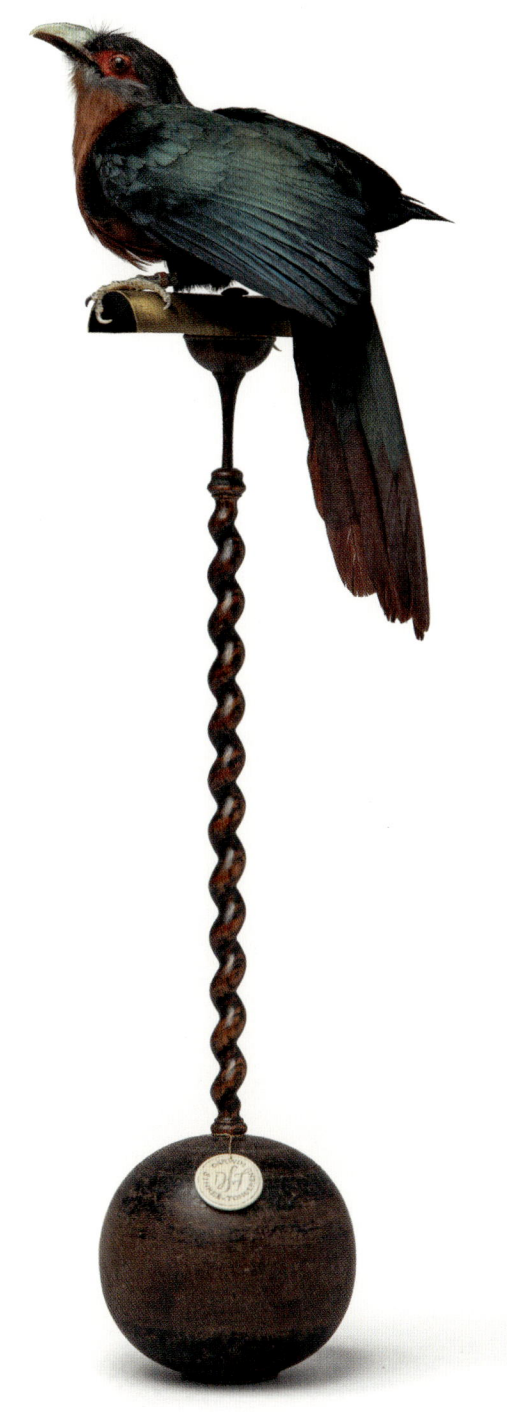

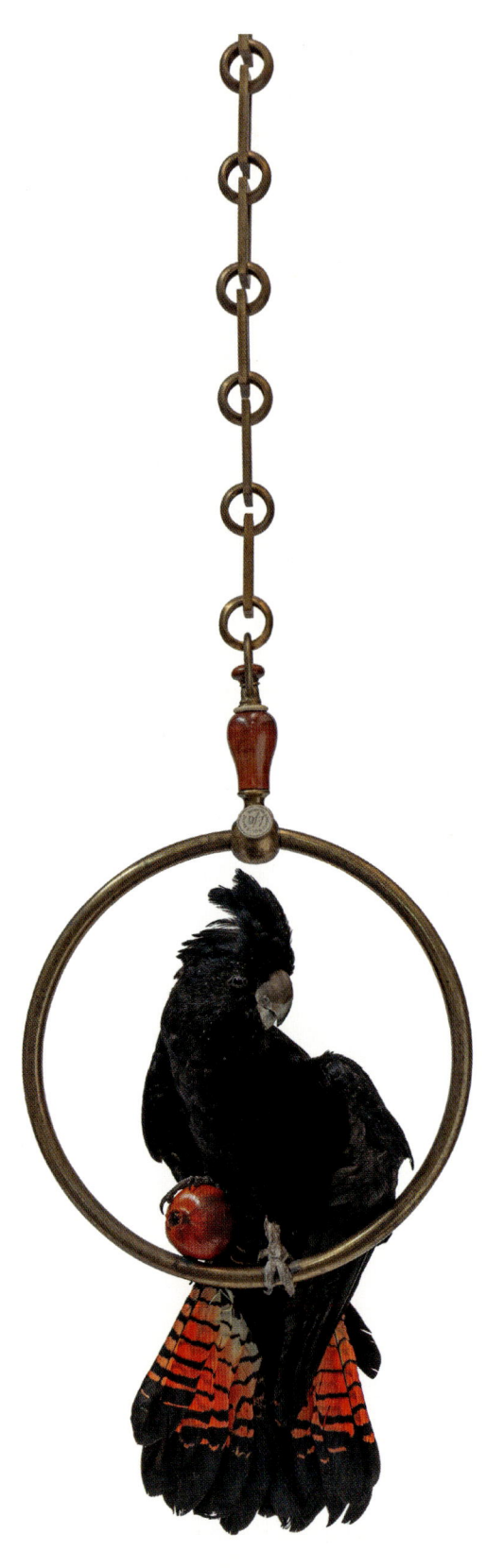

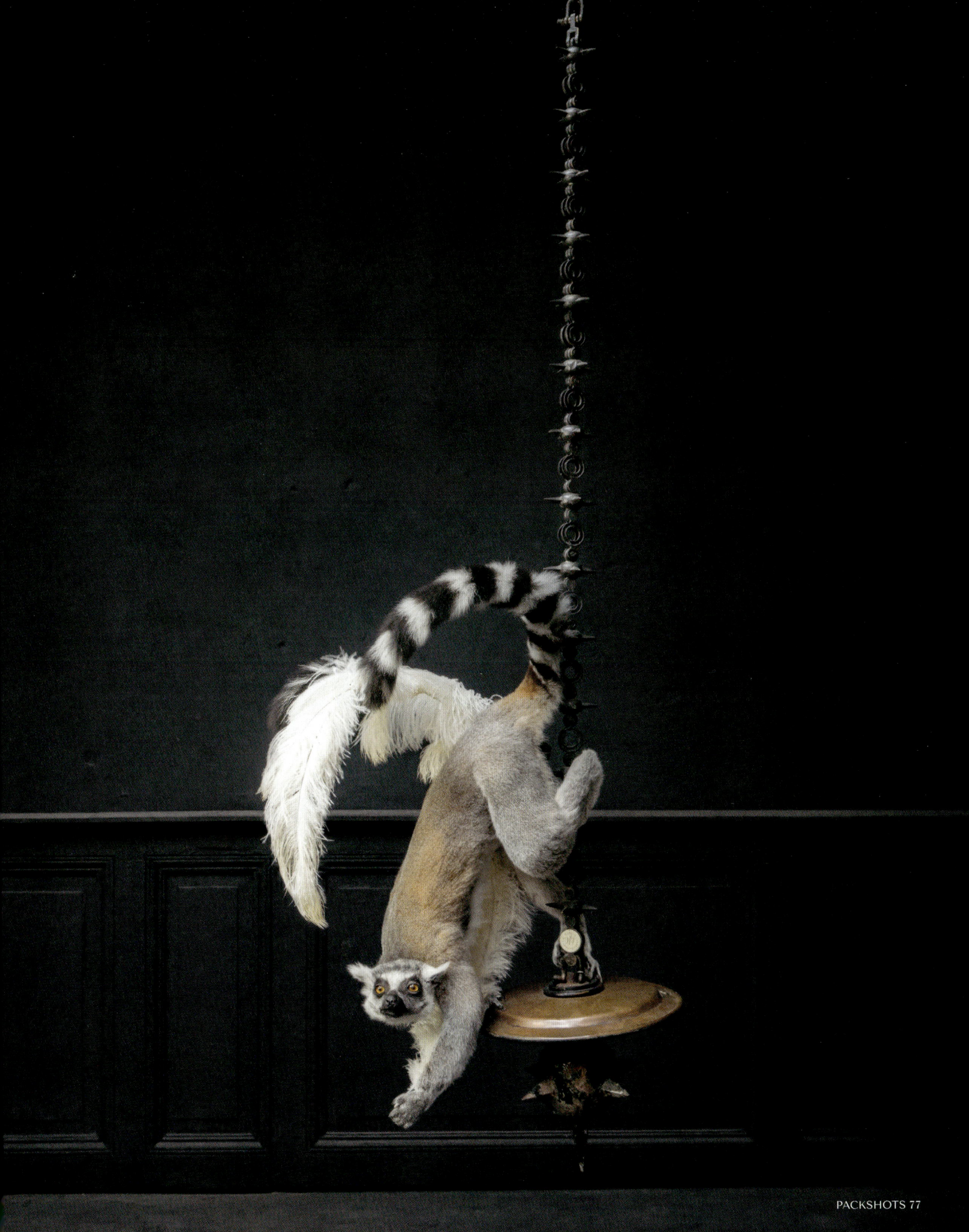

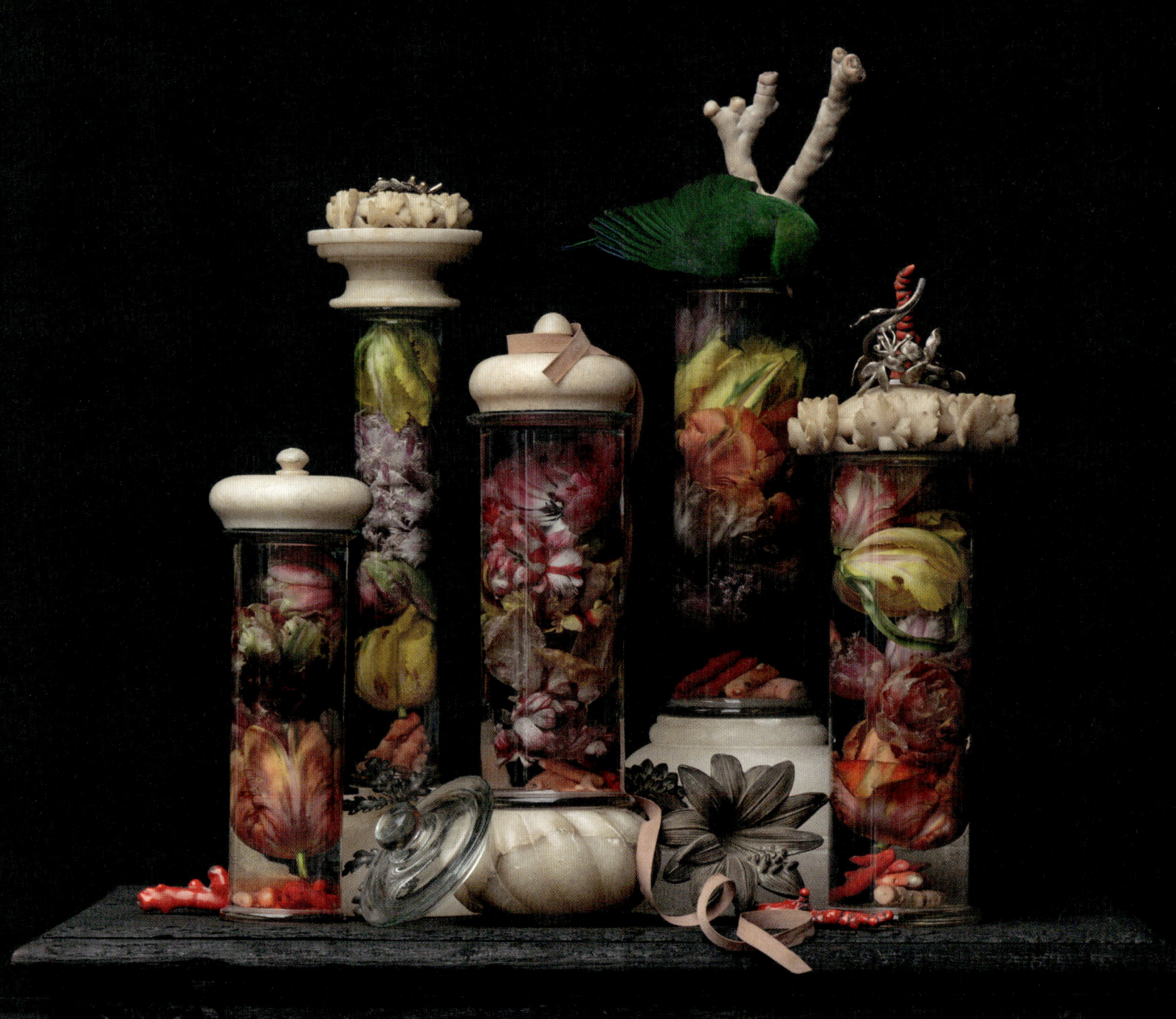

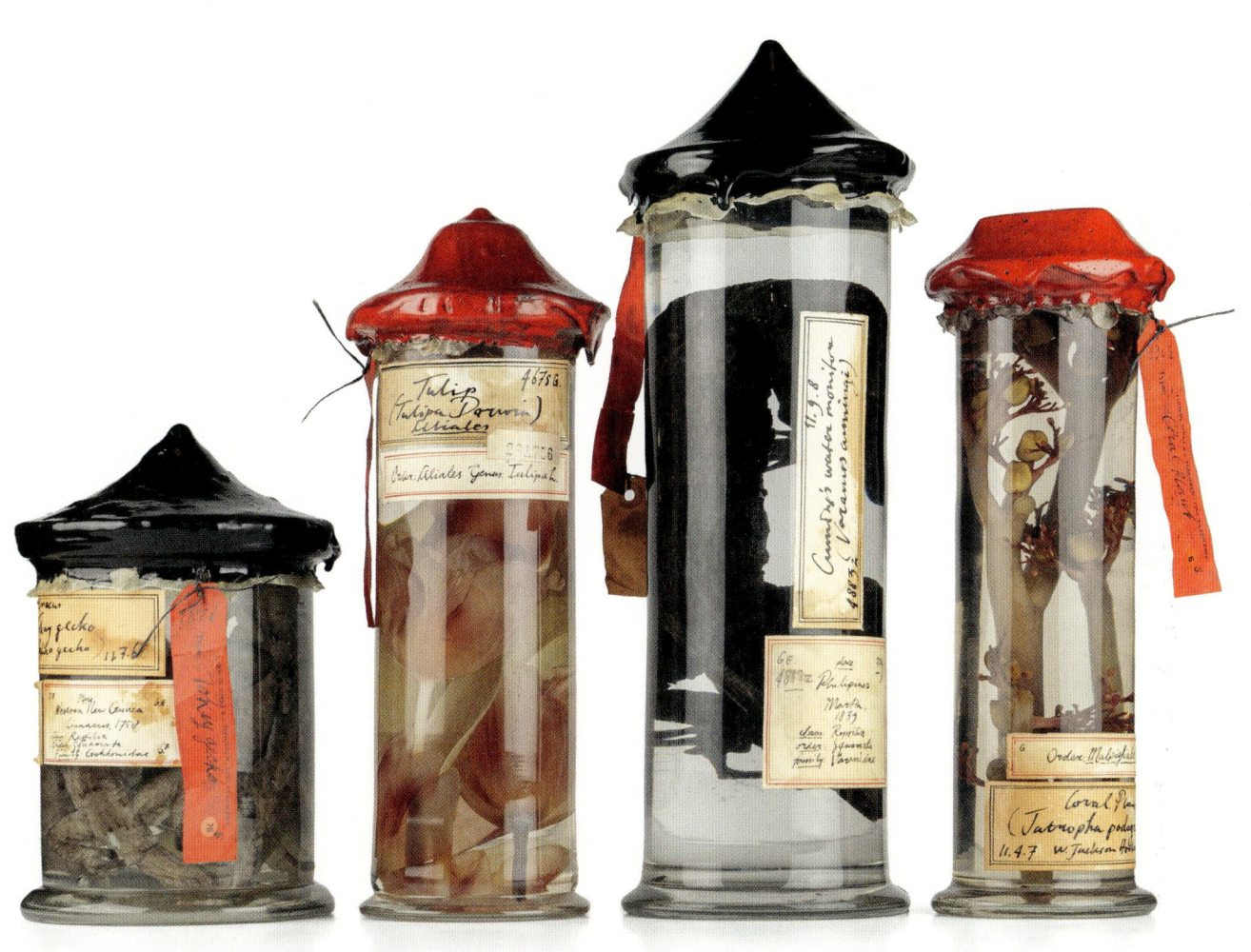

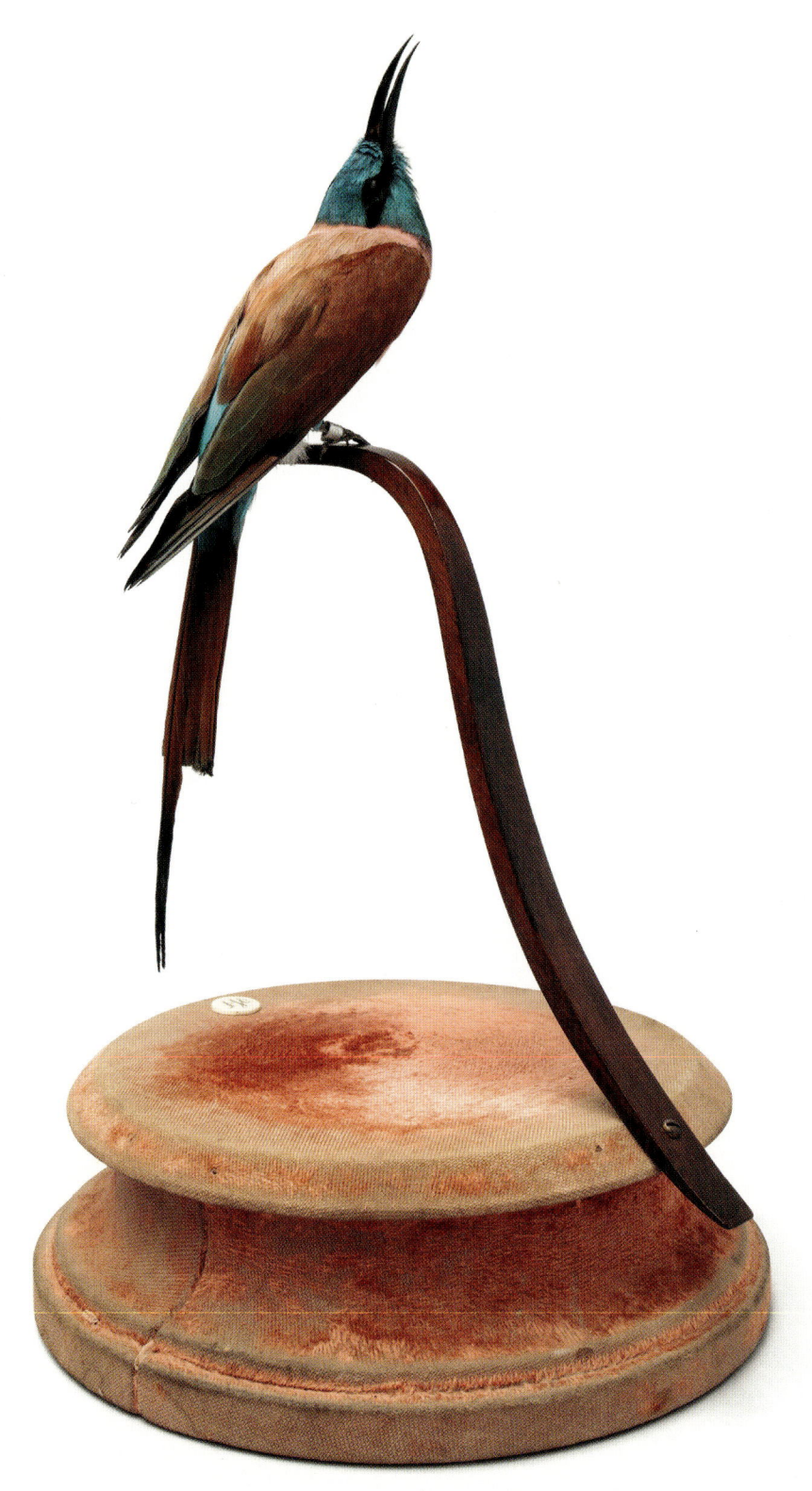

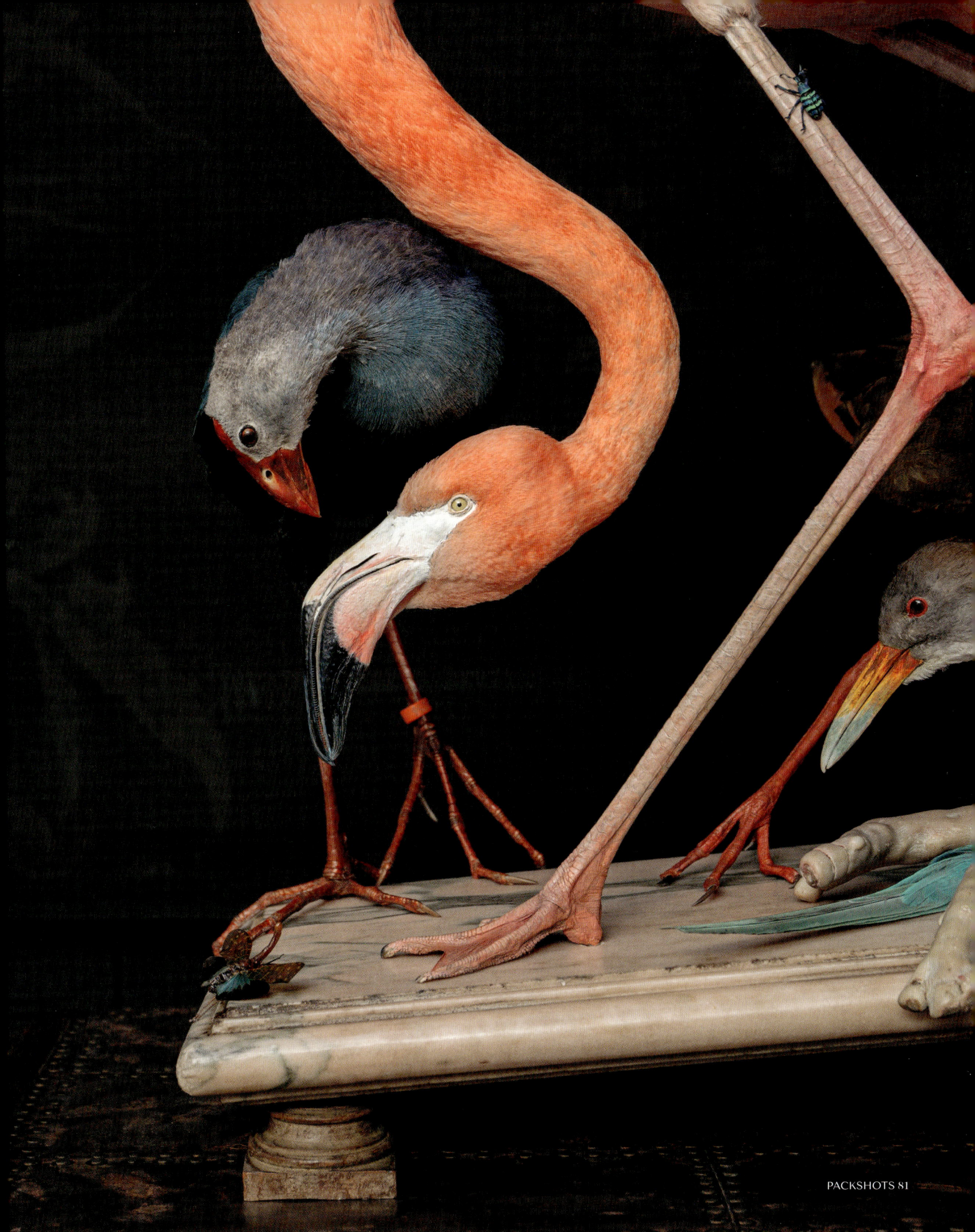

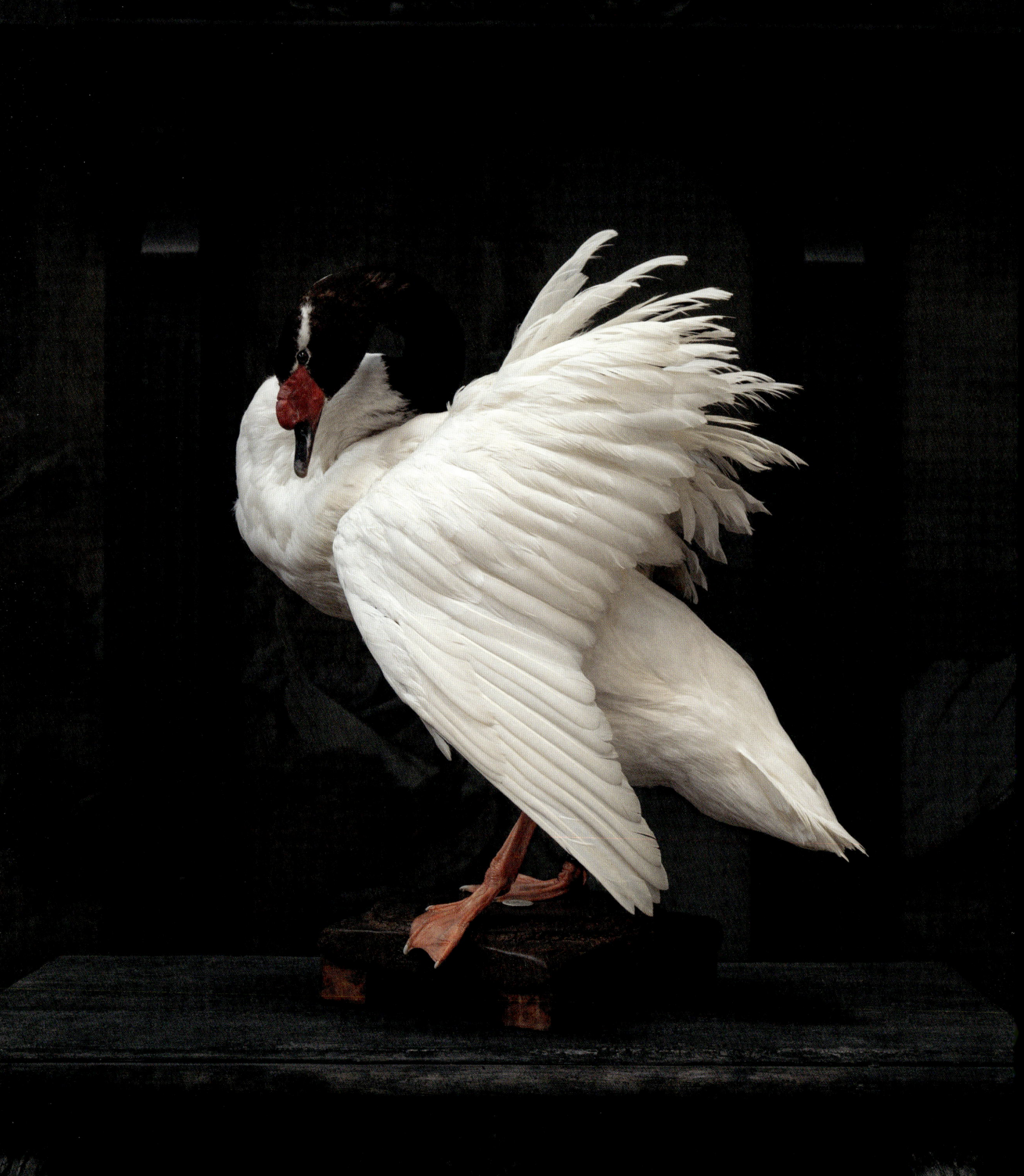

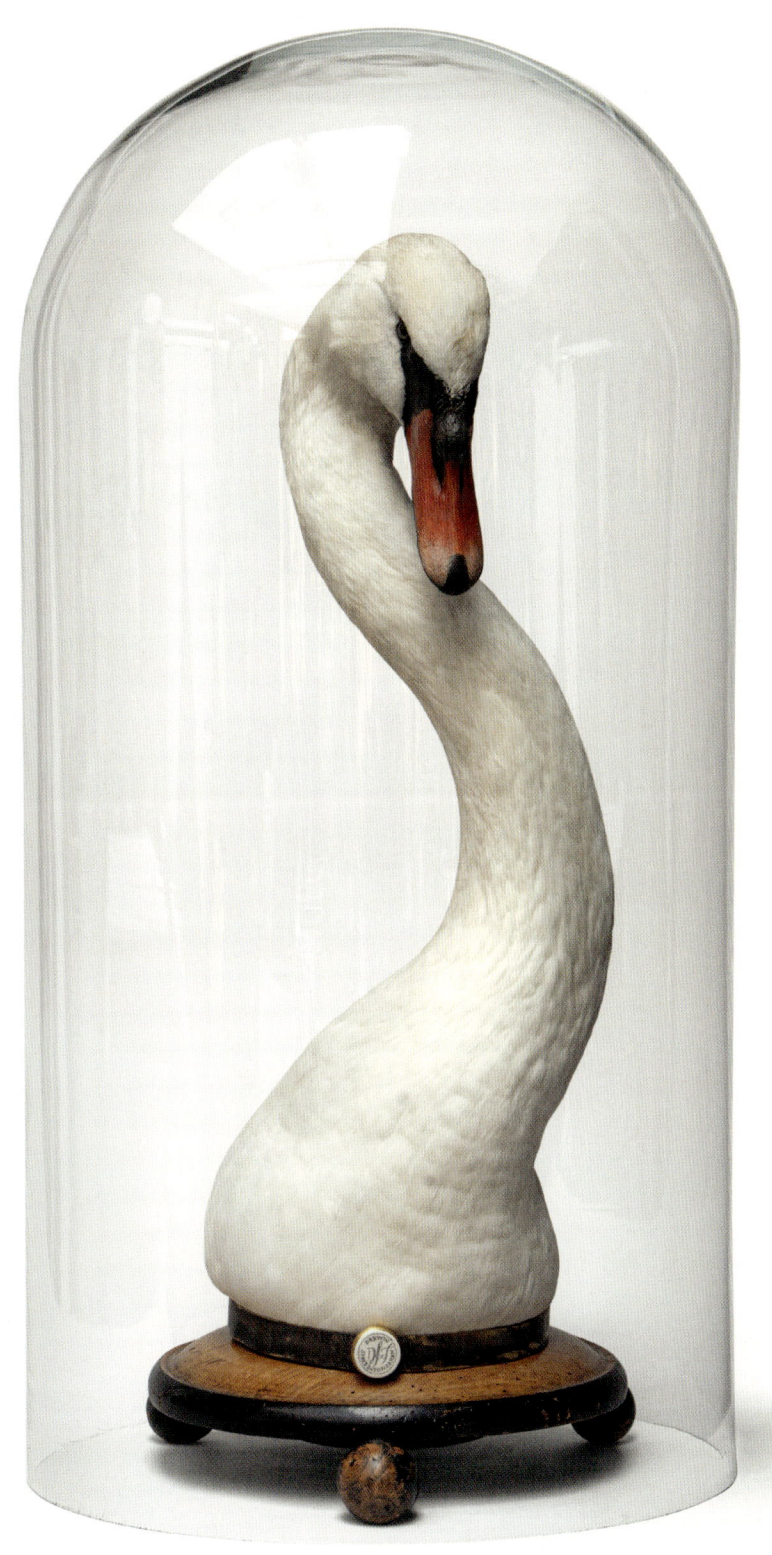

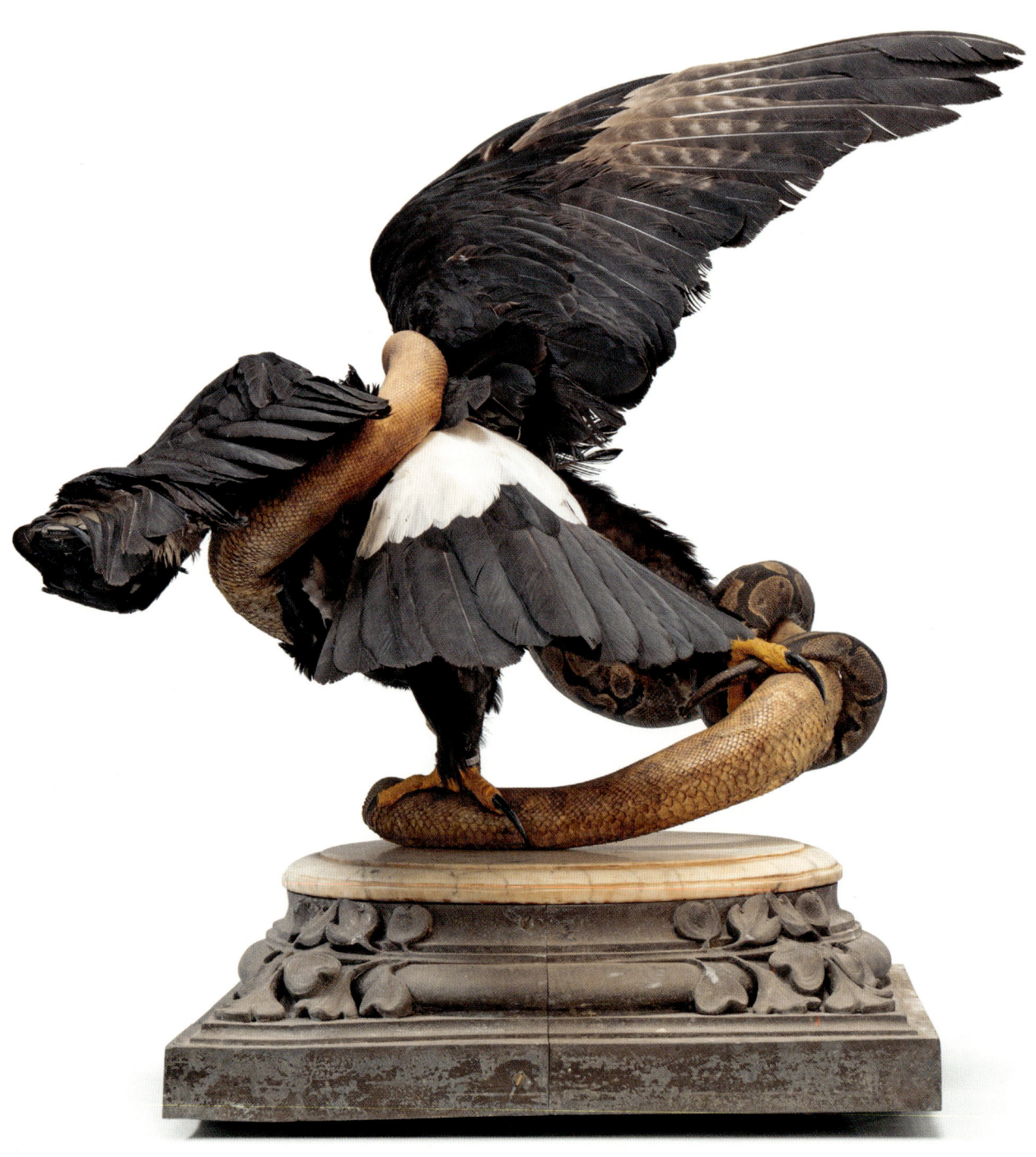

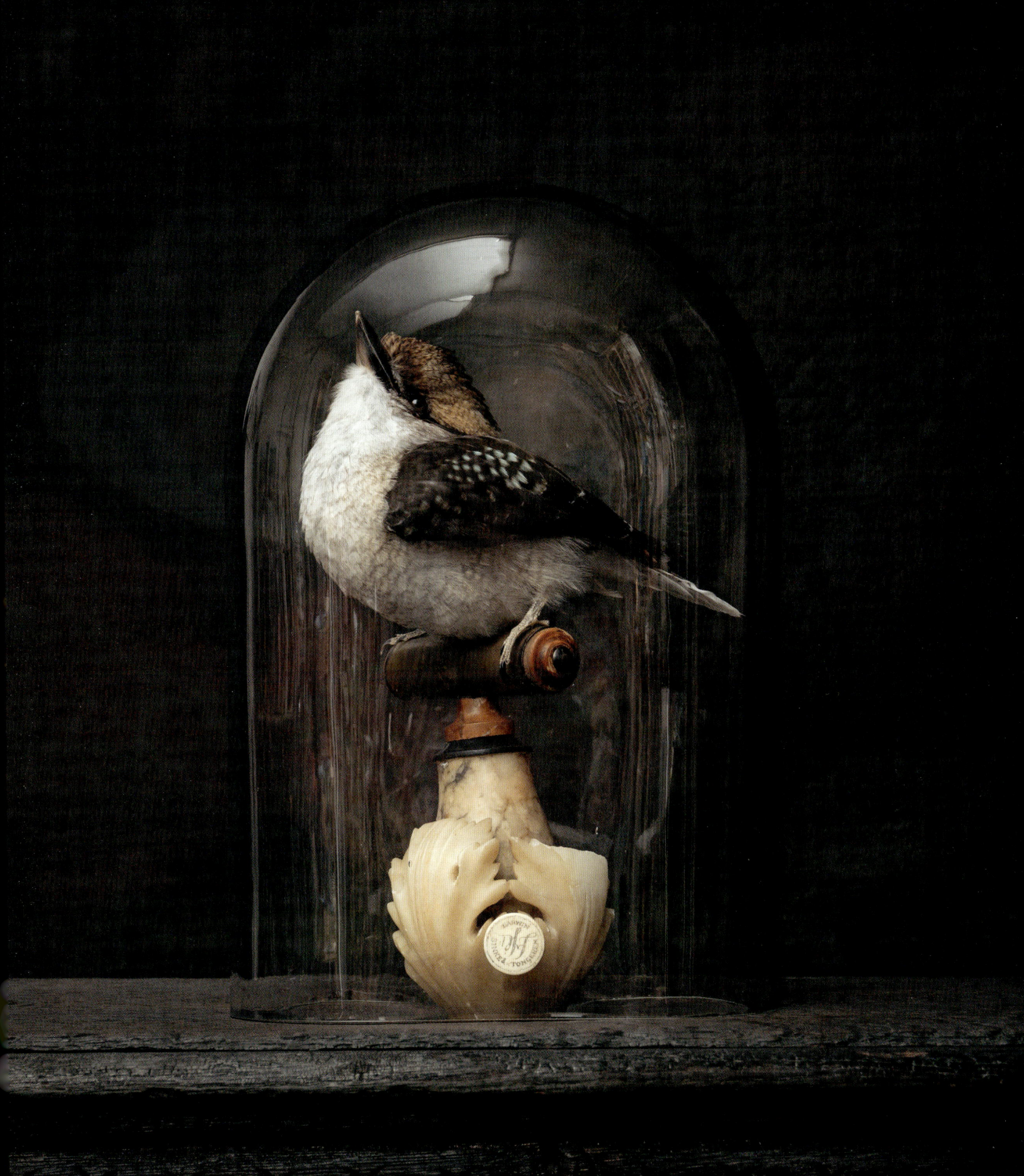

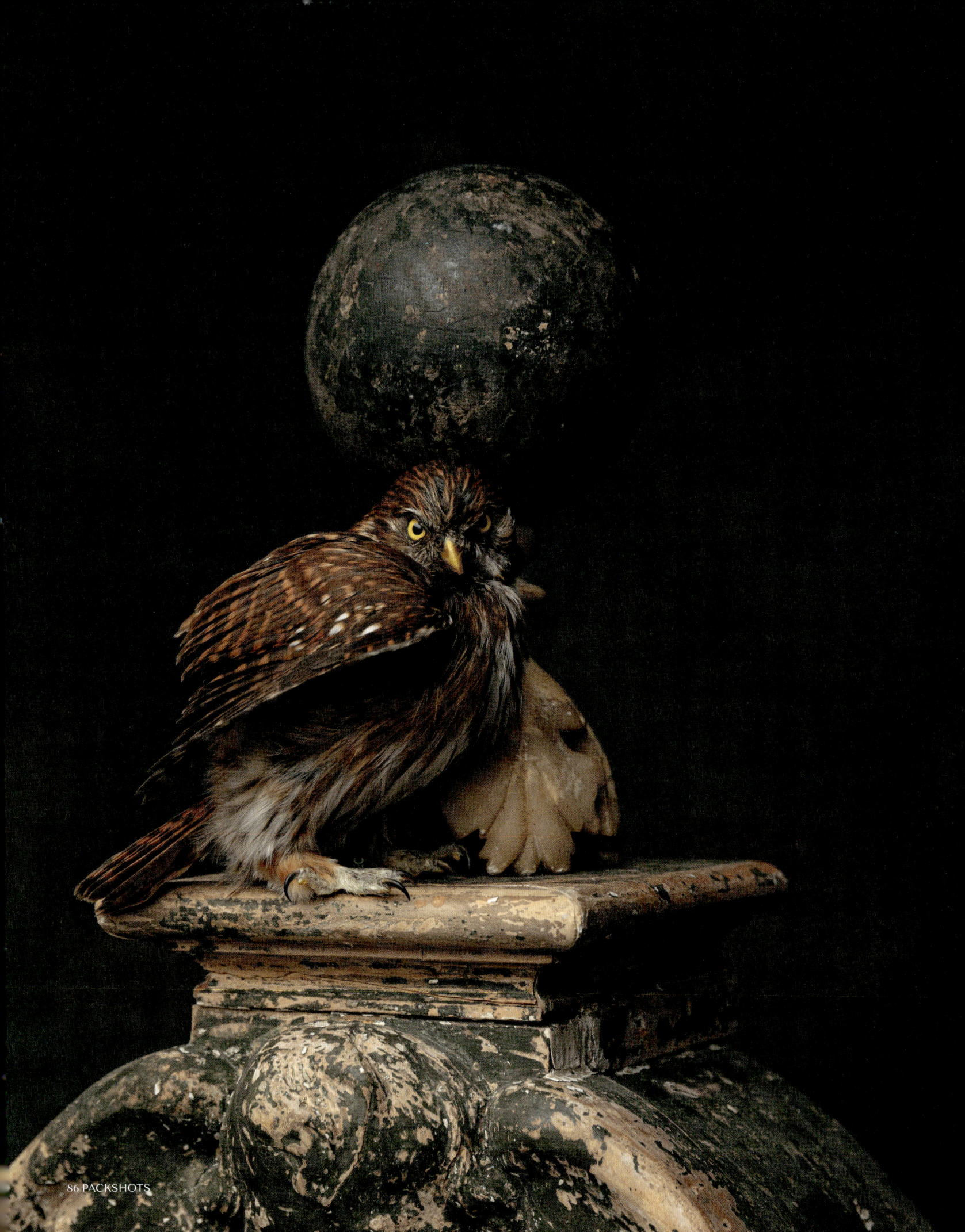

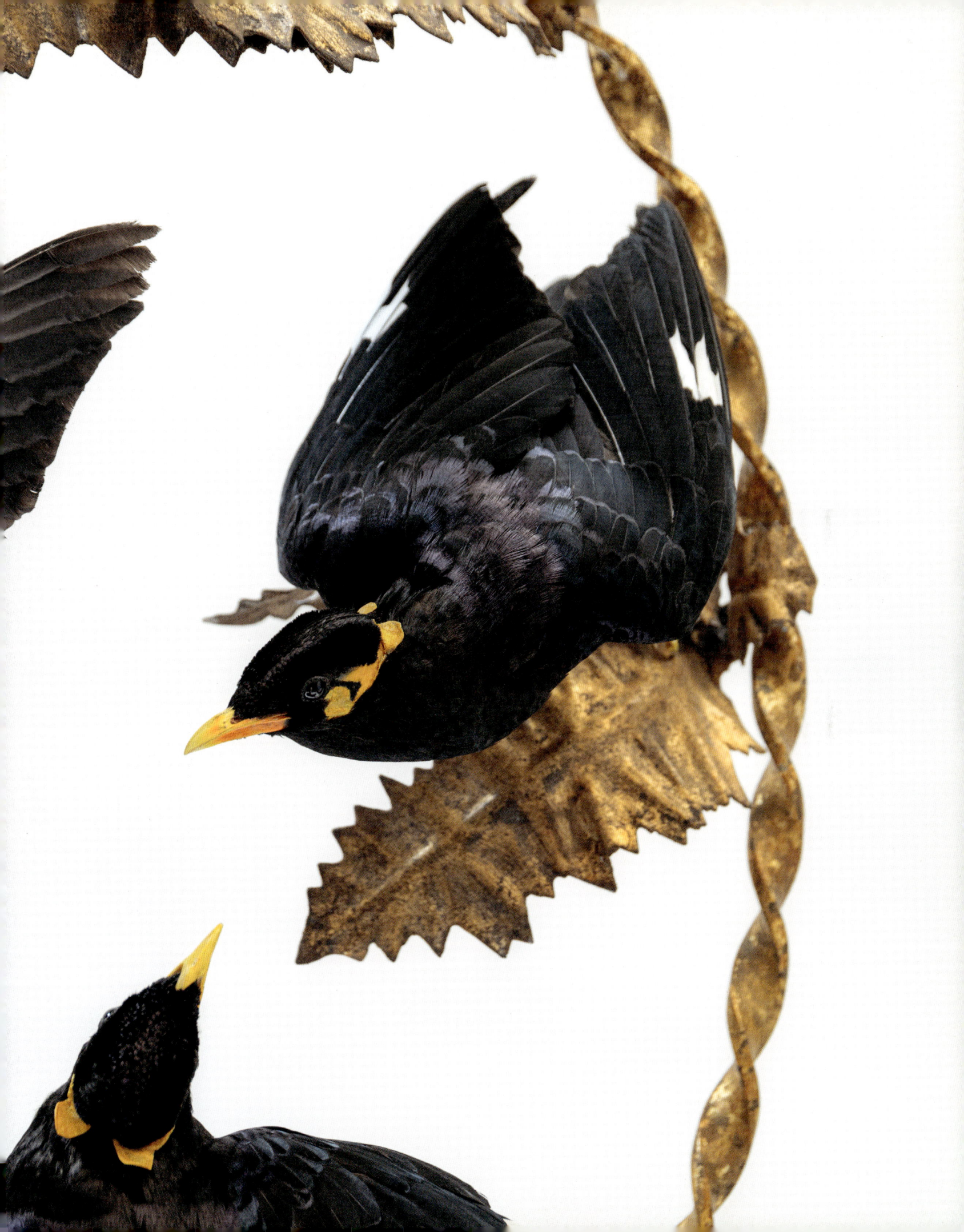

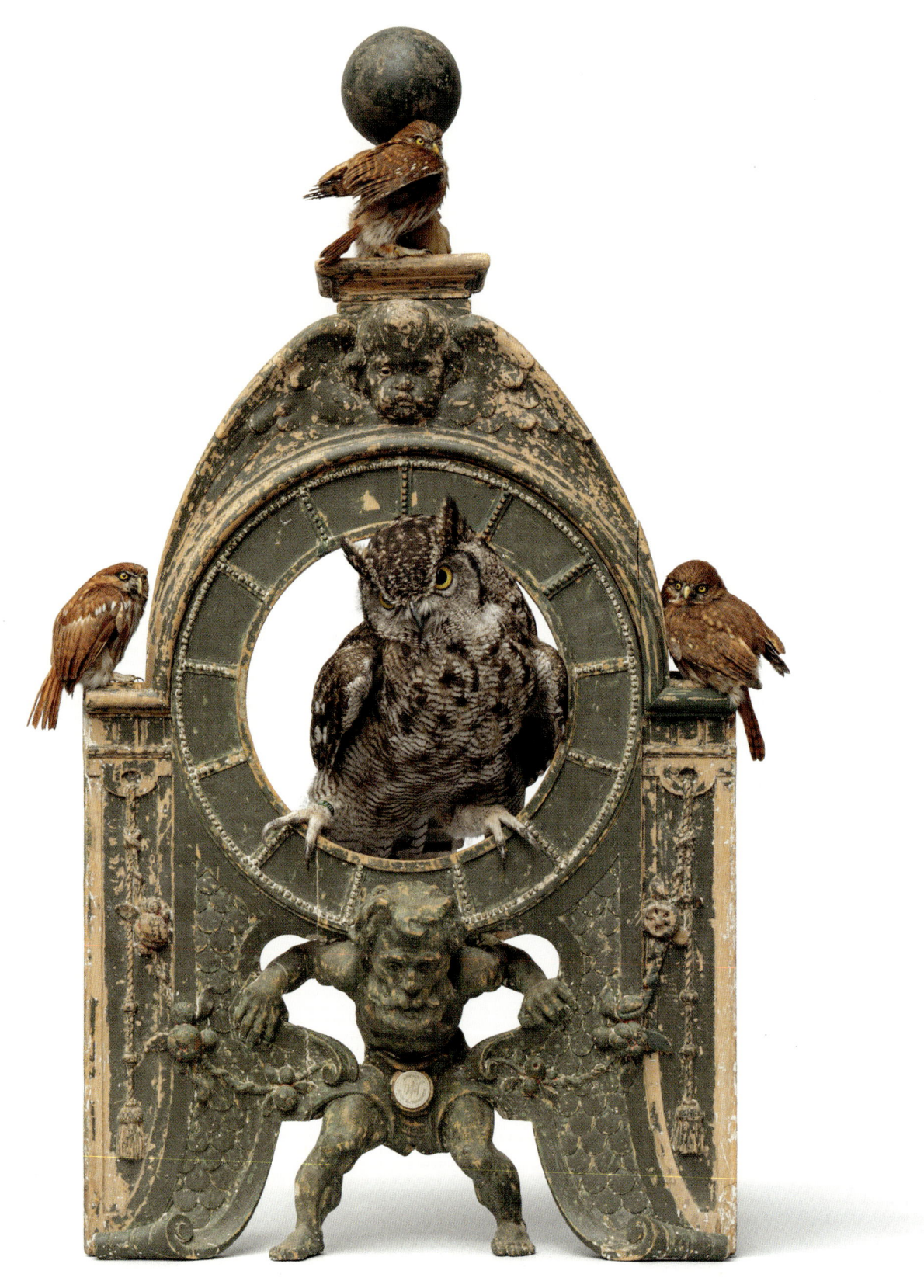

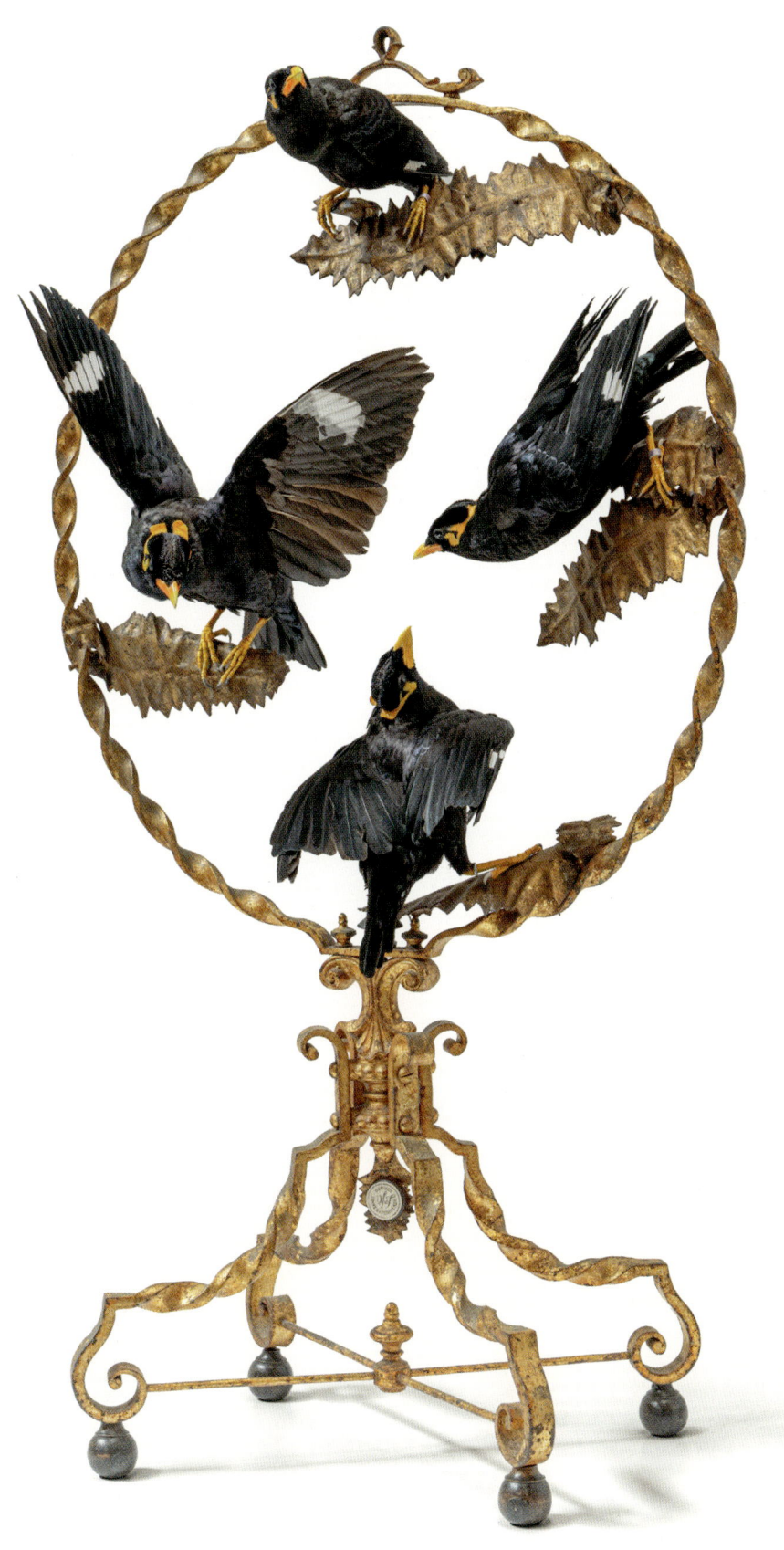

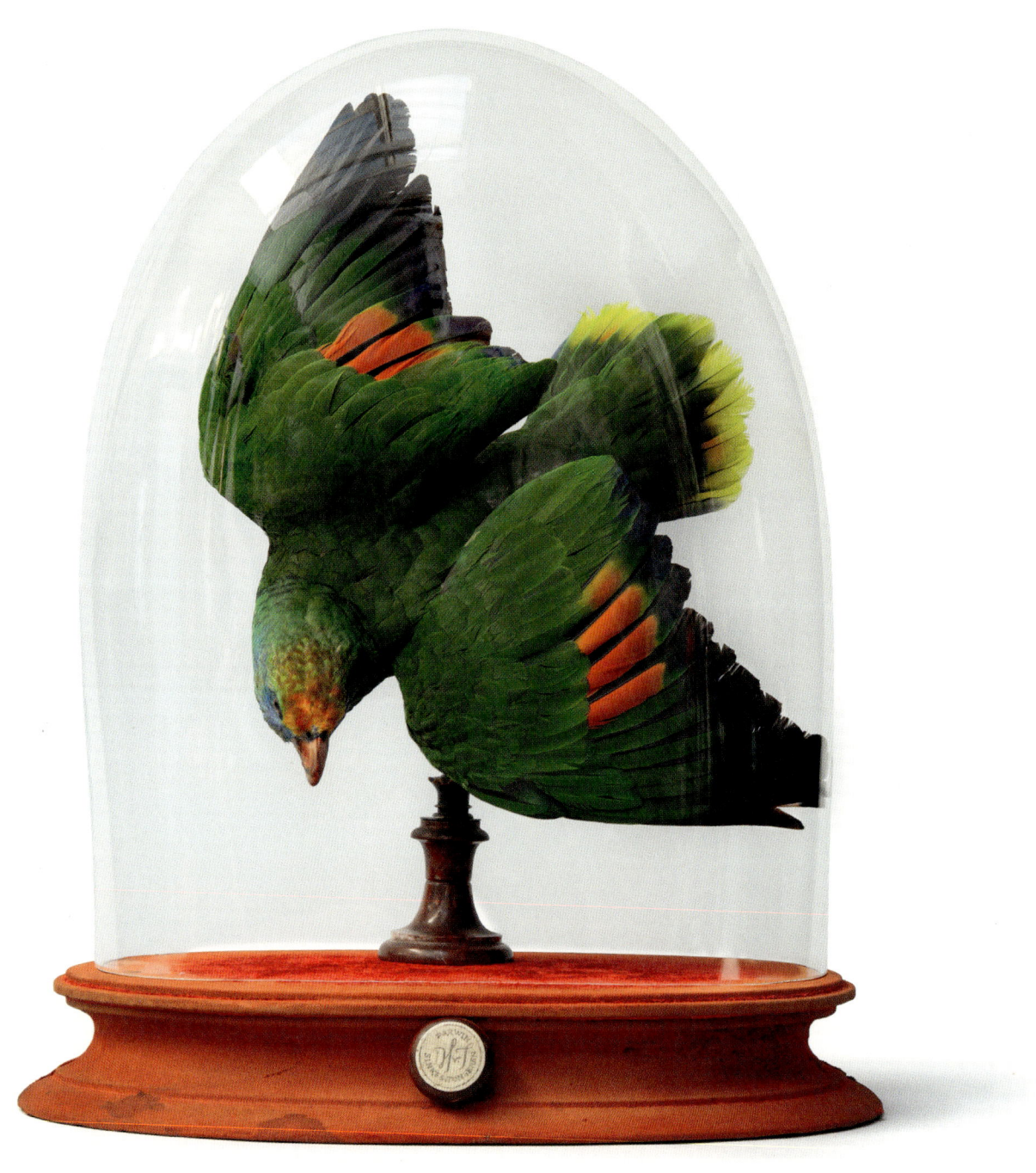

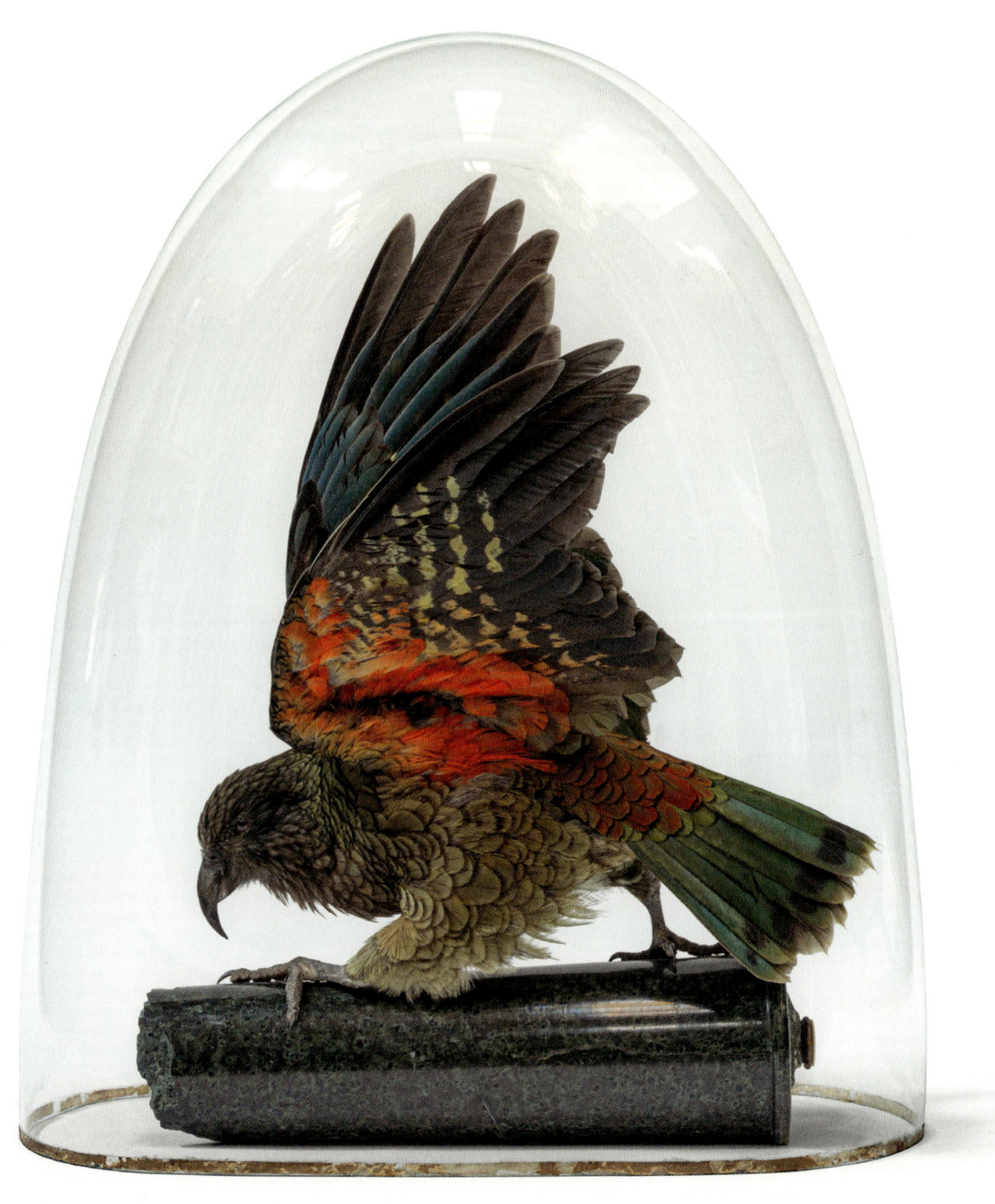

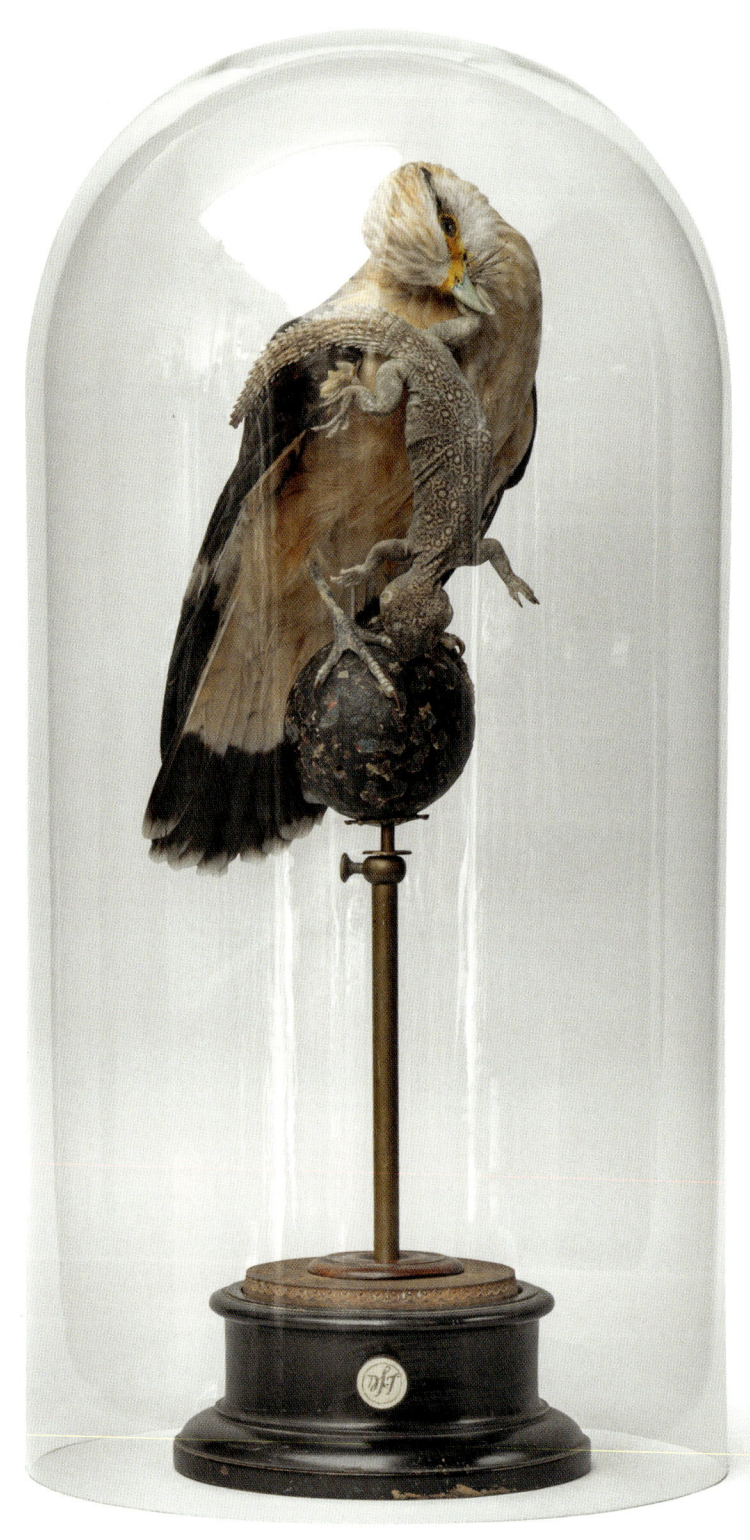

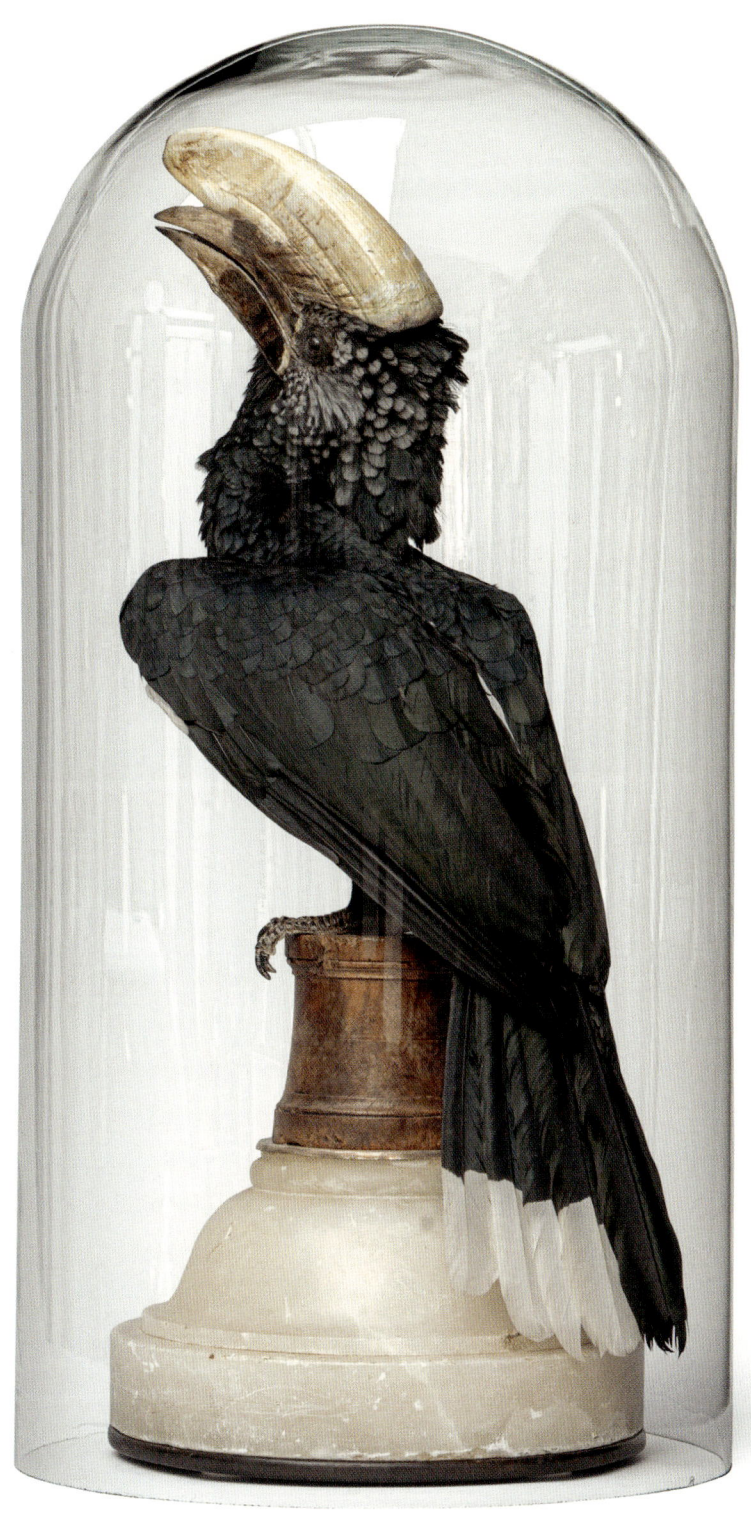

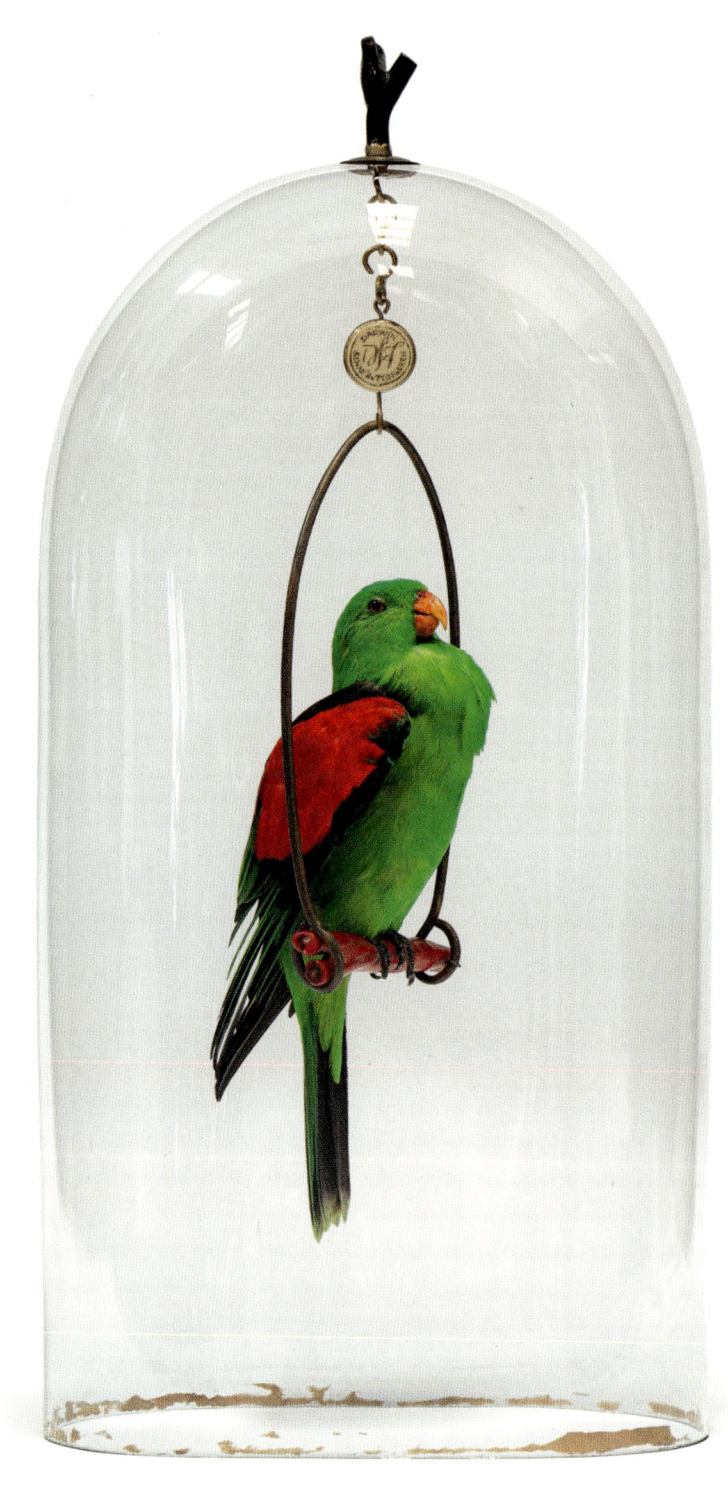

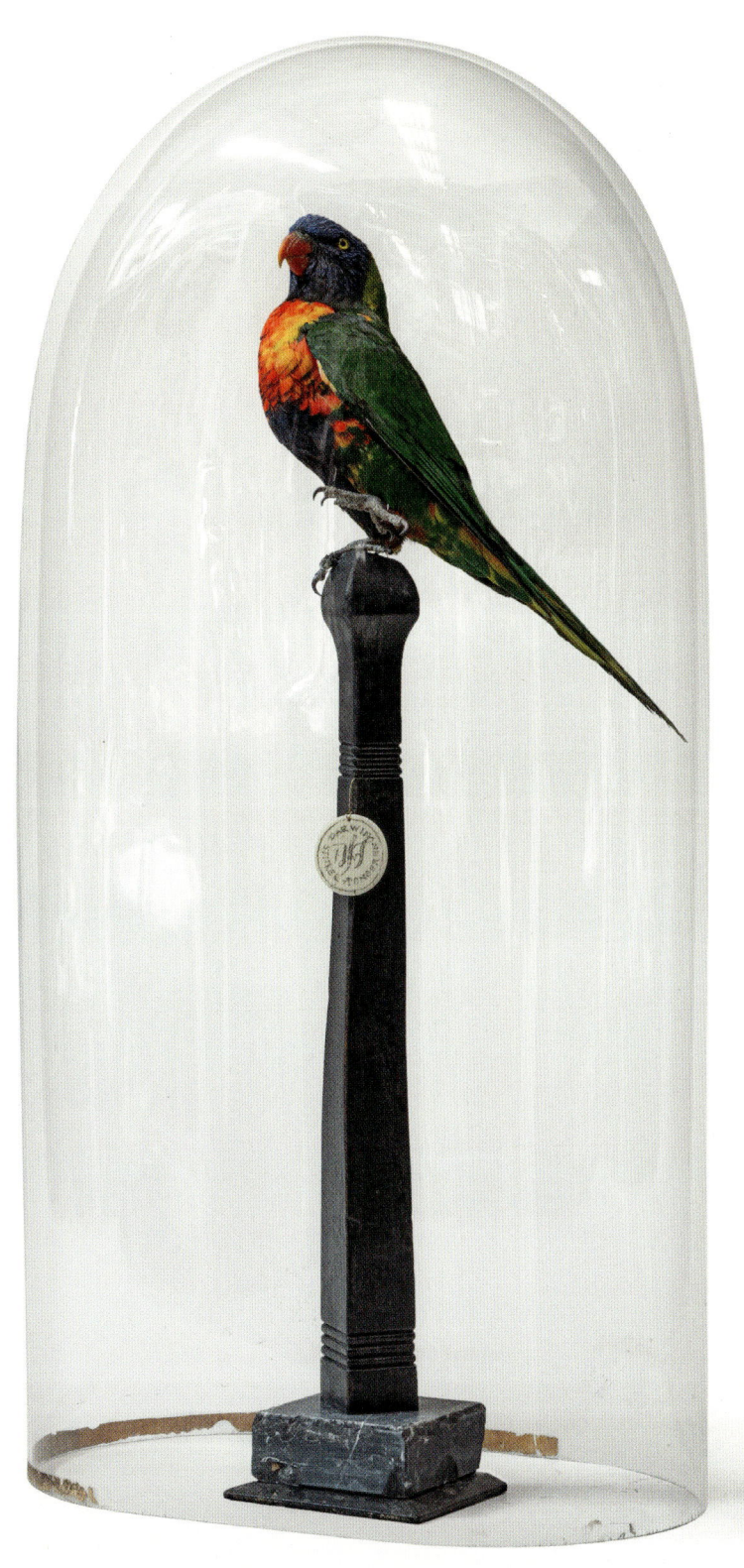

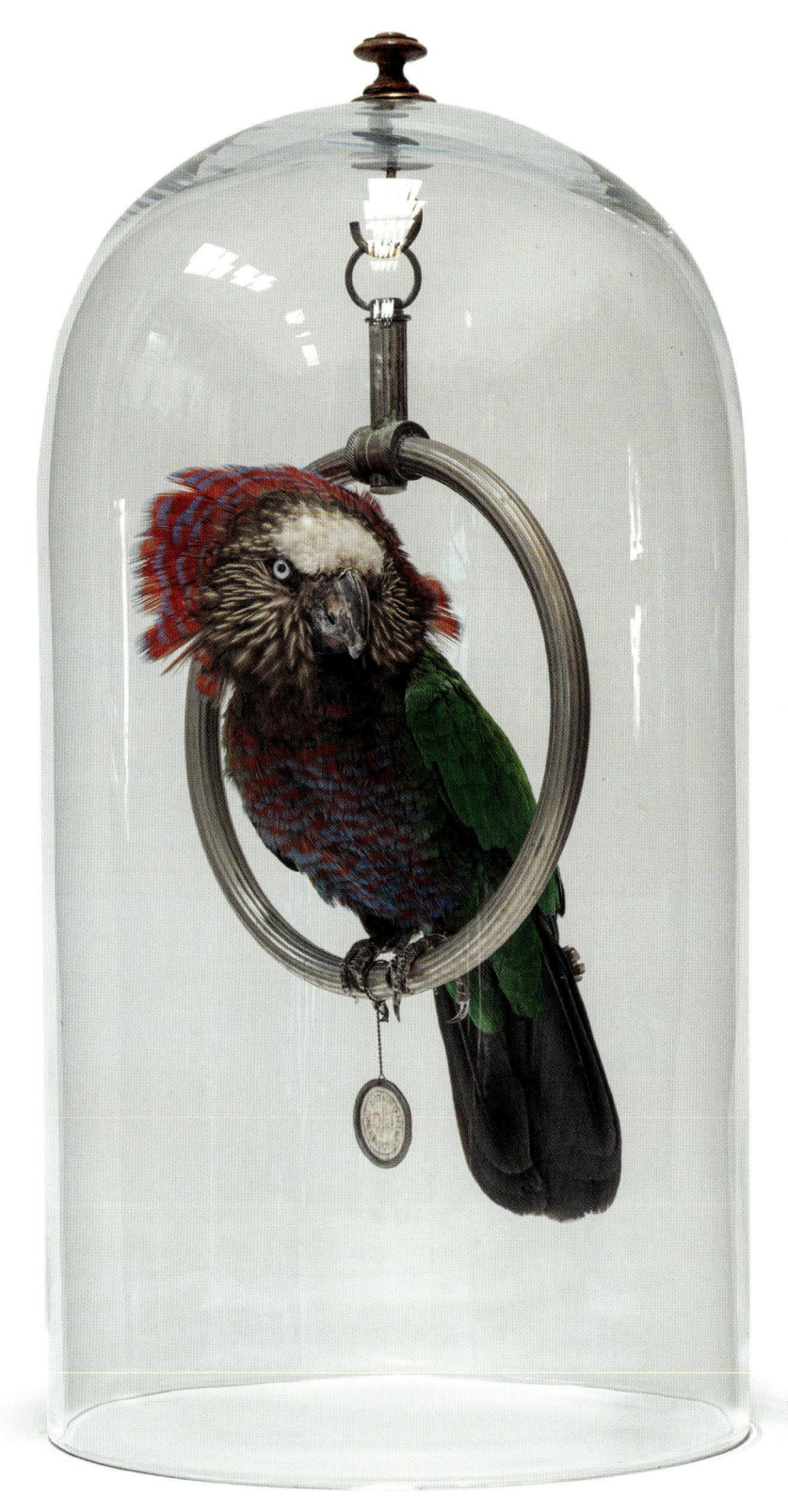

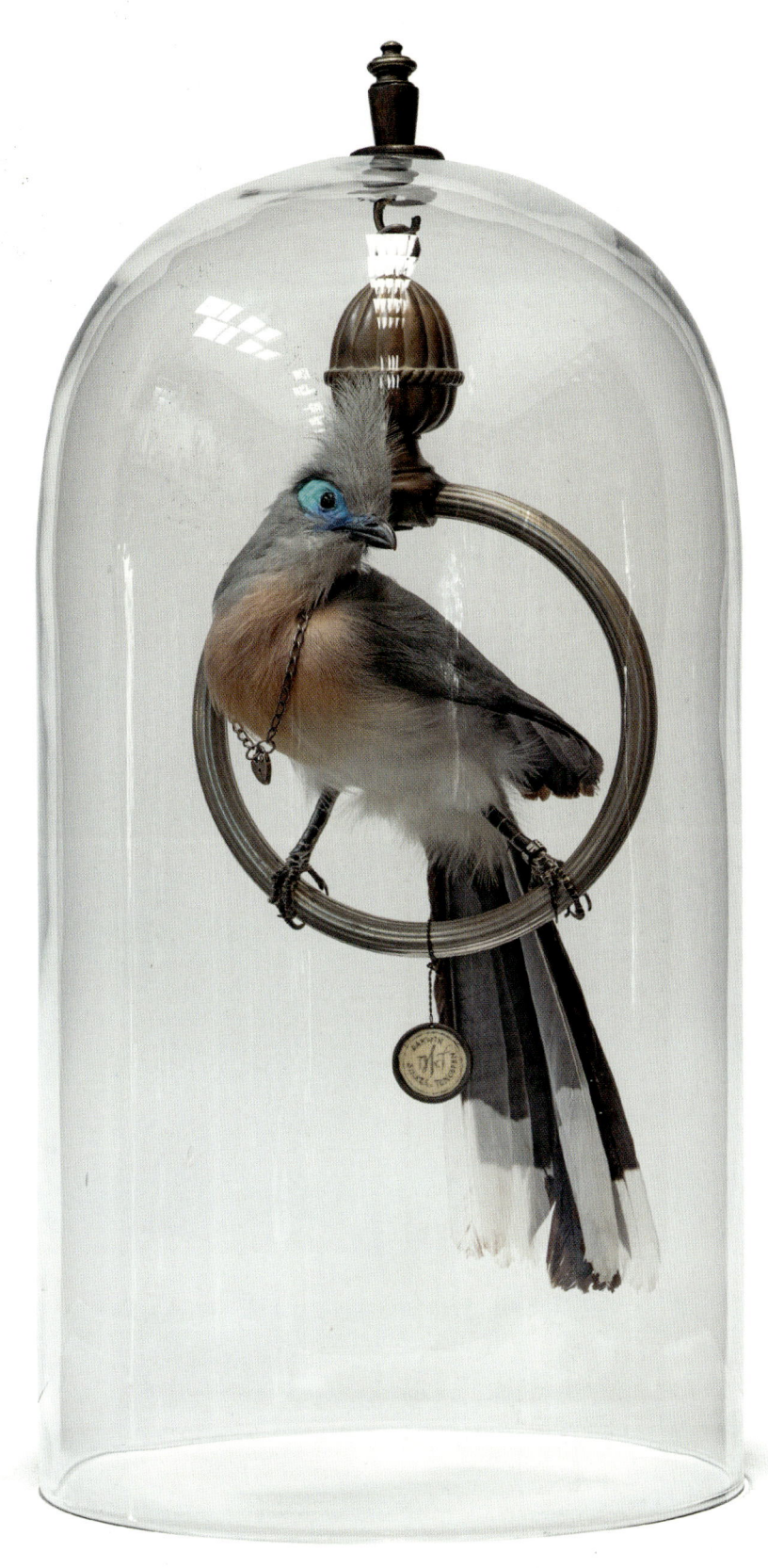

PACKSHOTS 97

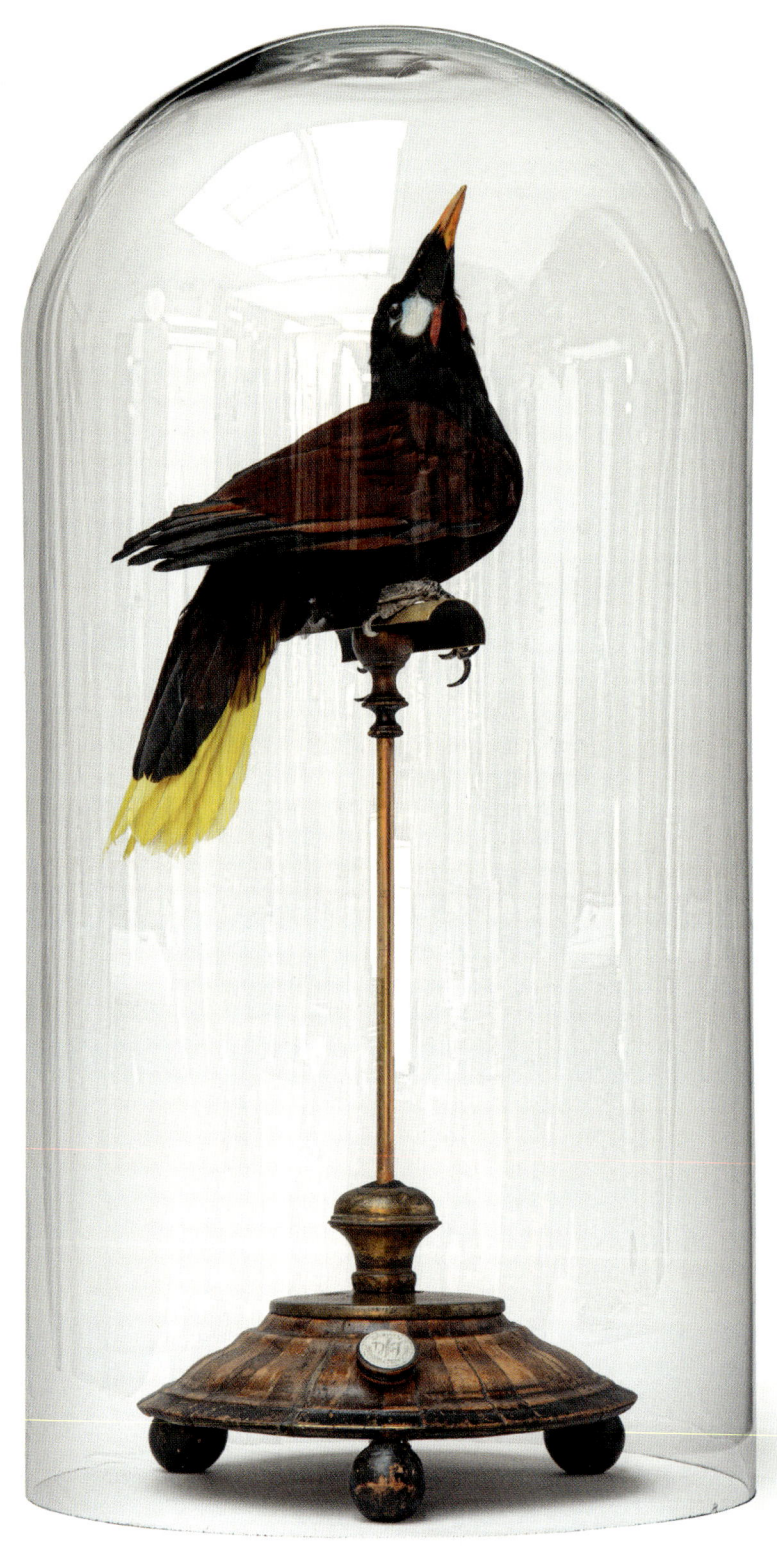

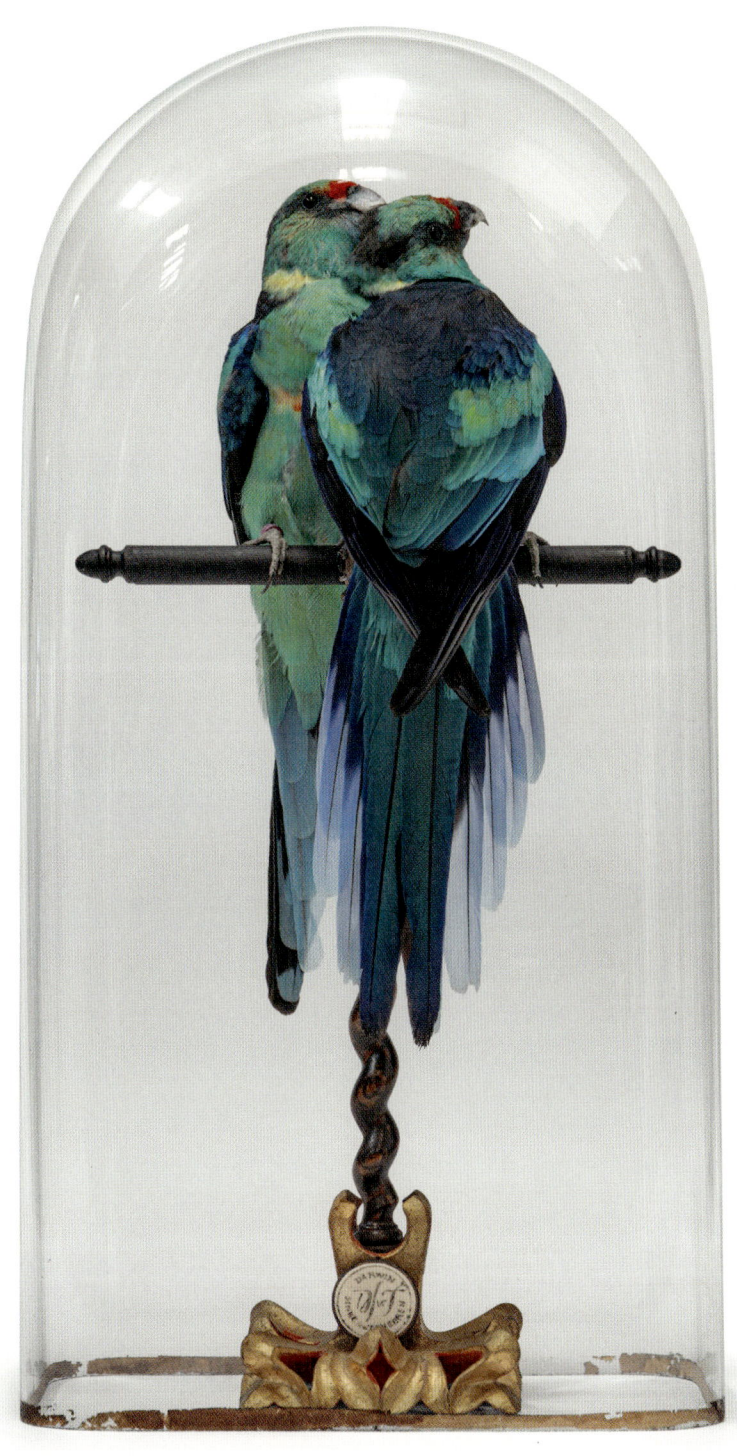

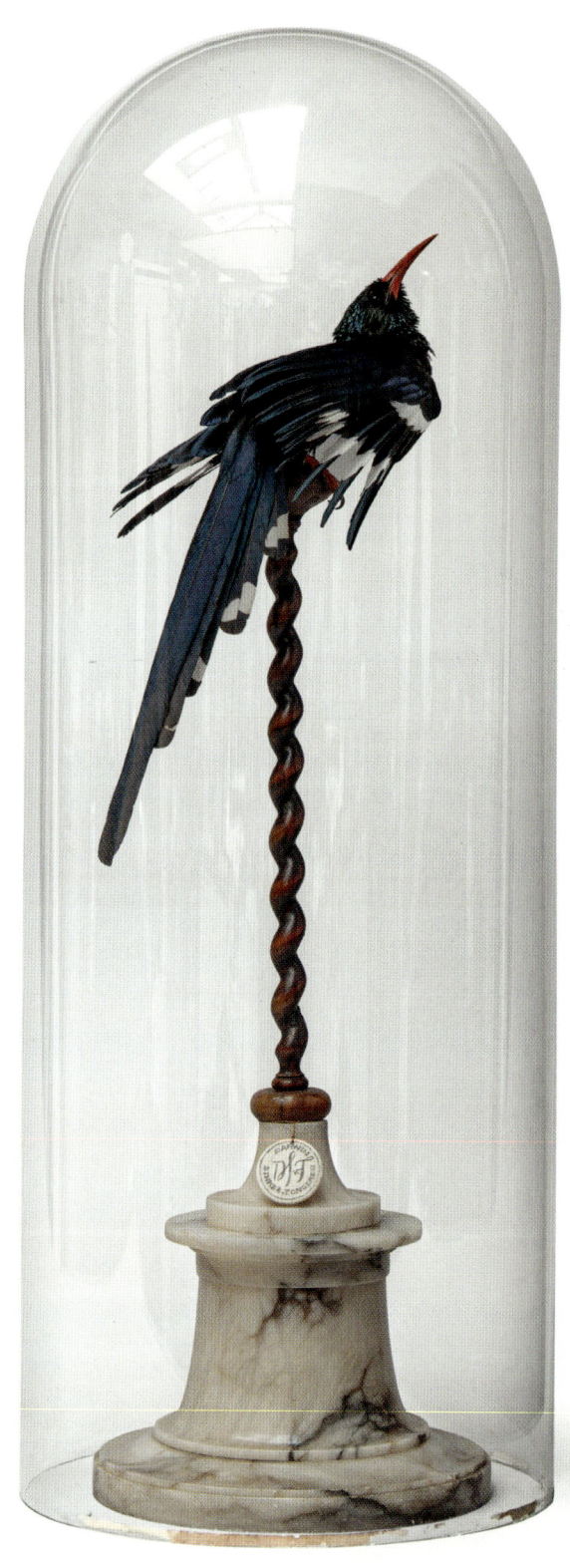

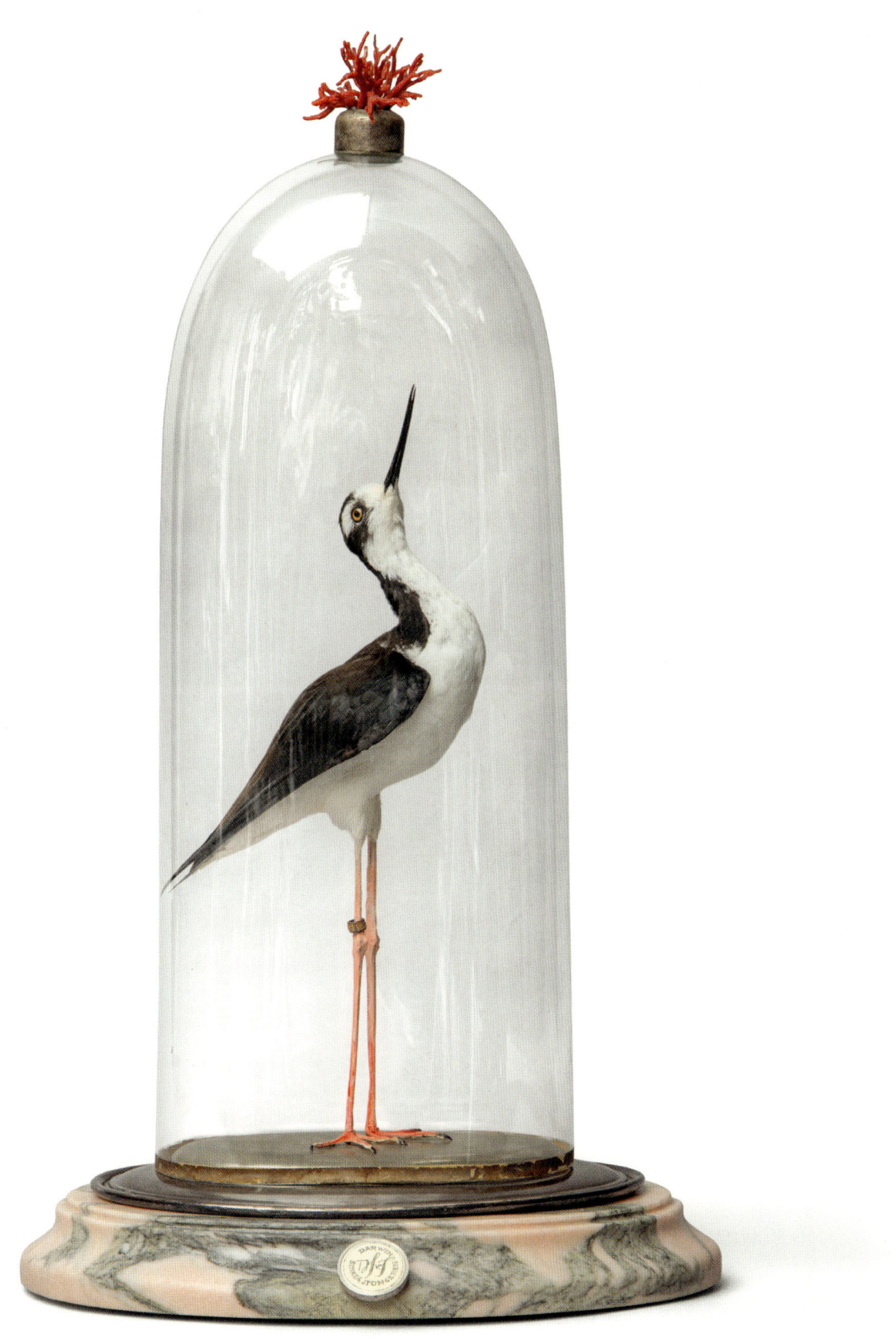

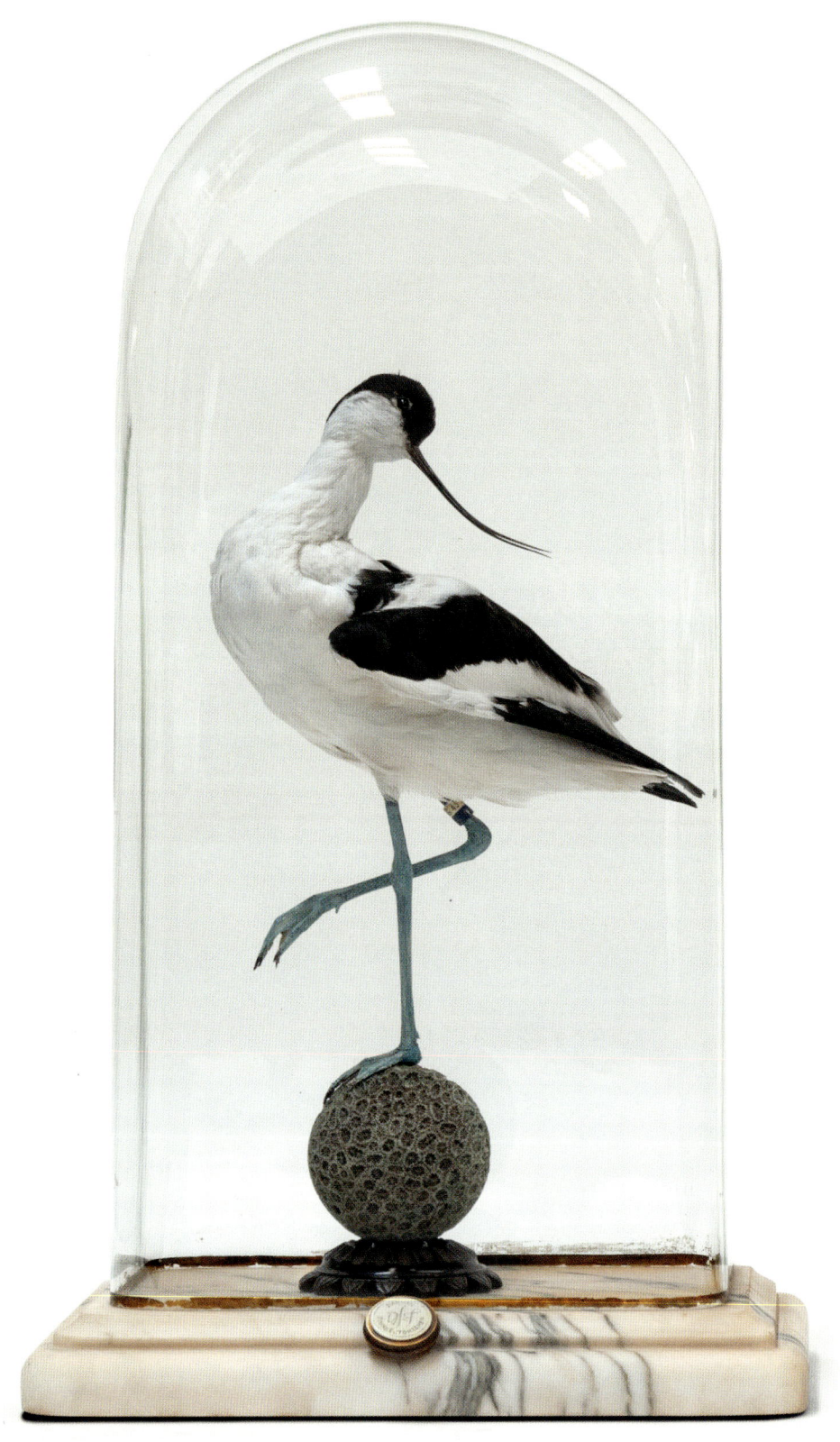

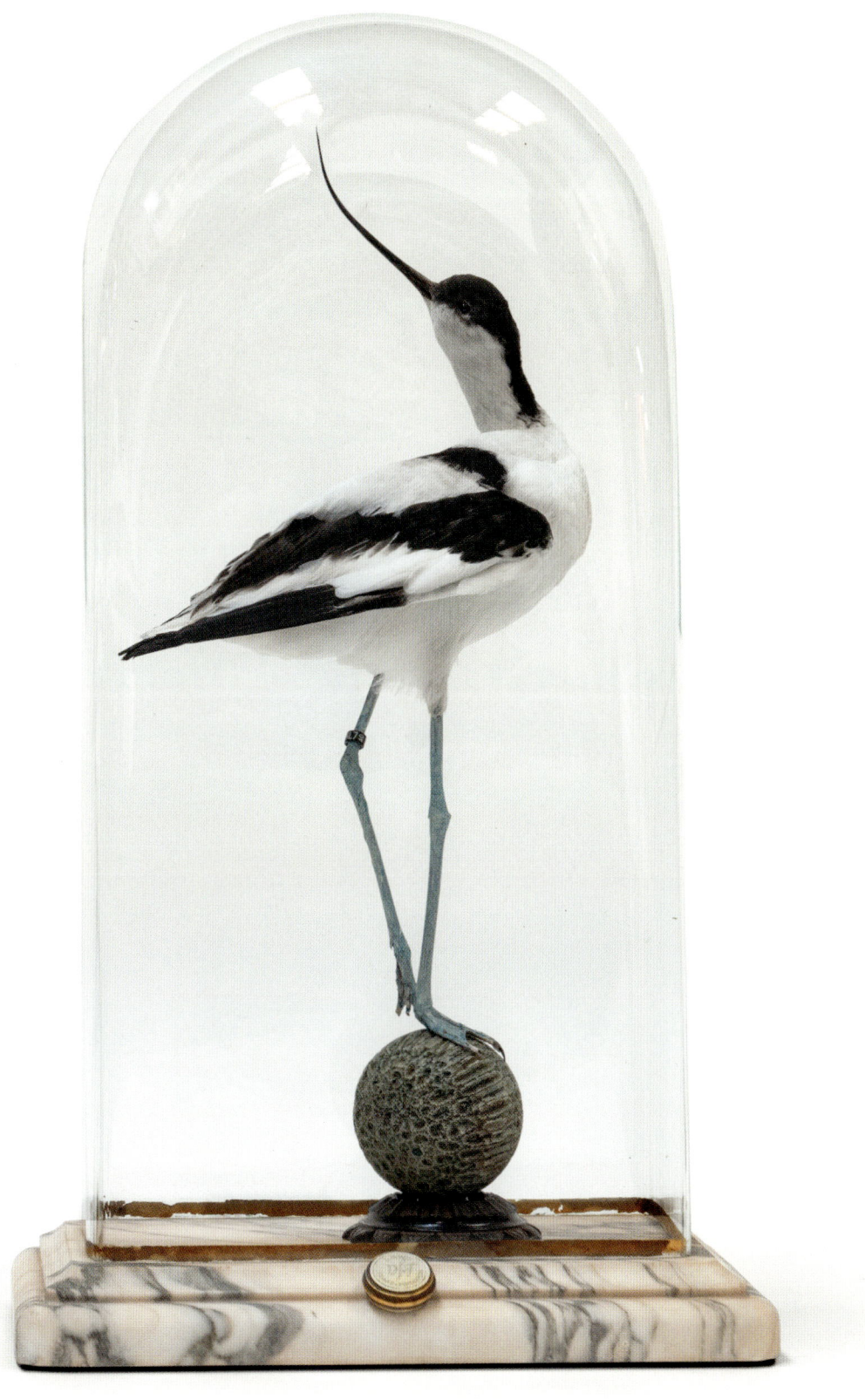

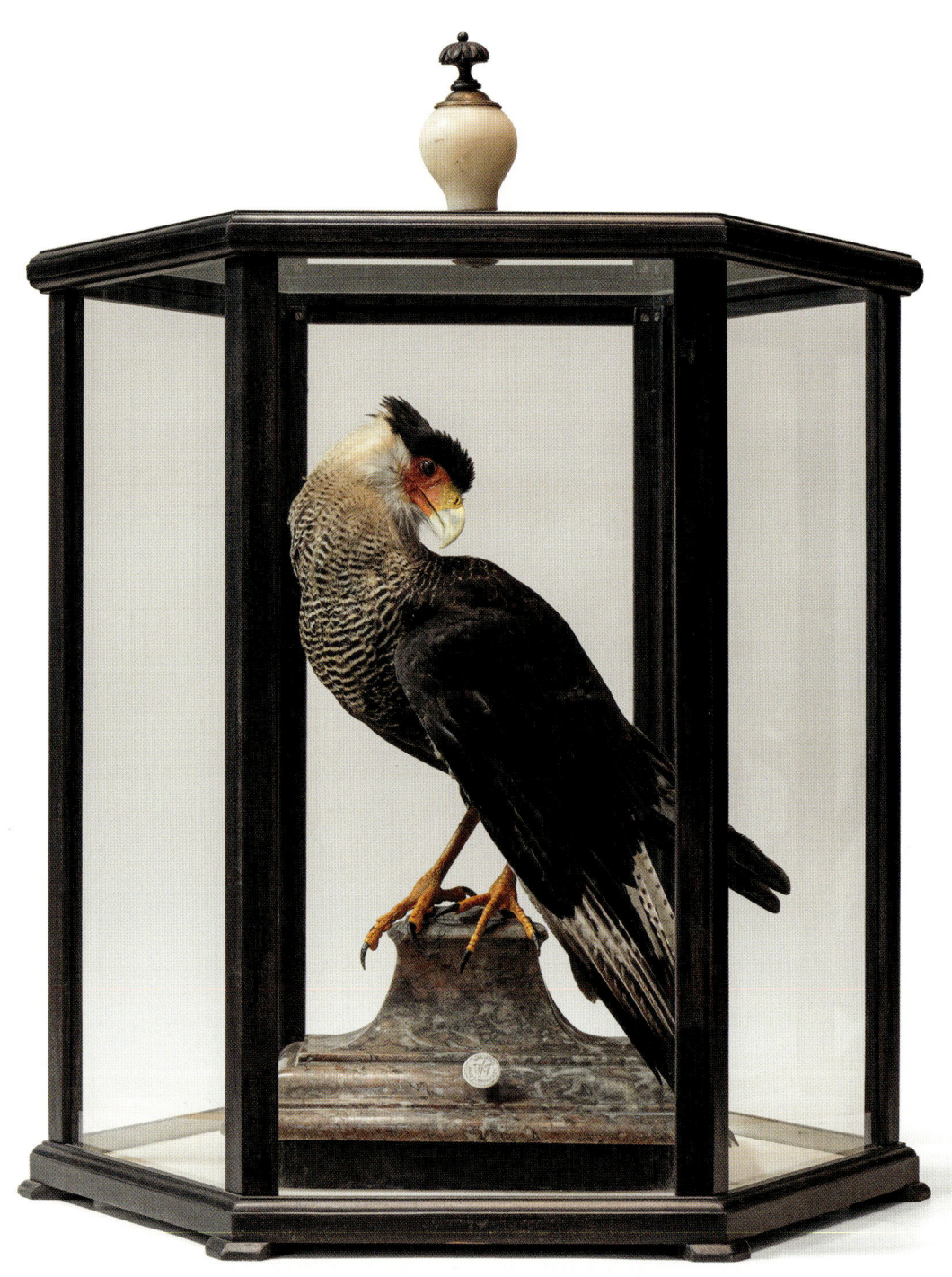

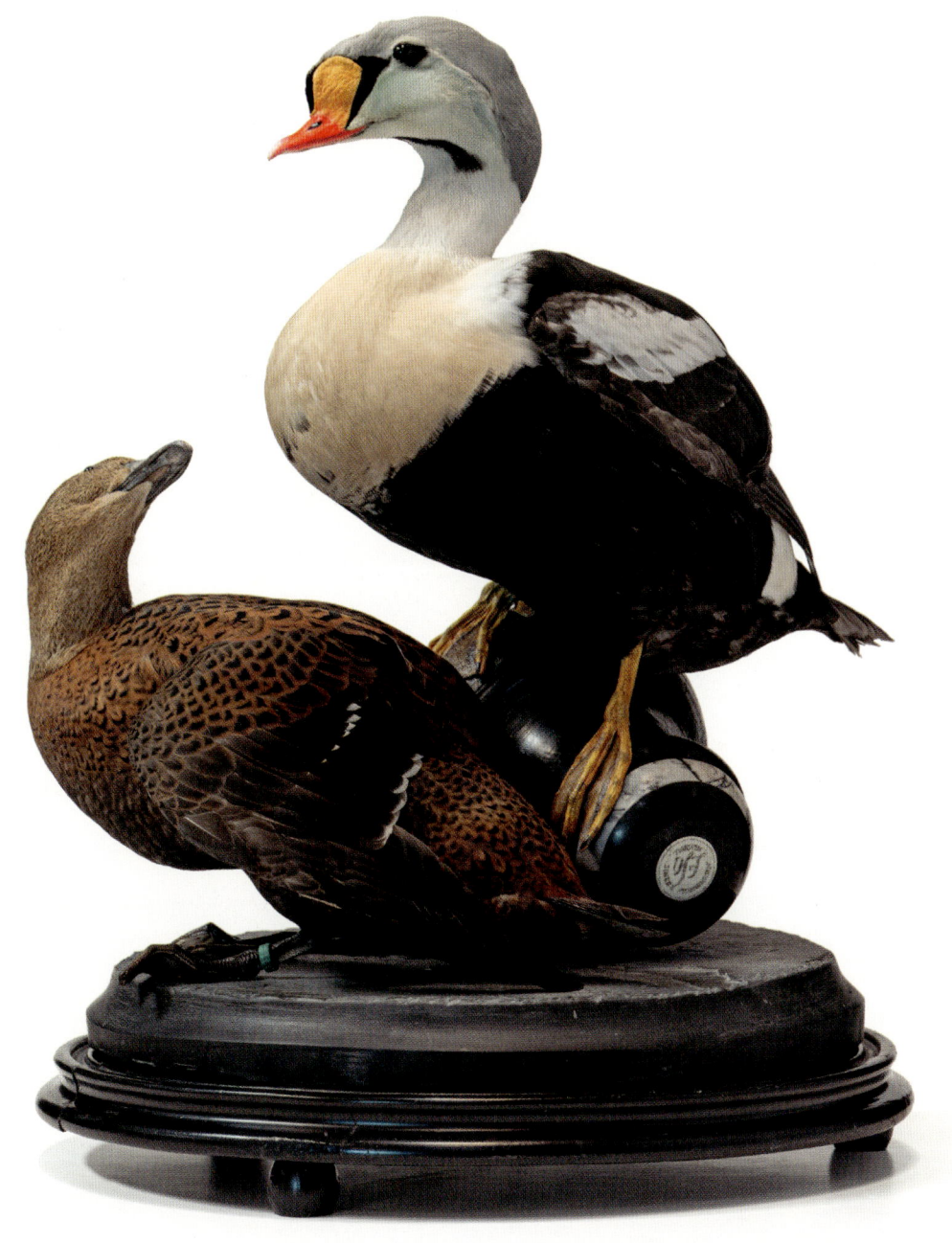

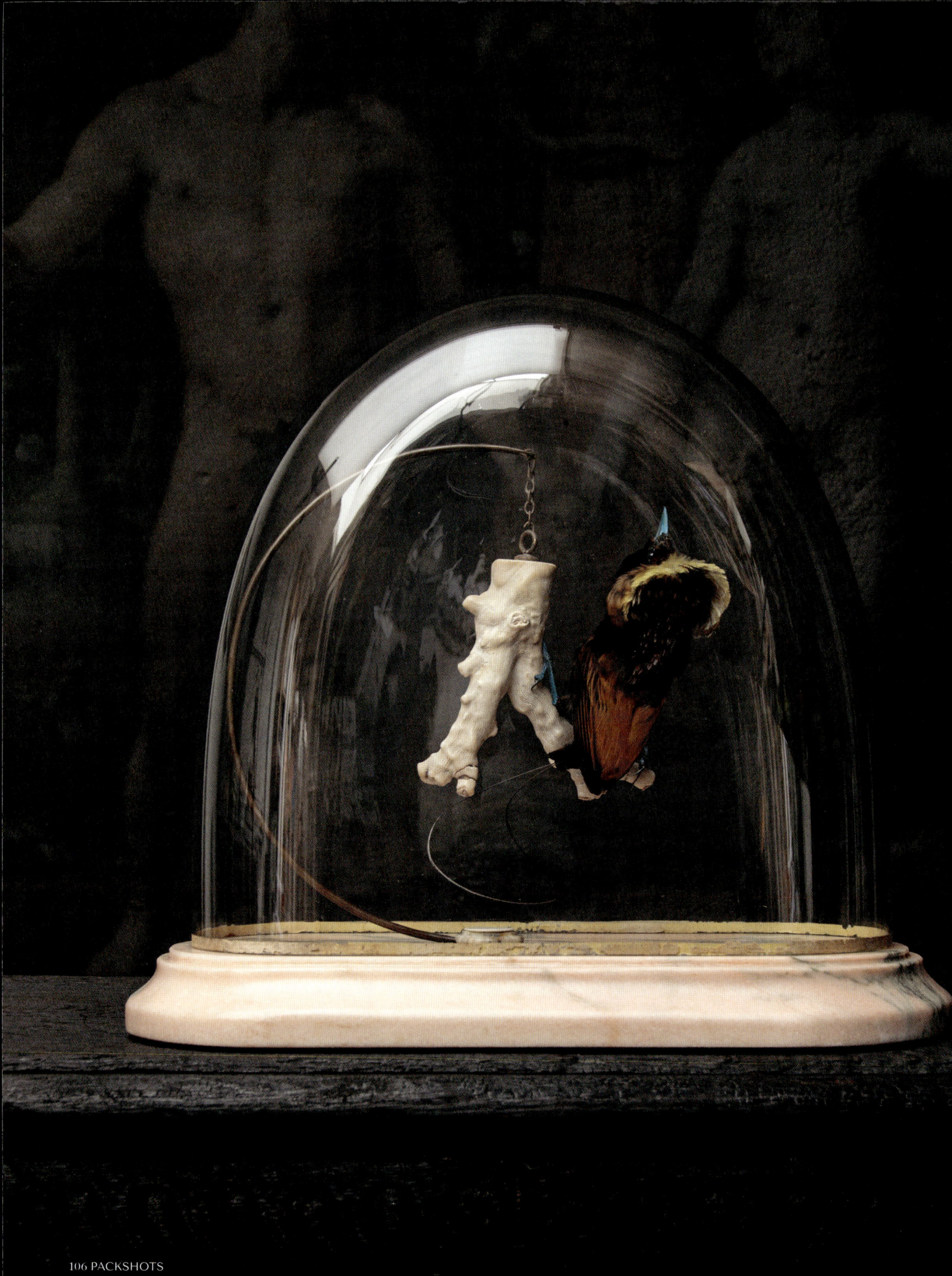

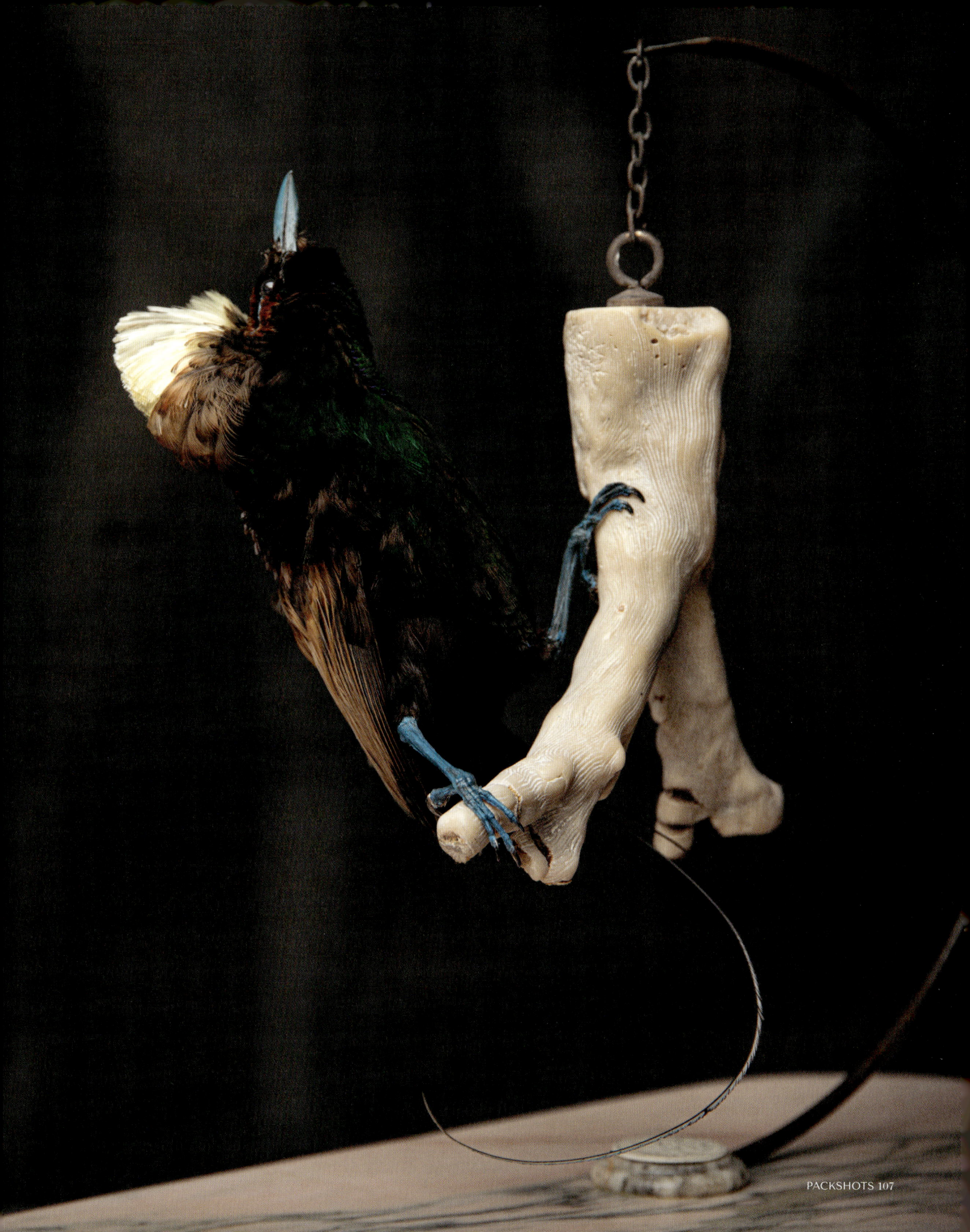

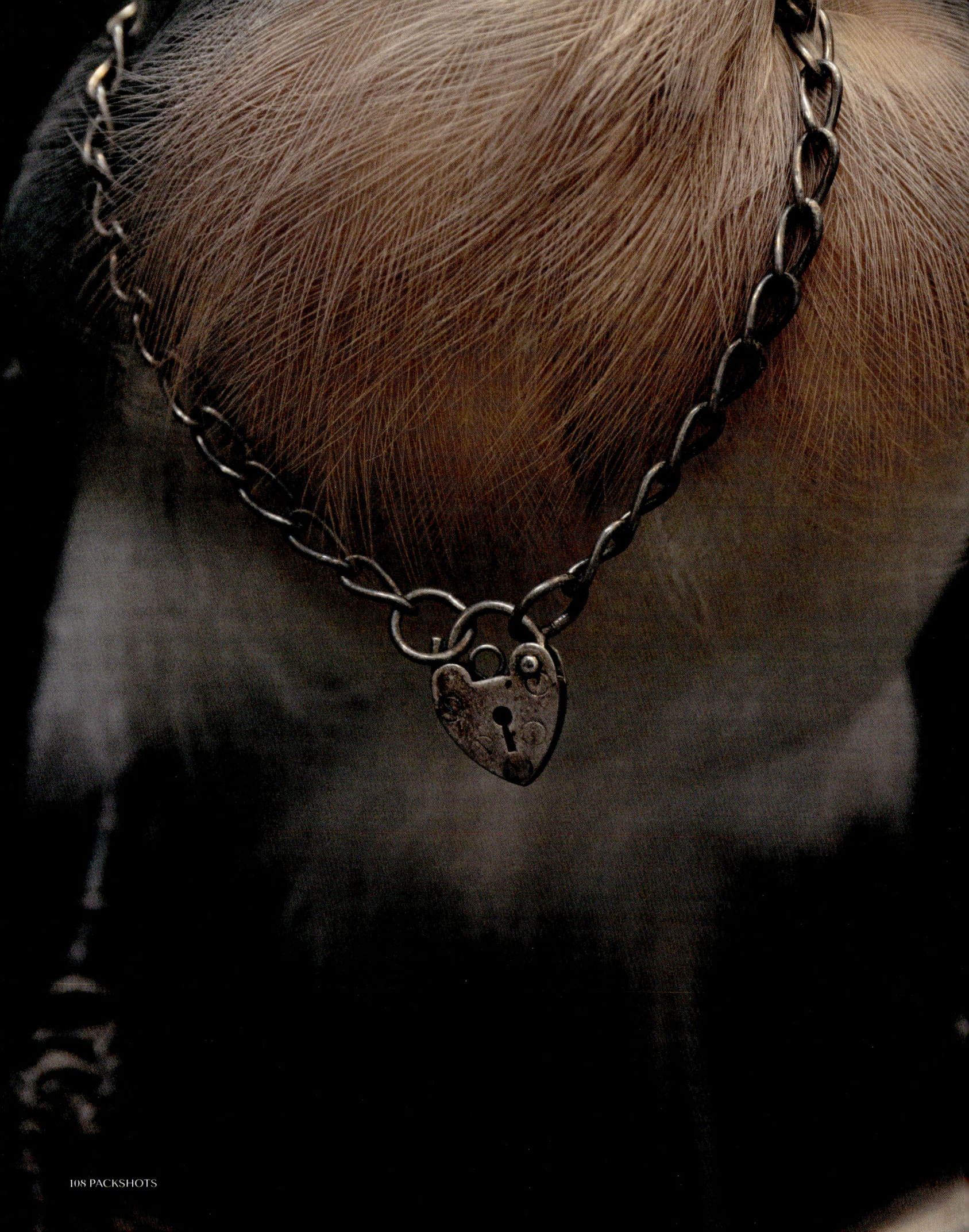

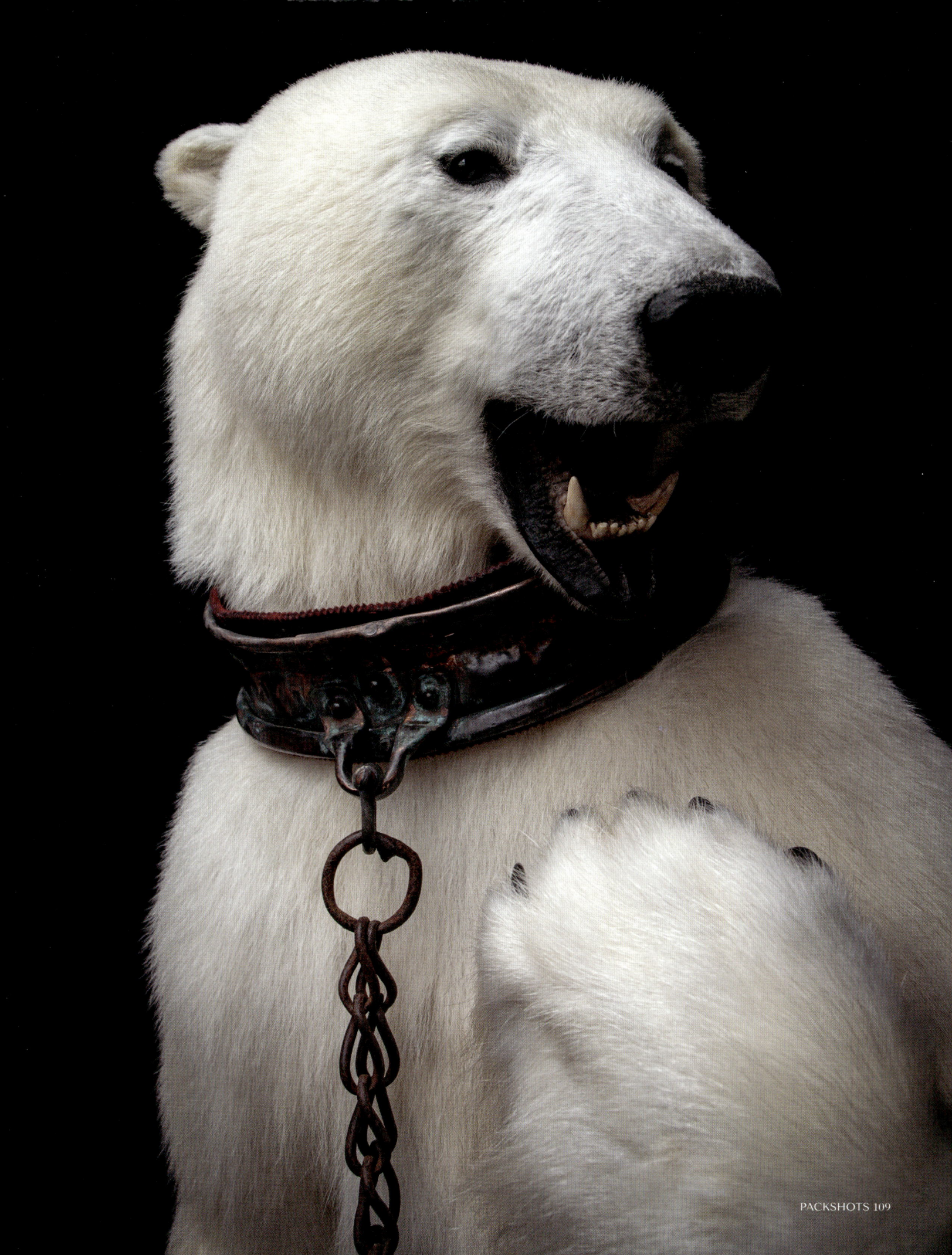

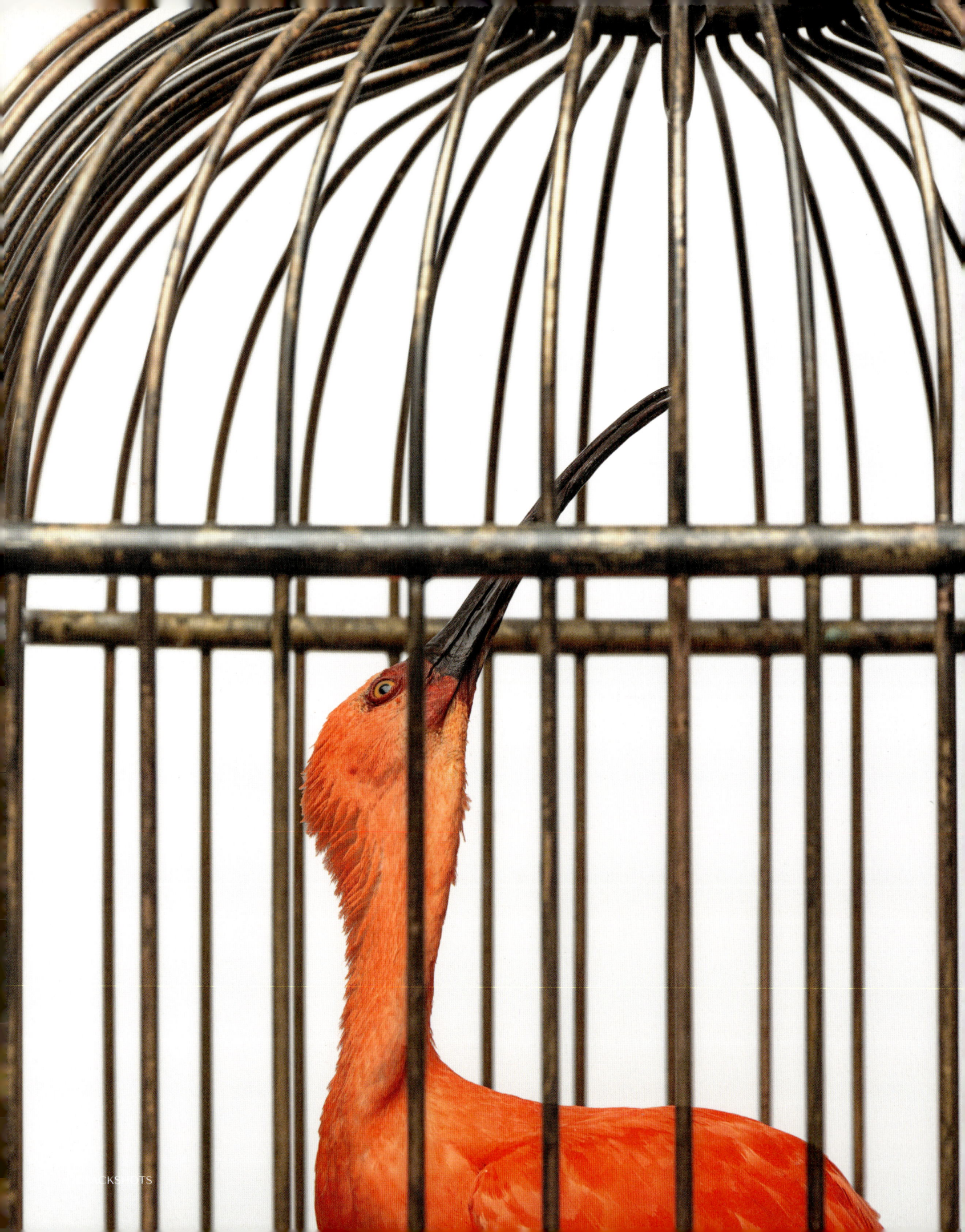

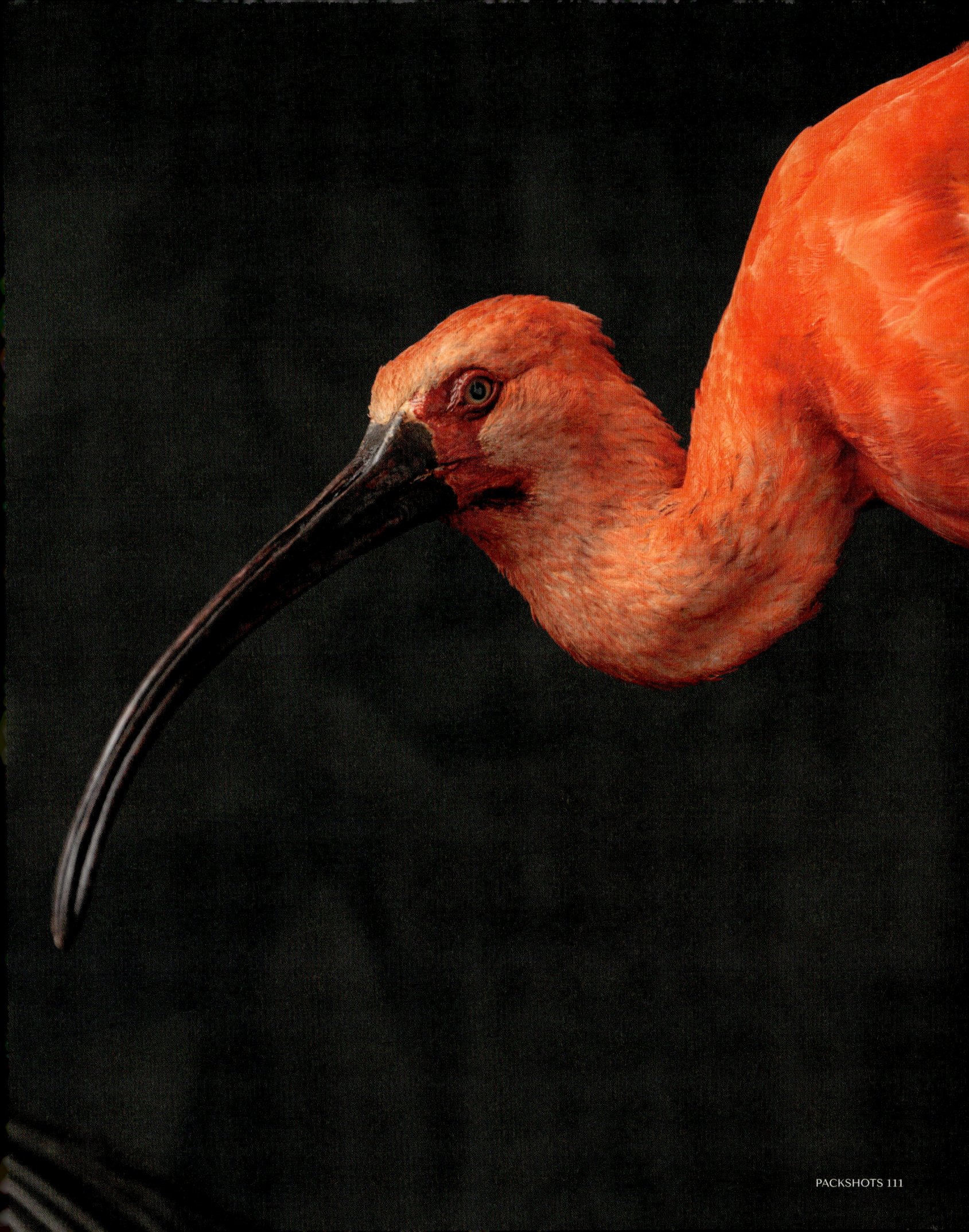

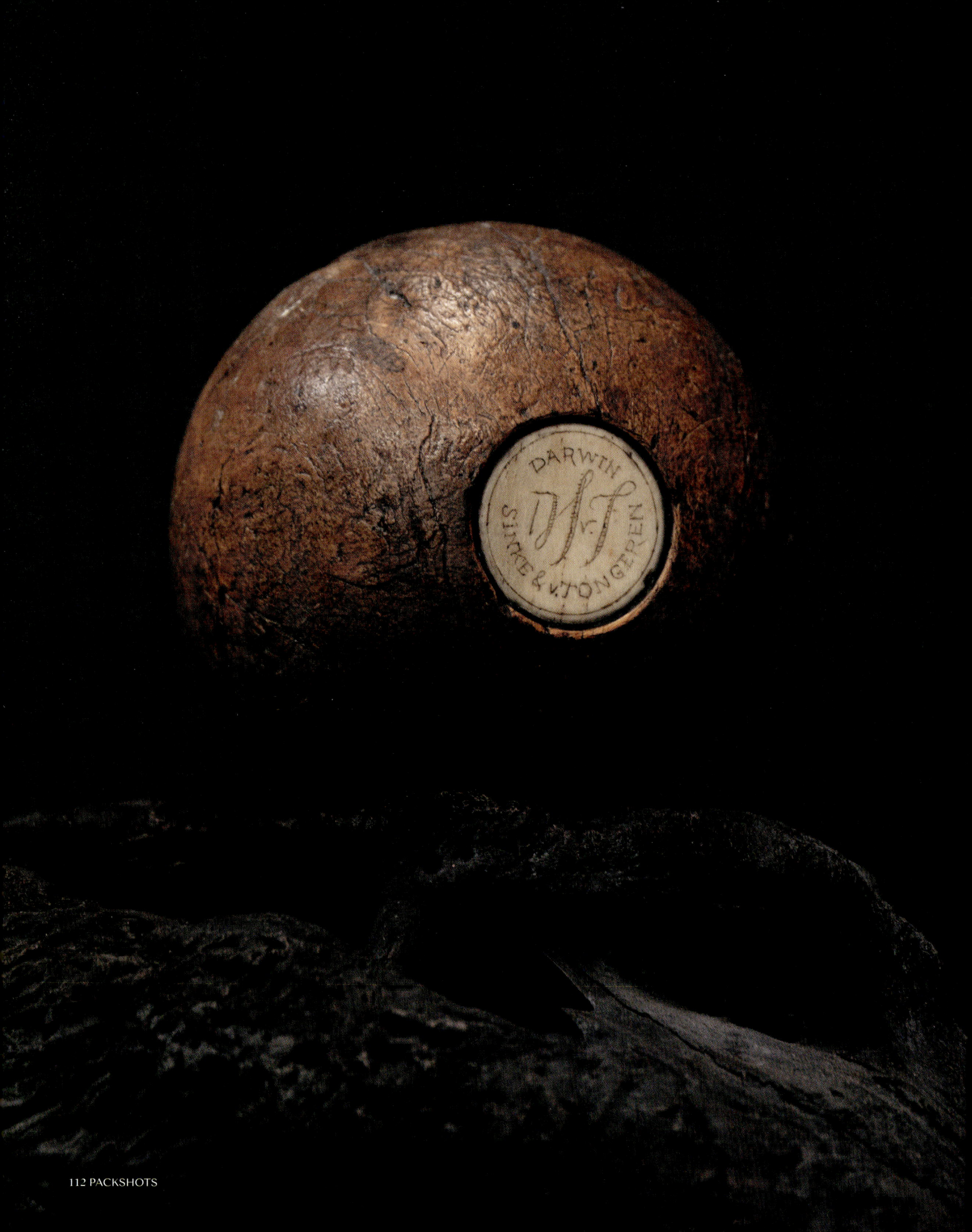

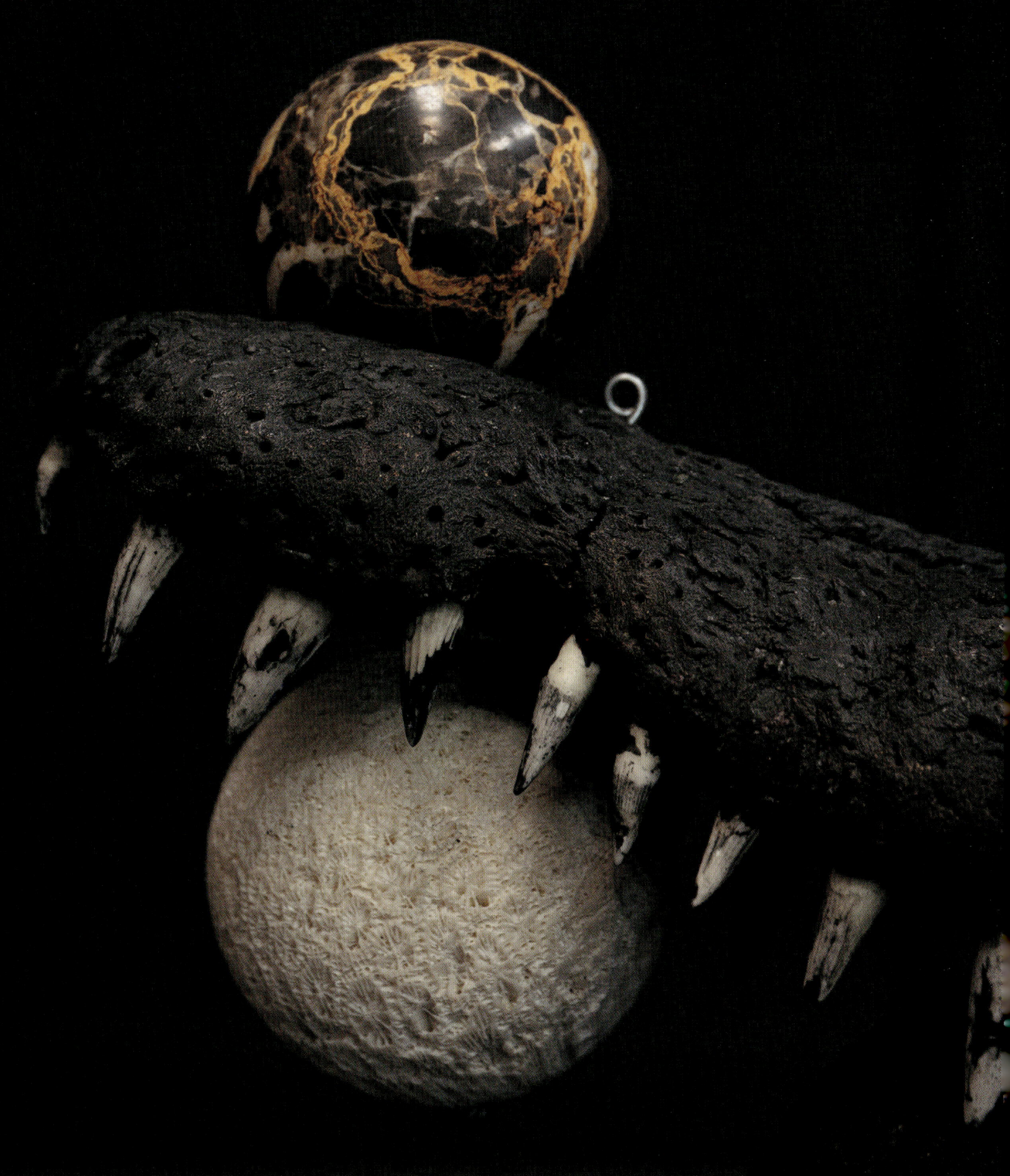

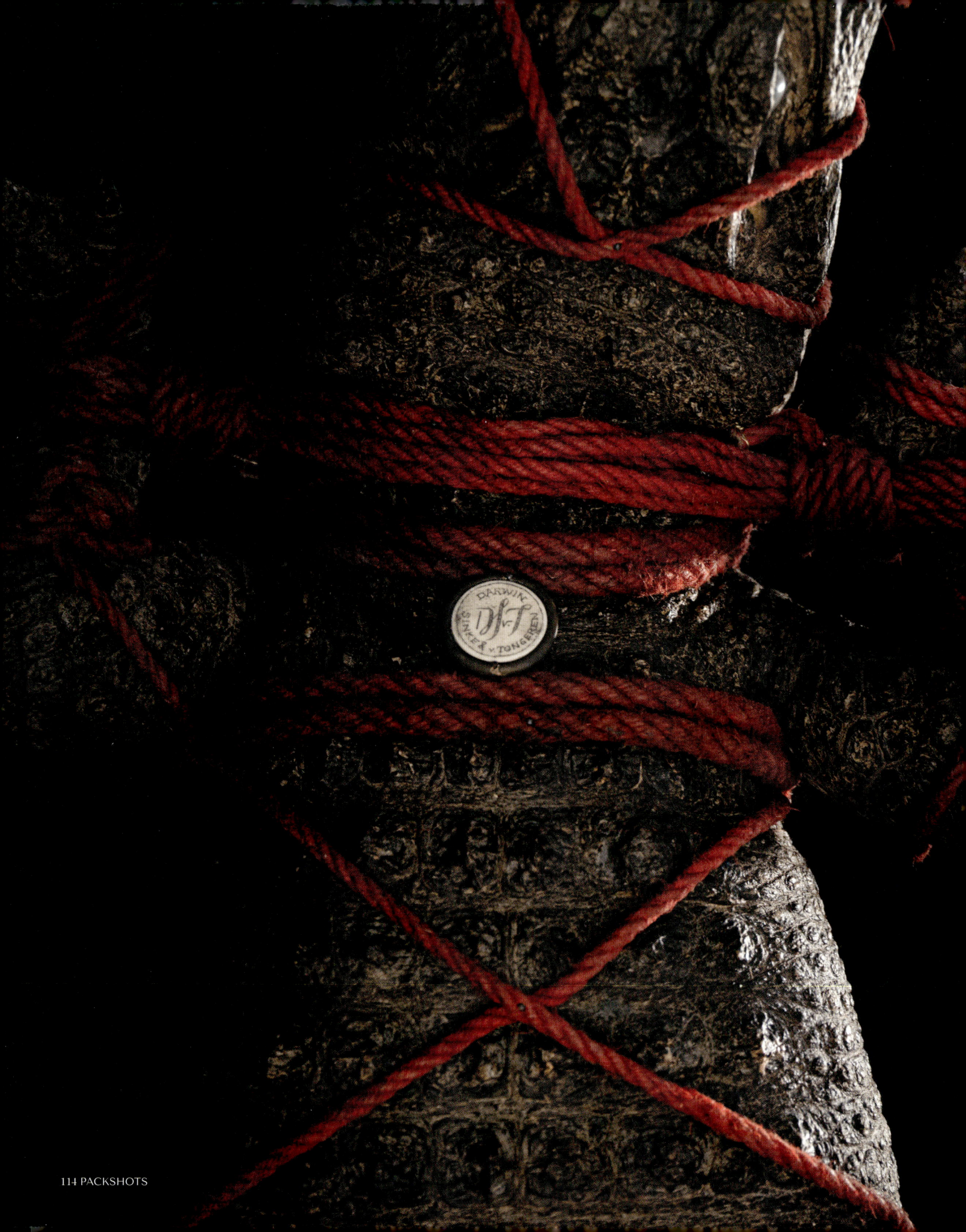

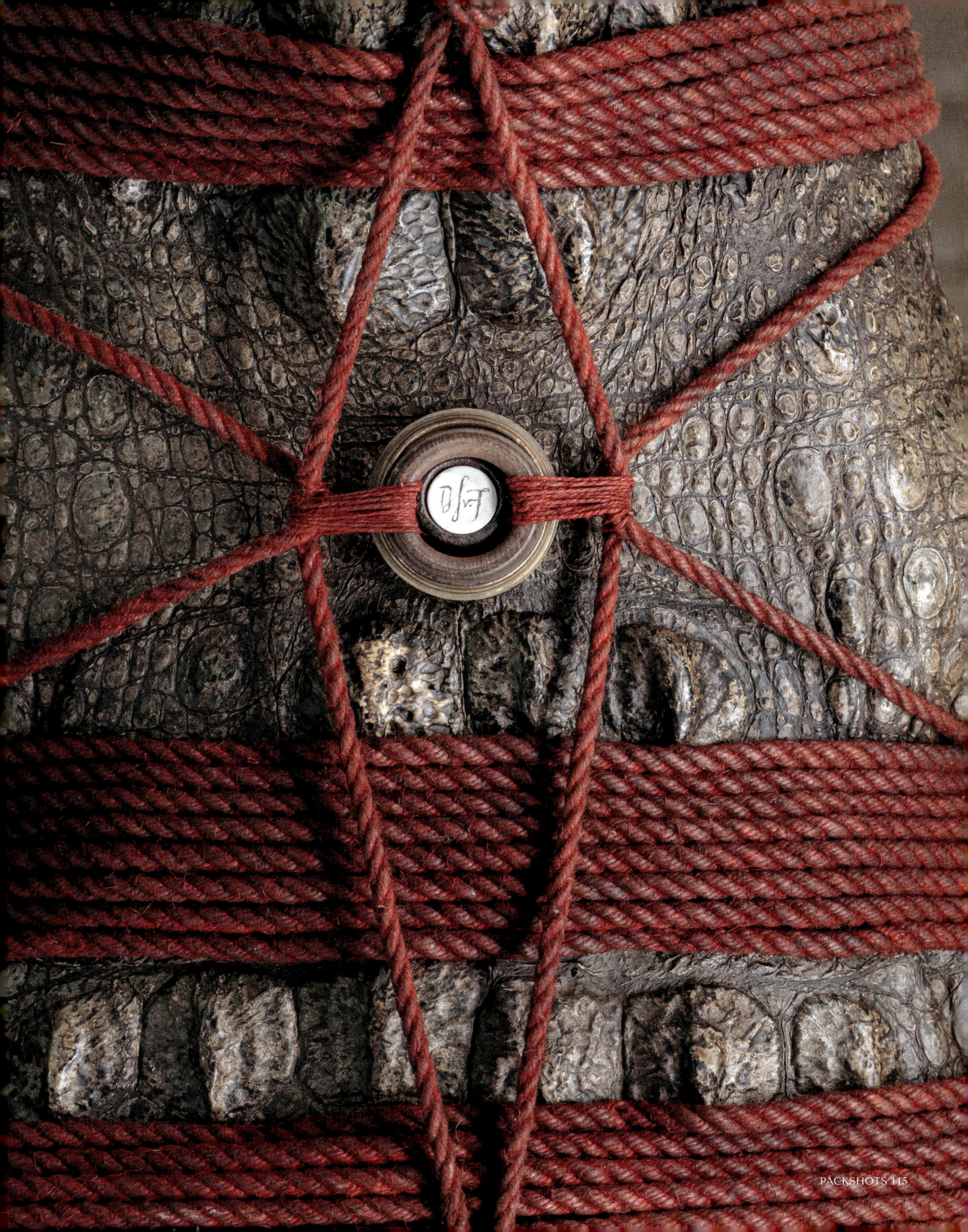

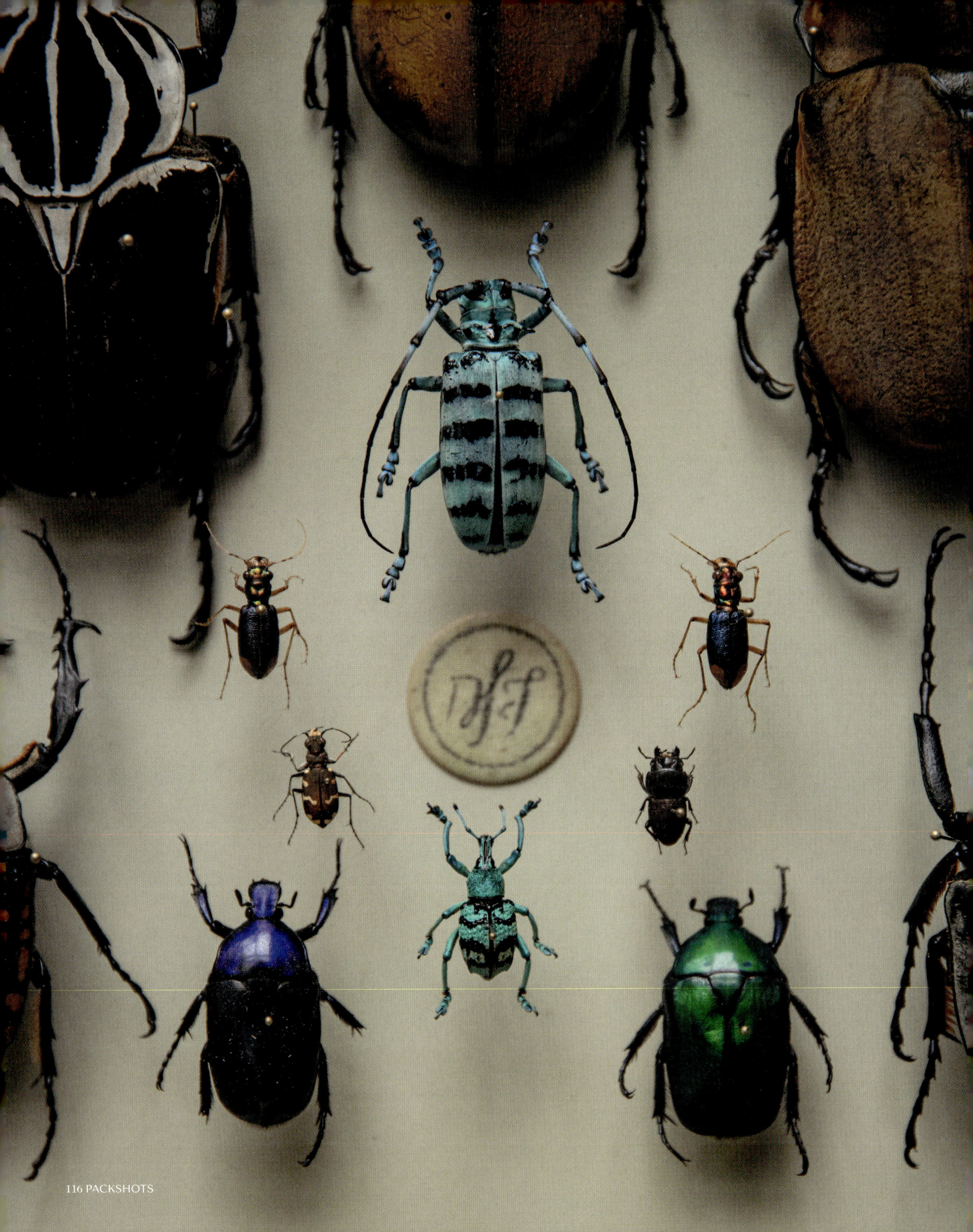

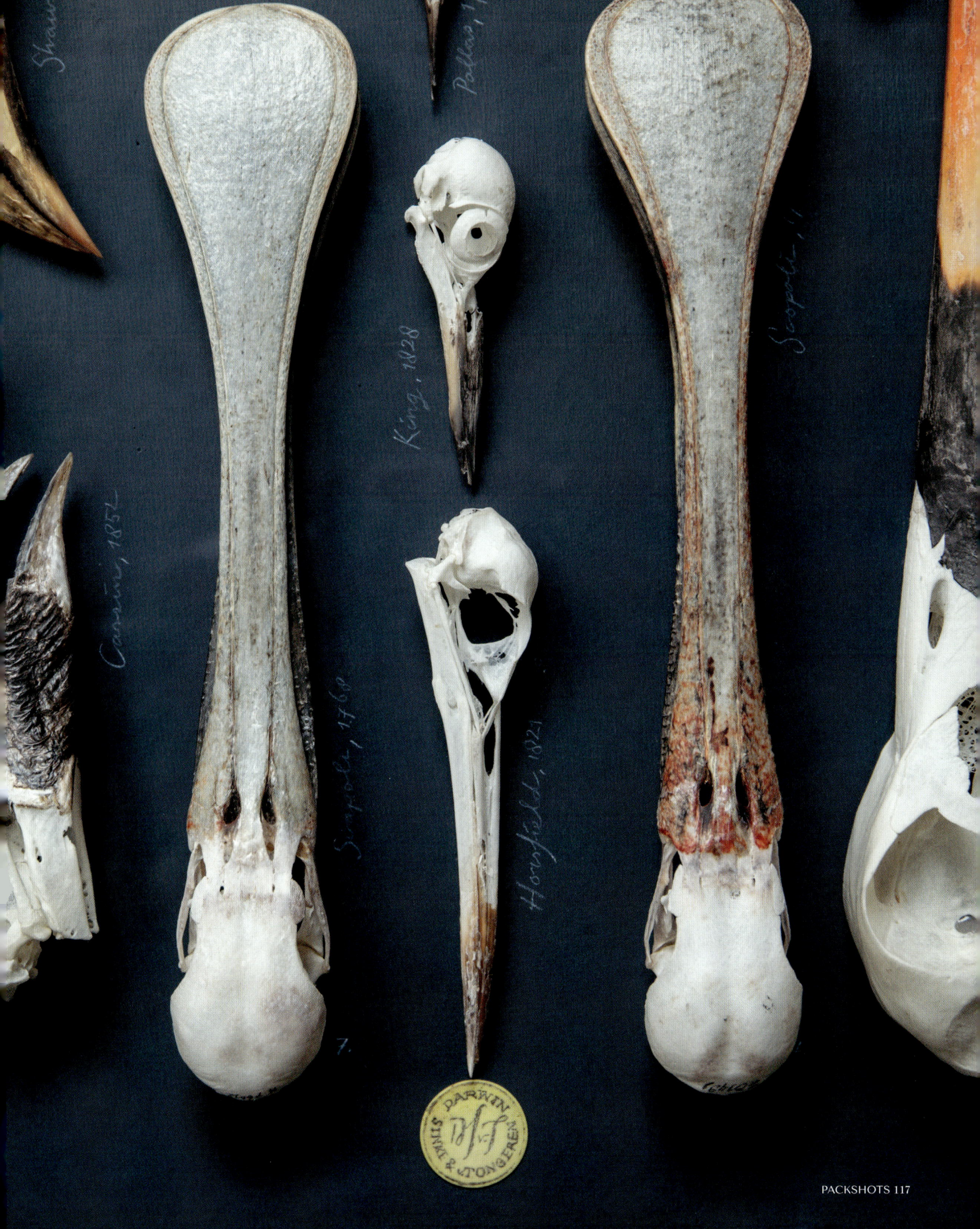

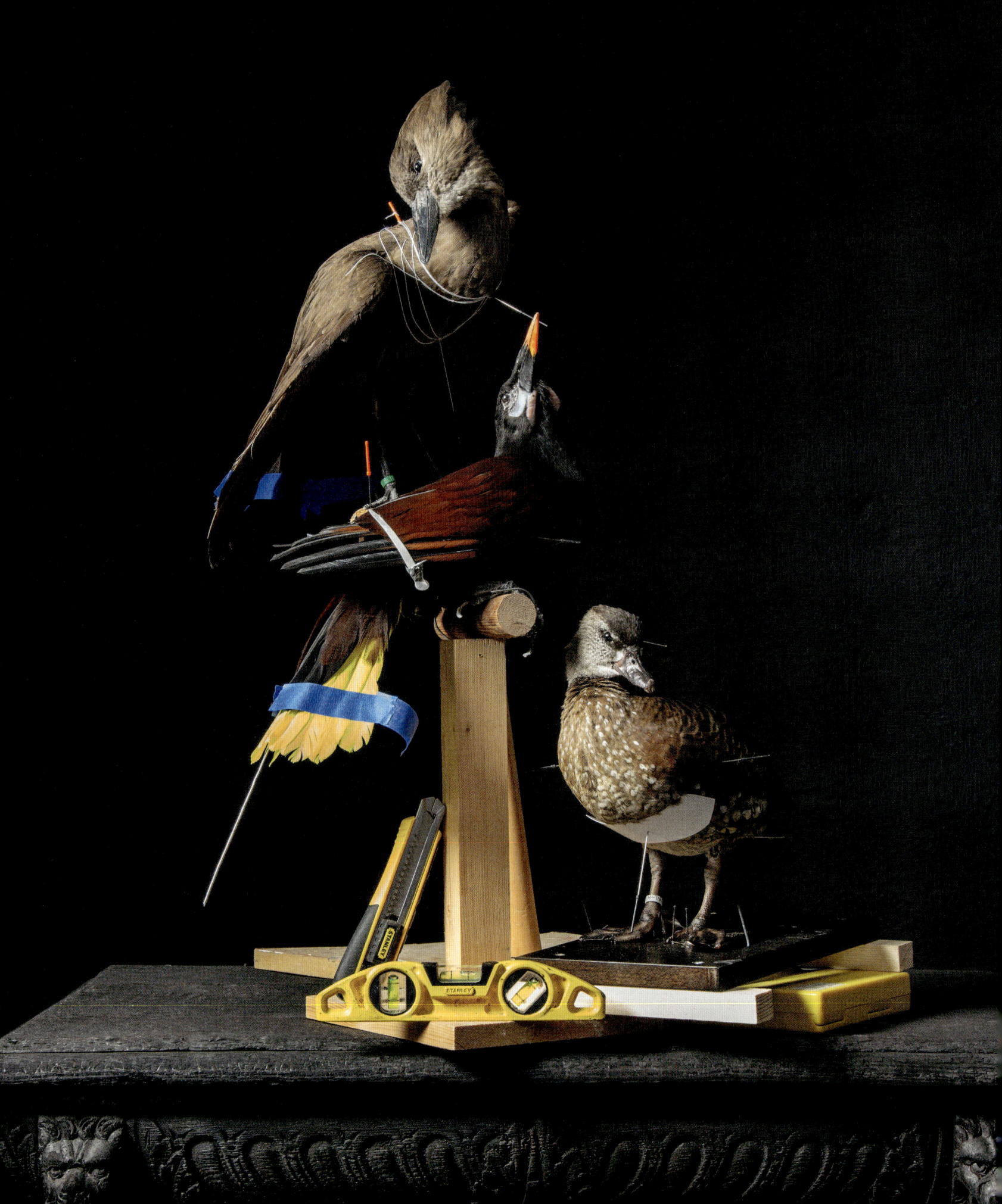

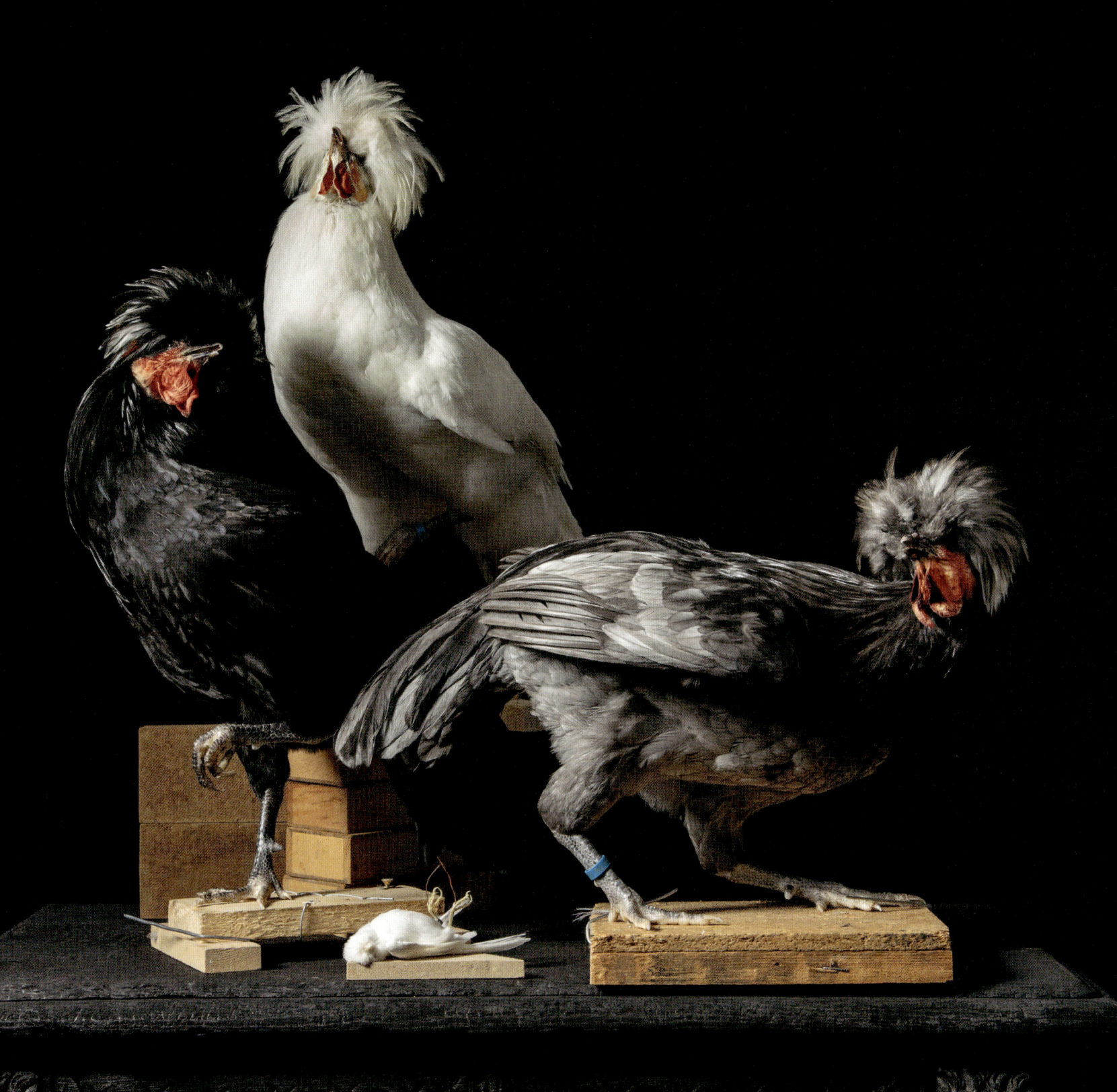

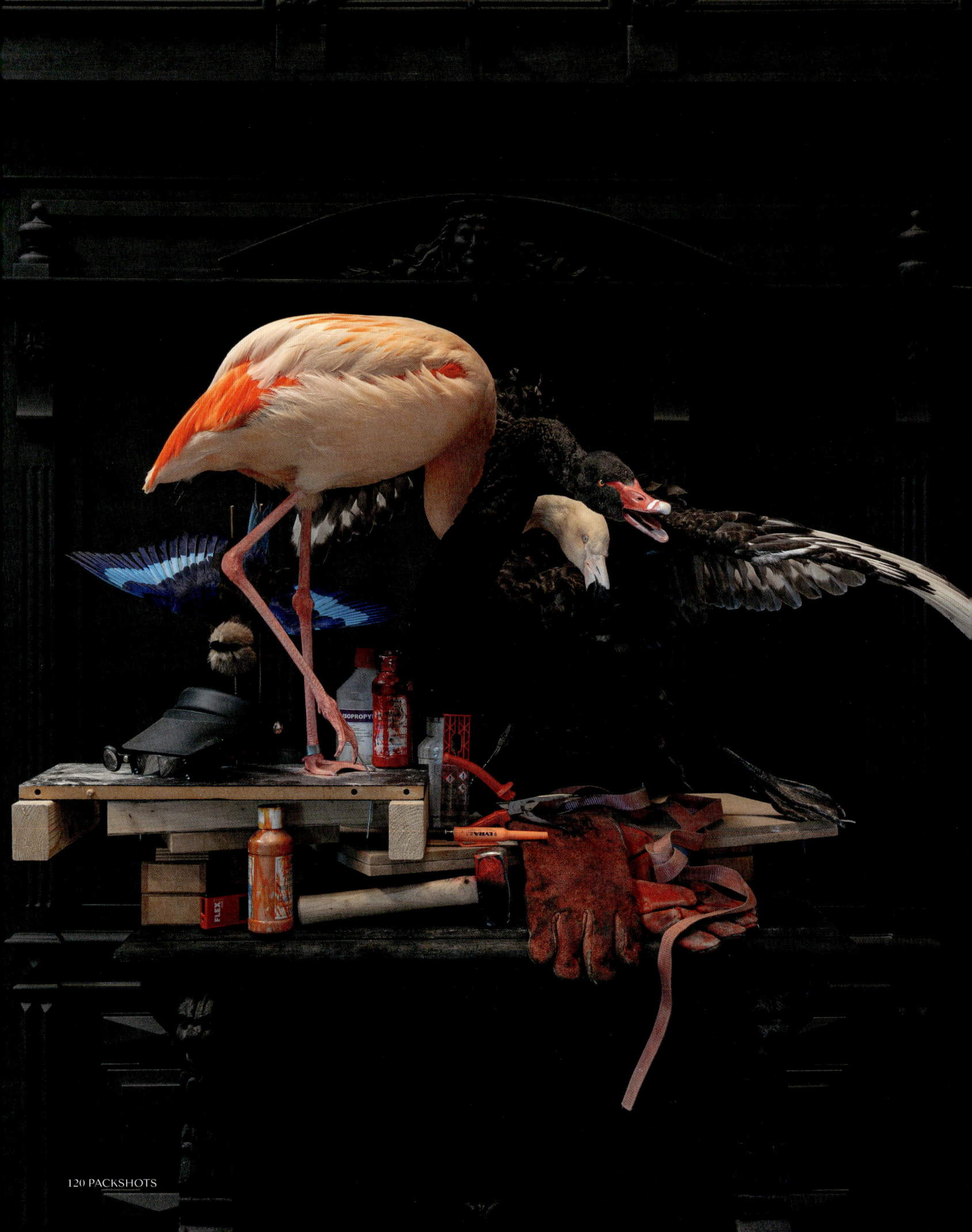

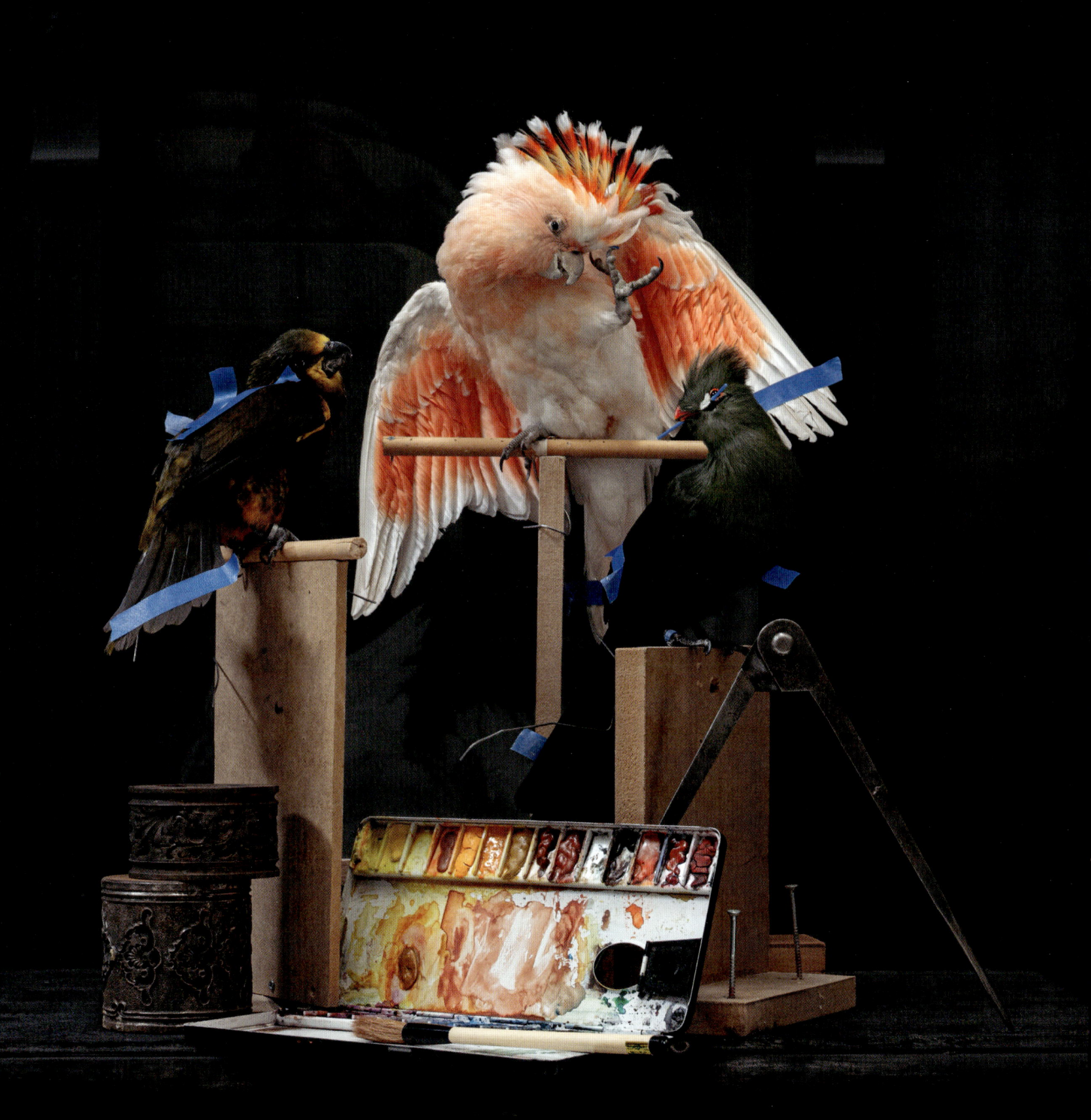

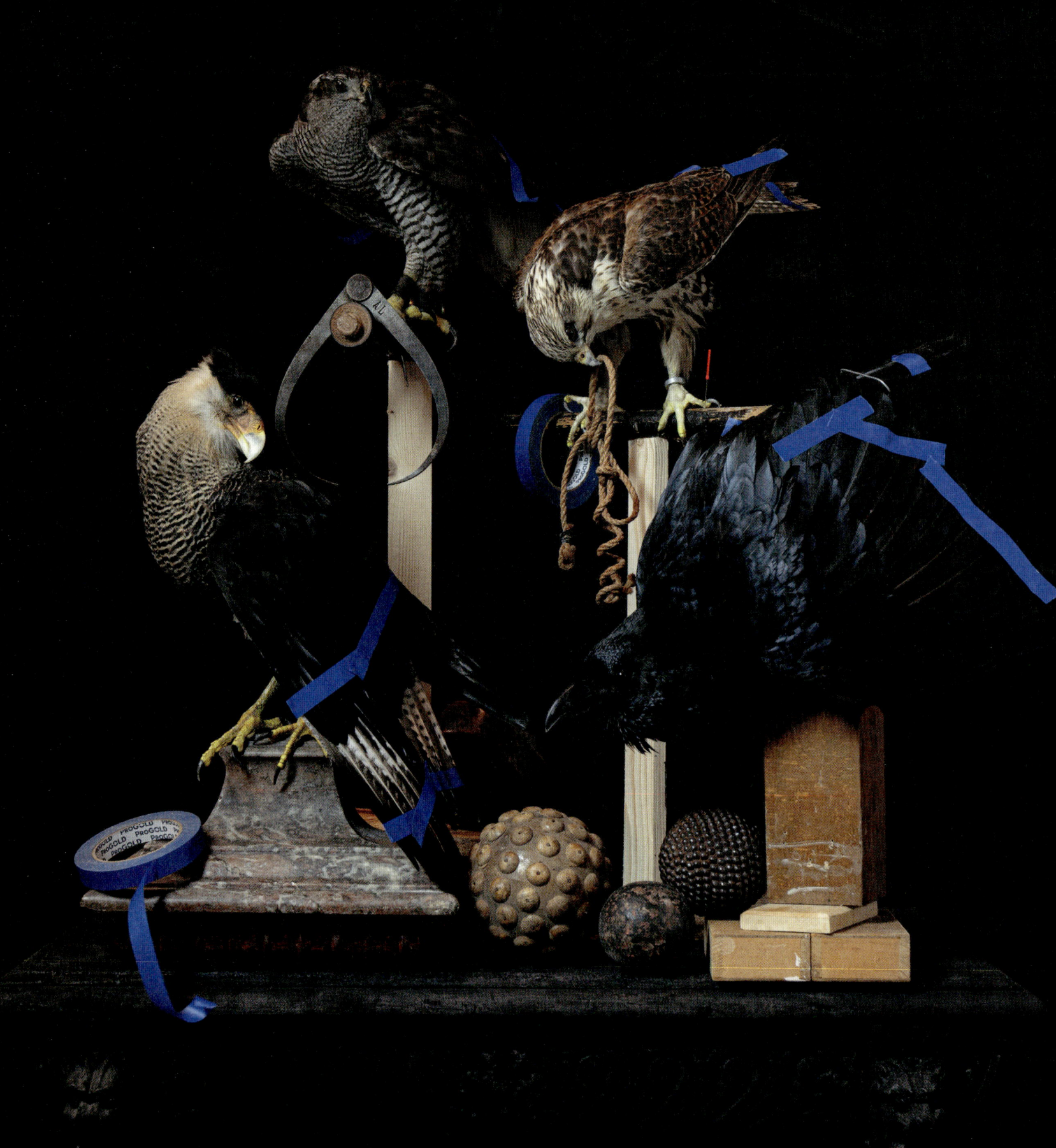

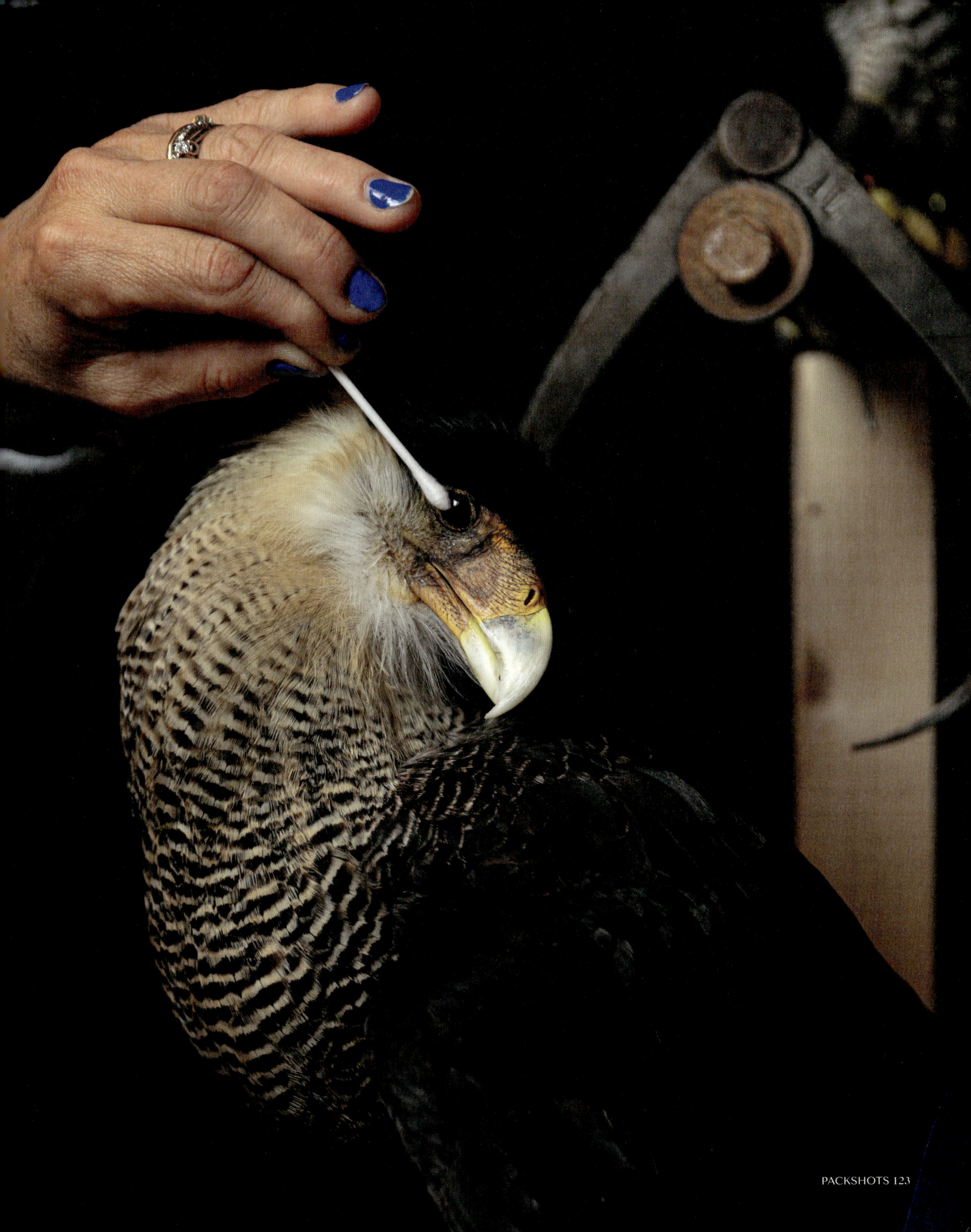

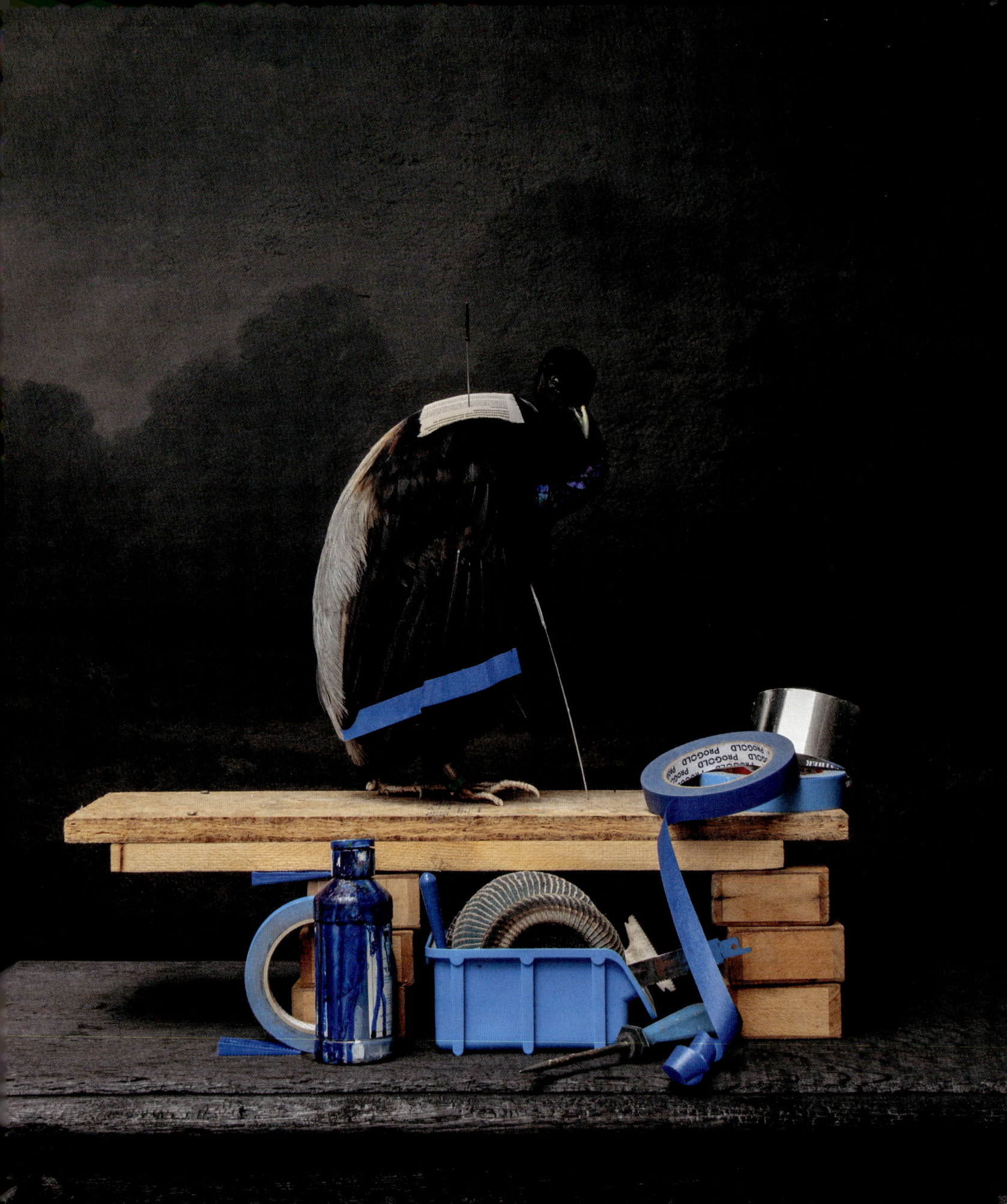

124 PACKSHOTS

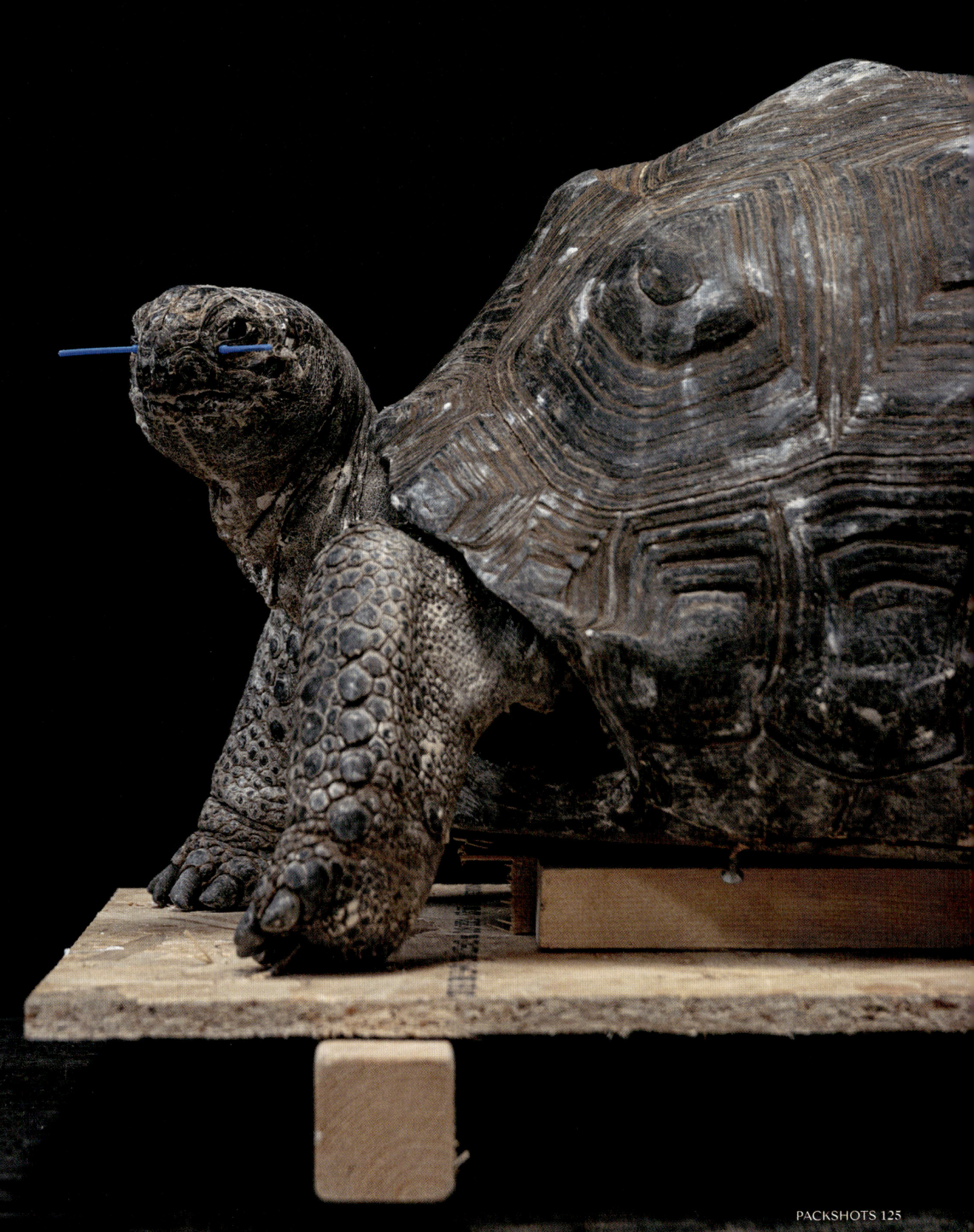

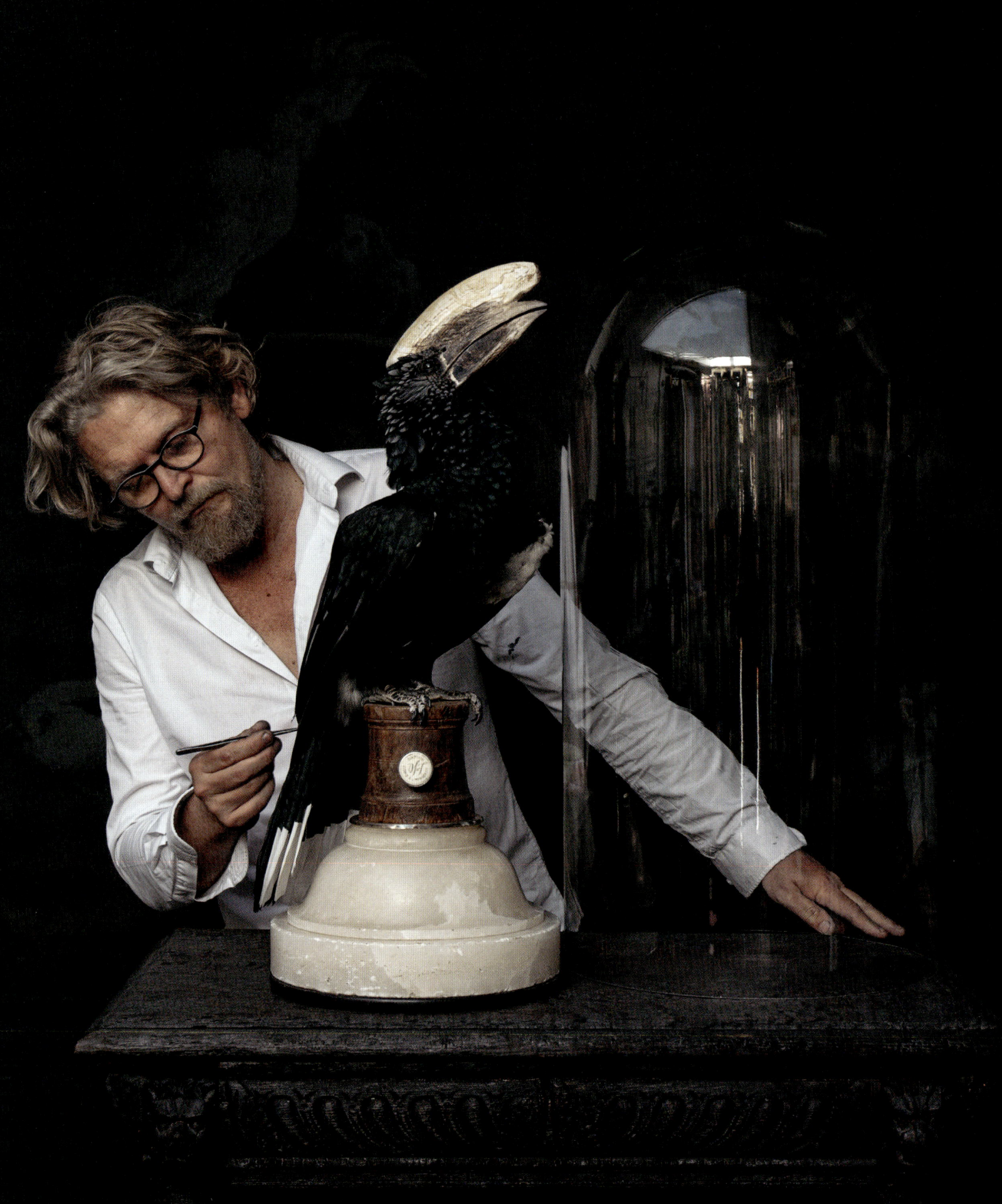

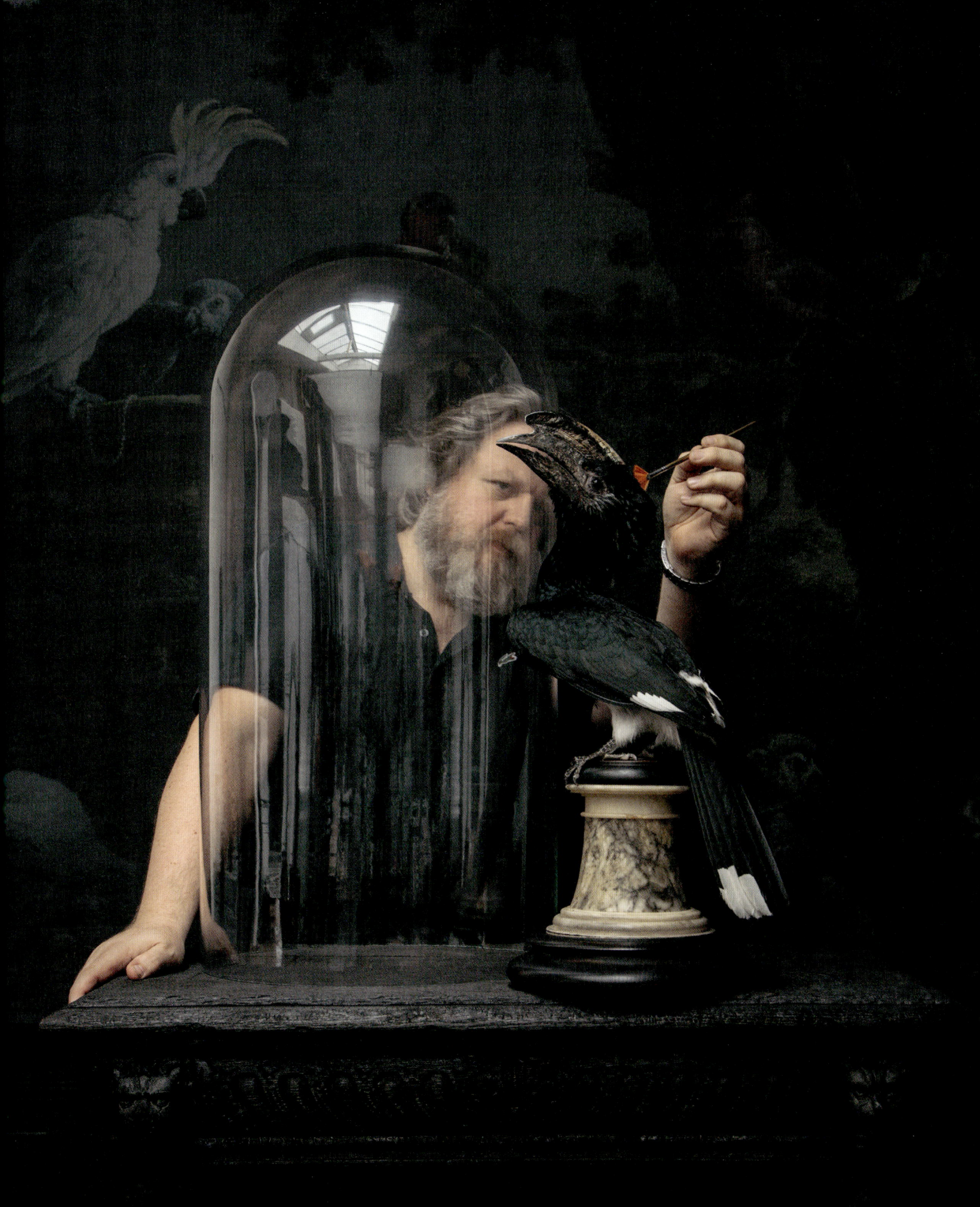

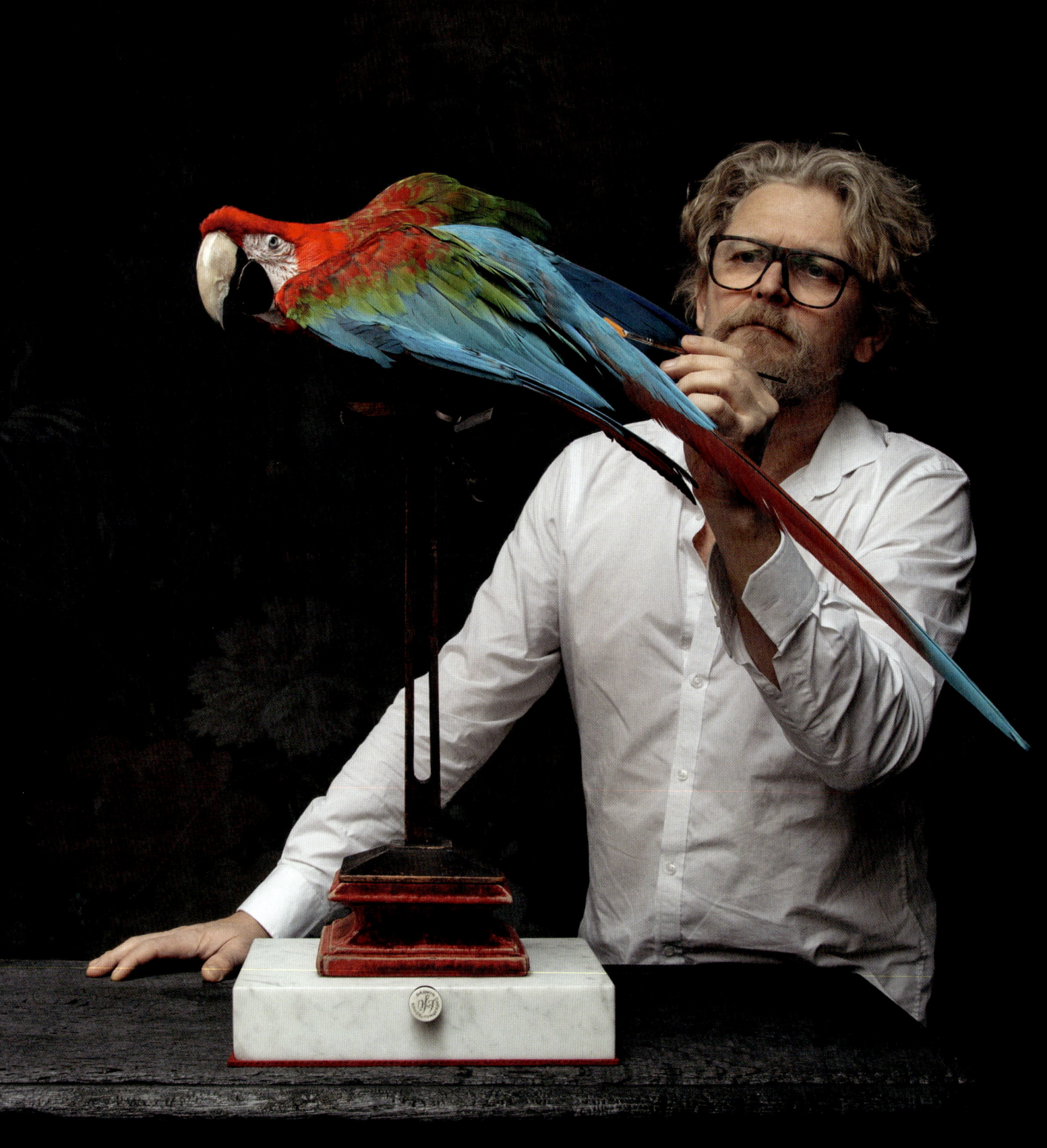

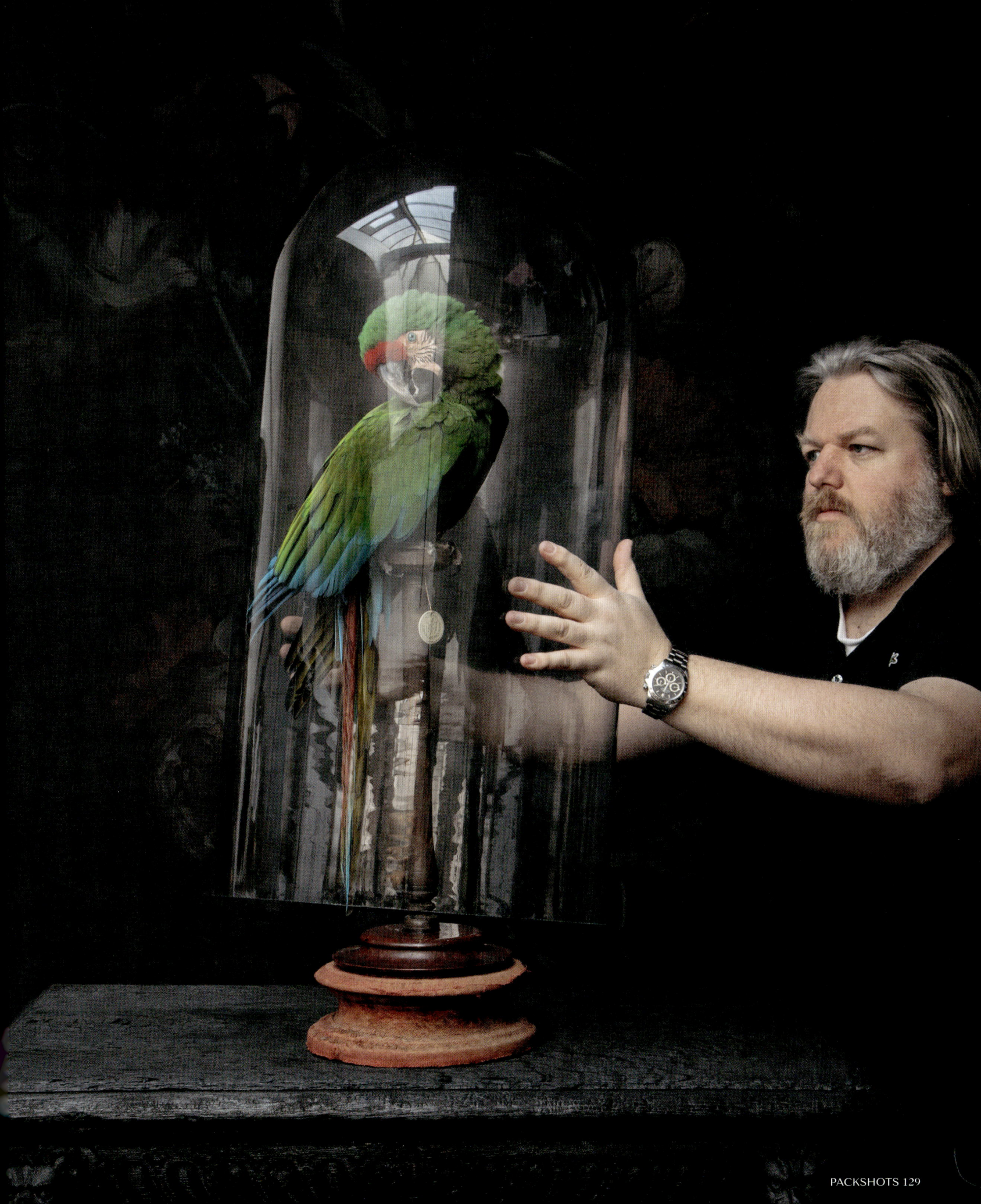
PACKSHOTS 129

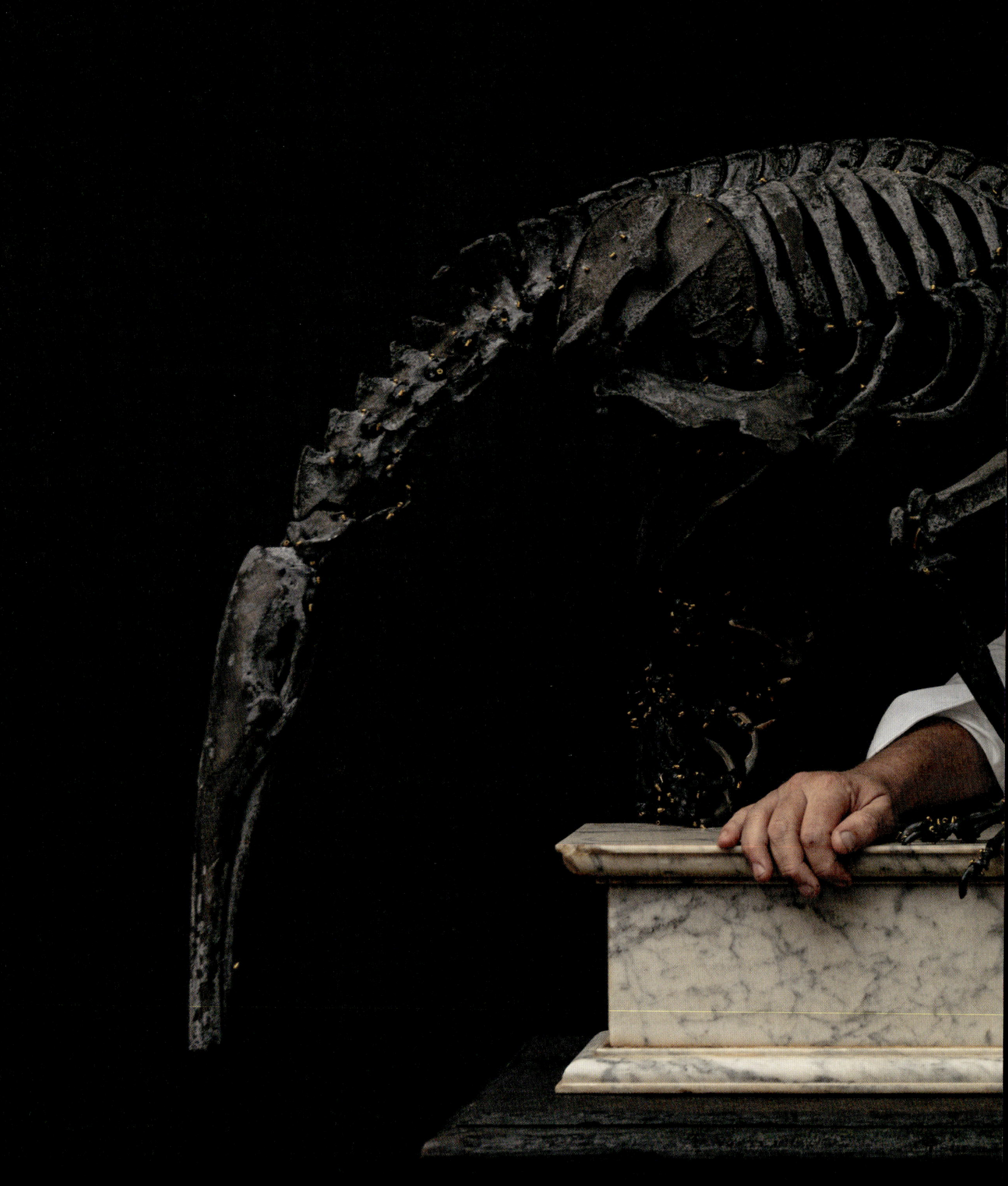

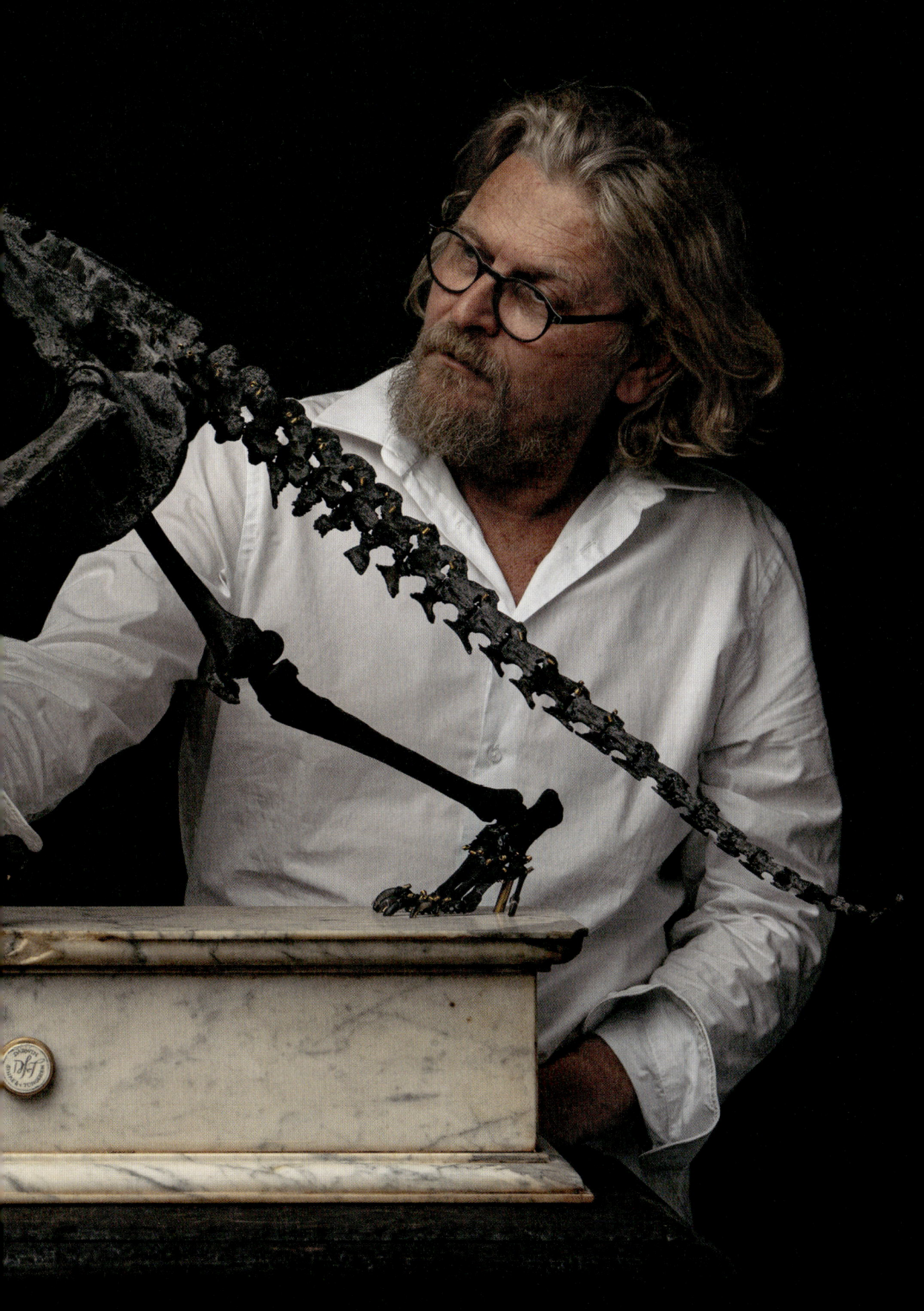

PACKSHOTS 131

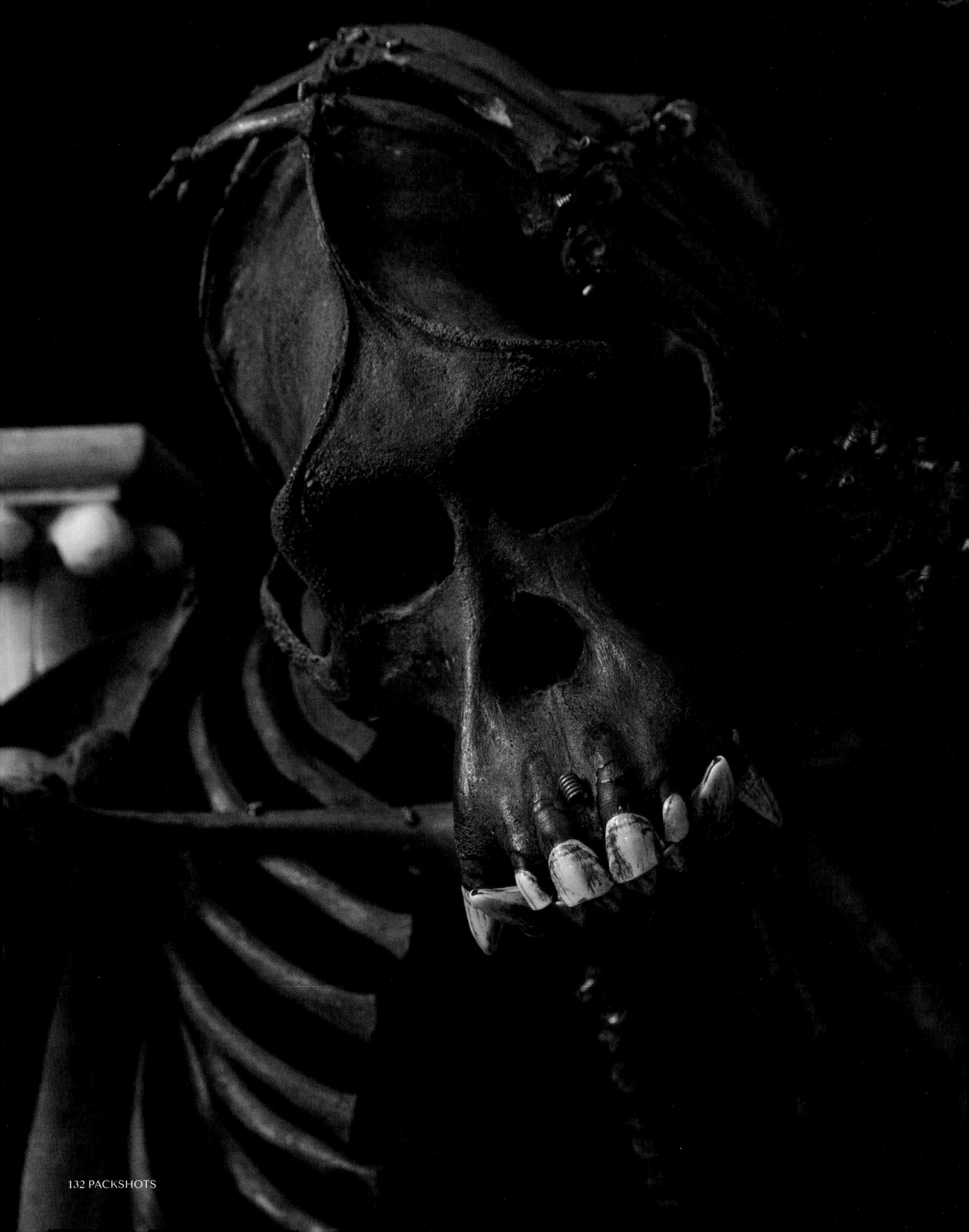

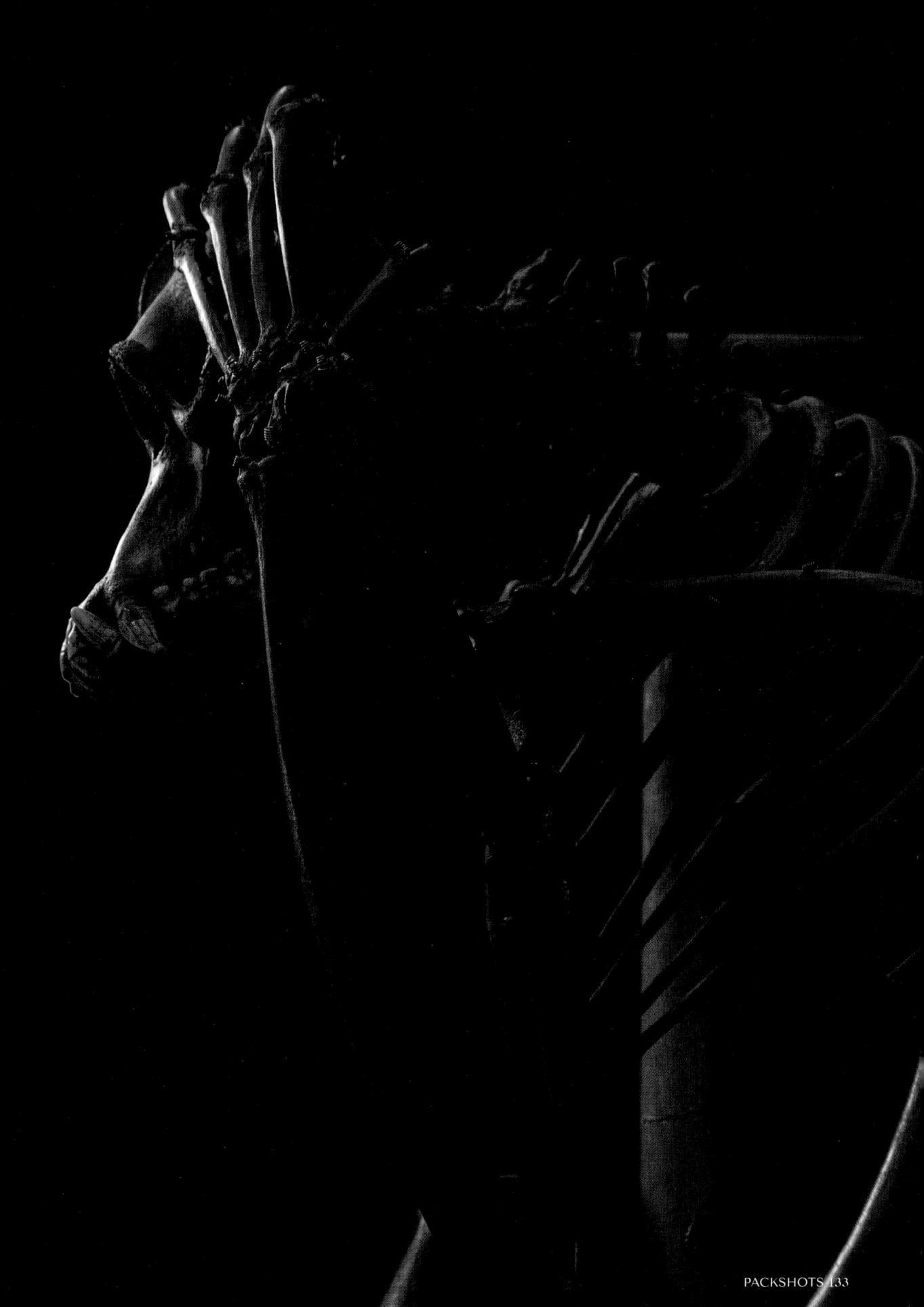

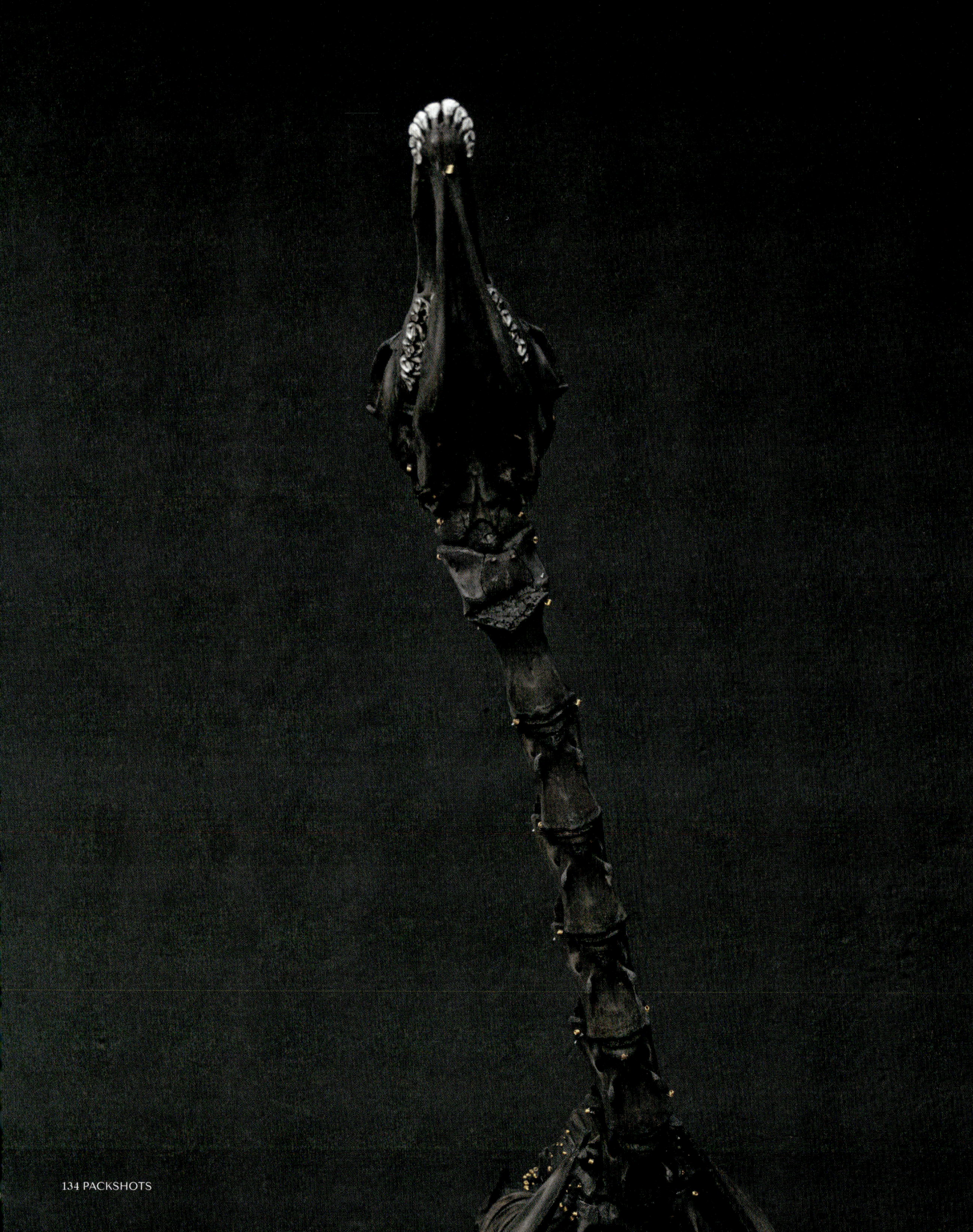

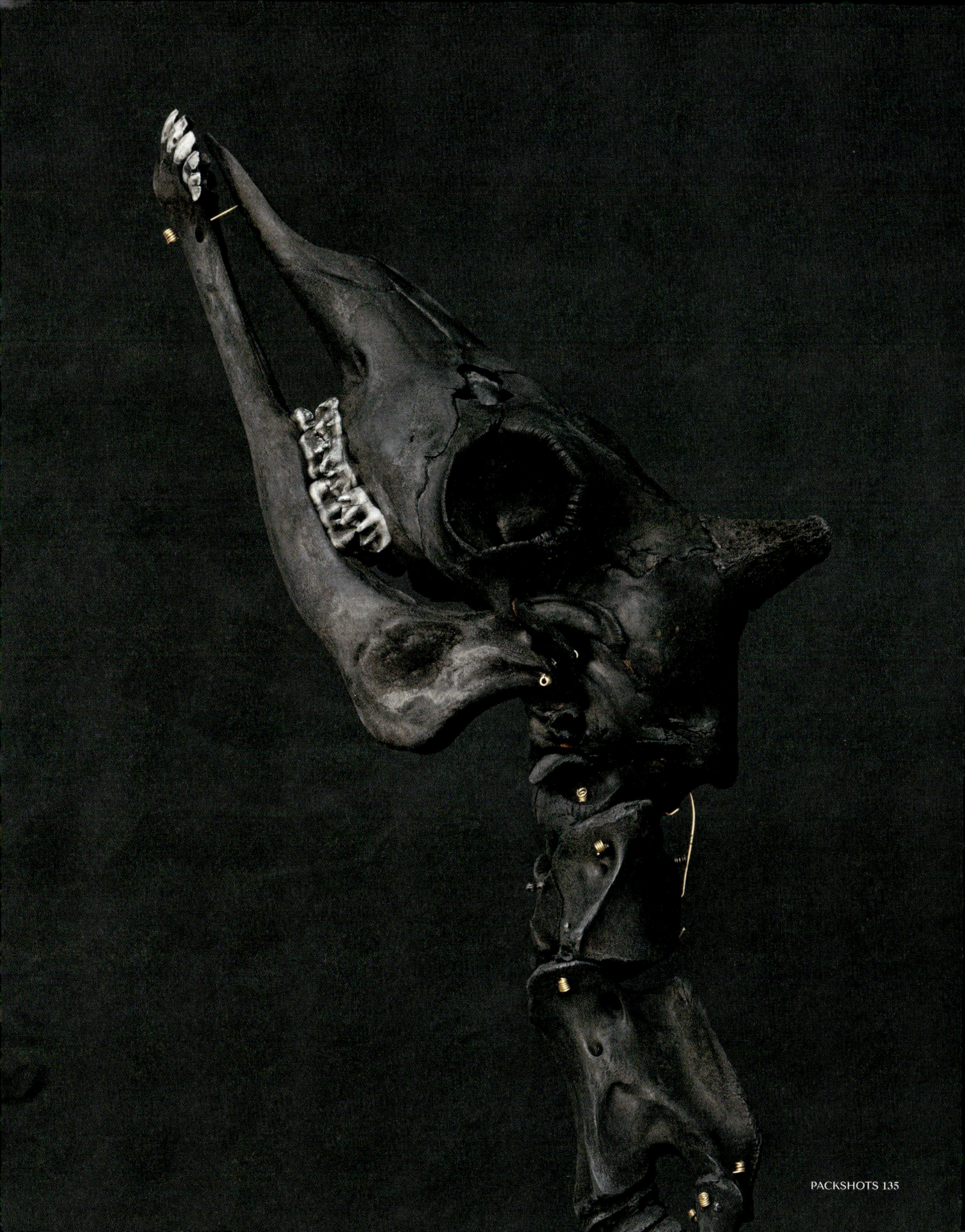

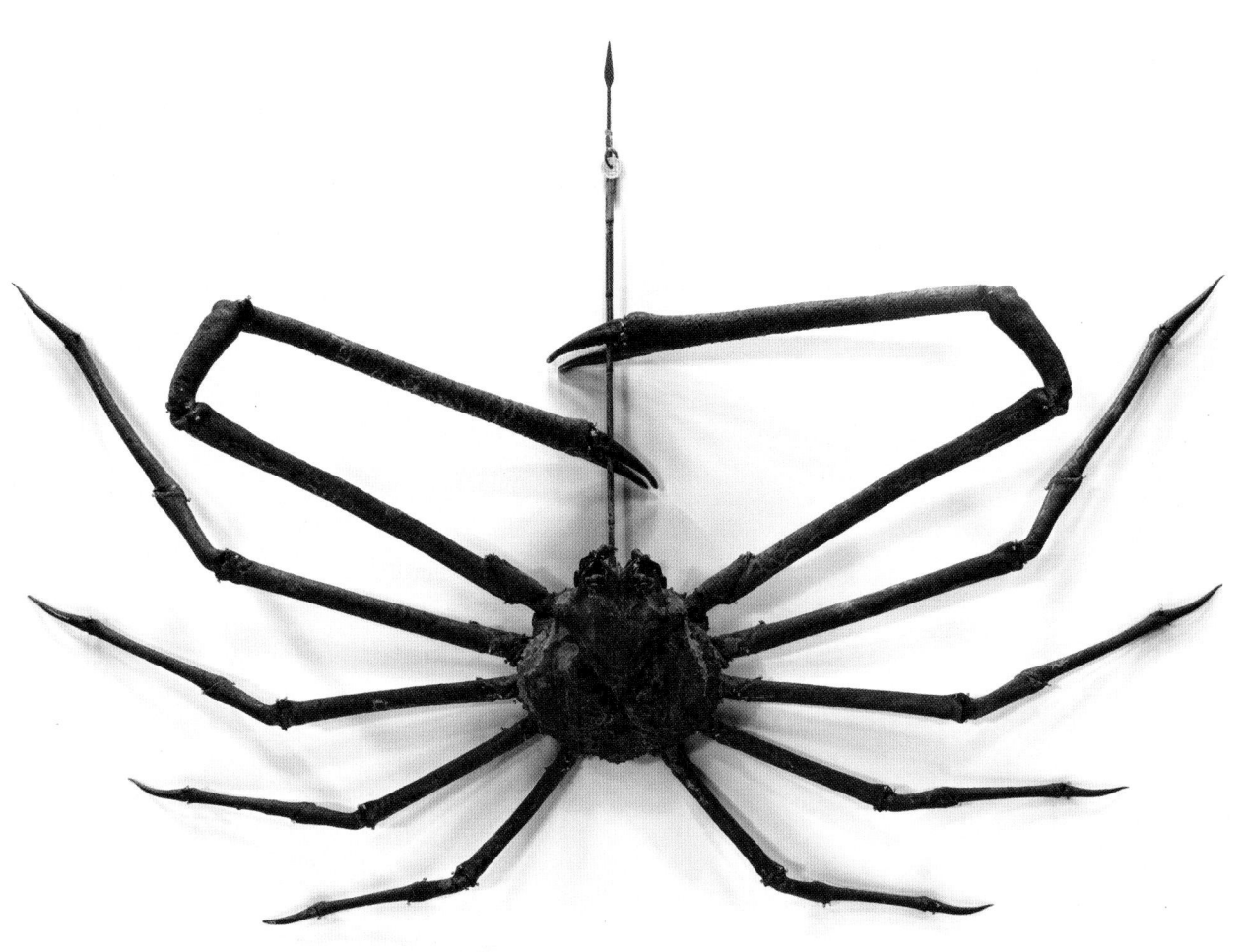

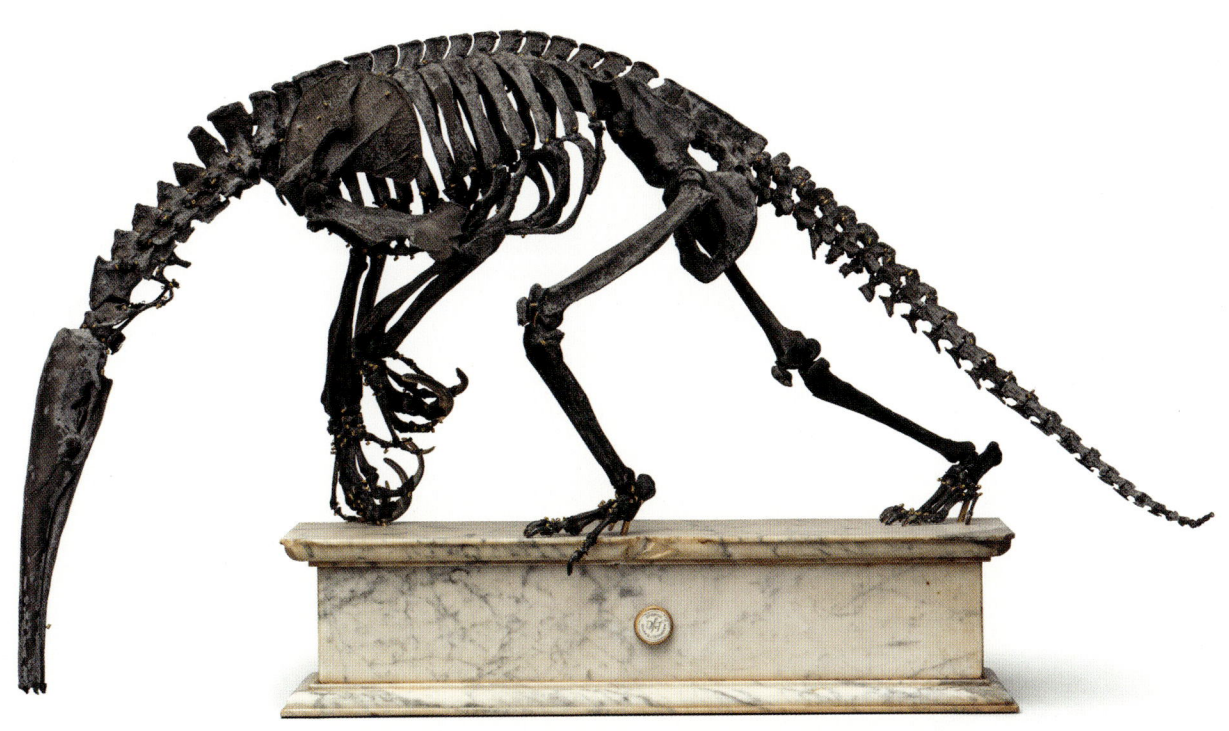

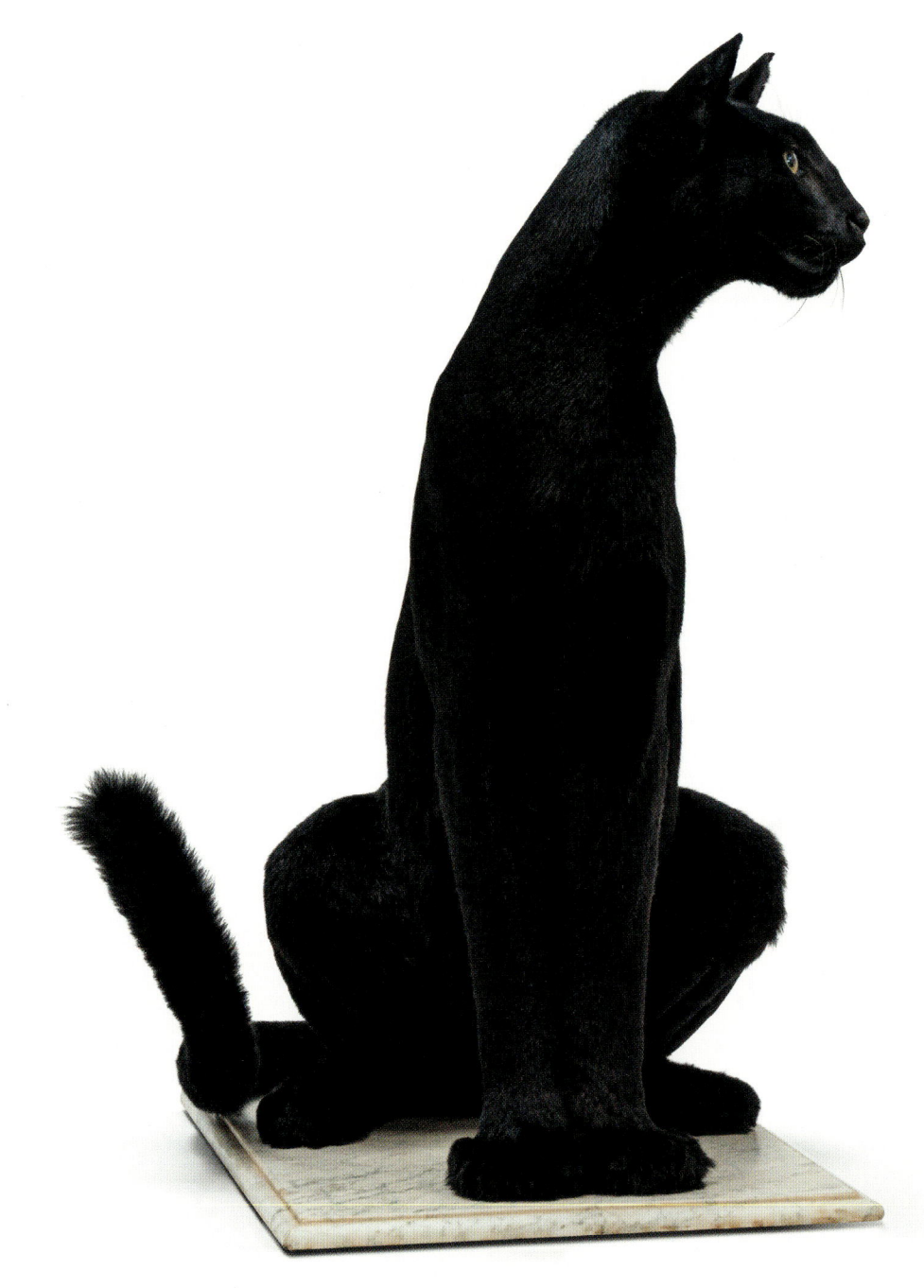

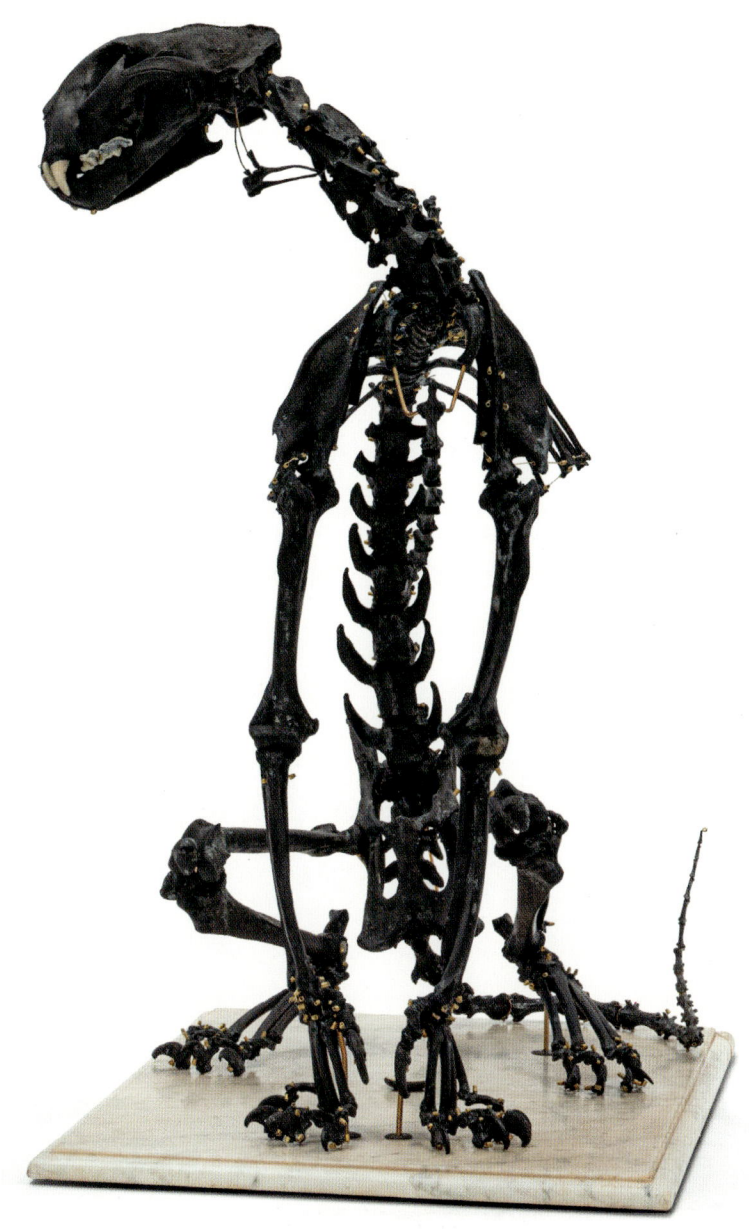

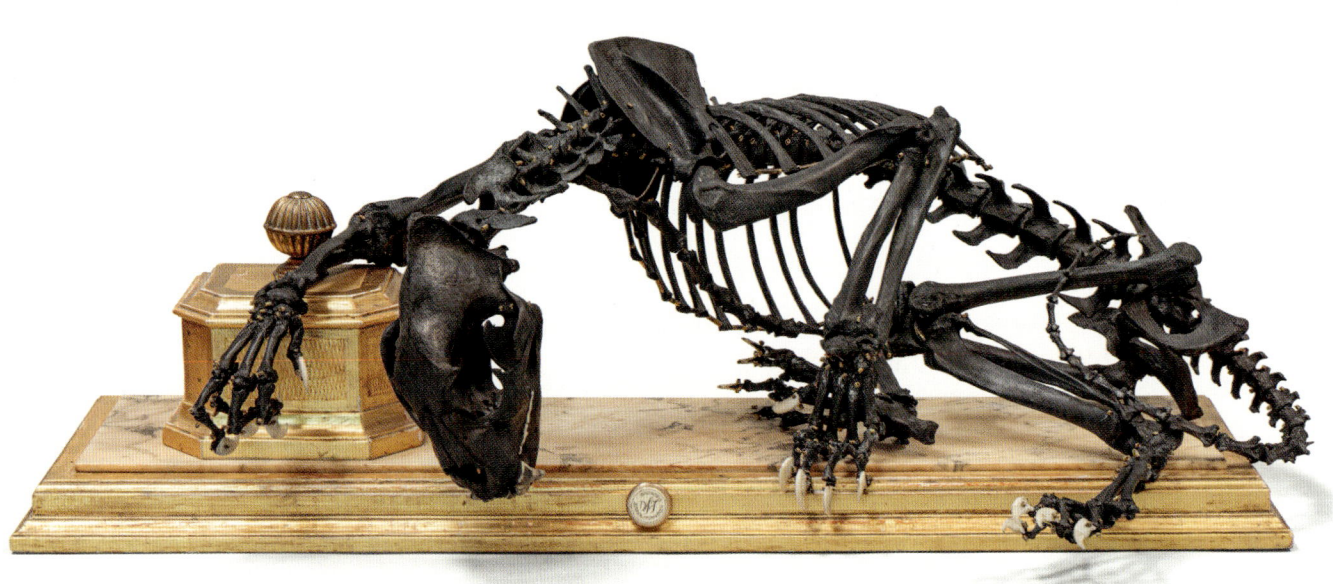

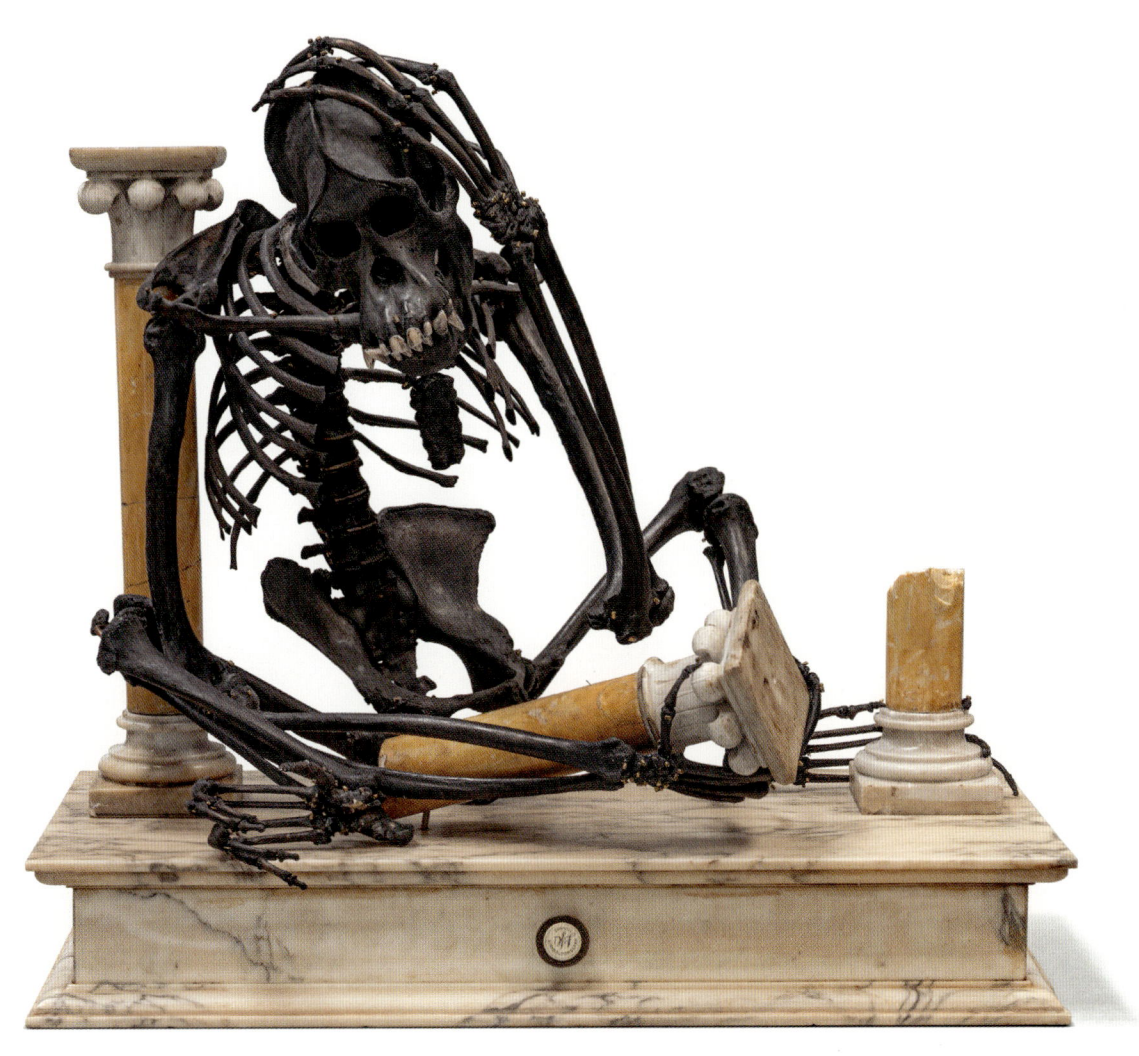

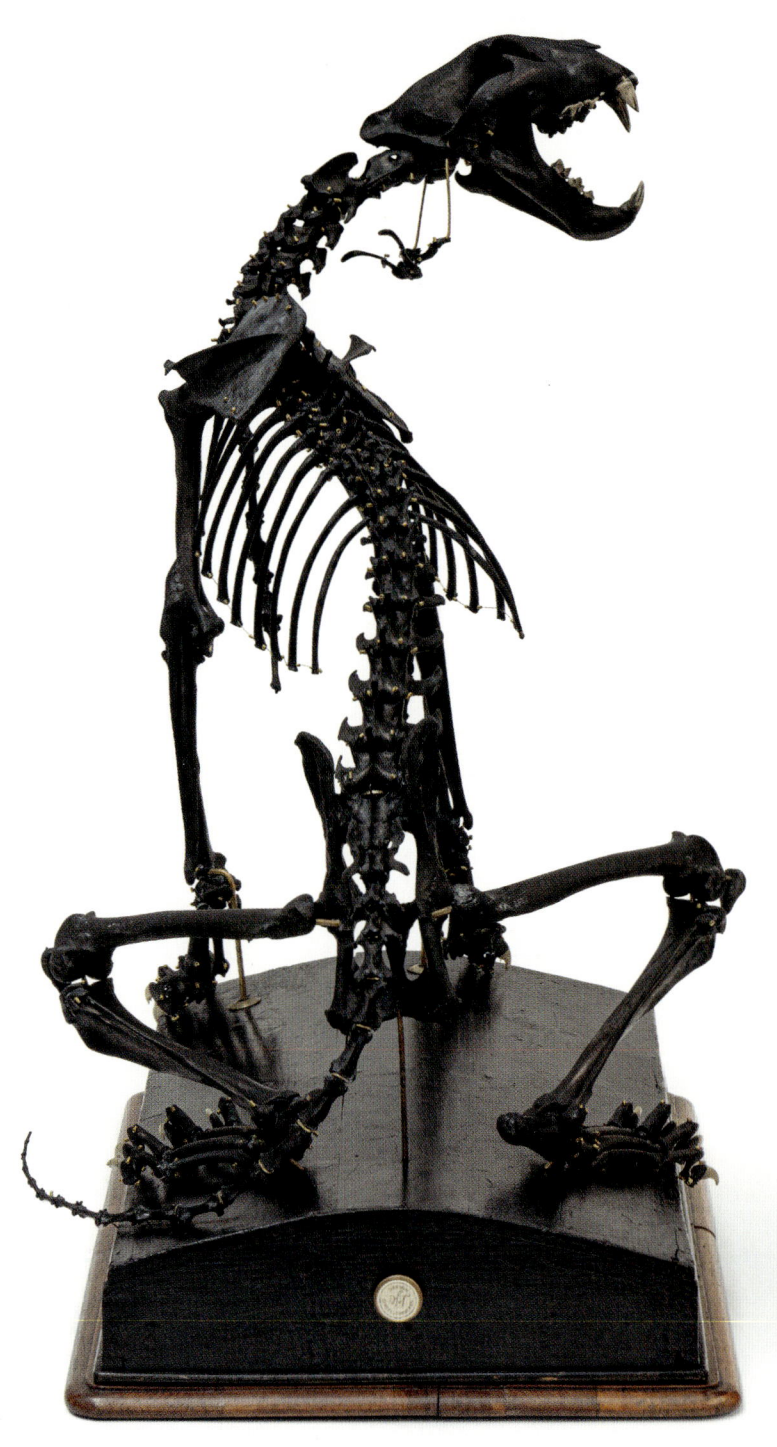

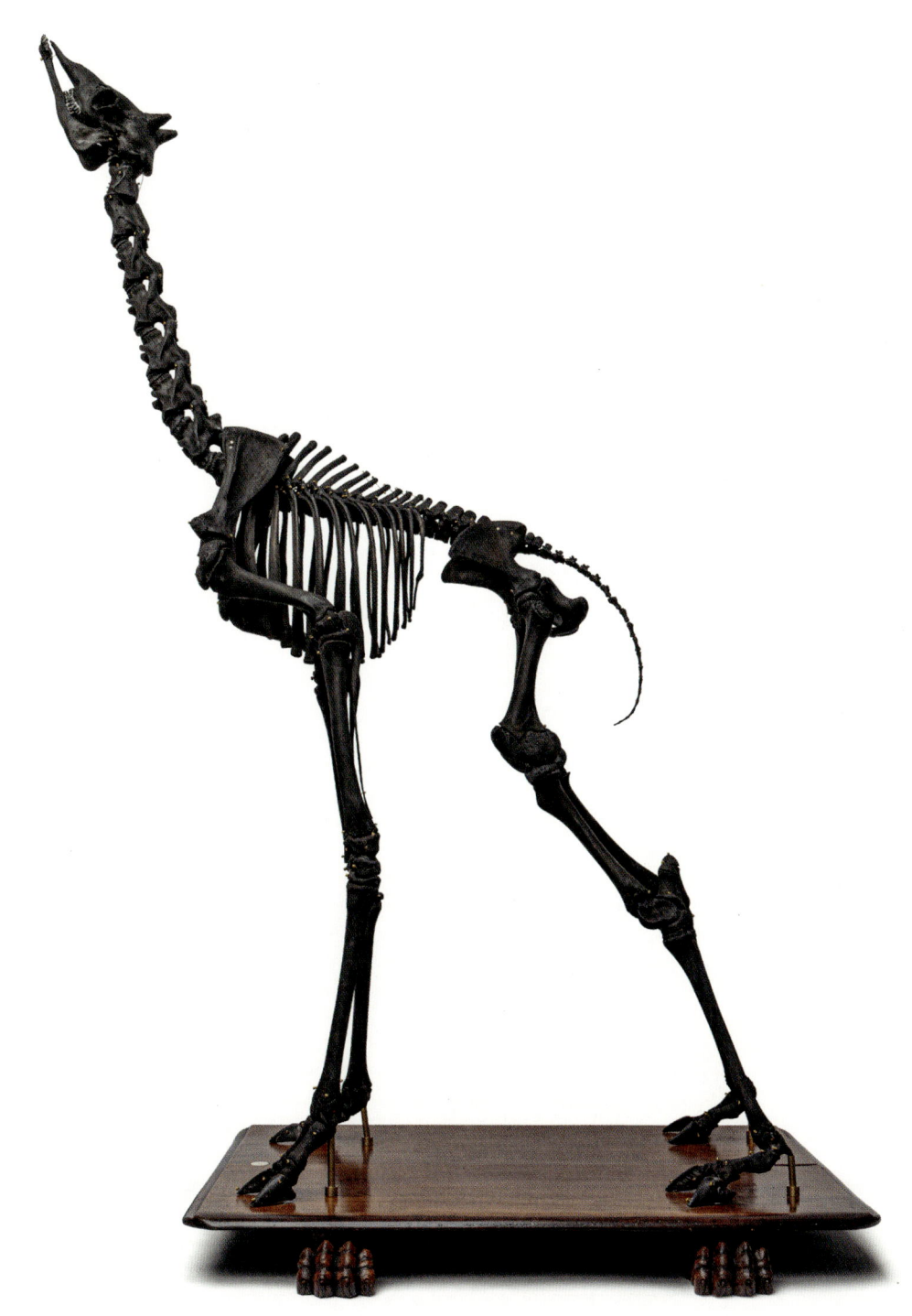

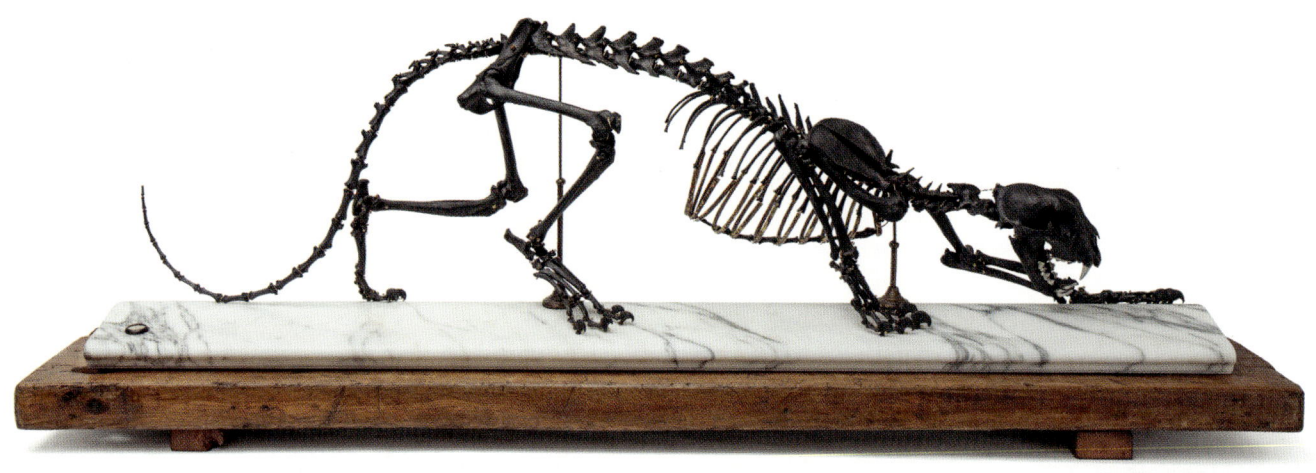

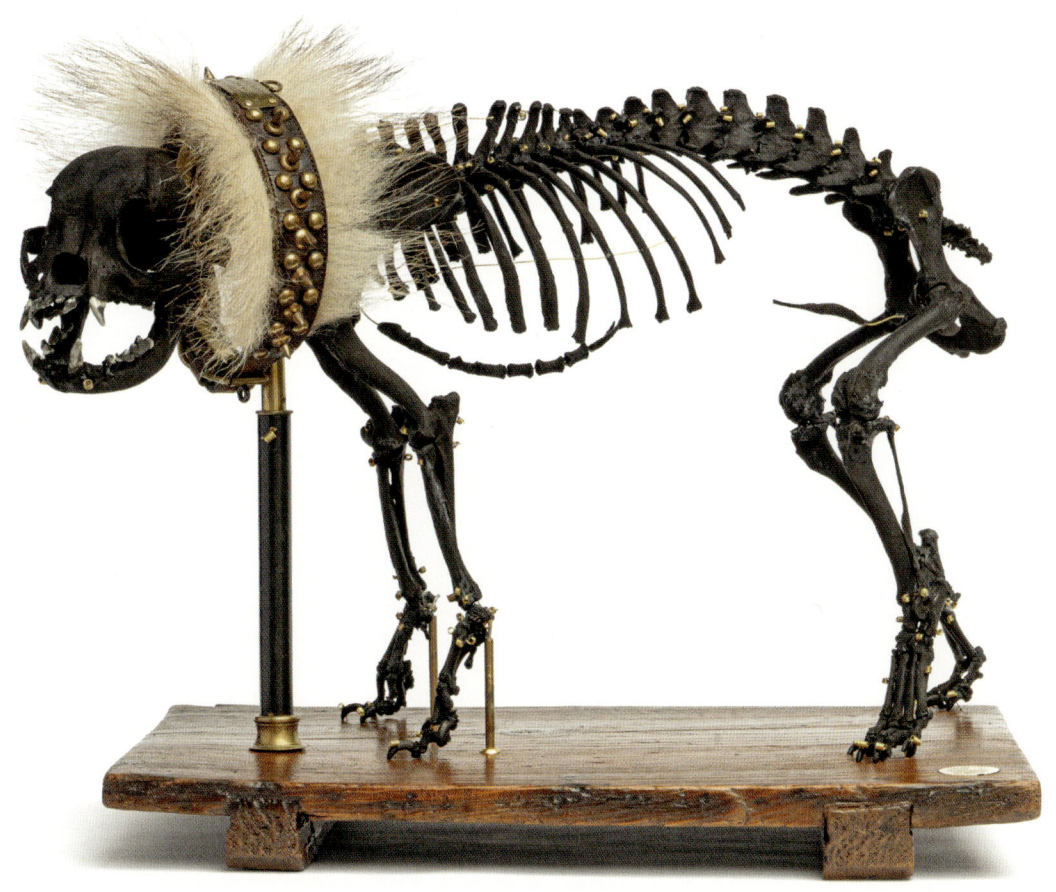

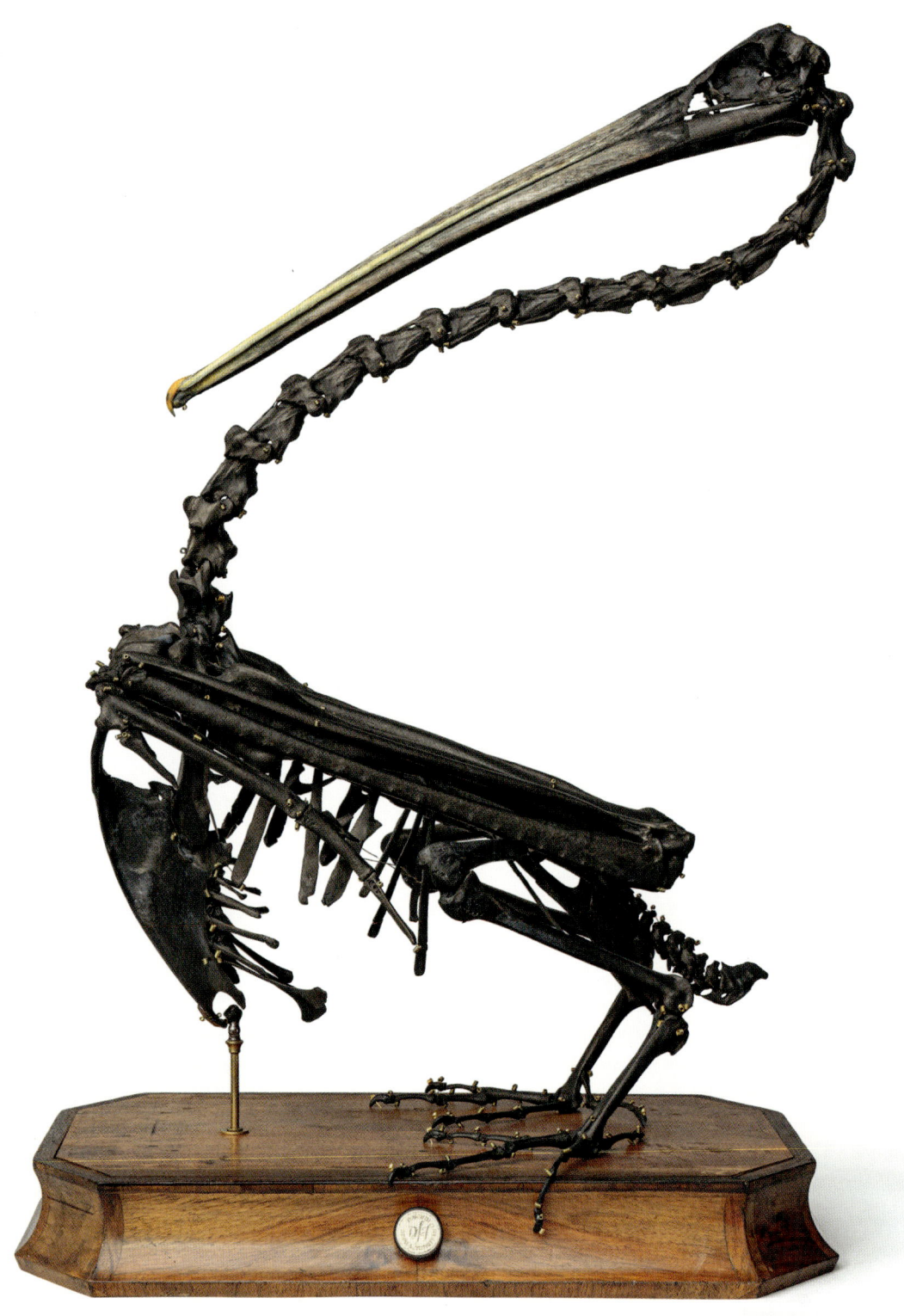

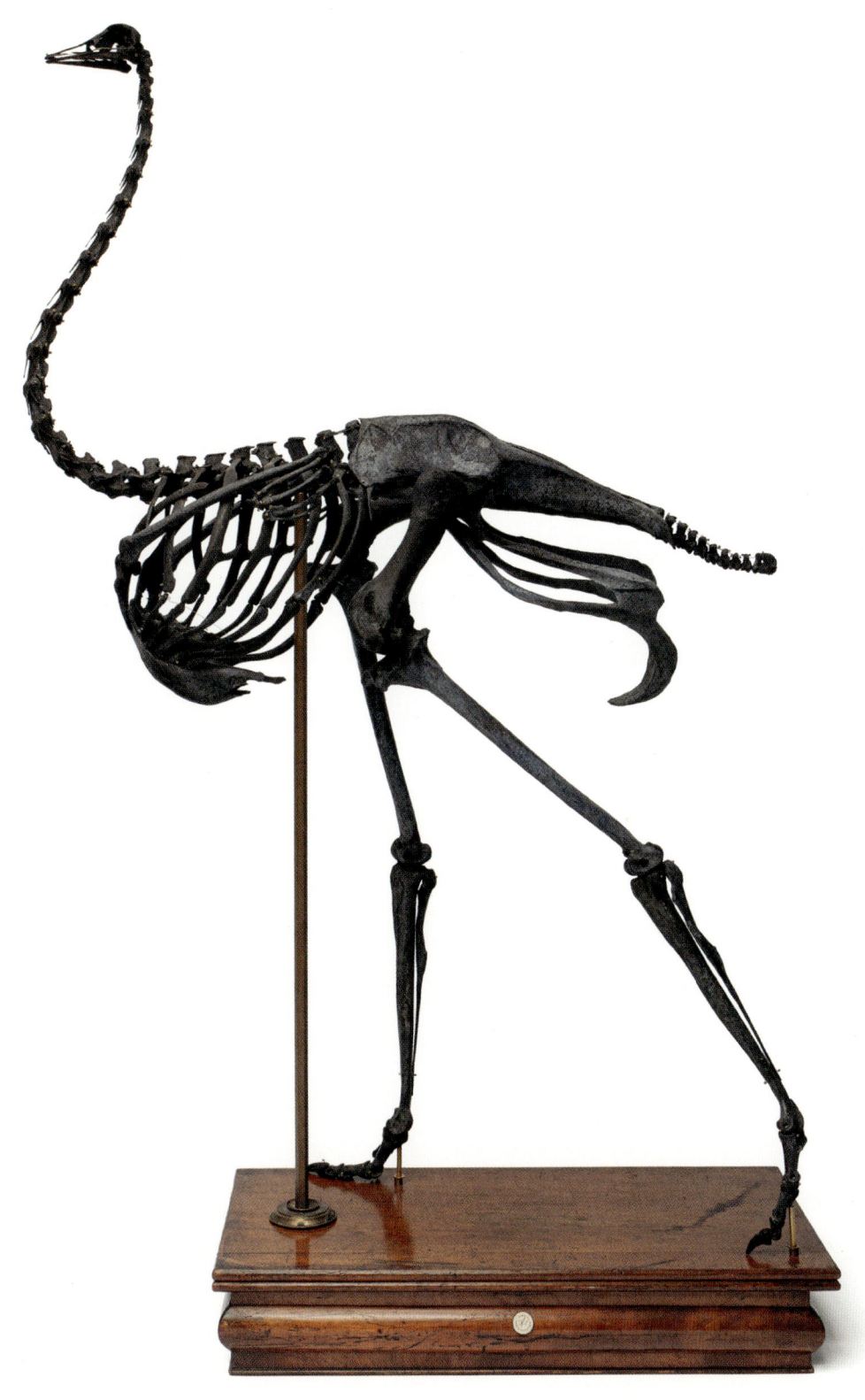

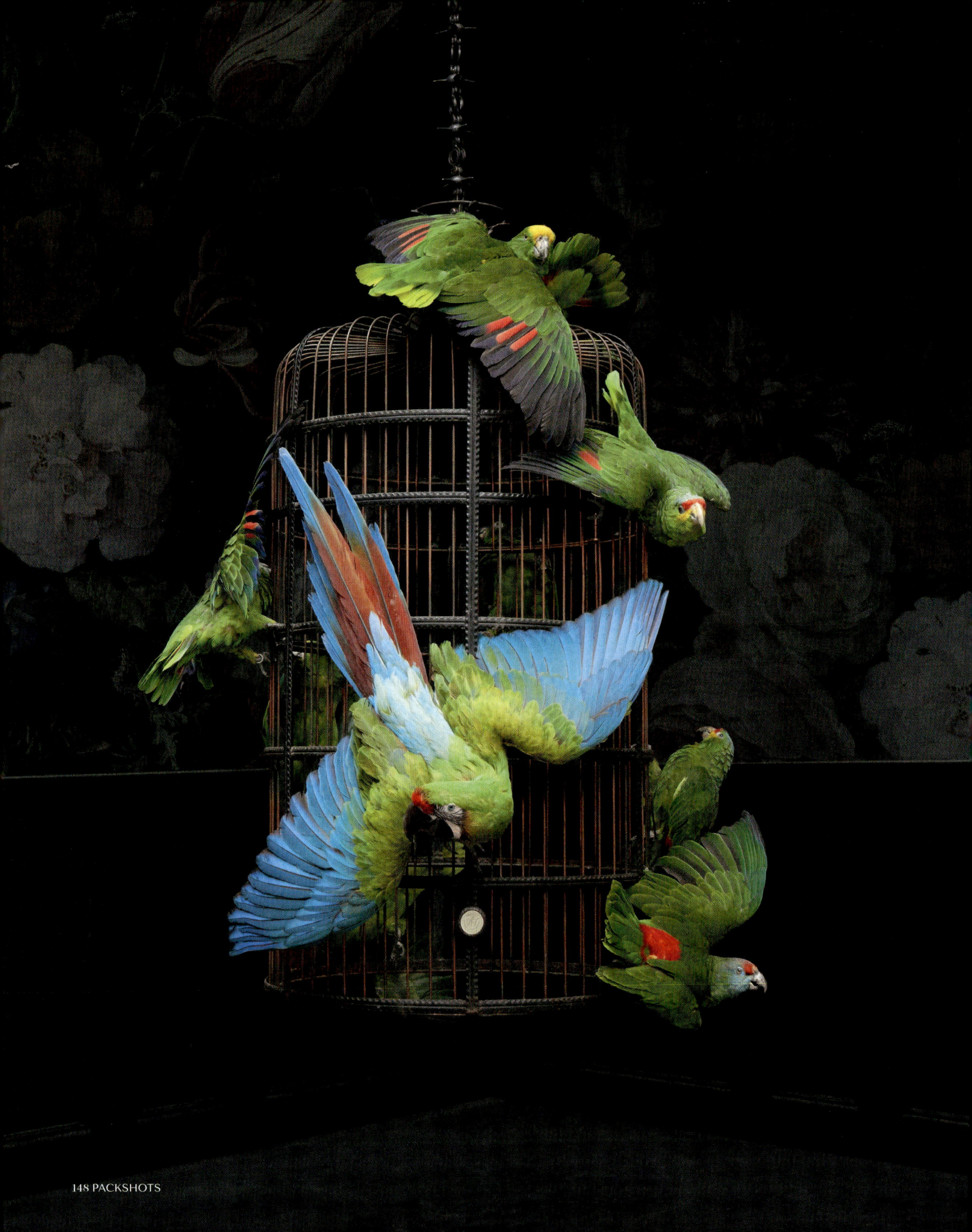

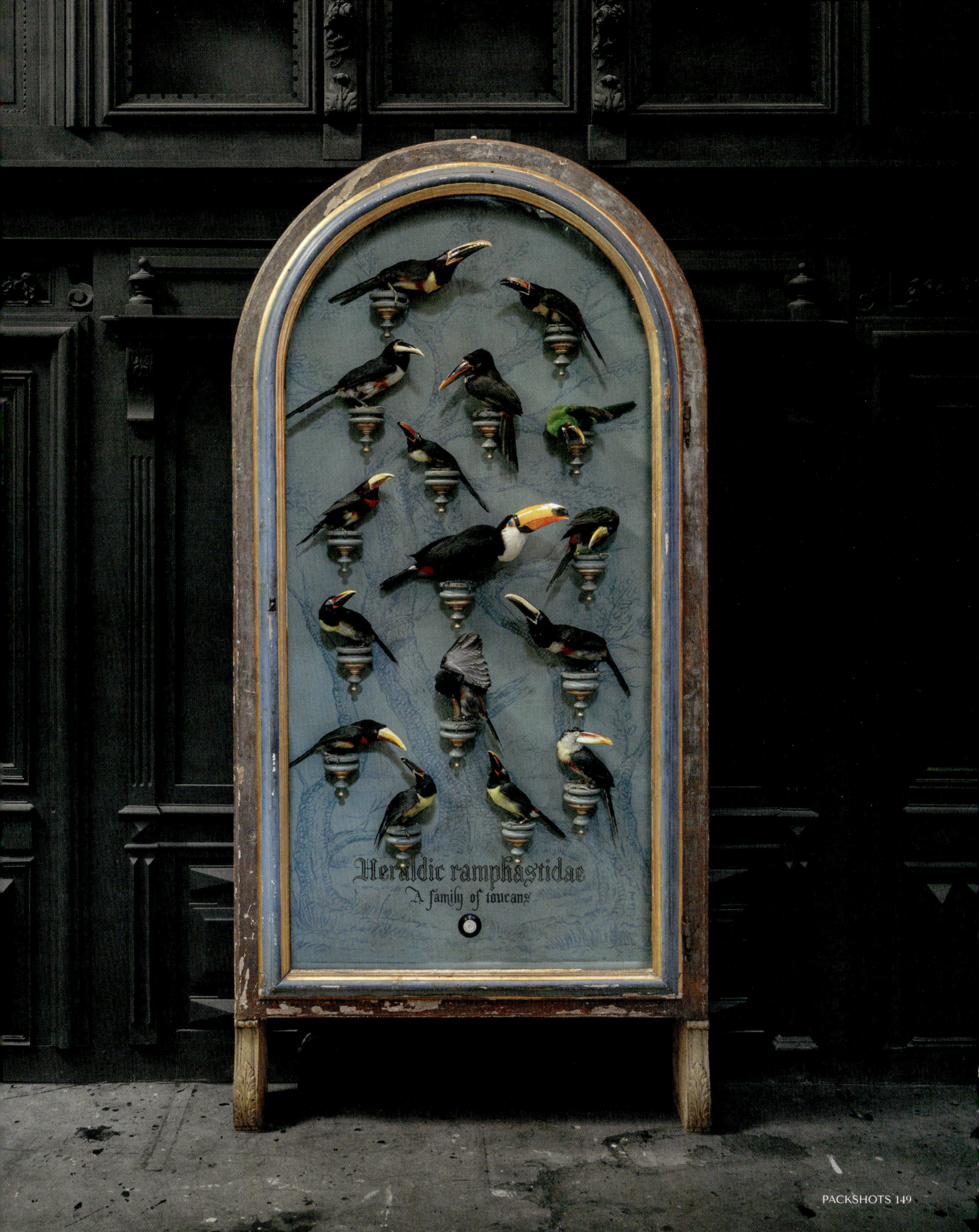

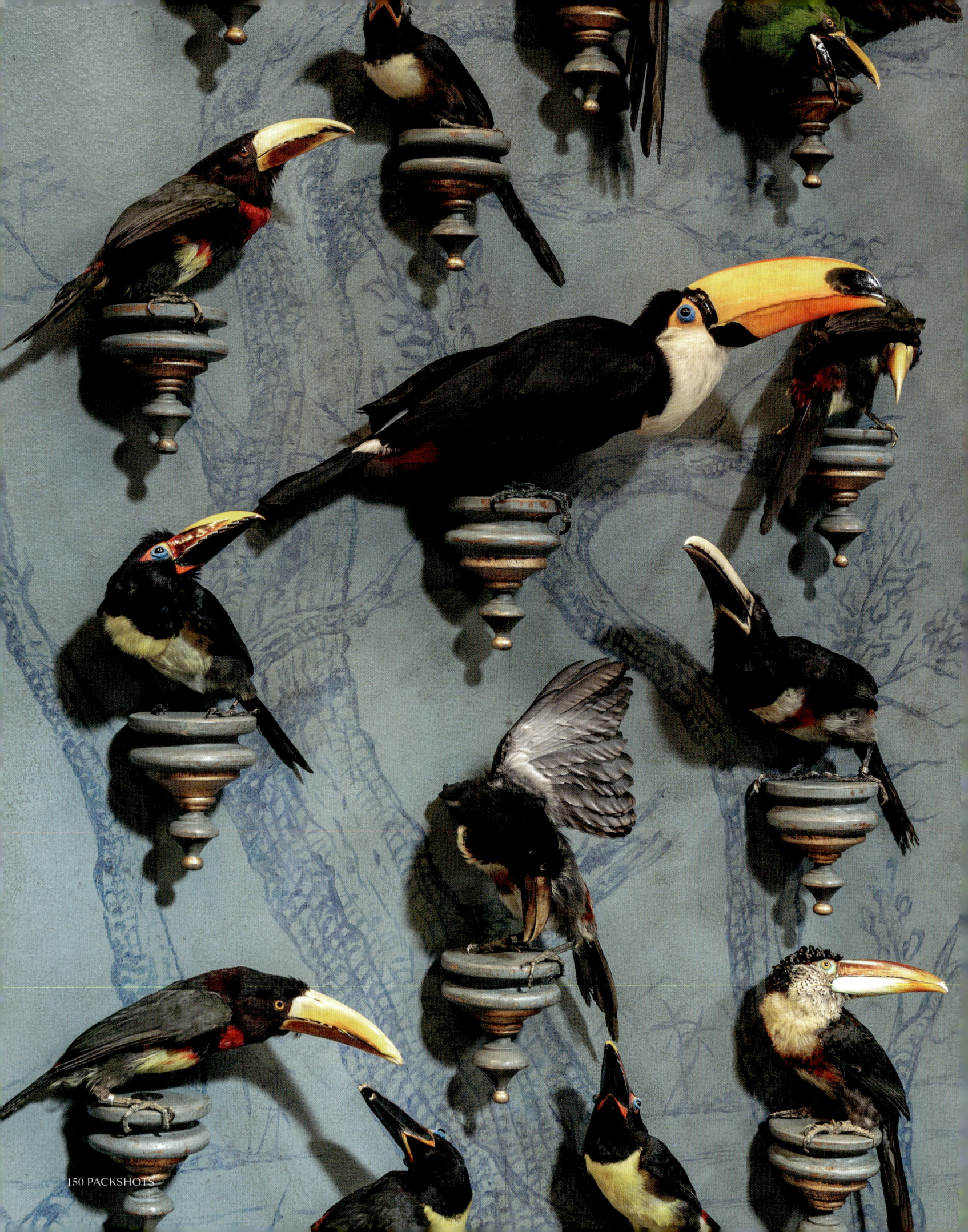

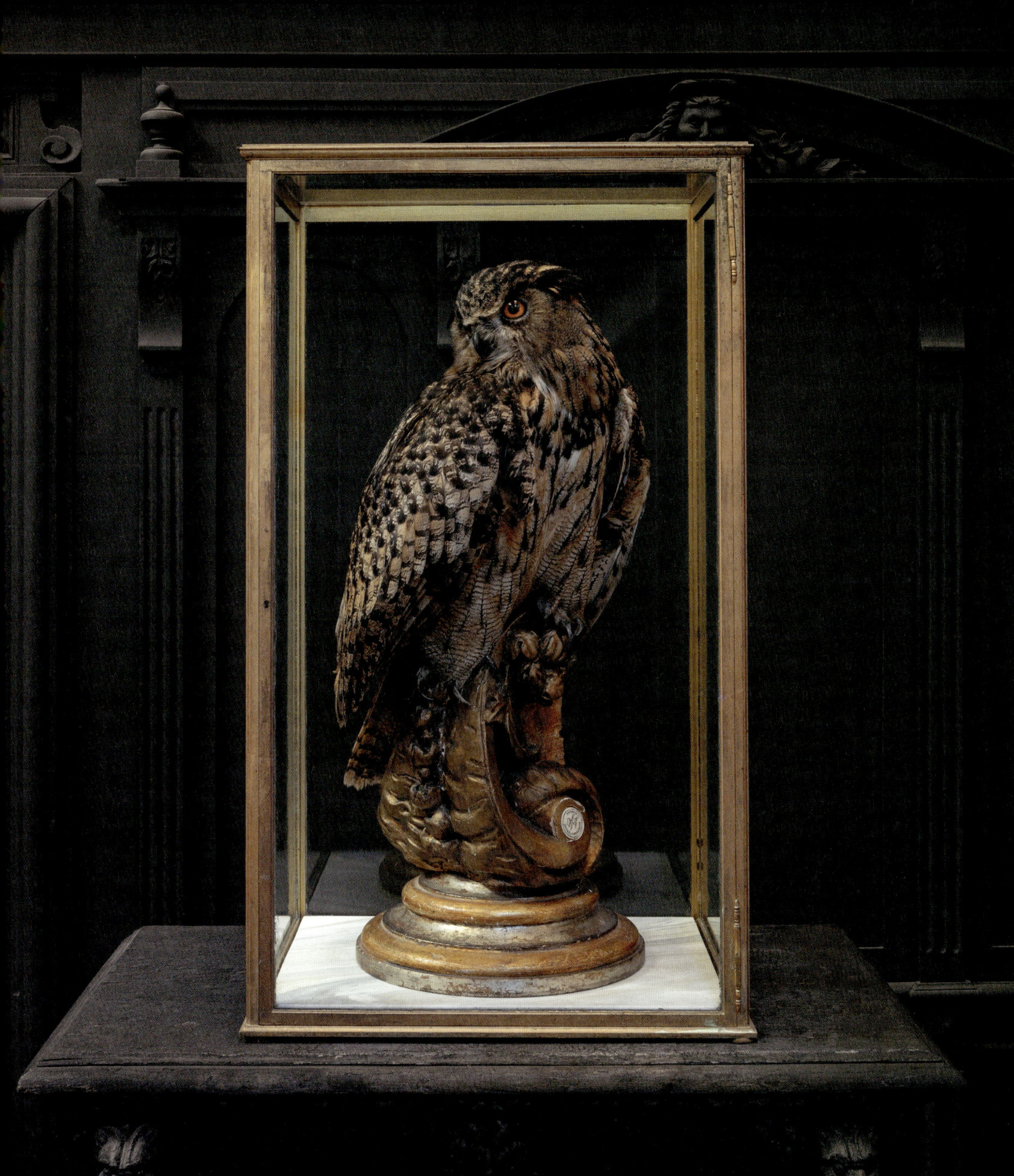

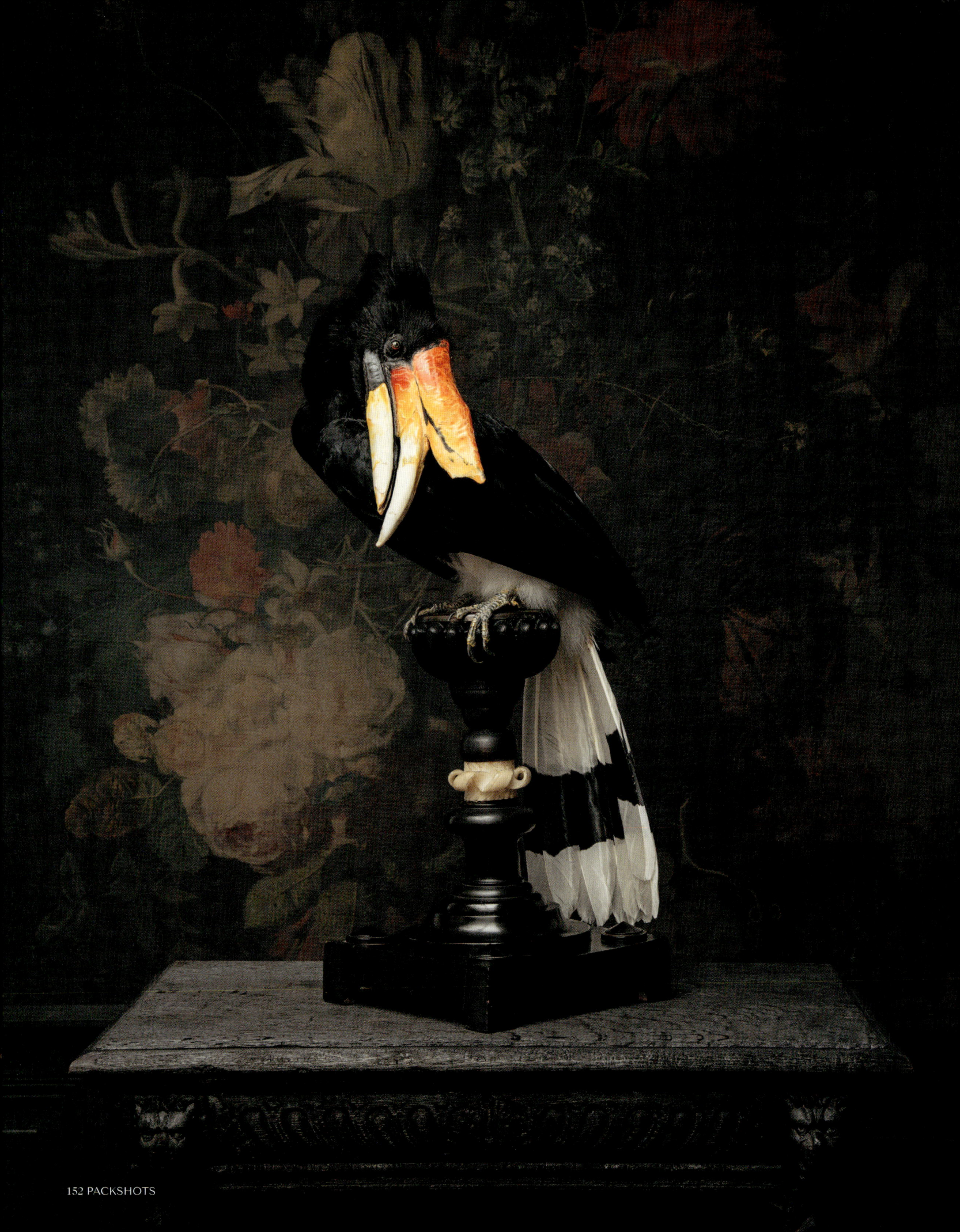

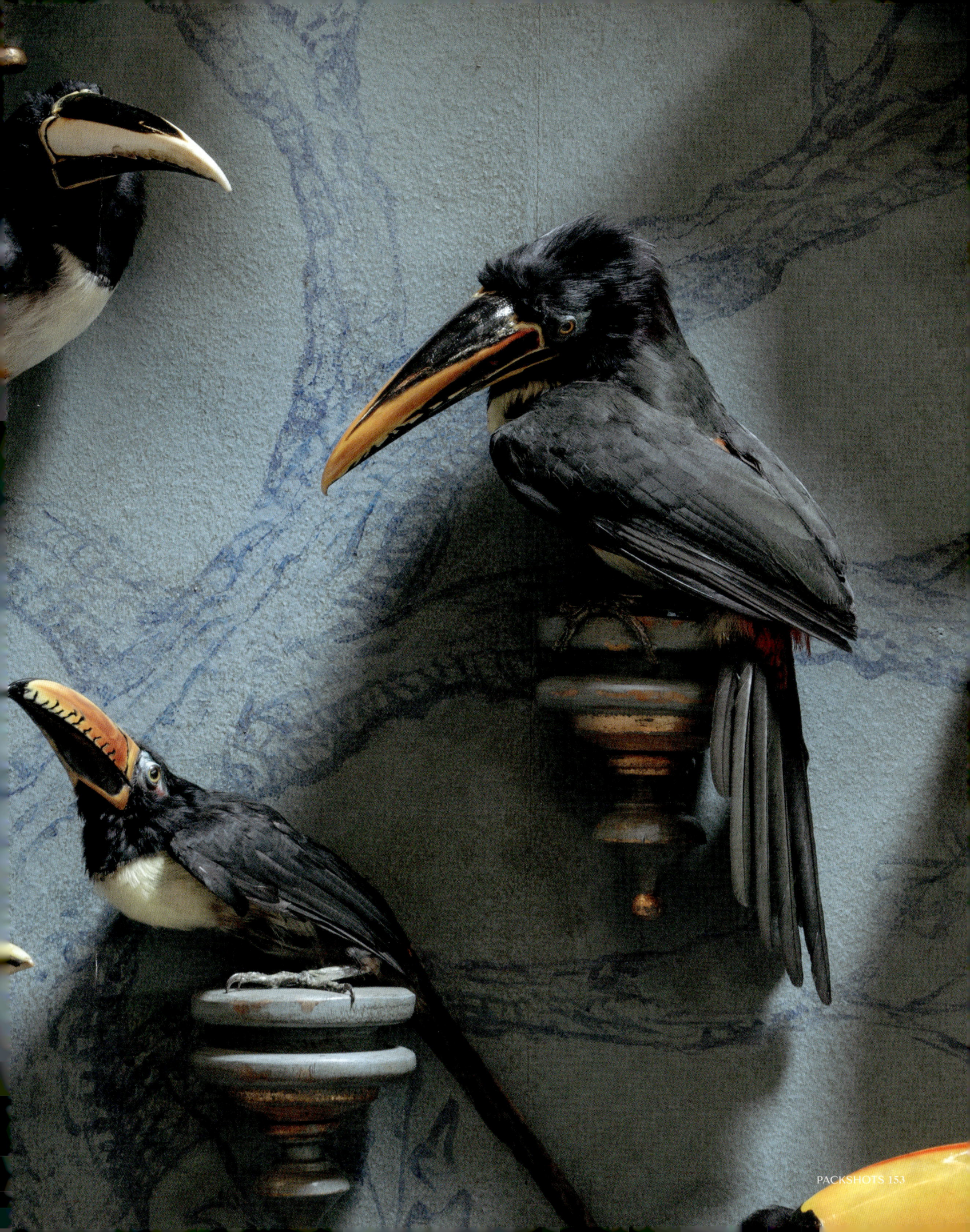

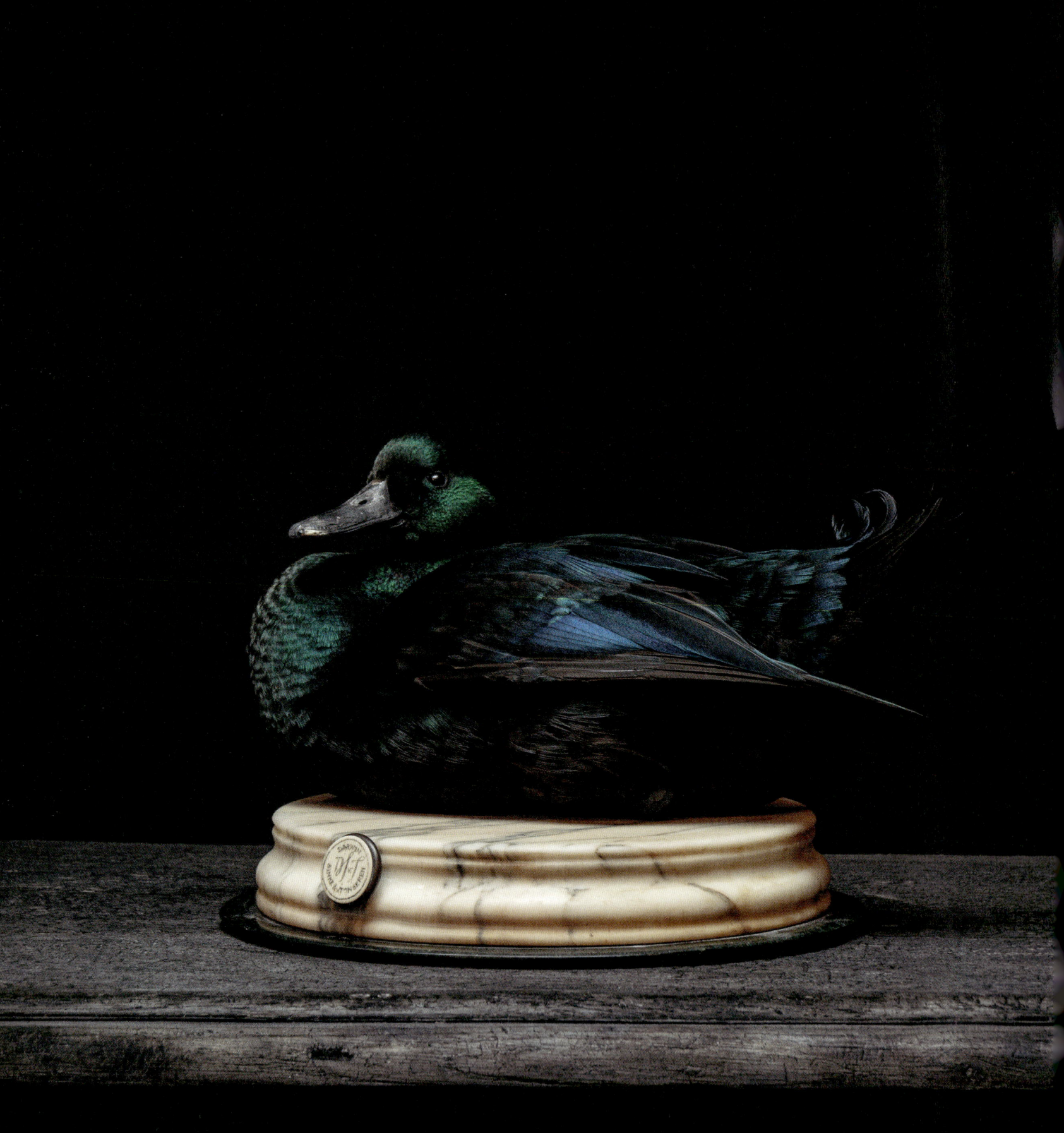

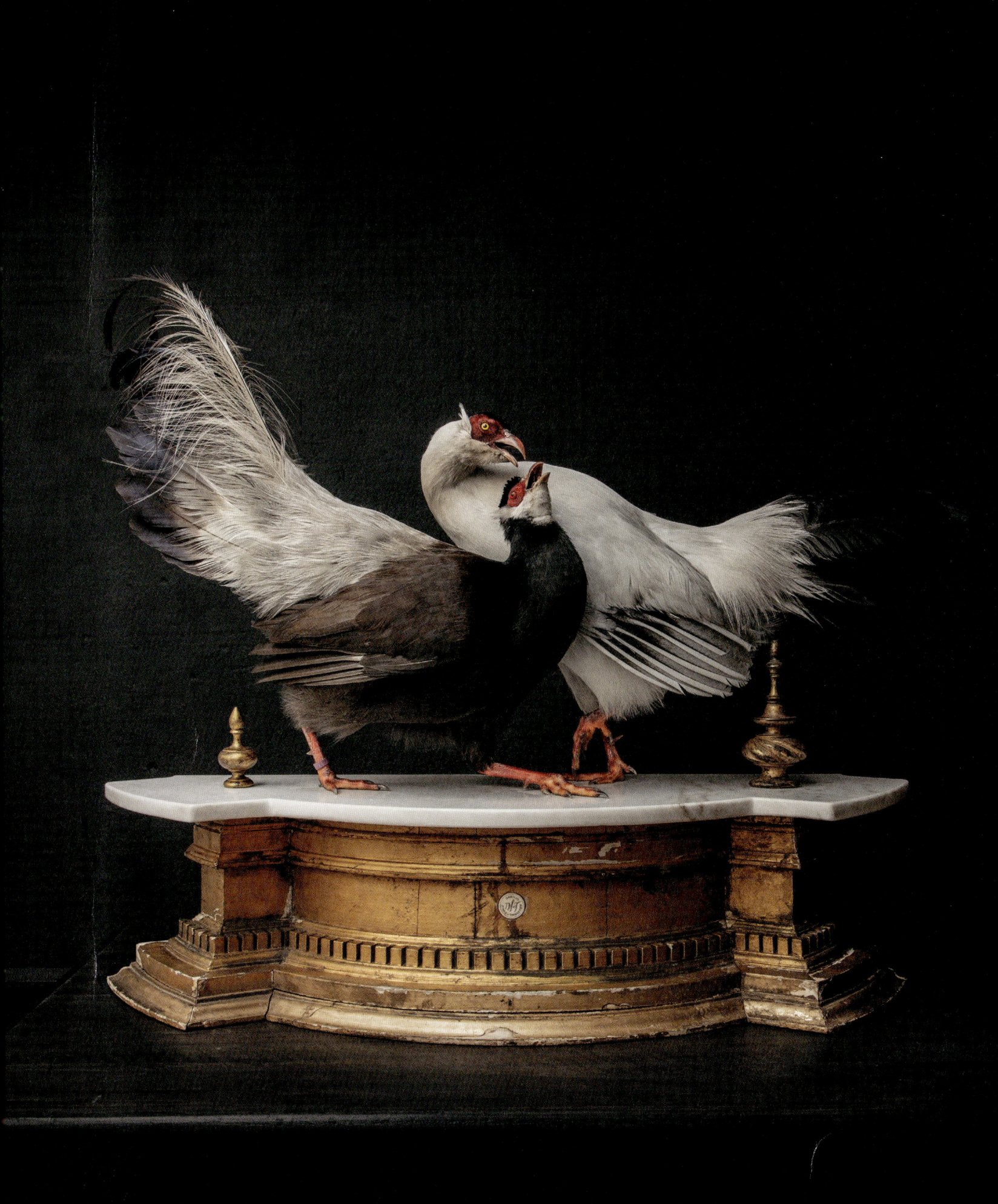

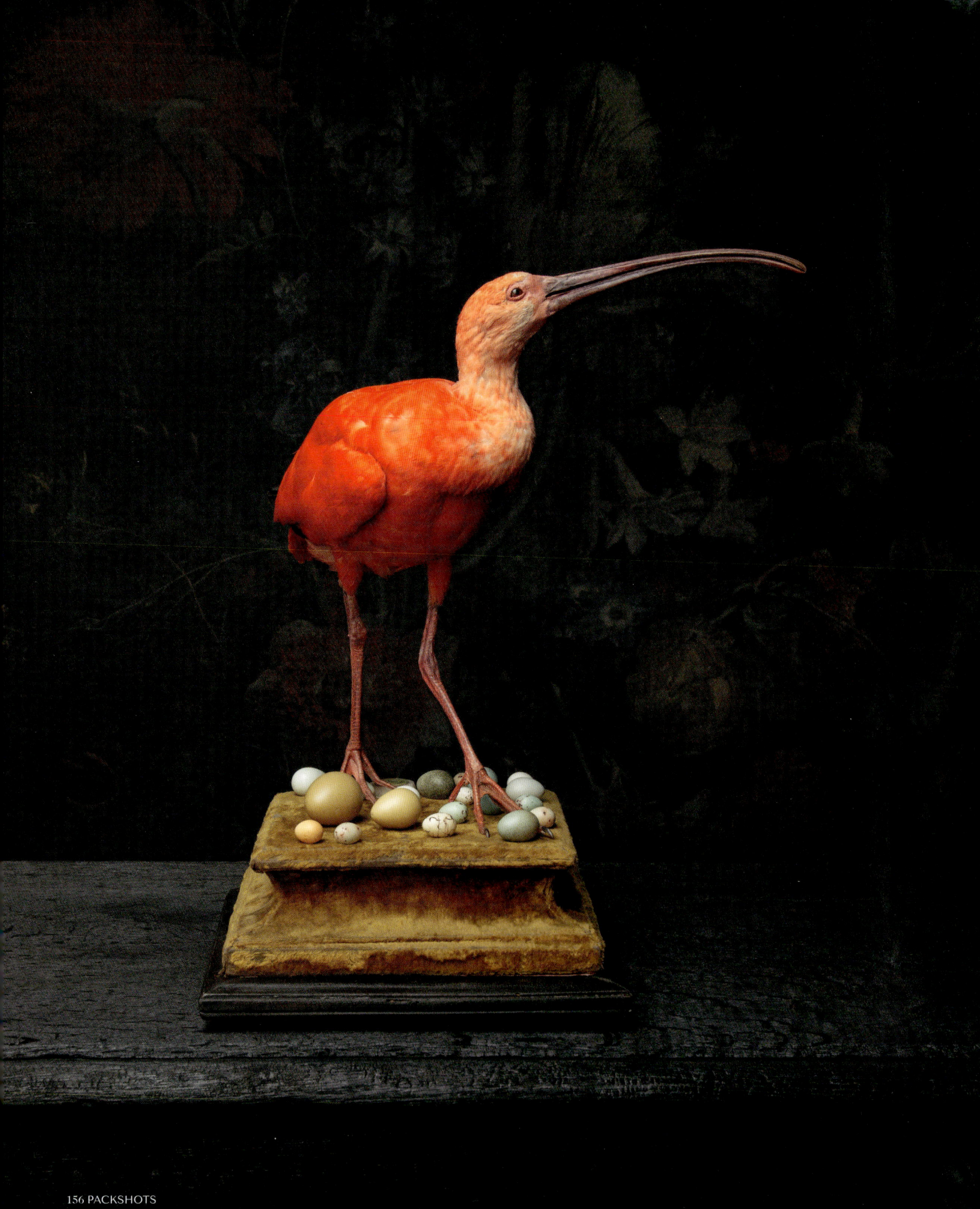

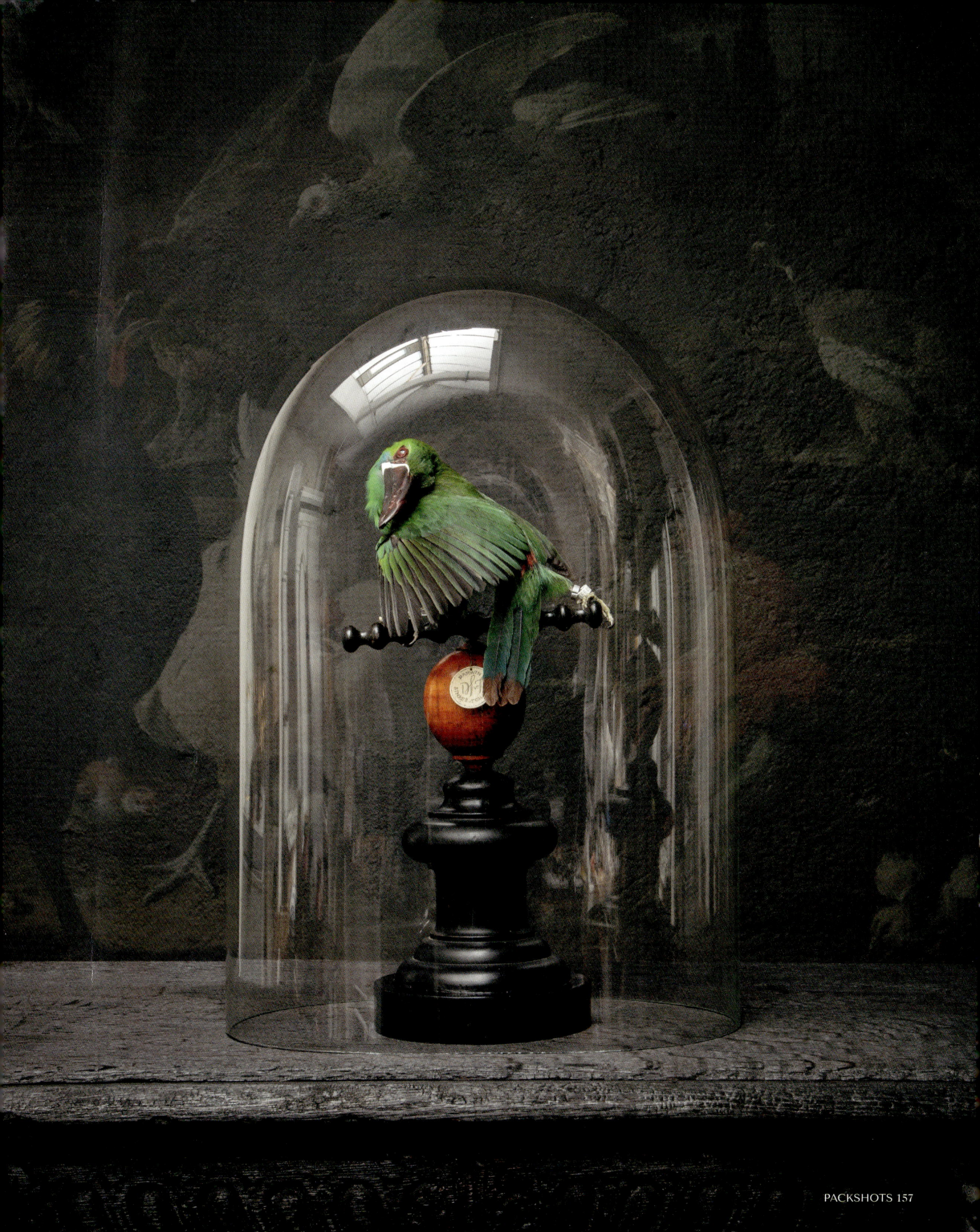

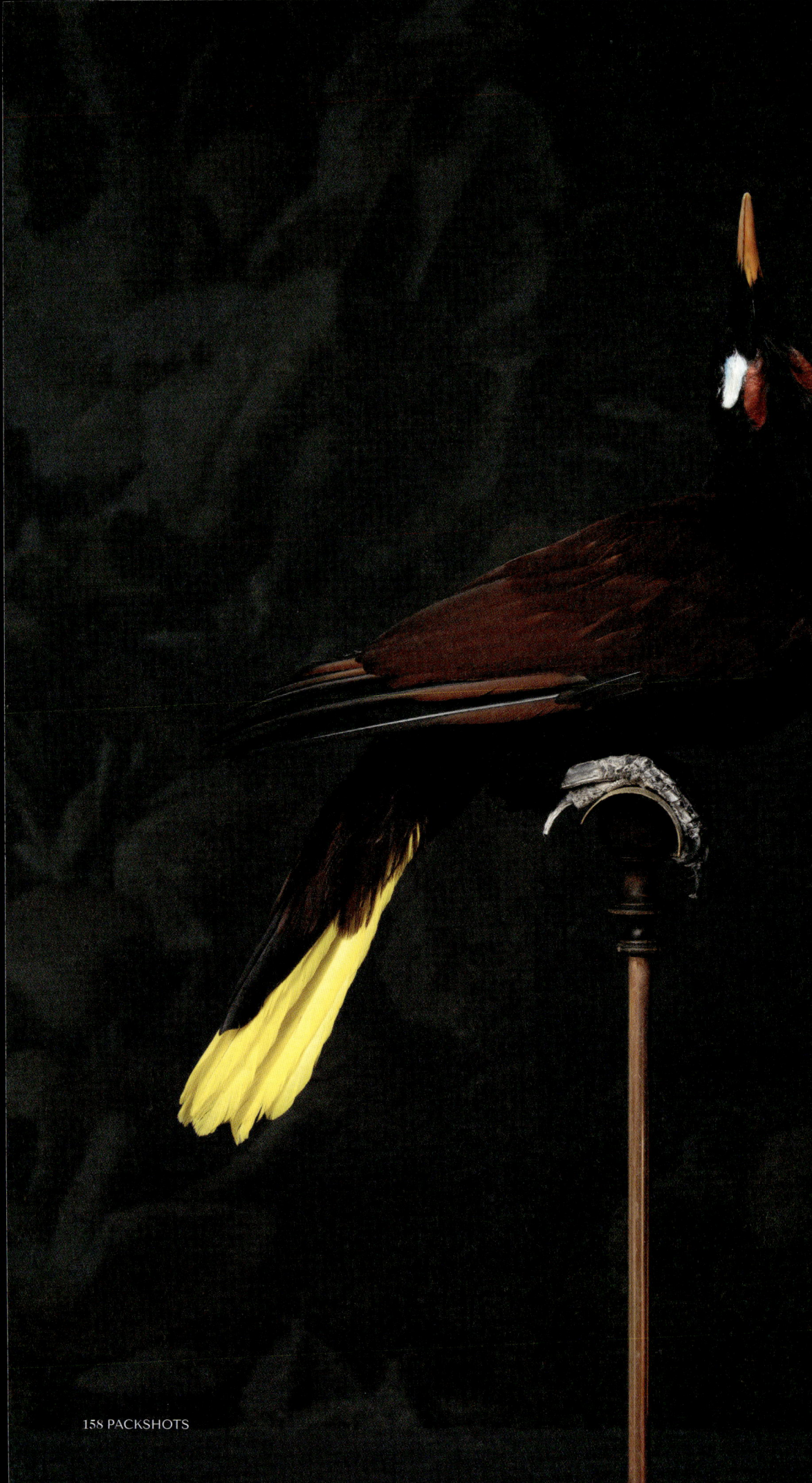

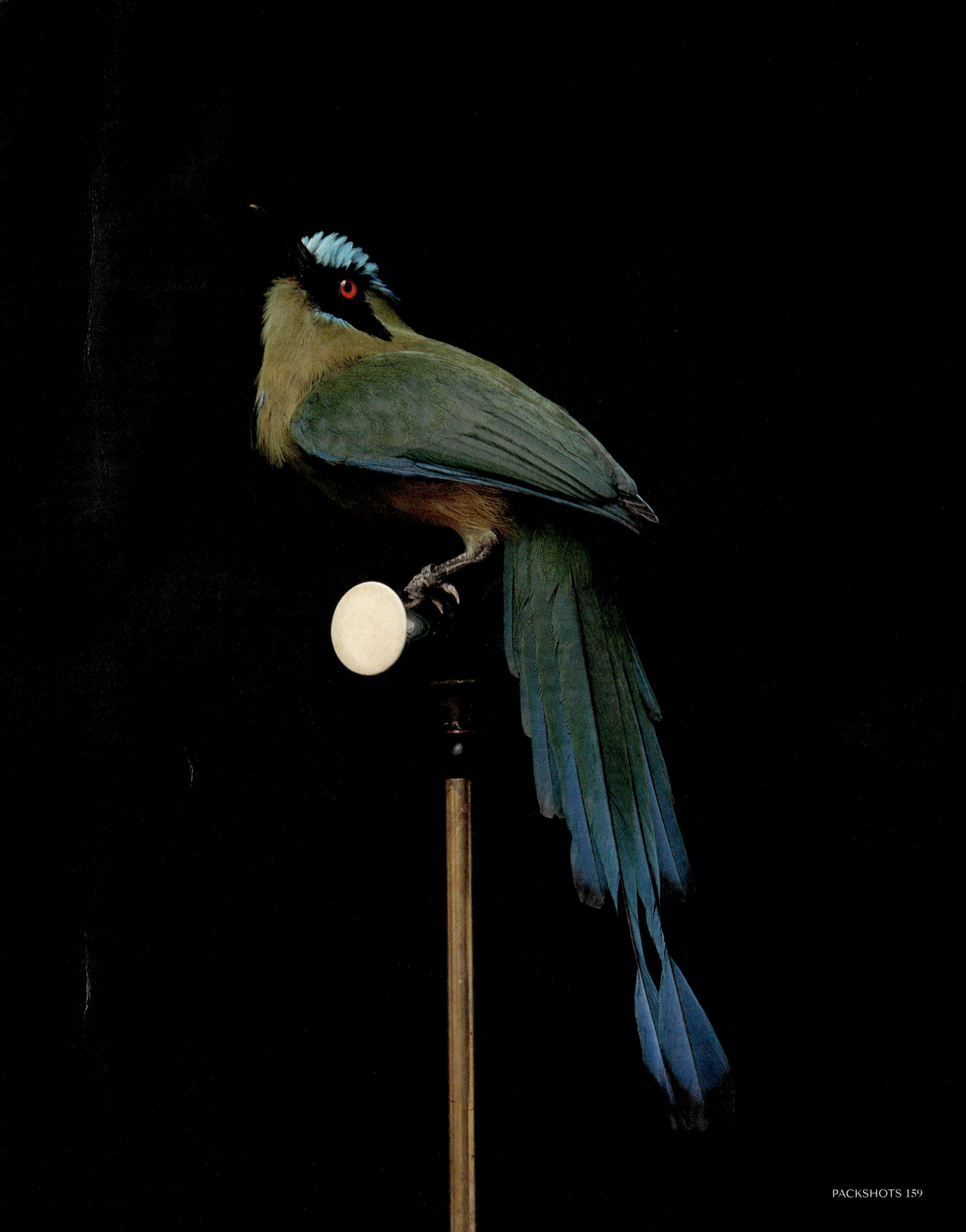

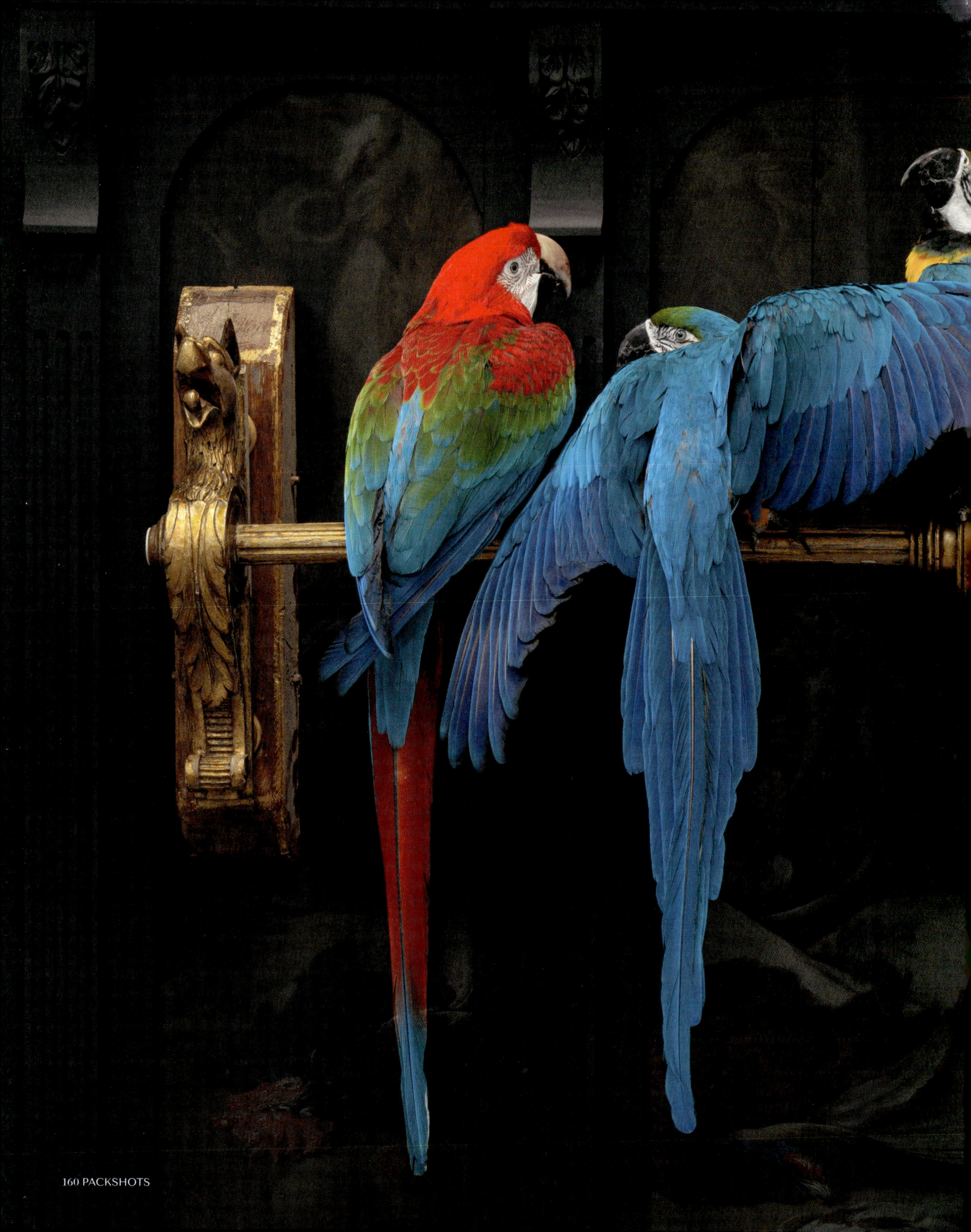

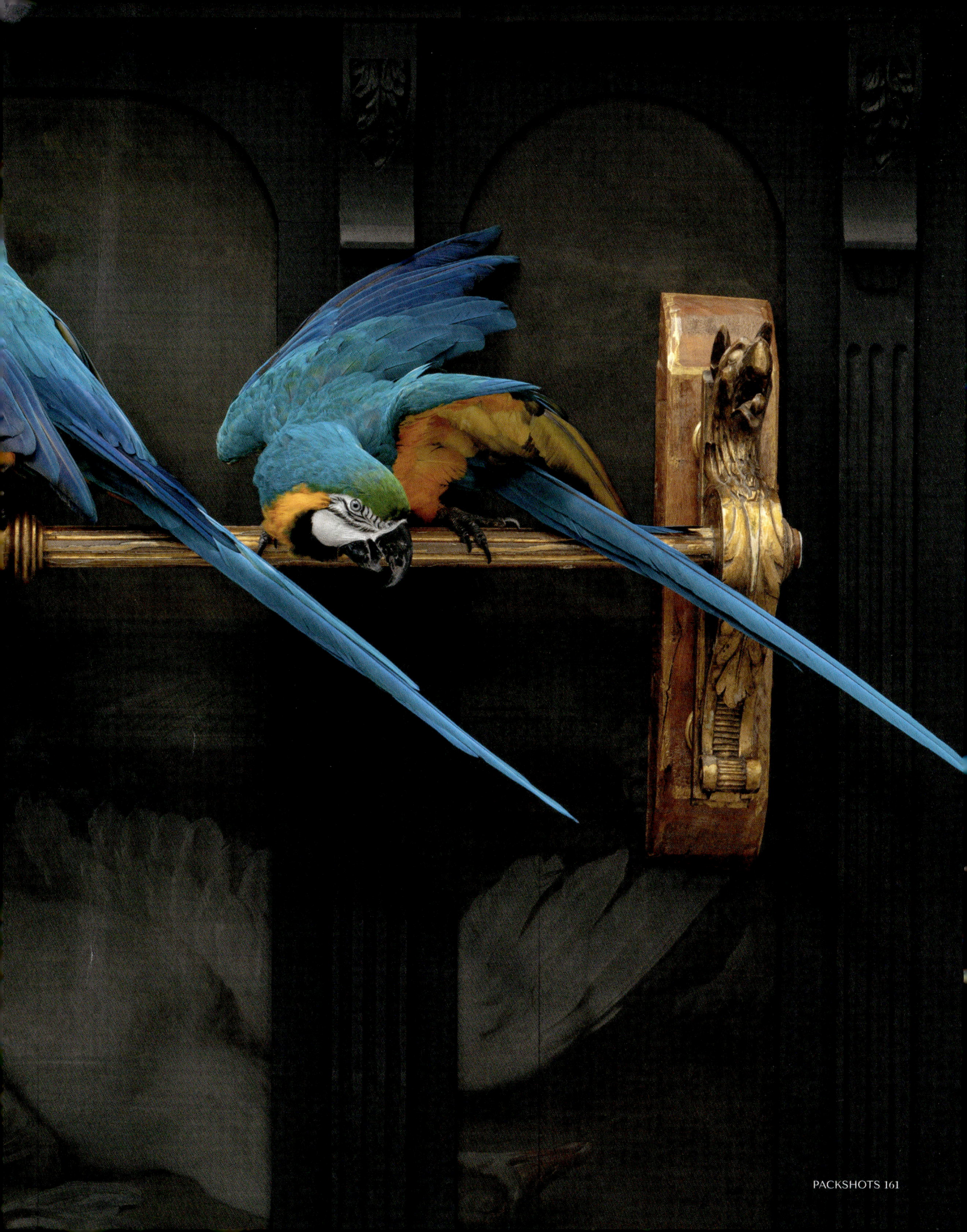

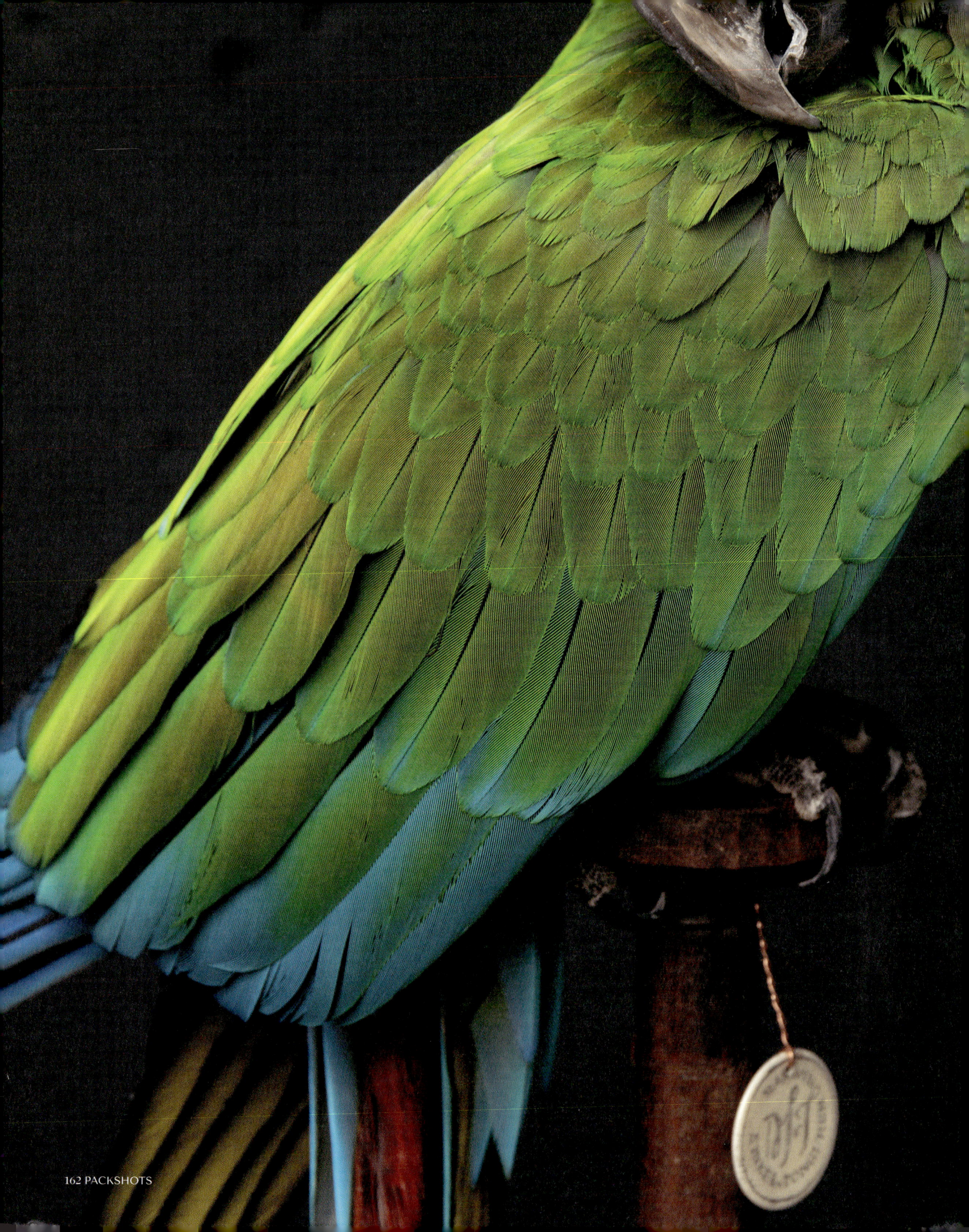

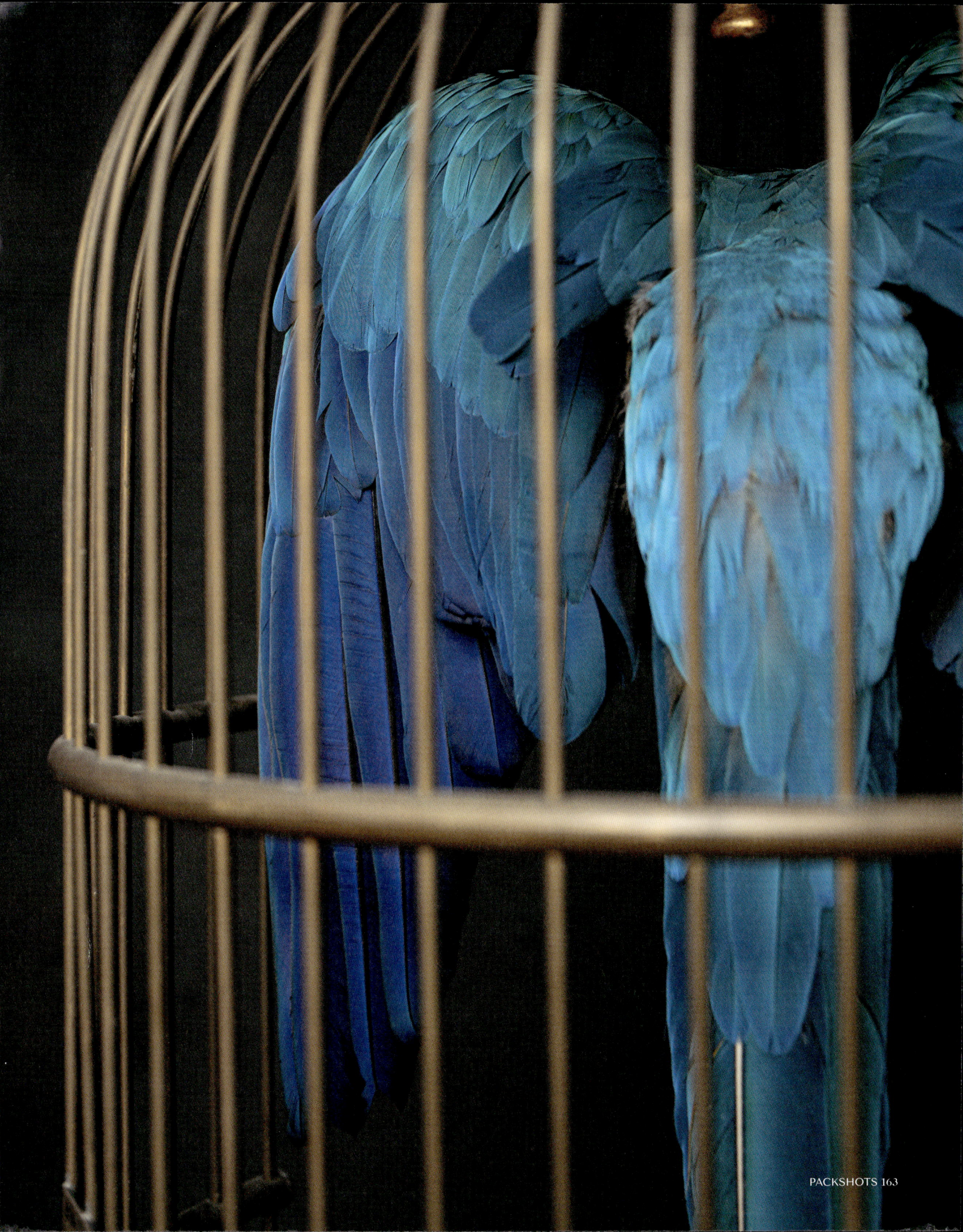

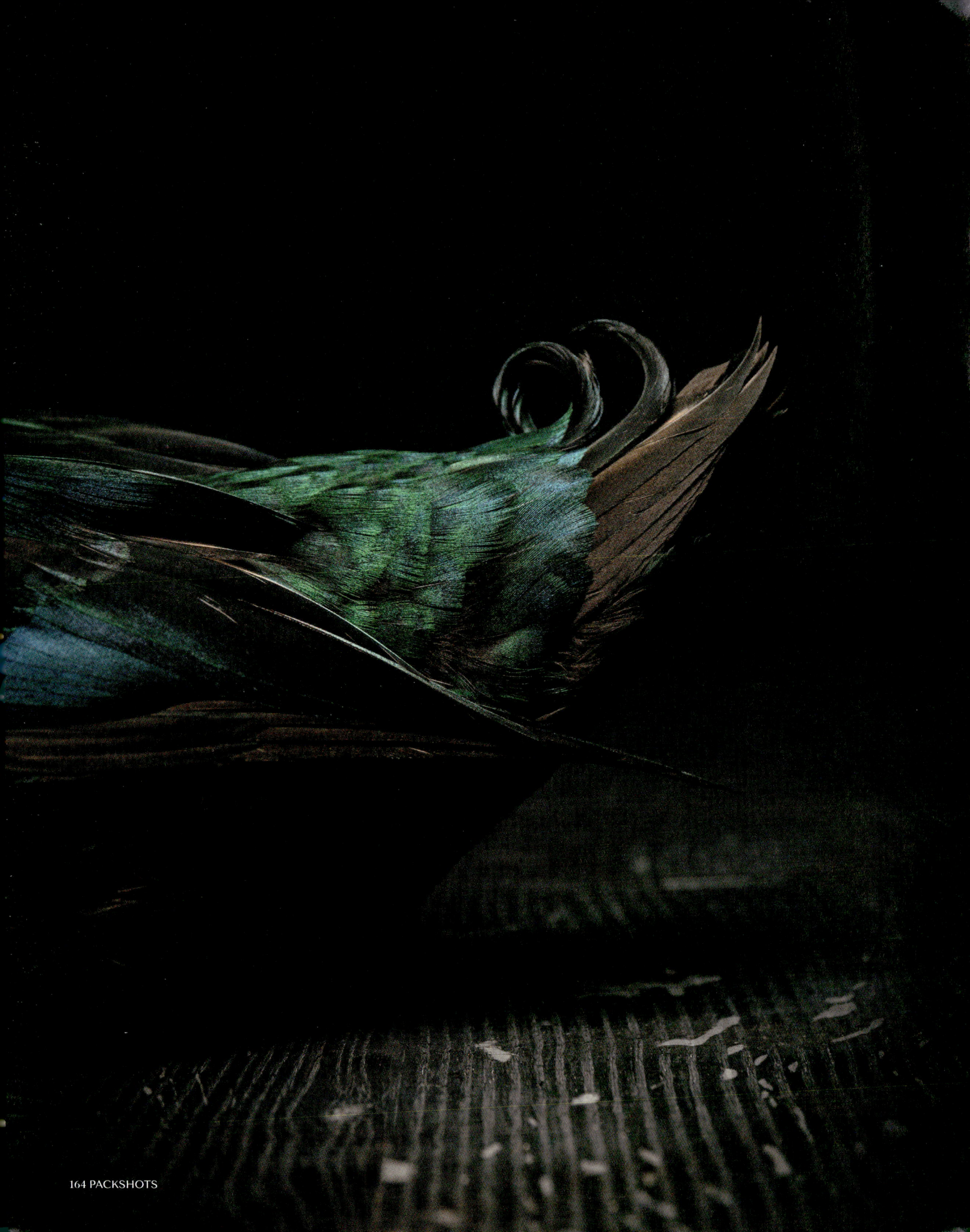

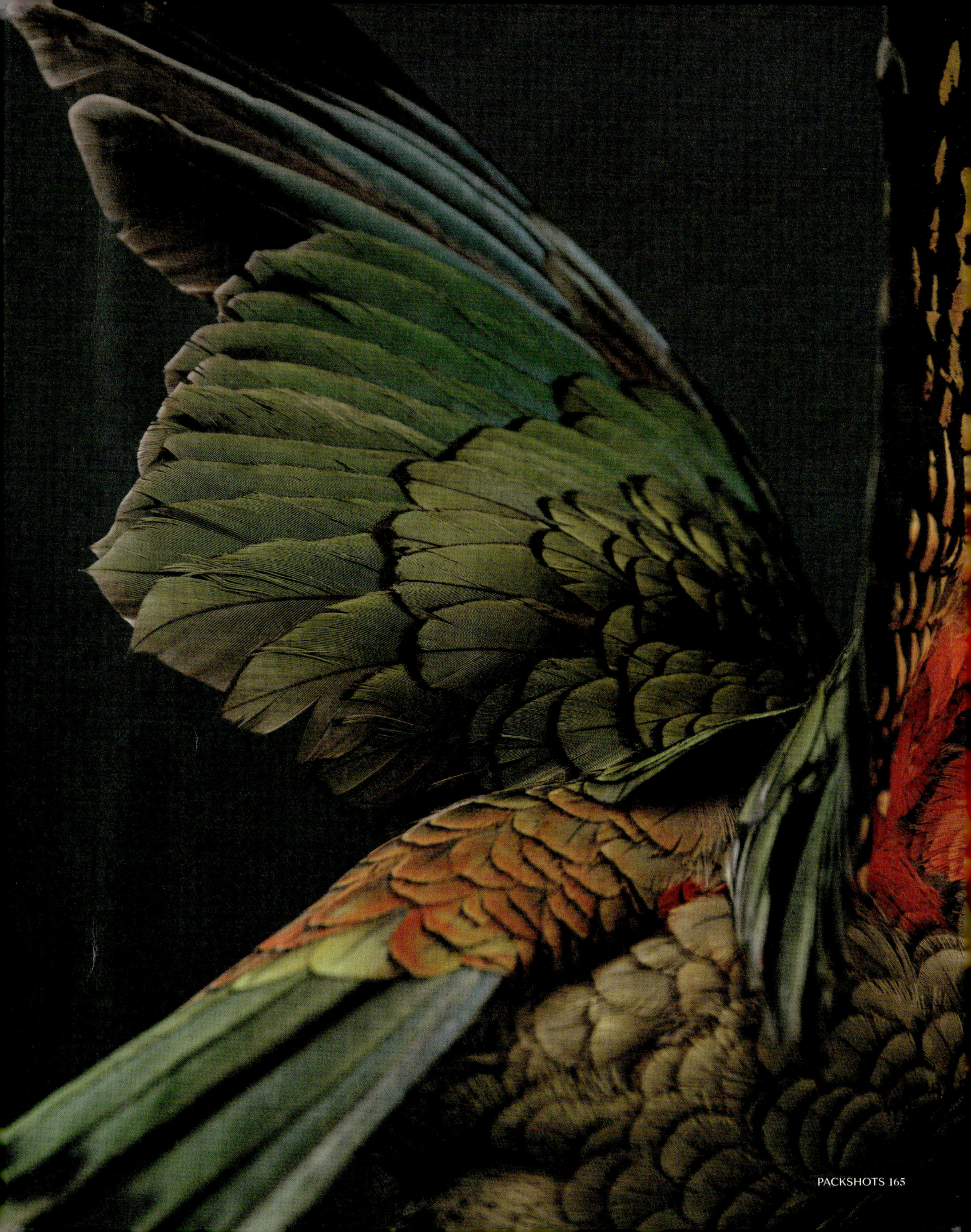

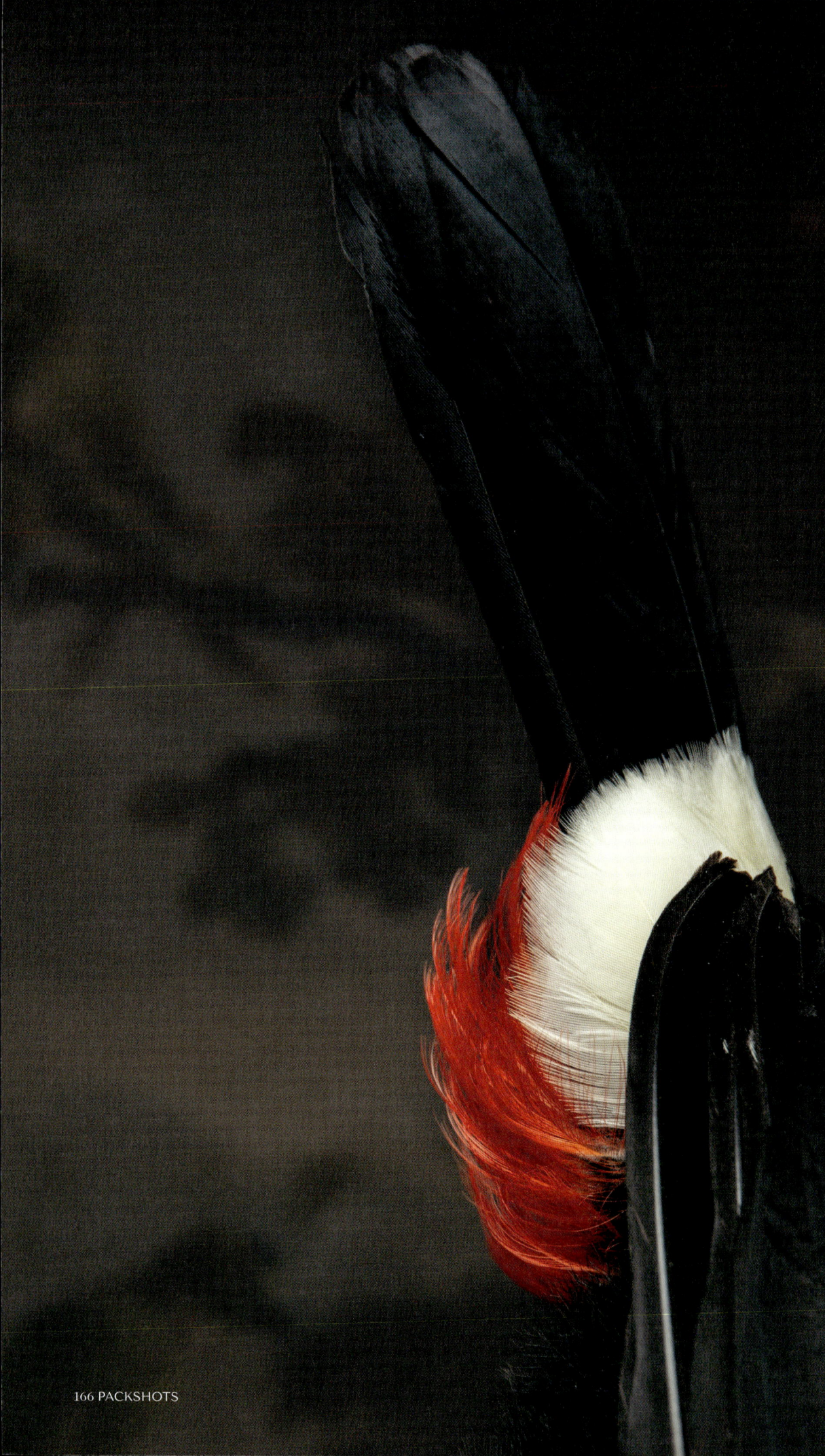

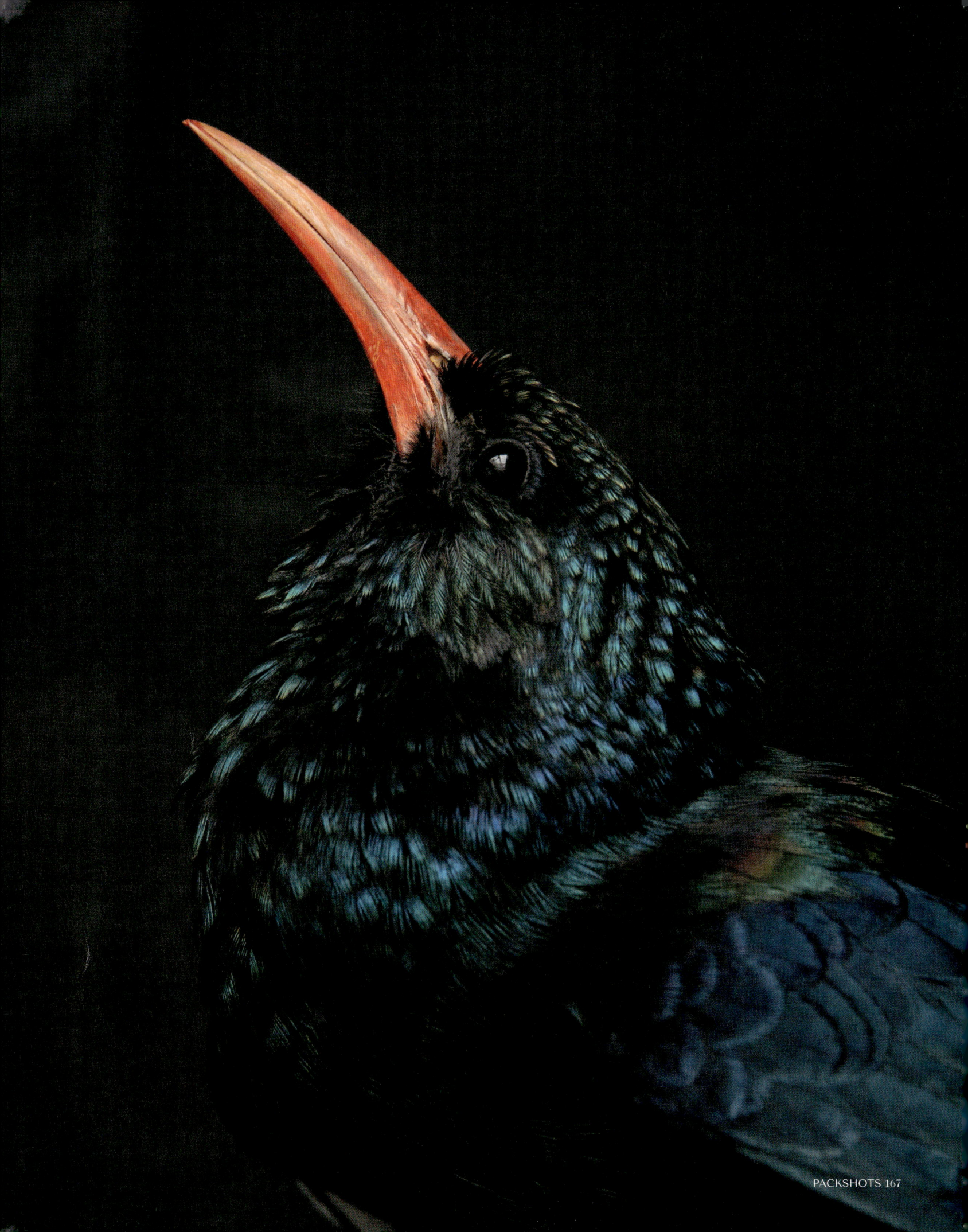

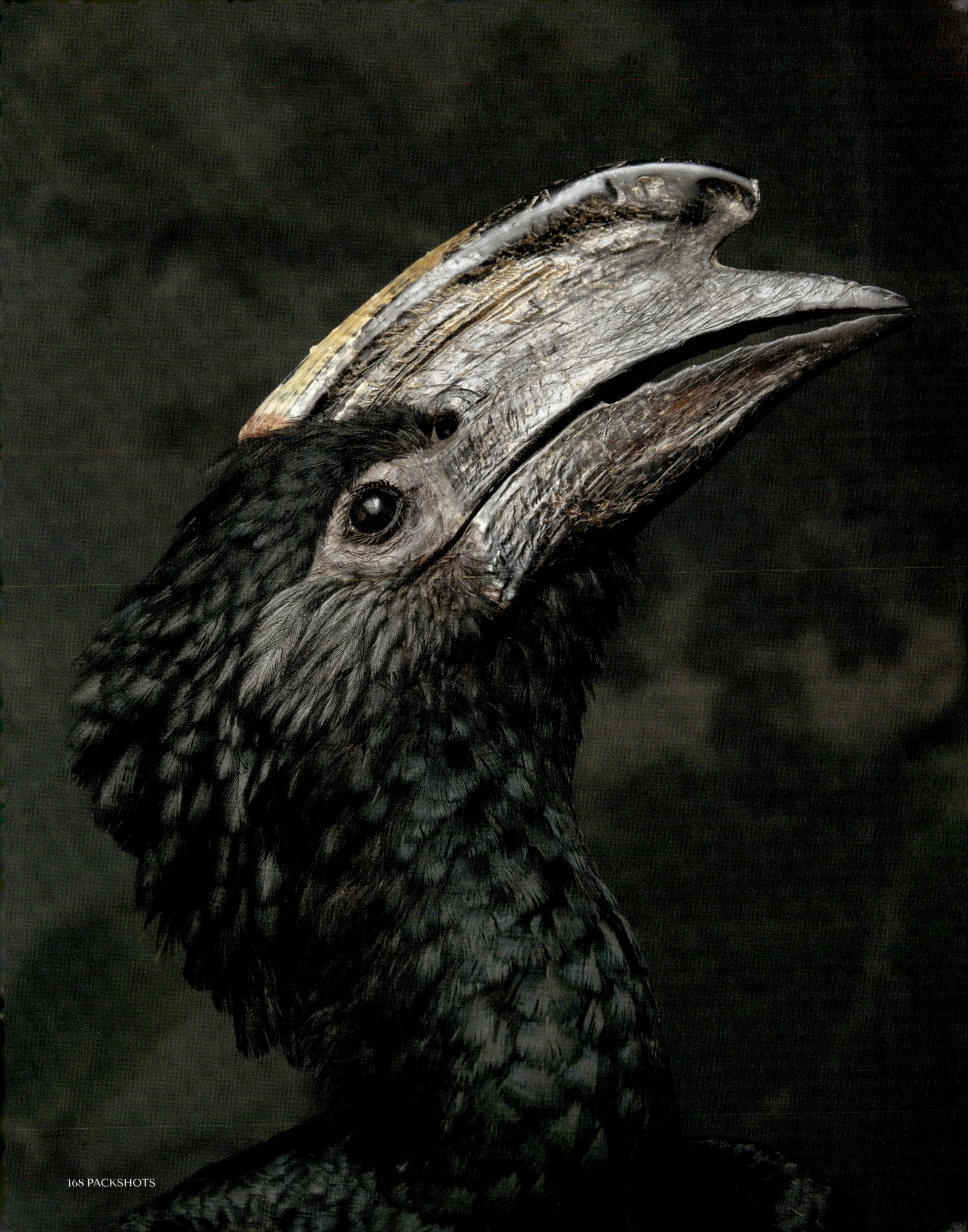

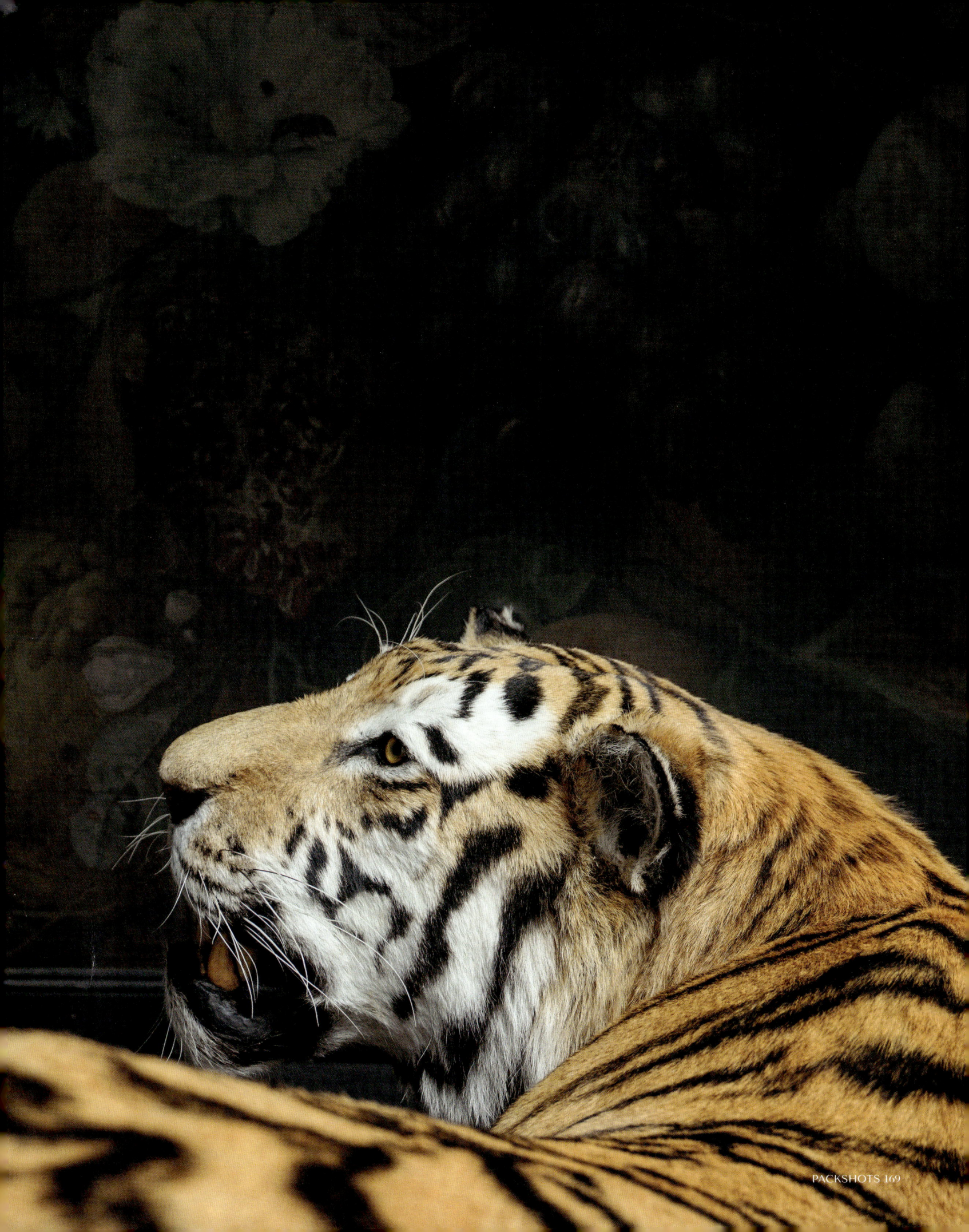

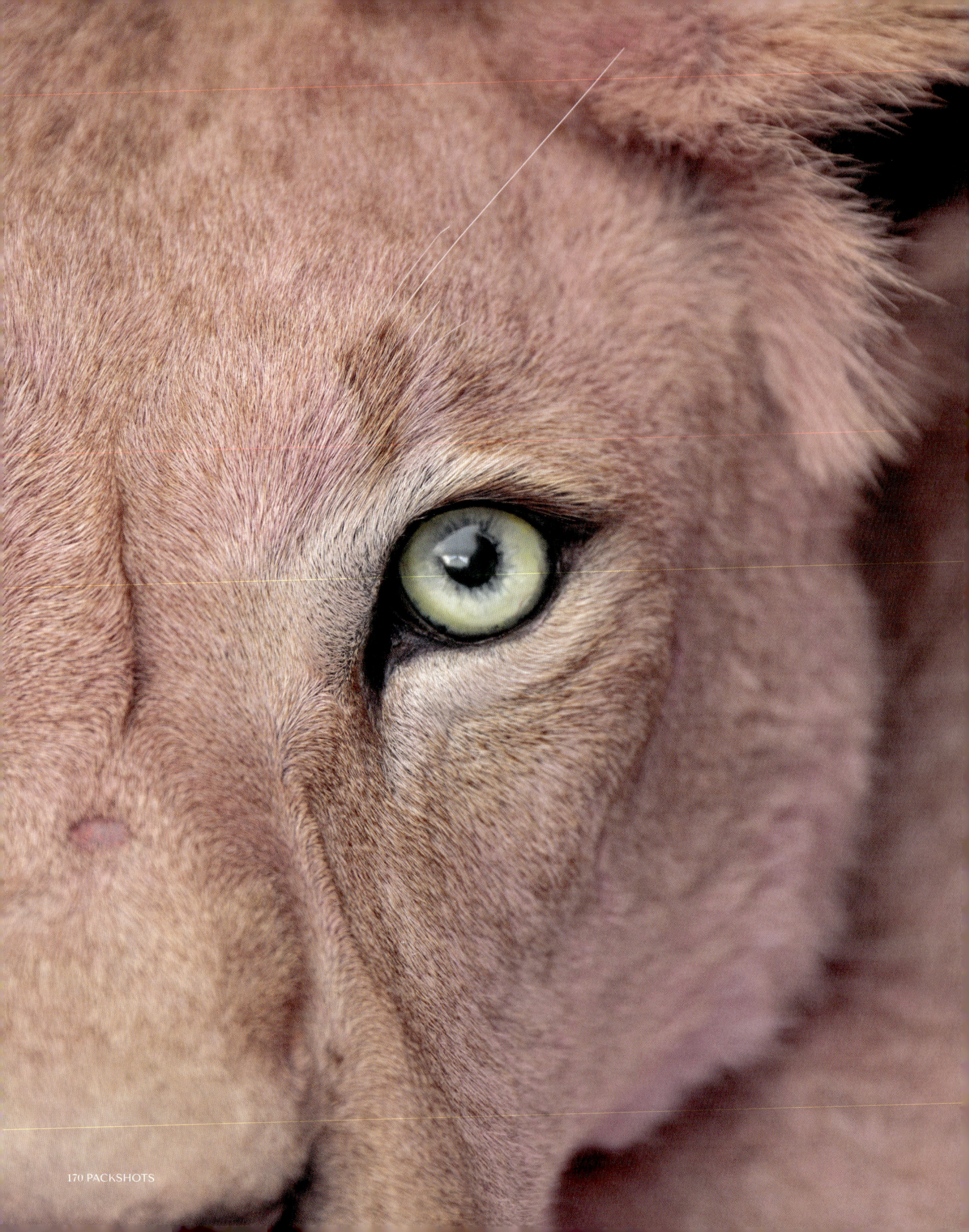

PACKSHOTS 171

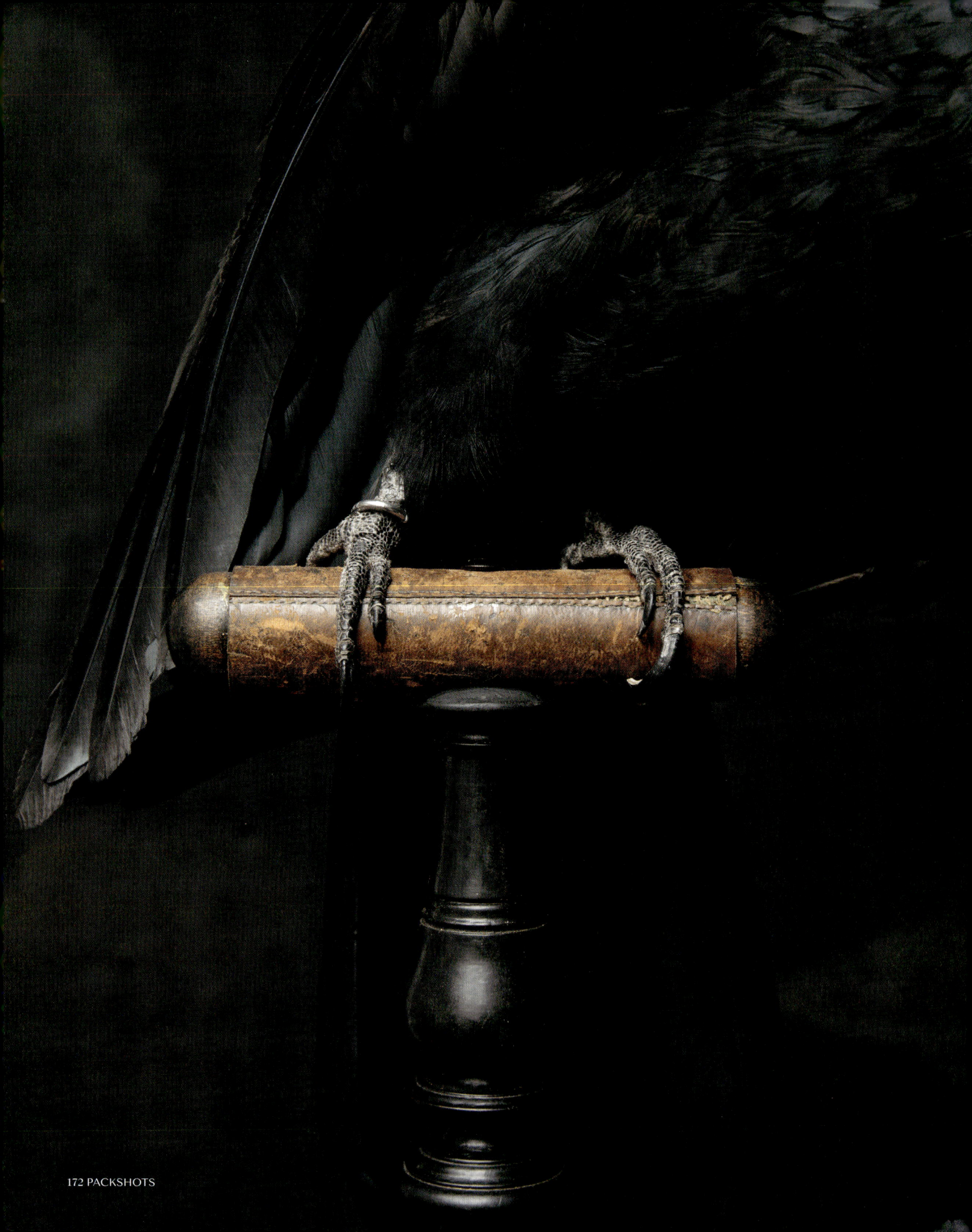

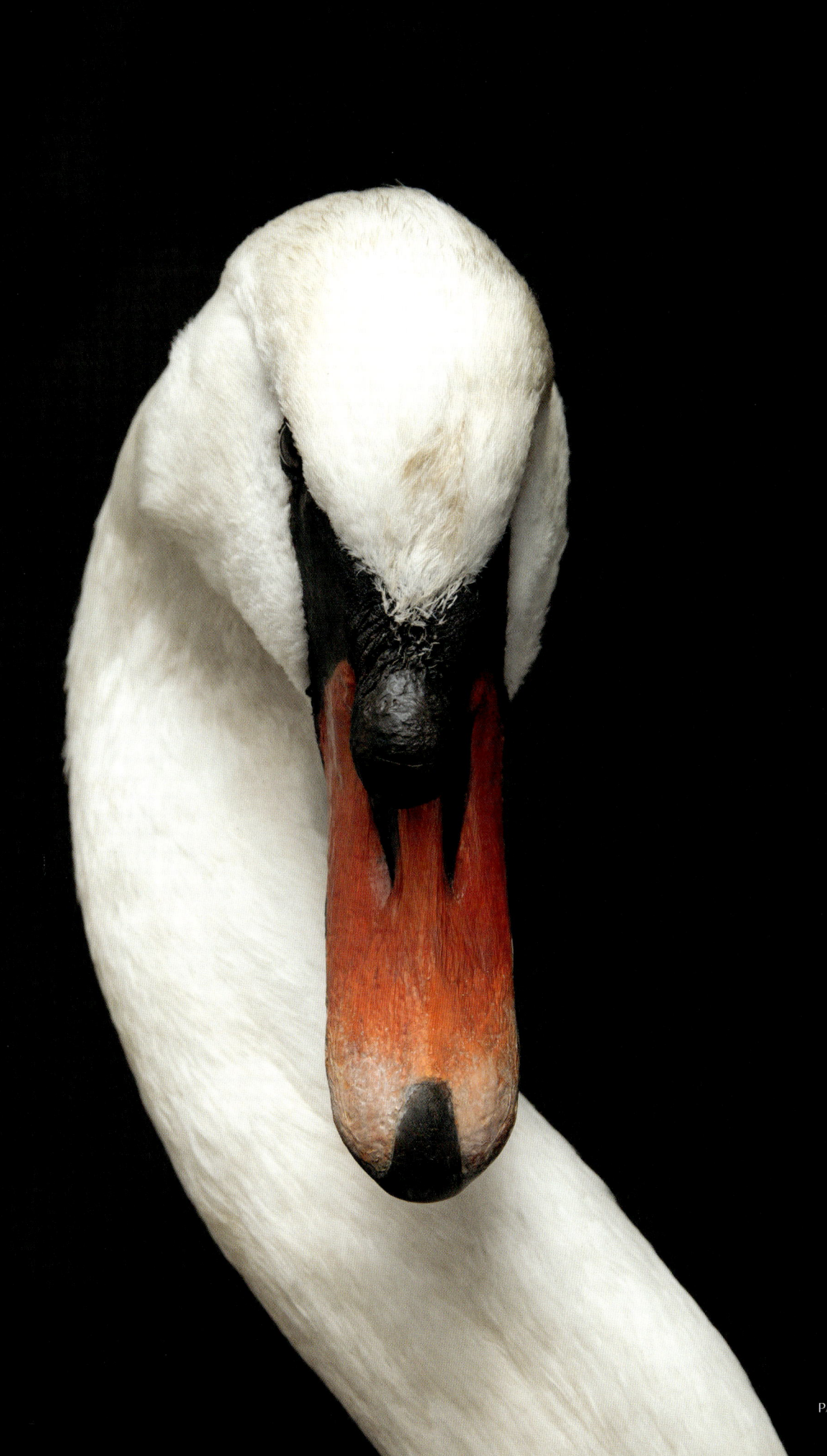

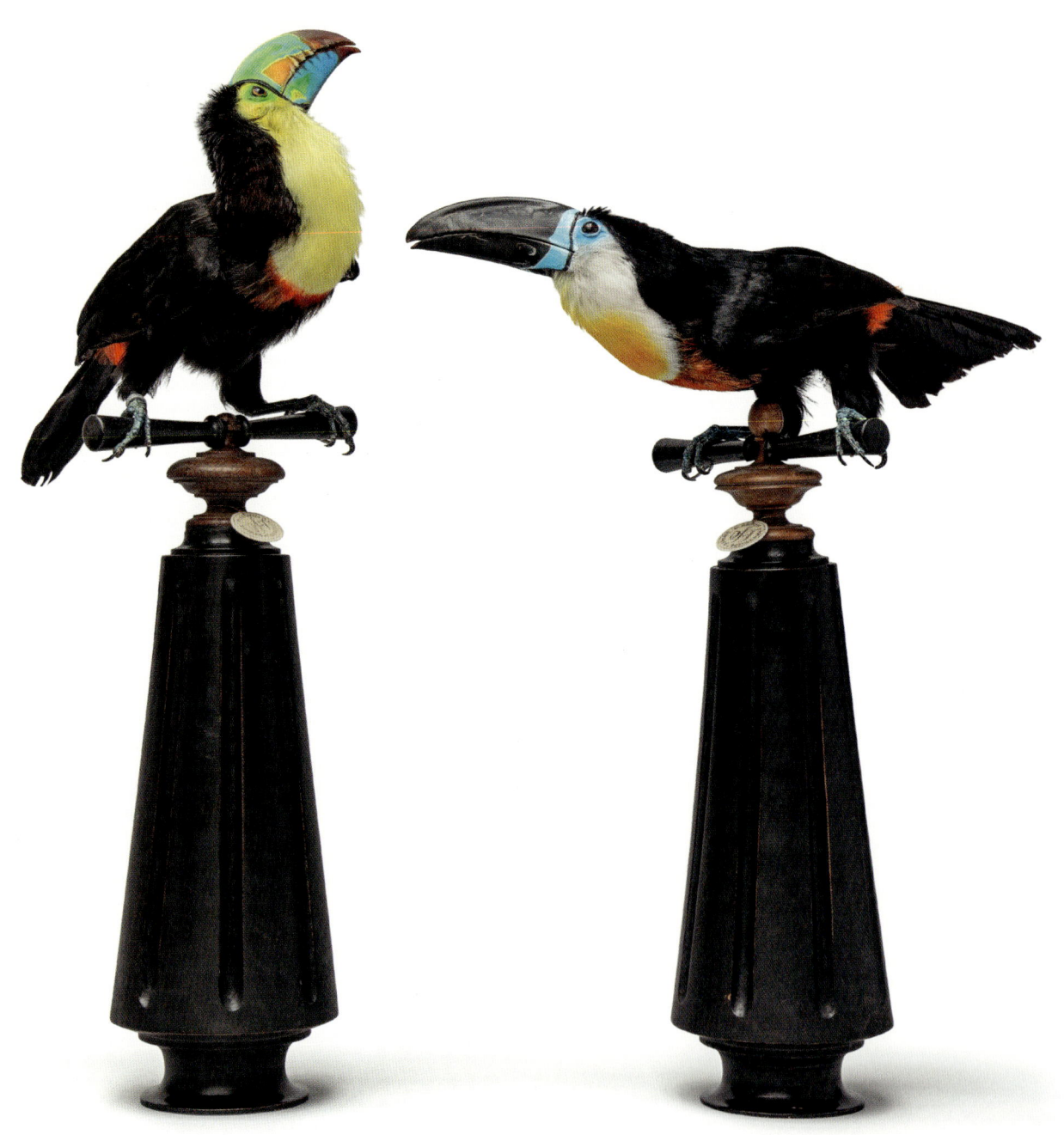

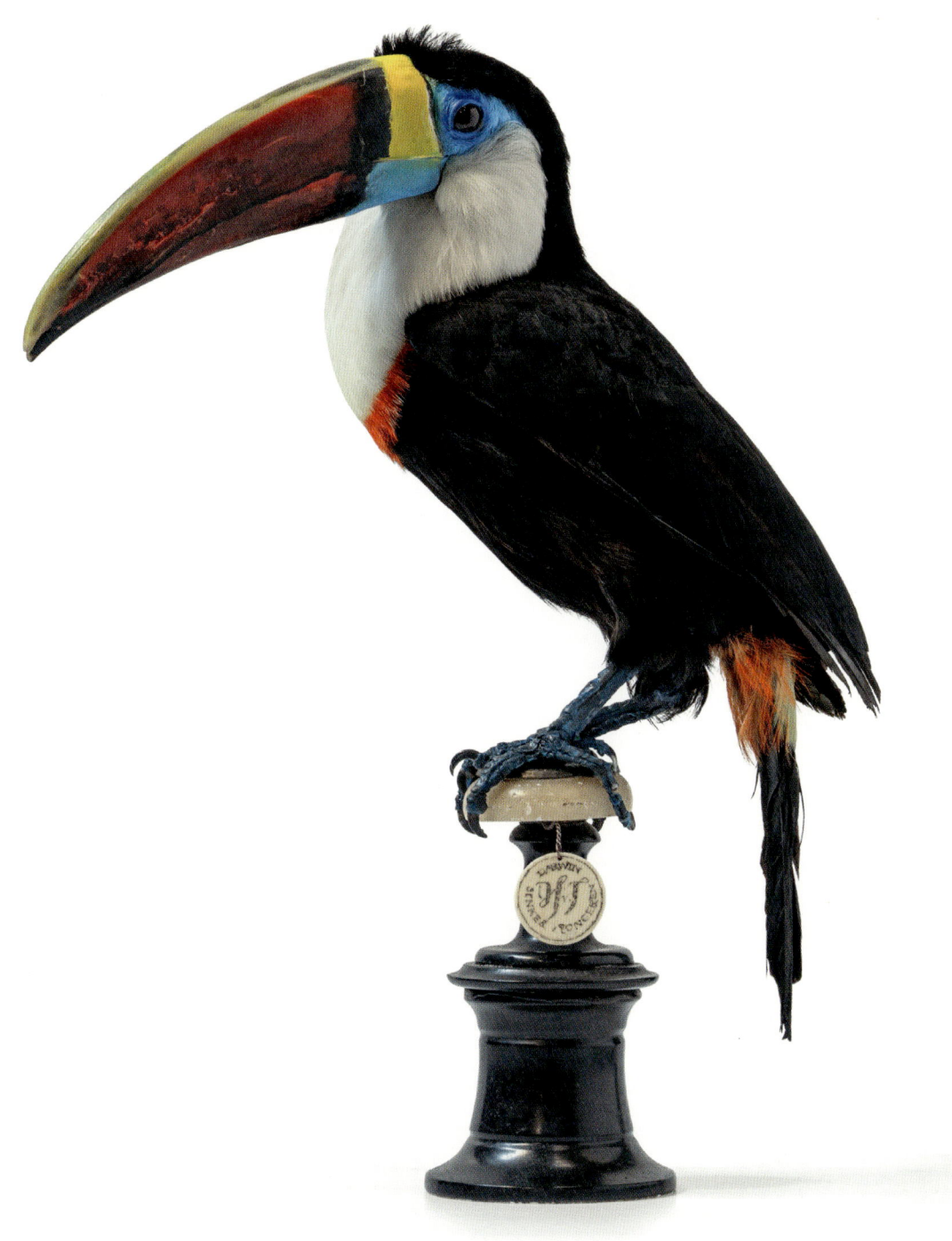

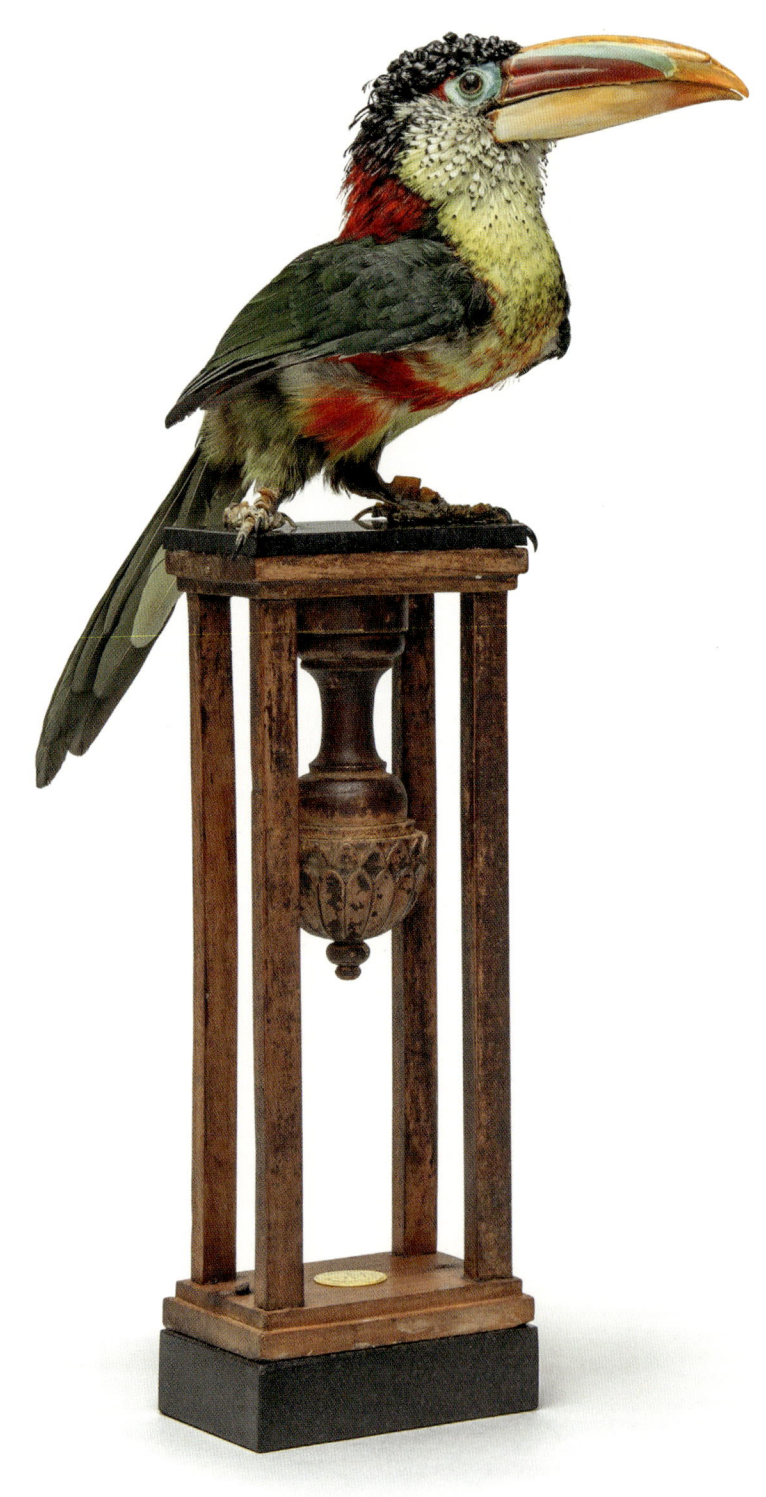

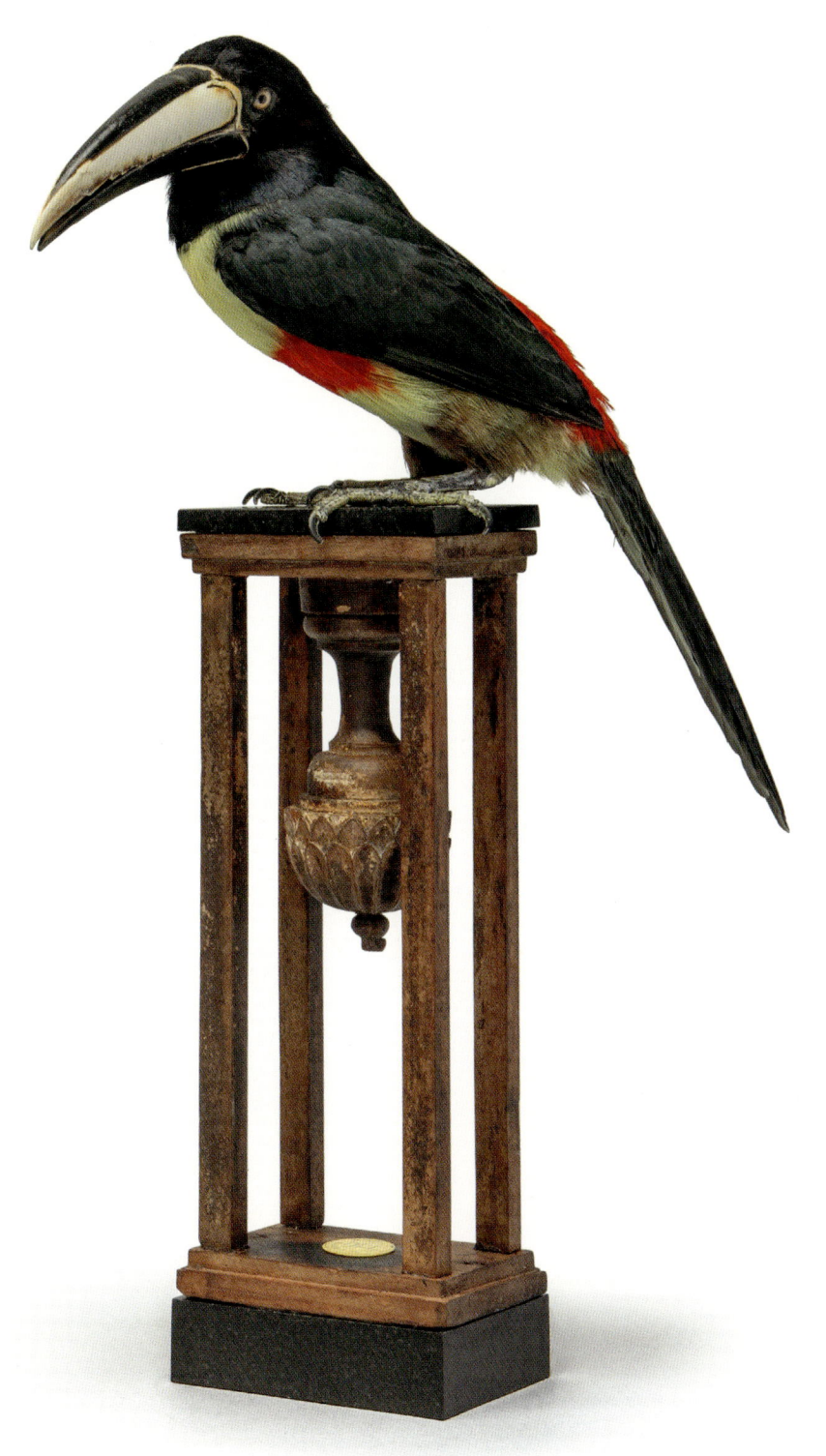

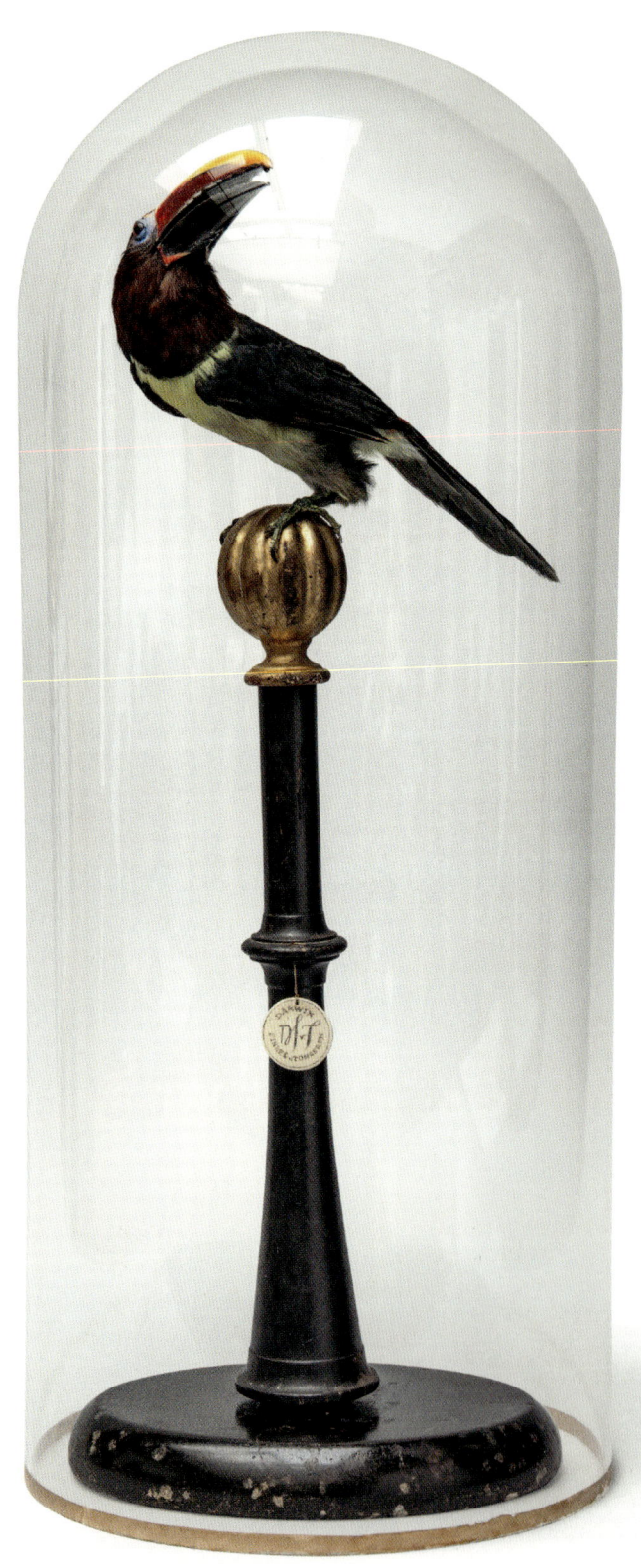

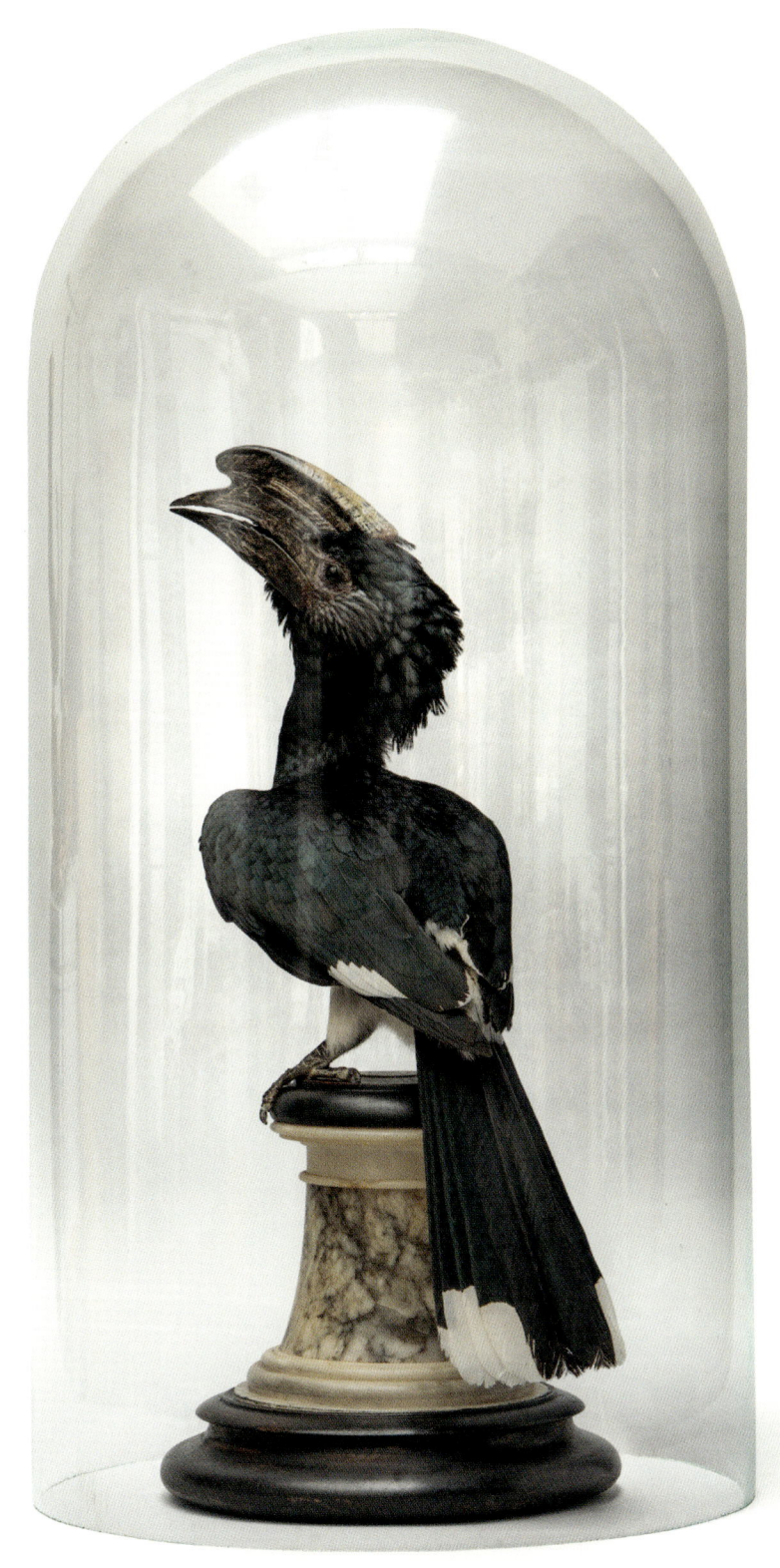

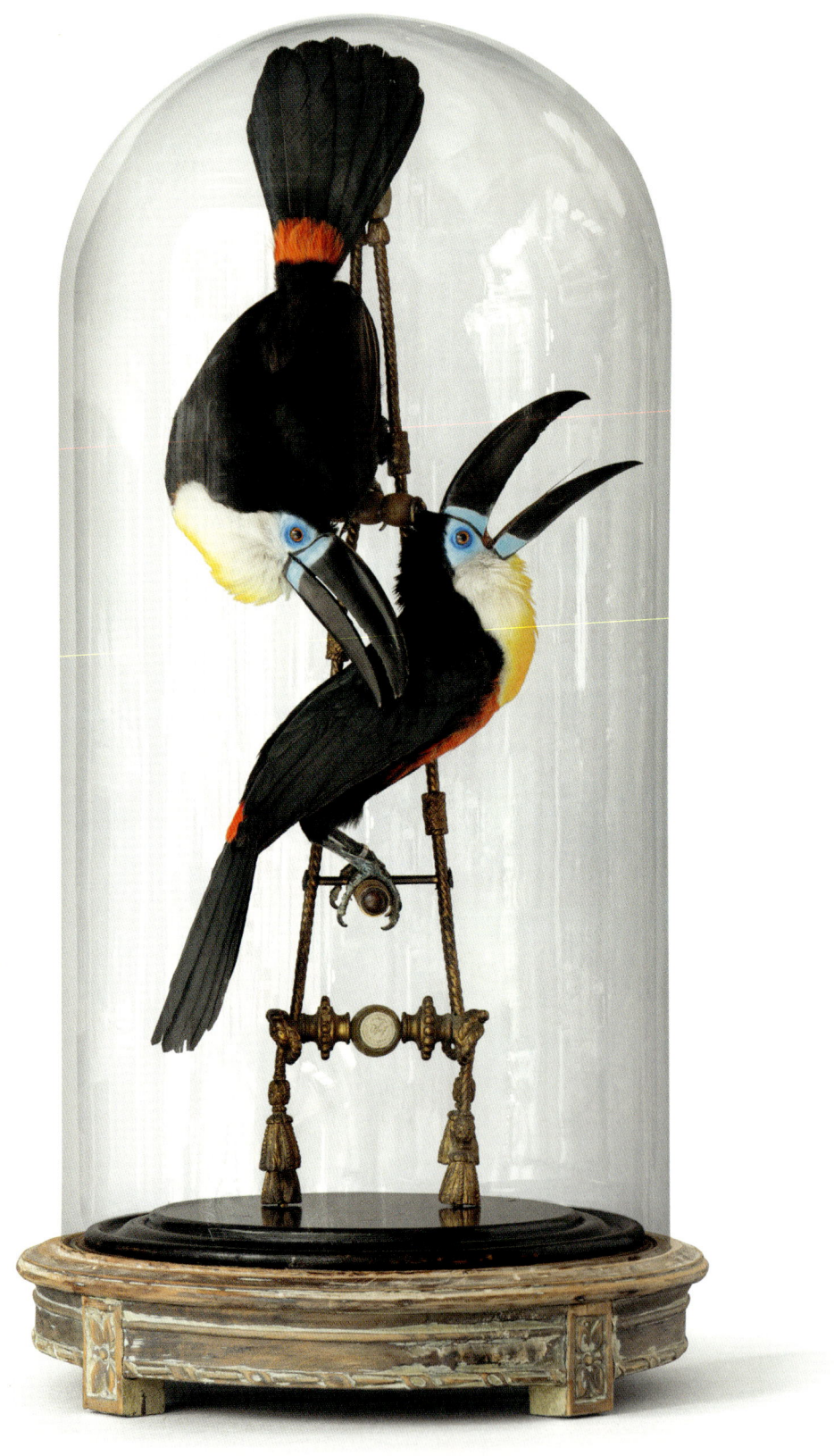

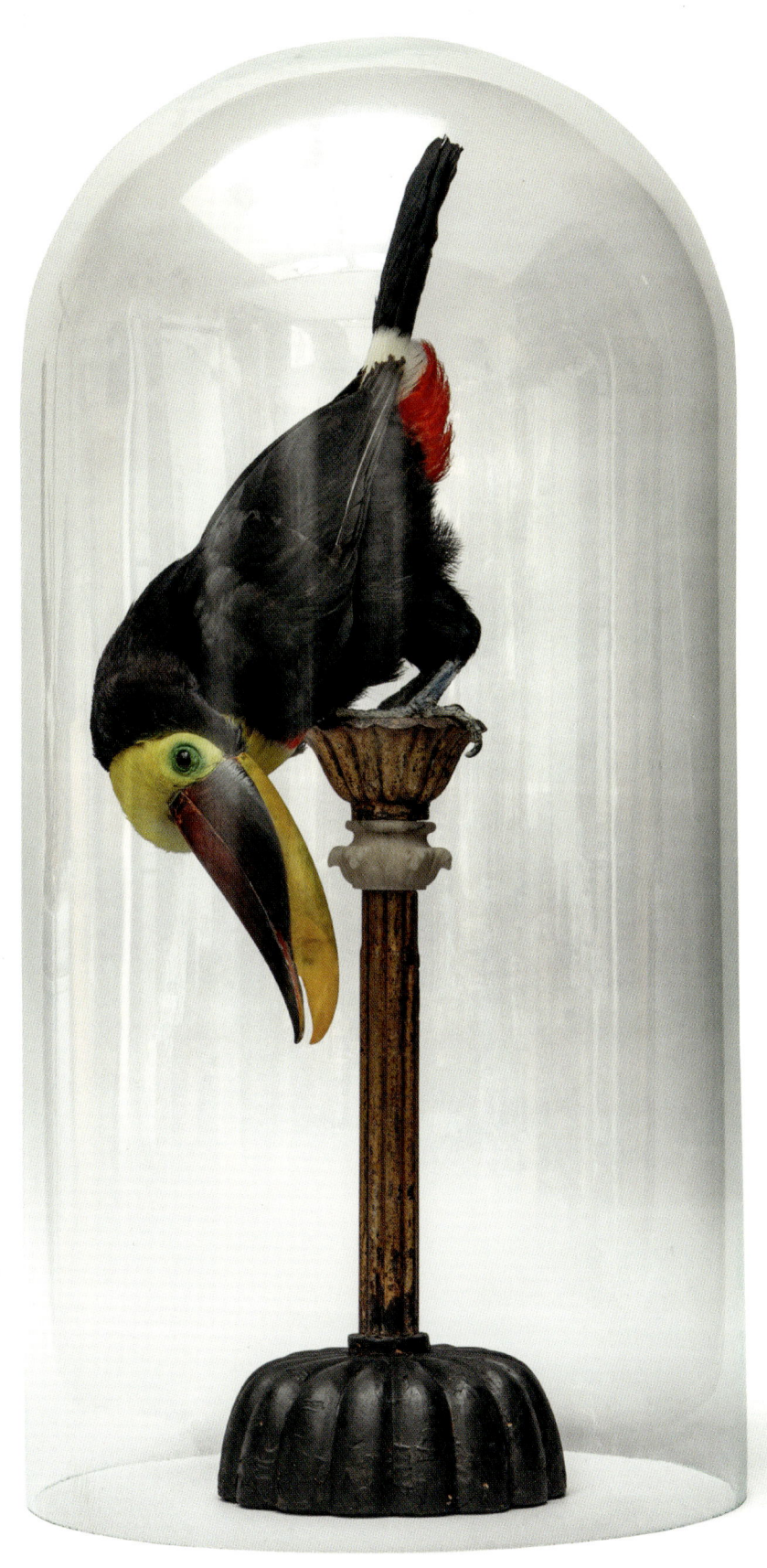

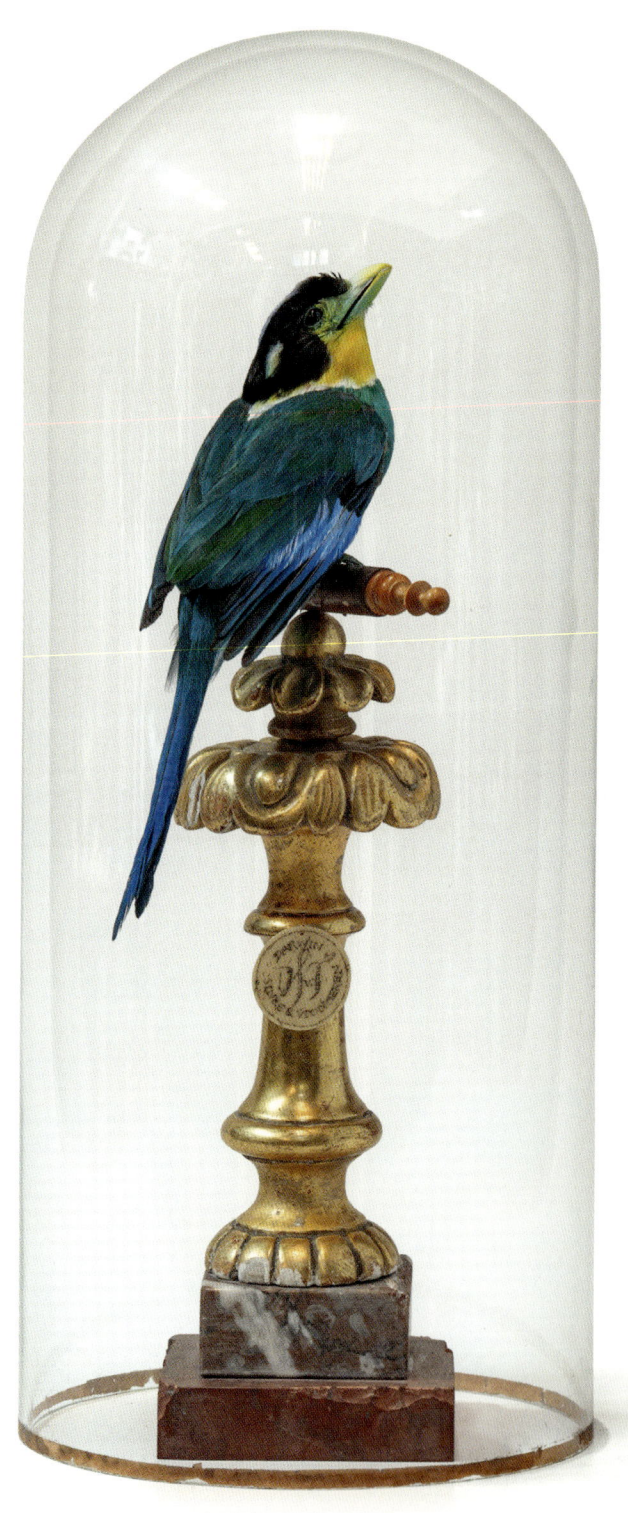

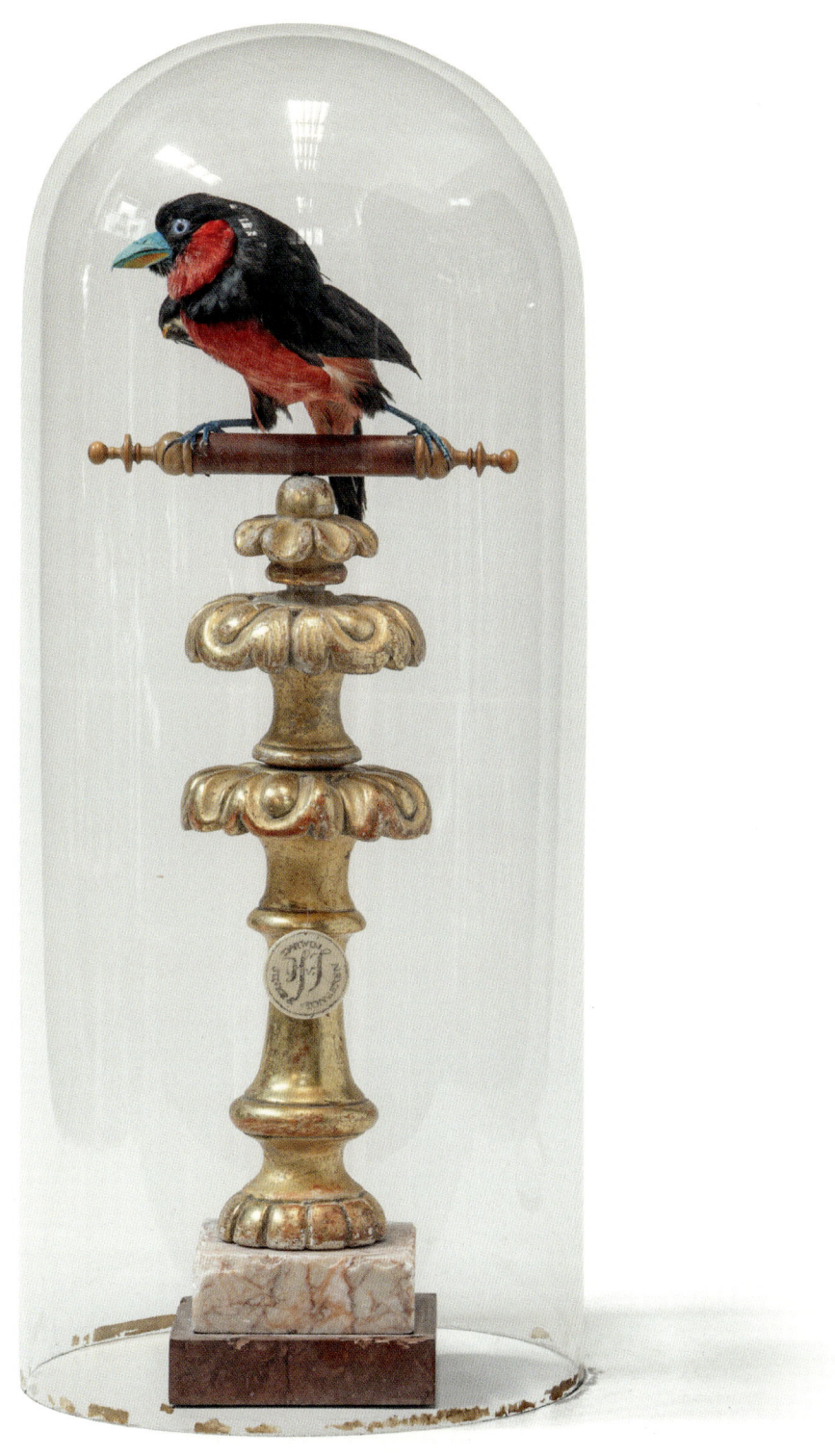

PACKSHOTS 183

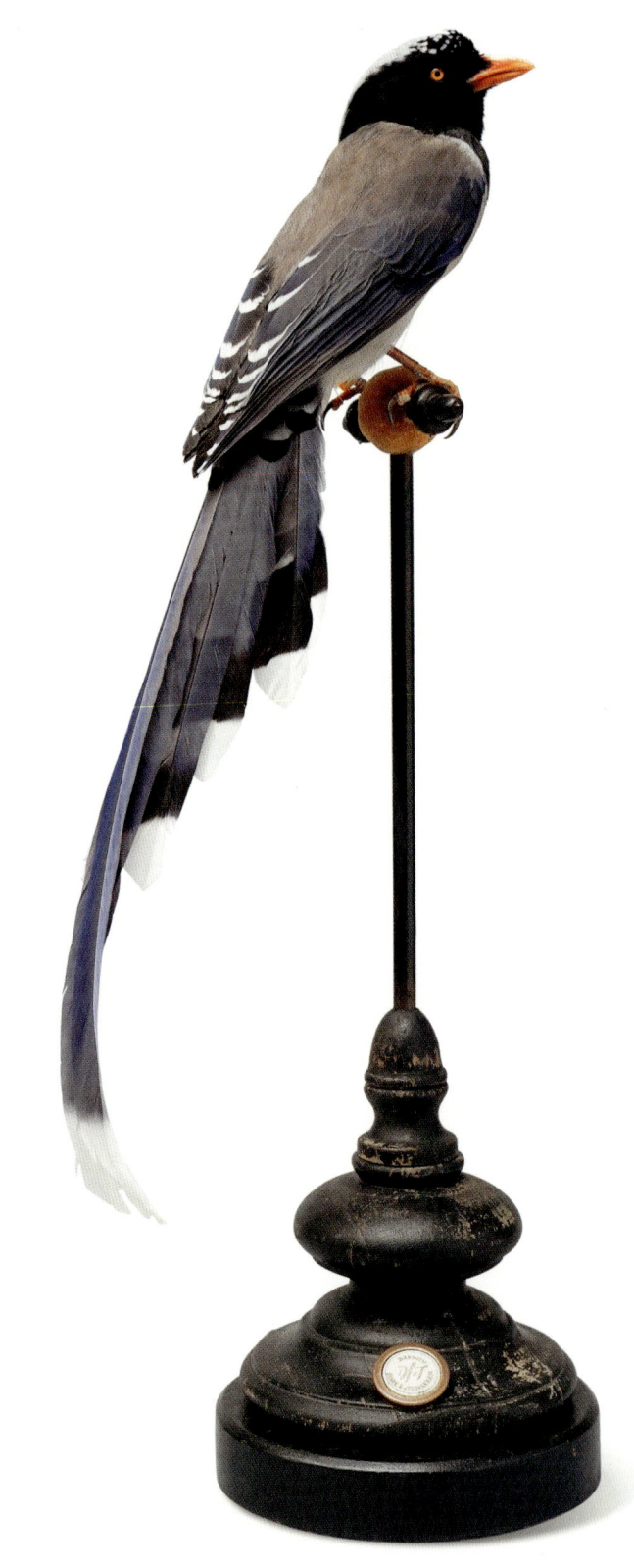

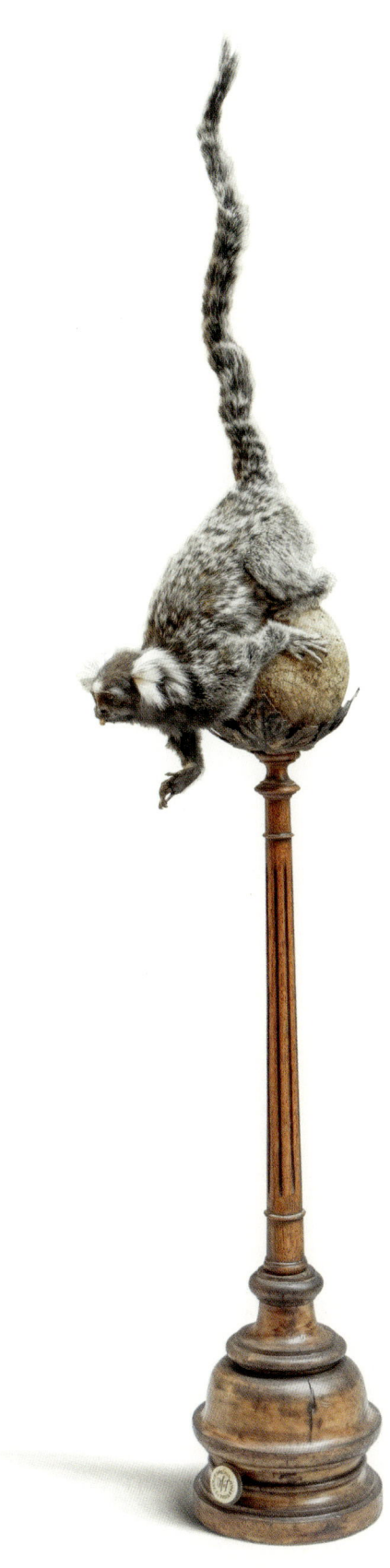

PACKSHOTS 185

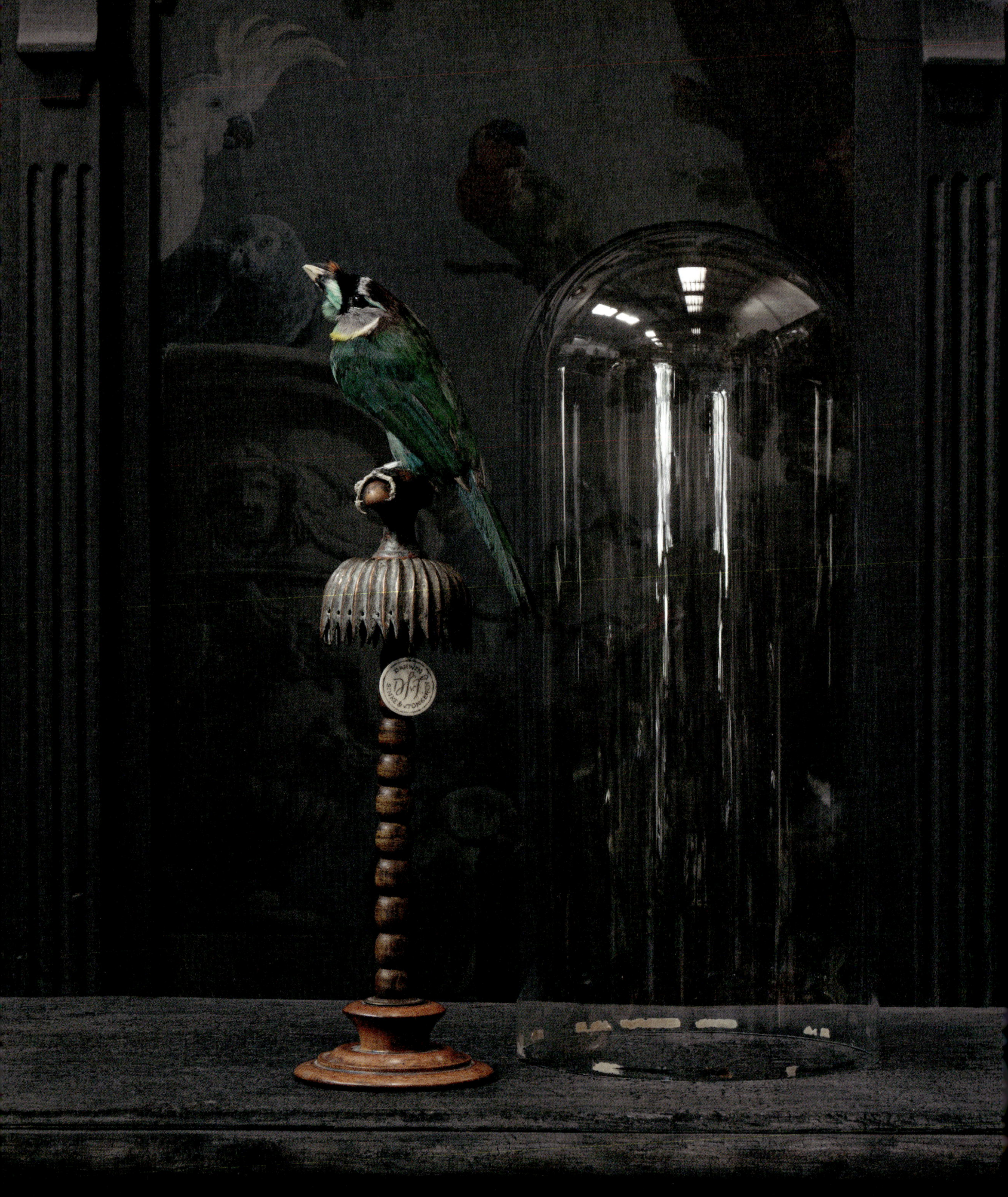

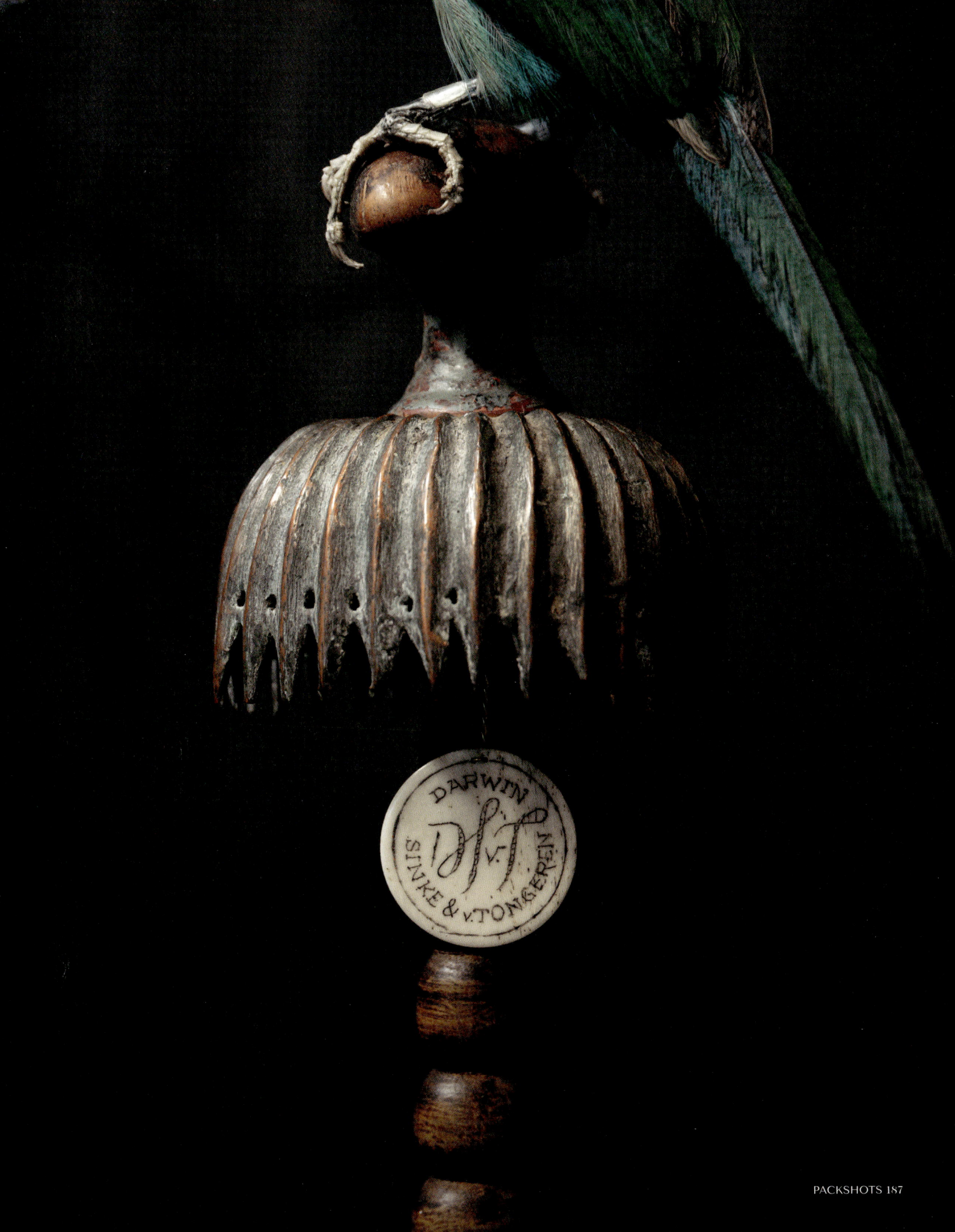

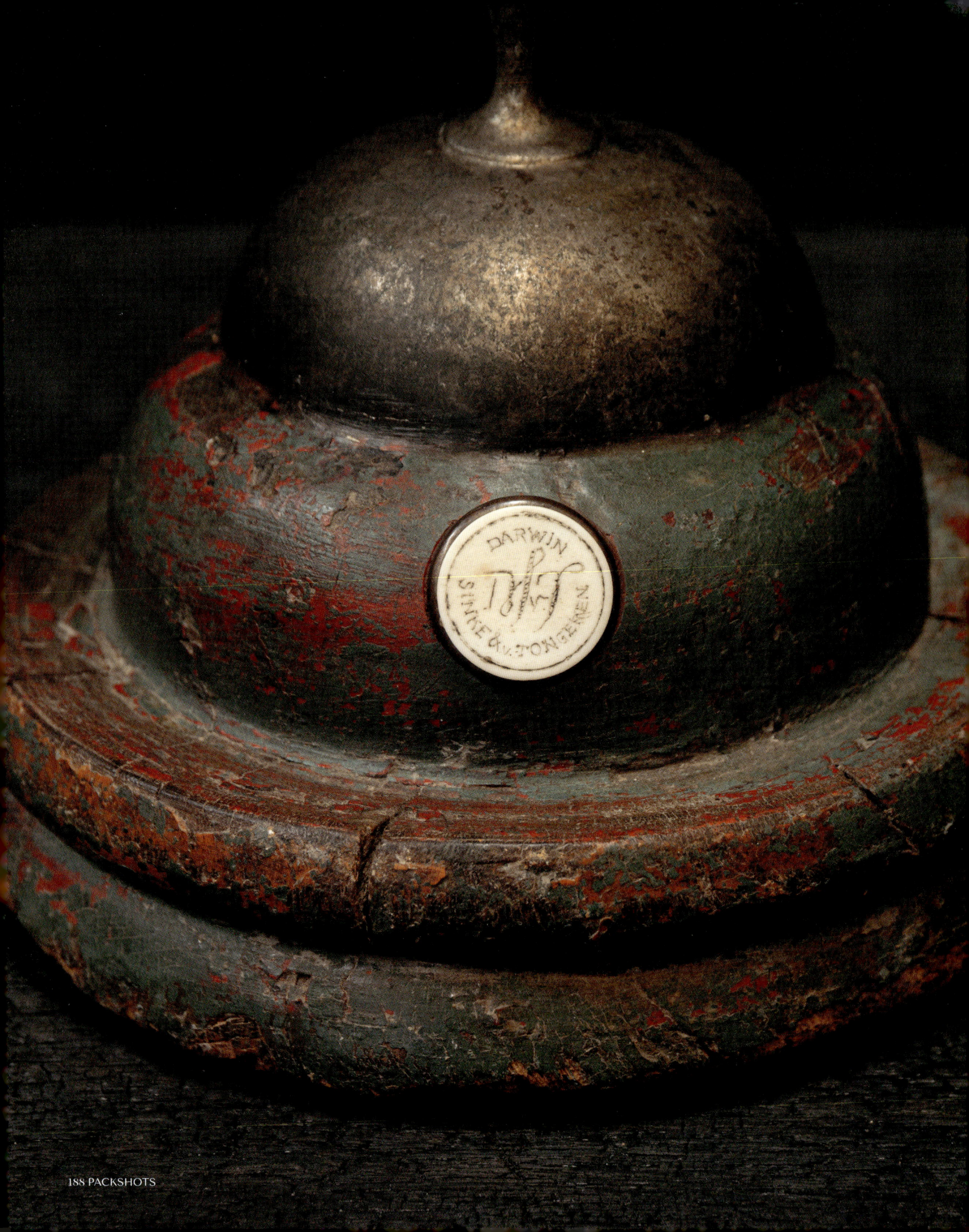

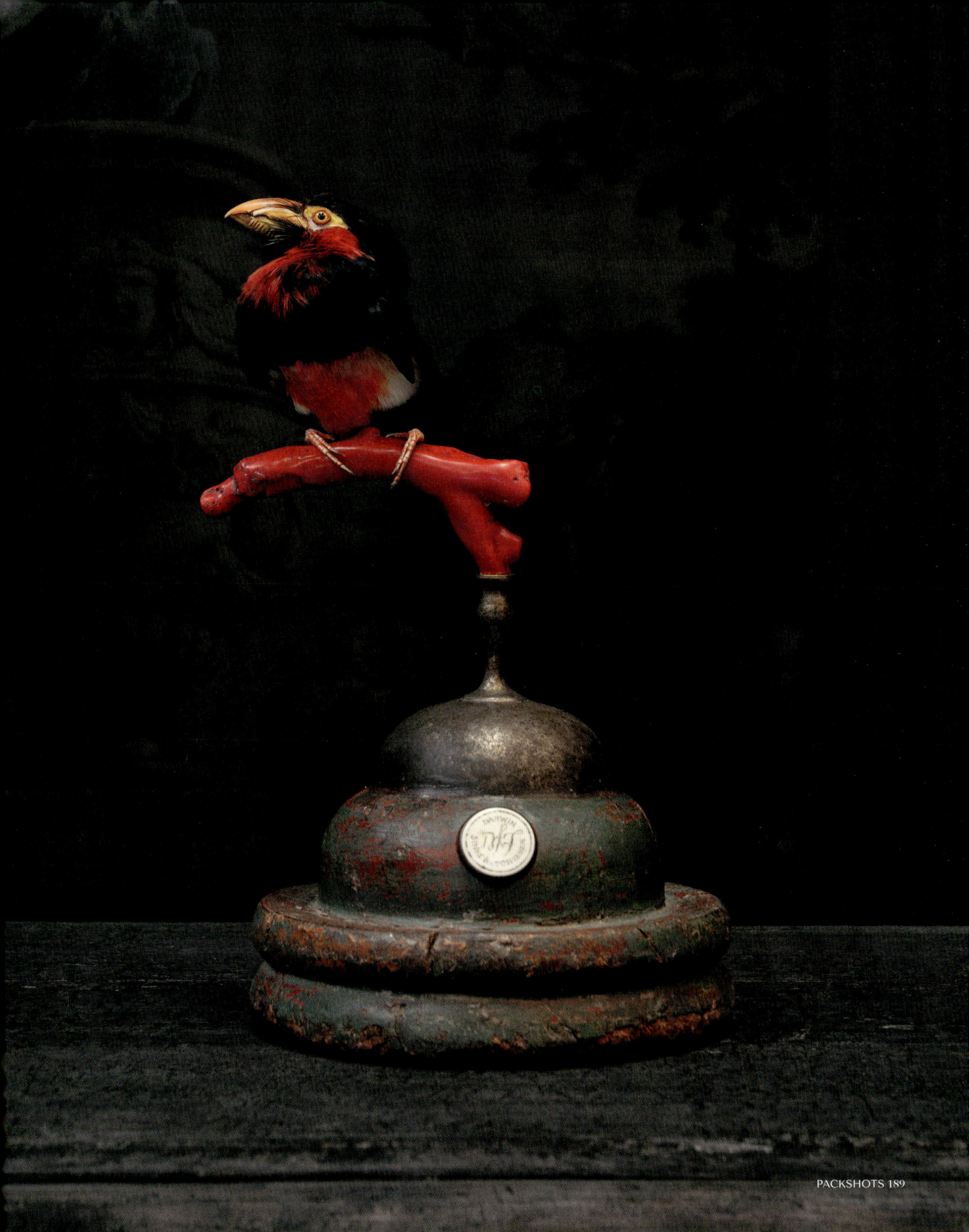

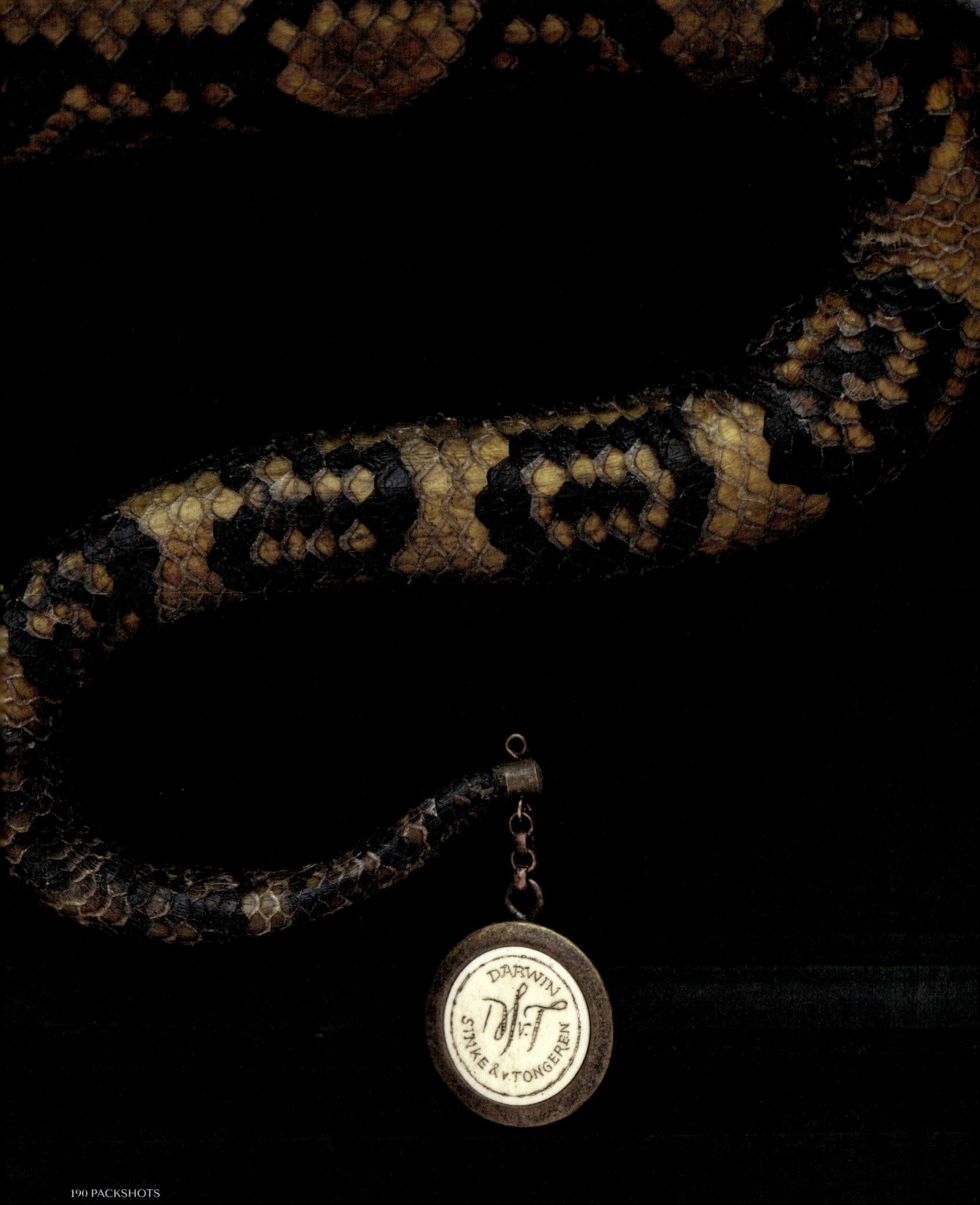

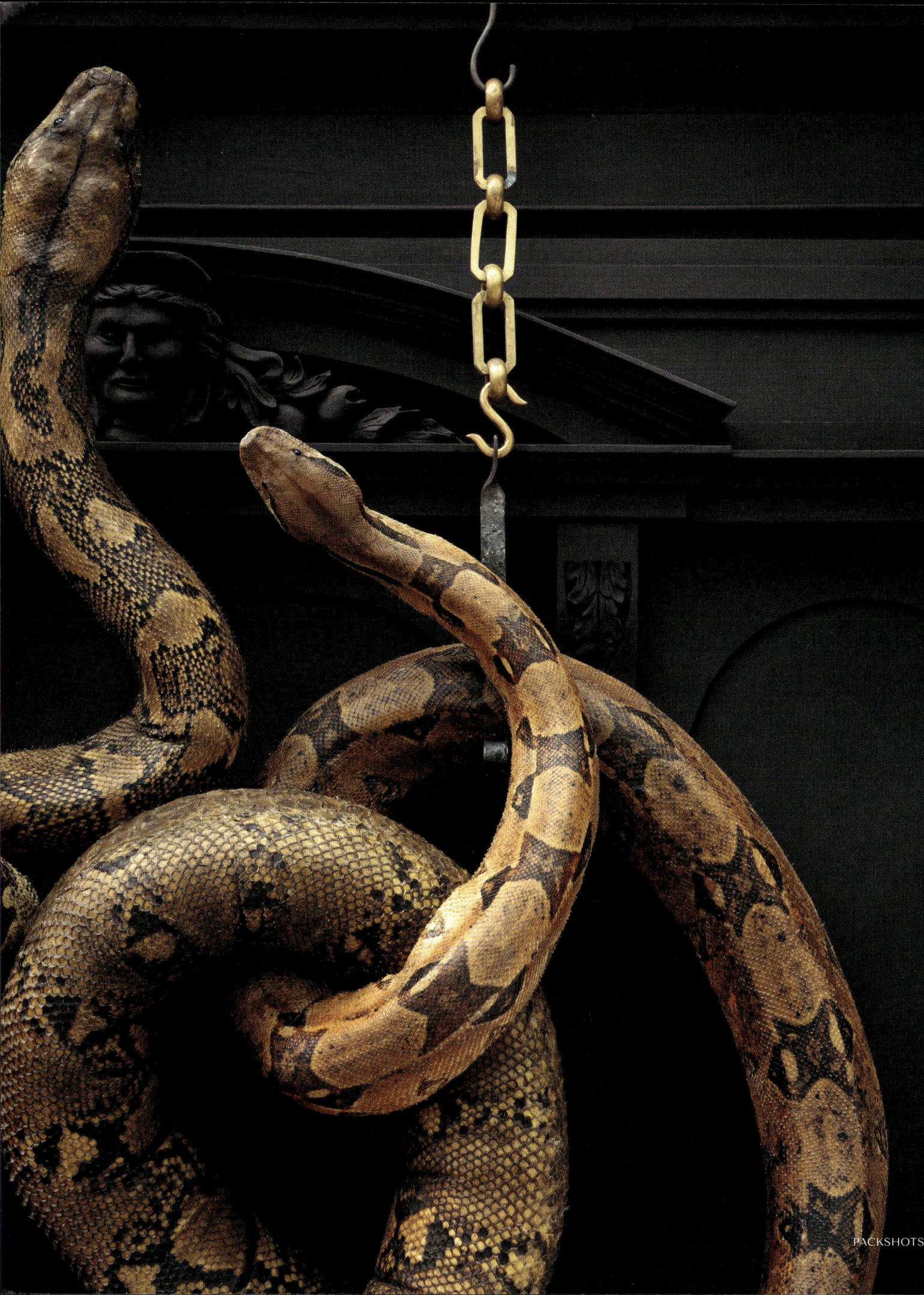
PACKSHOTS

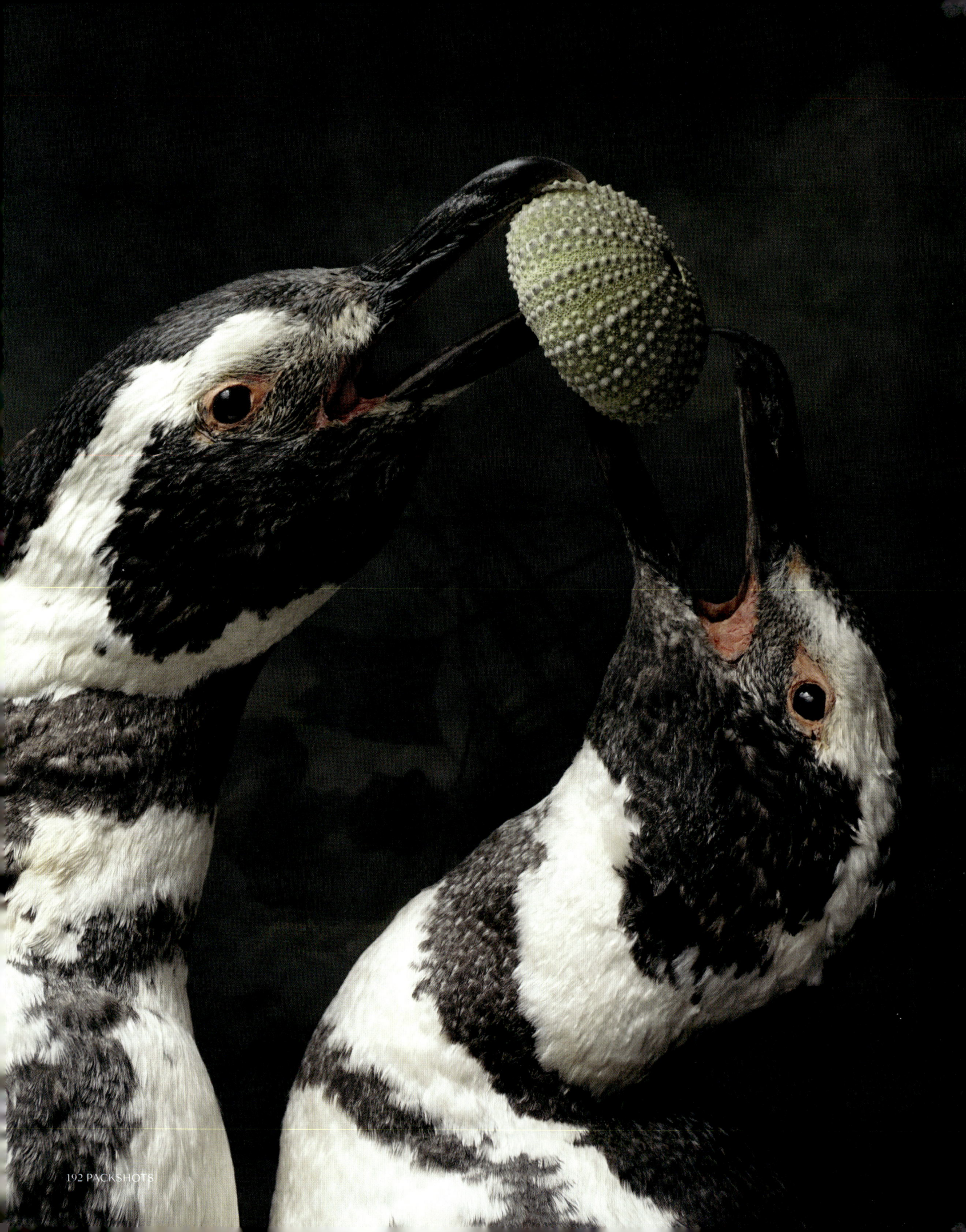

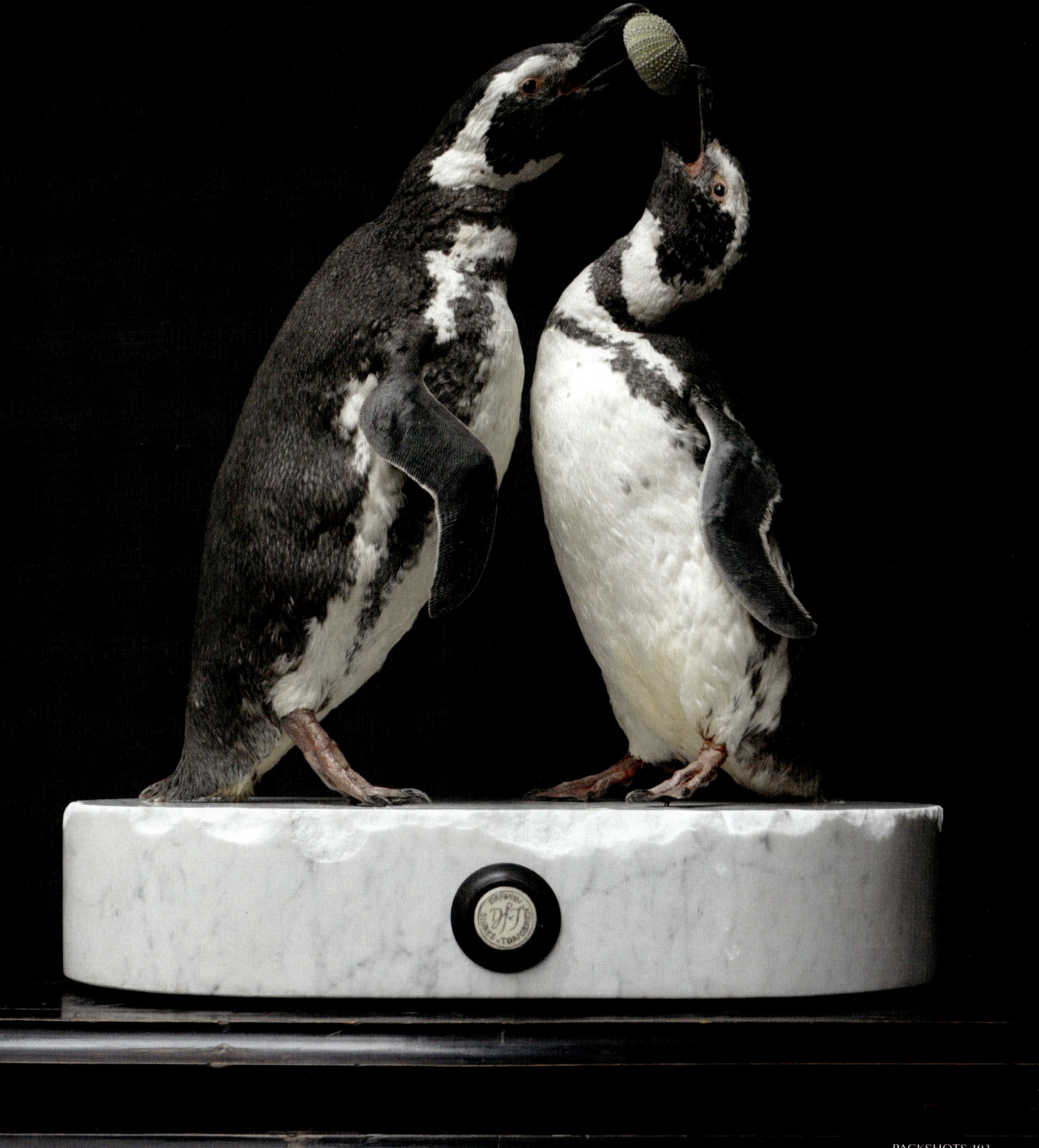

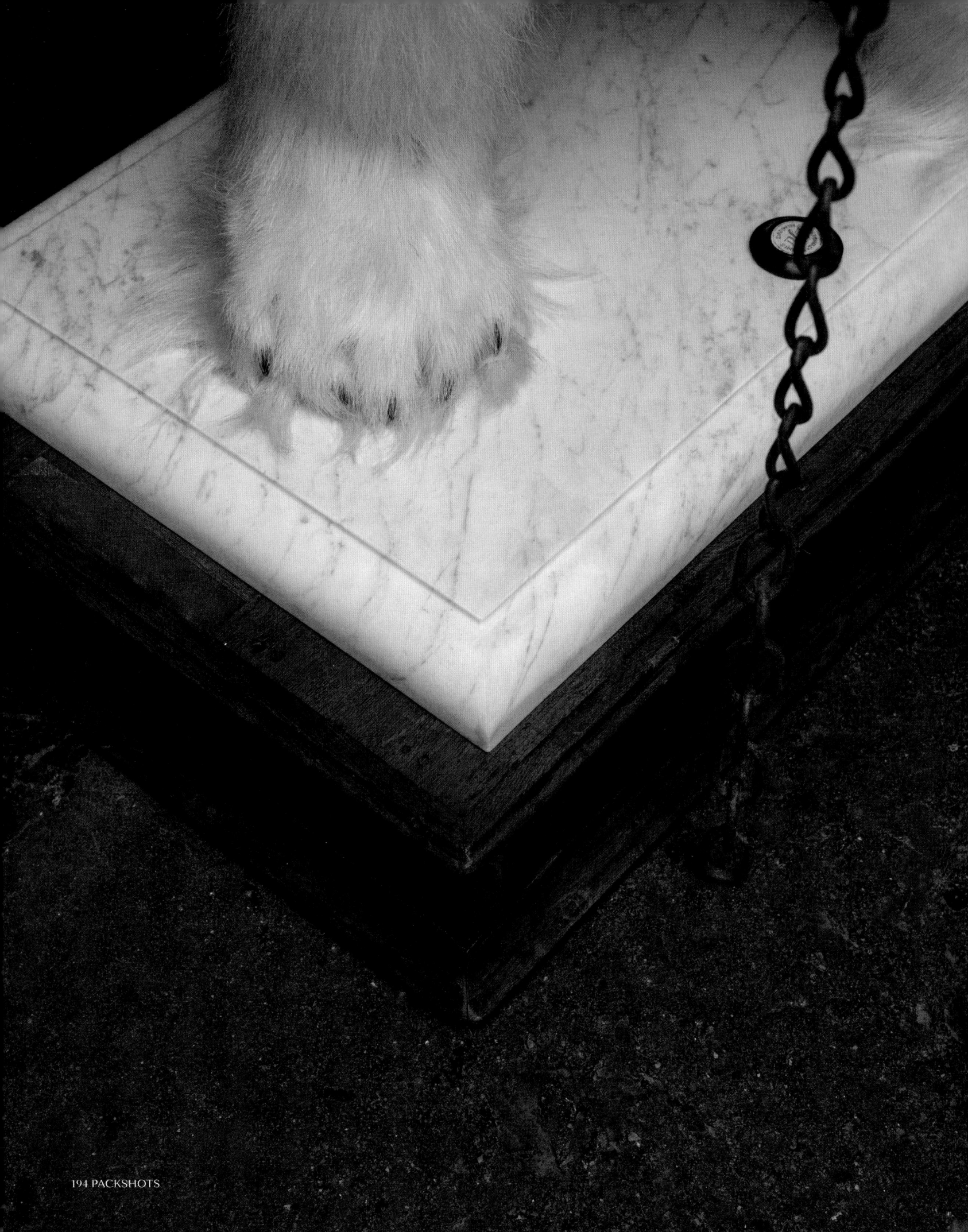

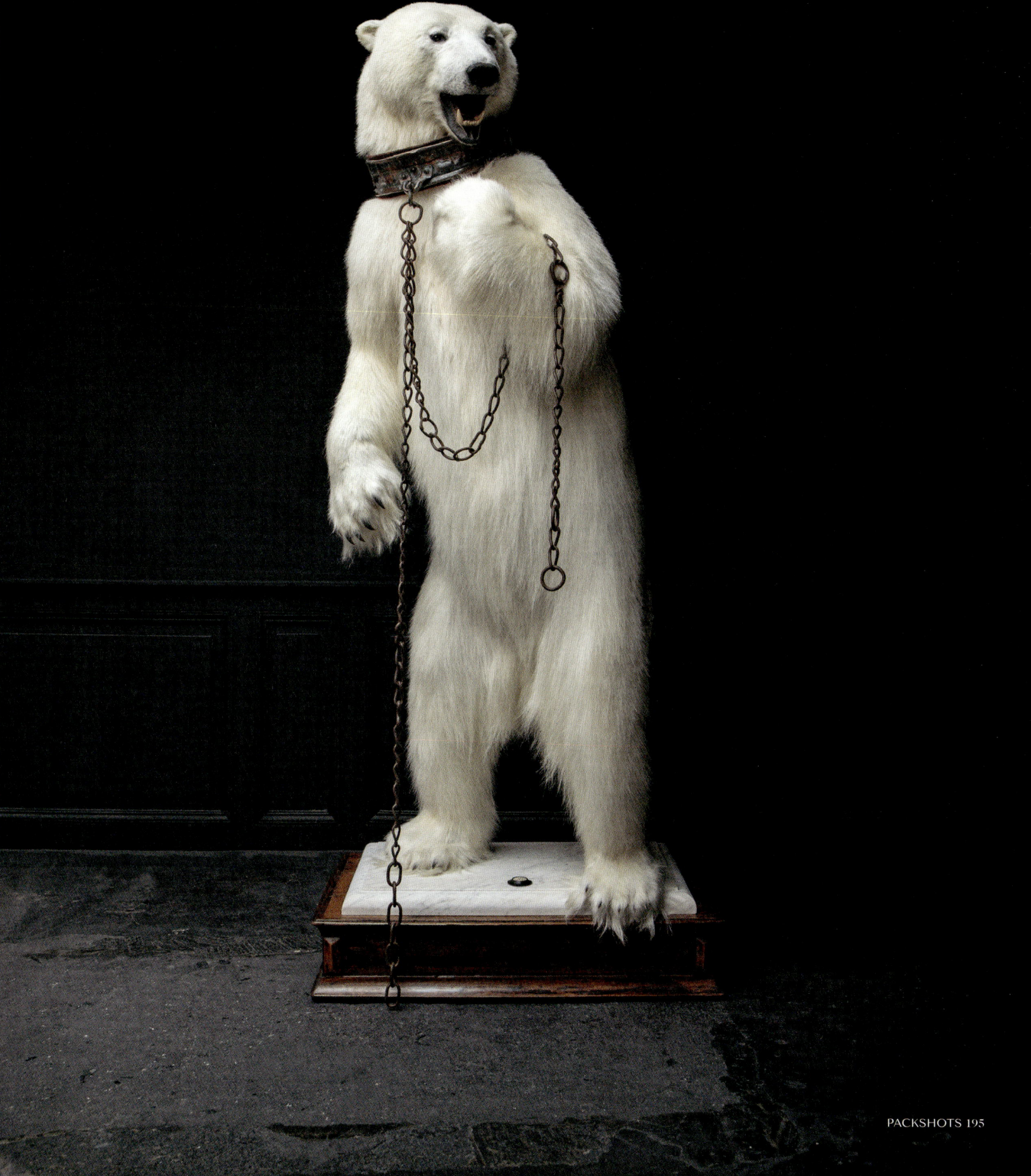

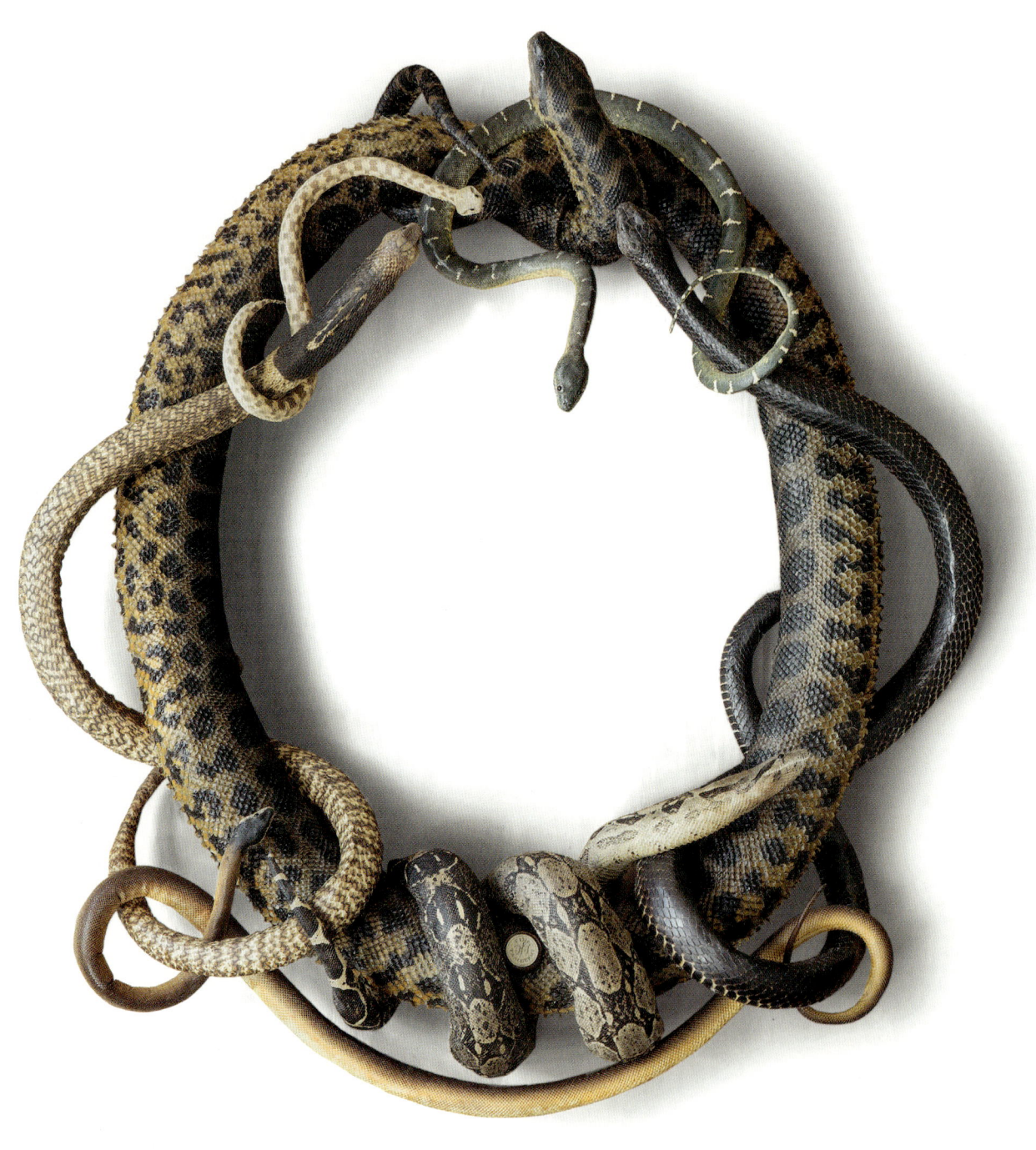

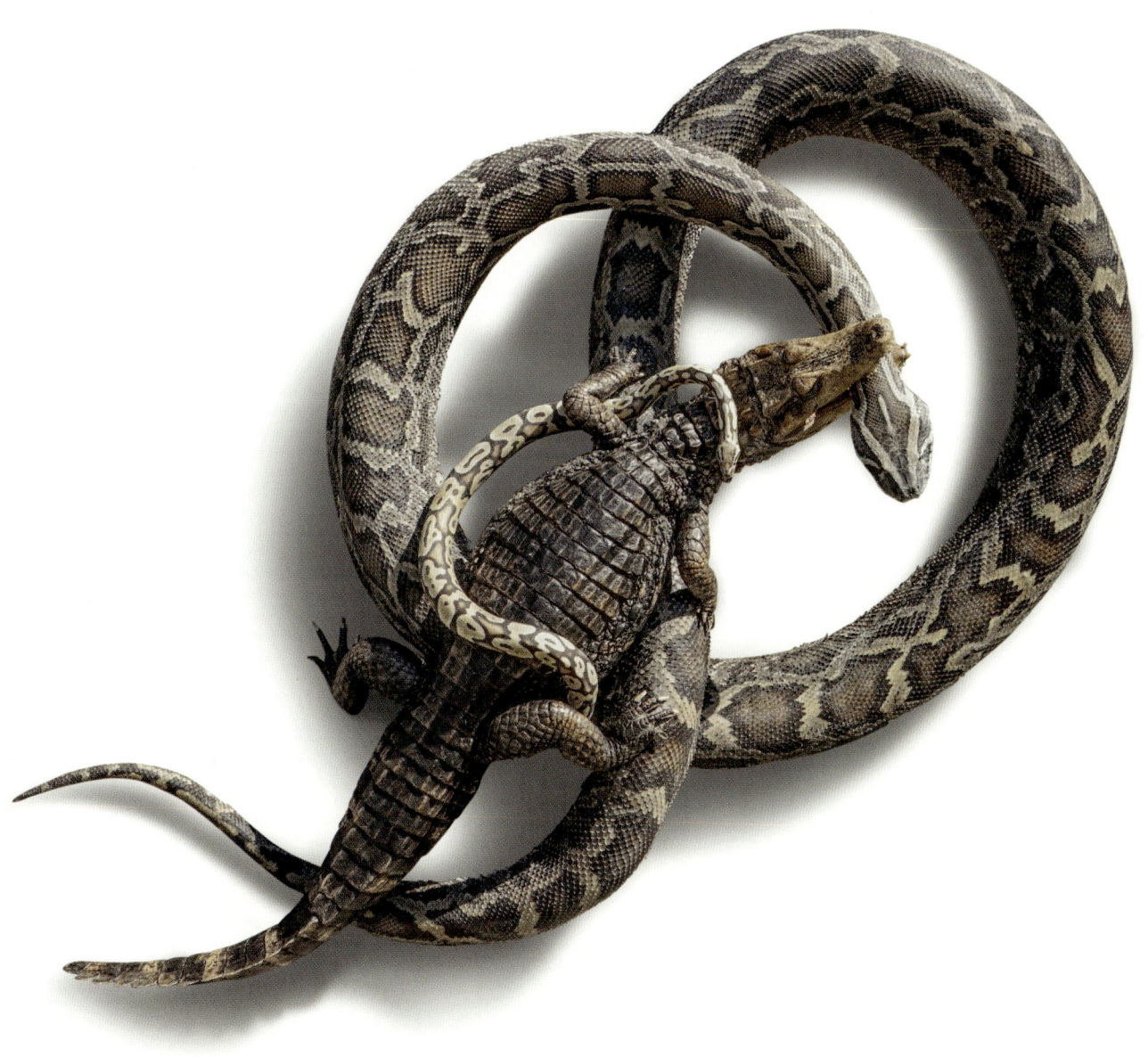

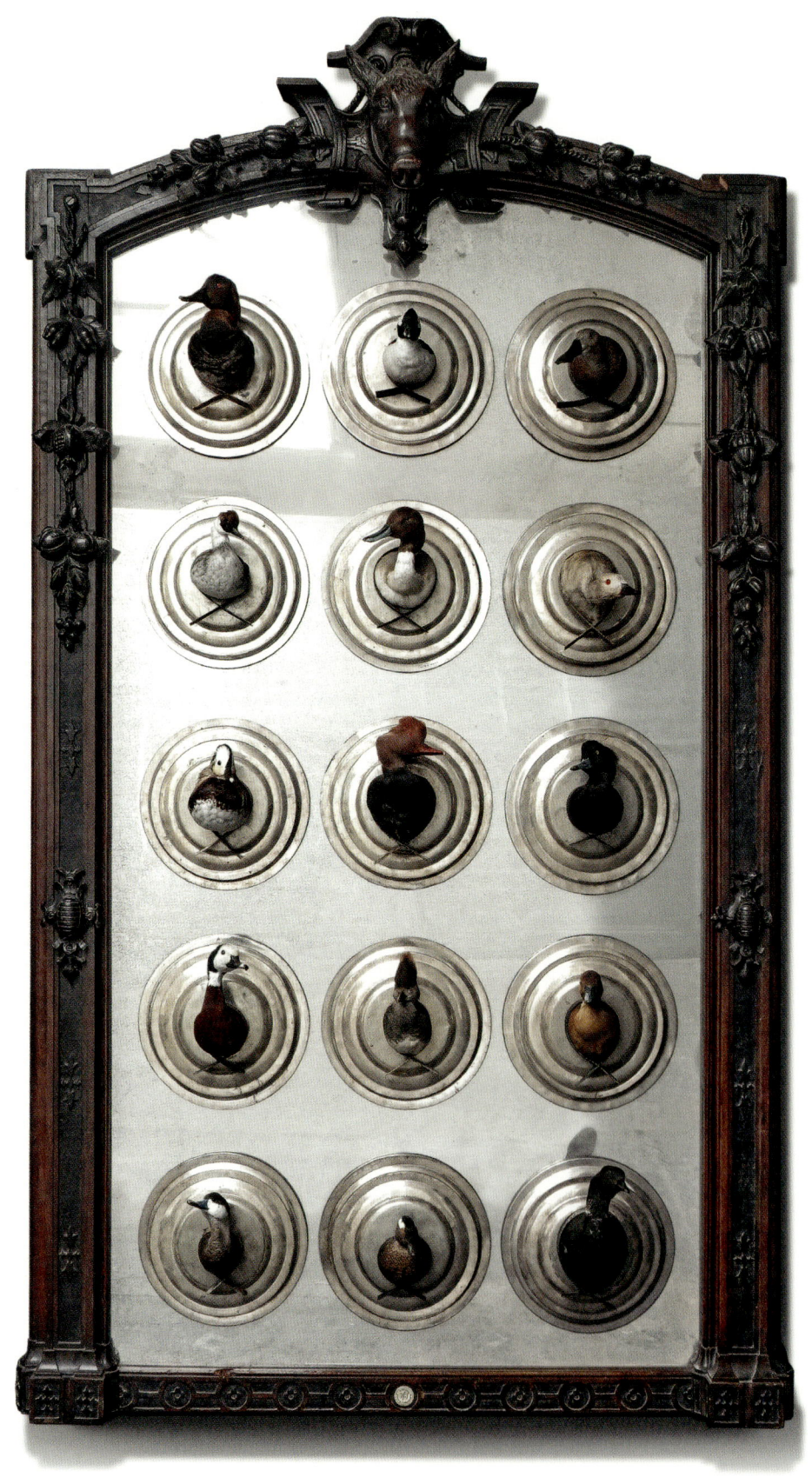

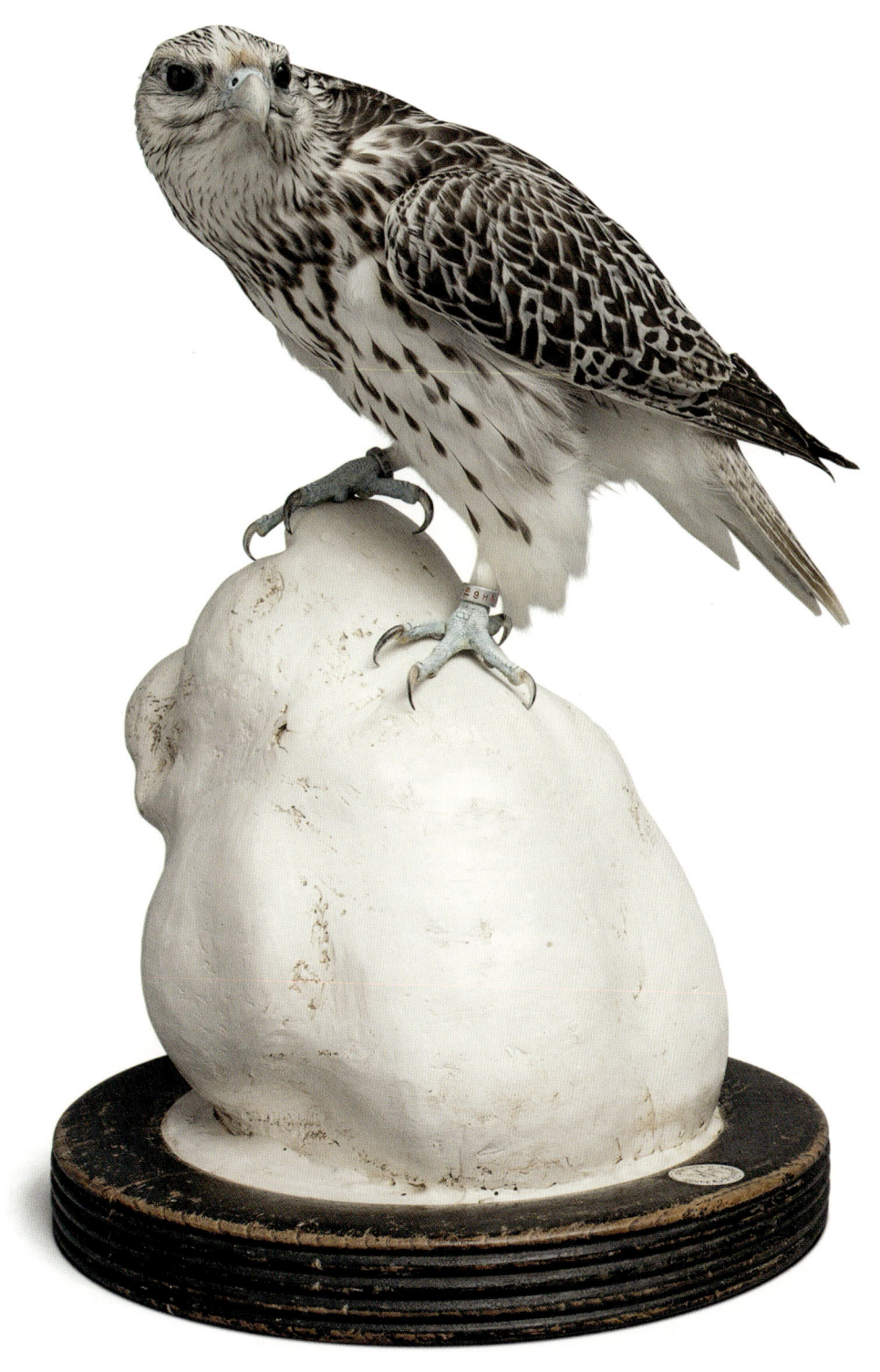

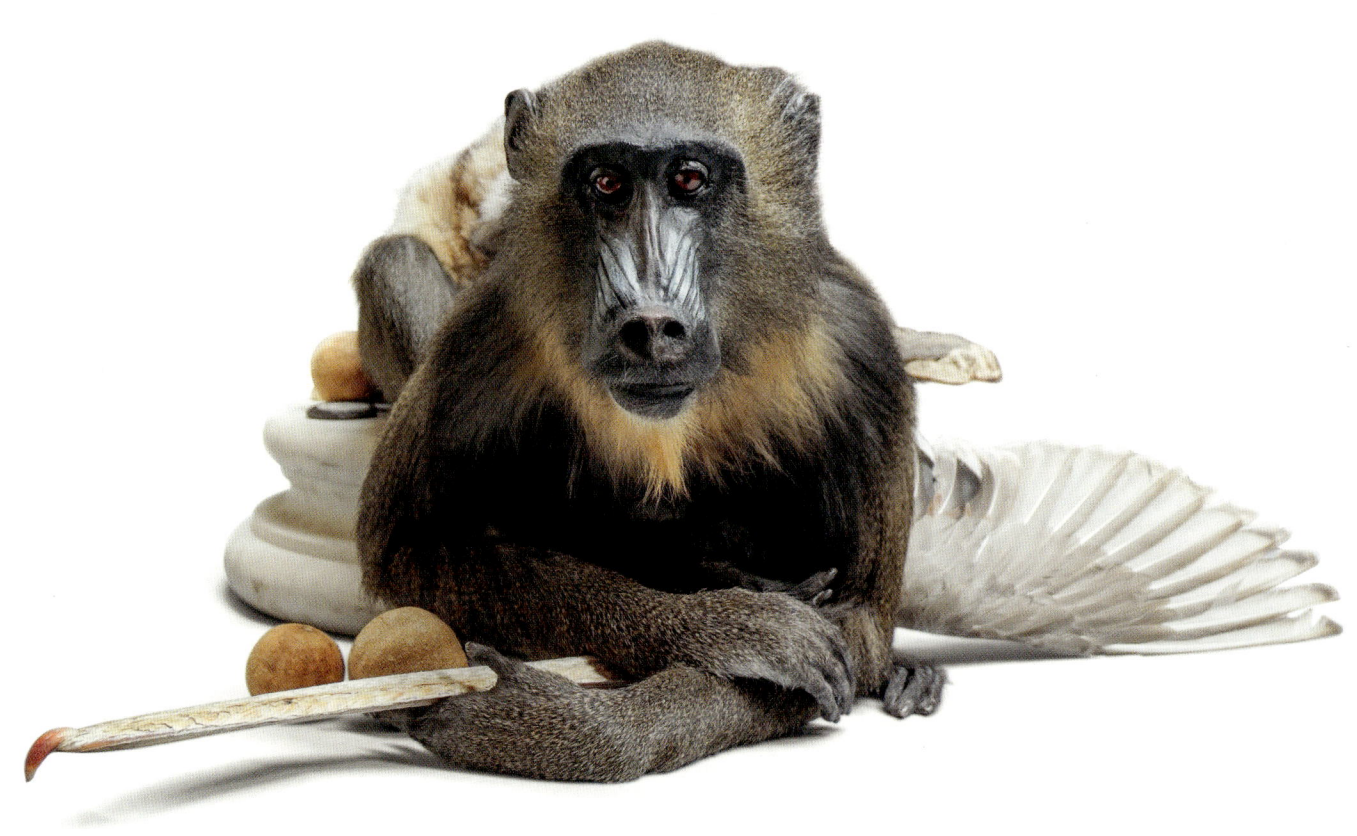

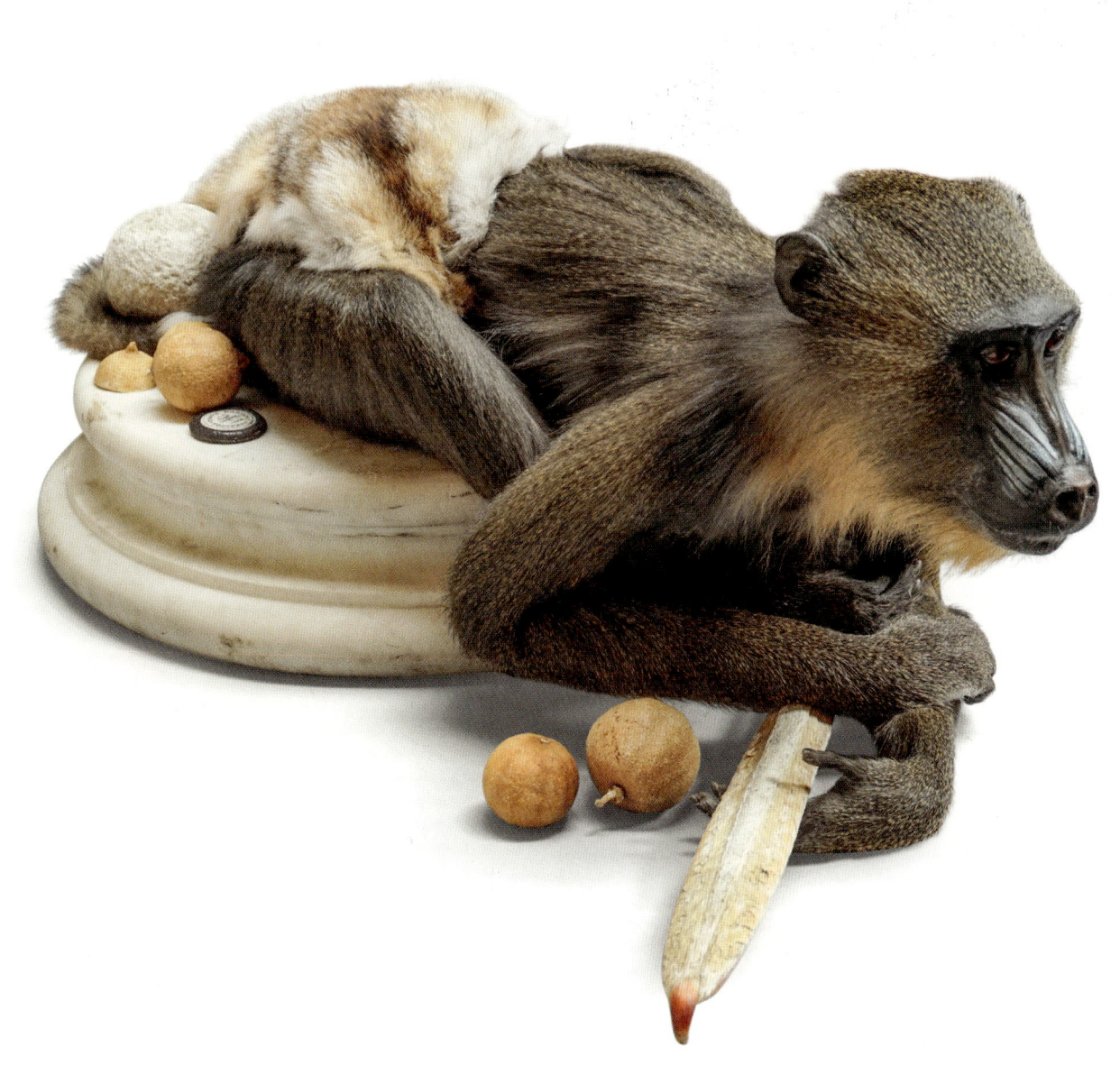

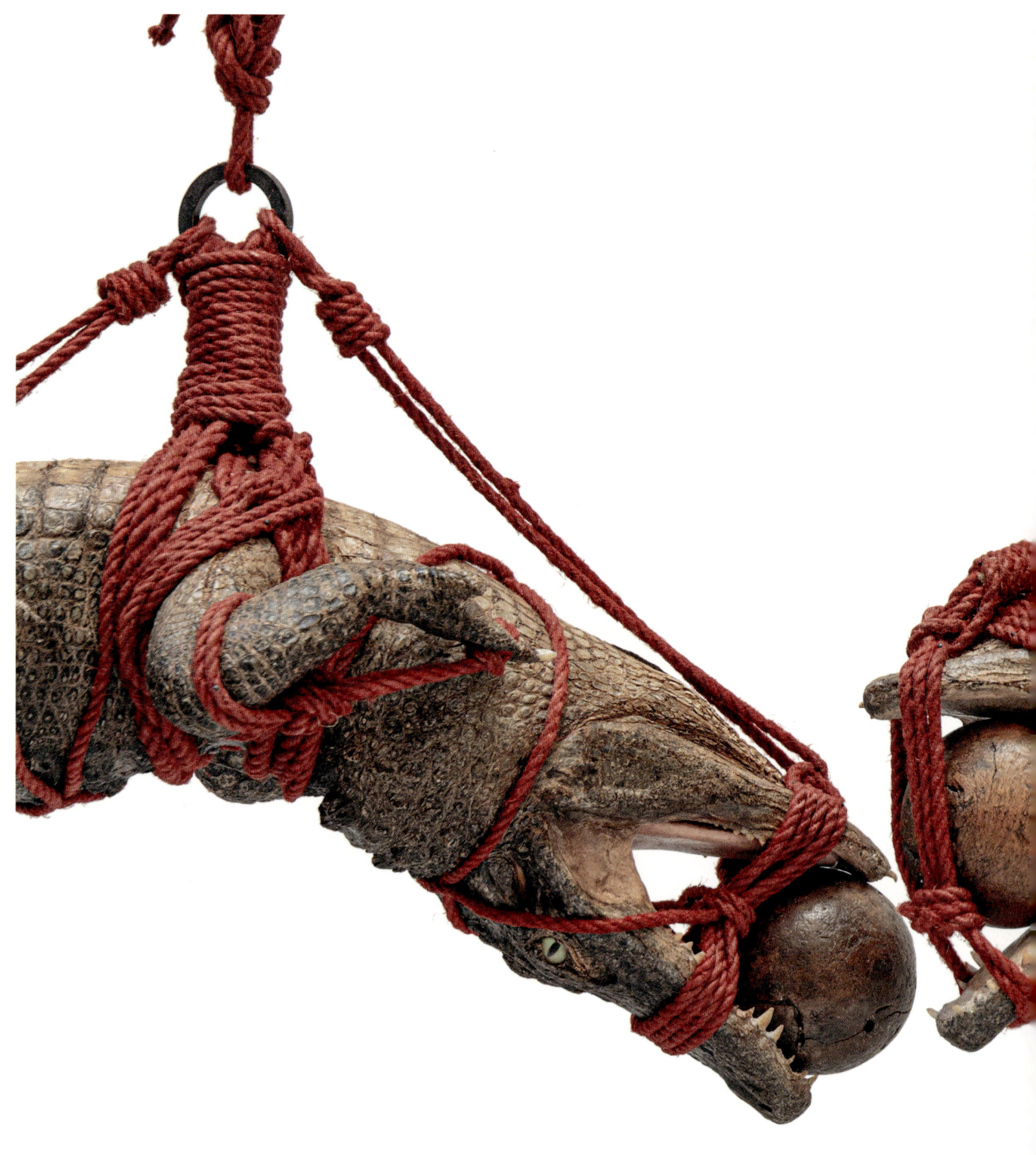

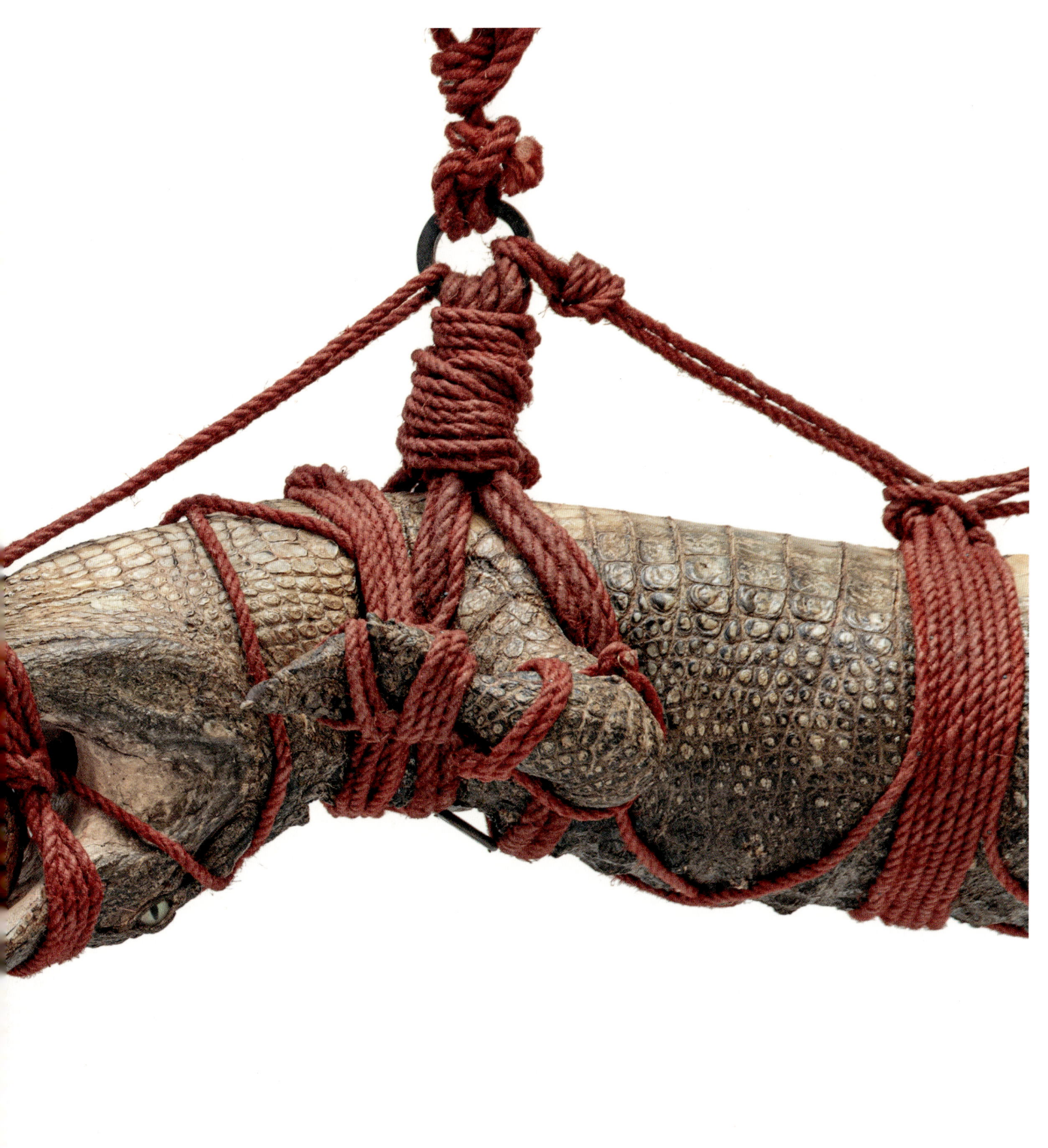

PACKSHOTS 203

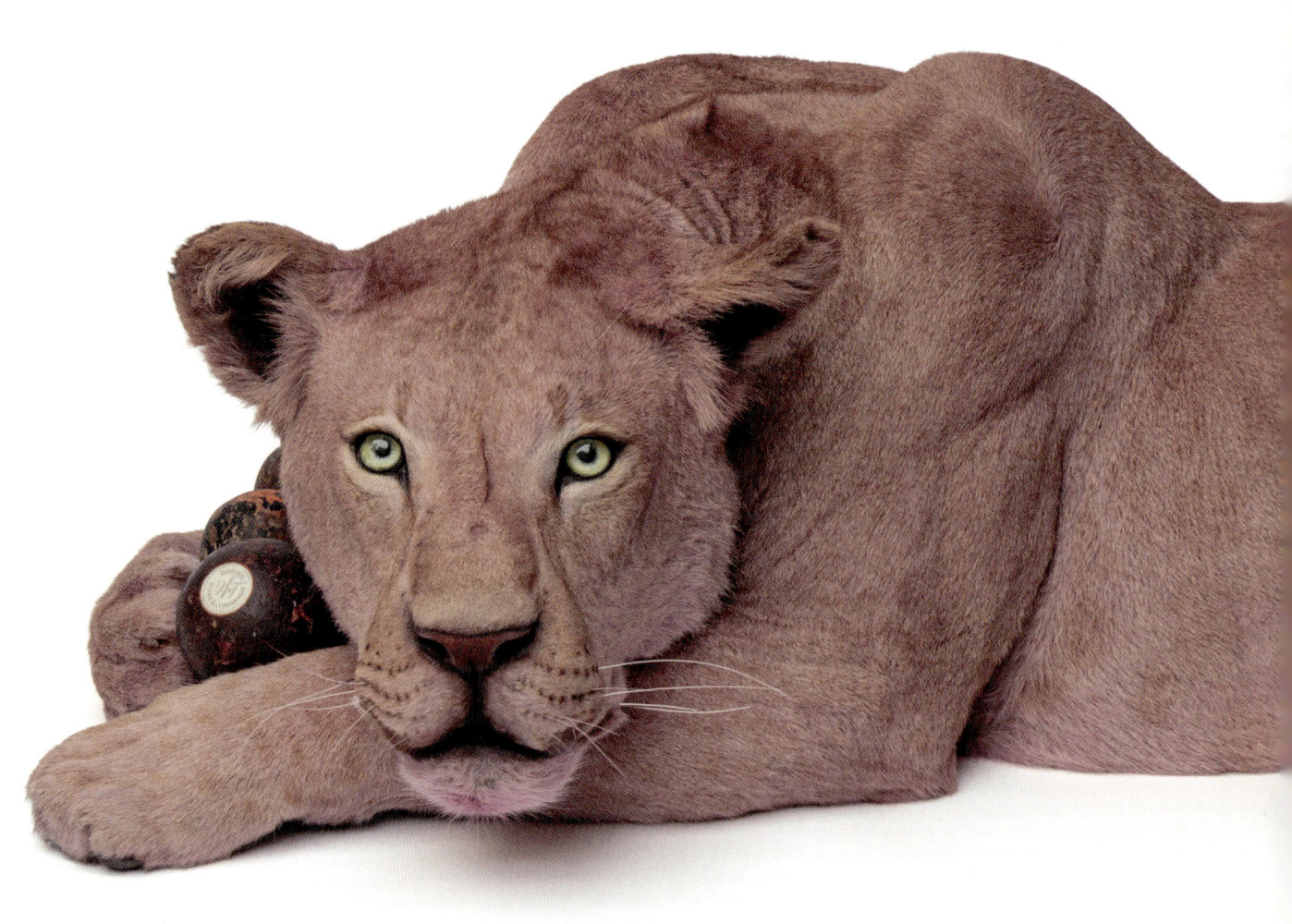

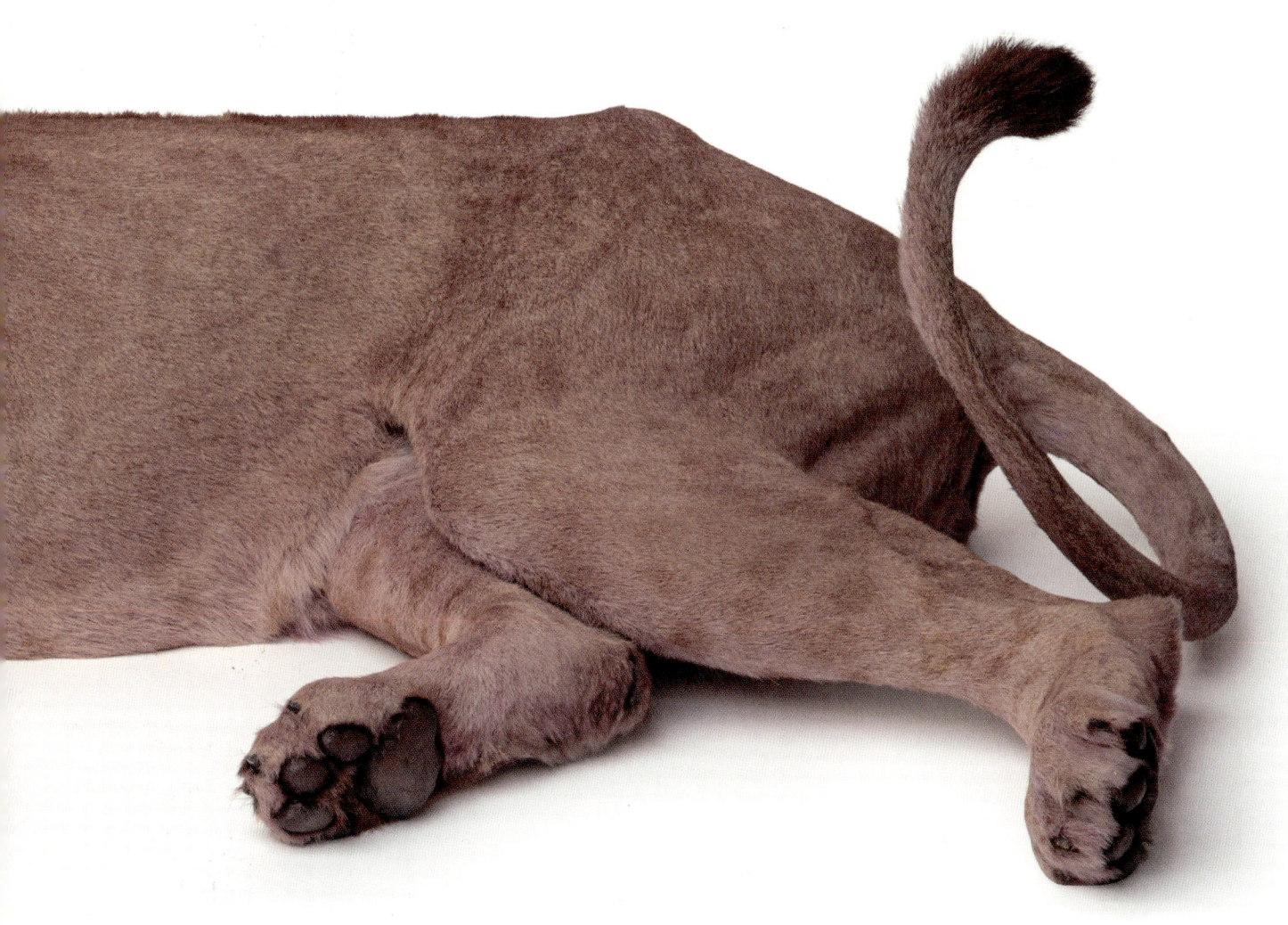

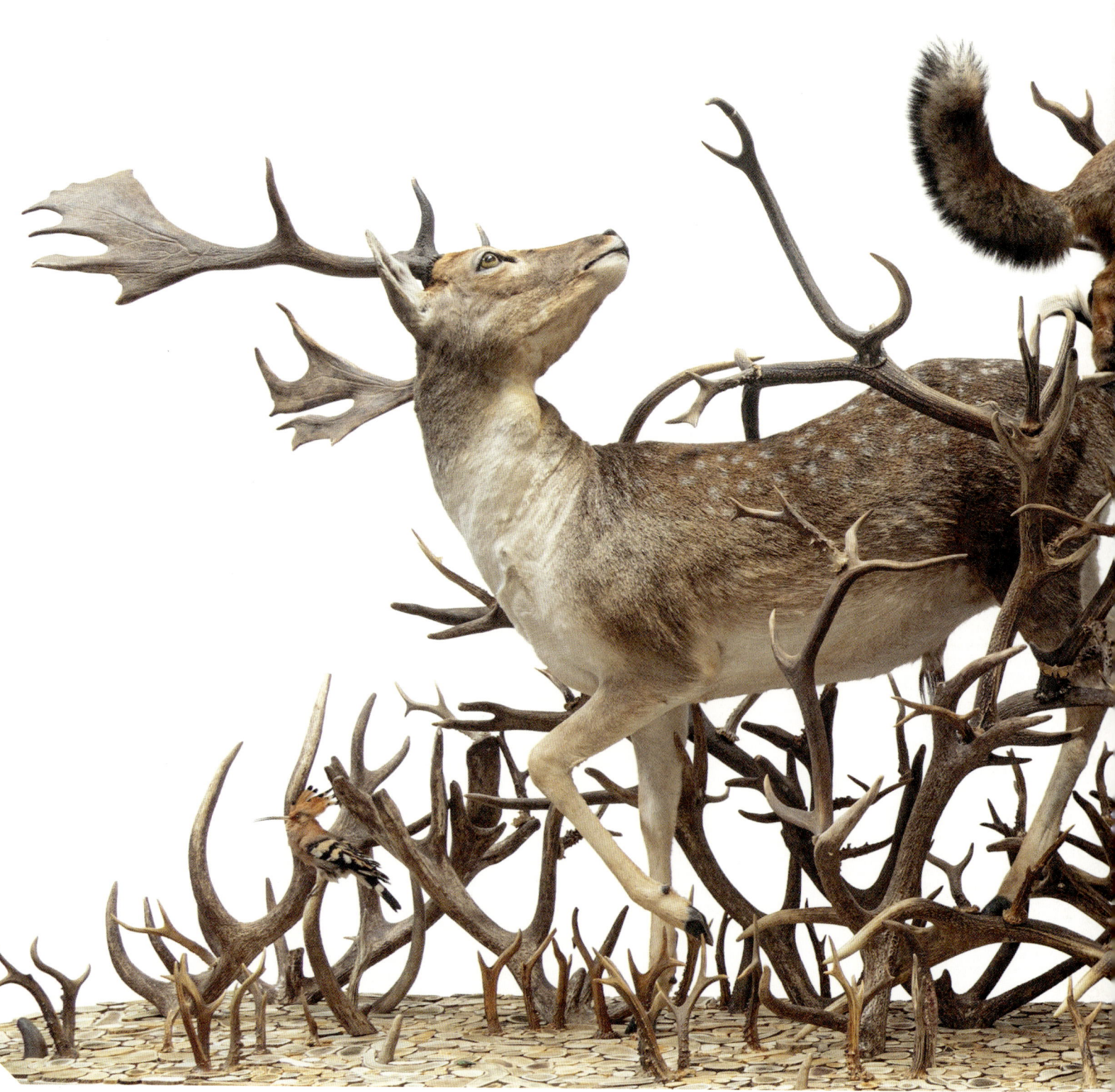

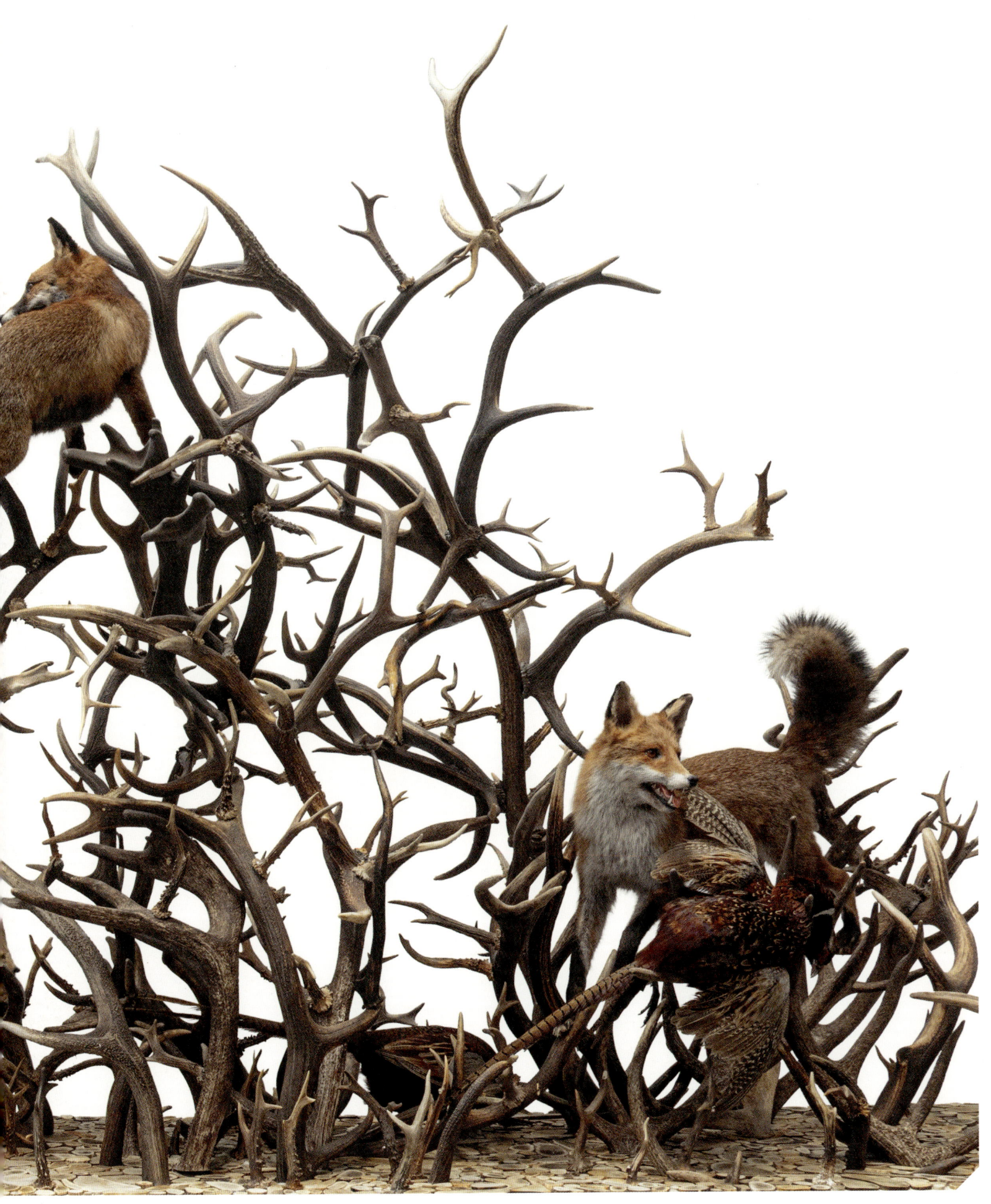

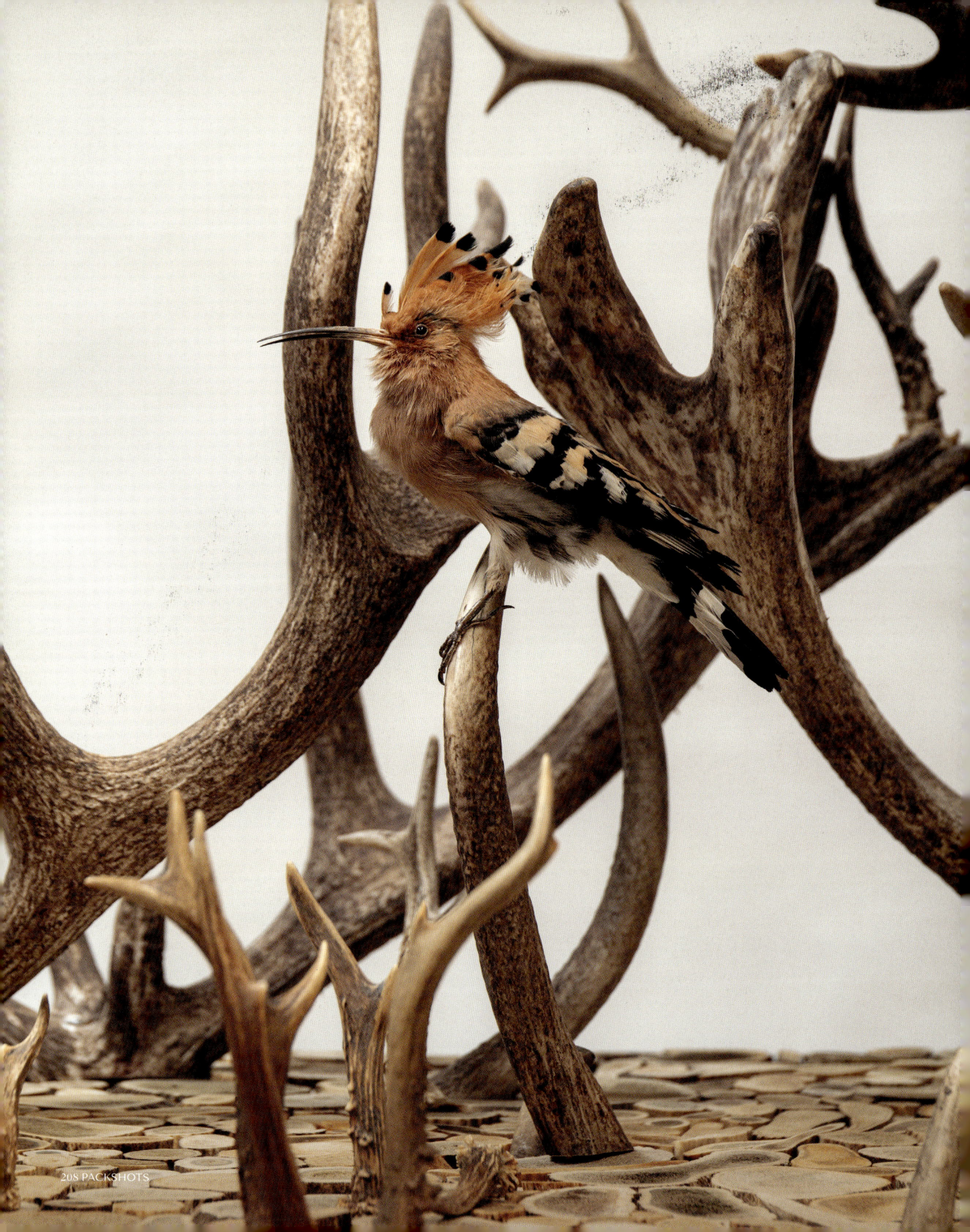

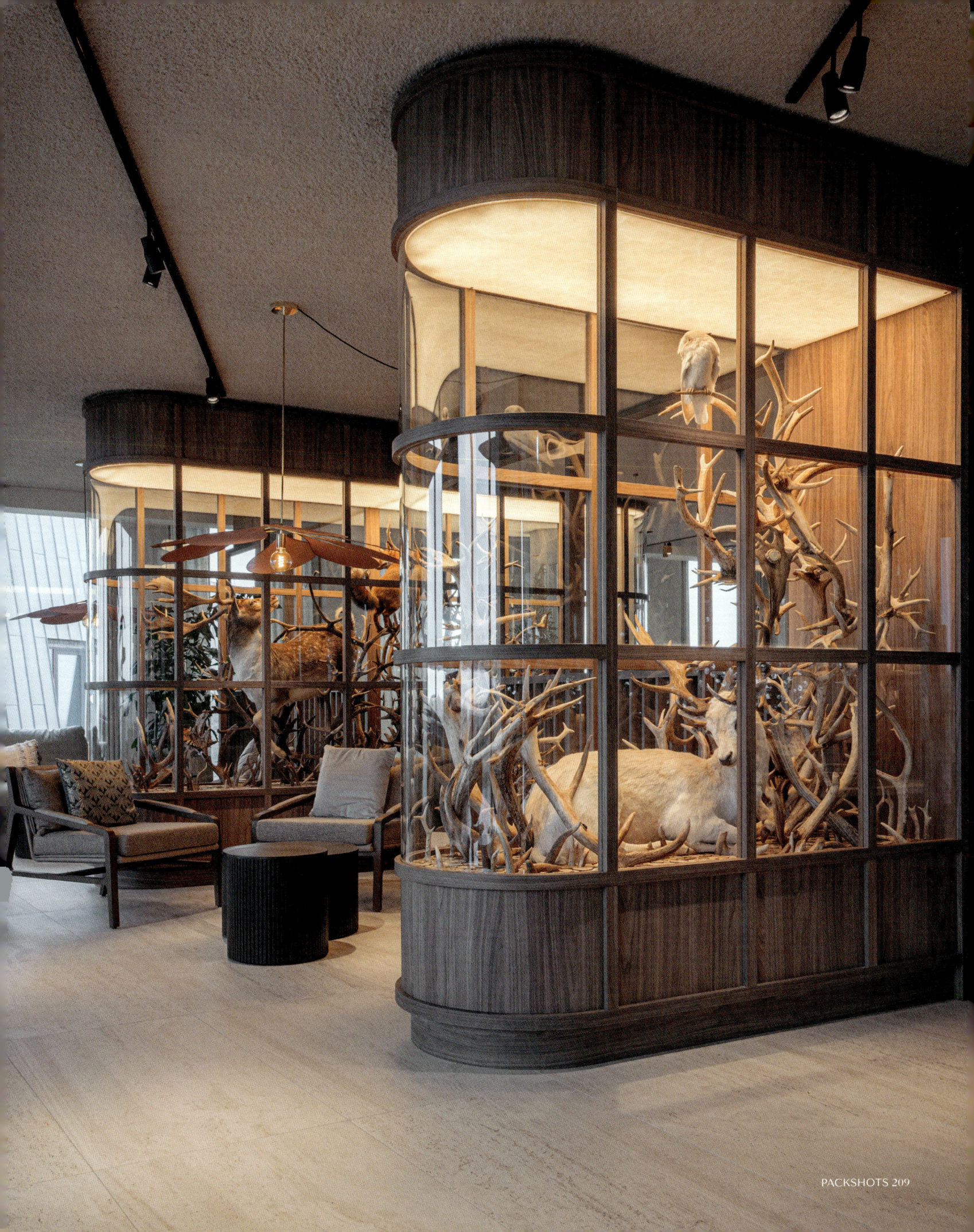

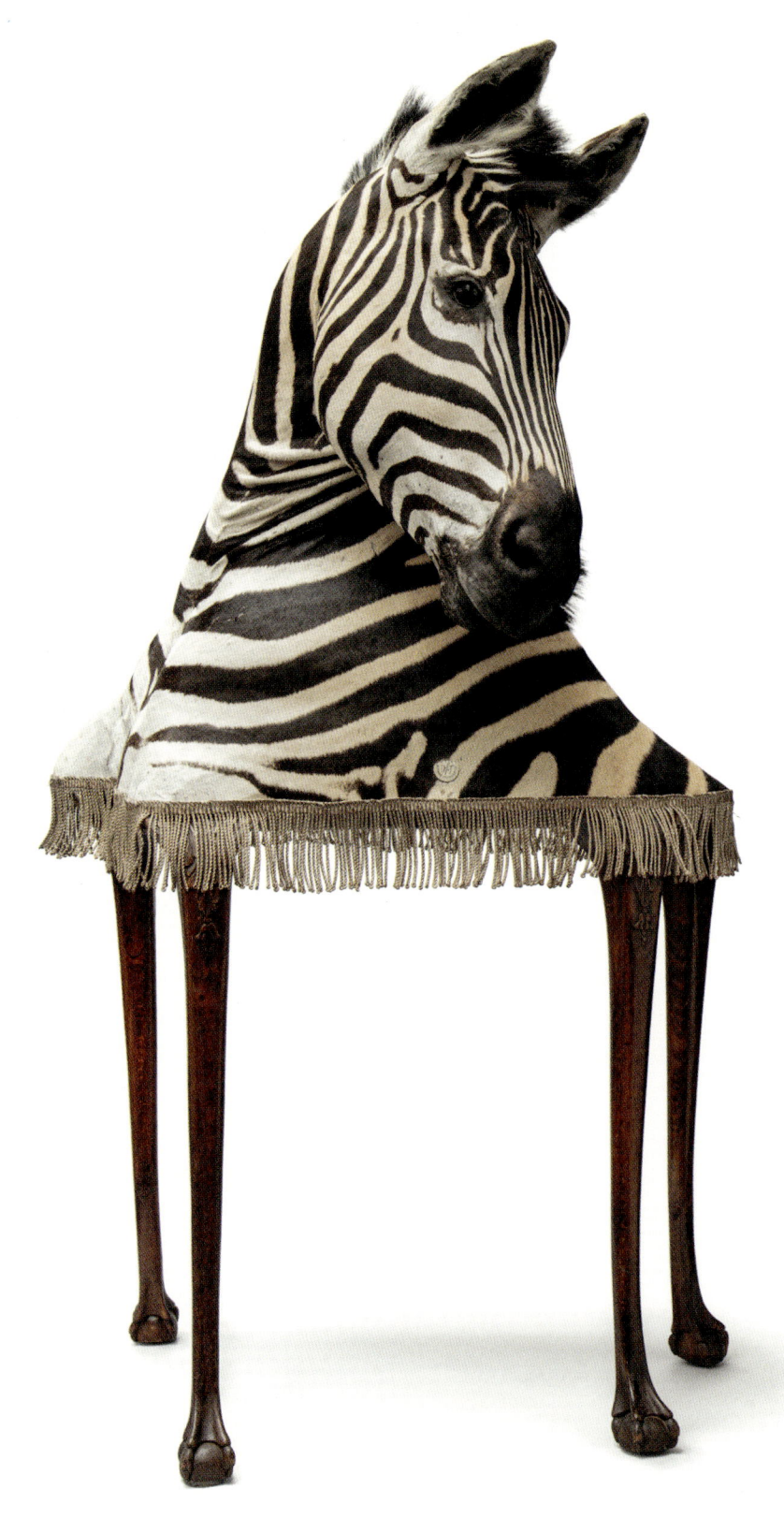

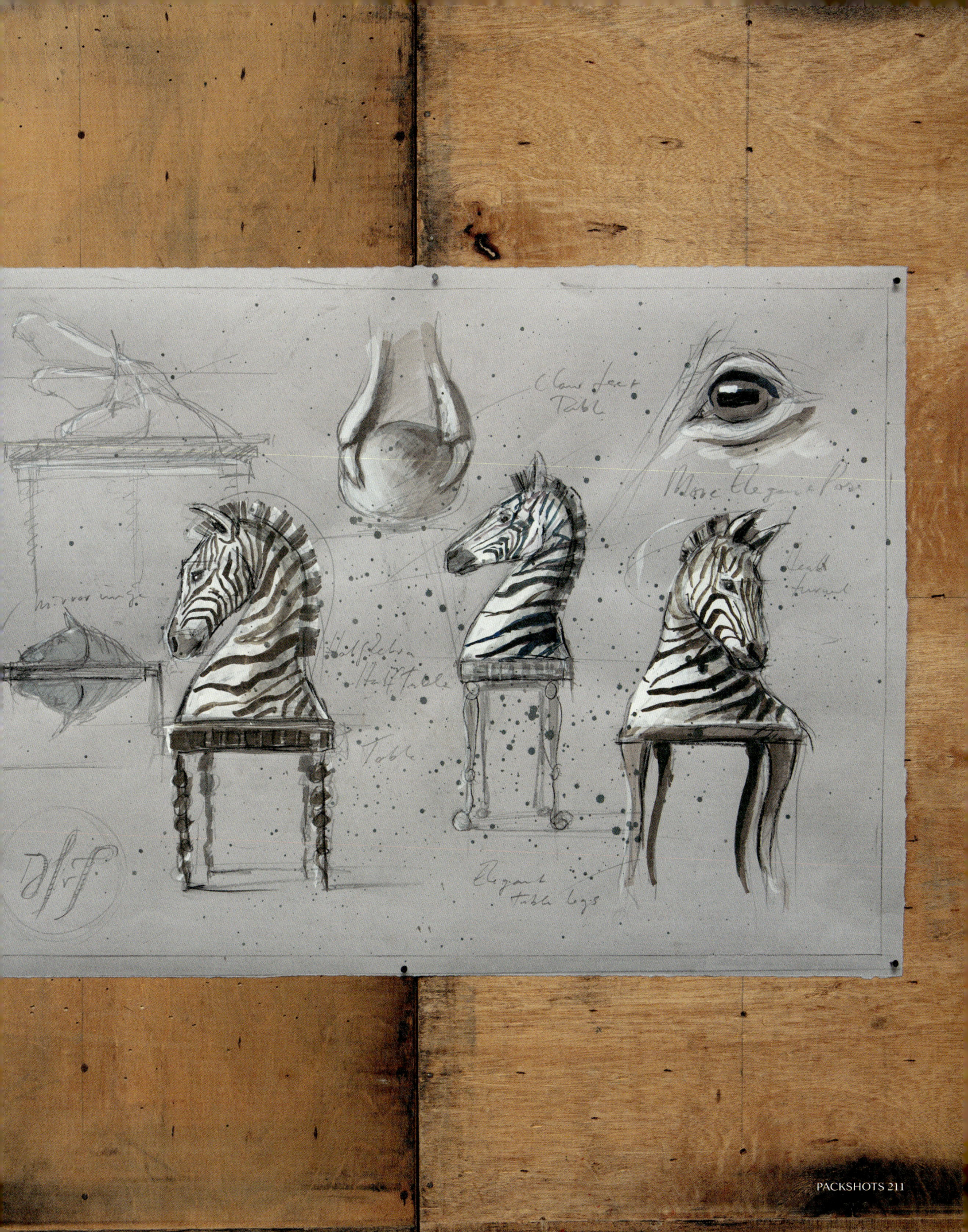

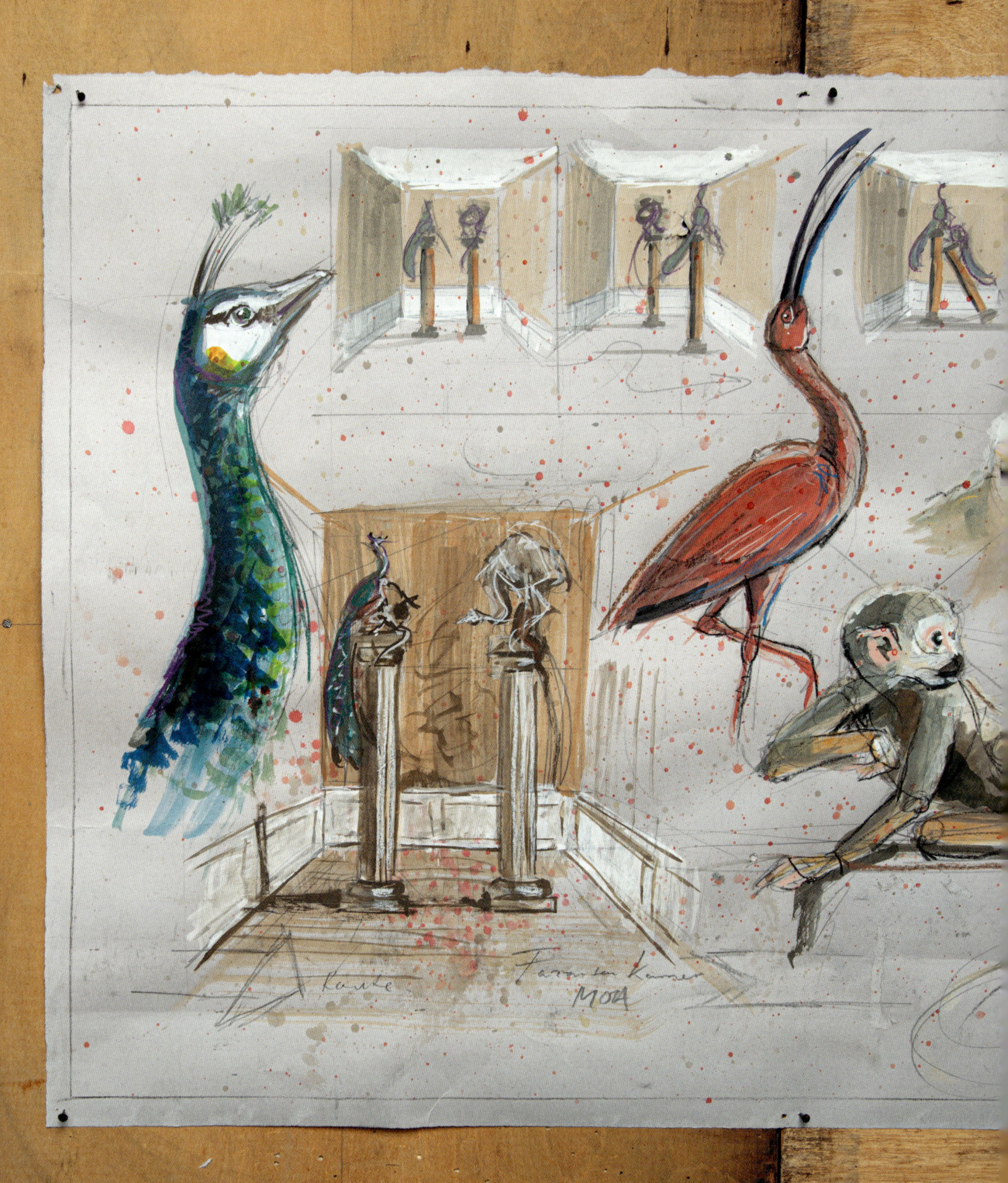

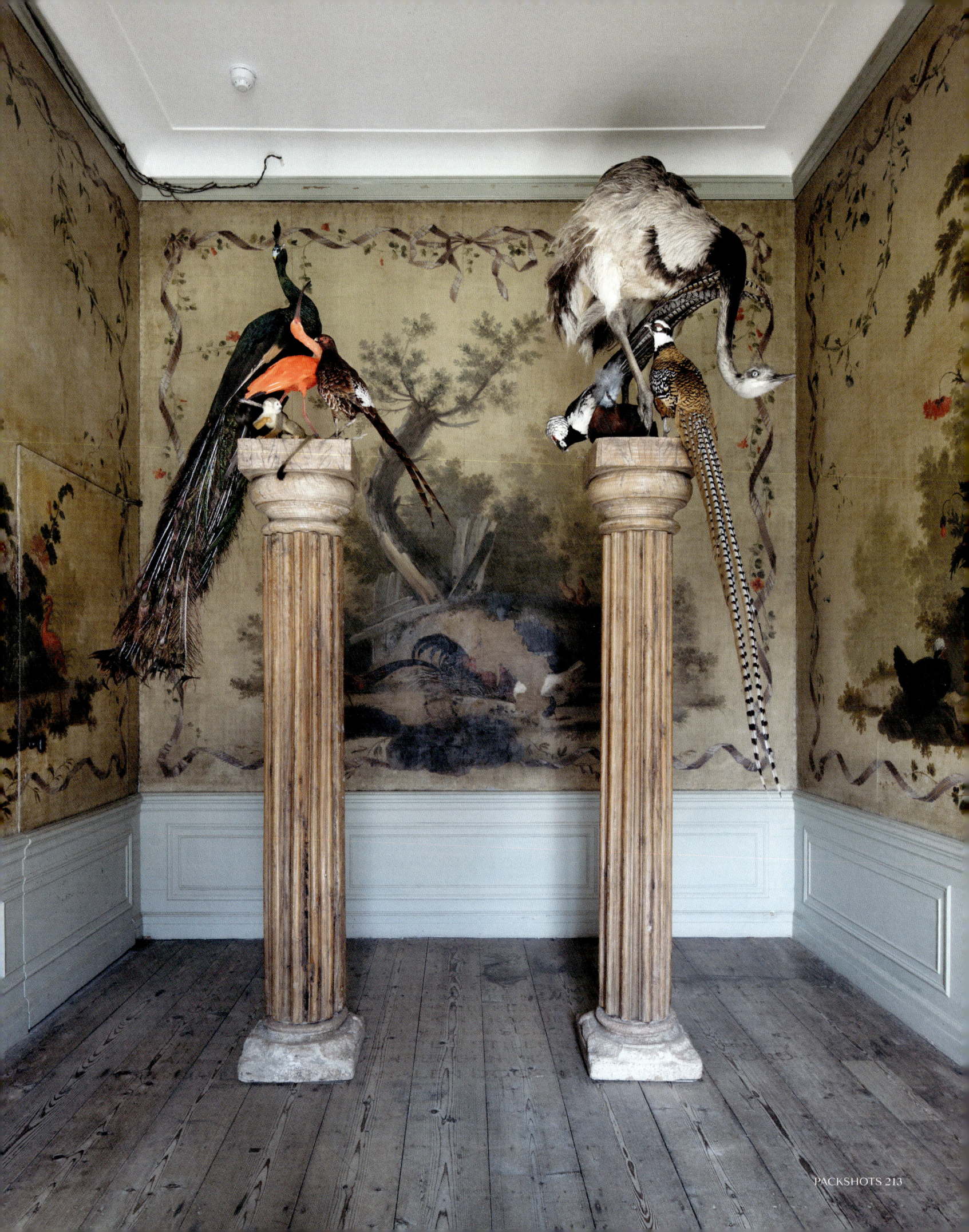

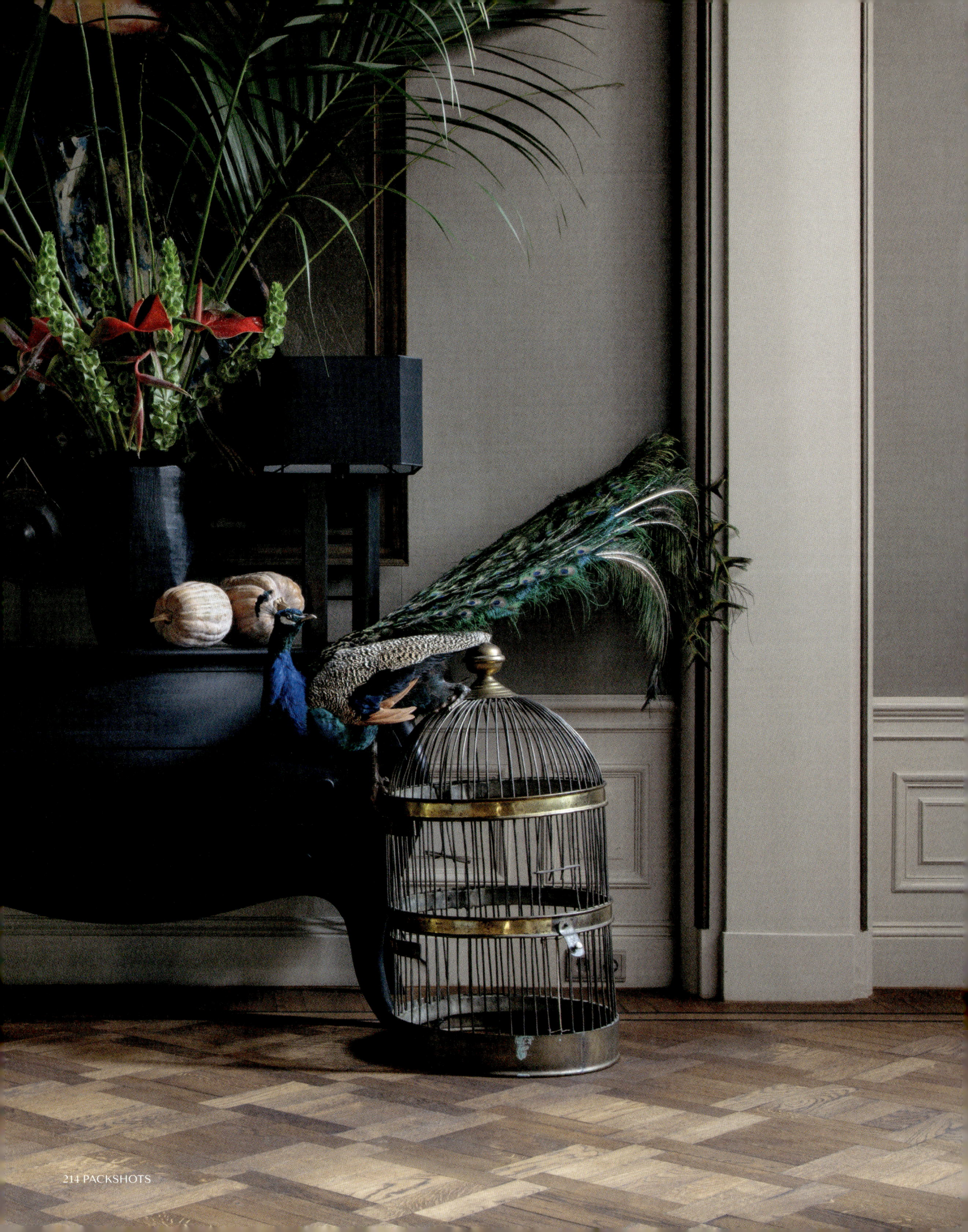

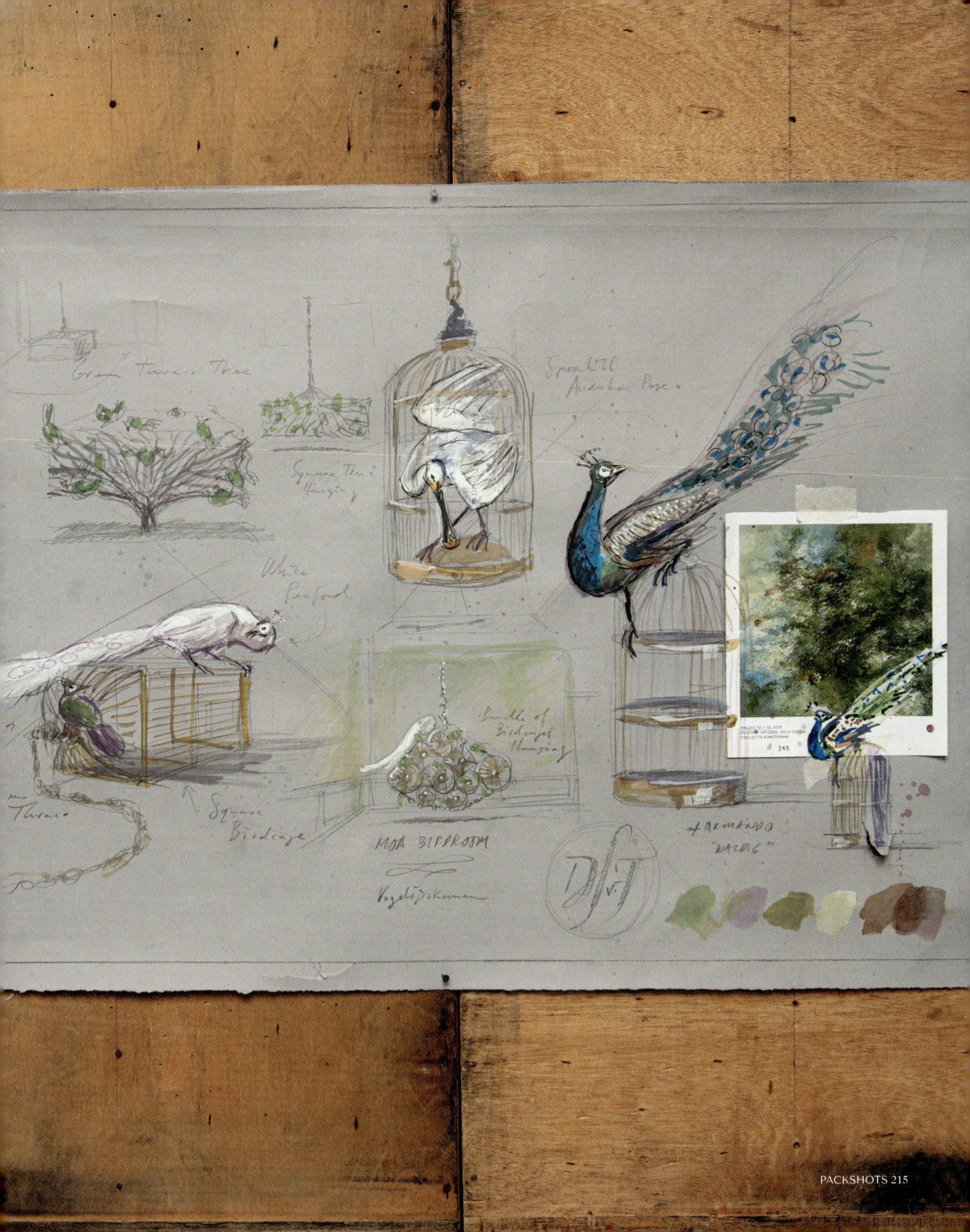

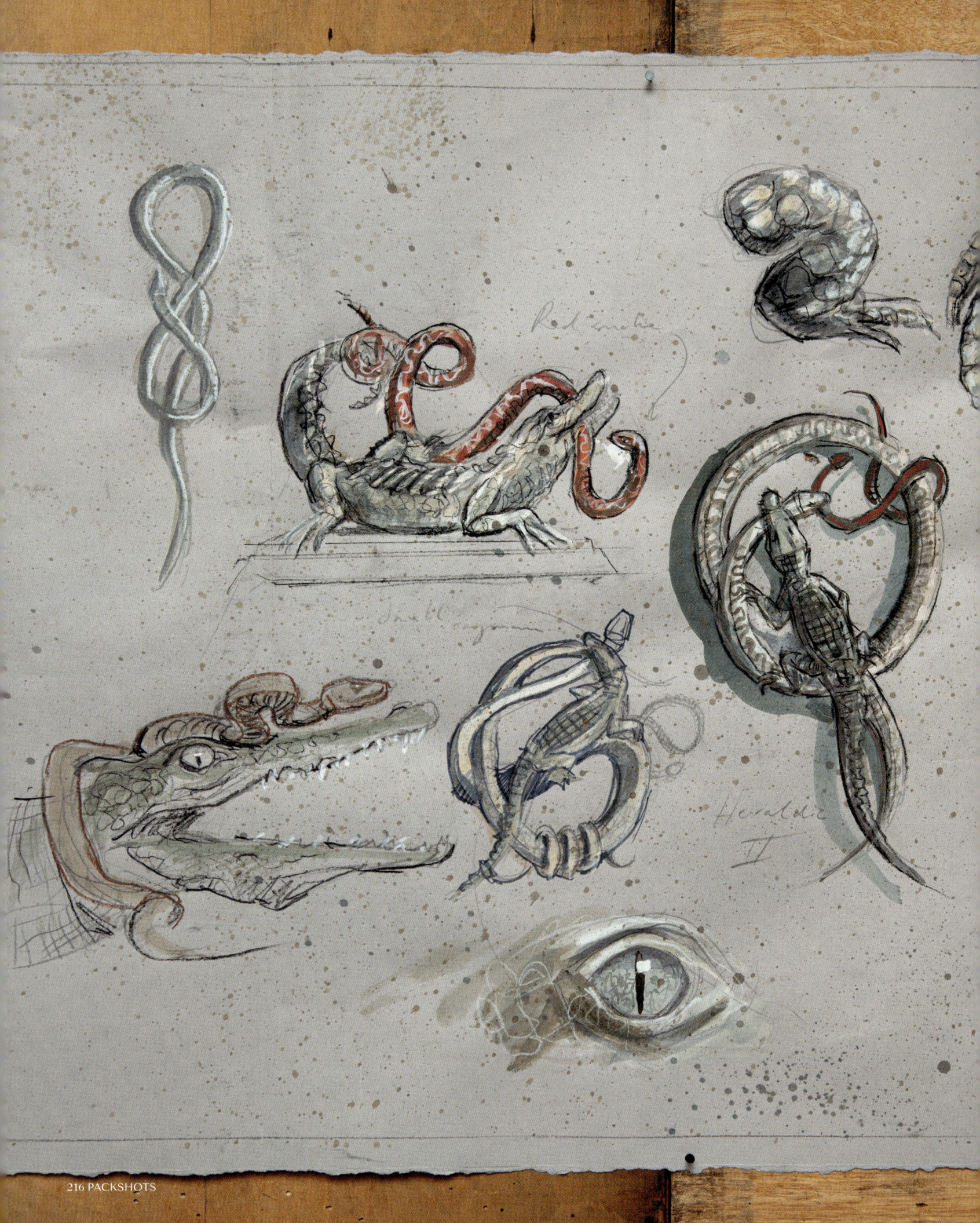

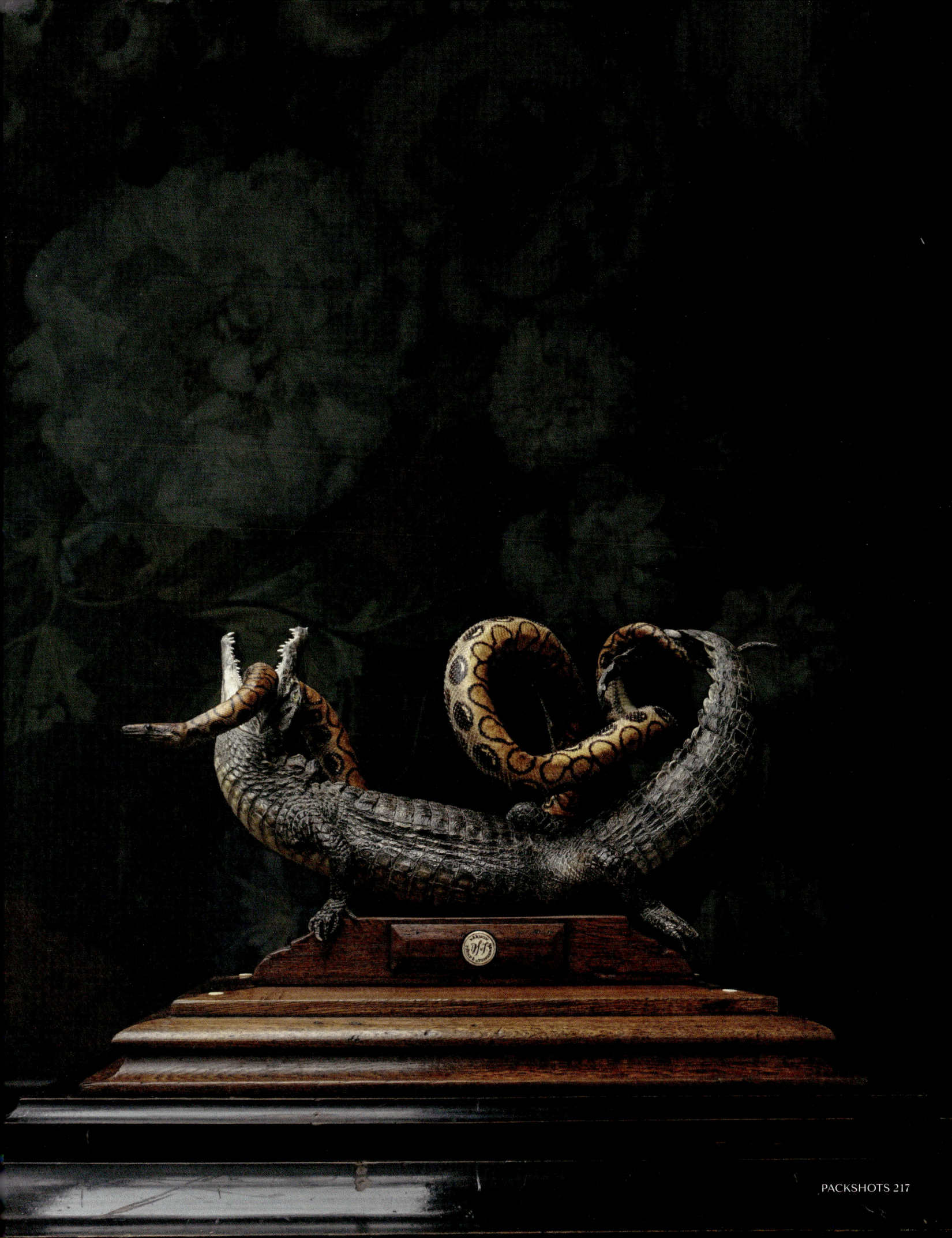

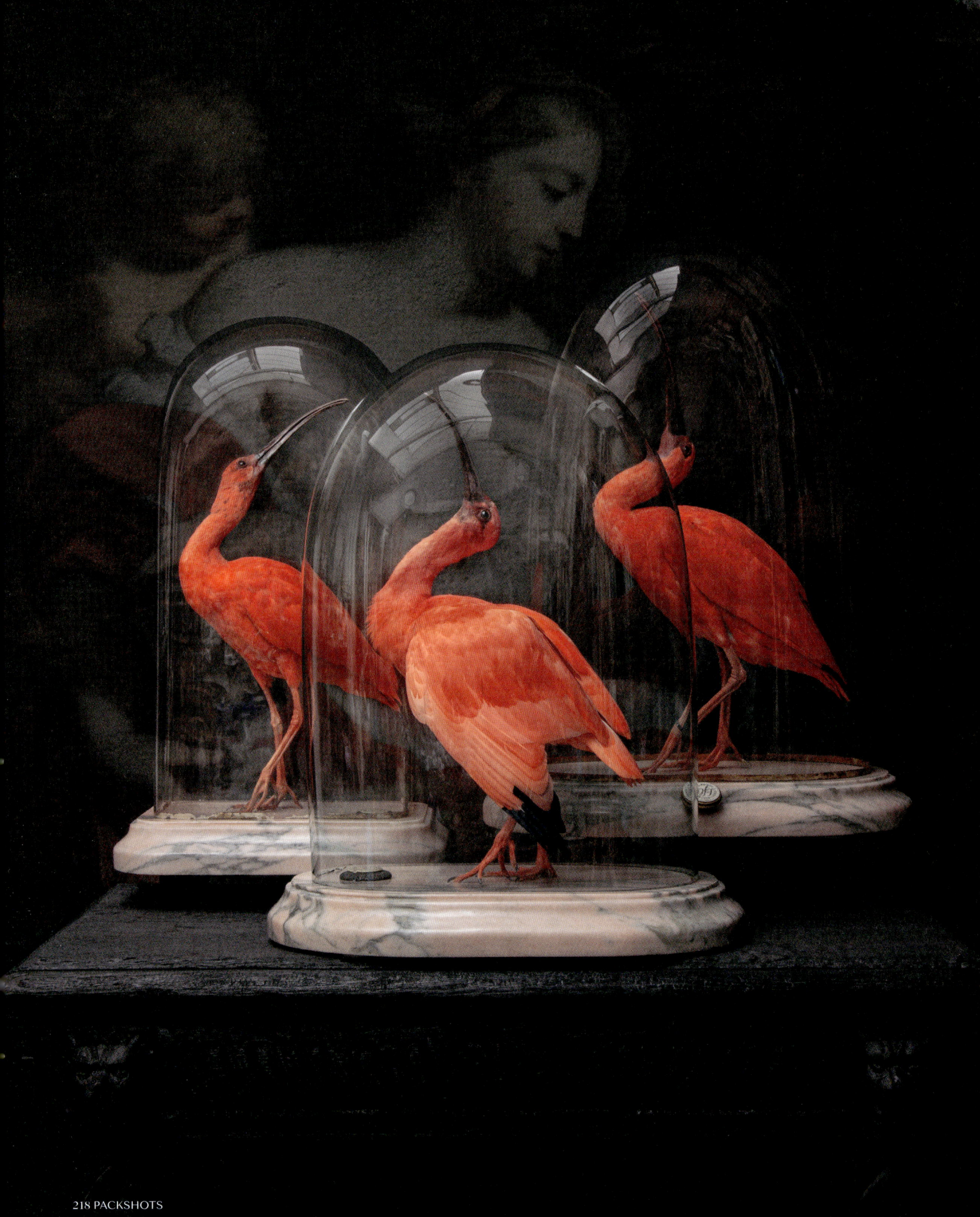

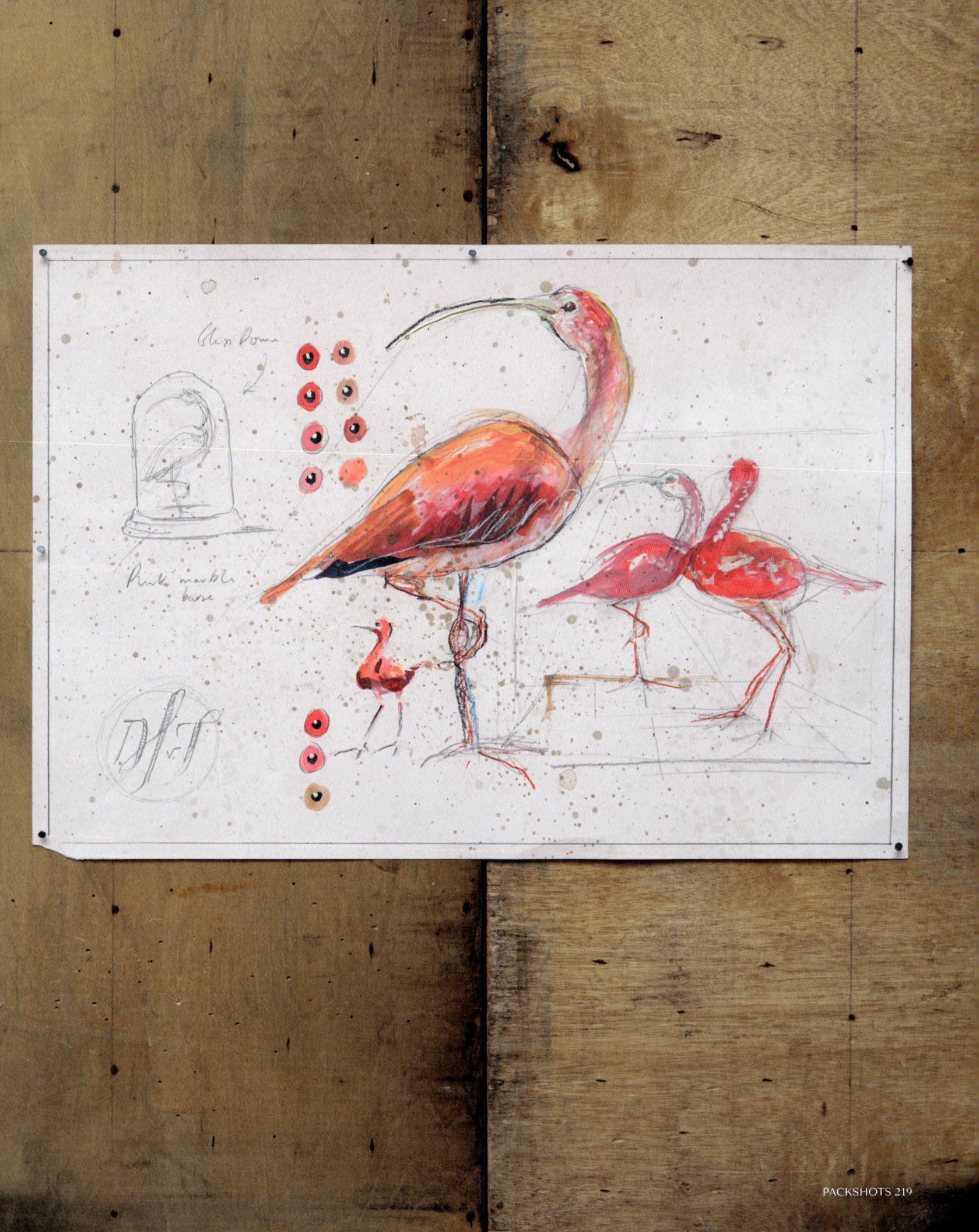

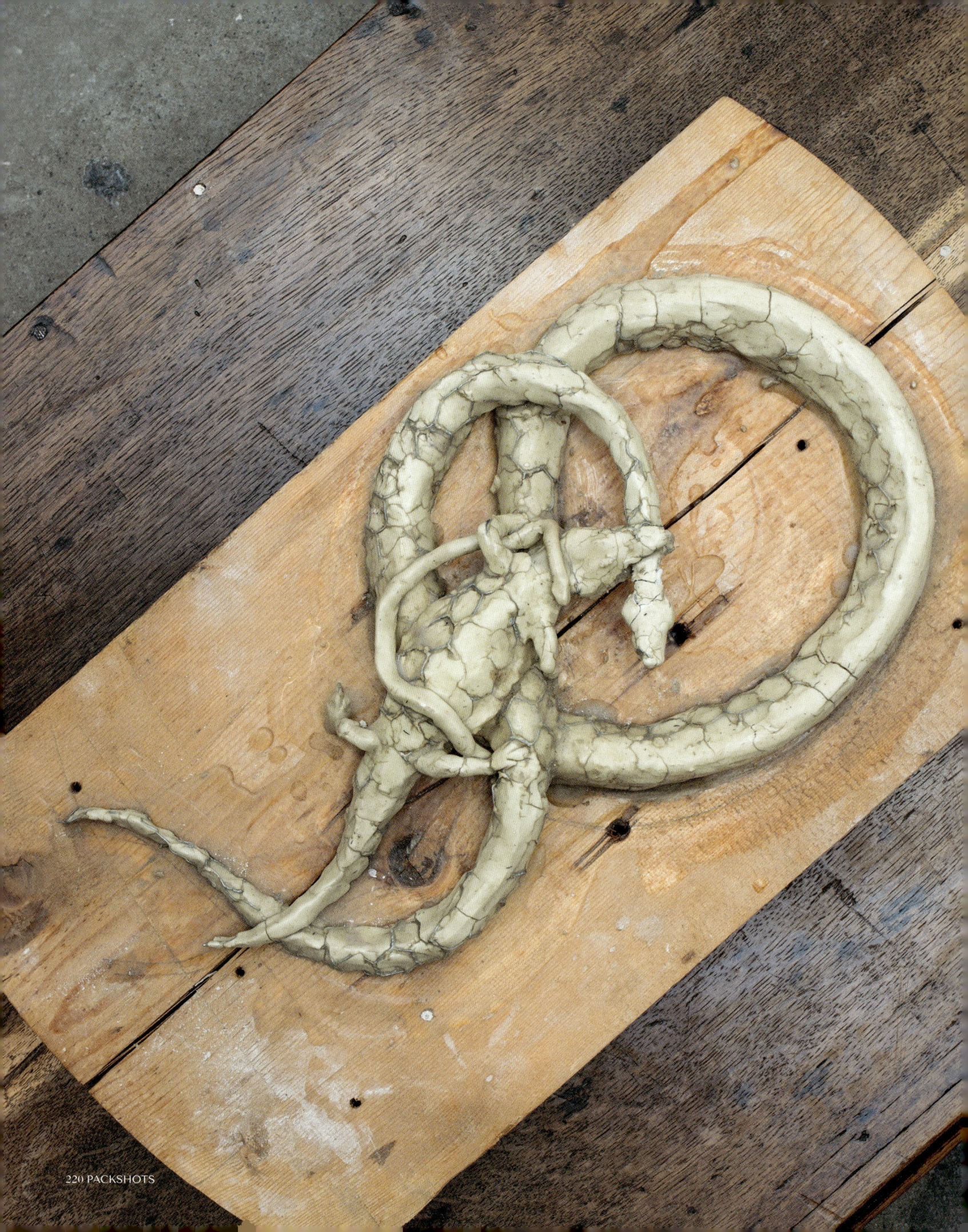

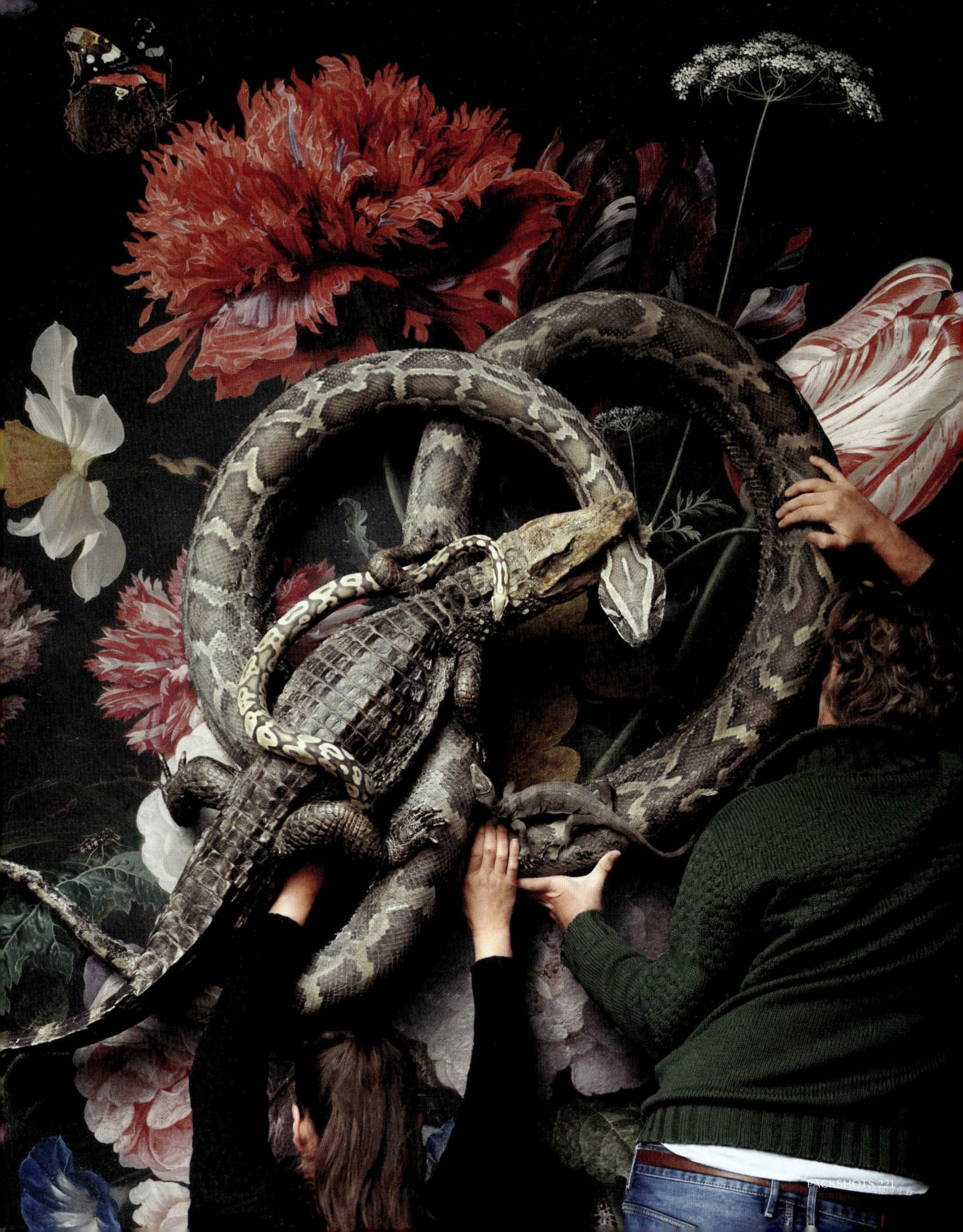

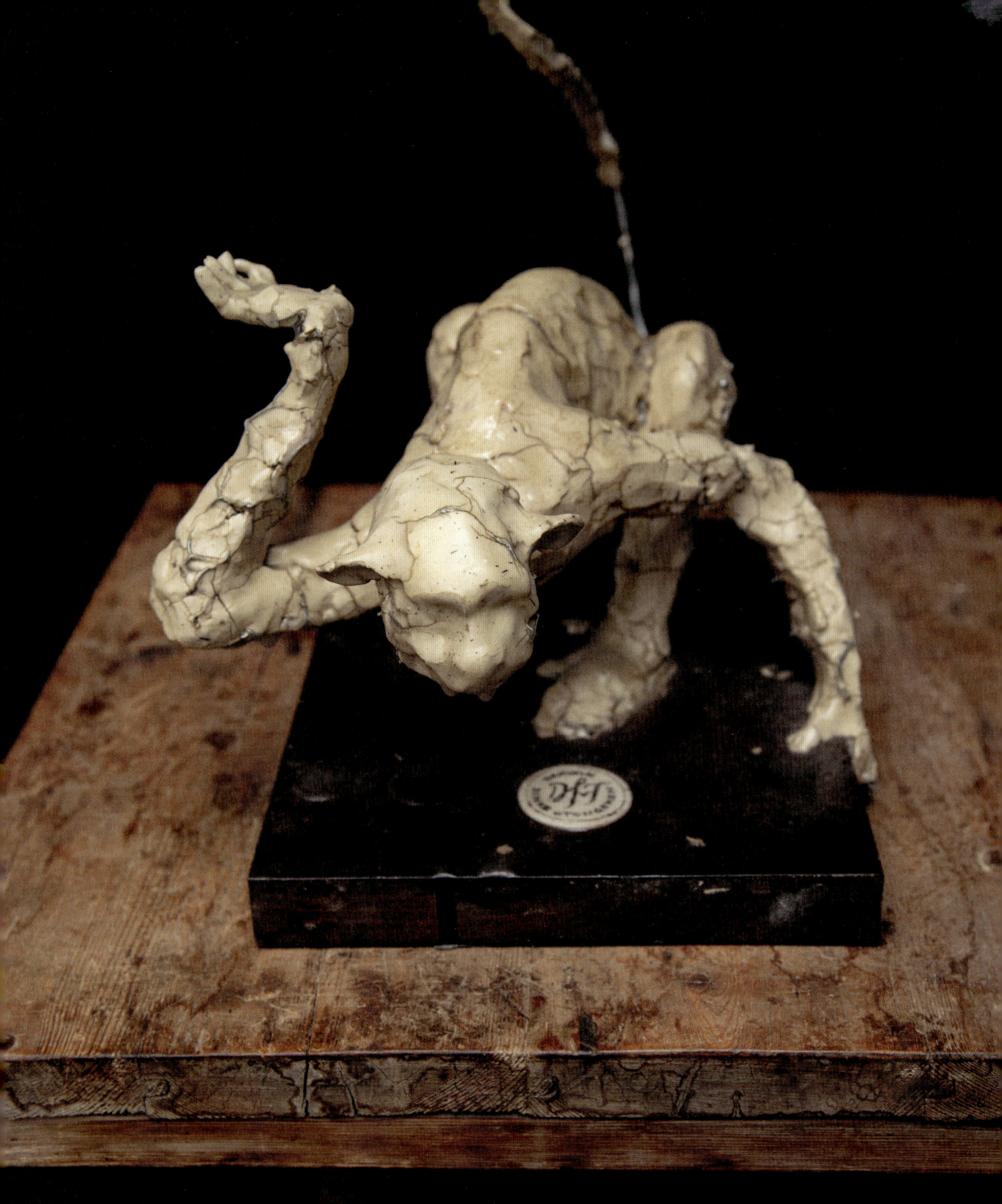

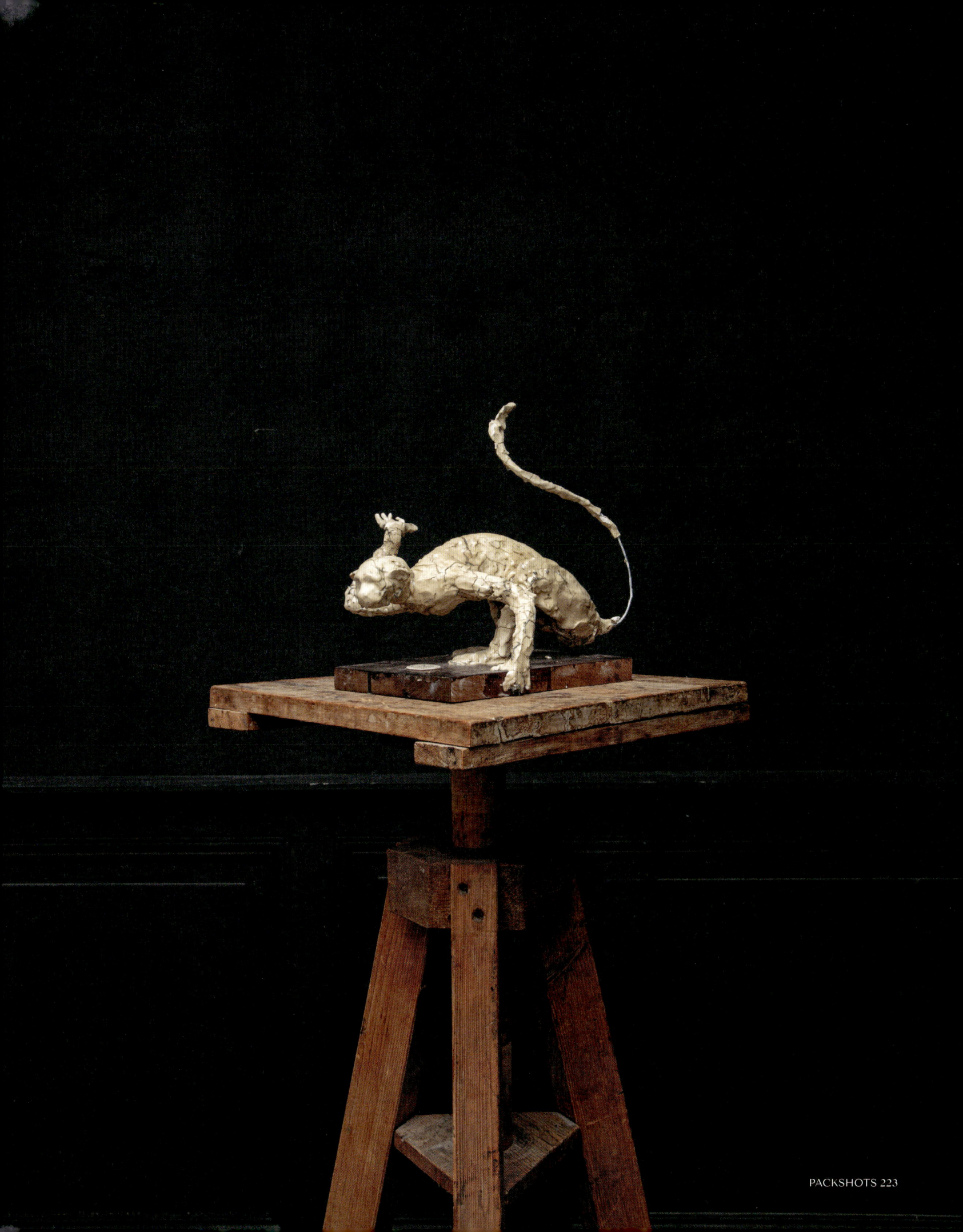

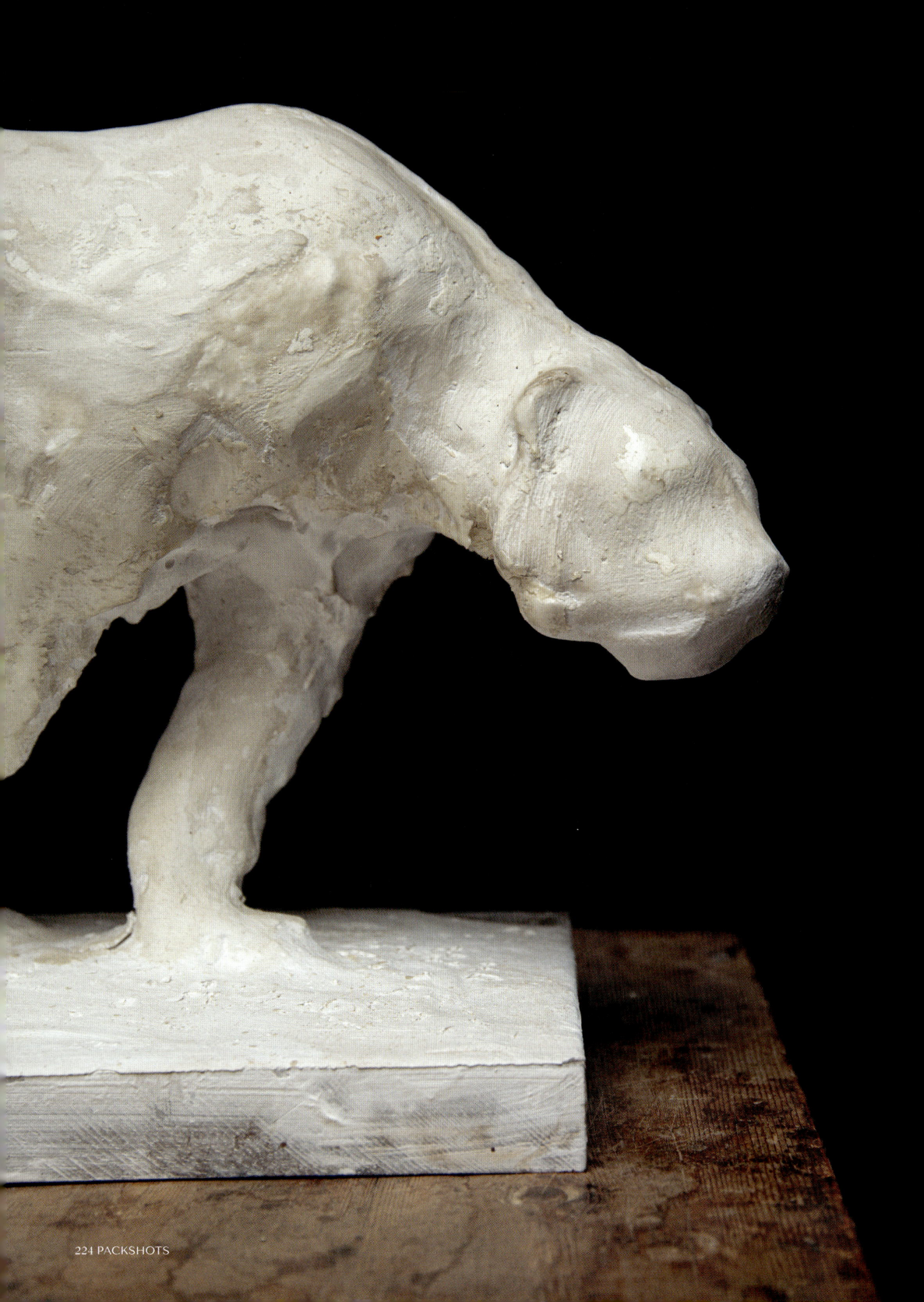

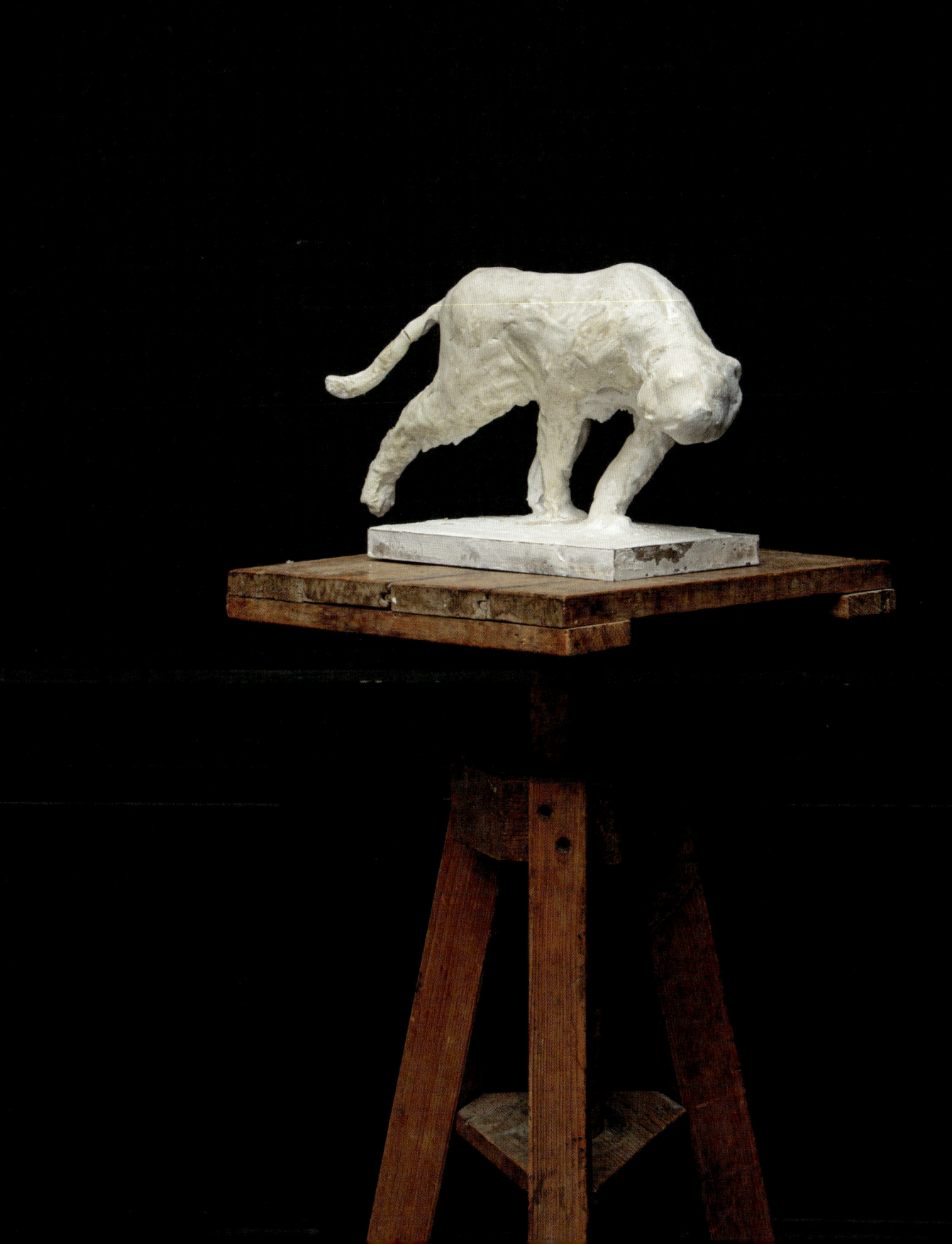

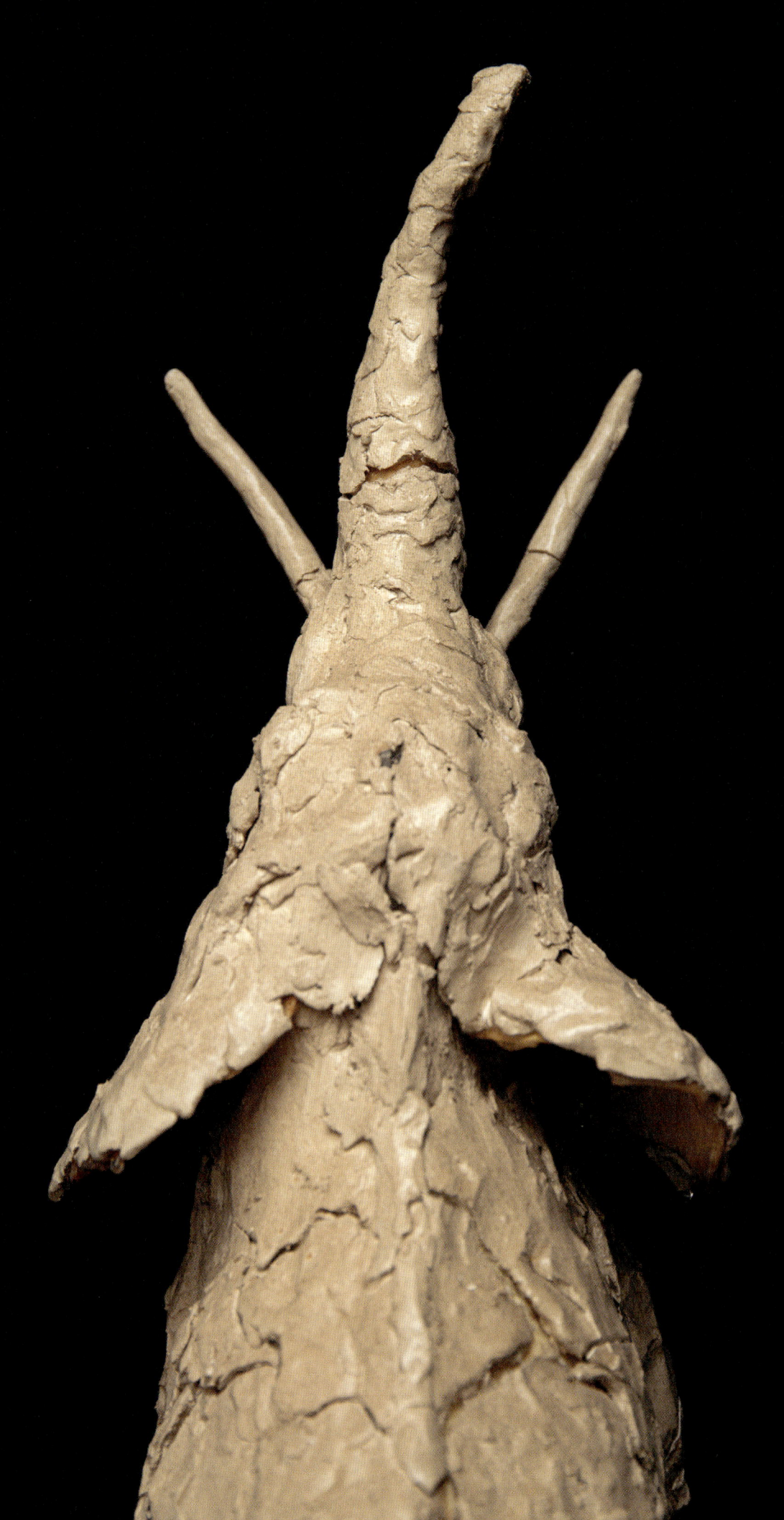

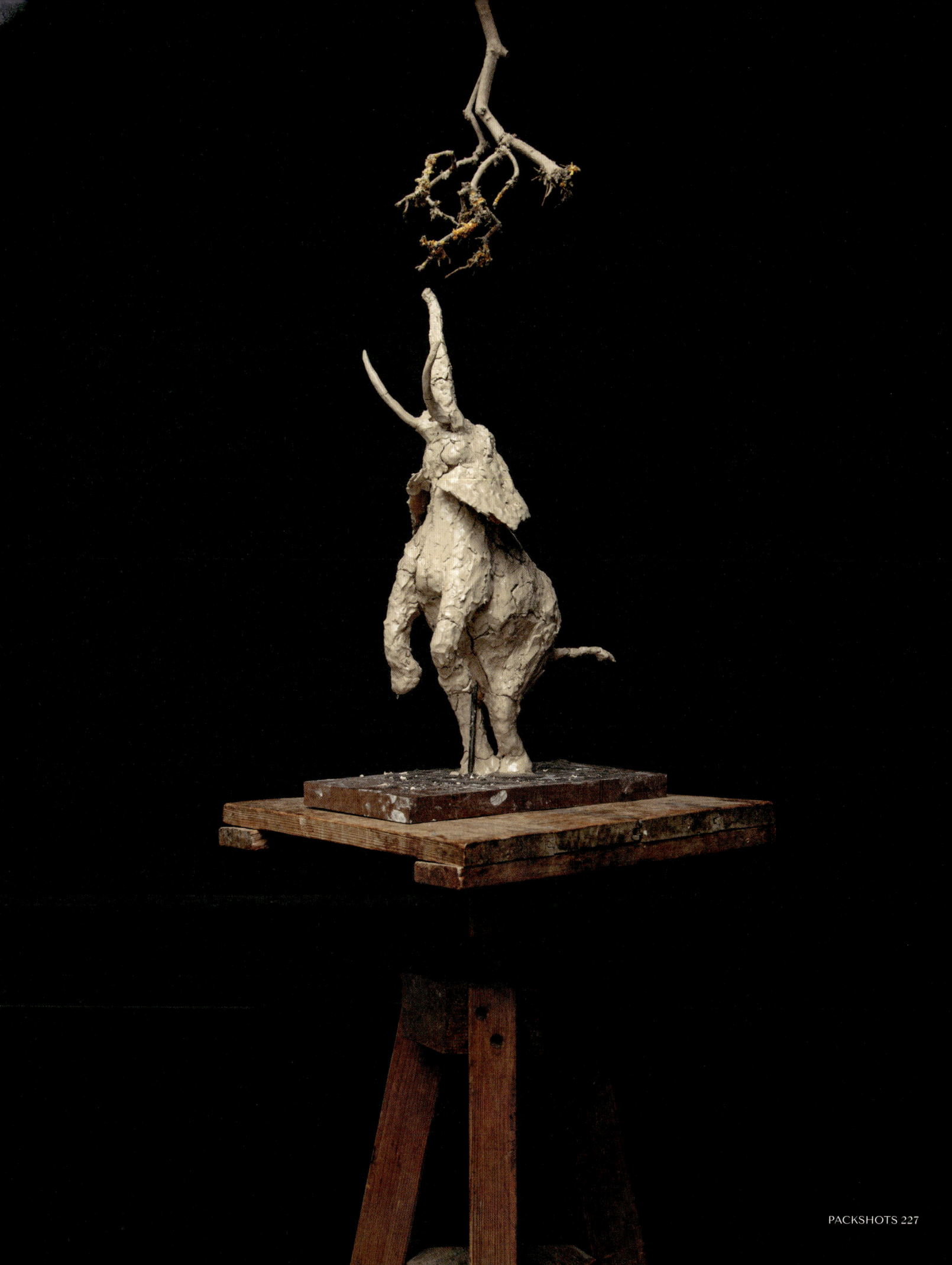

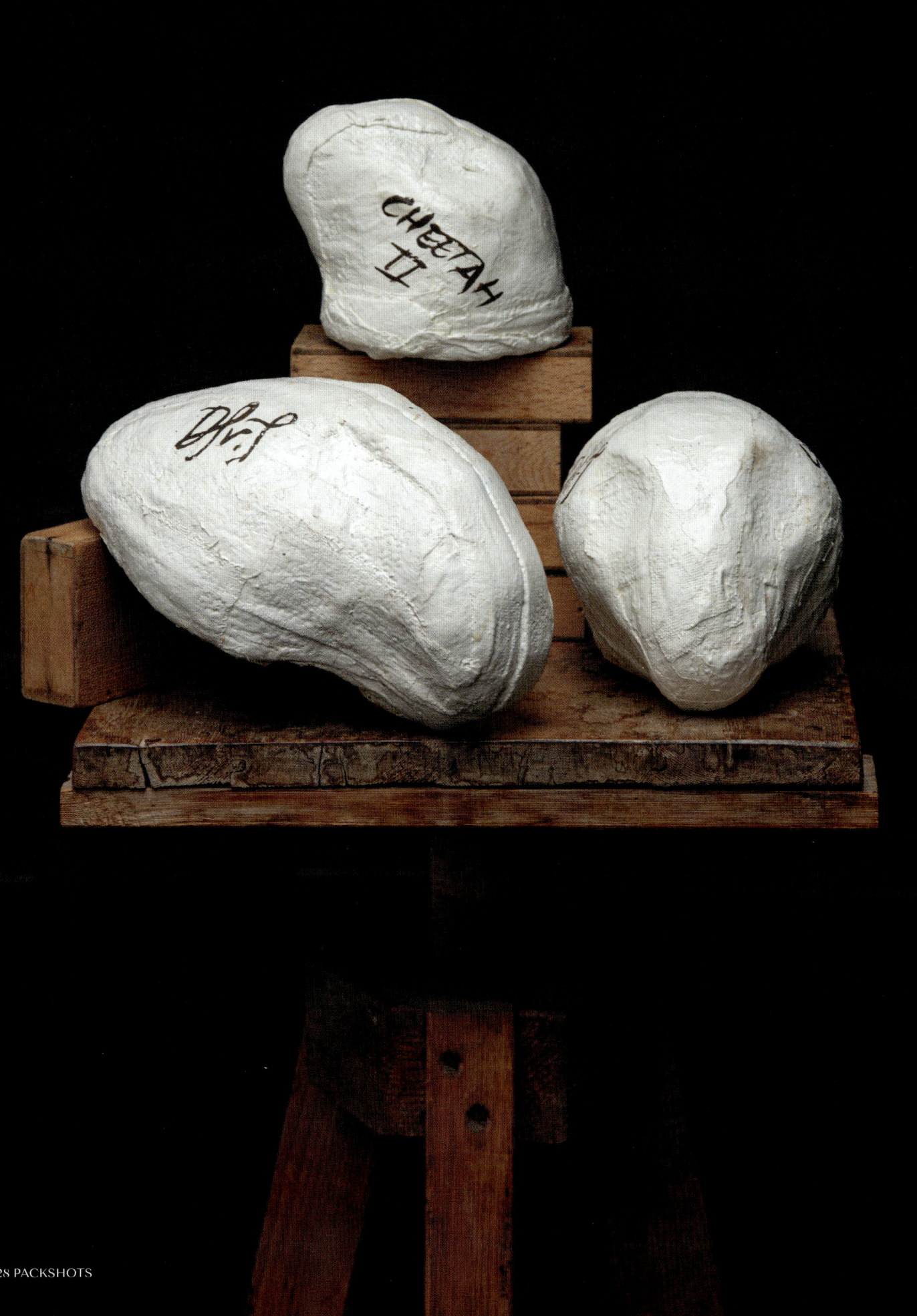

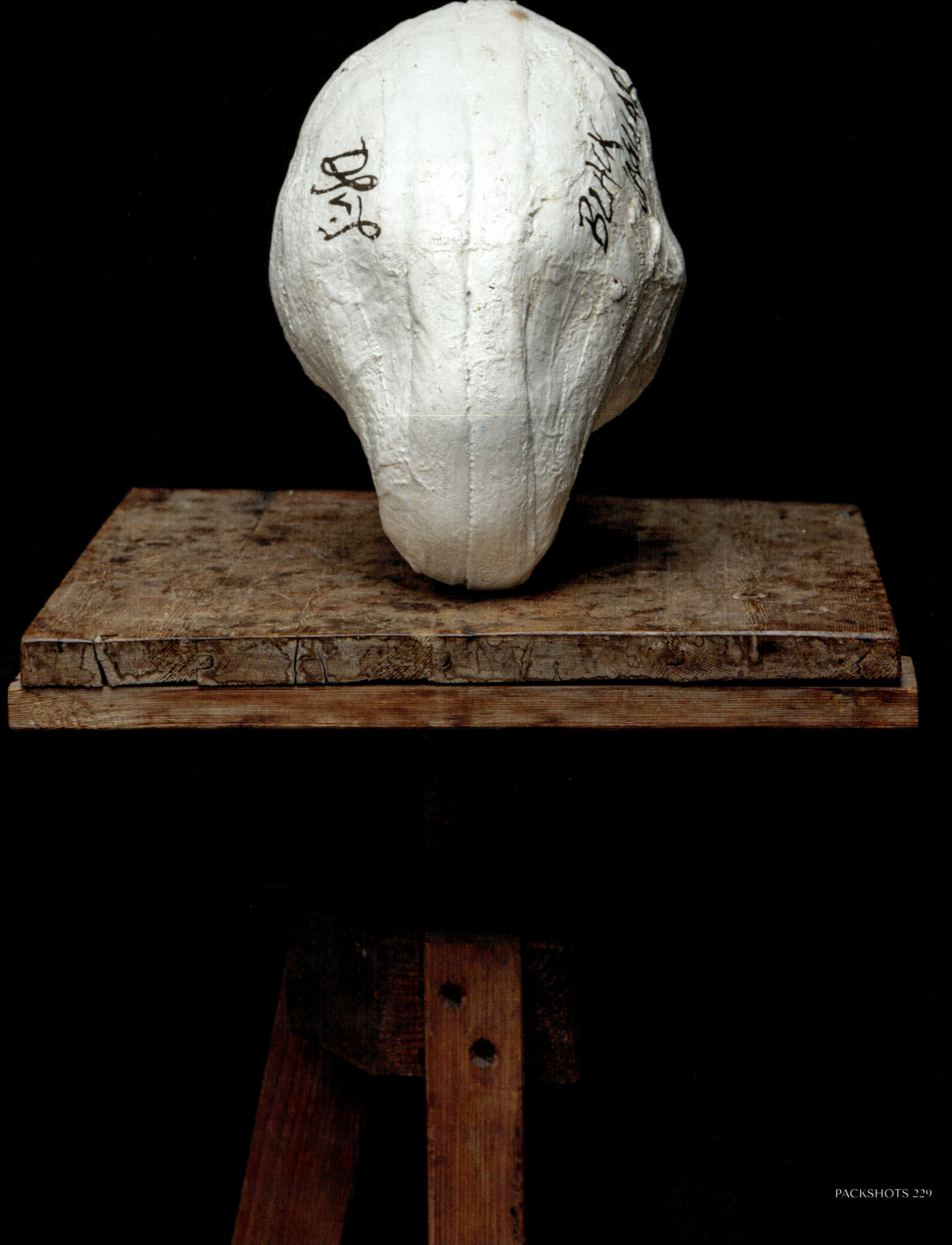

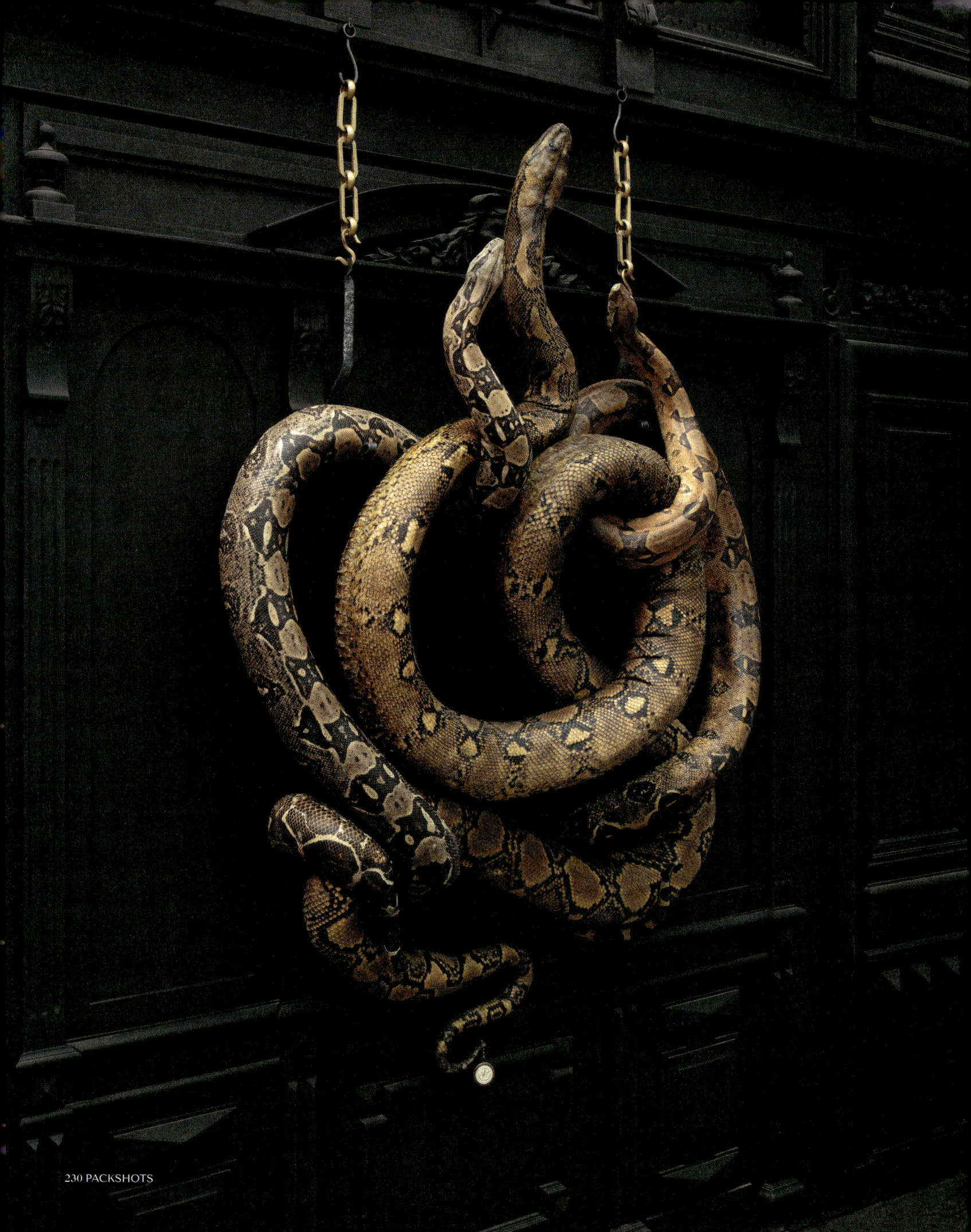

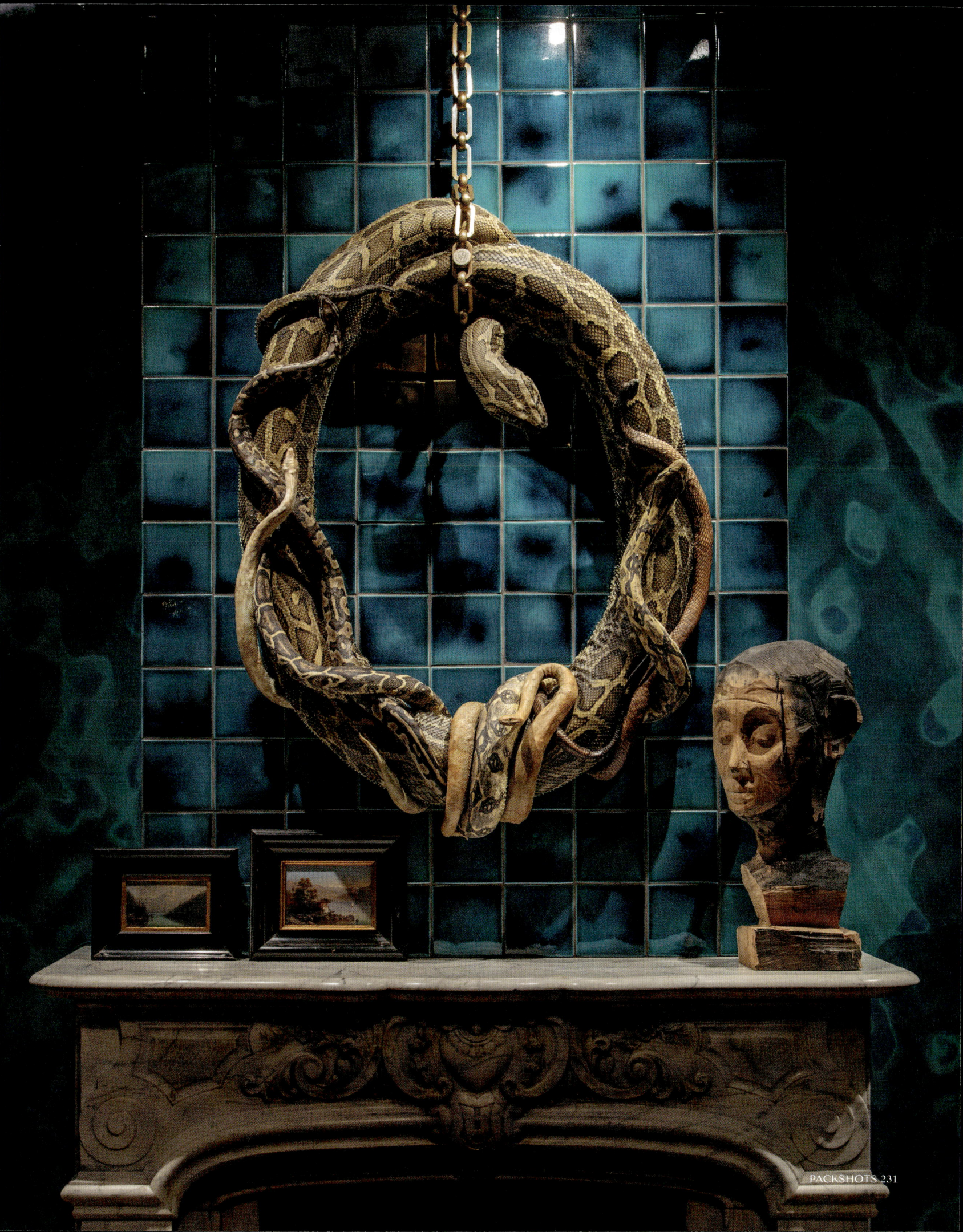

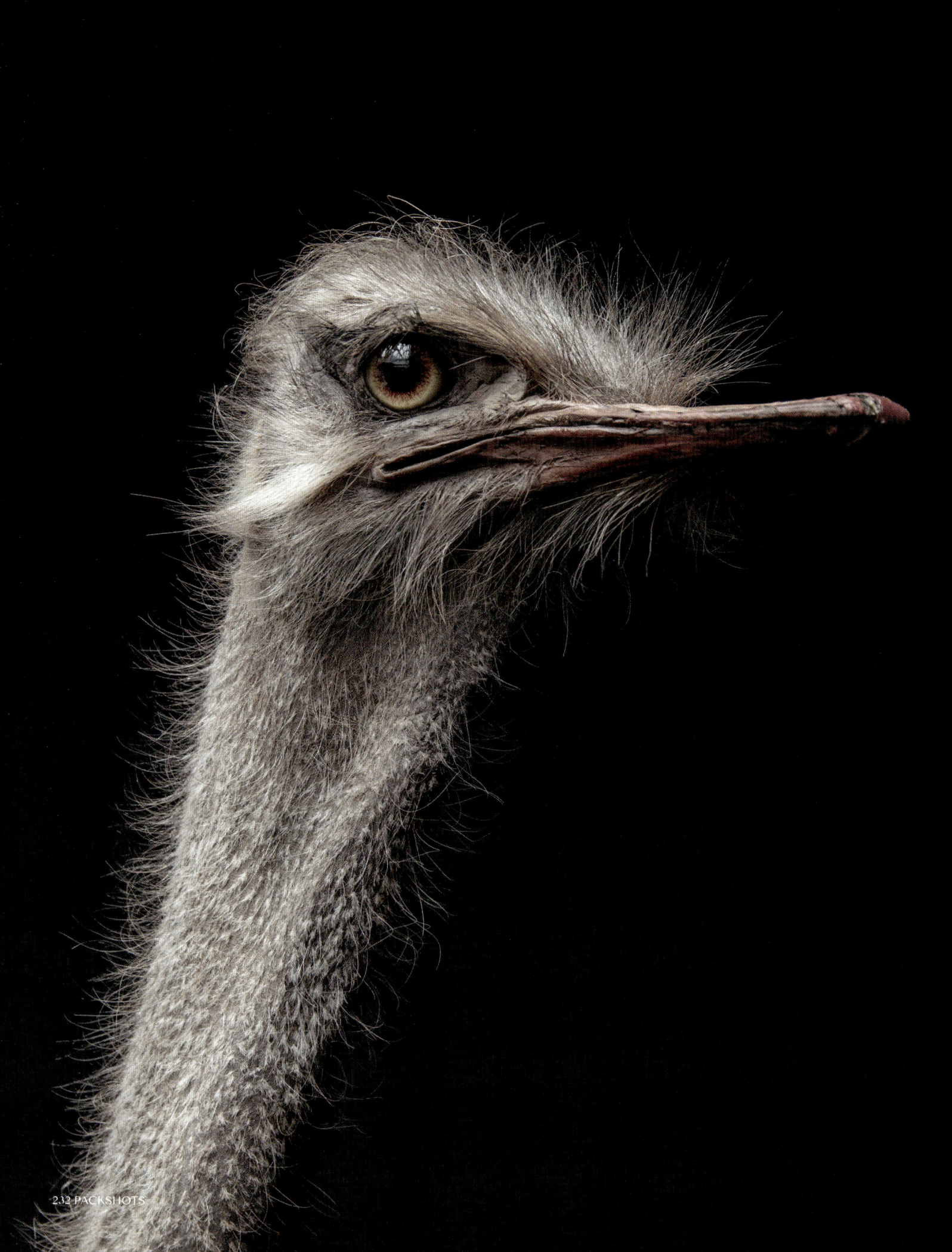

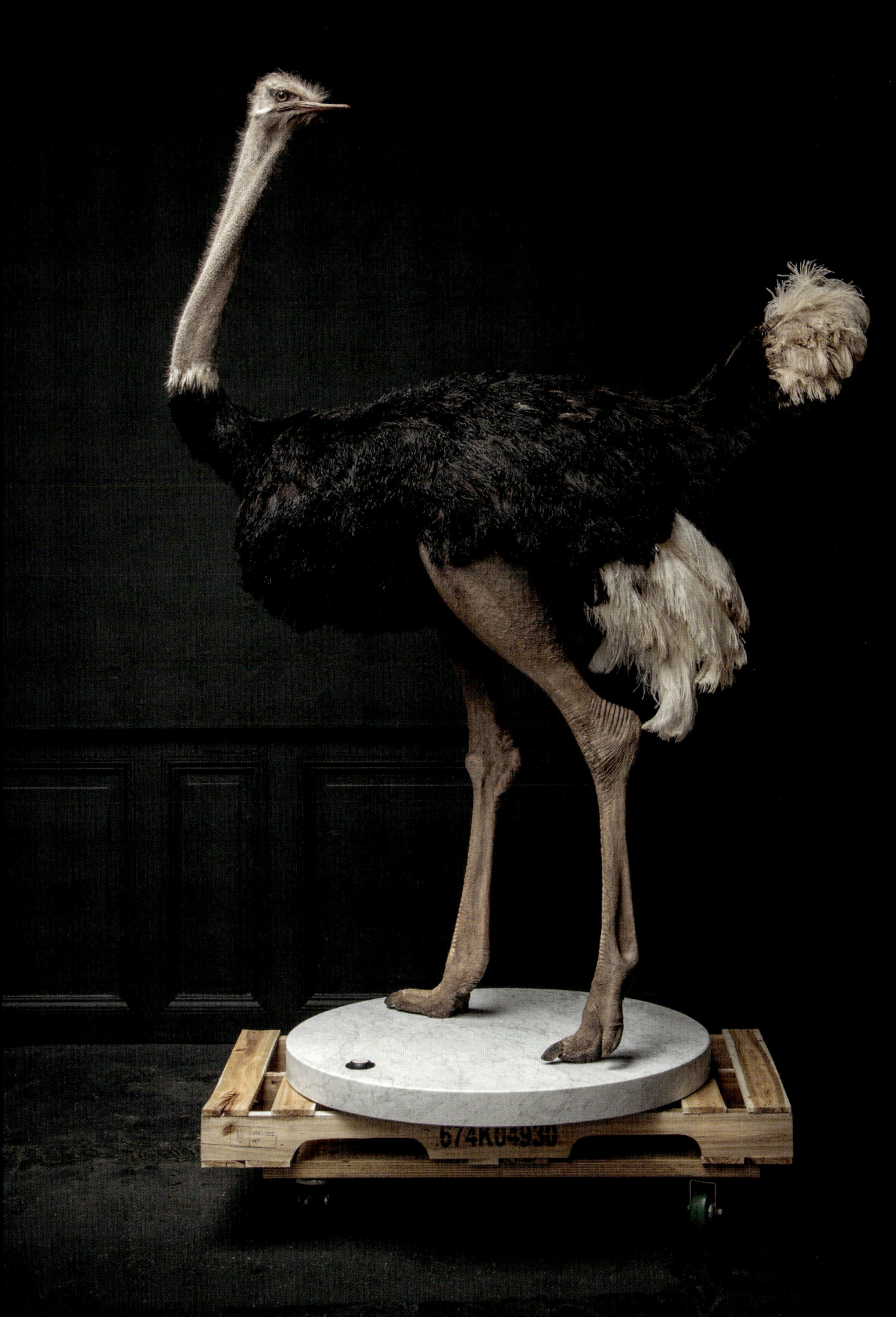

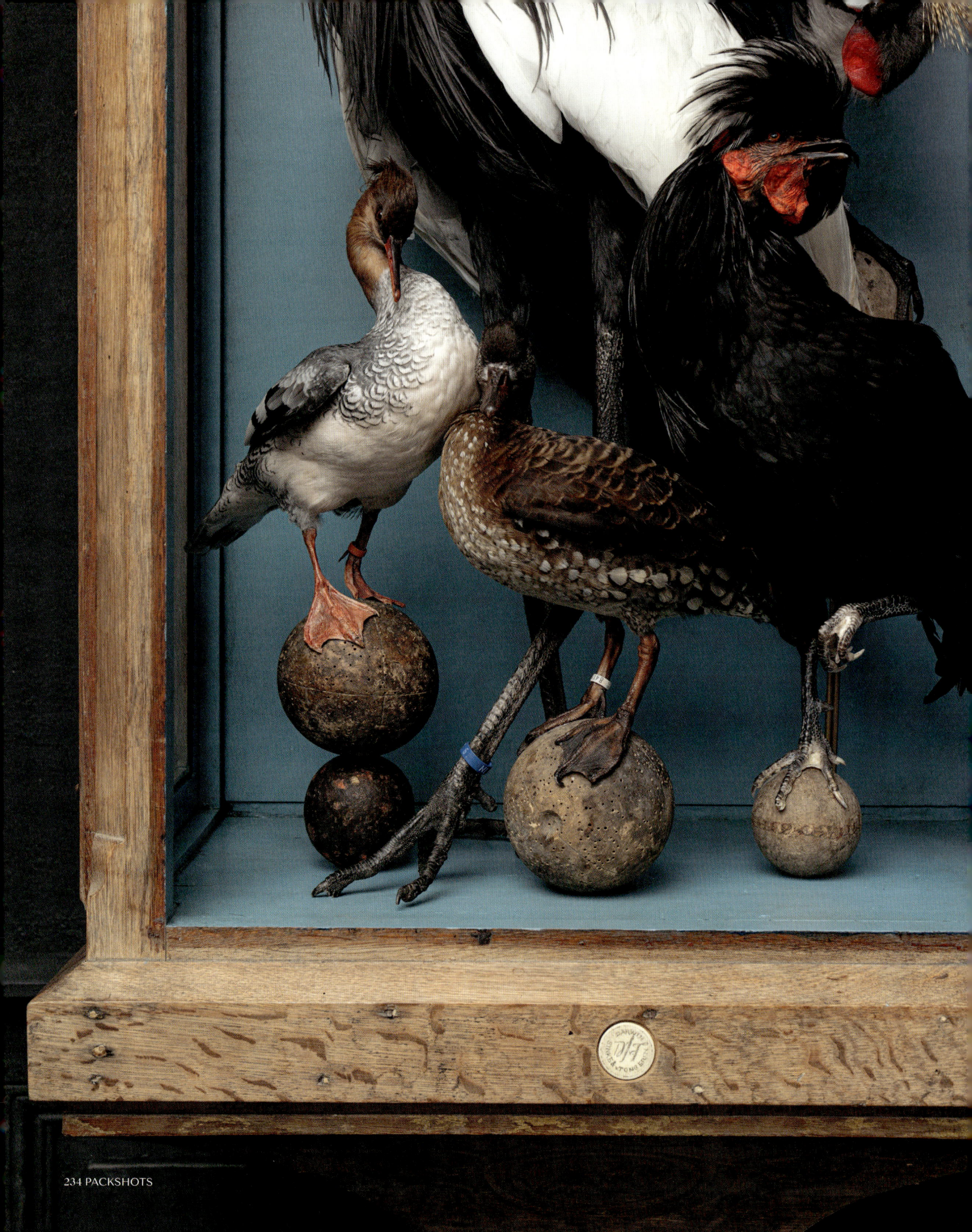

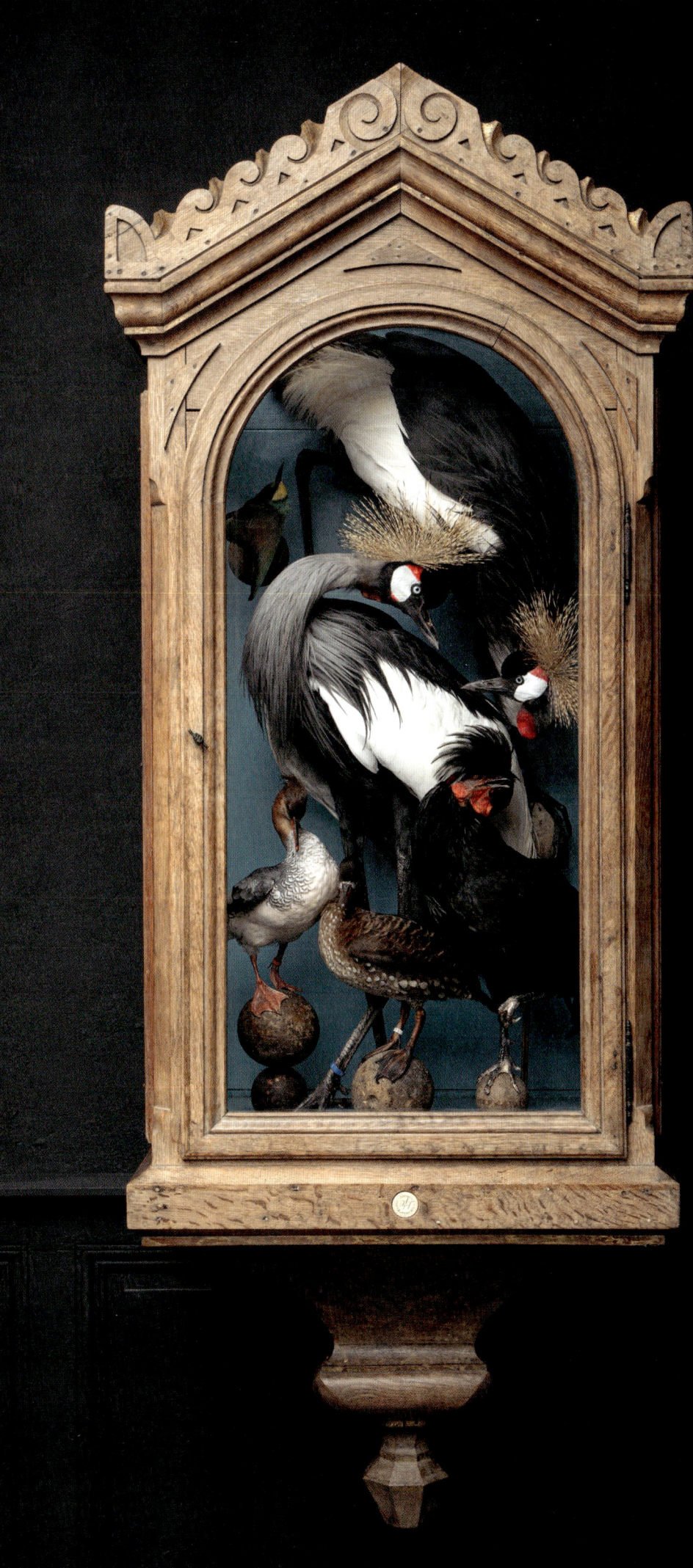

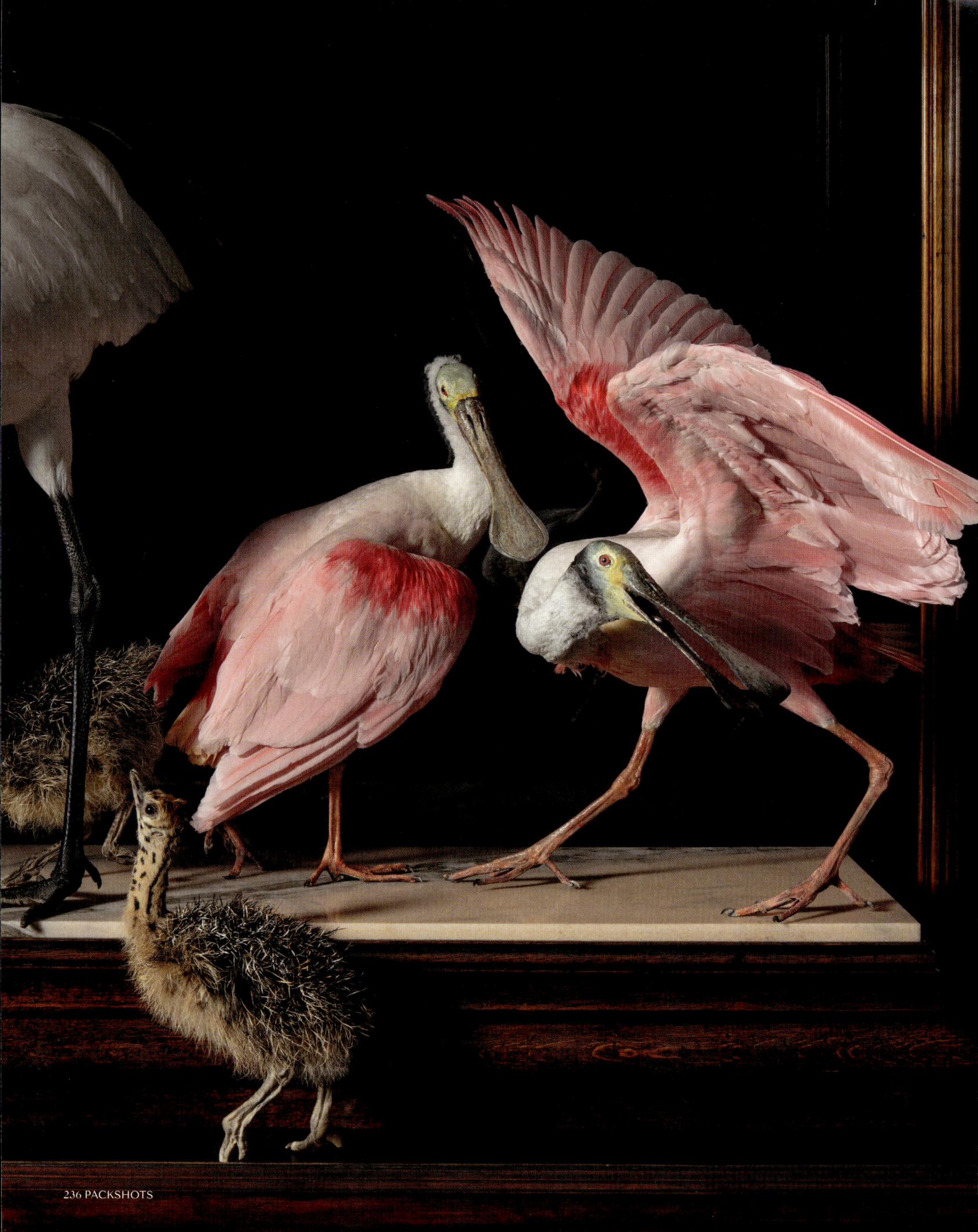

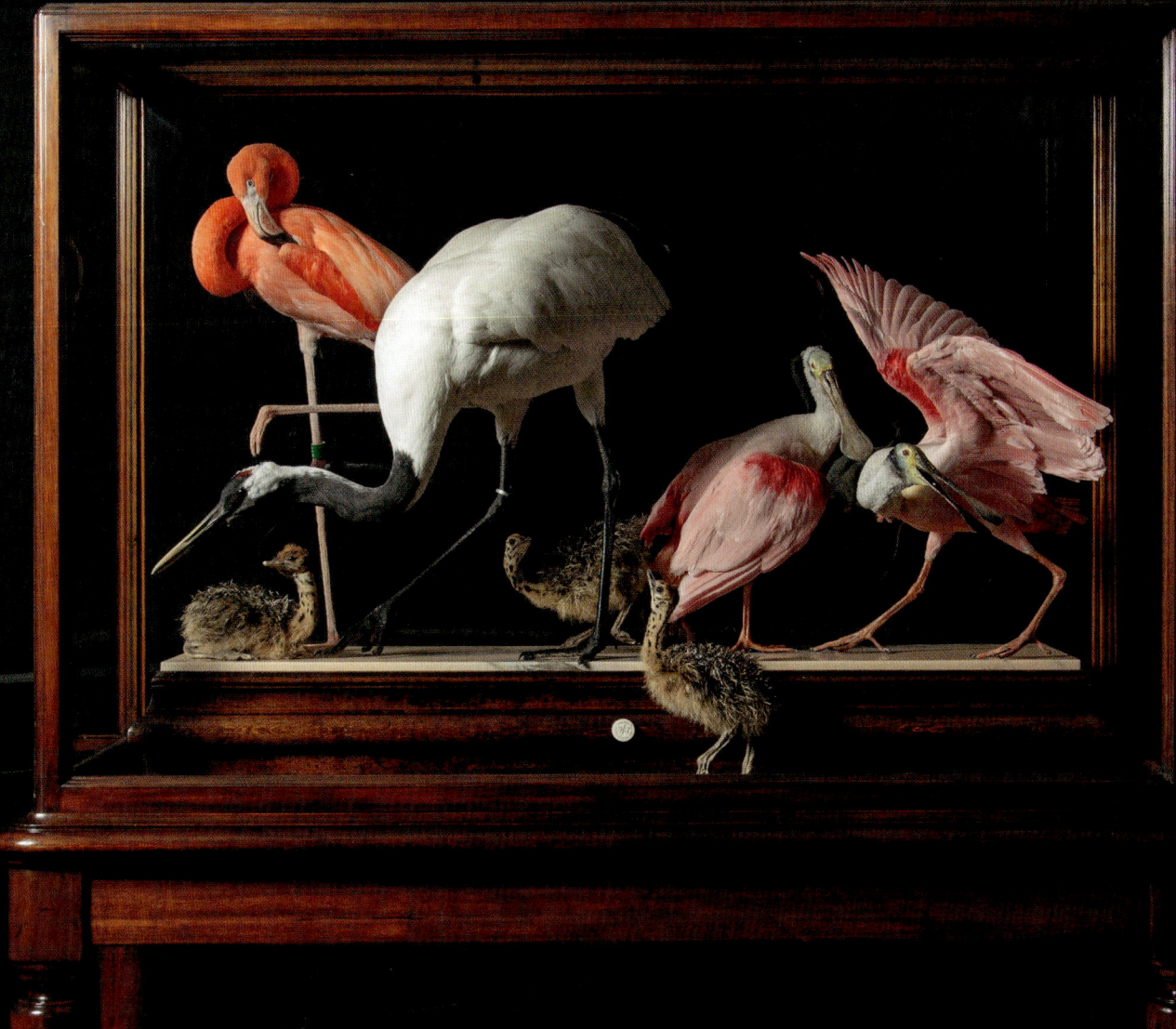

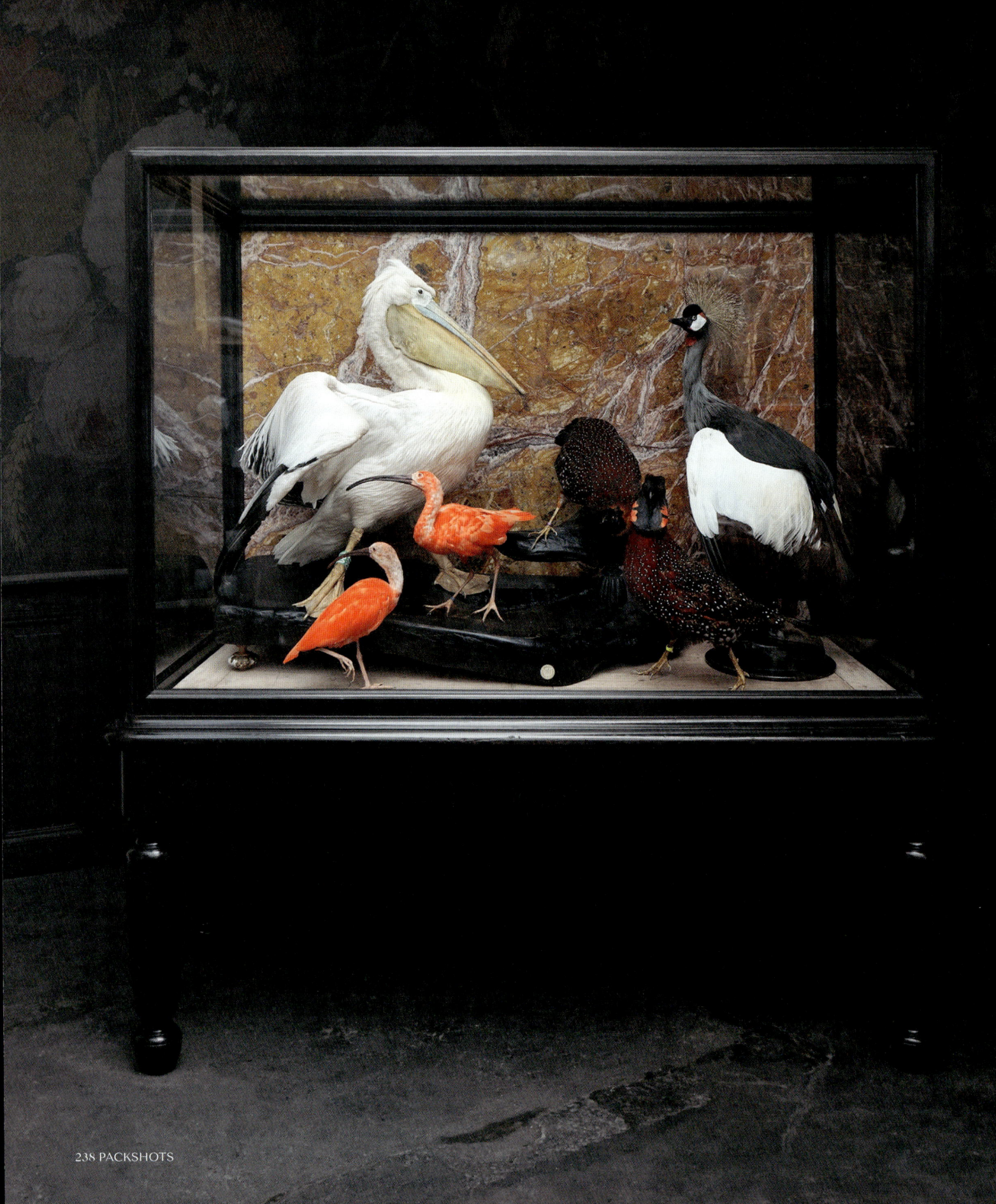

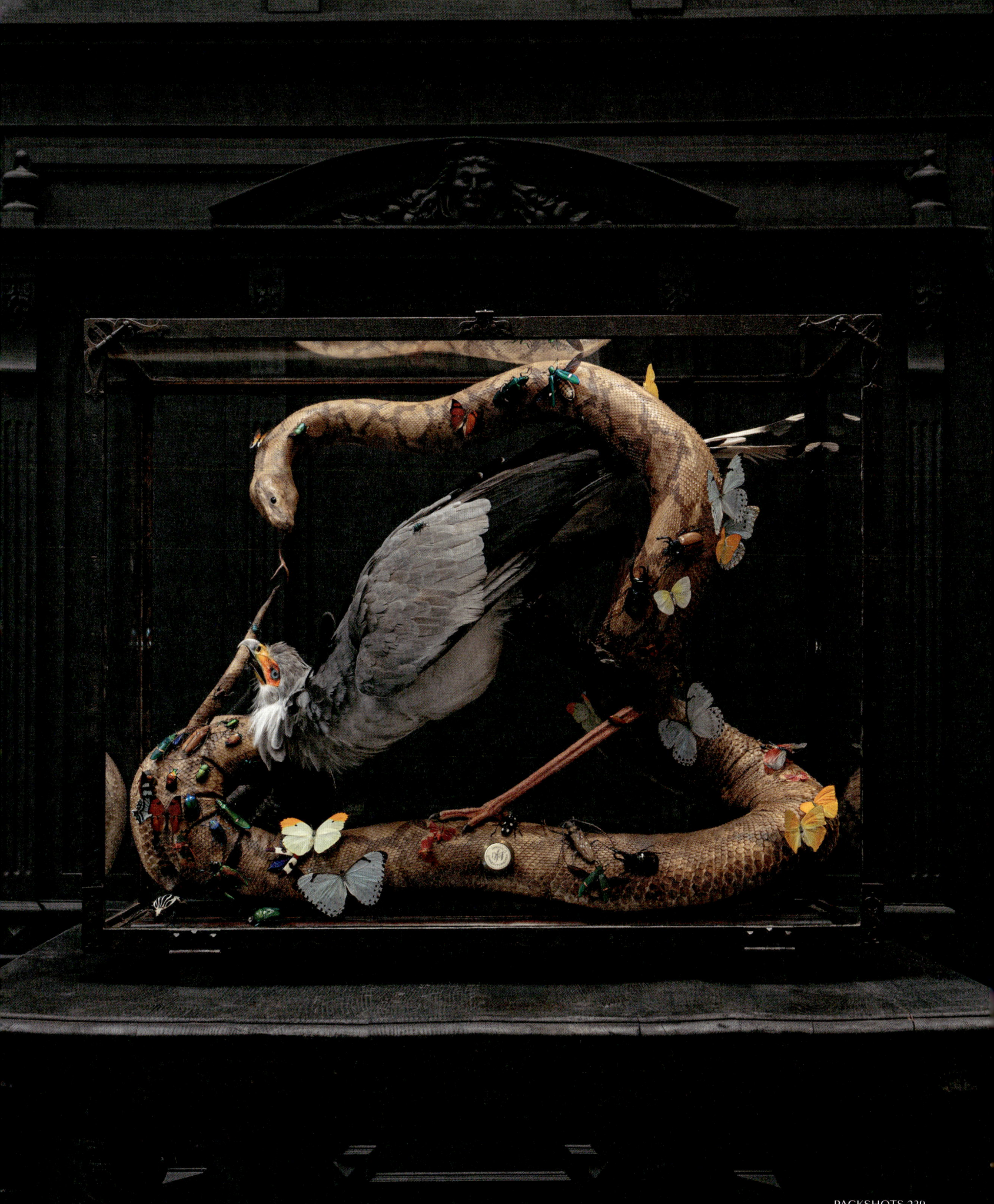

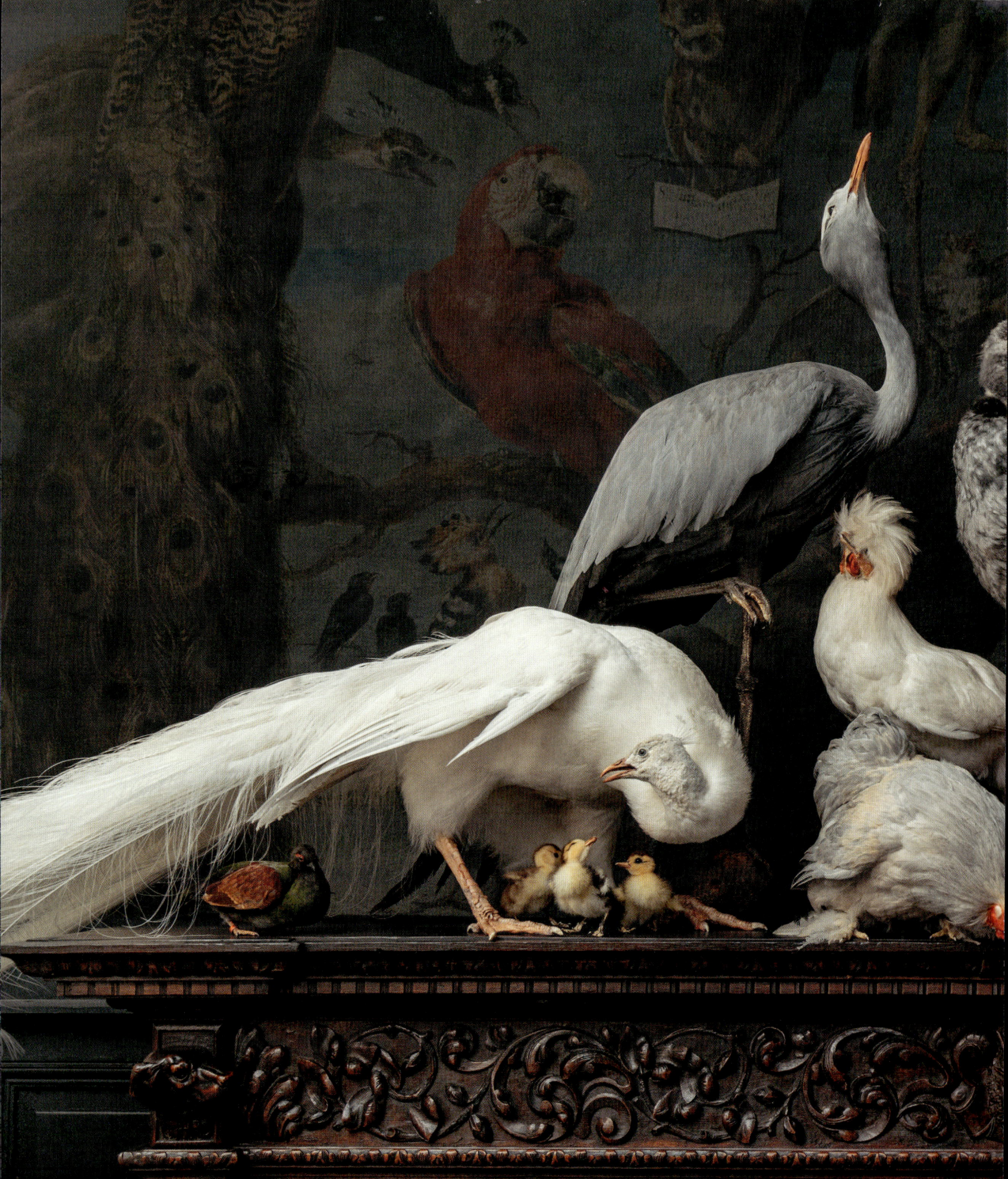

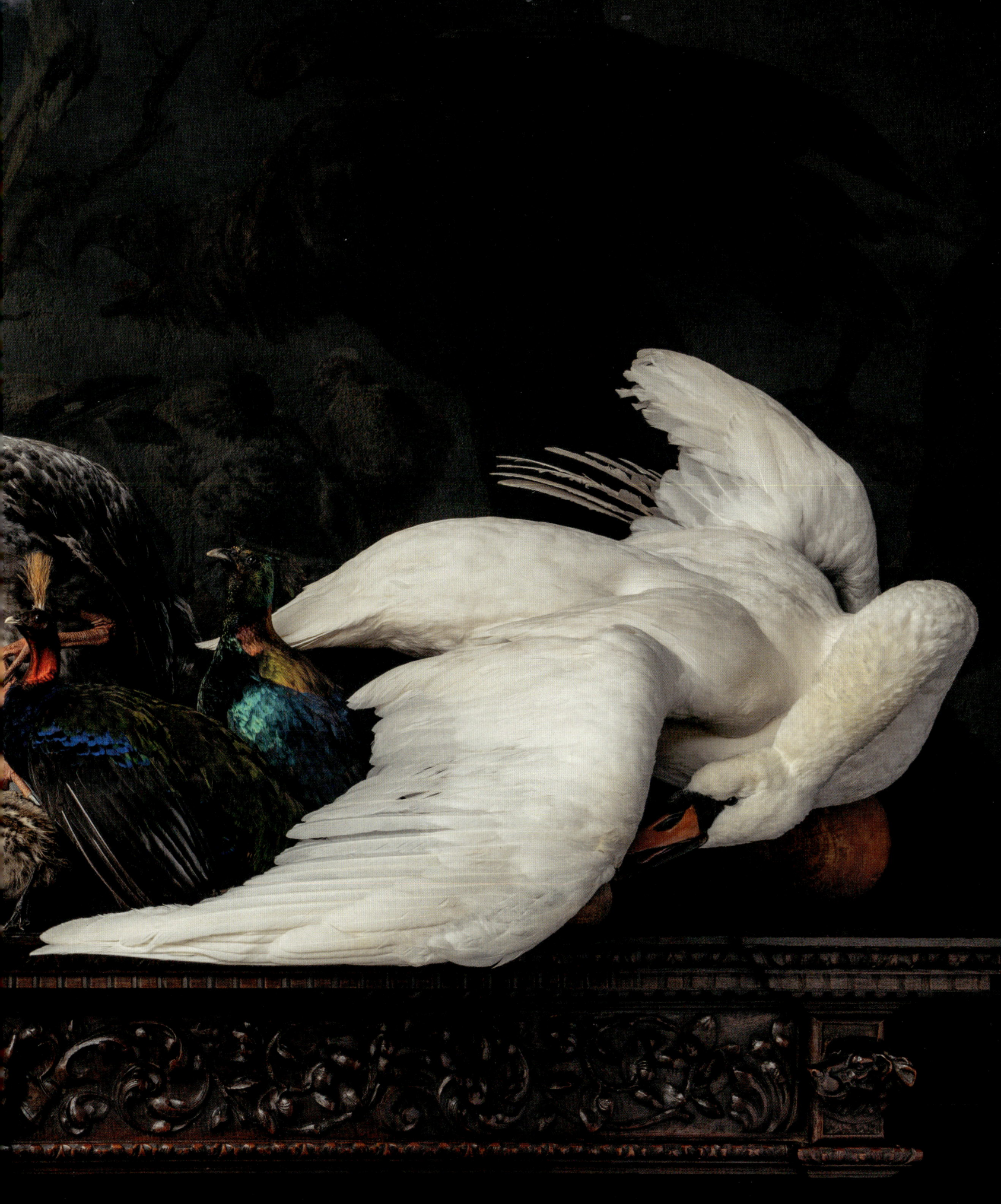

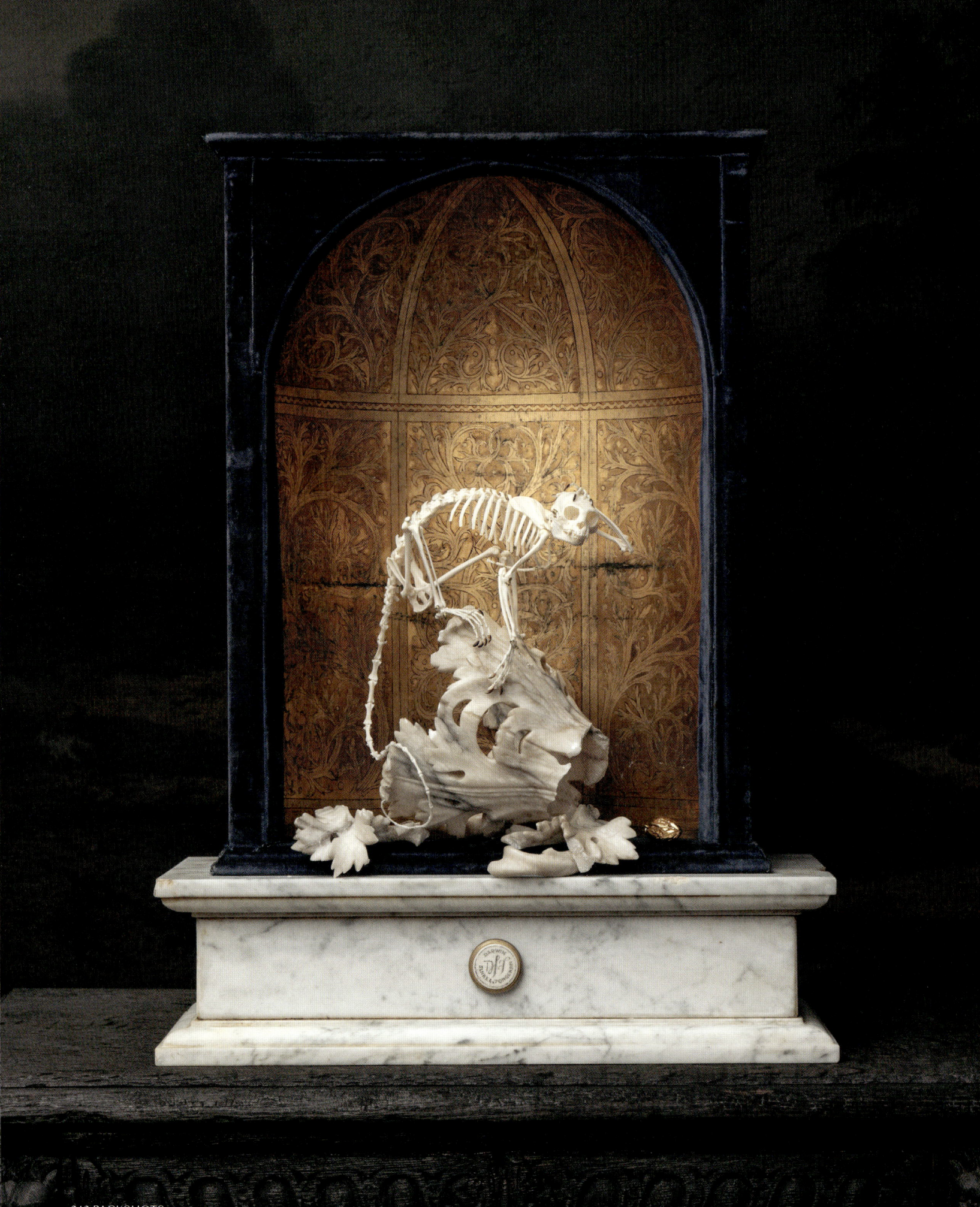

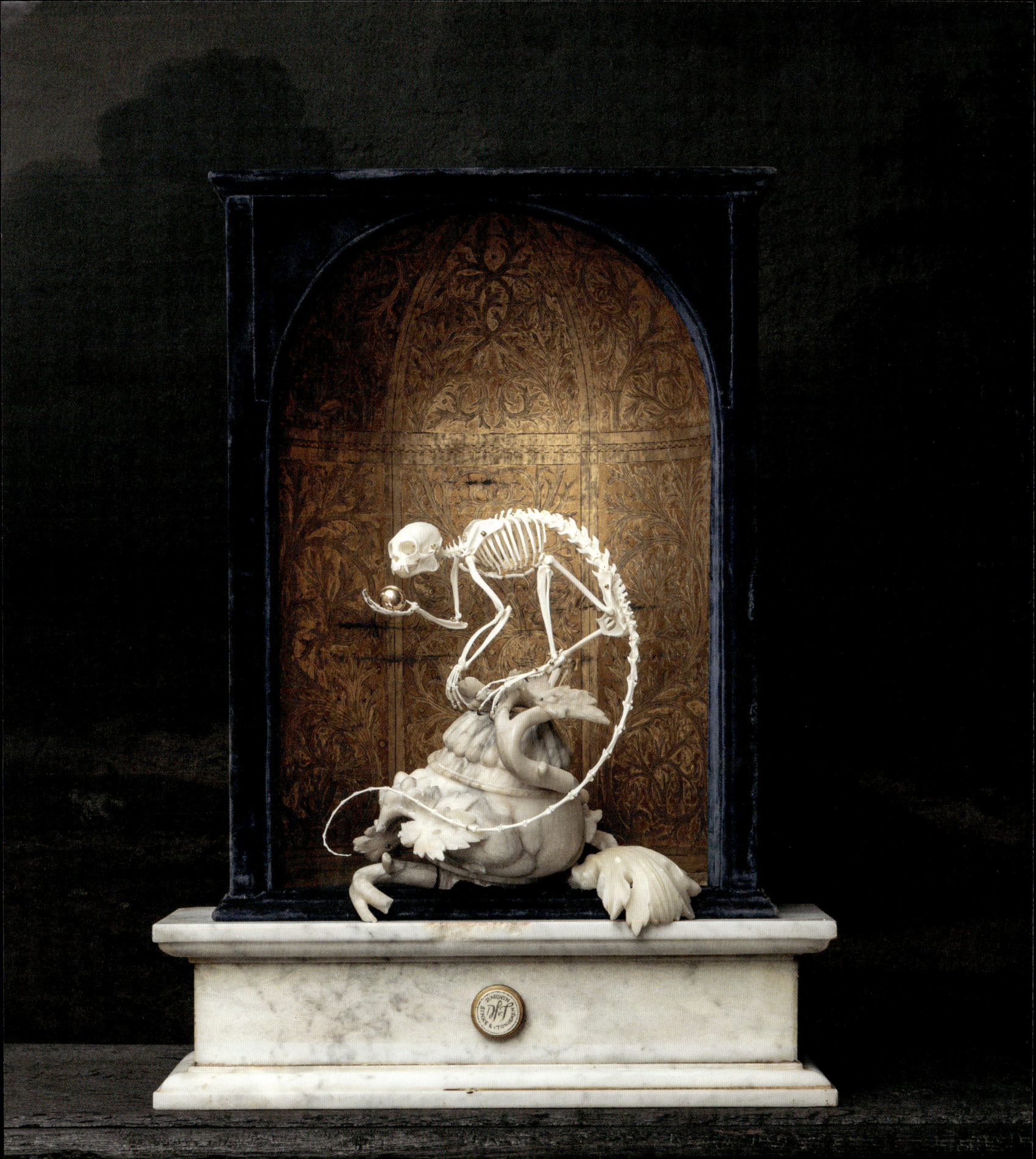

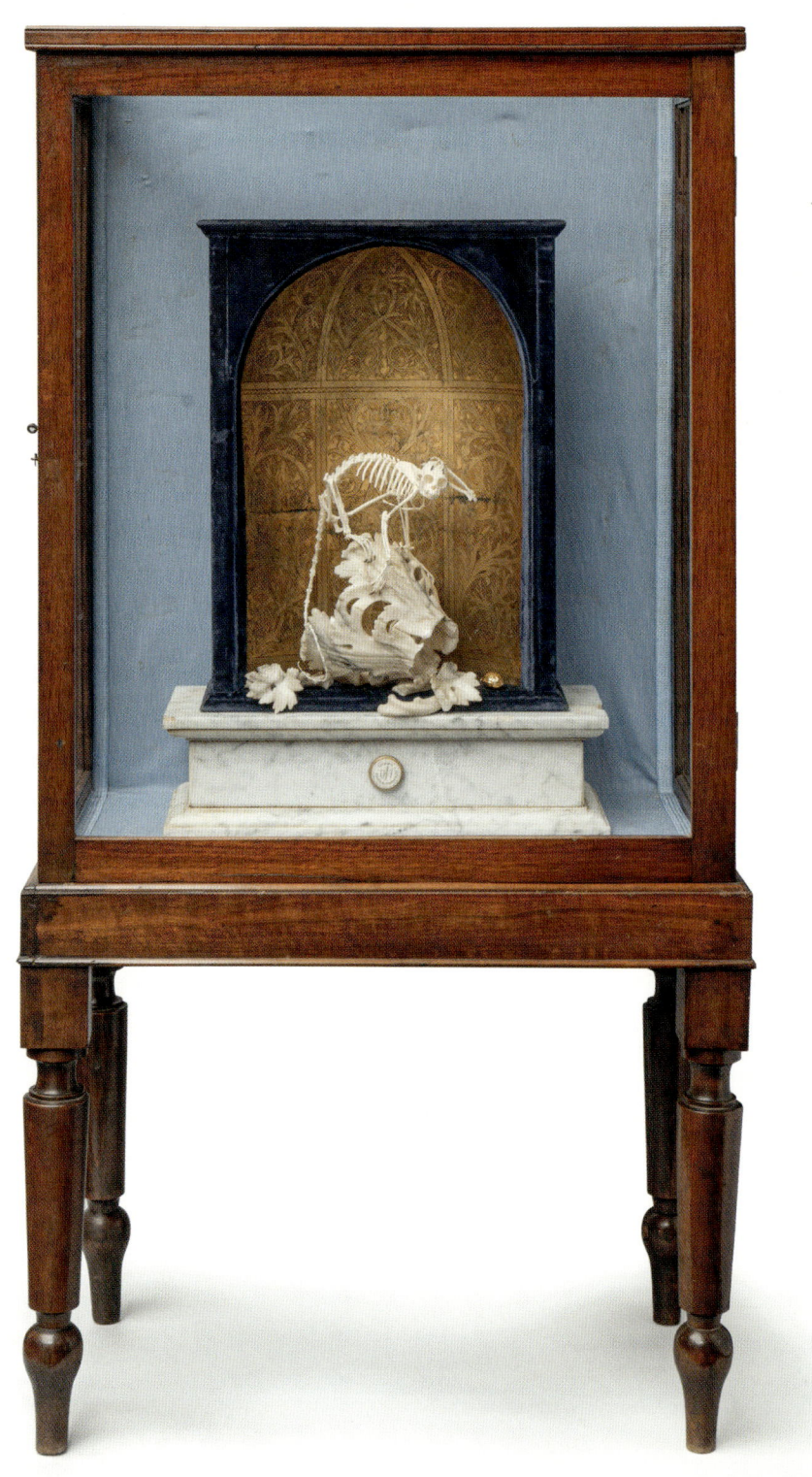

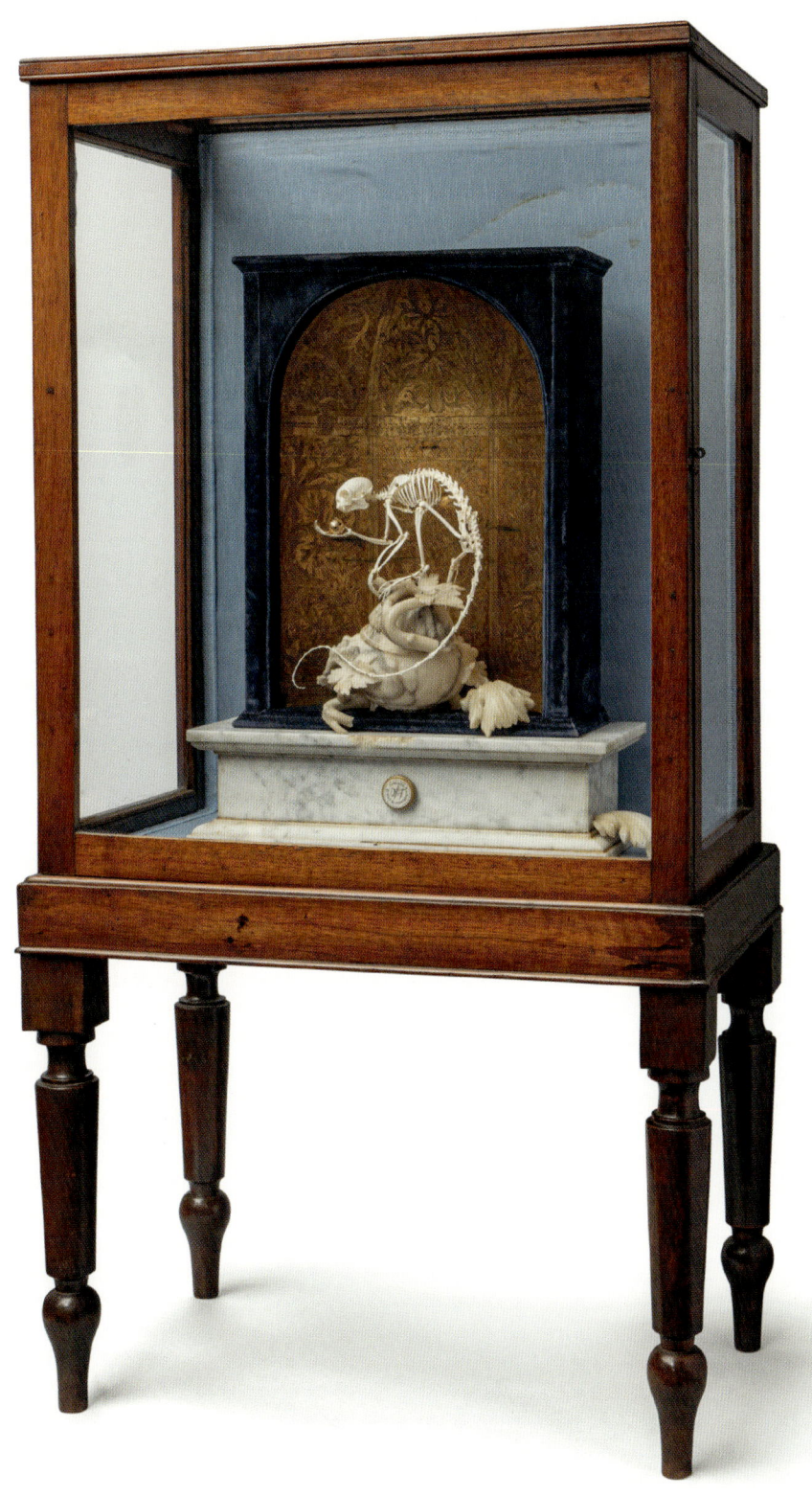

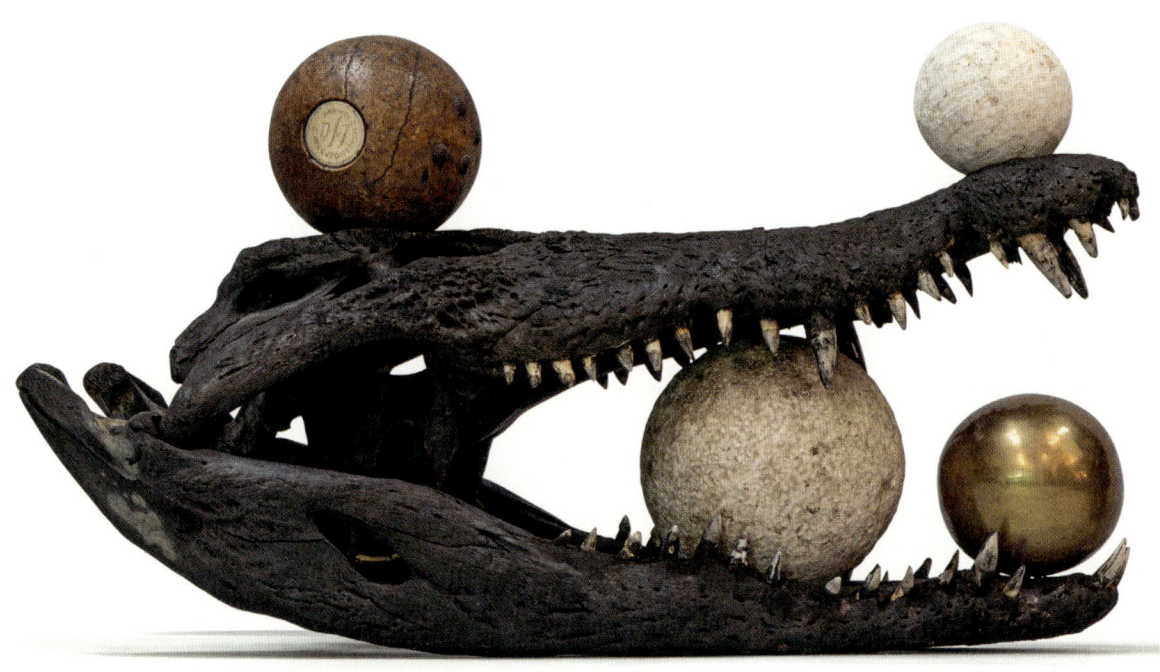

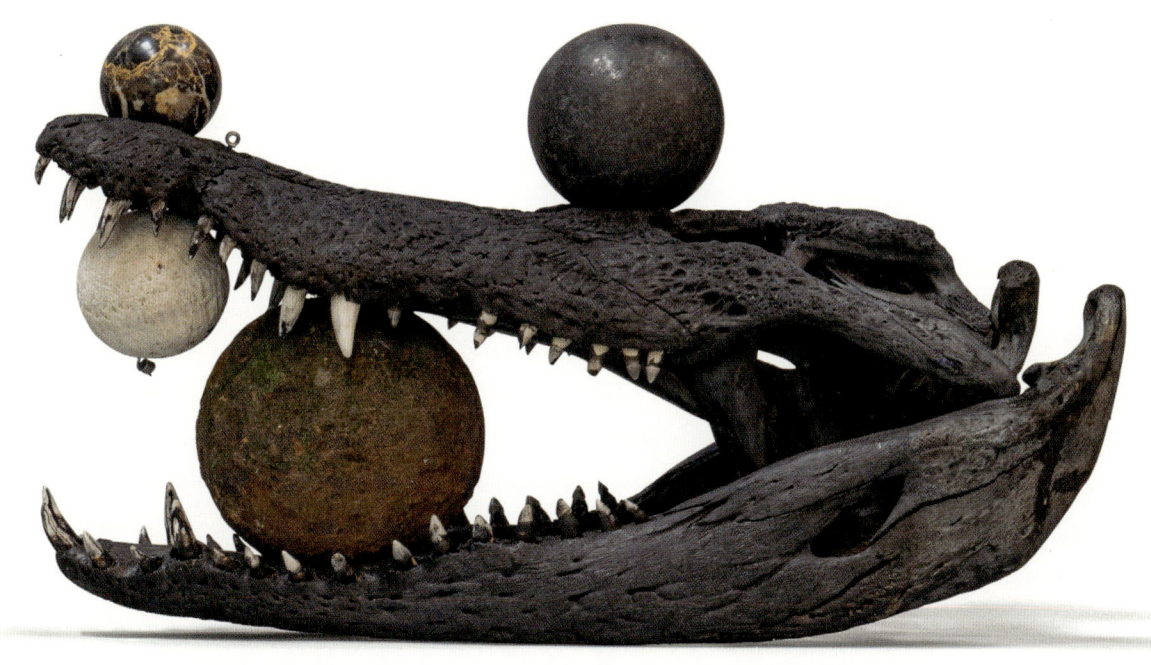

PACKSHOTS 247

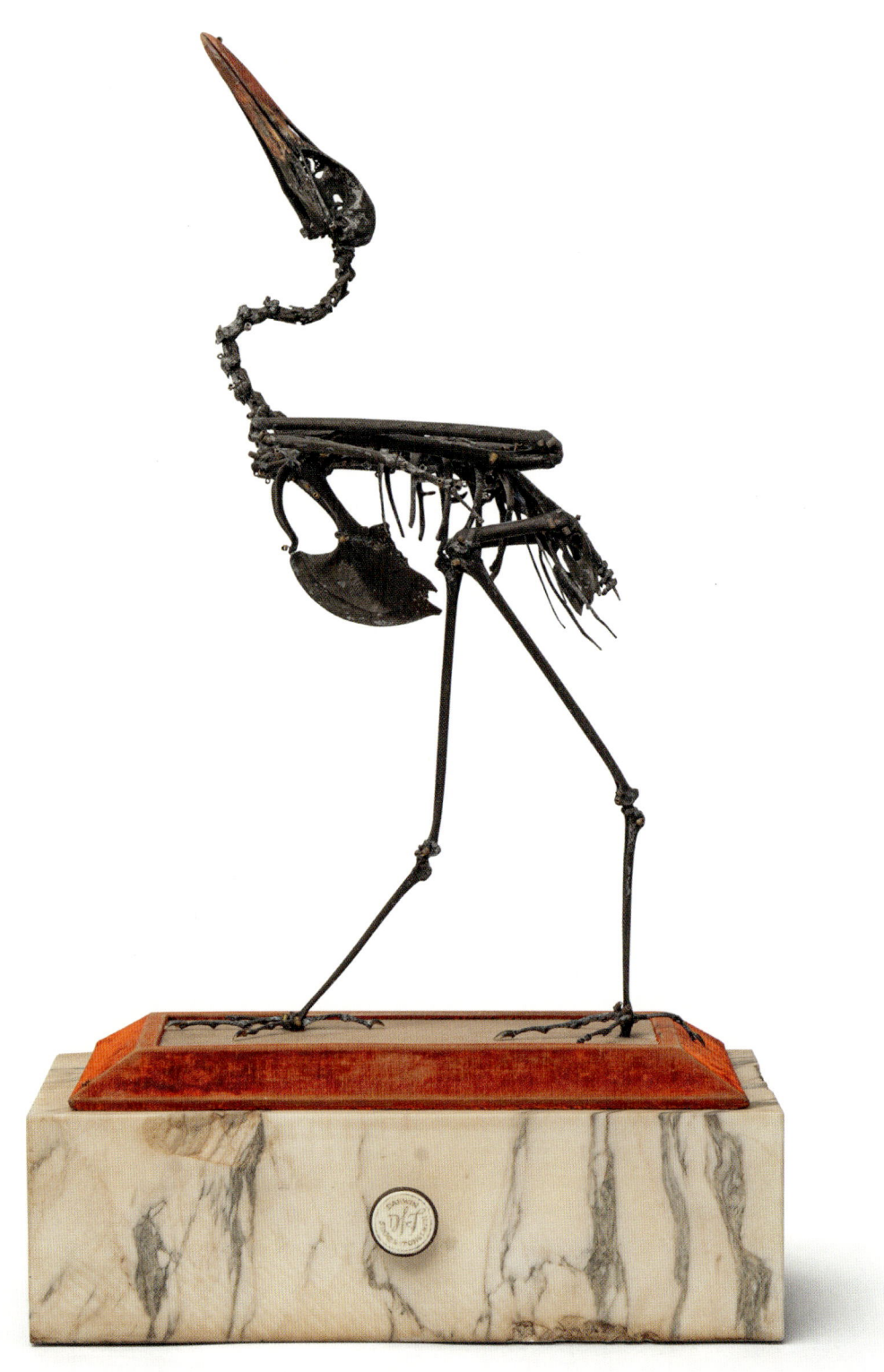

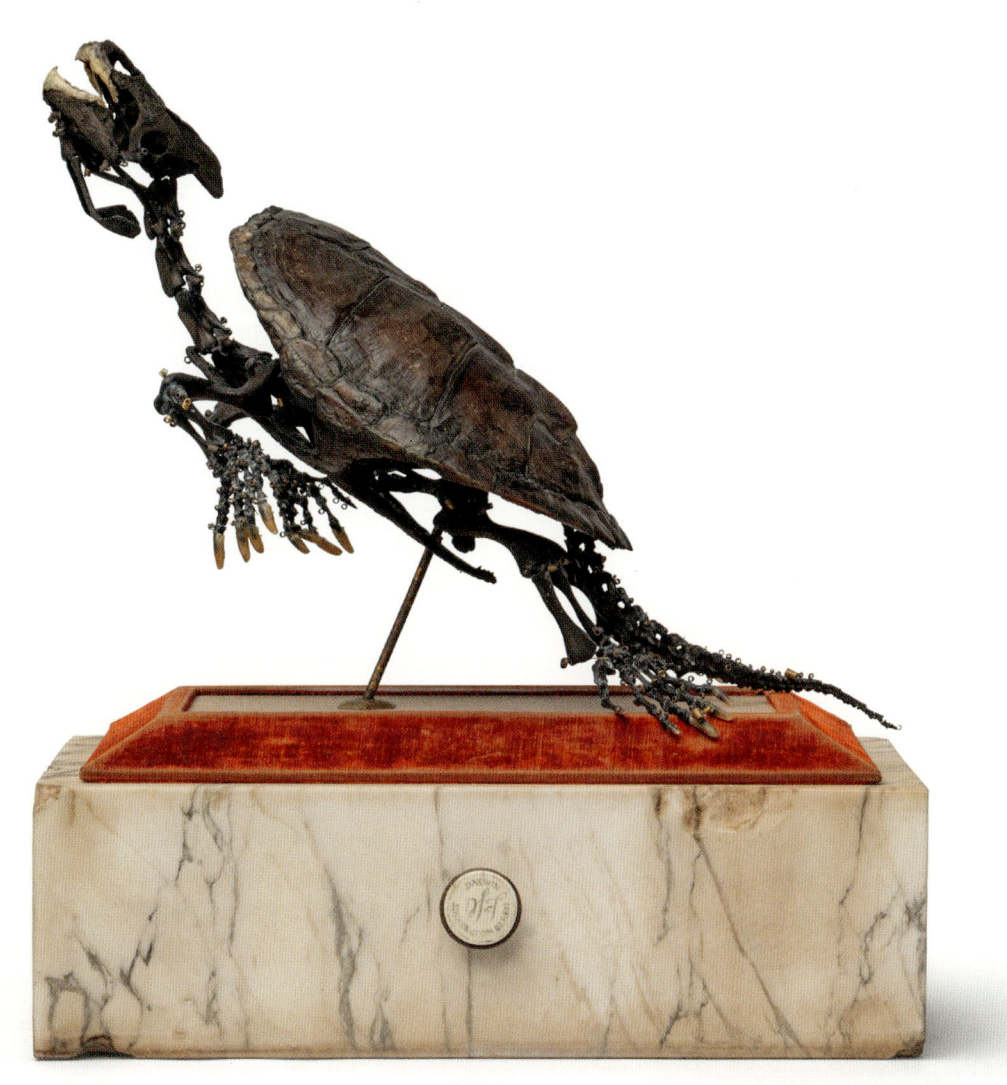

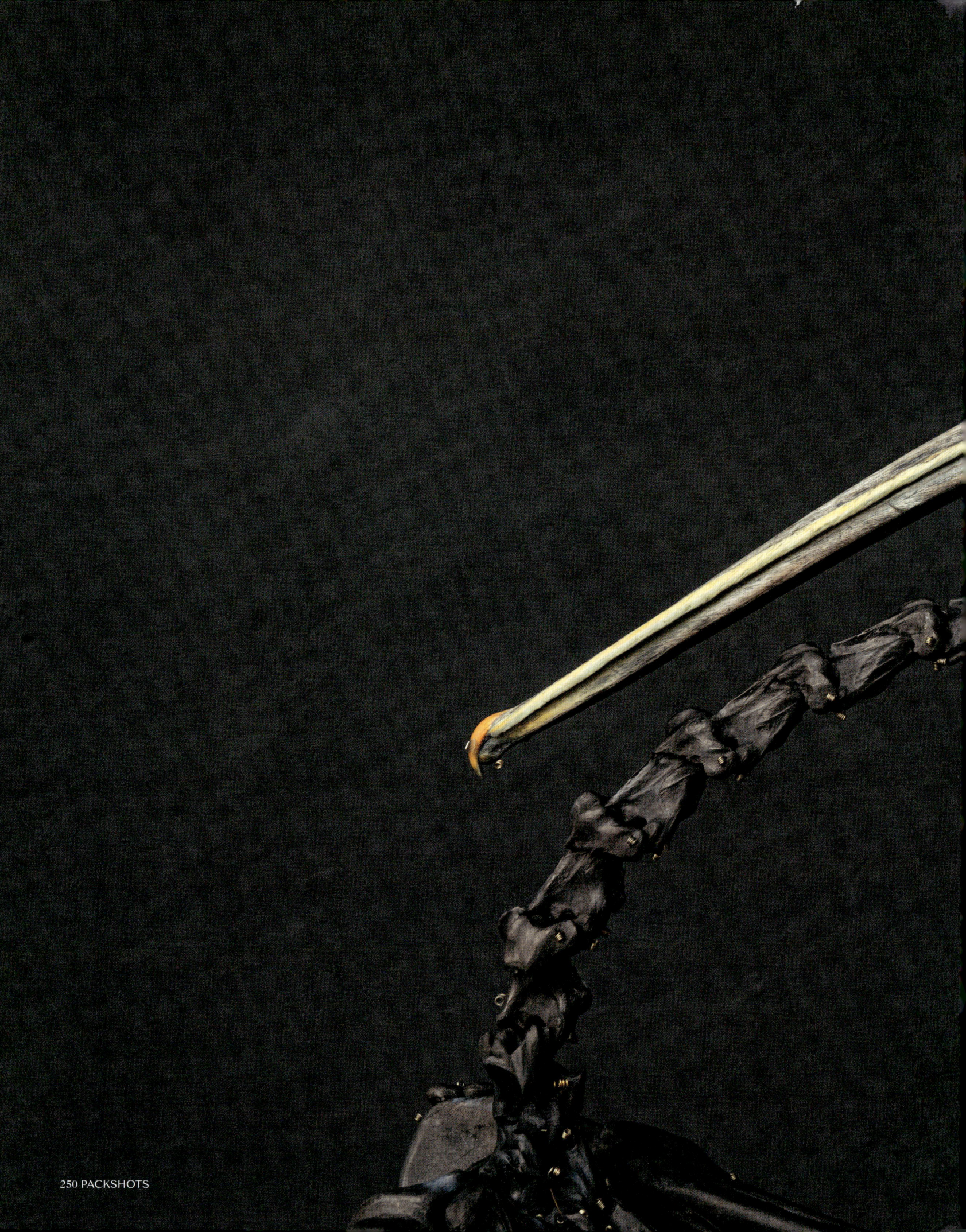

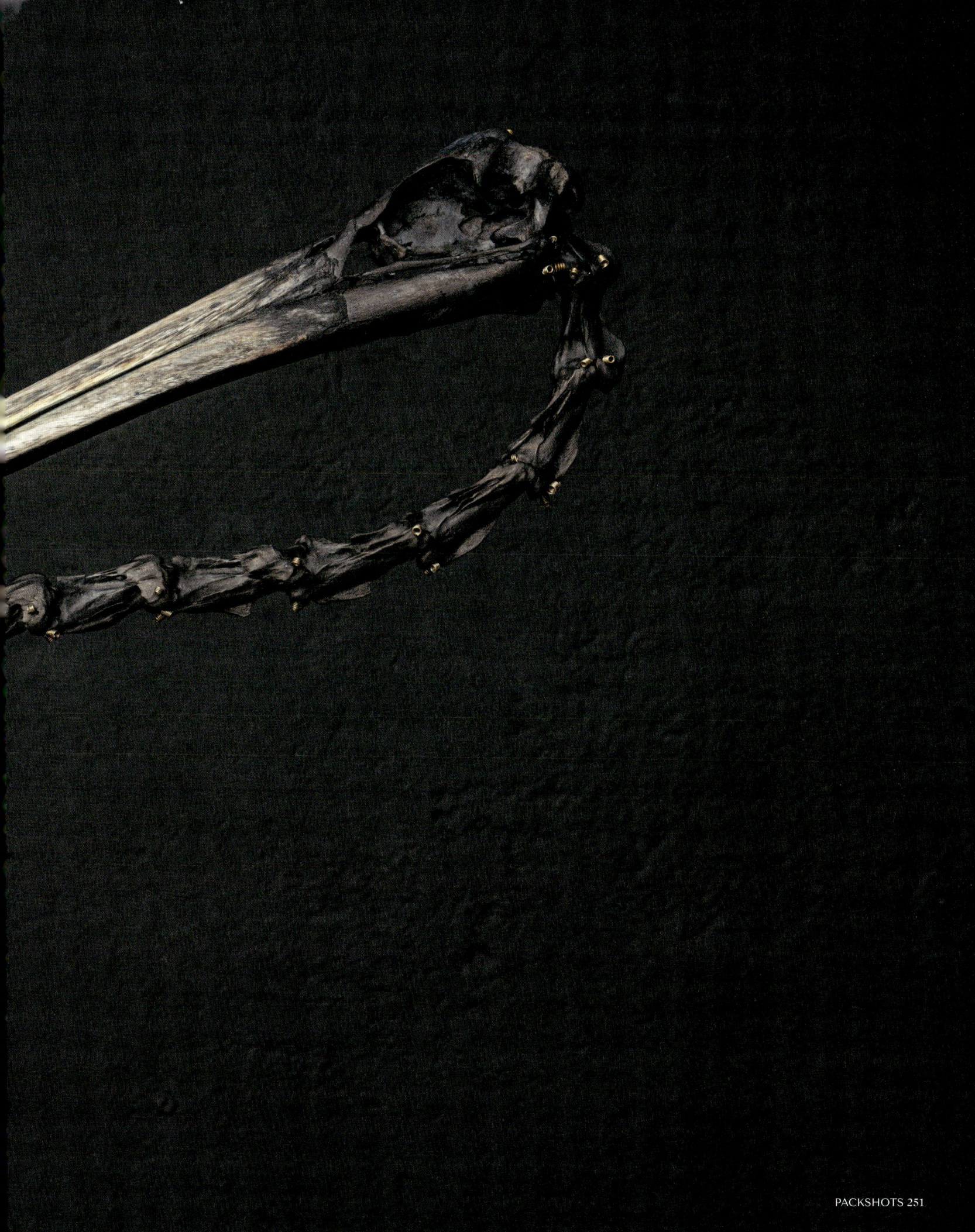

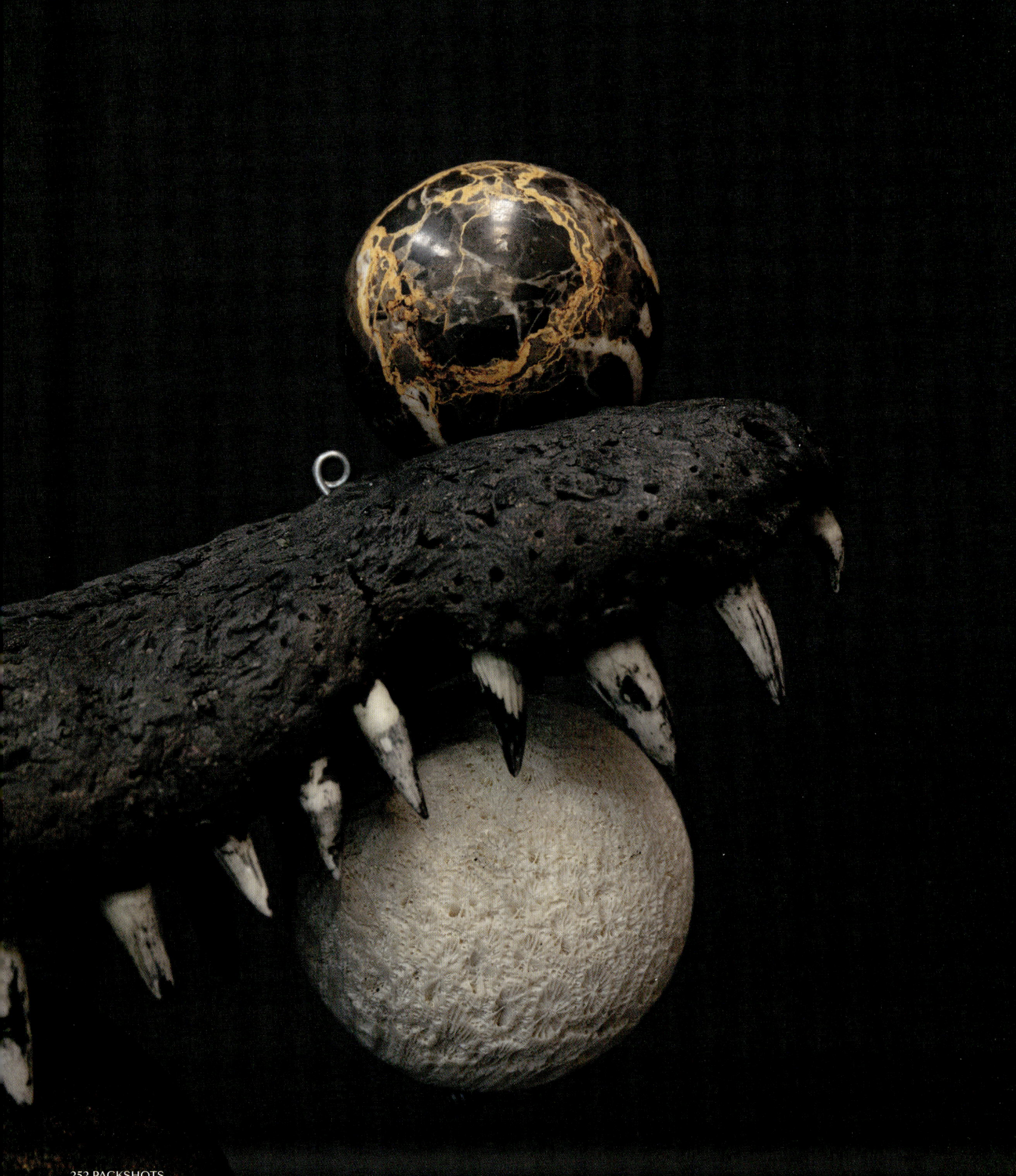

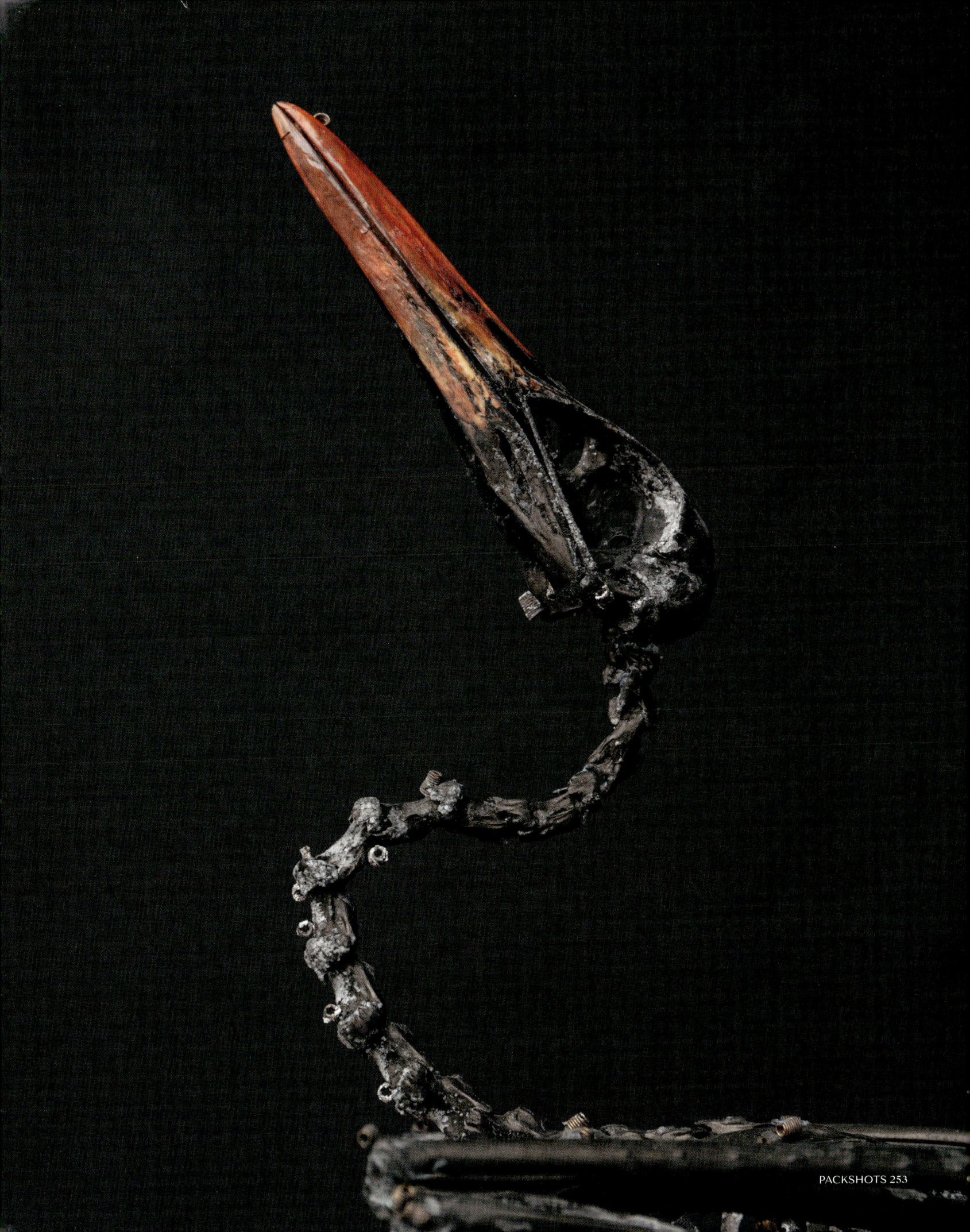

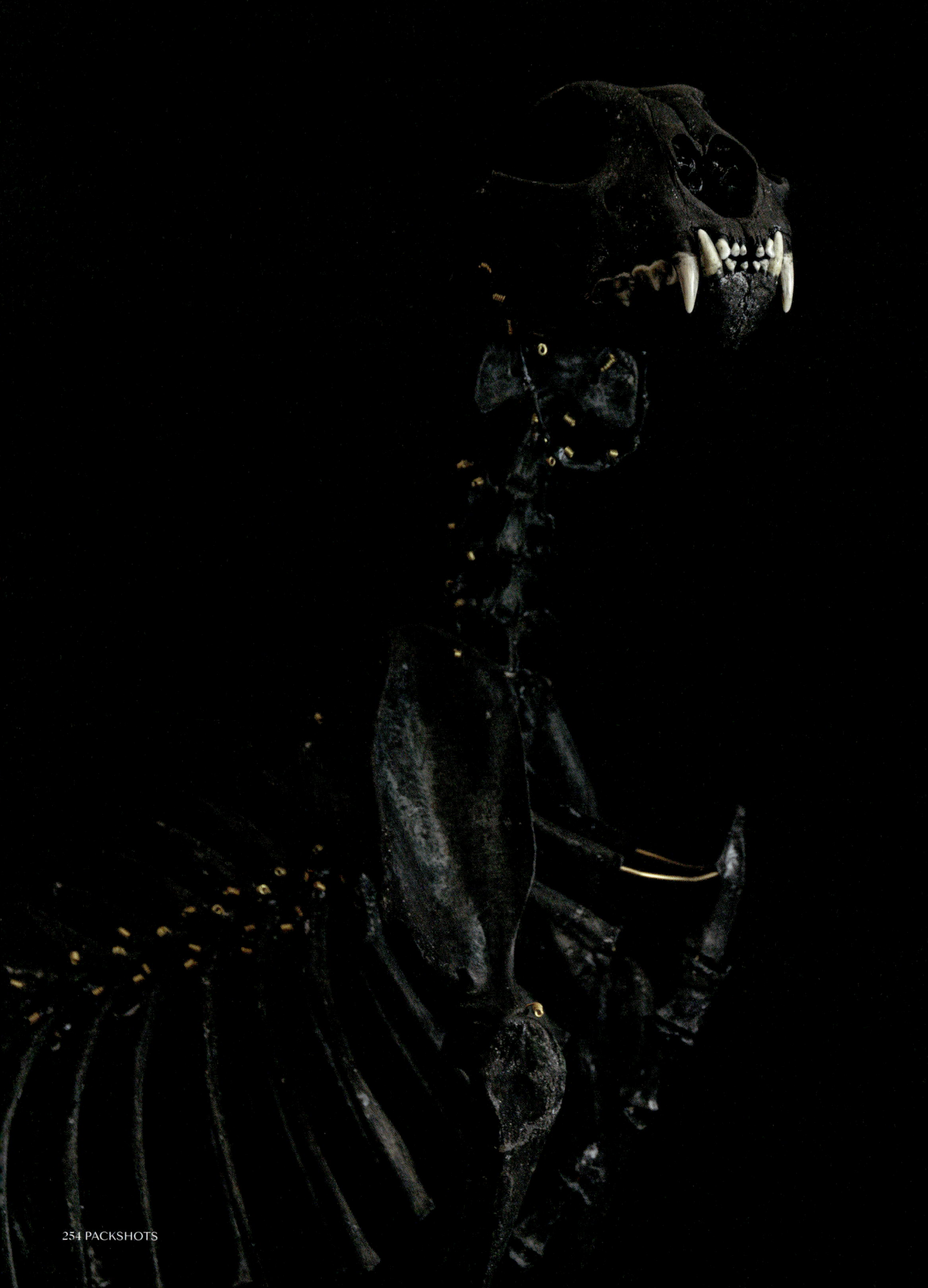

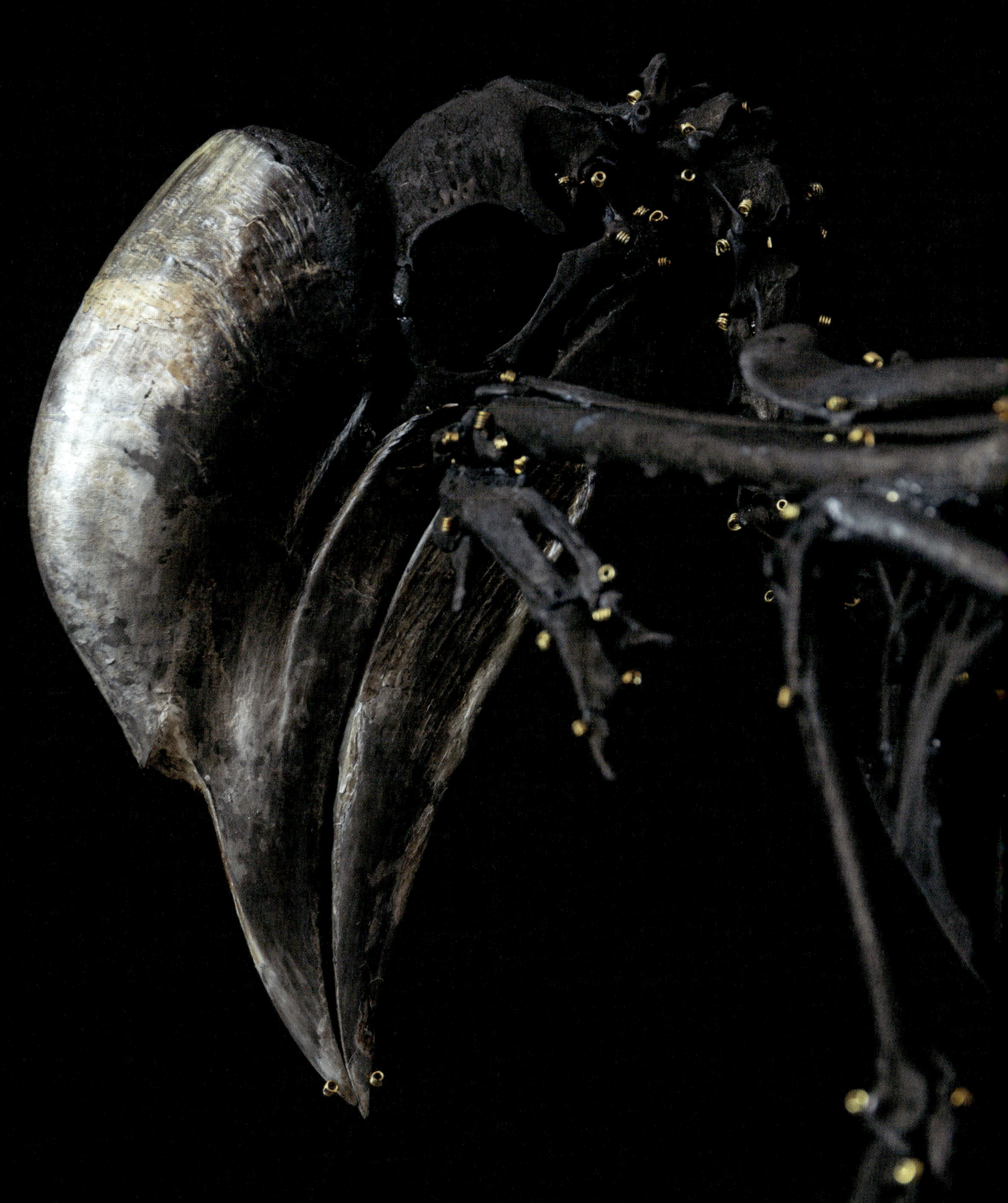

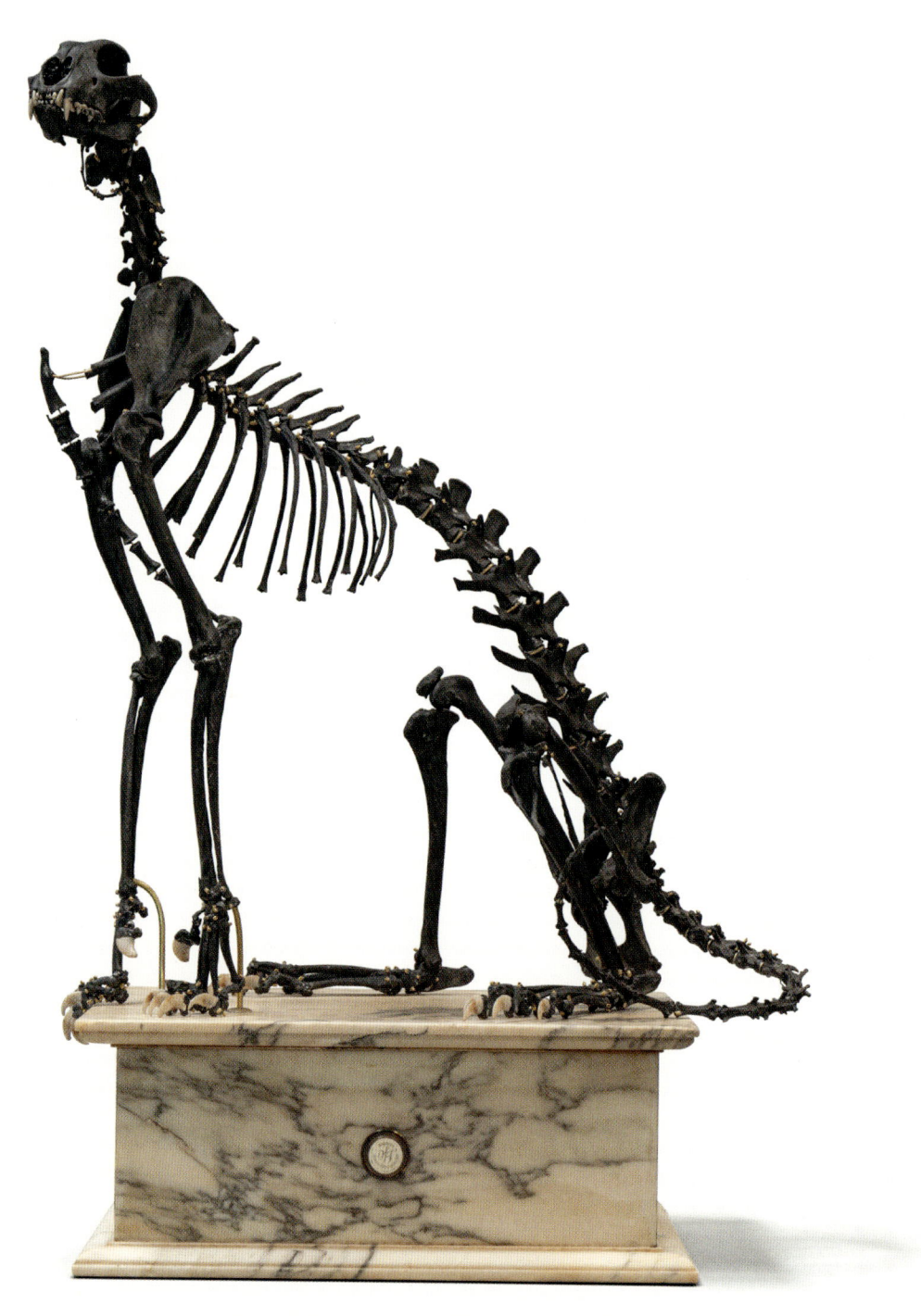

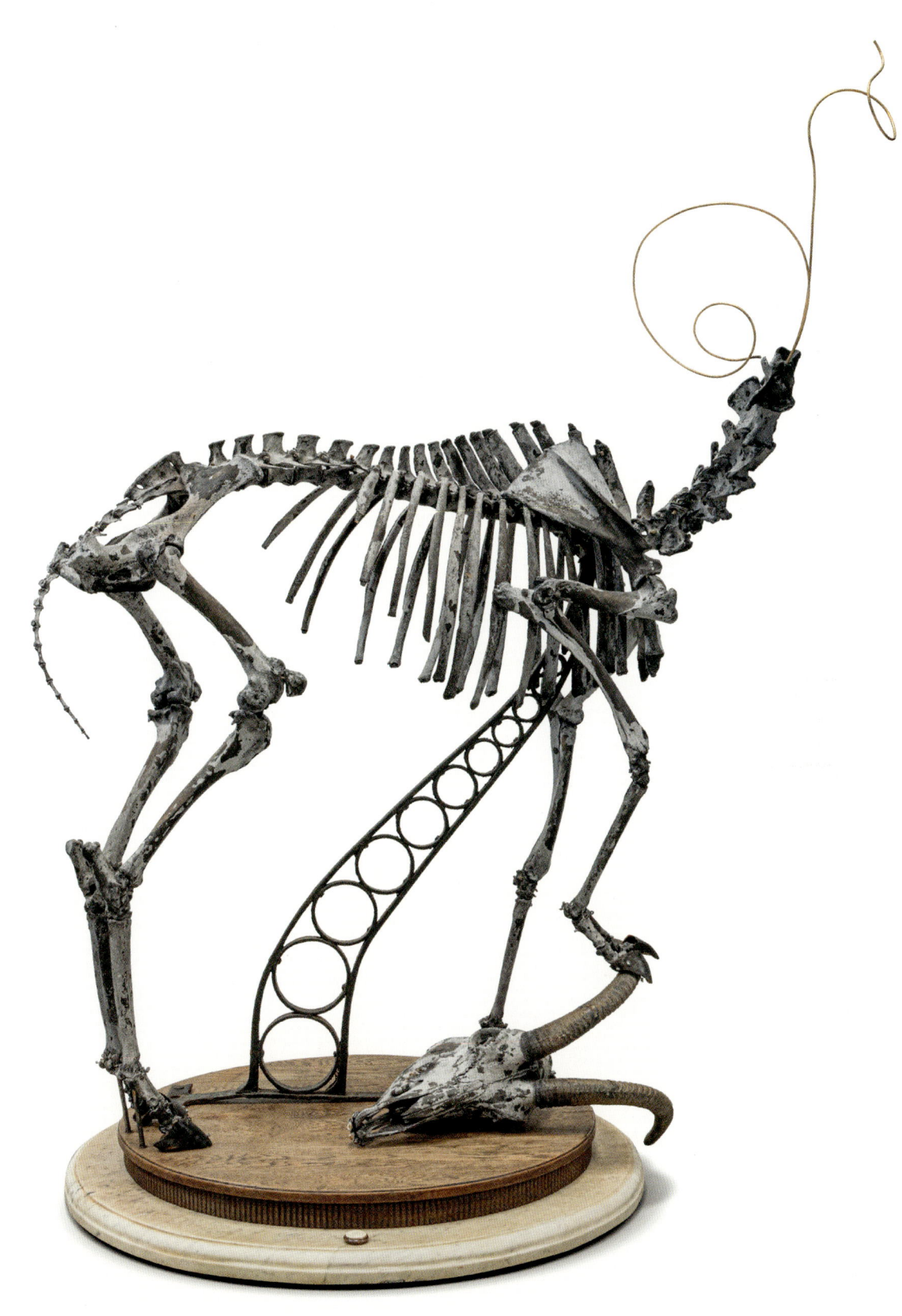

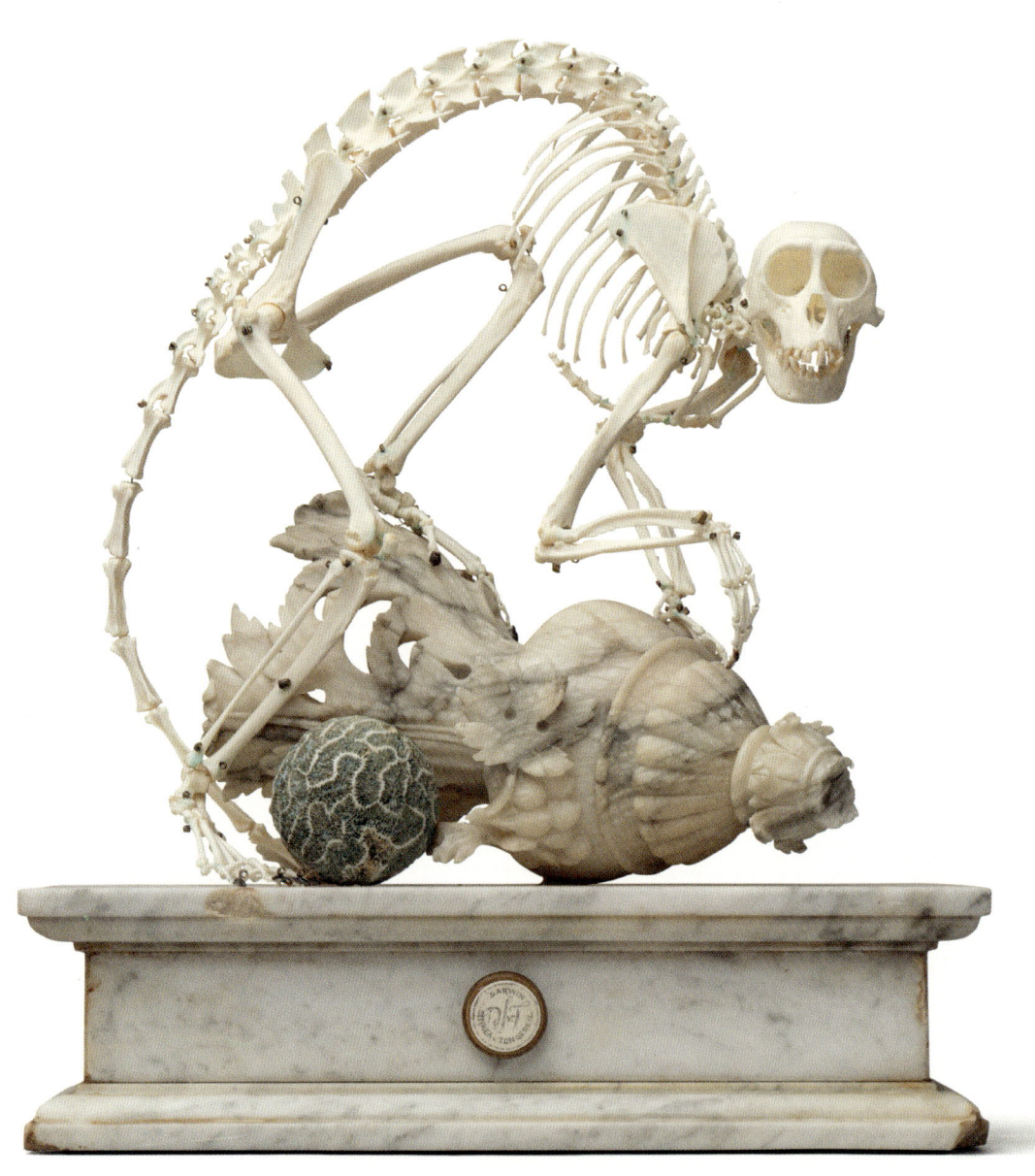

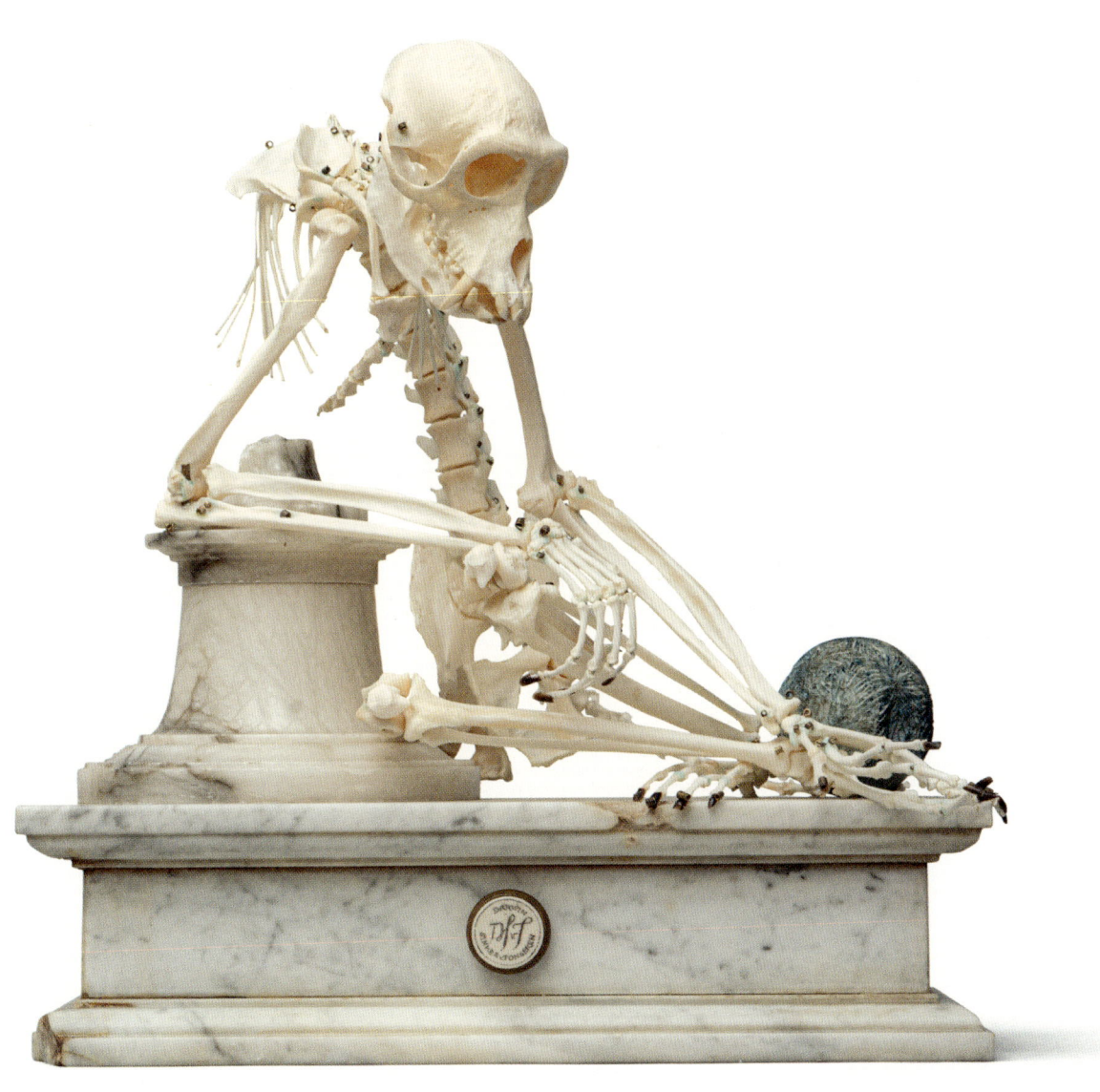

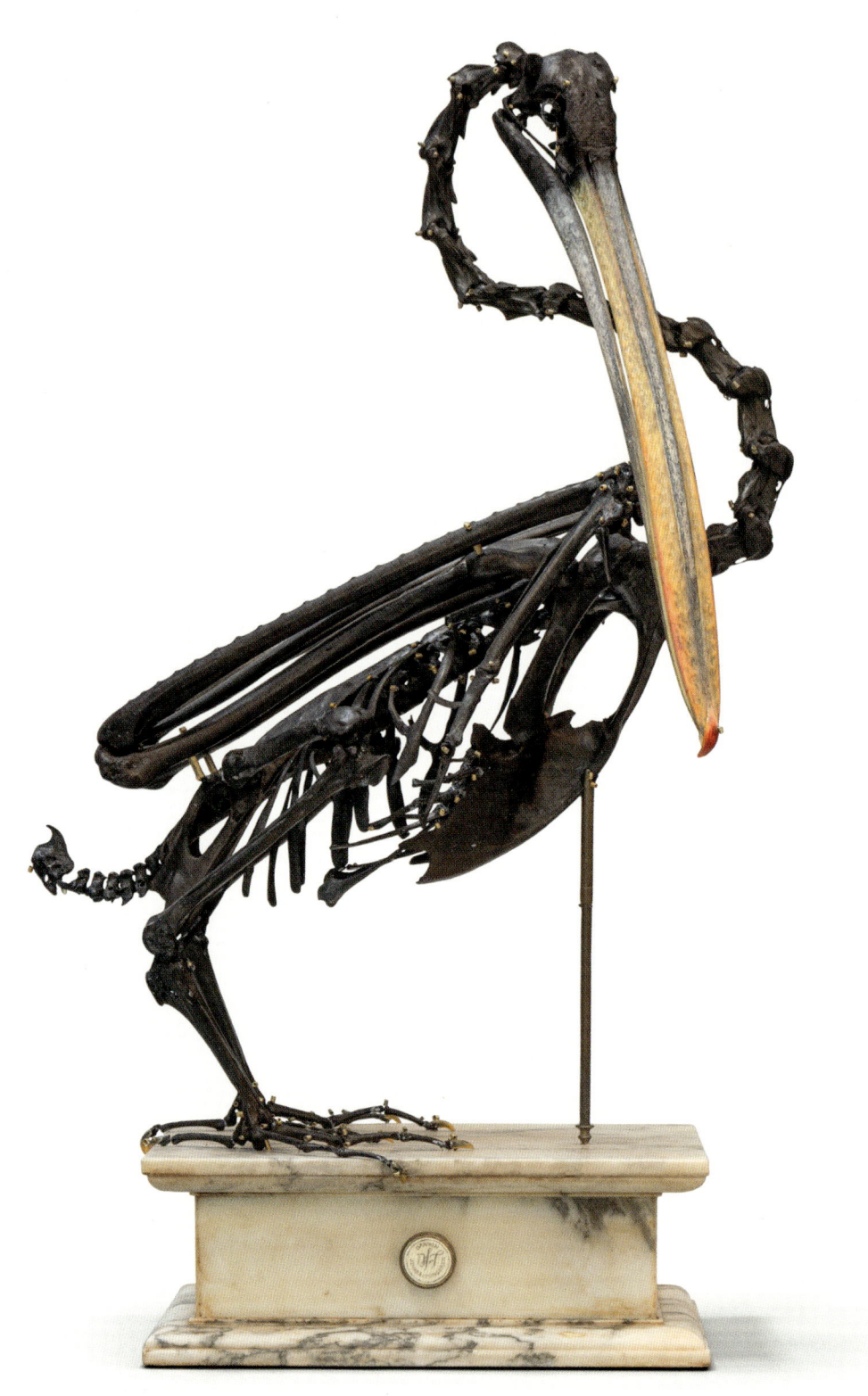

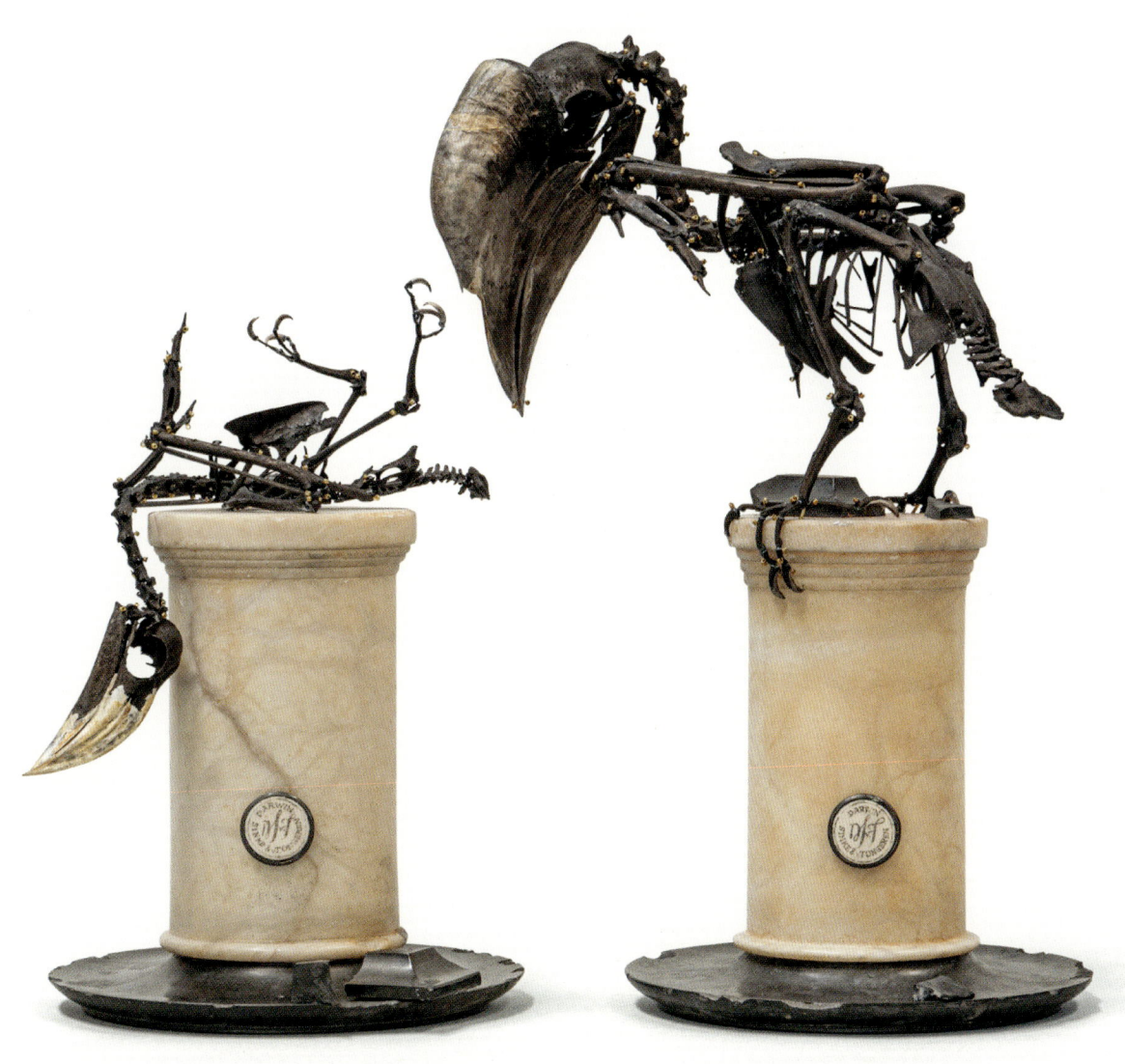

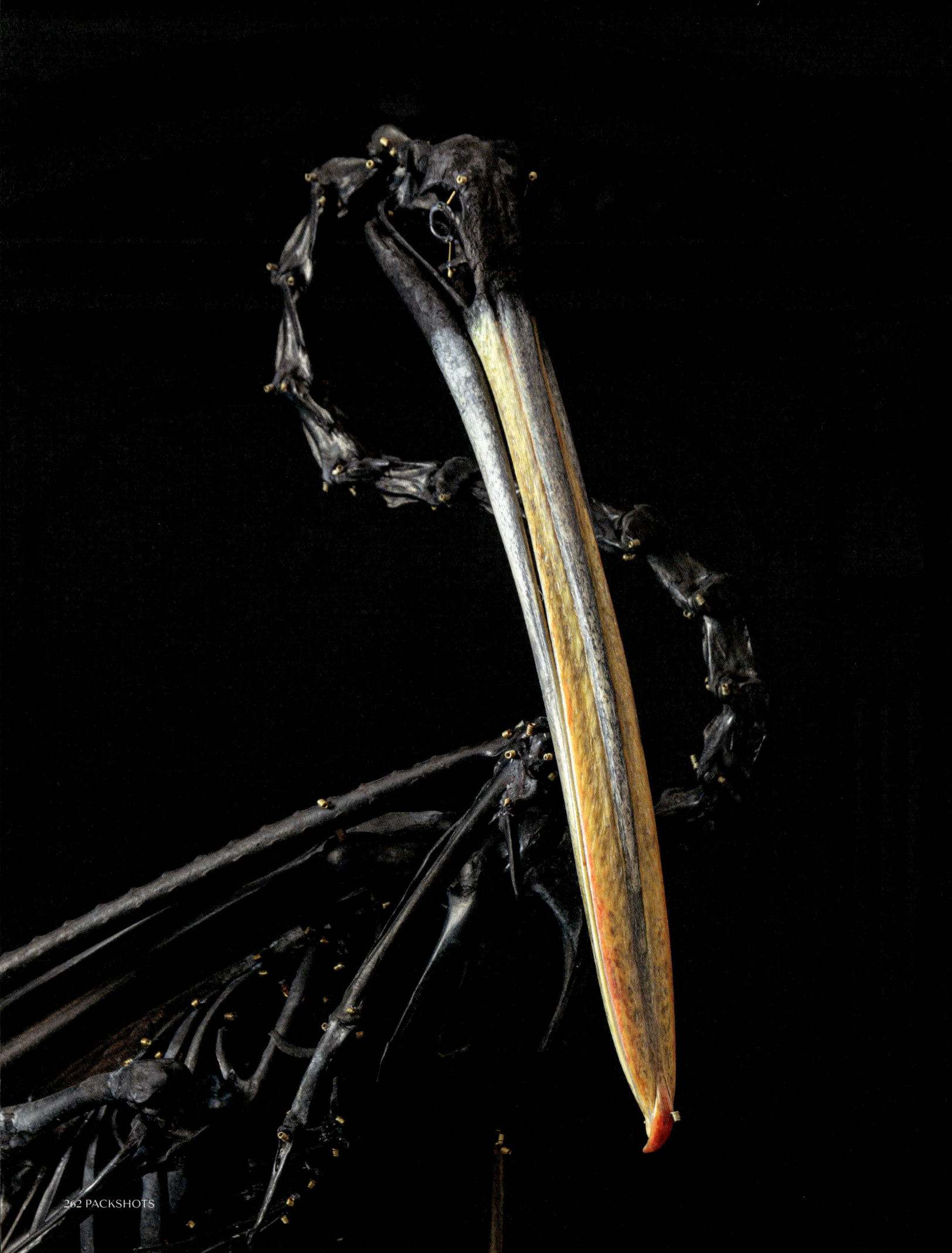

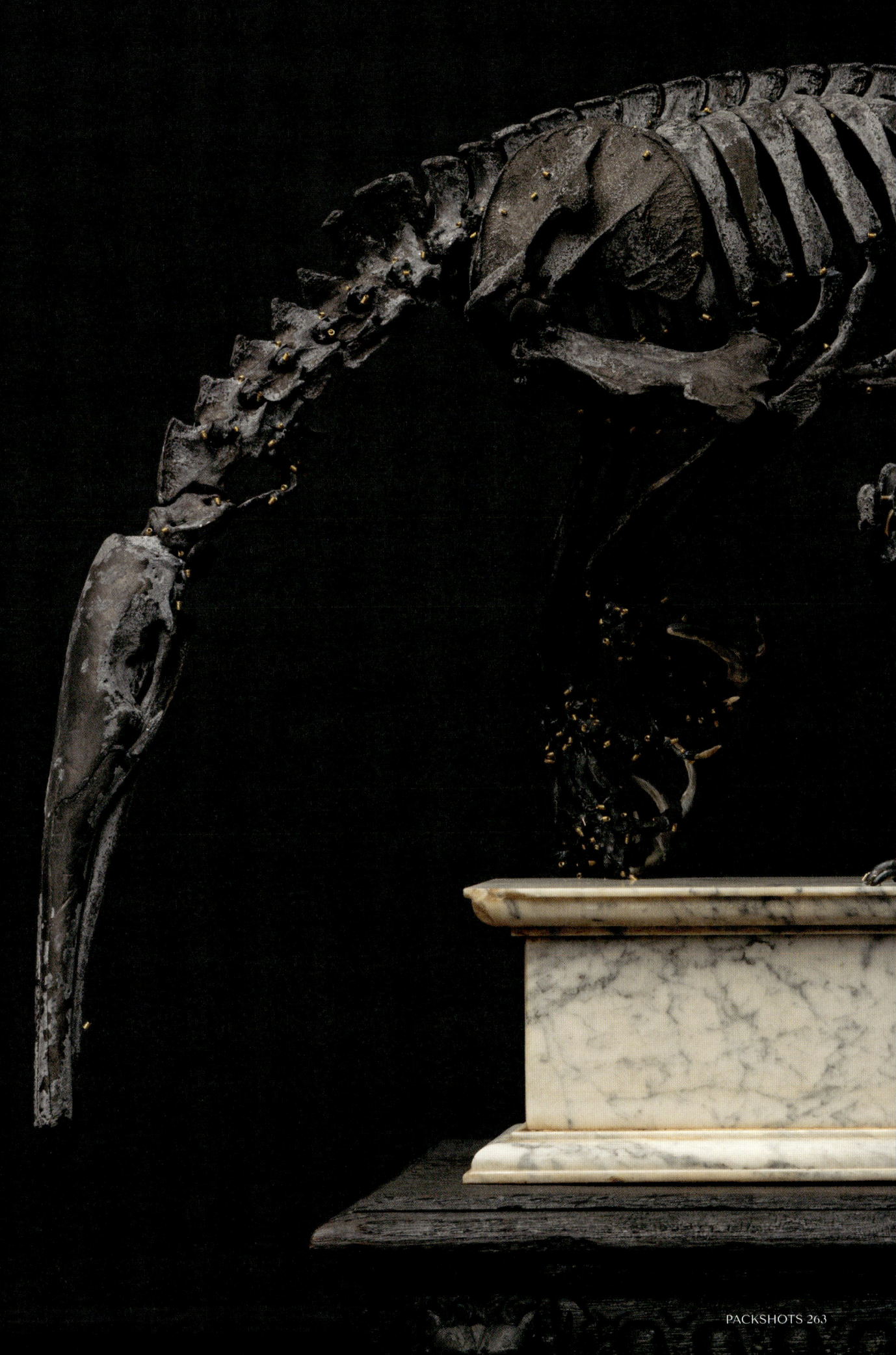

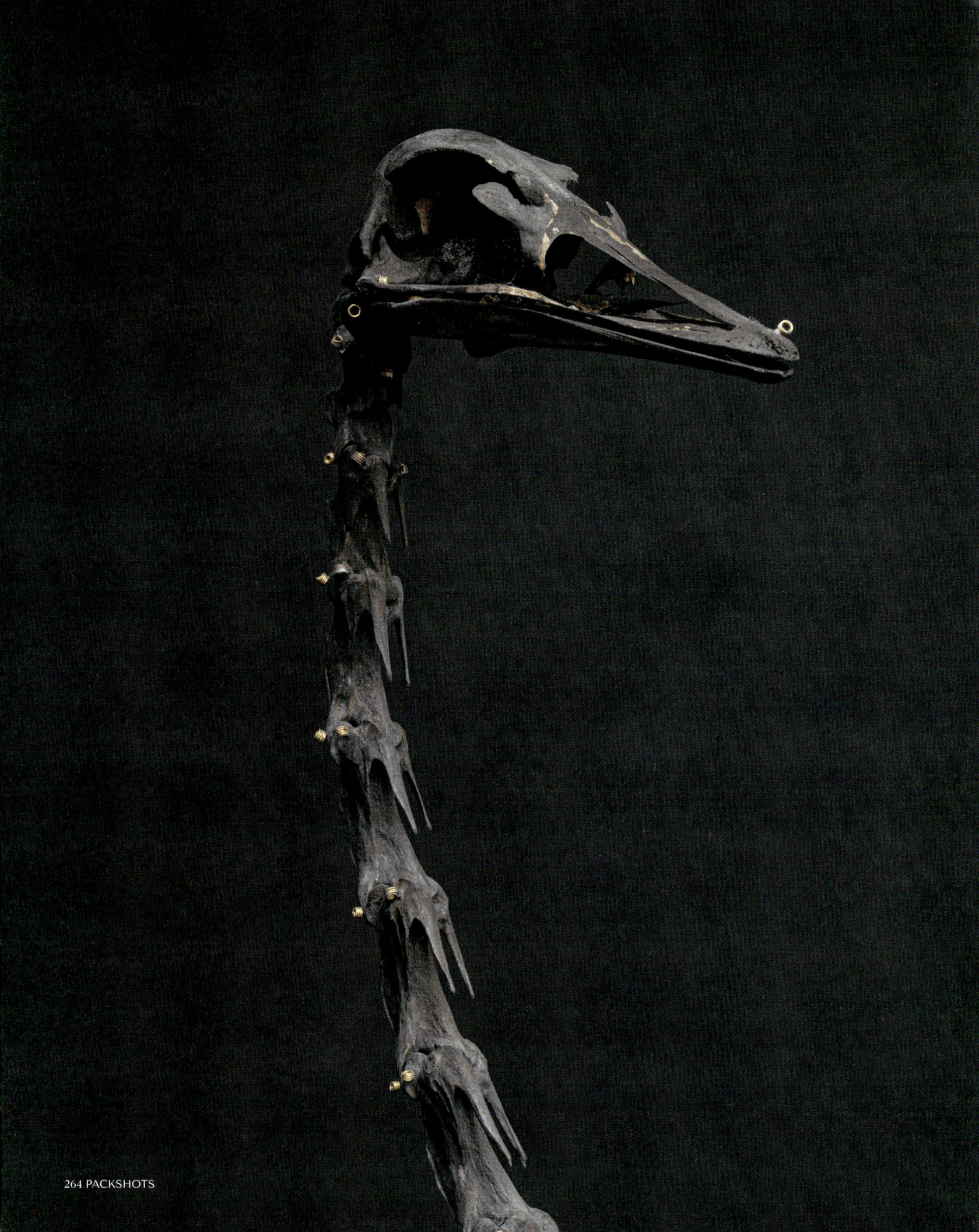

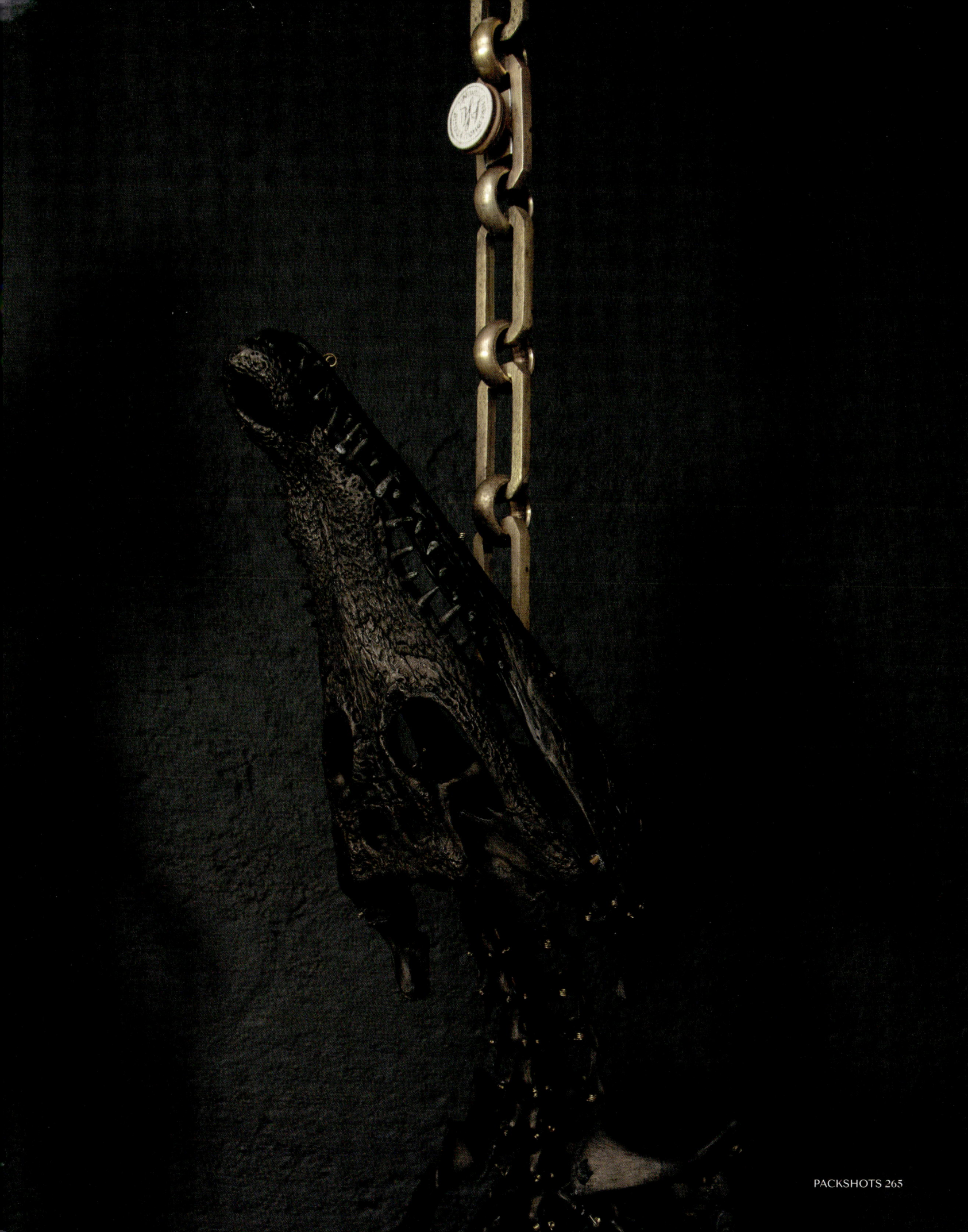

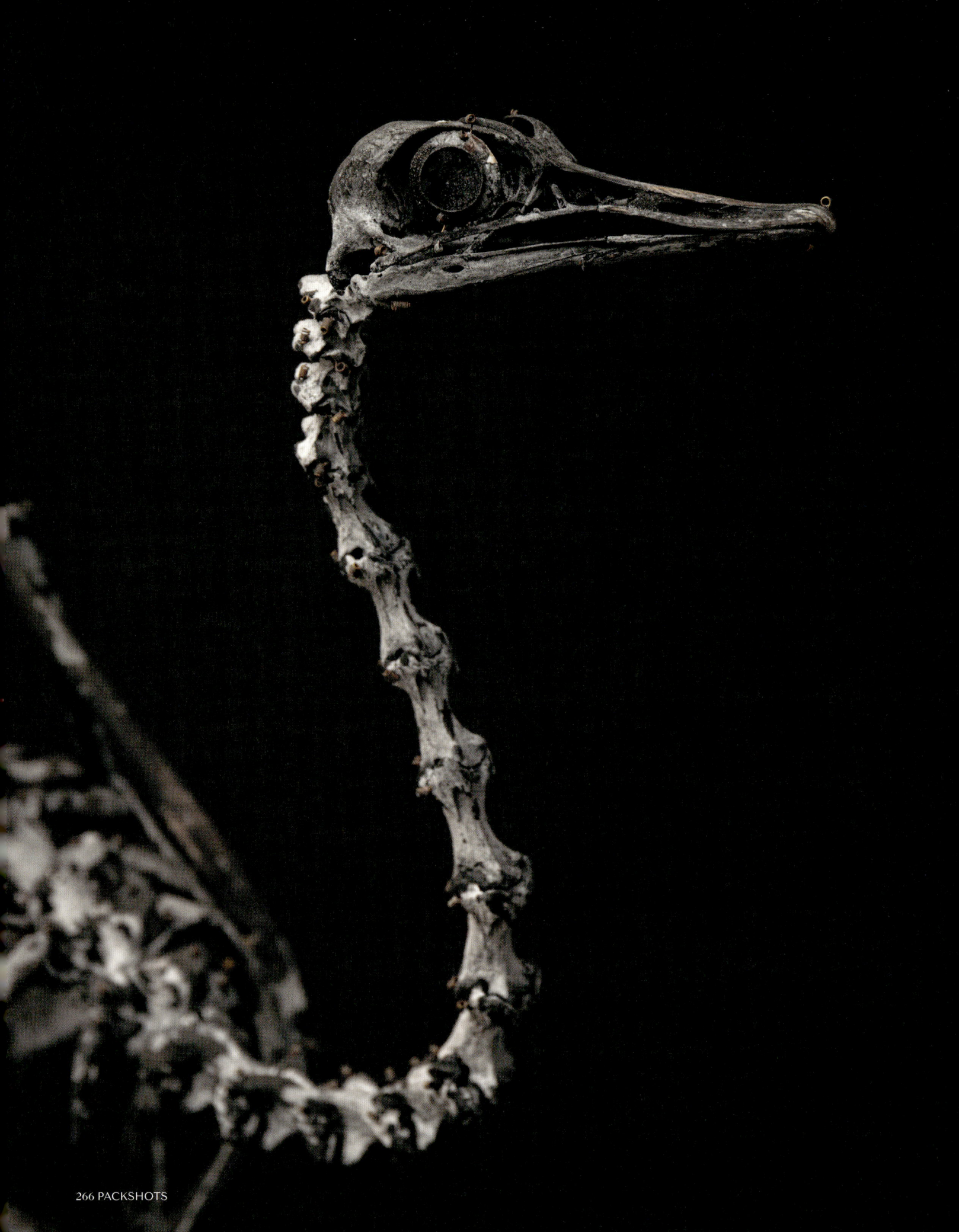

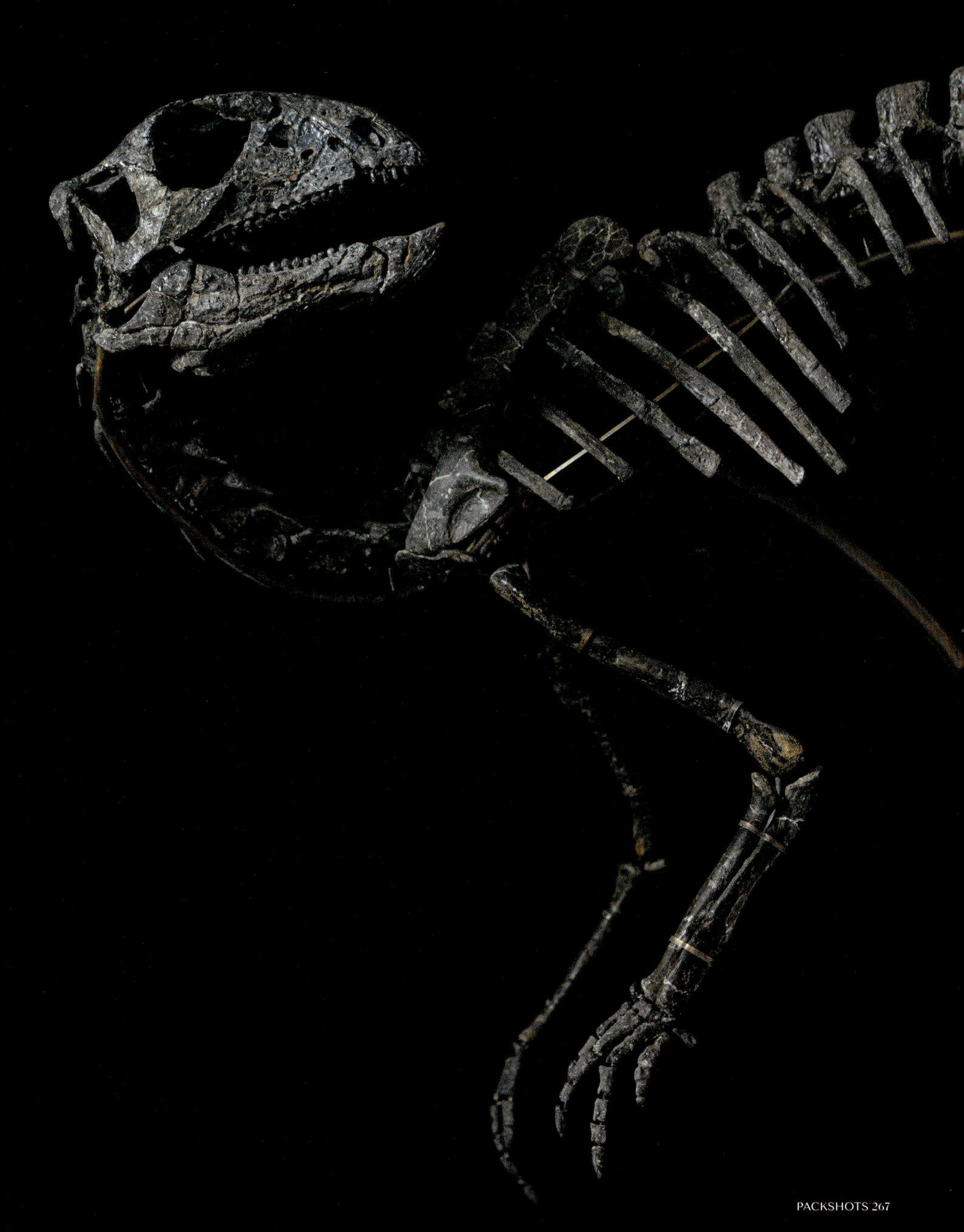

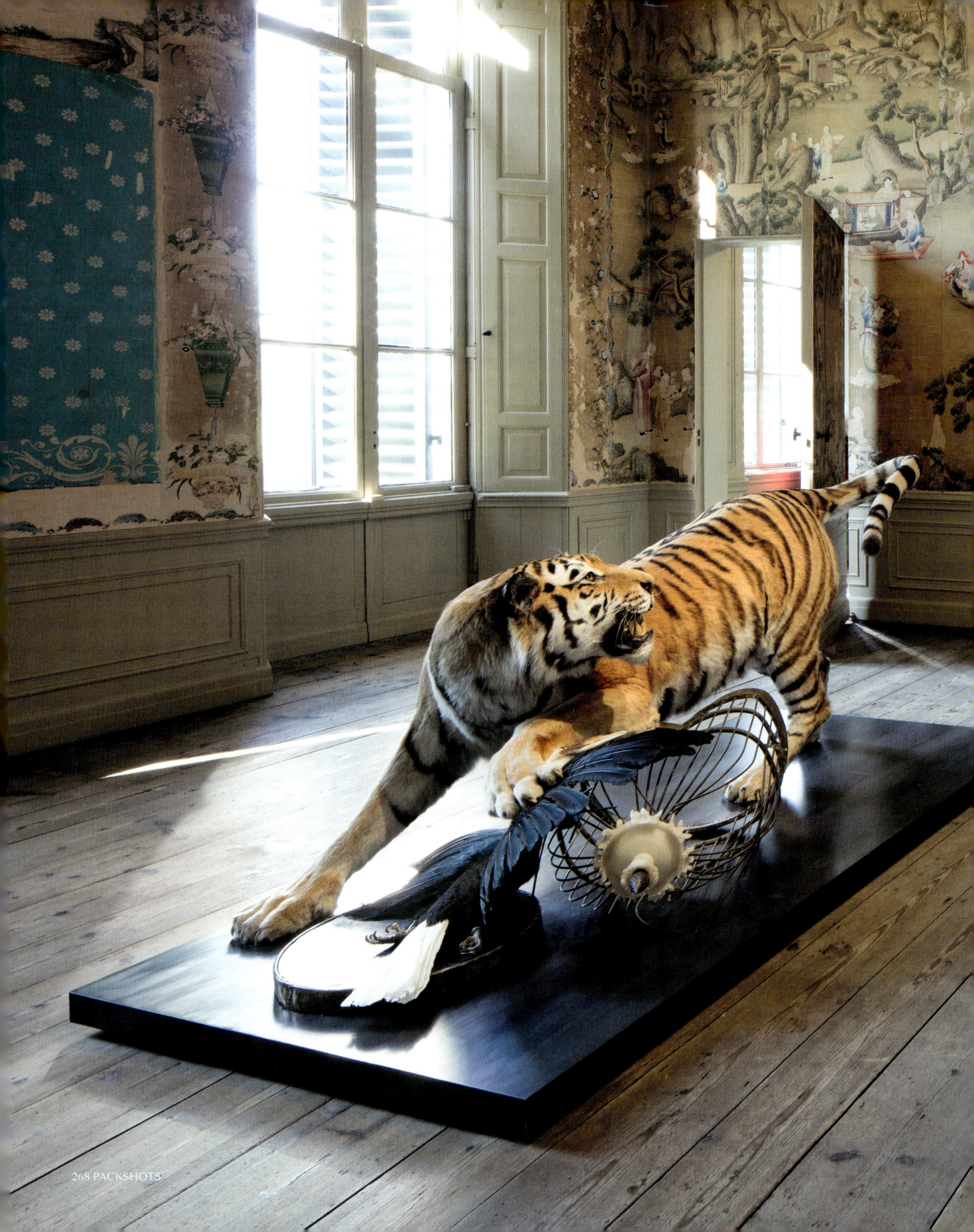

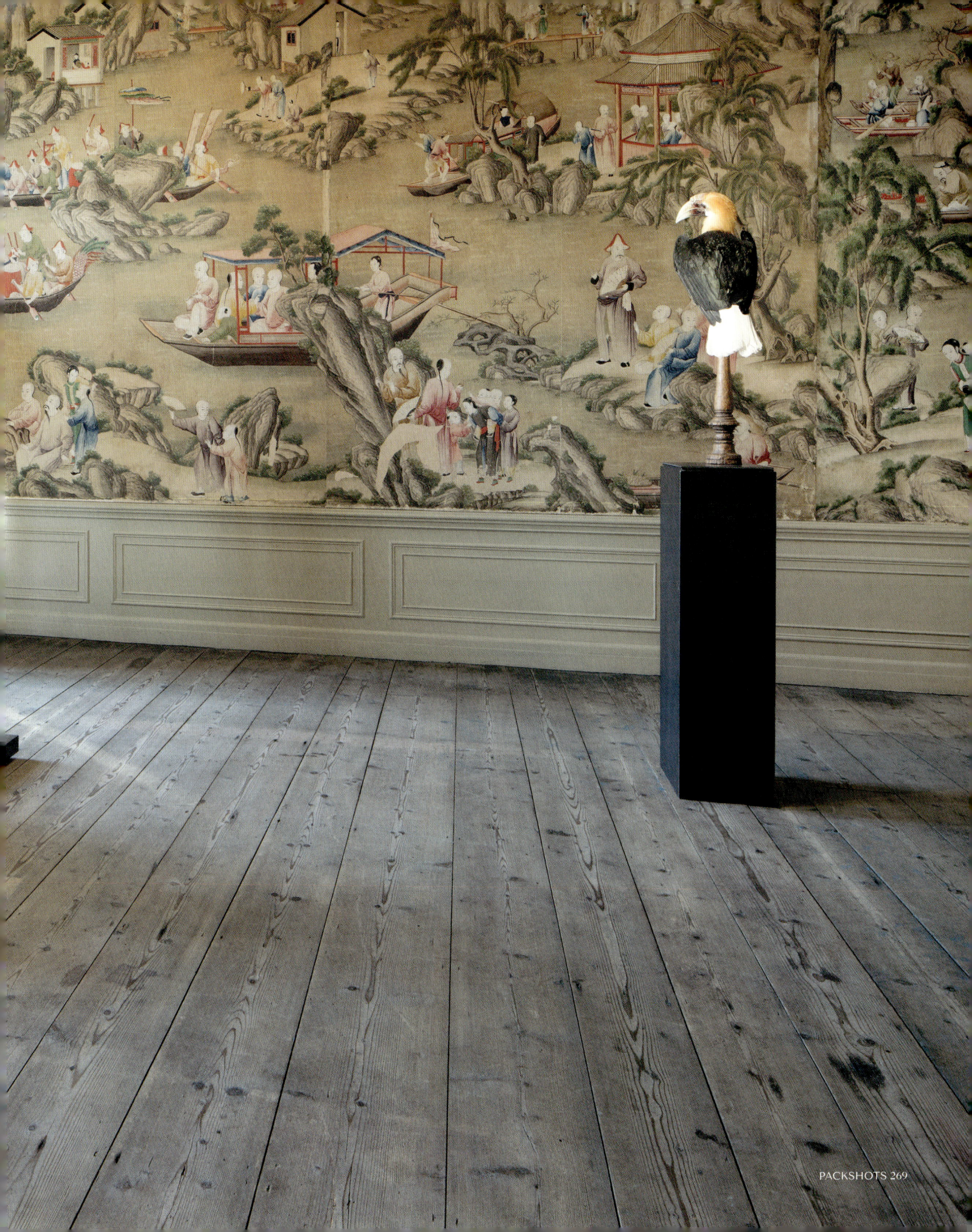

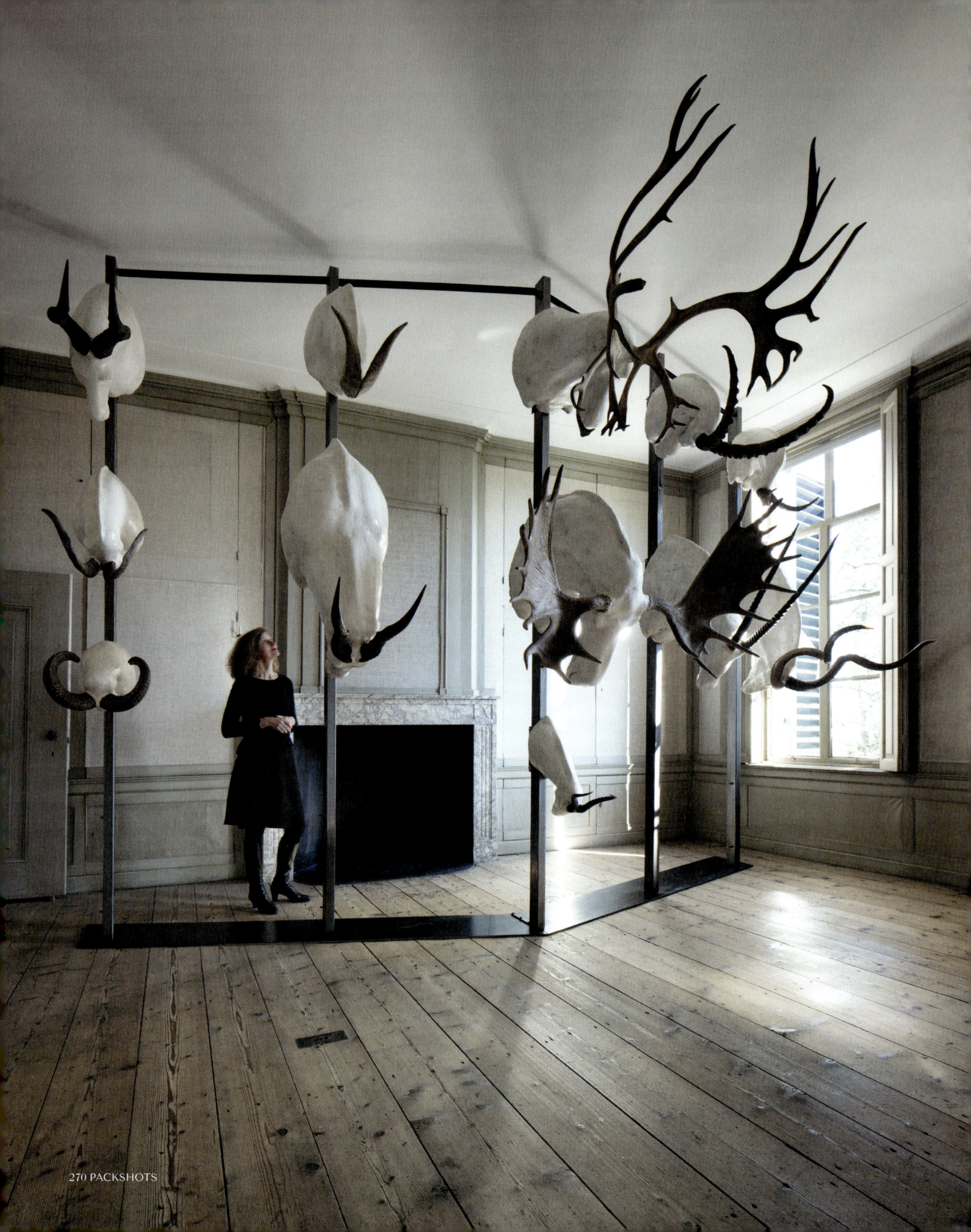

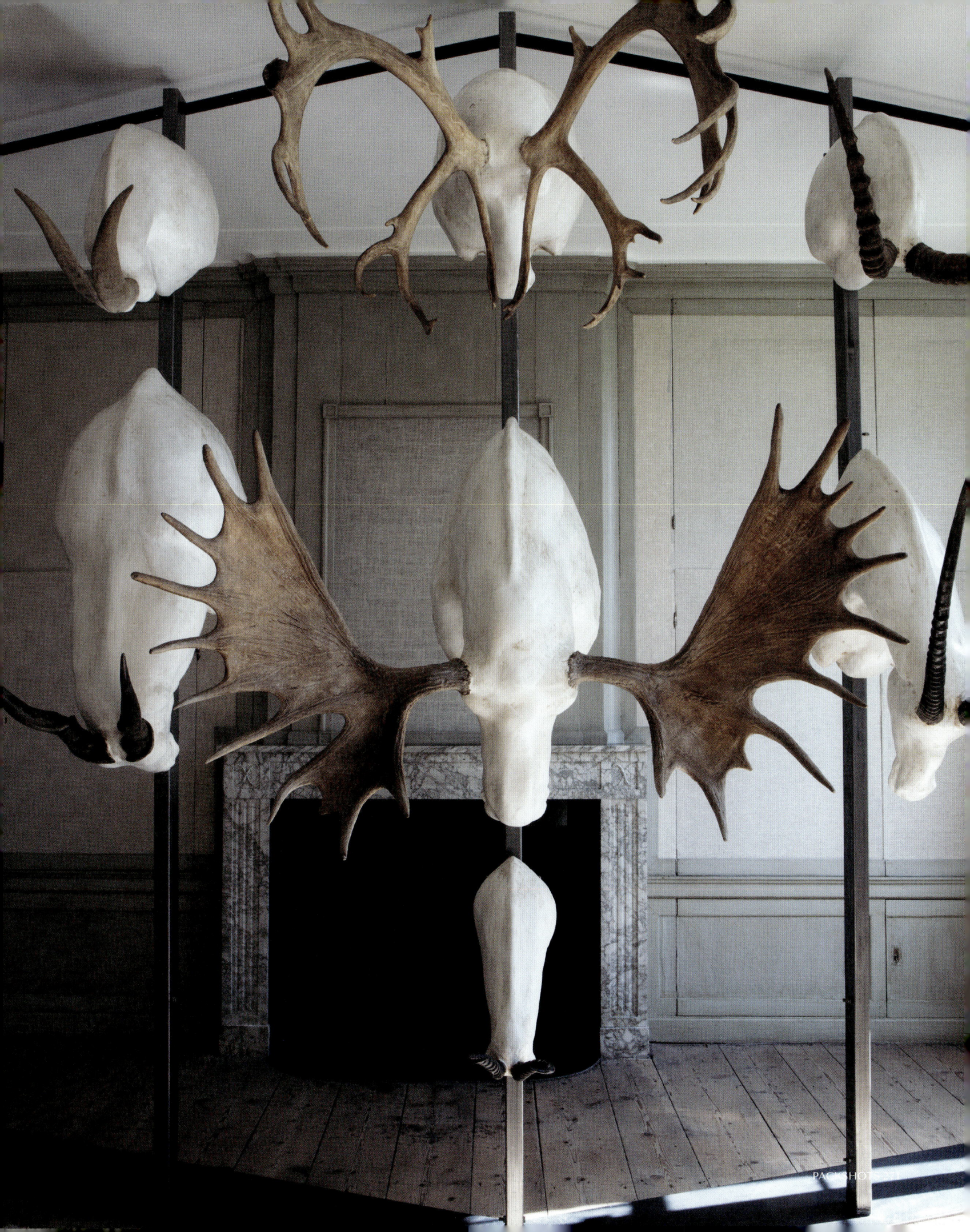

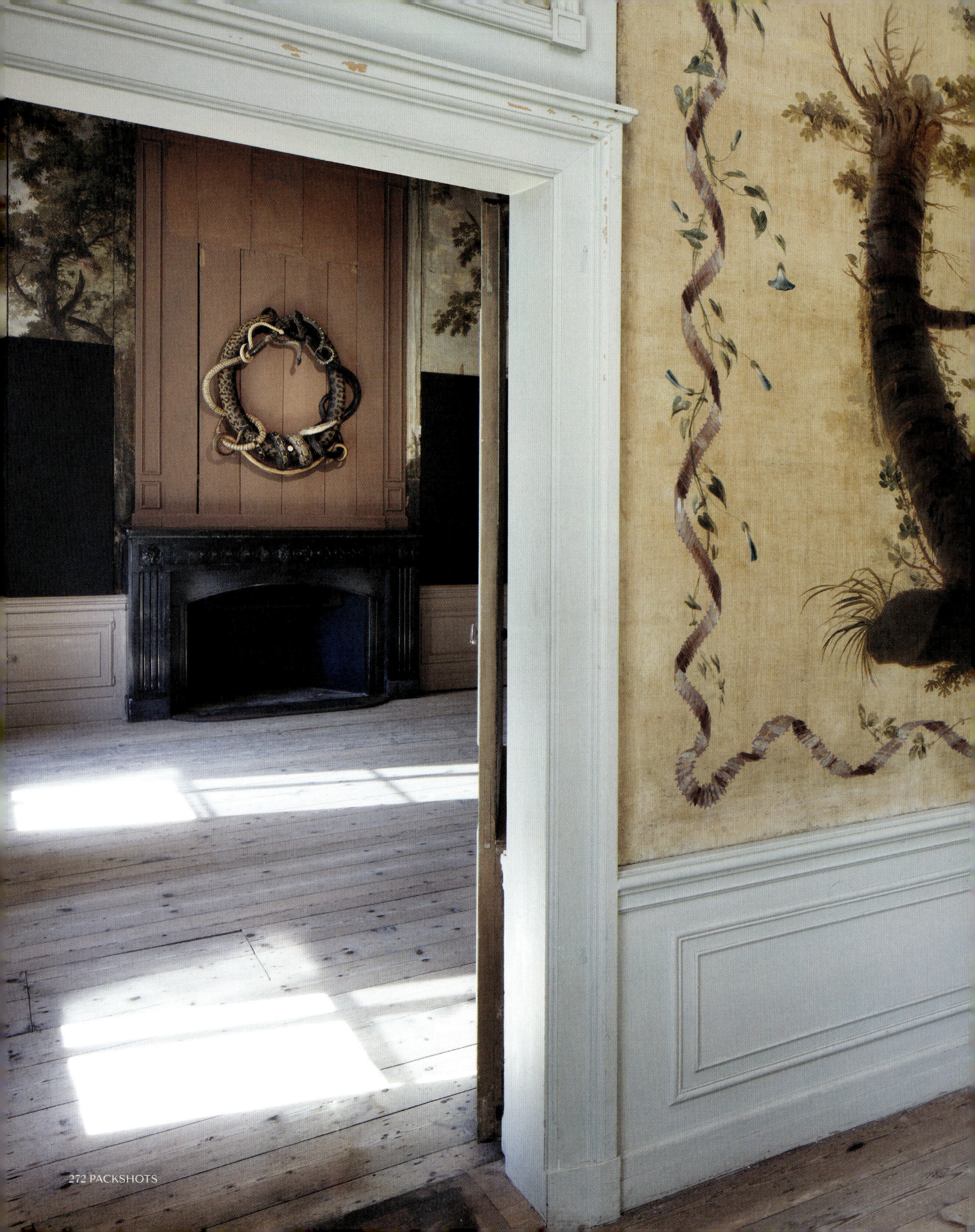

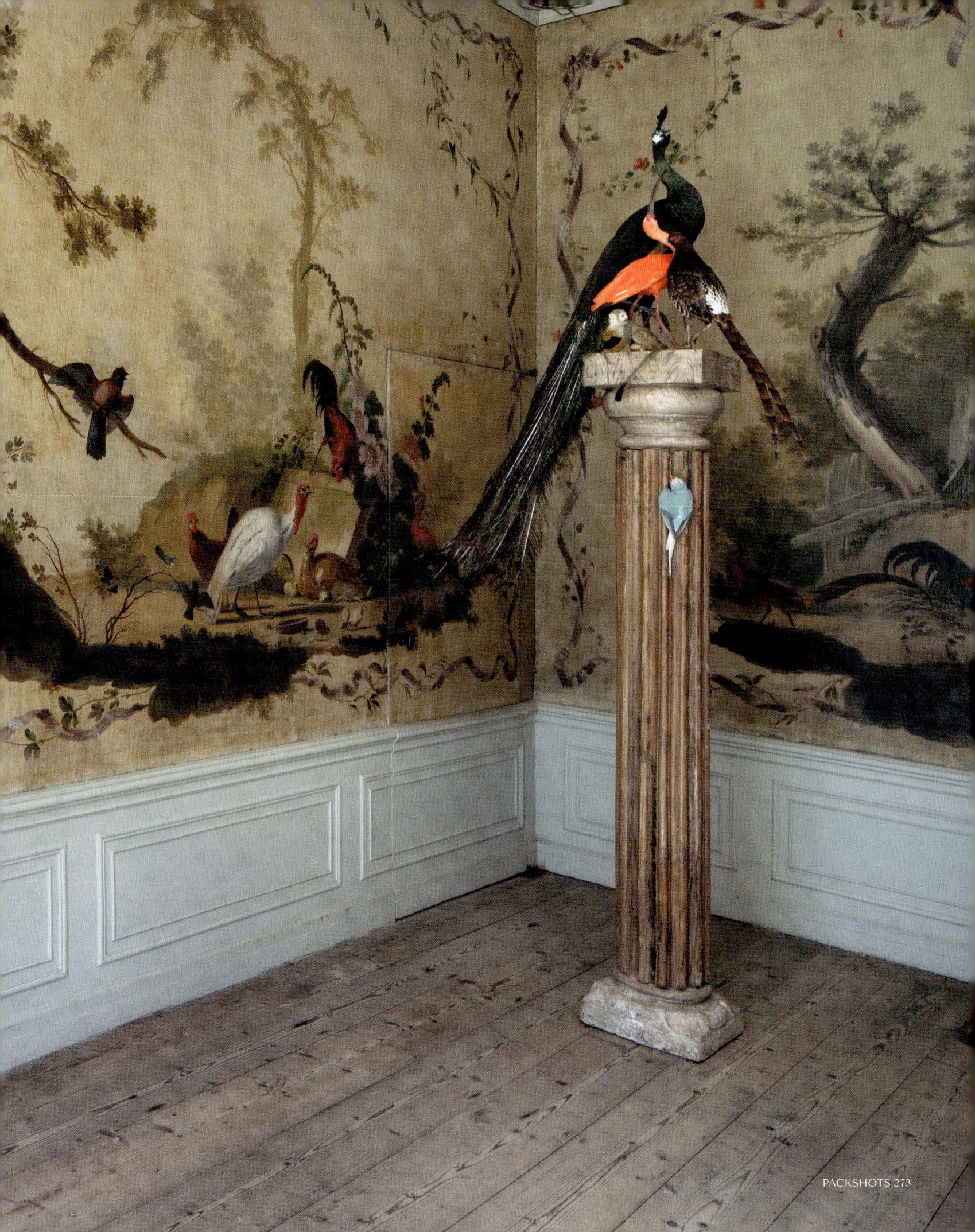

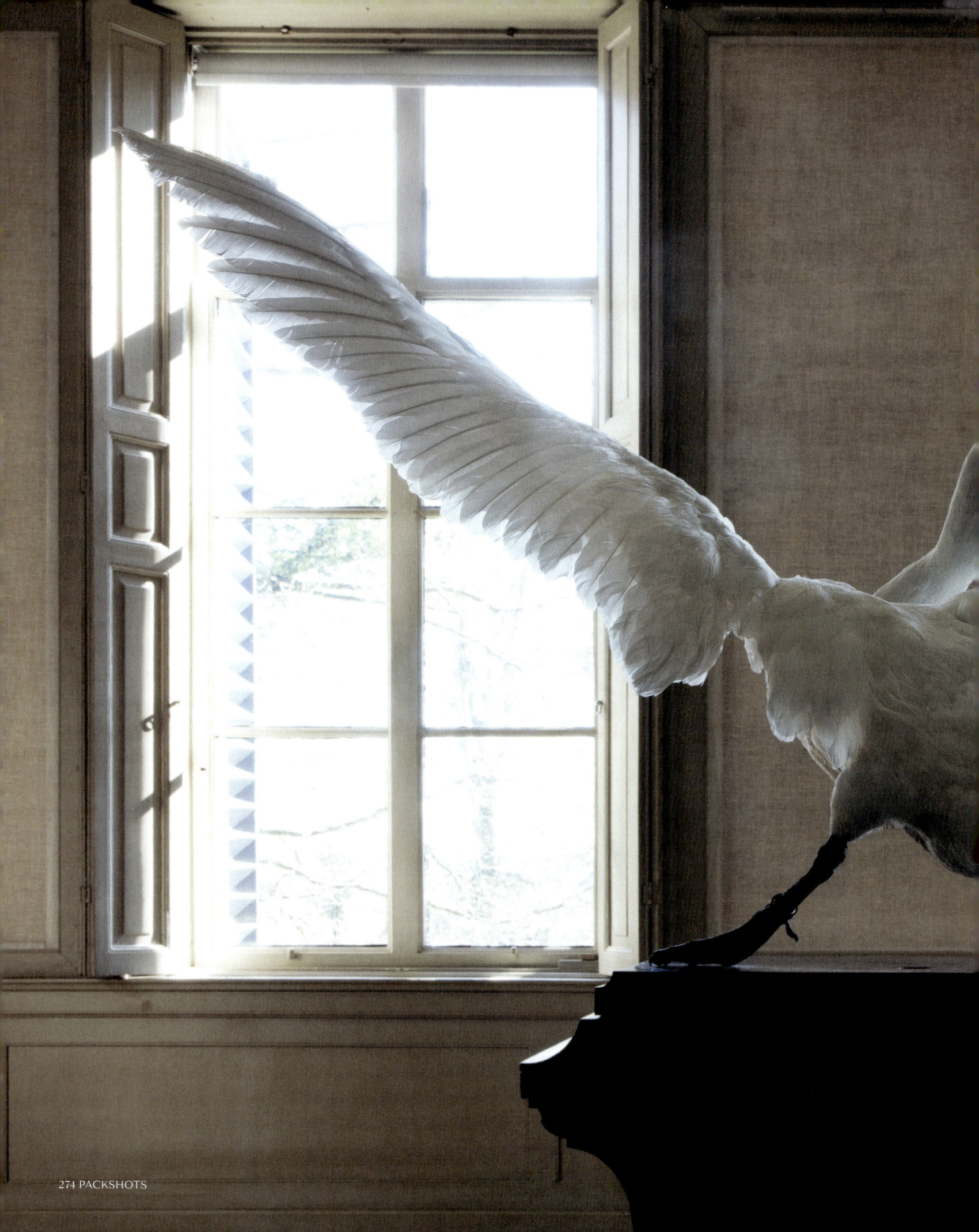

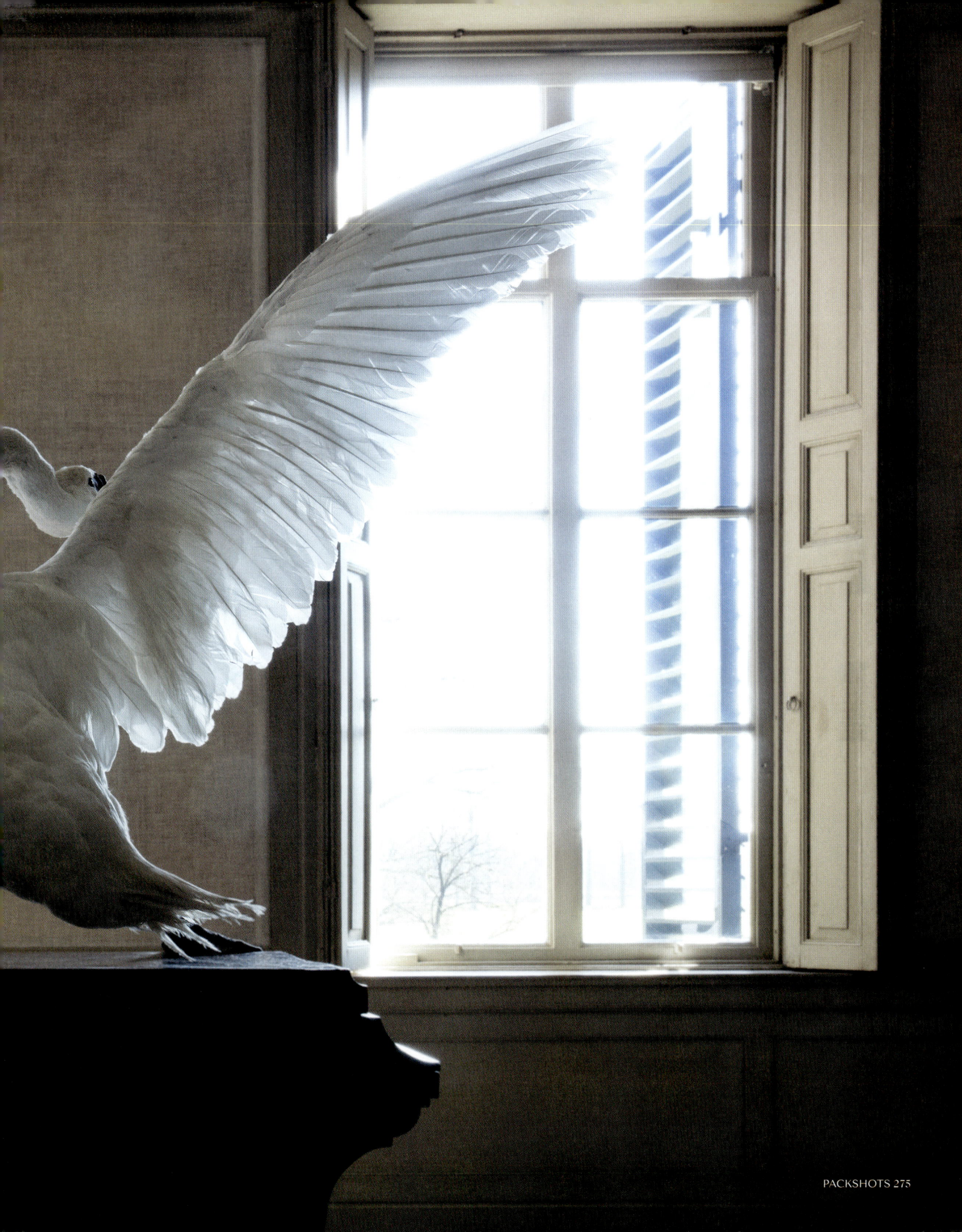

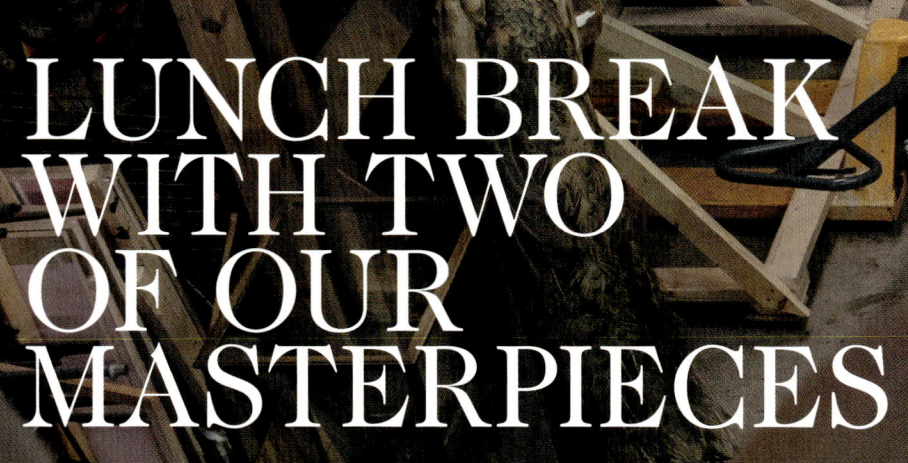

LUNCH BREAK WITH TWO OF OUR MASTERPIECES

On 22 September 2024, we had lunch with our daughters Noor and Anna at the Darwin, Sinke & van Tongeren studio.

Photographs by Inga Powilleit

Guests at the table:

Noor van Tongeren, 16 (Daughter of Ferry)
First year / Preliminary exam at Amsterdam Business School. At the age of 12, she was skinning a Sumatran tiger with her father at the zoo.

Anna Sinke, 24 (Daughter of Jaap)
Graduated from Rotterdam University of Applied Sciences, specialising in Creative Marketing & Sales. Currently works at the Artist Driven Playground Brutus as Communication Strategist.

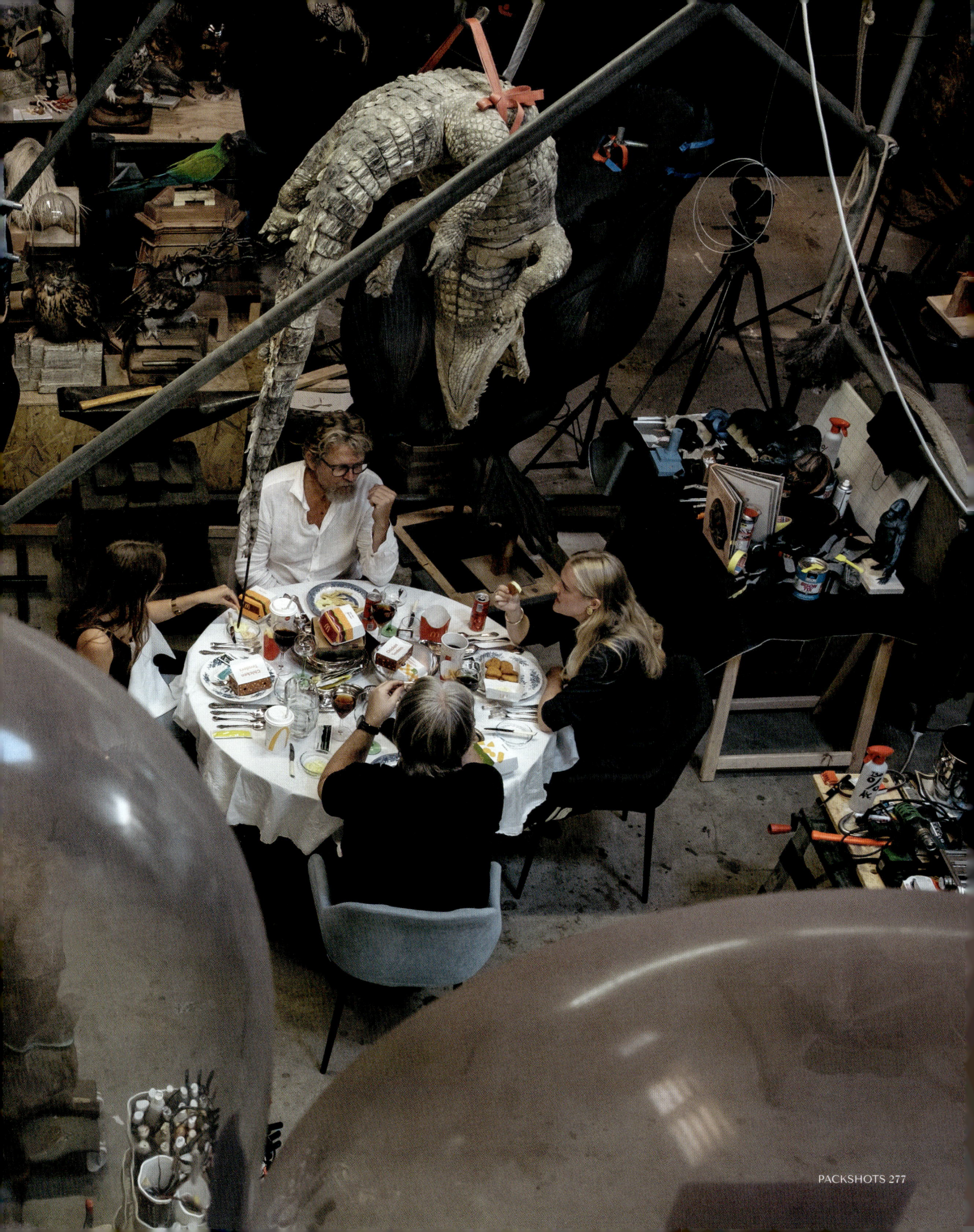

PACKSHOTS 277

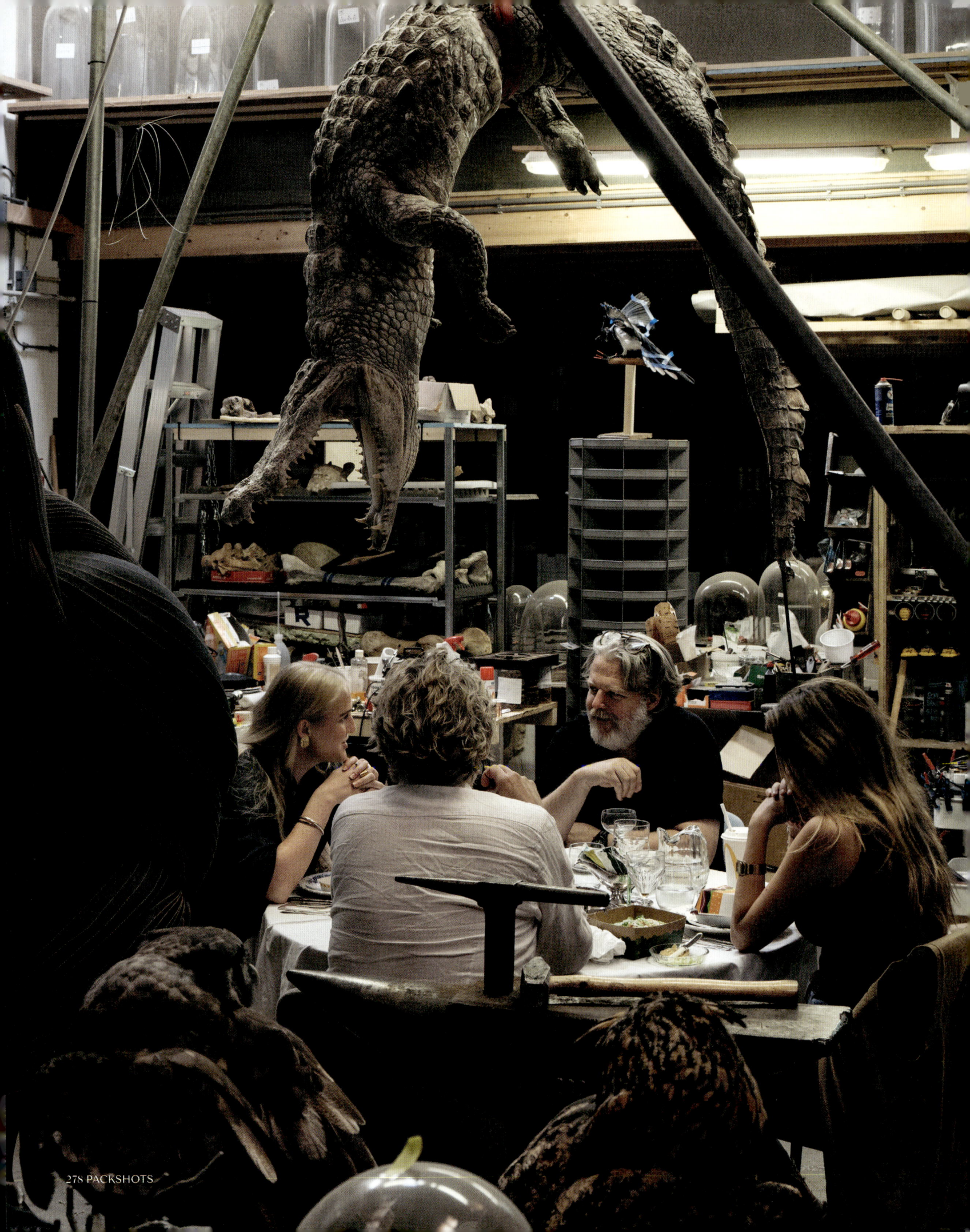

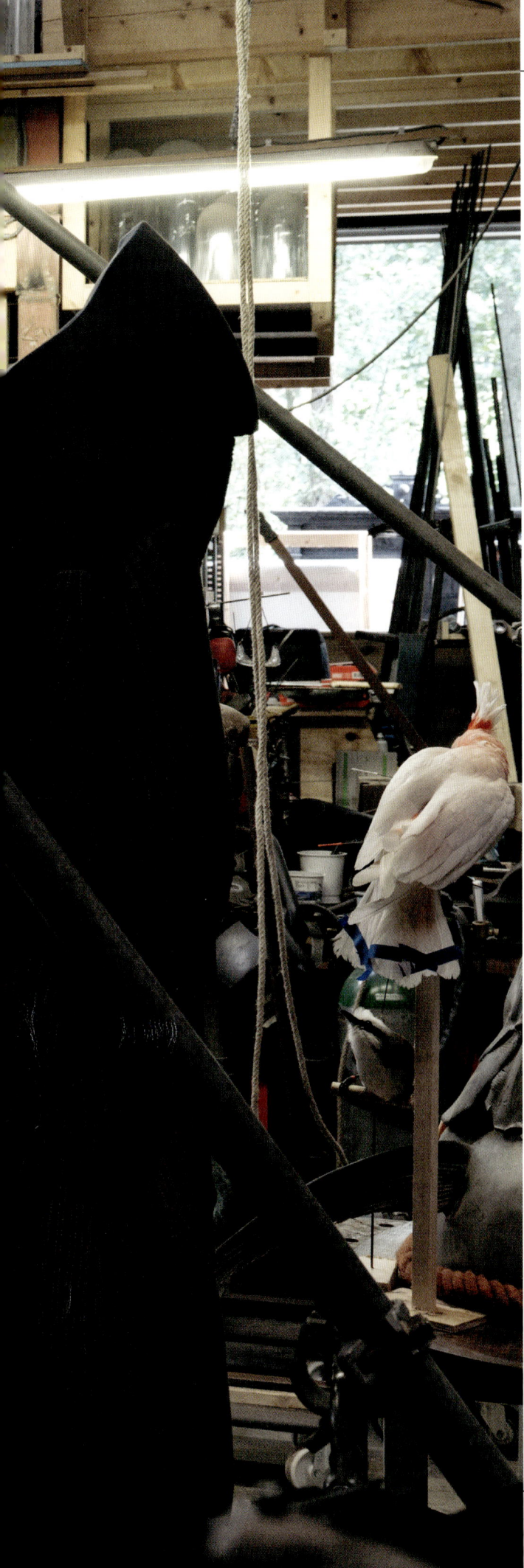

For this lunch meeting we set a beautiful table with damask table linens and a large set of silver cutlery. We had crystal glasses and silver candelabra. It all looked out of place, set up in our workshop under the unfinished, mounted Nile crocodile and surrounded by all these animals in progress. For our children the table setting was more surprising than all the animals together. For them, our workshop is a habitat they grew up in. And it all fell into place when the doorbell rang and McDonald's bags were delivered.

FERRY: Have you thought a bit about questions? I mean, we also have some questions, but we'll just see how it goes, right? It's a bit of a strange situation...

ANNA: Did you deliberately place the cutlery the other way around? They always do that to show how rich you are. That way, you can see the brand and the silver marks on the back. That's how it is in certain circles. That's etiquette or something.

FERRY: Is that so? I thought that etiquette was specifically designed to make others feel comfortable.

ANNA: Do you remember when you exhibited at Royal Dutch Palace Soestdijk? There was also a table that was set backwards like that!

FERRY: Speaking of the palace and etiquette, I once read a story about Queen Juliana. She once hosted a state visitor, and they had dinner together. Shrimp were served, and bowls with

> "Every animal we use is actually discarded by breeders and zoos. We're basically recyclers."
> *Jaap*

lemon in warm water were placed to clean your hands after peeling. The head of state didn't know that and picked up the bowl, put it to his mouth, and drank it. The people at the table started to feel uncomfortable, but Juliana picked up her bowl and drank it too.

NOOR: Really?

FERRY: Yes, really. The point is that all etiquette was invented to avoid discomfort for the other person, or at least that's how I remember it.

NOOR: Beautiful.

JAAP: We ordered all the salads and vegetarian burgers for you, Anna. But how vegetarian are you, actually?

ANNA: I'm very vegetarian. I've also stopped eating fish.

JAAP: And does that influence how you view our work?

ANNA: Not really. I mean, you don't kill the cows to stuff them.

JAAP: No, we don't kill anything. And we don't have anything killed either. Everything we use is actually discarded by breeders and zoos. Animals that would otherwise just be thrown away or burned. We're basically recyclers. Would that resonate well with your peers in the woke scene? Are there opinions about what we do among your generation that we don't hear about?

ANNA: Woke isn't necessarily about vegetarianism or opinions about animal cruelty and such. Woke is more about cultural differences and how you think about politics and so on. But… I'm the only one in my circle who's vegetarian so far. And I've never heard any negative comments about you or your work.

FERRY: Great. Luckily. Though I'm willing to engage in any discussion about the ethical aspects of what we do. I can defend everything.

ANNA: It also really depends on how you tell it. Because when I tell people that you stuff animals, they immediately think you kill them. When you then explain that's not the case, they see it very differently. Although you do have people who think it's all very gross, that you're scooping the animals out with spoons or something.

NOOR: Yes, I get that a lot too. I often notice that there's a prejudice. That it's really dirty work.

FERRY: Yes, people often don't understand how we do it. We sort of take off the skin instead of hollowing out the animal. If we do it right, not a drop of blood is involved. But Noor, I remember when you were younger. You were much more embarrassed about what I did. Especially in front of your friends.

NOOR: No, that wasn't so bad. I just found it hard to explain. And at school, they thought for a long time that you were a taxi driver!

ANNA: Taxi driver?

NOOR: Yes. In primary school, we had a career week. They asked everyone what their parents did. And I said "taxidermist" because I thought it was really cool that I already knew that word in primary school. And then the teacher thought I said taxi driver. I wanted to correct her and say "no, not taxi driver." But she cut me off, so she always thought my dad was a taxi driver.

JAAP: That's a good one.

FERRY: But I also know about you and Jip [*Noor's brother*]. When your friends came to our house, where of course there's all kinds of stuff, you found it exciting too.

NOOR: Yes. Many of my friends found it scary to sleep over at our place. Which I understand when you're young. And there are all these animals

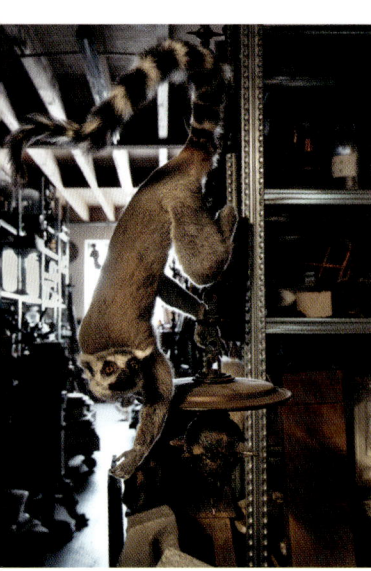

hanging on the walls. They also asked me if I dared to walk through the house at night. Haha.

ANNA: You know what I found the scariest thing at your house? That collection of corned beef cans!

FERRY: What?!

NOOR: I've never had any comments about that from friends.

ANNA: In your kitchen, a whole row of those cans with squashed meat. Really disgusting.

FERRY: Haha. Well, I didn't expect that out of everything in our house you found the corned beef the worst. Let me tell you where that comes from. I was in advertising for nearly 25 years with your father, and we travelled a lot. I discovered that corned beef is a worldwide phenomenon. Asia, South America, Africa — everywhere has corned beef. So, I decided to buy a can in every country. Because they all look a little different.

NOOR: Some people collect stamps, but my dad collects corned beef. Yeah, that works.

FERRY: I've never eaten it! I actually find it a disgusting product. But the packaging is often quite beautiful.

ANNA: That's such a strange hobby! Didn't you also keep a roadkill diary during your world trip?

NOOR: Yes! Everywhere we encountered roadkill, we had to stop, and then you would take a picture! That's pretty weird.

FERRY: It is quite weird, yes. But we started the trip in Borneo. And there was so much roadkill and such extraordinary species. Monkeys, snakes, civet cats. I found that fascinating. Later, I learned that it was because of all those palm oil plantations. Due to deforestation, all the wildlife was displaced and ended up in front of cars. That realisation was the big bang for Darwin, Sinke & van Tongeren. That roadkill made me curious about taxidermy.

JAAP: It's funny how things can go. Did you also have that, Anna, when friends came over?

ANNA: No. But we don't have dead animals at home. People always ask me: "Oh, are there lots of animals at your house?" That's not the case. But it is hard to explain what you guys actually do. It's not just taxidermy; it's art. A lot of people are familiar with taxidermy. And then it gets vague. People don't initially see it as art.

FERRY: And what do you say then?

ANNA: Well, I usually try to end the conversation. I'm not really in the mood for it.

FERRY: I get that. Neither am I. I generally hate talking about our work. But I think the difference is that a traditional taxidermist takes biology or nature as a starting point. Jaap and I are art directors by background, with a focus on art history. So we actually take art history as a starting point. We work towards those old paintings, or we strive to recreate the poses like the old Italian and Greek sculptors made. Our animals tell stories.

JAAP: And we also create compositions with animals based on what we think is beautiful. Not based on the habitat where those animals are found. We don't really care about that.

ANNA: And the next question is always: who buys them?!

NOOR: I say "famous rich people". It's true, right?

FERRY: Definitely. But also museums, artists, interior designers and collectors. People with taste. But that immediately sounds a bit arrogant.

JAAP: Do people your age know Damien Hirst?

ANNA: Oh, yes.

NOOR: I don't think so.

JAAP: Well, I think Anna says yes because she's

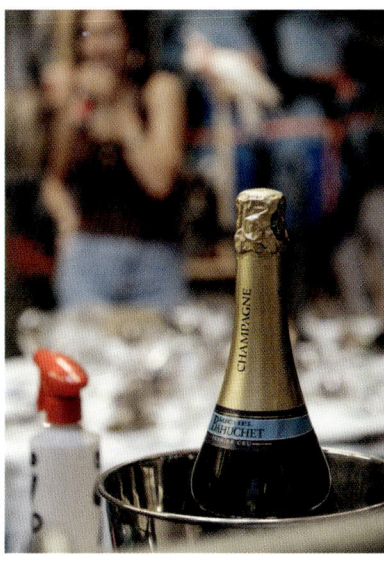

"Many of my friends found it scary to sleep at our place, with all those animals hanging on the walls."
Noor

> "I didn't like antique markets when I was young, but I do like them a lot now."
> *Anna*

more into art. I had a whole group of elderly people visiting for a tour of the studio and someone asked who the third partner was. Darwin, our inspiration and "silent" partner. And they didn't know Damien Hirst either.

FERRY: But, anyway. If people want to understand, I quickly show them our Instagram page. That saves a lot of talking. Once people see it, they immediately understand what we do. Hey Noor, changing the subject for a bit. We've been on many trips together for my work. Which trip did you like the most? What do you remember the most?

ANNA: Noor has also been to skin animals after they died at the zoo, right?

NOOR: Yes. I really liked that trip to the zoo, with the tiger. But that's also because we usually go on holiday afterwards.

FERRY: And the antique trips to England, you liked those a lot too, right?

NOOR: Yes, I really liked England too. But there were also a lot of boring parts for my age. Like all those antique markets.

JAAP: You *did* love those antique markets, didn't you, Anna?

ANNA: I didn't like them much back then, but I do like them a lot now.

NOOR: Oh, really?

ANNA: Yes. You get hooked.

FERRY: And you used to always go to antique auctions with me. You liked it at first, but later it became too boring. I get why the zoo is more fun.

NOOR: Yes, at the zoo it's just fun when we're all working there, and I get to go with those people to feed the animals. I've fed giraffes and lemurs.

FERRY: When you're young, that's really special, of course.

NOOR: Yes — like feeding the monkeys. I thought it was really cool that I got to go inside the enclosure while people were watching, to see them being fed. And I was inside with the animals.

ANNA: That's really great. Did you go to London as well?

NOOR: Yes, quite a few times for the show at Jamb [*the London gallery where we had our first exhibition*].

ANNA: One of my favourite memories was that exhibition opening you had with the food truck.

NOOR: Yes, I remember. That was in Amsterdam. That's also a fun memory. That we got to stand in the food truck.

FERRY: That was our first solo exhibition at a gallery in Amsterdam. And it turned out that the guy hadn't arranged anything for catering. So, at the last minute, we rented a food truck, raced to Sligro Supermarket, and bought a few hundred meatballs.

ANNA: They were delicious! I still ate meat back then.

FERRY: Yeah, the meatballs weren't anything special, really. But we also bought a ton of coriander, chopped it up, and rolled the meatballs in soy sauce first and then in the coriander bits. And suddenly, it looked like something fancy. Everyone still talks about the meatballs. Damn, that was a real race against the clock. And it was also a relief for me because I could focus on making the meatballs instead of talking about my work inside the gallery.

NOOR: But I think I was five or six years old then. Probably five. I got to stay up late too.

FERRY: Do you remember any specific work that stuck with you?

NOOR: I think that work in Switzerland, where I got to go along. With those people with the huge dogs.

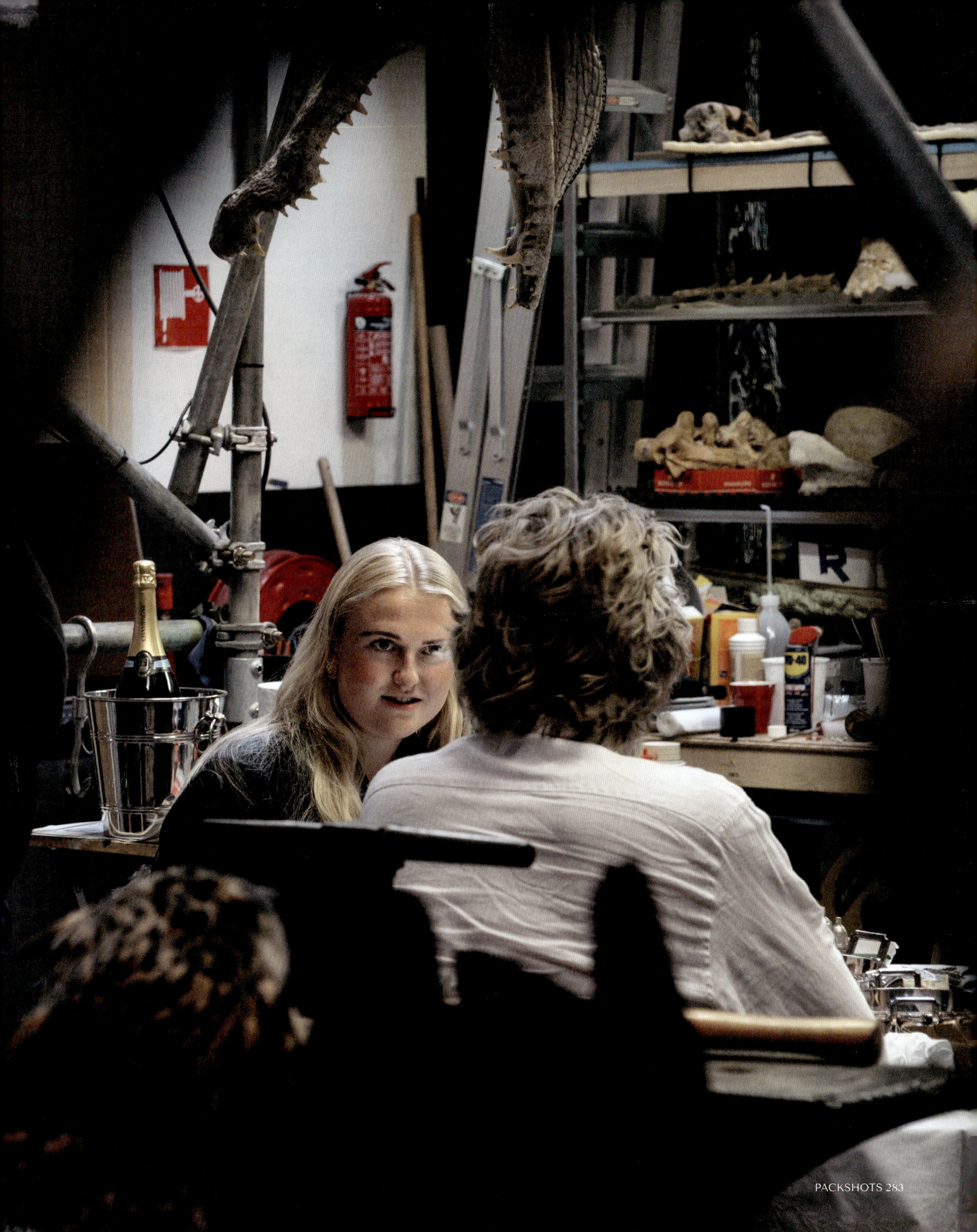

> "The fact that Damien Hirst bought an entire collection of ours automatically put us into the art scene."
> *Ferry*

Yeah. And they had a lift for the dogs. I loved that. I think that was my favourite trip too.

ANNA: Oh, yeah?

NOOR: Those people were so kind.

FERRY: But I was asking about the work, not the trip.

NOOR: It was a cage with birds. Yeah, it was a cage. You had to install it, all the way at the top of that big house. It was so much fun. I remember being there with you, and we had rented a Mini Cooper. That's my favourite car, so that made it even better.

FERRY: So, it's mostly about the trip for you, huh, Noor? Haha. Well, my favourite trip was to Yorkshire. Do you remember, Jaap? We once delivered some work to Yorkshire. It was in some nature reserve. We arrived too early, so we were just wandering around a bit. We were driving through the Yorkshire Dales in a van. And then, suddenly... we saw a Jeep with soldiers inside. But they were Asian. And they actually came to check us out. It turned out they were part of a private army of our client. They had their own soldiers for protection. And those people were really old. In the middle of nowhere. Such a bizarre experience! When we finally went back at the right time, those same soldiers were standing behind the gate. And there was another Jeep full of soldiers. We had to install the artwork there because it was really large. So, we were busy for quite a while. There was a butler, and at some point, he said: "Lunch, gentlemen." So we had to go downstairs. It was really like one of those old English series, where the servants sit downstairs in the kitchen. While we were sitting there eating and chatting with the butler, the man suddenly realised something. He stammered, "So... you are the artists?" And we said, "Yes, we are." He immediately panicked, grabbed the phone in the next room and called the lady of the house. He came back, took all the food away from us and said, "I'm deeply sorry. If you gentlemen could follow me to the dining room upstairs!"

JAAP: They thought we were the delivery guys. But we didn't mind eating downstairs, of course.

NOOR: Maybe even nicer.

JAAP: Yeah, maybe. They were really gossiping about those people too. The staff, among themselves. That's probably why they were so shocked.

ANNA: But you've both seen some really special places and had some quite remarkable clients. You've sold large pieces and all that. But it hasn't really gone to your heads, or at least, that's the impression I get. Do you think so?

JAAP: I don't know. You'd probably know better.

ANNA: No, definitely not! But I was thinking about it recently, and I wondered: do you now see yourselves as true artists, or still more as commercial admen?

FERRY: Actually, neither. You see, when we started, we just had the idea that you could do much cooler things with taxidermy. And that's what we wanted to do. And the fact that Damien Hirst bought up that whole collection for his art museum kind of automatically put us into the art scene. But we never had the dream of becoming artists. We only had the dream of making really cool stuff.

ANNA: I didn't actually know that.

FERRY: And... well, I don't really feel like an artist. When I have to fill out what my profession is on a plane or something, I feel really uncomfortable writing "artist".

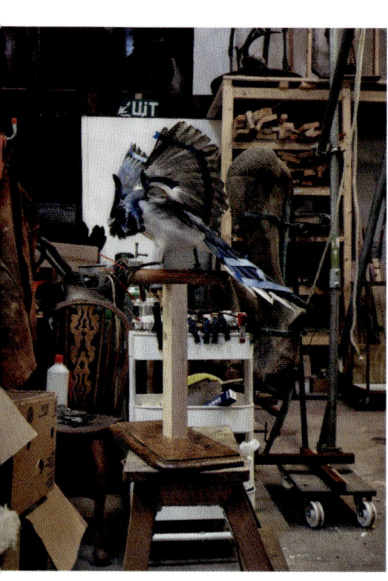

NOOR: Then just write taxi driver!

FERRY: Because there's such a wide range of different kinds of artists, and most of them I wouldn't want to be associated with. I actually prefer not to belong anywhere.

NOOR: But you guys do dress like artists.

FERRY: Hahaha, really? You mean unkempt? Homeless, artist — it's a fine line.

ANNA: They dress more like, "I couldn't care less." No frills. And that's also a sign that it hasn't gone to your heads. You're not out there chasing fame either.

FERRY: No, definitely not. I actually think it's the worst part of what we do — like, an exhibition opening.

NOOR: Really?

FERRY: By far. Well, no, the absolute worst for me is dealing with the government, the laws and customs. The pointless hassle of the procedures. But second place goes to the opening of a show. I often tell Jaap that it's bizarre how hard we work for attention that we don't even want. I don't want to be in the spotlight at all.

NOOR: No, that's true.

FERRY: I actually think it's a shame that you always have to do those kinds of things to get known, to be able to sell and to make a living from it. Yeah. One-on-one with a client, I often really enjoy that. But in a room full of people? Brrr.

ANNA: An opening with your own work! Come on… isn't that fun?! Well, okay, I guess I'm really a marketer at heart. I think it should be big; you need to know who the face is and tell the stories behind it.

JAAP: So… is that your advice to artists? That they should clearly show who the face behind the work is?

ANNA: I do think a lot of artists act really secretive. I don't know if it's because they don't really know what they're doing themselves or if they just don't feel comfortable with it, like you. But it's a shame because you create something really beautiful. Personally, I find it much more interesting to know how something was made, how the process went, who's behind it, who made it. Those museum-like texts they often use are awful too. I read them and think, what am I even reading? It's like some AI that always spits out the same texts. I think it's much more fun when there's a personal face to it — someone you can actually talk to.

FERRY: Well, I have to say, that's why I think it's good that we're doing this — this lunch conversation. Because it allows us to talk more relaxed, openly and honestly. And what you were saying about those texts that artists put next to their works — we both often find them really embarrassing.

ANNA: Trying to sound interesting. It's like they're forcing themselves to sound intelligent.

FERRY: I completely agree. So yeah, I think we're always very open and honest. And we don't give some kind of bullshit story about our work, right Noor?

NOOR: Except that the idea for this lunch was only thought up three days ago.

ANNA: Yeah, but what difference does that make? I just find it funny. That's kind of typical of artists, I think.

FERRY: We thought the texts in the last book were a bit too slick, and we were brainstorming how to do it differently. Then the idea of having a conversation with our daughters came up, and it immediately fit with what we wanted to do differently. And I already feel like this works better for us. Much more natural.

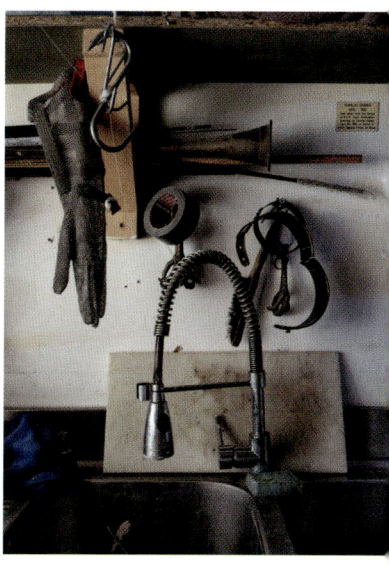

"A lot of artists act really secretive. It's a shame because you create something really beautiful."
Anna

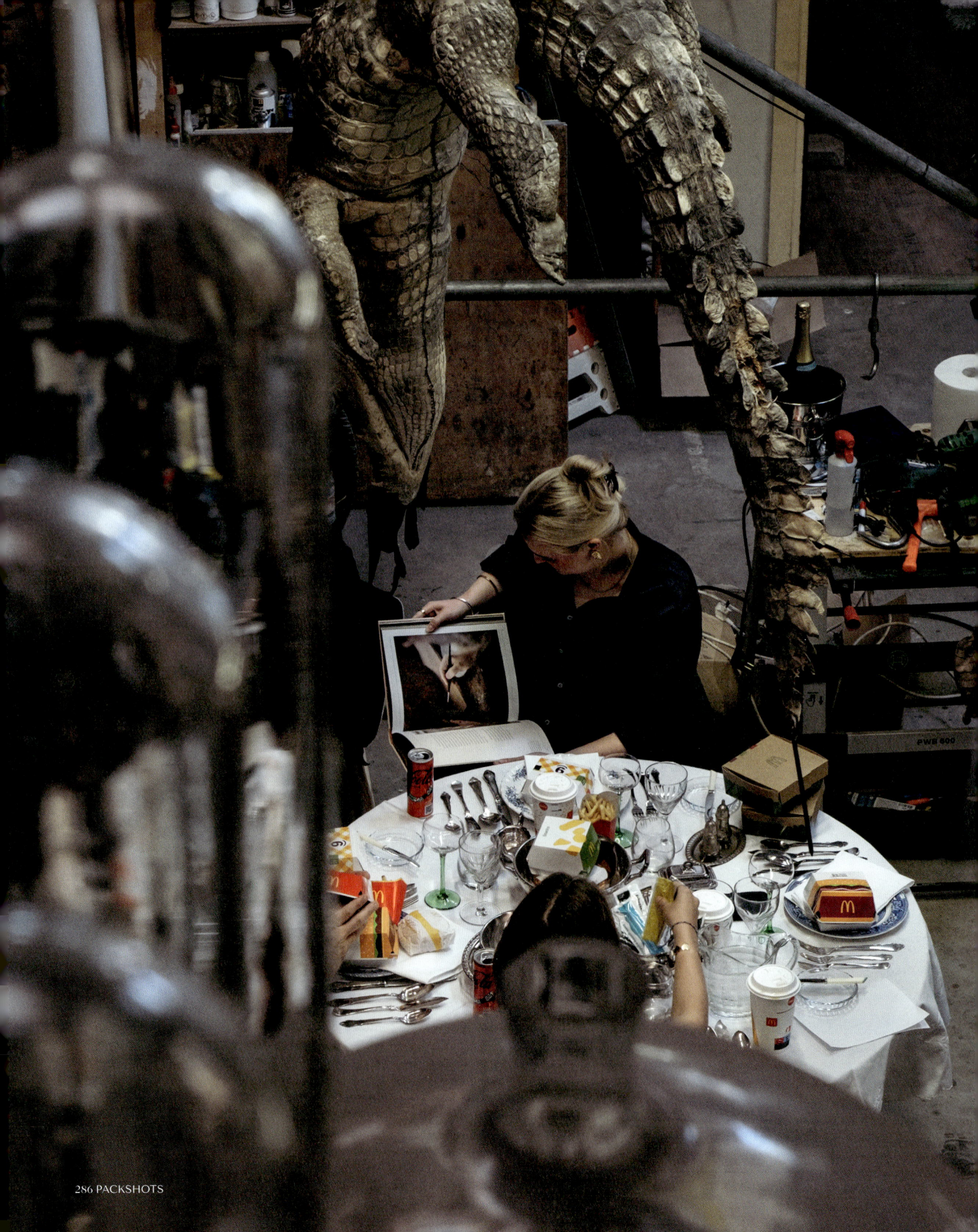

JAAP: Do you ever buy books, by the way? Art books?
ANNA: Me? Yeah. But not often. They're too expensive.
JAAP: And your friends? Do you know a lot of people who buy books?
ANNA: Yeah, Matej [*Anna's partner*] has a lot of those art books, but mostly photography. Ibi [*Anna's friend*] and I do too, but we often buy them at second-hand shops. Just a nice coffee table book.
JAAP: Ah, for the luxury?!
ANNA: Yeah, for styling. But I often find them too expensive. Plus, I still live in a student room, so I don't have a nice place to put them where you can leaf through them every now and then. But what do you think is your biggest achievement? Damien Hirst? Because that story always comes up in all the articles and books. Aren't you tired of talking about it?
FERRY: People who interview us always look back at previous interviews. And then they read, "Oh, Damien Hirst bought everything from these guys — that's interesting." And there's not much more to say about it. So they bring it up again, and we give the same answers. But yeah, it's not like we're the Obamas getting interviewed all day.
ANNA: True. But is there really nothing else to say about it?
FERRY: Well, it's funny. We always tell this story— that when the news came out that Hirst had bought the whole collection, we got two phone calls that day. One was from Wim Pijbes from the Rijksmuseum. He invited us over. And the other call was from the tax office. So pathetic. They had read the newspaper too, and we got an immediate audit! But somehow that part never makes it into the articles. Hahaha. But I'm not really sure what I'm most proud of. I think it keeps changing.
JAAP: I don't know.
FERRY: Well, I think our G-Star gorilla. We were asked by Dutch denim brand G-Star to create an artwork using their denim. We are in the process of making a huge sculpture of a gorilla. It is an anatomical muscle study called *écorché*: all muscles are covered with G-Star denim and stitching. It is a big thing. It's not finished yet, but I'm already proud of it. It's going to be really impressive.
JAAP: And the museum. We are opening our own museum in Amsterdam in 2025, featuring our taxidermy artworks in an Amsterdam canal house. The next big thing. Yeah.
FERRY: Well, we're in the middle of it right now, of course. And we can already envision it, but it still has to come together. And then we'll have to see if it attracts visitors. Because a museum on the Herengracht in Amsterdam is obviously not cheap. So that makes it pretty exciting.
NOOR: How did you actually get that place?
JAAP: You mean the museum? We were offered the space by the Vrije Academie. They're in that massive building and didn't really have the right purpose for the ground floor. They thought maybe a museum could work there, so they approached us. We have complete freedom to decide how to use the space.
FERRY: The owner knows we've been working for a long time on the idea of a museum — a sort of monument for endangered species. But that would need to be bigger than what we're doing now. This is more like a dress rehearsal. If we ever find the backers for this idea of "The Monument", that would be pretty much our ultimate goal.

"We are opening our own museum in Amsterdam in 2025."
Jaap

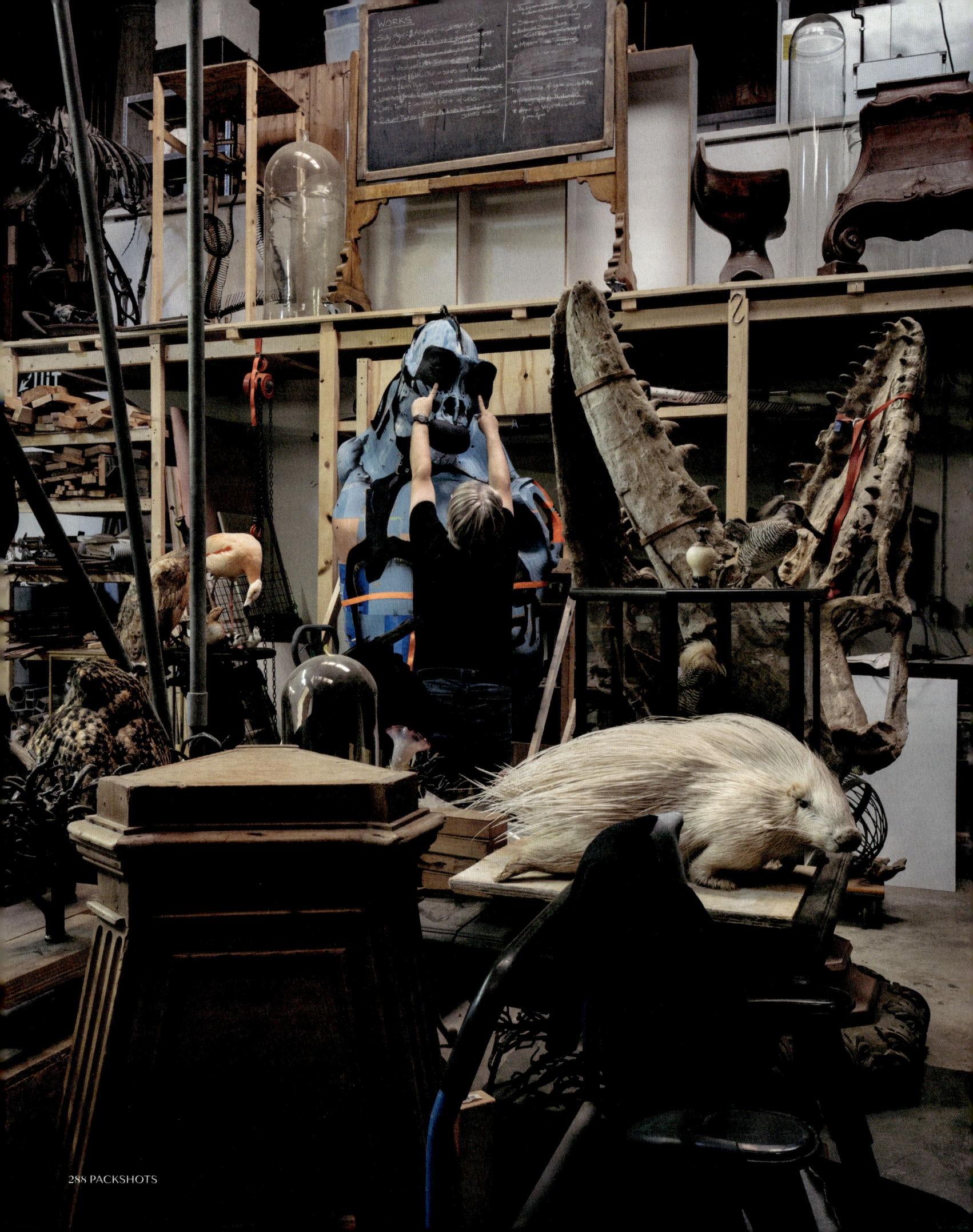

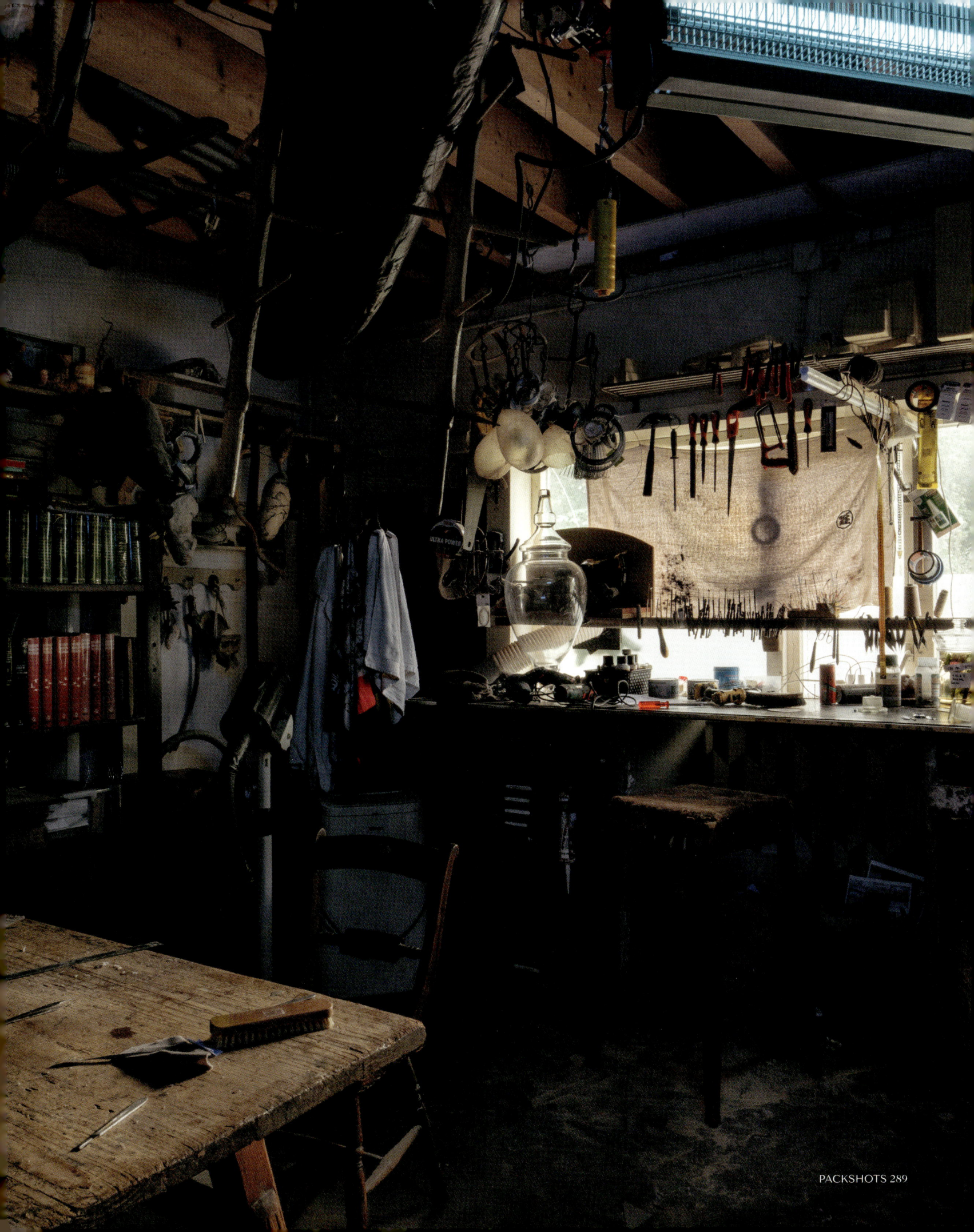

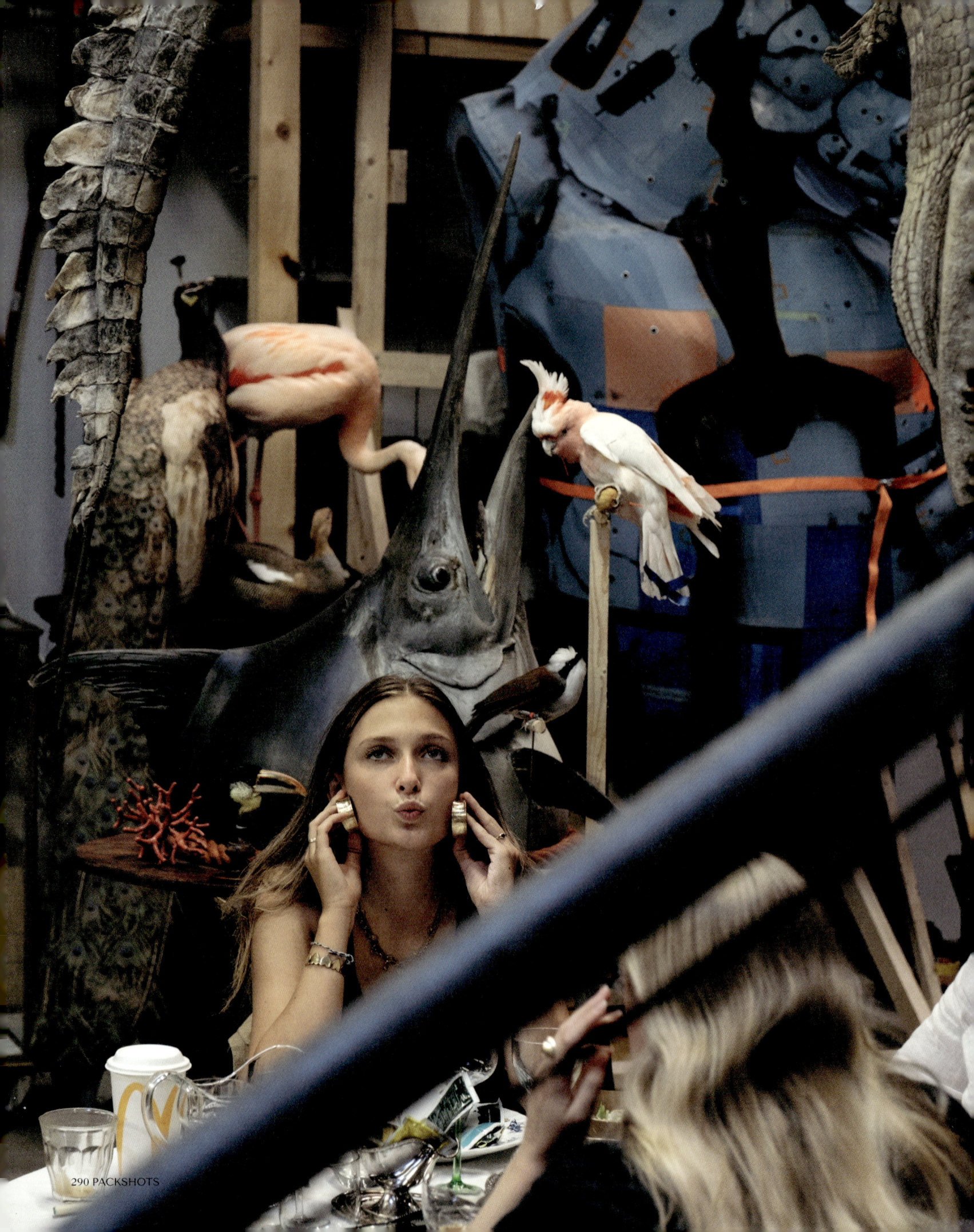

JAAP: But first, we need to get this museum off the ground!

FERRY: Hahaha. Yeah, we've still got a few weeks and weekends of work ahead!

ANNA: You guys are such perfectionists!

JAAP: You think so?

ANNA: Well, yeah. But I mean that in a positive way. What I think is the most beautiful thing about you guys, and something that's a recurring theme in all your collections and work, is that it's always worked out in such detail. Like the furniture around it, or how it's displayed, or what kind of space it's in, or how it's maintained. I find that really special because, personally, I think it's funny to see that many artists just kind of... not rush it, but... It's all so beautifully framed, and you pay a lot for it, and then you still see one little hair in the frame. I just think it's beautiful that you guys perfect everything.

FERRY: I like that you notice that. Because that's absolutely our approach.

ANNA: Exactly, and I've also developed a critical eye for that myself. I really appreciate it when someone has thought about everything.

JAAP: Maybe because we're art directors by origin.

ANNA: But mum told me that you're doing something with cages in the museum.

JAAP: Yeah, cages are the central theme of the museum. We're making large Victorian aviary-style cages, and as a visitor you walk through the cages and all the animals are actually outside of them.

FERRY: And around that is a sort of wunderkammer with our work. But actually, the whole exhibition is a Gesamtkunstwerk or total artwork. There's also a room with a T-Rex skeleton. And a flower room with tulips in formaldehyde.

ANNA: Interesting for tourists!

NOOR: Yeah?

ANNA: Because tourists associate Amsterdam or the Netherlands with tulips. Then you're getting into that marketing side again.

FERRY: I don't see it as marketing. It's more like thinking commercially. We want to make those jars anyway — they're called 17th-century specimen jars. And yeah, it's commercial to think "let's do tulips". But I don't see anything wrong with that. Because ultimately, if no one comes, then we'd have to tear it all down. And it's far too expensive for that.

ANNA: Would you ever stuff an animal, Noor?

NOOR: I already have. The first one I stuffed, I was ten. It was a mole from grandma's garden. That was at the first studio in the bunker. And later I tried a pigeon at the second studio.

FERRY: The old horse slaughterhouse. We're at the third studio now.

NOOR: The bunker, the old studio and this one.

ANNA: I can still really remember the bunker. I had no idea what you were doing there, actually. How old was I back then? Well, that was ten years ago. You had a sort of ramp leading down and below that was water.

NOOR: And it was full of stinging nettles. One time, I fell and rolled down that slope. But it was a really cool place. Why did you guys leave?

FERRY: We once made an ostrich skeleton and it turned out that it couldn't fit through the door. The doorway was too narrow. But the walls were a metre thick, because it was a bunker. So, we had to take the skeleton apart again. Then we moved to the Burgwal.

NOOR: Yeah, I was there a lot.

FERRY: You were there very often, yeah.

NOOR: I used to do my homework there after school.

"When I was ten, I stuffed a mole from grandma's garden."
Noor

FERRY: And here, too. It's funny, when we were in the bunker, we left and we thought, okay, the new studio needs to have a doorway big enough for an elephant. Because that ostrich could never fit through. So, then we got the Burgwal, which had a kind of carriage entrance. So, an elephant could fit through that. Then, when we started the dinosaur project, we left that place. And we said, "in the new studio, we need to be able to fit a dinosaur". Because we had that 15-metre dinosaur.

NOOR: How did that get in here?

FERRY: In parts. So, it also went out in parts. But it fit, for sure.

NOOR: And those big papier-mâché bears. They were for MOA, your first museum exhibition, right?

ANNA: No, those were for San Francisco.

FERRY: Yeah. We did that too. But that was still at the Burgwal. Everyone helped out with that, I think.

ANNA: You didn't go to San Francisco, did you?

NOOR: No. Oh, I really wanted to go.

JAAP: Yeah, Anna went. I'm actually curious — can we hear from Anna how she found San Francisco? She had to organise everything. You were our producer for that trip, right? As part of a school project.

ANNA: I had to do a senior thesis. And I had decided that I wanted to do something with art, but I didn't know what. It was about how to manage projects for big museums. How exhibitions are set up from start to finish. And then suddenly, you mentioned that I should just come along. We were leaving for San Francisco the next day! I think that was the coolest trip ever. The house and that space there.

FERRY: Yeah, that was a great trip for you. Personally, I found it one of the less enjoyable ones. But shall we wrap it up, guys? I really need to use the bathroom.

ANNA: Well, I had one more question. A bit silly, but where do you see yourselves in ten years?

FERRY: Wow. That's a tough one… I hope that in ten years we've found a patron and we're building The Monument museum. Right, Jaap?

JAAP: Definitely!

> "I hope that in ten years we've found a patron and we're building The Monument, our dream project."
> *Ferry*

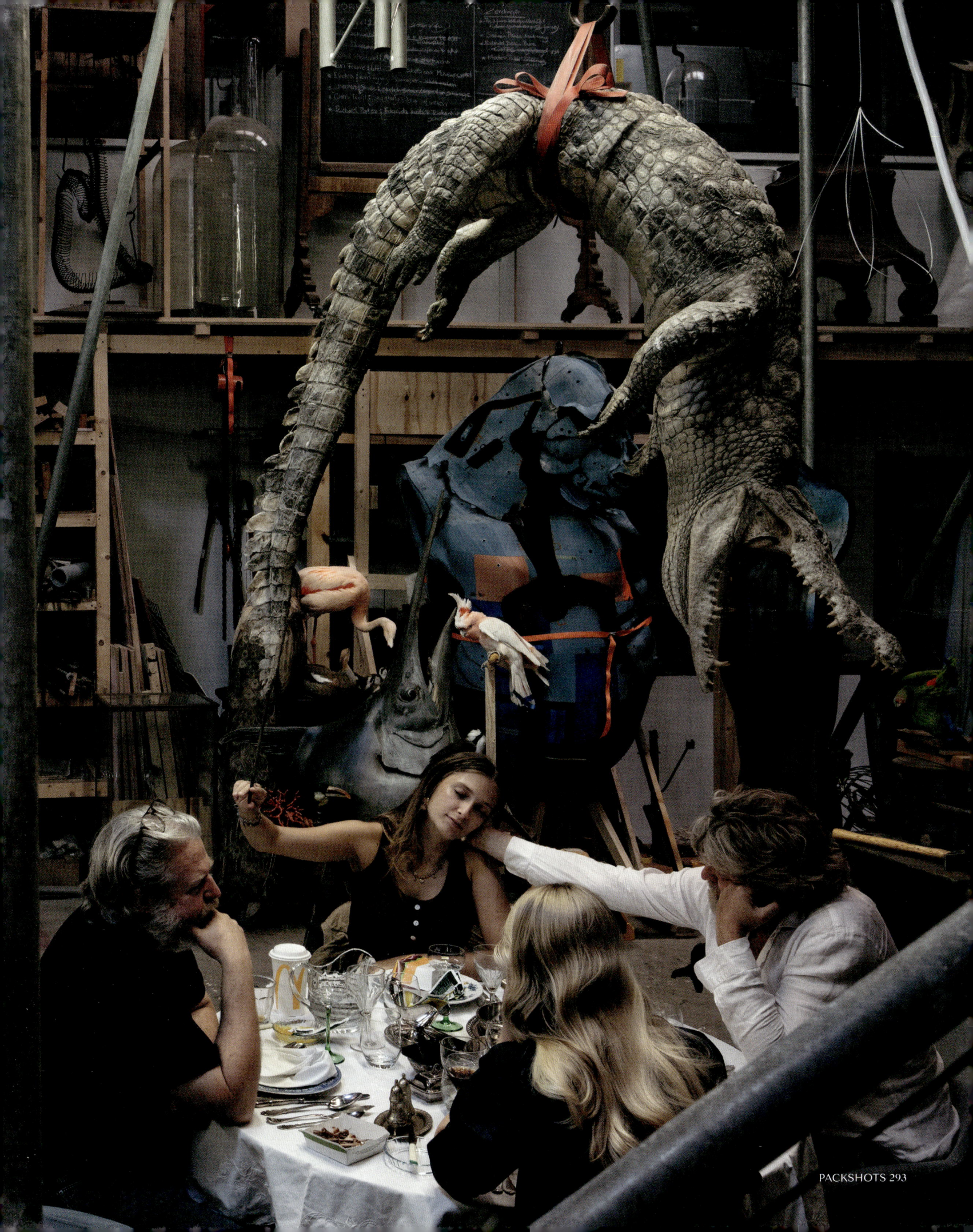

Page Index

COVER.	African sacred ibis *(Threskiornis aethiopicus)*
2.	Title: **Inferno Equus**
	Horse *(Equus ferus caballus)* 3x
4–5.	Title: **Turacages**
	Great blue turaco *(Corythaeola cristata)*
	Guinea turaco *(Tauraco persa)*
	Livingstone's turaco *(Tauraco livingstonii)*
	Purple crested turaco *(Gallirex porphyreolophus)*
	Red-crested turaco *(Tauraco erythrolophus)*
	Schalow's turaco *(Tauraco schalowi)*
	White-crested turaco *(Tauraco leucolophus)*
6.	Title: **Colonne Comme Bachelier**
	Common squirrel monkey *(Saimiri sciureus)*
	Copper pheasant *(Syrmaticus soemmerringii)*
	Green peafowl *(Pavo muticus)*
	Rose-ringed parakeet *(Psittacula krameri)*
	Scarlet ibis *(Eudocimus ruber)*
7.	Title: **Enraged Vari According to D'Hondecoeter**
	American flamingo *(Phoenicopterus ruber)*
	American white ibis *(Eudocimus albus)*
	Black-and-white ruffed lemur *(Varecia variegata)*
	Black crowned crane *(Balearica pavonina)*
	Black-necked aracari *(Pteroglossus aracari)*
	Green-winged macaw *(Ara chloropterus)* 2x
	Grey crowned crane *(Balearica regulorum)*
	Himalayan monal *(Lophophorus impejanus)*
	Scarlet ibis *(Eudocimus ruber)*
8–9.	Title: **Threatened Swan Inspired by Asselijn**
	Mute swan *(Cygnus olor)*
10–11.	Title: **The Hornbill That Got Away**
	Siberian tiger / Amur tiger *(Panthera tigris tigris)*
	Blyth's hornbill *(Rhyticeros plicatus)*
18.	Blue-eared pheasant *(Crossoptilon auritum)*
	European bee-eater *(Merops apiaster)* 3x
	Lilac-breasted roller *(Coracias caudatus)* 2x
19.	Title: **Snake Heraldry I**
	Green anaconda *(Eunectes murinus)*
	Spectacled cobra *(Naja naja)*
	Black mamba *(Dendroaspis polylepis)*
	Western rat snake *(Pantherophis obsoletus)*
	Reticulated python *(Malayopython reticulatus)*
	Emerald tree boa *(Corallus caninus)*
	Saharan horned viper *(Cerastes cerastes)*
20.	Title: **C'est Un Vol Vert Extraordinaire**
	Alexandrine parrot *(Psittacula eupatria)*
	Cuban amazon *(Amazona leucocephala)*
	Finsch's parakeet *(Psittacara finschi)*
	Hybrid ara ararauna *(Ara chloropterus)*
	Monk parakeet *(Myiopsitta monachus)*
	Mountain parakeet *(Psilopsiagon aurifrons)*
	Orange winged amazon *(Amazona amazonica)*
	Ring necked parakeet – juvenile *(Psittacula krameri)*
	Rose-ringed parakeet *(Psittacula krameri)*
	Rosy faced lovebird *(Agapornis roseicollis)*
	Superb parrot *(Polytelis swainsonii)*
	Swift parrot *(Lathamus discolor)*
	Turquoise-fronted amazon *(Amazona aestiva)* 2x
	Twenty-eight parrot *(Barnardius zonarius semitorquatus)*
21.	Title: **The King of the Museum**
	Nile crocodile *(Crocodylus niloticus)*
22.	Great blue turaco *(Corythaeola cristata)*
	Purple-throated mountaingem *(Lampornis calolaemus)*
	Red-legged honeycreeper *(Cyanerpes cyaneus)*
	White-necked jacobin *(Florisuga mellivora)*
23.	African sacred ibis *(Threskiornis aethiopicus)*
24.	Black mamba *(Dendroaspis polylepis)*
	Ural owl *(Strix uralensis)*
25.	Japanese spider crab *(Macrocheira kaempferi)*
26.	Major Mitchell's cockatoo *(Cacatua leadbeateri)*
27.	Scarlet ibis *(Eudocimus ruber)*
28.	Hamerkop *(Scopus umbretta)*
29.	American white ibis *(Eudocimus albus)*
30.	Andean Cock of the Rock male and female *(Rupicola peruvianus)*
31.	Red-tailed black cockatoo *(Calyptorhynchus banksii)*
32.	Snowy owl *(Bubo scandiacus)*
33.	Eurasian eagle-owl / Uhu *(Bubo bubo)*
34.	Great grey owl *(Strix nebulosa)*
35.	Barn owl *(Tyto alba)*
36.	Blue-and-gold macaw *(Ara ararauna)*

Page Index

37.	Title: **Turacages**
	Great blue turaco *(Corythaeola cristata)*
	Guinea turaco *(Tauraco persa)*
	Livingstone's turaco *(Tauraco livingstonii)*
	Purple crested turaco *(Gallirex porphyreolophus)*
	Red-crested turaco *(Tauraco erythrolophus)*
	Schalow's turaco *(Tauraco schalowi)*
	White-crested turaco *(Tauraco leucolophus)*
38.	Aldabra giant tortoise *(Aldabrachelys gigantea)*
39.	Aldabra giant tortoise *(Aldabrachelys gigantea)*
40.	Bald eagle *(Haliaeetus leucocephalus)*
41.	Verreaux's eagle *(Aquila verreauxii)*
42.	Blyth's hornbill *(Rhyticeros plicatus)*
43.	Mute swan *(Cygnus olor)*
44.	Horse *(Equus ferus caballus)* 3x
45.	Northern raven *(Corvus corax)*
	Hermit crab *(Paguroidea)*
46.	Toco toucan *(Ramphastos toco)*
47.	Rhinoceros hornbill *(Buceros rhinoceros)*
48.	Black-necked swan *(Cygnus melancoryphus)*
49.	Curl-crested aracari *(Pteroglossus beauharnaisii)*
50.	Red panda *(Ailurus fulgens)*
51.	Ural owl *(Strix uralensis)*
52.	Great blue turaco *(Corythaeola cristata)*
53.	Palm cockatoo *(Probosciger aterrimus)*
54.	American alligator *(Alligator mississippiensis)* 2x
55.	Northern raven *(Corvus corax)*
56.	Red-crested turaco *(Tauraco erythrolophus)*
57.	Crested cockerel *(Gallus gallus domesticus)*
	European bee-eater *(Merops apiaster)*
	Grey crowned crane *(Balearica regulorum)* 2x
	Scaly-sided merganser *(Mergus squamatus)*
	Spotted whistling duck *(Dendrocygna guttata)*
58.	Title: **The Birds of DSvT by John James Audubon**
	American flamingo *(Phoenicopterus ruber)*
	Giant wood rail *(Aramides ypecaha)*
	Grey-headed swamphen *(Porphyrio poliocephalus)*
59.	Chilean flamingo *(Phoenicopterus chilensis)*
60–61.	Scarlet ibis *(Eudocimus ruber)*
62–63.	Title: **Songbird Orchestra No. 1**
	Blue-bellied roller *(Coracias cyanogaster)*
	Brahminy starling *(Sturnia pagodarum)*
	Brown-breasted barbet *(Lybius melanopterus)*
	Buffon's green turaco *(Tauraco persa buffoni)*
	Cayenne jay *(Cyanocorax cayanus)*
	Golden-breasted starling *(Lamprotornis regius)* 2x
	Inca jay *(Cyanocorax yncas)*
	Lady Ross's turaco *(Musophaga rossae)*
	Long-tailed fiscal *(Lanius cabanisi)*
	Paradise tanager *(Tangara chilensis)*
	Purple roller *(Coracias naevius)* 2x
	Red-billed blue magpie *(Urocissa erythroryncha)*
	Rufous-vented laughingthrush *(Pterorhinus gularis)*
	Spotted laughingthrush *(Ianthocincla ocellata)*
	White-crested laughingthrush *(Garrulax leucolophus)*
	White-winged redstart *(Phoenicurus erythrogastrus)*
	Yellow-crowned gonolek *(Laniarius barbarus)*
	Yellow-faced myna *(Mino dumontii)*
64.	Eurasian spoonbill *(Platalea leucorodia)*
65.	Title: **Snake Heraldry IV**
	Boa constrictor *(Boa constrictor)*
	Boa imperator *(Boa constrictor imperator)*
	Reticulated python *(Malayopython reticulatus)*
66.	Helmeted guineafowl *(Numida meleagris)*
67.	Helmeted guineafowl *(Numida meleagris)*
68.	Red-and-green macaw *(Ara chloropterus)*
69.	Red-and-green macaw *(Ara chloropterus)*
70.	Hybrid ara ararauna *(Ara chloropterus)*
71.	Hybrid ara ararauna *(Ara chloropterus)*
72.	Tayra *(Eira barbara)*
73.	Palm cockatoo *(Probosciger aterrimus)*
74.	Blue-crowned motmot *(Momotus coeruliceps)*

Page Index

75.	Chestnut-breasted malkoha *(Phaenicophaeus curvirostris)*	99.	Mallee ringneck *(Barnardius zonarius barnardi)* 2x
76.	Red-tailed black cockatoo *(Calyptorhynchus banksii)*	100.	Green wood hoopoe *(Phoeniculus purpureus)*
77.	Ring-tailed lemur *(Lemur catta)*	101.	Black-necked stilt *(Himantopus mexicanus)*
78.	Specimen jars with flowers	102.	Pied avocet *(Recurvirostra avosetta)*
79.	Specimen jars with flowers & reptiles	103.	Pied avocet *(Recurvirostra avosetta)*
80.	Southern carmine bee-eater *(Merops nubicoides)*	104.	Crested caracara *(Caracara plancus)*
81.	Title: **The Birds of DSvT by John James Audubon** American flamingo *(Phoenicopterus ruber)* Giant wood rail *(Aramides ypecaha)* Grey-headed swamphen *(Porphyrio poliocephalus)*	105.	King eider male and female *(Somateria spectabilis)*
		106.	Magnificent bird-of-paradise *(Diphyllodes magnificus)*
		107.	Magnificent bird-of-paradise *(Diphyllodes magnificus)*
82.	Black-necked swan *(Cygnus melancoryphus)*	108.	Crested coua *(Coua cristata)*
83.	Mute swan neck *(Cygnus olor)*	109.	Polar bear *(Ursus maritimus)*
84.	Verreaux's eagle *(Aquila verreauxii)*	110.	Scarlet ibis *(Eudocimus ruber)*
85.	Laughing kookaburra *(Dacelo novaeguineae)*	111.	Scarlet ibis *(Eudocimus ruber)*
86.	Ferruginous pygmy owl *(Glaucidium brasilianum)*	112.	Siamese crocodile – skull *(Crocodylus siamensis)*
87.	Common hill myna *(Gracula religiosa)*	113.	Siamese crocodile – skull *(Crocodylus siamensis)*
88.	Title: **The Tower of Strigiformes** Ferruginous pygmy owl *(Glaucidium brasilianum)* 3x Spotted eagle-owl *(Bubo africanus)*	114.	American alligator *(Alligator mississippiensis)*
		115.	Nile crocodile *(Crocodylus niloticus)*
89.	Common hill myna *(Gracula religiosa)* 4x	116.	Beetle & insect collection in Victorian display case
90.	Blue-cheeked amazon *(Amazona dufresniana)*	117.	Bird – skull collection in Victorian display case
91.	Kea *(Nestor notabilis)*	118.	Note: Works under construction Hamerkop *(Scopus umbretta)* Montezuma oropendola *(Psarocolius montezuma)* Spotted whistling duck *(Dendrocygna guttata)*
92.	Bent's spiny-tailed lizard *(Uromastyx benti)* Yellow-headed caracara *(Milvago chimachima)*		
93.	Silvery-cheeked hornbill *(Bycanistes brevis)*	119.	Note: Works under construction Crested cockerel *(Gallus gallus domesticus)* White canary *(Serinus canaria forma domestica)*
94.	Red-winged parrot *(Aprosmictus erythropterus)*		
95.	Rainbow lorikeet *(Trichoglossus moluccanus)*	120.	Note: Works under construction Black swan *(Cygnus atratus)* Blue-bellied roller *(Coracias cyanogaster)* Chilean flamingo *(Phoenicopterus chilensis)*
96.	Red-fan parrot *(Deroptyus accipitrinus)*		
97.	Crested coua *(Coua cristata)*		
98.	Montezuma oropendola *(Psarocolius montezuma)*		

Page Index

121.	Note: Works under construction Buffon's green turaco *(Tauraco persa buffoni)* Major Mitchell's cockatoo *(Cacatua leadbeateri)* Duyvenbode's lory *(Chalcopsitta duivenbodei)*
122.	Note: Works under construction Crested caracara *(Caracara plancus)* Eurasian goshawk *(Astur gentilis)* Northern raven *(Corvus corax)* Saker falcon *(Falco cherrug)*
123.	Note: Works under construction Crested caracara *(Caracara plancus)*
124.	Note: Works under construction Grey-winged trumpeter *(Psophia crepitans)*
125.	Note: Works under construction Aldabra giant tortoise *(Aldabrachelys gigantea)*
126.	Silvery-cheeked hornbill *(Bycanistes brevis)*
127.	Trumpeter hornbill *(Bycanistes bucinator)*
128.	Red-and-green macaw *(Ara chloropterus)*
129.	Military macaw *(Ara militaris)*
130–131.	Giant anteater – skeleton *(Myrmecophaga tridactyla)*
132.	Bornean orangutan – skeleton *(Pongo pygmaeus)*
133.	Bornean orangutan – skeleton *(Pongo pygmaeus)*
134.	Northern giraffe – skeleton *(Giraffa camelopardalis)*
135.	Northern giraffe – skeleton *(Giraffa camelopardalis)*
136.	Japanese spider crab *(Macrocheira kaempferi)*
137.	Giant anteater – skeleton *(Myrmecophaga tridactyla)*
138.	Cougar *(Puma concolor)*
139.	Cougar – skeleton *(Puma concolor)*
140.	Black jaguar – skeleton *(Panthera onca)*
141.	Bornean orangutan – skeleton *(Pongo pygmaeus)*
142.	Sumatran tiger – skeleton *(Panthera tigris sondaica)*
143.	Northern giraffe – skeleton *(Giraffa camelopardalis)*
144.	Snow leopard – skeleton *(Panthera uncia)*
145.	Pug dog – skeleton *(Canis lupus familiaris)*
146.	Great white pelican – skeleton *(Pelecanus onocrotalus)*
147.	Common ostrich – skeleton *(Struthio camelus)*
148.	Title: **C'est Un Vol Vert** Military macaw *(Ara militaris)* And a selection of different Amazon birds
149.	Title: **Heraldic Ramphastidæ** Black-necked aracari *(Pteroglossus aracari)* 2x Black-necked aracari – juvenile *(Pteroglossus aracari)* Black-throated toucanet *(Aulacorhynchus atrogularis)* Chestnut-eared aracari *(Pteroglossus castanotis)* 2x Collared aracari *(Pteroglossus torquatus)* Curl-crested aracari *(Pteroglossus beauharnaisii)* Green aracari *(Pteroglossus viridis)* 3x Ivory-billed aracari *(Pteroglossus azara)* 3x Lettered aracari *(Pteroglossus inscriptus)* Toco toucan *(Ramphastos toco)*
150.	Title: **Heraldic Ramphastidæ** (Detail) Black-necked aracari *(Pteroglossus aracari)* Black-necked aracari – juvenile *(Pteroglossus aracari)* Black-throated toucanet *(Aulacorhynchus atrogularis)* Chestnut-eared aracari *(Pteroglossus castanotis)* Curl-crested aracari *(Pteroglossus beauharnaisii)* Green aracari *(Pteroglossus viridis)* 3x Ivory-billed aracari *(Pteroglossus azara)* 3x Lettered aracari *(Pteroglossus inscriptus)* Toco toucan *(Ramphastos toco)*
151.	Eurasian eagle-owl / Uhu *(Bubo bubo)*
152.	Rhinoceros hornbill *(Buceros rhinoceros)*
153.	Title: **Heraldic Ramphastidæ** (Detail) Black-necked aracari *(Pteroglossus aracari)* Chestnut-eared aracari *(Pteroglossus castanotis)* Lettered aracari *(Pteroglossus inscriptus)*
154.	Emerald duck *(Anas platyrhynchos)*
155.	White eared pheasant *(Crossoptilon crossoptilon)* Brown eared pheasant *(Crossoptilon mantchuricum)*
156.	Scarlet ibis *(Eudocimus ruber)*
157.	Crimson-rumped toucanet *(Aulacorhynchus haematopygus)*

Page Index

158.	Montezuma oropendola (*Psarocolius montezuma*)
159.	Blue-crowned motmot (*Momotus coeruliceps*)
160–161.	Red-and-green macaw (*Ara chloropterus*) Blue-and-gold macaw (*Ara ararauna*) 3x
162.	Military macaw (*Ara militaris*)
163.	Blue-and-gold macaw (*Ara ararauna*)
164.	Emerald duck (*Anas platyrhynchos*)
165.	Kea (*Nestor notabilis*)
166.	Choco toucan (*Ramphastos brevis*)
167.	Green wood hoopoe (*Phoeniculus purpureus*)
168.	Trumpeter hornbill (*Bycanistes bucinator*)
169.	Siberian tiger / Amur tiger (*Panthera tigris tigris*)
170.	Lion female (*Panthera leo*)
171.	Cougar (*Puma concolor*)
172.	Palm cockatoo (*Probosciger aterrimus*)
173.	Mute swan (*Cygnus olor*)
174.	Channel-billed toucan (*Ramphastos vitellinus*) Keel-billed toucan (*Ramphastos sulfuratus*)
175.	White-throated toucan (*Ramphastos tucanus*)
176.	Curl-crested aracari (*Pteroglossus beauharnaisii*)
177.	Black-necked aracari (*Pteroglossus aracari*)
178.	Green aracari (*Pteroglossus viridis*)
179.	Trumpeter hornbill (*Bycanistes bucinator*)
180.	Channel-billed toucan (*Ramphastos vitellinus*)
181.	Choco toucan (*Ramphastos brevis*)
182.	Long-tailed broadbill (*Psarisomus dalhousiae*)
183.	Black-and-red broadbill (*Cymbirhynchus macrorhynchos*)
184.	Red-billed blue magpie (*Urocissa erythroryncha*)
185.	Common marmoset (*Callithrix jacchus*)
186.	Fire-tufted barbet (*Psilopogon pyrolophus*)
187.	Fire-tufted barbet (*Psilopogon pyrolophus*)
188.	Detail of stand for bearded barbet (*Pogonornis dubius*)
189.	Bearded barbet (*Pogonornis dubius*)
190.	Boa imperator (*Boa constrictor imperator*)
191.	Boa imperator (*Boa constrictor imperator*)
192.	Magellanic penguin (*Spheniscus magellanicus*) 2x
193.	Magellanic penguin (*Spheniscus magellanicus*) 2x
194.	Polar bear (*Ursus maritimus*)
195.	Polar bear (*Ursus maritimus*)
196.	Title: **Snake Heraldry I** Black mamba (*Dendroaspis polylepis*) Emerald tree boa (*Corallus caninus*) Green anaconda (*Eunectes murinus*) Reticulated python (*Malayopython reticulatus*) Spectacled cobra (*Naja naja*) Western rat snake (*Pantherophis obsoletus*)
197.	Burmese python (*Python bivittatus*) Curvier's caiman (*Paleosuchus palpebrosus*) Royal python (*Python regius*)
198.	15 duck heads on hunting mirror mirror
199.	Gyrfalcon (*Falco rusticolus*)
200.	Mandrill female (*Mandrillus sphinx*)
201.	Mandrill female (*Mandrillus sphinx*)
202–203.	American alligator (*Alligator mississippiensis*) 2x
204–205.	Lion female (*Panthera leo*)
206–207.	Large installation for the Dutch Hotel Blenin Bloemendaal Common pheasant (*Phasianus colchicus*) Eurasian hoopoe (*Upupa epops*) European fallow deer (*Dama dama*) Red fox (*Vulpes vulpes*) 2x
208.	Eurasian hoopoe (*Upupa epops*)

Page Index

209.	Large installation for the Dutch Hotel Blenin Bloemendaal
210.	Burchell's zebra (*Equus quagga burchellii*)
211.	First sketches for Burchell's zebra (*Equus quagga burchellii*)
212.	First sketches for **Colonne Comme Bachelier**
213.	Title: **Colonne Comme Bachelier** Common squirrel monkey (*Saimiri sciureus*) Copper pheasant (*Syrmaticus soemmerringii*) Greater rhea (*Rhea Americana*) Green peafowl (*Pavo muticus*) Lady Amherst's pheasant (*Chrysolophus amherstiae*) Reeves's pheasant (*Syrmaticus reevesii*) Rose-ringed parakeet (*Psittacula krameri*) Scarlet ibis (*Eudocimus ruber*) Western crowned pigeon (*Goura cristata*)
214.	Blue peafowl (*Pavo cristatus*)
215.	First sketches for works with birdcages
216.	First sketches for heraldic works
217.	Rainbow boa (*Epicrates cenchria*) Spectacled caiman (*Caiman crocodilus*)
218.	Scarlet ibis (*Eudocimus ruber*) 3x
219.	First sketches for various scarlet ibis poses
220.	Clay sketch for heraldic work with caiman & snakes
221.	Burmese python (*Python bivittatus*) Cuvier's caiman (*Paleosuchus palpebrosus*) Royal python (*Python regius*)
222.	Common squirrel monkey – clay study (*Saimiri sciureus*)
223.	Common squirrel monkey – clay study (*Saimiri sciureus*)
224.	Siberian tiger / Amur tiger – clay study (*Panthera tigris tigris*)
225.	Siberian tiger / Amur tiger – clay study (*Panthera tigris tigris*)
226.	African bush elephant – clay study (*Loxodonta africana*)
227.	African bush elephant – clay study (*Loxodonta africana*)
228.	Cheetah – head cast 2x (*Acinonyx jubatus*) Black jaguar – head cast (*Panthera onca*)
229.	Black jaguar – head cast (*Panthera onca*)
230.	Title: **Snake Heraldry IV** Boa constrictor (*Boa constrictor*) Boa imperator (*Boa constrictor imperator*) Reticulated python (*Malayopython reticulatus*)
231.	Title: **Snake Heraldry III**
232.	Common ostrich (*Struthio camelus*)
233.	Common ostrich (*Struthio camelus*)
234.	Crested cockerel (*Gallus gallus domesticus*) Scaly-sided merganser (*Mergus squamatus*) Spotted whistling duck (*Dendrocygna guttata*)
235.	Crested cockerel (*Gallus gallus domesticus*) European bee-eater (*Merops apiaster*) Grey crowned crane (*Balearica regulorum*) 2x Scaly-sided merganser (*Mergus squamatus*) Spotted whistling duck (*Dendrocygna guttata*)
236.	Common ostrich chick (*Struthio camelus*) 2x Roseate spoonbill (*Platalea ajaja*) 2x
237.	American flamingo (*Phoenicopterus ruber*) Common ostrich chick (*Struthio camelus*) 3x Red-crowned crane (*Grus japonensis*) Roseate spoonbill (*Platalea ajaja*) 2x
238.	Great white pelican (*Pelecanus onocrotalus*) Grey crowned crane (*Balearica regulorum*) Scarlet ibis (*Eudocimus ruber*) 2x Temminck's tragopan (*Tragopan temminckii*) 2x
239.	Title: **Secretary Bird Memento Mori** Reticulated python (*Malayopython reticulatus*) Secretary bird (*Sagittarius serpentarius*)
240–241.	Title: **Quoting Charles Darwin No. 1** Crested partridge (*Rollulus rouloul*) Brahma chicken (*Gallus gallus domesticus*) Congo peafowl (*Afropavo congensis*) Crested cockerel (*Gallus gallus domesticus*) Emu chick (*Dromaius novaehollandiae*) Himalayan monal (*Lophophorus impejanus*) Mallard chicks (*Anas platyrhynchos*) Mute swan (*Cygnus olor*) Southern screamer (*Chauna torquata*) Stanley crane (*Grus paradisea*) White peafowl (*Pavo cristatus*)
242.	White-lipped tamarin – skeleton (*Saguinus labiatus*)
243.	Golden-handed tamarin – skeleton (*Saguinus midas*)

Page Index

244.	White-lipped tamarin – skeleton *(Saguinus labiatus)*
245.	Golden-handed tamarin – skeleton *(Saguinus midas)*
246.	Siamese crocodile – skull *(Crocodylus siamensis)*
247.	Siamese crocodile – skull *(Crocodylus siamensis)*
248.	Abdim's stork – skeleton *(Ciconia abdimii)*
249.	Snapping turtle *(Chelydra serpentina)*
250–251.	Great white pelican – skeleton *(Pelecanus onocrotalus)*
252.	Siamese crocodile – skull *(Crocodylus siamensis)*
253.	Abdim's stork – skeleton *(Ciconia abdimii)*
254.	Cheetah – skeleton *(Acinonyx jubatus)*
255.	Black-casqued hornbill – skeleton *(Ceratogymna atrata)*
256.	Cheetah – skeleton *(Acinonyx jubatus)*
257.	Roan antelope *(Hippotragus equinus)*
258.	De brazza's monkey – skeleton *(Cercopithecus neglectus)*
259.	Bonnet macaque – skeleton *(Macaca radiata)*
260.	Great white pelican – skeleton *(Pelecanus onocrotalus)*
261.	Black-casqued hornbill – skeleton *(Ceratogymna atrata)* Congo pied hornbill – skeleton *(Lophoceros fasciatus)*
262.	Great white pelican – skeleton *(Pelecanus onocrotalus)*
263.	Giant anteater – skeleton *(Myrmecophaga tridactyla)*
264.	Common ostrich – skeleton *(Struthio camelus)*
265.	American crocodile – skull *(Crocodylus acutus)*
266.	Greater rhea – skeleton *(Rhea americana)*
267.	Othnielosaurus mounted by DSvT
268–269.	Title: **The Hornbill That Got Away** Siberian tiger / Amur tiger *(Panthera tigris tigris)* Blyth's hornbill *(Rhyticeros plicatus)*
270.	Title: **Trophees Defence** An impressive set of 12 sculptures creating a wall of weaponry. Real antique horns and antlers facing the viewer and forcing them into defence. From left to right and top to bottom: Hartebeest *(Alcelaphus buselaphus)*, Billy goat *(Capra aegagrus hircus)*, Caribou *(Rangifer tarandus caribou)*, Alpine ibex *(Capra ibex)*, Bezoar goat *(Capra aegagrus)*, Goat *(Capra aegagrus hircus)*, Common eland *(Taurotragus oryx)*, Moose *(Alces alces)*, Oryx *(Oryx gazella)*, Greater kudu *(Tragelaphus strepsiceros)*, Mouflon *(Ovis orientalis orientalis)*, Springbok *(Antidorcas marsupialis)*
271.	Title: **Trophees Defence**
272.	Title: **Snake Heraldry I** Green anaconda *(Eunectes murinus)* Spectacled cobra *(Naja naja)* Black mamba *(Dendroaspis polylepis)* Western rat snake *(Pantherophis obsoletus)* Reticulated python *(Malayopython reticulatus)* Emerald tree boa *(Corallus caninus)* Saharan horned viper *(Cerastes cerastes)*
273.	Title: **Colonne Comme Bachelier** Common squirrel monkey *(Saimiri sciureus)* Copper pheasant *(Syrmaticus soemmerringii)* Green peafowl *(Pavo muticus)* Rose-ringed parakeet *(Psittacula krameri)* Scarlet ibis *(Eudocimus ruber)*
274–275.	Title: **Threatened Swan Inspired by Asselijn** Mute swan *(Cygnus olor)*

Species Index

A.

Abdim's stork – skeleton	248, 253
African bush elephant – clay study	226, 227
African sacred ibis	cover, 23
Aldabra giant tortoise	38, 39, 125
Alexandrine parrot	20
American alligator	54, 114, 202, 203
American crocodile – skull	265
American flamingo	7, 58, 81, 237
American white ibis	7, 29
Amur tiger / Siberian tiger	10, 11, 169, 268, 269
Amur tiger / Siberian tiger – clay study	224, 225
Andean Cock of the Rock male and female	30

B.

Bald eagle	40
Barn owl	35
Bearded barbet	189
Beetle & insect collection	116
Bents's spiny-tailed lizard	92
Black crowned crane	7
Black jaguar – head cast	228, 229
Black jaguar – skeleton	140
Black mamba	19, 24, 196, 272
Black swan	120
Black-and-red broadbill	183
Black-and-white ruffed lemur	7
Black-casqued hornbill – skeleton	255, 261
Black-necked aracari	7, 149, 150, 153, 177
Black-necked aracari – juvenile	149, 150
Black-necked stilt	101
Black-necked swan	48, 82
Black-throated toucanet	149, 150
Blue peafowl	214
Blue-and-gold macaw	36, 160, 161, 163
Blue-bellied roller	62, 63, 120
Blue-cheeked amazon	90
Blue-crowned motmot	74, 159
Blue-eared pheasant	18
Blyth's hornbill	10, 11, 42, 268, 269
Boa constrictor	65, 230
Boa imperator	65, 191, 230
Bonnet macaque – skeleton	259
Bornean orangutan – skeleton	132, 133, 141
Brahma chicken	240, 241
Brahminy starling	62, 63
Brown eared pheasant	155
Brown-breasted barbet	62, 63
Buffon's green turaco	62, 63, 121
Burchell's zebra	210
Burmese python	197, 221

C.

Canary – white	119
Cayenne jay	62, 63
Channel-billed toucan	174, 180
Cheetah – head cast	228
Cheetah – skeleton	254, 256
Chestnut-breasted malkoha	75
Chestnut-eared aracari	149, 150, 153
Chilean flamingo	59, 120
Choco toucan	166, 181
Collared aracari	149
Common hill myna	87, 89
Common marmoset	185
Common ostrich	232, 233
Common ostrich chick	236, 237
Common ostrich – skeleton	147, 264
Common pheasant	206, 207
Common squirrel monkey	6, 213
Common squirrel monkey – clay study	222, 223
Congo peafowl	240, 241
Congo pied hornbill – skeleton	261
Copper pheasant	6, 213
Cougar	138, 171
Cougar – skeleton	139
Crested caracara	104, 122, 123
Crested cockerel	57, 119, 234, 235, 240, 241
Crested coua	97, 108
Crested partridge	240, 241
Crimson-rumped toucanet	157
Cuban amazon	20
Curl-crested aracari	49, 149, 150, 176
Curvier's caiman	197, 221

D.

De brazza's monkey – skeleton	258
Duyvenbode's lory	121

E.

Emerald duck	154, 164
Emerald tree boa	19, 196
Emu chick	240, 241
Eurasian eagle-owl / Uhu	33, 151
Eurasian goshawk	122
Eurasian hoopoe	206, 208
Eurasian spoonbill	64
European bee-eater	18, 57, 235
European fallow deer	206, 207, 209

Species Index

F.

Ferruginous pygmy owl	86, 88
Finsch's parakeet	20
Fire-tufted barbet	186, 187

G.

Giant anteater – skeleton	130, 131, 137, 263
Giant wood rail	58, 81
Golden-breasted starling	62, 63
Golden-handed tamarin – skeleton	243, 245
Great blue turaco	4, 5, 22, 37, 52
Great grey owl	34
Great white pelican	238
Great white pelican – skeleton	146, 250, 251, 260, 262
Greater rhea	213
Greater rhea – skeleton	266
Green anaconda	19, 196, 272
Green aracari	149, 150, 178
Green peafowl	6, 213, 273
Green wood hoopoe	100, 167
Green-winged macaw	7
Grey crowned crane	7, 57, 235, 238
Grey-headed swamphen	58, 81
Grey-winged trumpeter	124
Guinea turaco	4, 5, 37
Gyrfalcon	199

H.

Hamerkop	28, 118
Helmeted guineafowl	66, 67
Hermit crab	45
Himalayan monal	7, 240, 241
Horse	2, 44
Hybrid ara ararauna	20, 70, 71

I.

Inca jay	62, 63
Ivory-billed aracari	149, 150

J.

Japanese spider crab	25, 136

K.

Kea	91, 165
Keel-billed toucan	174
King eider male and female	105

L.

Lady Amherst's pheasant	213
Lady Ross's turaco	62, 63
Laughing kookaburra	85
Lettered aracari	149, 150, 153
Lilac-breasted roller	18
Lion – female	170, 204, 205
Livingstone's turaco	4, 5, 37
Long-tailed broadbill	182
Long-tailed fiscal	62, 63

M.

Magellanic penguin	192, 193
Magnificent bird-of-paradise	106, 107
Major Mitchell's cockatoo	26, 121
Mallard chicks	240, 241
Mallee ringneck	99
Mandrill – female	200, 201
Military macaw	129, 148, 162
Monk parakeet	20
Montezuma oropendola	98, 118, 158
Mountain parakeet	20
Mute swan	8, 9, 43, 173, 240, 241, 274, 275
Mute swan neck	83
Nile crocodile	21, 115

N.

Northern giraffe – skeleton	134, 135, 143
Northern raven	45, 55, 122

O.

Orange winged amazon	20
Othnielosaurus	267

P.

Palm cockatoo	53, 73, 172
Paradise tanager	62, 63
Pied avocet	102, 103
Polar bear	109, 194, 195
Pug dog – skeleton	145
Purple crested turaco	4, 5, 37
Purple roller	62, 63
Purple-throated mountaingem	22

Q.

Species Index

R.

Rainbow boa	217
Rainbow lorikeet	95
Red fox	206, 207
Red panda	50
Red-and-green macaw	68, 69, 128, 160, 161
Red-billed blue magpie	62, 63, 184
Red-crested turaco	4, 5, 37, 56
Red-crowned crane	237
Red-fan parrot	96
Red-legged honeycreeper	22
Red-tailed black cockatoo	31, 76
Red-winged parrot	94
Reeves's pheasant	213
Reticulated python	19, 65, 196, 230, 239, 272
Rhinoceros hornbill	47, 152
Ring necked parakeet – juvenile	20
Ring-tailed lemur	77
Roan antelope	257
Rose-ringed parakeet	6, 20, 213, 273
Roseate spoonbill	236, 237
Rosy faced lovebird	20
Royal python	197, 221
Rufous-vented laughingthrush	62, 63

S.

Saharan horned viper	19, 272
Saker falcon	122
Scaly-sided merganser	57, 234, 235
Scarlet ibis	6, 7, 27, 60, 61, 110, 111, 156, 213, 218, 238, 273
Schalow's turaco	4, 5, 37
Secretary bird	293
Siamese crocodile – skull	112, 113, 246, 247, 252
Siberian tiger / Amur tiger	10, 11, 169, 268, 269
Siberian tiger / Amur tiger – clay study	224, 225
Silvery-cheeked hornbill	93, 126
Snapping turtle – skeleton	249
Snow leopard – skeleton	144
Snowy owl	32
Southern carmine bee-eater	80
Southern screamer	240, 241
Spectacled caiman	217
Spectacled cobra	19, 196, 272
Spotted eagle-owl	88
Spotted laughingthrush	62, 63
Spotted whistling duck	57, 118, 234, 235
Stanley crane	240, 241
Sumatran tiger – skeleton	142
Superb parrot	20
Swift parrot	20

T.

Tayra	72
Temminck's tragopan	238
Toco toucan	46, 149, 150
Trumpeter hornbill	127, 168, 179
Turquoise-fronted amazon	20
Twenty-eight parrot	20

U.

Uhu / Eurasian eagle-owl	33, 151
Ural owl	24, 51

V.

Verreaux's eagle	41, 84

W.

Western crowned pigeon	213
Western rat snake	19, 196, 272
White eared pheasant	155
White peafowl	240, 241
White-crested laughingthrush	62, 63
White-crested turaco	4, 5, 37
White-lipped tamarin – skeleton	242, 244
White-necked jacobin	22
White-throated toucan	175
White-winged redstart	62, 63

X.

Y.

Yellow-crowned gonolek	62, 63
Yellow-faced myna	62, 63
Yellow-headed caracara	92

Z.

CREDITS

Foreword:	Nimi & Anton Corbijn
Texts:	Darwin, Sinke & van Tongeren
Interview:	Noor van Tongeren & Anna Sinke
Editing:	Léa Teuscher
Book Design:	Darwin, Sinke & van Tongeren

© Darwin, Sinke & van Tongeren | Lannoo Publishers, 2025
D/2025/45/146 NUR 640/653
ISBN 978 90 209 2021 5

Darwin, Sinke & van Tongeren
www.finetaxidermy.com
Instagram: @finetaxidermy
www.lannoo.com

If you have any questions or comments about the material in this book, please do not hesitate to contact our editorial team: art@lannoo.be.

All rights reserved. No part of this publication may be reproduced or transmitted in any form or by any means, electronic or mechanical, including photocopy, recording or any other information storage and retrieval system, without prior permission in writing from the publisher and Darwin, Sinke & van Tongeren.

Every effort has been made to trace copyright holders. If, however, you feel that you have been inadvertently overlooked, please contact the publishers.

Photography:	Tim Mintiens	p. 2–11
	Morleigh Steinberg	p. 12
	Ernst Moritz	p. 268–275
	Inga Powilleit	p. 276–293
	All other photography	
	© Darwin, Sinke & van Tongeren	

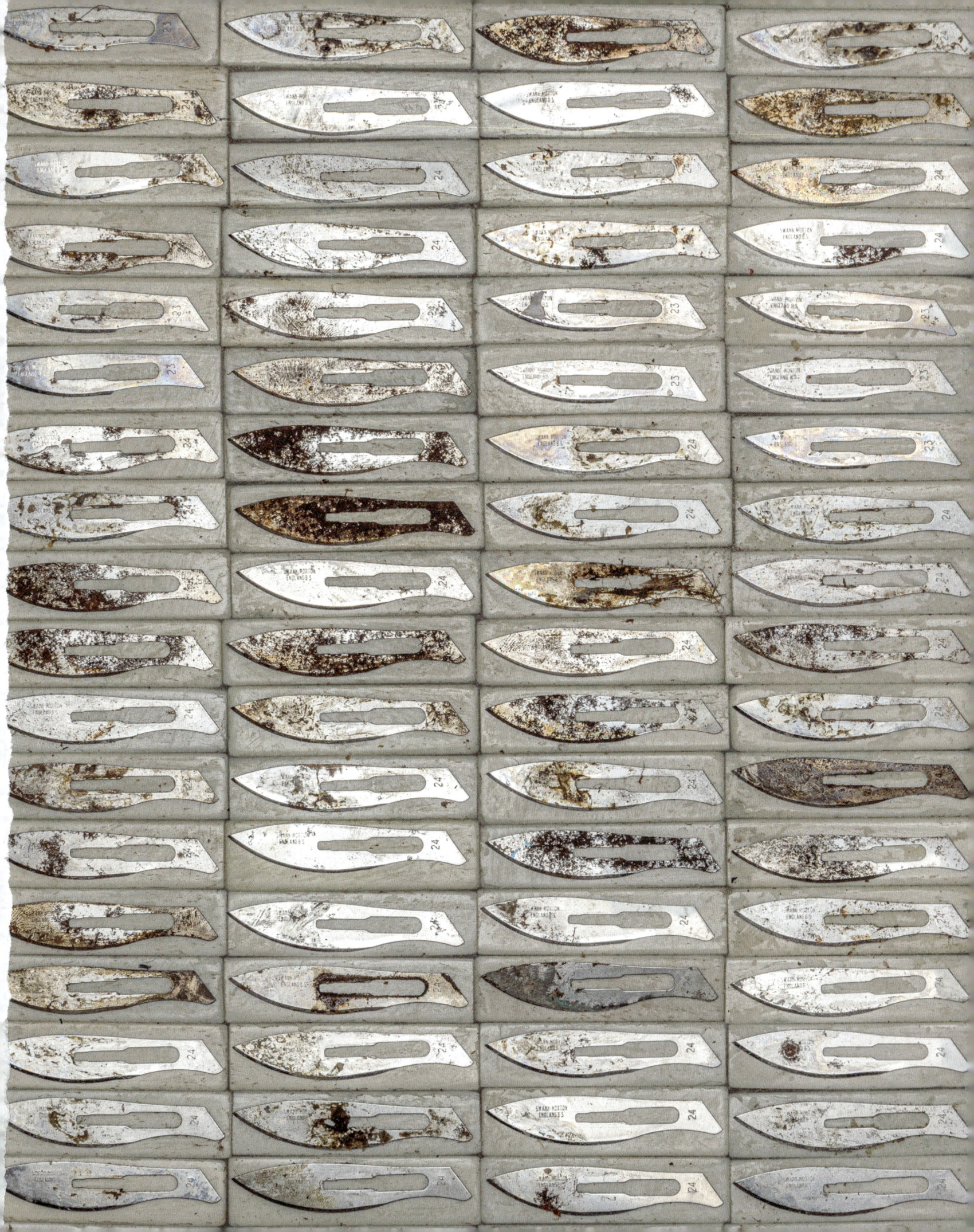

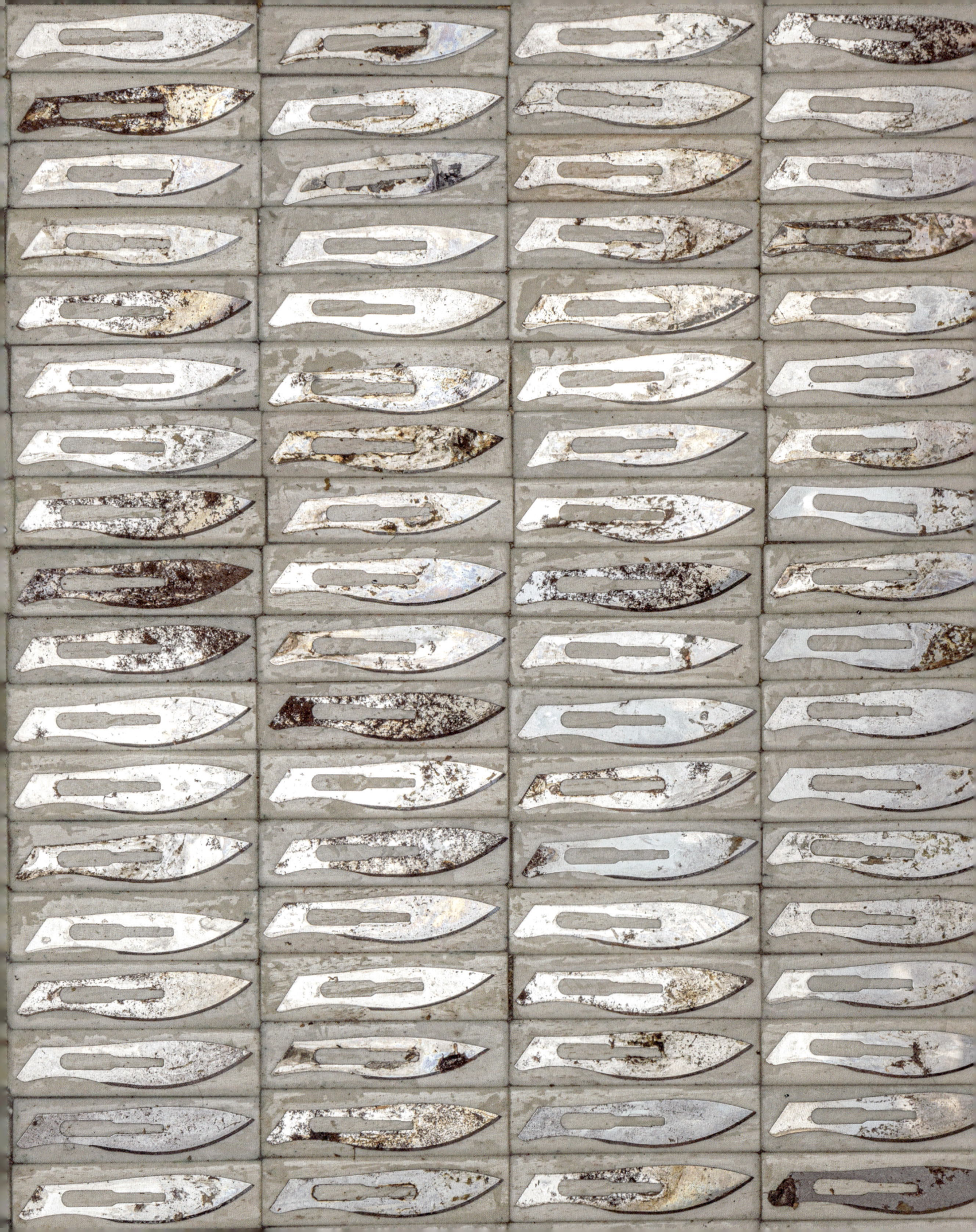